MĀYĀ DIVINE AND HUMAN

MĀYĀ DIVINE AND HUMAN

A study of magic and its religious foundations in Sanskrit texts, with particular attention to a fragment on Viṣṇu's Māyā preserved in Bali.

TEUN GOUDRIAAN

MOTILAL BANARSIDASS
Delhi :: Varanasi :: Patna

© MOTILAL BANARSIDASS
Indological Publishers and Booksellers
Head Office : BUNGALOW ROAD, JAWAHAR NAGAR, DELHI-7
Branches : 1. CHOWK, VARANASI-1 (U.P.)
2. ASHOK RAJPATH, PATNA-4 (BIHAR)

First Edition : Delhi, 1978
Price : MLBD
Rs 300.00

Printed in India
BY SHANTILAL JAIN AT SHRI JAINENDRA PRESS, A-45, PHASE-I, INDUSTRIAL AREA, NARAINA, NEW DELHI-28 AND PUBLISHED BY SUNDARLAL JAIN, FOR MOTILAL BANARSIDASS, BUNGALOW ROAD, JAWAHAR NAGAR, DELHI-7

Certainly, my children, you must have
come here with some object in view.
I have never known you to come
without one.

Earthmaker to the Winnebago (Radin, p. 216)

CONTENTS

PREFACE

The following pages owe their origin to a desire to reflect upon the Sanskrit fragment edited as No. 450 in the collection of Balinese hymns and fragments "Stuti and Stava". This fragment of 21 ślokas interspersed by prose mantras, called Mahāmāyā, describes the supranormal effects of a meditation upon Viṣṇu's Māyā, here to be understood as that god's ability to change his appearance at will. I did not succeed in finding its Indian place of origin, although it very probably originally formed part of some Tantra or Āgama. Perhaps it will some day be recognized by an expert in the field. In essence, the present book is a commentary on this fragment grown out of size.

It might be asked whether the large amount of relevant material which has been adduced from Sanskrit sources did not lead to a regrettable disturbance of coherence. For instance, the connecting thread between the first chapter and the rest of the book is not always visible, because emphasis has been laid here upon features (like form changing as an aspect of Māyā) which play only a very restricted role in the later chapters. I have tried to minimize this evil by including a number of cross-references. Perhaps there occurred a contamination of two aims: a thorough elucidation of a small Sanskrit text and an introductory survey of magical lore in Ancient Indian religious literature. The original plan, however, to build up the book round a single fragment as nucleus seems to have kept its value at the completion of this study. The governing idea is that the supranormal powers of human practitioners have been ultimately derived from, and shaped after the form of, divine examples revealed in mythology.

Another setback might be the desire to write for historians of religion as well as for indologists. This has led to the side-by-side existence of rather technical parts (especially in chs. 3 and 6) and many pages the contents of which will be familiar to any student of Ancient Indian culture. But Indologists are few in number and India is admittedly one of the most fertile fields of exploitation for those interested in the religious side of human experience.

The division of the book into six chapters has evolved in a natural way from the grouping of the material. The third chapter serves as a nucleus: it contains a new edition and translation of the Mahāmāyā text, accompanied by a philological commentary. The first two chapters contain data which were originally meant to be introductory; but their size has outgrown that qualification. The chapters 4, 5 and 6 deal with subjects which clarify the background of the Mahāmāyā fragment but which were far too large to be included in the commentary in ch.3.

A short survey of the contents of the chapters might be desirable.

Chapter 1 discusses some instances of the Māyā as supernatural power wielded by the Vedic and Brahmanical gods for various ends. Particular attention has been paid to shape changing and an-ethical, seemingly irresponsible behaviour. Sometimes the execution of such Māyā has been compared in the texts to the activities of malicious magicians, while its effects have been expressed in terms of magic. The figure of Viṣṇu-Kṛṣṇa has been studied in the first place, but also Indra and Śiva come to the foreground. Although the material included in this chapter (which is certainly not exhaustive) is generally known, it constitutes an aspect of Māyā which seems to have been comparatively neglected in monographs on the subject. Such monographs tend to emphasize the Māyā's philosophical side.

Chapter 2 deals with the appropriation of supranormal power by means of intense meditation. In its Indian form, presupposed by the Mahāmāyā fragment, this is the self-identification by a human performer, a Tantric adept or magician, with a particular deity. In the course of the process the performer is assisted by potent utterances, the mantras or bījas, considered to be identical with the deity and bearers of the desired powers. Special emphasis has been laid upon the aims with which such processes were to be carried out according to the sources.

Chapter 3 mentions, besides the discussion of the Mahāmāyā fragment, a few other instances of meditation on Viṣṇu and the Māyā. A special section has been included on the role of the Aghoramantra.

Chapter 4 contains a study of the role of the colours in meditations of the kind described in the preceding chapters. It appears that they play an important role as determinants in a stereotyped pattern of division of reality and of gradation of human objectives. Very often the colours serve to enhance the potency of mantra, power of thought and sacred object.

In *Chapter* 5 some remarks are given on the nature of the magic described in Vedic and Sanskrit texts, with some emphasis upon the magician as impersonating divine faculties and upon the aims striven after by him. It seemed necessary to include such a chapter in the absence of a badly needed general history of Sanskritized magic.

Chapter 6 has grown to disproportionate size on account of the abundance of the material which has, however, not at all been exhausted. Its aim was to study the place in Sanskrit (especially Tantric) literature of some terms of magic which occur in the Mahāmāyā fragment; it became a systematical discussion of the Tantric performances generally known as the Six Acts. The chief angle of vision has again been that of the aims for which the magical powers were considered applicable. It has been shown that these aims most often were similar to those sought at present by humanity by means of greatly improved technical resources. Also the claims of the Tantric wonder-workers were for the greater part based upon, and motivated by, the prevailing social and economic circumstances.

In some cases it has been deemed of interest to add references to, or short discussions of, comparable phenomena in other cultures or to the findings of the history of religion. They have, however, been intentionally restricted; it must be conceded that they are often due to accidental familiarity with the subject. The same holds good for comparisons with data taken from the India of modern times. An exception has to be made, however, for passages from Balinese hymns which I have often tried to involve in the discussion. This has been done with the twofold aim to promote research into the background of Balinese Sanskrit literature and to make some corrections to the edition and translation in "Stuti and Stava". The interested reader is therefore referred to Appendix 3 where the passages from "Stuti and Stava" discussed in the present book have been systematically registered.

A remark on the method of presentation : in order to restrict the number and size of the notes, the relevant literature has often been referred to within the text by means of the author's name between brackets. The bibliographical particulars can be found in the Bibliography under that author's name. Numbers put in the text between square brackets refer to the Sanskrit text of a passage which can be found in Appendix 1.

This book claims no originality; many sources of inspiration to which I should have expressed gratitude remained unnamed. Let me mention at least a few of them: in the first place Professor C. Hooykaas who disclosed to me the Balinese field of study; my colleagues Sanjukta Gupta, George Champarathy, Karel van Kooy and Tillman Vetter; the students at Nijmegen who enabled me to read their excerpts of two important articles; and my wife who by her solidarity greatly facilitated the completion of this book.

ABBREVIATIONS

ABORI	Annals of the Bhandarkar Oriental Research Institute, Poona.
ASS	Ānandāśrama Sanskrit Series, Poona.
BEFEO	Bulletin de l'Ecole Française d'Extrême-Orient, Paris.
BI	Bibliotheca Indica, Calcutta.
BSOAS	Bulletin of the School of Oriental and African Studies, London.
BTLV	Bijdragen tot de Taal-, Land- en Volkenkunde, Leiden.
CHI	The Cultural Heritage of India, Calcutta.
GOS	Gaekwad's Oriental Series, Baroda.
HOS	Harvard Oriental Series, Cambridge, Mass.
IIJ	Indo-Iranian Journal, Leiden.
JAOS	Journal of the American Oriental Society, Chicago, III.
JOIB	Journal of the Oriental Institute of Baroda, Baroda.
JRAS	Journal of the Royal Asiatic Society, London (if not specified otherwise).
KSS	Kāśī Sanskrit Series, Benares.
ms	manuscript.
NSP	Nirṇaya-Sāgara Press, Bombay.
OJ	Old Javanese
PD	St. Petersburg Dictionary by Böhtlingk and Roth (cf. the Bibliography).
PIFI	Publications de l'Institut Francais d'Indologie à Pondichêry.
PTS	Pali Text Society, London.
Pur.	Purāṇa.
Skt.	Sanskrit.
SVOS	Śrī Veṅkaṭeśvara Oriental Series, Tirupati.
TrivSS	Trivandrum Sanskrit Series, Trivandrum.
Up.	Upaniṣad.

VKAW	Verhandelingen van de Koninklijke Akademie van Wetenschappen, Afd. Letteren, N.R.
WZKSOA	Wiener Zeitschrift für die Kunde Süd- und Ostasiens und Archiv für Indische Philosophie, Wien.
ZDMG	Zeitschrift der deutschen Morgenländischen Gesellschaft, München.

1. THE MĀYĀ OF THE GODS

1. *Māyā in the Veda*

From the earliest sources onwards the idea of *māyā* is present as an important element in Indian religious history. It is unnecessary to present here a detailed study, or even a rapid survey, of the various applications of this word in the Ṛgveda and other Vedic literature. It may suffice to refer to Gonda's study[1] and to repeat his conclusion that all the applications and shades of meaning which this term has acquired during the many centuries of Indian religious history have not essentially changed. The central meaning of māyā is, in Gonda's words, "an incomprehensible wisdom and power enabling its possessor, or being able itself, to create, devise, contrive, effect, or do something".[2] While presenting this definition, Gonda also referred to P. D. Shastri,[3] who circumscribed the term māyā as follows (for the Ṛgveda): "a wondrous, supernatural power, an extraordinary skill," and, further on[4]: "supernatural power, mysterious will-power." Almost the same circumscription was already given by Oldenberg[5]: "Māyā ist, wie bekannt (in note 2 Oldenberg refers to earlier literature), die an sich guten wie bösen Wesen beilegbare geheime Kraft und Kunst, Wunderwirkungen zu erzielen, die dem allgemeinen Können und Verstehen unbegreiflich sind...".

In the ṚV. there is a strong "magical" connotation to the word māyā. By executing māyā, for example, one is able to trick one's adversaries. This connotation still more clearly emerges from the AV. This is not to say that māyā originally was no other thing than "magic", but only that in the non-speculative mind the ideas connected with it were liable to gravitate around that focus; while its execution became associated with magical processes.

In our view, this "magical" tradition has been often overshadowed by māyā's "metaphysical" traits, yet it has never since lost its ground in Hindu religious history. It is the object of the present study to trace something, however casually and superficially, of this non-speculative side of the idea of māyā. In the present chapter, the attention will be chiefly directed to mythological subjects, because "mythology establishes the validity of the belief in witchcraft".[6]

As we concentrate upon this aspect of māyā, a certain onesidedness will be unavoidable. We emphasize in the first place, then, that very often in the Veda the word māyā stands for the creation of a real, material form, be it human or non-human, by means of which the creator of that form shows his incomprehensible power.[7] The wondrous power may be wielded by either gods or counter-gods (as we shall henceforth call the Asuras). It may be noticed further that the creator of the māyā in question always has some end in view when he executes his power—an obvious statement, but perhaps not unnecessary to be expressed here. For example, Indra tries to overpower the counter-gods (ṚV. 1, 11, 7; 1, 32, 4); the counter-gods use their māyā against Indra (PVBr. 13, 6, 9) or try to conquer the world; the Ādityas make use of it in order to harm their foes (ṚV. 2, 27, 16). Accordingly, for the present purpose Gonda's definition may be paraphrased and narrowed as follows: "(māyā is) a wondrous power which is used in order to create some unexpected or novel appearance with a certain end in view".

In itself the māyā is a neutral force; not for good nor for evil. It all depends on who makes use of it. From an anthropocentrical point of view—and which other point of view would be imaginable ?—the māyā is a force for good when it is used by the gods—hence they may be called *sumāya*—and an evil threat when it originates from the counter-gods.[8] In both cases, however, the common feature is that something is placed before the eyes of ordinary creatures which they cannot understand. Also human beings can acquire a māyā; for example that of Soma by producing the soma (ṚV. 9, 83, 3). But in the human environment māyā is liable to degenerate into "deceit", as in Praśna Up. 1, 16: *na yeṣu jihmam anṛtaṃ na māyā ca* "in whom there is no crookedness, lie or deceit"; or into "illusionist tricks" (Oldenberg, l.c.).

The god, counter-god or demon who applies māyā can do this in two ways: he may cause some novel appearance to originate as it were spontaneously, out of nothing (for example, Varuṇa's māyā which appears from the fact that there is an ocean which always remains the same although the rivers continue to flow into it, and that there is an earth anchored and stabilized in a mysterious way: ṚV. 5, 85); or he can apply his creative power to himself, so that he appears in another form as before, in a disguise the real nature of which remains unperceived by a mortal (cf. Gonda, 1965, p. 168). The most famous instance is Indra (*purumāyá*—in ṚV. 6, 18, 12) who "goes around in many forms by means of his powers of māyā" (ṚV. 6, 47, 18). In ṚV. 3, 53, 8 the poet says: *rūpáṃ rūpaṃ Maghávā bobhavīti māyā́ḥ kṛṇvānás tanúaṃ pári svā́m* "the Generous One repeatedly appears in different forms, executing feats of māyā on his own body". And in ṚV. 10, 54, 2: *yád ácaras tanúā vāvṛdhānó bálānīndra prabruvāṇó jáneṣu/māyét sá te....* "when Thou walkedst around, constantly growing in size, proclaiming Thy powers among the people, O Indra, that was a māyā of Thine..". Of this miraculous power, some instances will be described now, taken from the Veda and more recent literature.

Beforehand one should note that the "philosophical' application of this motif has become one of the leading facets of Upaniṣadic speculation : the Primeval Lord became the cause of creation by disguising himself in other forms. Probably the oldest occurrence of the word māyā in the Upaniṣads is BAUp. 2, 5, 19 where it is said that Prajāpati "became corresponding in every form to every form. This (world) is to be looked upon as a form of him"; and after these words the Upaniṣad cites the passage just mentioned from the Ṛgveda (6, 47, 18 on Indra). Kaṭha Up. 5, 12 speaks of "the Inner Essence of all things..which makes Its unique form manifold".[9] On the other side, ŚvetUp. 6, 10 asserts that the Lord conceals himself by means of his māyā within his primordial material manifestation (*pradhānam*) just like a spider within its threads. But it is not the speculative use of the word māyā that interests us here in the first place (we refer to Gonda, 1965, p. 168ff.).

In the Veda the word māyā can stand for various aspects of the process involved: the power which creates a new appearance, the creation of that appearance as an abstract performance, and the result of the process, i.e. the created form itself. The power, its manifestation and its result are not distinguished by name; nor does it matter if the result is real or illusory from our standpoint. In the meaning "outward appearance" the word māyā occurs e.g. in ṚV. 6, 58, 1. This use is frequent in post-Vedic texts. In a philosophical context it is only a small step to apply it to the phenomenal world, which is in deepest sense no other thing than an incomprehensible or (if one prefers the word) magical creation by the Supreme God (ŚvetUp. 4, 10: *māyāṃ tu prakṛtiṃ vidyāt*).

As "power", the māyā can be compared to or equated with *śakti*; as "material form", it can be identified with *prakṛti*. In Sāṃkhya philosophy, prakṛti or māyā remains in a primordial state by means of an equilibrium of the three guṇas: *sattva* (white of colour), *rajas* (red of colour) and *tamas* (black of colour). When the Supreme God, Who is Unique, seems to appear in multiple forms this can be speculatively expressed in this way that the *niṣkala* becomes *sakala* (the indivisible aspect of the godhead becomes divisible) and creates the phenomena of nature. The mythological counterpart of this is that God is able to appear in many different or identical forms.

In non-speculative sense, māyā as "created form" can stand for the creation of a form by a magician. ṚV. 7, 104, 24 (=AV. 8, 4, 24) contains an address to Indra who is invoked against the māyā of sorcerers who present themselves in the guise of wild animals—a well-known feat of such people.[10] In later sources, the form created in this way is most often only illusory. When in the epic Indra conjures up a terrible vision of an imaginary character in order to trick a person (Mbh. 18, 3, 34; Gonda, 1965, p. 173), this vision is called a māyā. The same holds good in the epics when the god or demon applies the māyā to himself. In the Rāmāyaṇa of Vālmīki (Rām 3, 41, 7) Rāma and his companions are confronted with the notorious gazelle which is the demon Mārīca in another form: *māyaiṣā hi na saṃśayaḥ* "without any doubt this is a māyā". In st. 6: *asya māyāvido māyāmṛgarūpam idaṃ kṛtaṃ gandharvapurasaṃnibham* "this illusory manifestation of a deer has been created by that knower of māyā; it is like a *fata morgana*".

In Mbh. 3, 80, 126 Rudra manifests himself in ten million forms in order to end a quarrel between ten million sages. This feat is described with the help of the word yoga:

> *Tato yogeśvareṇāpi yogam āsthāya bhūpate teṣāṃ manyupraṇāśārtham ṛṣiṇāṃ bhāvitātmanām* (127) *sṛṣṭā koṭis tu Rudrāṇām ṛṣiṇām agrataḥ sthitā*

2. *Indra's disguises*

The motif of the god who walks on earth in a disguised shape is a famous one and we need not enlarge upon it here. The European peoples knew it from ancient times onwards. That the Greek gods with Zeus in the first place sometimes disguised themselves is a thing familiar to all students of classical literature. Among the Germanic peoples Woden has been said to possess such powers.[11] The Balinese have their legend of the "divine guest".[12]

In Vedic literature it is the god Indra in the first place who possesses a marked ability to change himself into all kinds of living beings of human as well as animal shape. Some of Indra's appearances as an animal have been memorized by Oertel.[13] Thus the ṢaḍvBr 1, 1, 18, in a passage which enumerates some of Indra's characteristic designations, calls him "a rutting buffalo" who emerges out of the wood in order to drink the soma. Very often in the Ṛgvedic hymns he is called a bull. But these are only literary comparisons. There are other places which allude to real transformations of the god's shape. As a monkey, Indra stole the sacrificial cake and thus disturbed the sacrifice prepared by the sages in the Naimiṣa wood.[14] In JaimBr 2, 79 he appears as a ram who drank Medhātithi's soma (*Medhātither ha meṣo bhūtvā rājānaṃ papau*), and the same is alluded to in JaimBr. 3, 233: *teṣāṃ (Vibhindukīyānām) ha smendro Medhātither meṣasya rūpaṃ kṛtvā somaṃ vratayati.* Sāyaṇa mentions the same feat in his commentary on ṚV. 1, 51. 1 and adds that since then Indra is called a ram. Of course, sometimes words like "bull" or "ram" may be applied in poetic figurative language, but Hillebrandt[15] was certainly right in pointing out that real animal appearances will have to be admitted as manifestations of Indra's māyā. He is even right, in our opinion, when he asserts that such passages as ṚV. 6, 47, 18 (*Indro māyā́bhiḥ pururū́pa īyate*) or ṚV. 3, 53, 8 refer to such theriomorphic appearances in the first place, despite the later "philosophical" explanation by the commentators and the Upaniṣads.

Oertel, o.c., does not refer to the other version of the Indra-as-ram story which goes back to ṚV. 8, 2, 40 and is recorded in ṢaḍvBr. 1, 1, 15. According to these sources Indra as a ram took Medhātithi with him to heaven (cf. Bollée, p. 18).

There are still other animal manifestations of Indra mentioned by Oertel, o.c. According to Sāyaṇa on ṚV. 10, 119, Indra applied that hymn in order to regain his own shape after he had been caught on the spot by the sages when he tried to drink the soma in the form of a quail (*Indro labarūpam āsthāya somapānaṃ kurvan...*). In TĀr. 1, 5, 2 there is a tale of Indra appearing as an ant. He becomes a horsetail in ṚV. 1, 32, 12 (*áśvyo vắro abhavaḥ*) and a leech in JaimBr. 1, 125f. On the same place he becomes a parrot and perhaps a caterpillar. There is also a connection between Indra and the falcon or eagle (*śyena-*) to which he is likened in ṚV. 1, 32, 14 and ṚV. 10, 99, 8 but also other gods, such as Soma, are likened to or identified with this bird.[16] According to TS. 6, 2, 4, 4 Indra conquered the earth from the asuras by making three steps in the guise of a *sālāvṛkī* (jackal ?) : *sá Indraḥ sālāvṛkīrūpáṃ kṛtvémāṃ trìḥ sarvátaḥ páryakrāmat.*[17]

In later texts Indra still adds to these marvellous feats by becoming a peacock (Rām. 7, 18), and a cat (i.a. Kathās. 3, 17, 140) during the Ahalyā episode.

These animal manifestations are a very real and important part of Indra's power. It is just these manifestations which are alluded to in BAUp. 2, 5, 19 when it is said that he (Prajāpati) became corresponding in every form to every form. The same Upaniṣad seems to present this in more detail in 1, 4, 4 by describing how the Primeval Being created a female out of himself; this female tried to evade him by changing herself into various animal shapes. The male being copulated with her in all these respective animal shapes, and thus created the animated world. The typically magical power of changing oneself into an animal for purposes of one's own has here been incorporated into the speculations on the incomprehensible feat of the origin of existence.

Indra also appeared in human form in order to meddle with human affairs for various purposes. Probably best known is his role in the famous tale of Śunaḥśepa. In the version as told in AitBr. 7, 15 Rohita the son of king Hariścandra has been pledged by his father as a sacrifice to Varuṇa. The boy resents this, says "no" and takes to the wood. But when he hears that his father has been punished by the angry god with dropsy, he resolves to return and offer himself to be sacrificed. Now Indra appears; he meets Rohita on the way in the guise of a man and causes him to change his mind by reciting a stanza in praise of the life of a wanderer.[18] According to this stanza, the best thing a man can do is to practise the homeless life, because "Indra is the wanderer's friend" (*Indra ic carataḥ sakhā*). Indra adds that a person who does not move from his place commits evil: *pāpo nṛṣadvaro janaḥ*, a statement which is in flat contradiction with the usual convictions as expressed e.g. in JaimBr. 2, 134: *padbhyāṃ pāpaṃ karoti yo janam eti* "a person who goes to foreign people commits a sin with his feet".

Next year, when Rohita has again resolved to return, Indra appears saying another stanza with the same result. The scene repeats itself during five successive years. Five impressive stanzas on the wandering life—and this probably means: the life of a religious mendicant—are proclaimed by Indra, who adds, by the way, that he heard them from a brahman. In one of these stanzas there is a comparison with the game of dice:

Kaliḥ śayāno bhavati saṃjihānas tu dvāparaḥ |
uttiṣṭhaṃs tretā bhavati kṛtaṃ sampadyate caran ||

"If one lies on his back he is Kali (the worst throw in the game); while springing up he is Dvāpara (the second worst throw); while standing upright he is Tretā (the second best throw); and while walking he constitutes Kṛta (the best throw)".

In the sixth year at last (according to a parallel version in the Śāṅkhāyana Śrautasūtra in the seventh year) Rohita on his wanderings finds the wretched brahman family of Ajīgarta who hands over to him after some deliberation his second son Śunaḥśepa to be sacrificed in Rohita's place. Śunaḥśepa's miraculous rescue lies outside the scope of the present study, the important fact for which is Indra's appearance in order to impart some (religious) instruction. This instruction contradicts the standards of fashionable and ethical behaviour: Rohita is advised to seek the wandering life and not to heed Varuṇa's wrath and his father's illness.

A reference to Indra's wanderings in a completely different context is discussed by Kane, 1962, p. 728, n.1156. When during the Pravargya ritual a "wild forest dog" (*ekavṛka-*) is heard barking, the priest should utter these words: *vi gā*

Indra vicaran spāśayasva "O Indra, observe the cows while you move about" (translation by Kane). Here Indra would be addressed as a kind of walking guardian. Kane interprets the passage as if Indra should look after the cows while he is on his routine wanderings. But another translation is presented by van Buitenen[19]: "Go around and make a tally of the cows, O Indra". In that case Indra's moving about would be only a consequence of the order given by the priests.

The ŚatBr. relates how Indra changed himself into an embryo and entered into the intercourse of Sacrifice and Speech, out of fear that from this intercourse a terrible monster would be born;[20] and a manifestation of Indra as child is alluded to in the same ŚatBr. when Indra is addressed in 3, 3, 4, 19 as Kauśika. Sāyaṇa in his commentary on ṚV. 1, 10, 11 tells us that Indra was born as Kuśika's son in order to comply with a desire of Kuśika that he would obtain a son equal to Indra.[21] This interpretation is open to question, but it illustrates the belief in Indra's manifestations in disguise.

On another occasion Indra furthered the cause of the gods by changing himself into the sage Gautama. The episode is told in ṢaḍvBr. 1, 1, 24: the gods and the counter-gods vied with each other. Between the two hostile camps the sage Gautama was absorbed in asceticism. Indra asked him to act as a spy for the gods out of his strategical position. When the holy man refused this, Indra proposed to change himself into Gautama's shape and take his seat on the seer's place. This was granted, and that is the reason why the priest uptill now during the Subrahmaṇyā litany calls Indra by the words: "O Thou Who callst Thyself Gautama !" (ṢaḍvBr. 1, 1, 23; according to the Jaiminīyas the sage in question was Kauśika).

By operating in this tricky way, Indra made the good cause to prevail. Involuntarily the scene of this god practising austerities and perhaps teaching as Gautama between two hostile armies is associated with the setting of the Bhagavad Gītā where Kṛṣṇa taught his fallacious doctrine to Arjuna between the armies of the Pāṇḍavas and the Kauravas on the eve of the Bhārata war.

Indra had some experience in acting as Gautama. It is a famous story how he seduced that sage's wife Ahalyā by appearing to her in her husband's guise during the hours before sunrise, when Gautama had gone to perform his morning religious duties. Some versions of this tale still add to Indra's versatility by relating how the god as a cock deceived Gautama by crowing too early before sunrise, while as a cat he tried to evade the sage's terrible wrath through the window.

The purpose for which the god applied his māyā is rather malevolent this time: bringing the wife of another man under his control. We know of Indra's amorous disposition by some other stories which need not be presented here. The legend of Indra and the wife of Gautama does not occur in the ṚV.; it is alluded upon in the first chapter of the ṢaḍvBr. mentioned before where Indra is invoked with various names in the cadre of the Subrahmaṇyā litany. In 1, 1, 19 the priest addresses him with the words: "Thou, Lover of Ahalyā!"

Sometimes Indra is told to covet demons' wives presumably in the cadre of the eternal strife between gods and their adversaries. Thus in the Veda he loves Vilisteṅgā (see below), in the Mbh. the wife of Bali (Mbh. 5, 15).[22] It is noted in passing that also Indra's wife, Indrāṇī, is able to destroy adversaries with a magical means (ṚV. 10, 145).

There may be an indication in the Veda of a surprising fact: the king of the gods, the bellowing bull, was able to assume the form of a woman. That a quality of female affection could be ascribed to him is proved by ṚV. 8, 1, 2 where the poet states his loving familiarity with his chosen deity:

> *Vaśyāṁ Indrāsi me pitúr utá bhrā́tur ábhuñjataḥ mātā́ ca me chadayathaḥ samā́ Vaso*

"Thou, Indra, art better for me than my father or my brother, who do not feed me; Thou pleasest me, being equal to a mother."

The place where Indra is called a wife or woman (ṚV. 1, 51, 13) is very obscure; one of those many allusions to unknown or very defectively known myths in which the Ṛgveda is so abundant. In the stanza mentioned it is said that "Thou gavest to the aged and staggering Kakṣīvant, when he pressed soma, a young girl Vṛcayā; thou becamest the Menā of Vṛṣaṇaśva, O ingenious One; all these (deeds) of Thine should be proclaimed at the sacrificial sessions" [1].

The ṢaḍvBr. 1, 1, 16 in the passage on the Subrahmaṇyā referred to above calls Indra also by the name "Menā of Vṛṣaṇaśva!" and offers as an explanation of this usage that Indra was in love with Menakā, the daughter of Vṛṣaṇaśva Menā—an unsatisfactory statement, for if this was the case, why should Indra have been said to become a Menā? Sāyaṇa on ṚV. 1, 51, 13 avoids this difficulty by asserting that Indra came to Menakā in the form of Menā who was a woman in Vṛṣaṇaśva's household. It is not clear what he means by this. Did Indra really assume Menā's form or did he only disguise himself as this woman as Geldner interprets ?[23]. That he really became Menā is said unambiguously in JaimBr. 2, 78: *Vṛṣaṇaśvasya ha Menā bhūtvā Maghavā kula uvāsa* "having become Menā, the Bounteous One lived in Vṛṣaṇaśva's household". In the same tradition stands MS 2, 5, 5 (p. 54, 7). KS 13, 5 (p. 186, 6) gives a similar story but with Vilisteṅgā in the leading part: *Indro vai Vilisteṅgāṃ dānavīm akāmayata, so 'sureṣv acarat. Stry eva strīṣv abhavat, pumān puṃsu* "Indra loved the demoness Vilisteṅgā. He lived among the Asuras. He became a woman among the women, a man among the men". This version points to temporary disguises assumed by the god in order to have unhampered access to his beloved—a motif which exists also later in Indian literature. Oertel[24] collected some instances from popular folklore and literature on the motif of a man who approaches his beloved by disguising himself as a woman; certainly they constitute interesting reading from the viewpoint of cultural history, but in our opinion they are of no avail for explaining the obscurity of the Ṛgvedic allusion to Menā. Oertel takes for granted the ṢaḍvBr author's assertion that Indra changed himself in order to win the king's daughter, but it is better to be sceptical about the trustworthiness of this tradition. Eggeling, while commenting on ŚatBr. 3, 3, 4, 17,[25] deems it likely that the myth in question had been forgotten in the time of the ṢaḍvBr. when a new version had come into existence. In any case we are not in a position to permit ourselves a definite judgment on the problem. Besides, the word *menā* is used also on other places in the ṚV. as a noun meaning "woman" or "wife".[26] And the place ṚV. 1, 51, 13 has been interpreted in a completely different way by Kane, 1962, p. 950f. This author, who tried to show on the pages mentioned that there existed in the Veda a lively tradition of devotion to Indra (Indra-bhakti), suggests that Indra's becoming a wife was done out of compassion: "It will be clear.... that he (Indra) assumed the form of a wife for the sake of a devotee..". After giving a few other instances of Indra's compassionate nature, the author says: "these stories...remind us of the stories in the works of the medieval sages".

It is very improbable that medieval themes can be transplanted as such into the Vedic age with its completely different social setting and economic background. But Kane's ascription of this feat of Indra to his compassion as motif does not at first sight seem impossible, the less so because in the same stanza Indra is said to have given Vṛcayā, apparently as a boon, to his worshipper the aged Kakṣīvant. Is it unthinkable that Indra became a human woman in order to gratify the wish of a privileged devotee? The motif of Menā—as an incarnation of Indra or not—would in that case be related to that of Urvaśī, the divine "nymph" who lived with king Purūravas. In later tradition Menakā—who seems to be a mythological double of Menā—indeed appears as an Apsaras and also (mostly with the name Menā) as the wife of the Himavant and the mother of Pārvatī.

The Menā problem is complicated still further when the question is posed who was the Vṛṣaṇaśva whose Menā Indra became. His name is mentioned only once in the ṚV. and thus there is no contemporary hint that he was even a king at all. And it is necessary to look with Geldner, l.c., to ṚV. 1, 121, 2b: *ánu svajáṃ mahiṣáś cakṣata vrā́ṃ ménām áśvasya pári mātáraṃ góḥ* "as a buffalo he desired the lusty female born from himself; the menā of the horse he made into the mother of the cow". And V 10, 111, 3b says: *ā́n ménāṃ kṛṇvánn ácyuto bhúvad gôḥ pátir diváḥ sanajā́ ápratītaḥ* "the Stable One, producing a menā of the cow, the Ancient One, he became the Lord of heaven, without adversaries". In the stanza cited first Indra seems to be presented as desiring his own daughter, a mare; he fecundates her with or changes her into a cow. In the second stanza the *menā* is said to be a cow herself; and it is noticed that Indra's marvellous feat assures him cosmical supremacy. The details are completely unclear, especially when it is remembered that the name Vṛṣaṇaśva means "bull-horse" or perhaps "stallion".

It seems as if the human and the animal element merge in this dim distance; and we wonder if the Menā has been conceived as a theriomorphic deity by appearing as whom Indra played an important creative role.

These allusions in the ṚV. remain obscure, but in any case Indra seems to have been thought of as changing himself into a female, be it of a human or an animal form. In the other Mantras and the Brāhmaṇas, however, there is the tradition, as we saw, that Indra might become a woman with selfish ends in view (we notice that according to ṚV. 8, 104, 24 a *yātudhāna* or sorcerer is able to appear both as a man or a woman). According to the ṢaḍvBr. l.c., Indra is called Menā because he loved Menakā. In the KS. l.c., it is said that he moves among the Asuras in order to make love in secret to their woman Vilistеṅgā, although we have to admit that according to AV. 7, 38, 2 the Asura woman forced him to come to her. No wonder that the texts recognize that Indra incurred grave dangers by behaving himself like this. The MS. 2, p. 54, 4 (according to Geldner l.c.) says that "by Nirṛti that woman is caught who possesses a male form, and also that man who possesses a female form", adding that when Indra became Vṛṣaṇaśva's Menā he was caught by Nirṛti. The ritual cadre in the MS. is that Indra succeeded in liberating himself by performing the subrahmaṇya sacrifice. Something similar is told in the KS. on the occasion of the Vilisteṅgā myth. Nirṛti chased away by Indra became a castrated animal. Thus, uptill now, the texts conclude, if a person feels caught by Nirṛti (impotent ? abnormally inclined ?), he should offer a castrated animal to Indra. It should be added that during this same ceremony the officiating priest himself is also called Subrahmaṇyā, that is he is addressed as a female.[27] Like his divine prototype, he acts by māyā, with natural human ends in view for himself or the sacrificer his client, and evades the dangers.

We add succinctly that in post-Vedic literature when Indra has lost his paramount position, he is still sometimes said to figure on earth in a human shape, usually to take human beings to test or to present some religious truth. In the story of Uttaṅka in Mbh 1, 3 the hero of the legend is presented by Indra, who appears on his way as a horseman, with startling difficulties, despite the fact that Uttaṅka was on a very urgent and delicate mission. In the cadre of this mission Uttaṅka's immediate goal appears to be that the serpent demons come under his power (*nāgā me vaśam īyur iti*), and Indra turns out to be the one who helps him realize this.[28] In Mbh. 1, 76, 4 during the tale of Yayāti it is told that Indra in the shape of Vāyu the god of Wind blows into confusion the clothes of bathing girls. One other instance, from the Kathās. 1, 7, 89: as a falcon (*śyena-*). Indra takes King Śibi to test. He pursues Dharma who has changed himself into the guise of a pigeon (*māyākapotavapuṣam*). The pigeon takes refuge with Śibi who offers to the falcon as much of his own flesh as the pigeon weighs. The pigeon keeps growing, and at last Śibi lays himself down on the scale. At that moment a divine voice cheers at him and Indra and Dharma again assume their usual form.

As a modern instance we mention a tale told by Swami Ramdas, in which Indra humiliates a deluded brahman.[29]

Having thus discussed a few instances of the application by the god Indra of his māyā or power of changing himself into another form, one may try to resume the methods applied by him and the goals which he aspires after. When Bergaigne points out[30] that in the Veda Indra is only benevolent in character because he always fights the demons, this may be true when seen out of the dualistic conception of the eternal strife of the Devas against the Asuras. But we can say something more. Both gods and counter-gods make use of their māyā, and both do this with their own ends in view. The fact that the human beings are on the side of the gods turns the latters' māyā, so to say, into "white" and that of the Asuras into "black." Morals do not exist in their own right in Vedic society; or, in any case, in another way than in our own times. The gods, when fighting the Asuras, take off the truth of their Speech and depose it with the Aśvins and with Pūṣan; after they have conquered the Asuras by untruth, they again obtain truth from the Aśvins and Pūṣan.[31] Also a human being, even when pursuing selfish goals from our point of view, may try to realize them by means of the māyā which is, of course, "white" for him. An instance is furnished by AV. 4, 38, 3, where luck in gambling is invoked by the aid of māyā (Devanandan, p. 21).

Turning now again to Indra, and applying ethical standards, we cannot say that this god uses his wonder-working power always in an honest way. On the contrary, he sometimes acts like a murderer and a deceiver. We shall overlook the fact that he is a drunkard; but he is invoked to bring the enemies out of their senses (AV. 3, 1, 5). He casts his net of magic (Indrajāla) over his adversaries (AV. 8, 8, 8; see below, Ch. 5) he tricks them into death by means of ignominious ruses. He kills Namuci while basing himself upon a flagrantly mischievous interpretation of their mutual treaty.[32] He steals the sun. He steals the Water-of-Life from the snakes (Mbh). He craves for another's wife. His behaviour became even too much for the gods themselves who decide to exclude him from the Soma draught because of his misdeeds against Viśvarūpa the son of Tvaṣṭar, against Vṛtra, the Yatis, the Arurmaghas and Bṛhaspati. Yet Indra gained access to the Soma by stealing it from Tvaṣṭar.[33]

The malicious sides of Indra's character are brought into the foreground by a younger Vedic text, the KauśBUp. (3, 1) where the god boastingly admits them himself during a remarkable discourse with Pratardana. "The supreme gift", Indra says there, "is to know me". In the next paragraph he expounds that he is to be considered as the prāṇa or life breath, but before that he gives a short survey of his mighty deeds [2]: "I killed the three-headed son of Tvaṣṭar (Viśvarūpa, his own domestic priest); I delivered the Arunmukha Yatis (?) to the Sālāvṛkas (jackals ? sorcerers or demons in the guise of wolves ?); by transgressing many treaties I crushed the sons of Prahlāda (these were millions of Asuras of great magical powers according to the Skt. commentary) in heaven; in the intermediate space (I crushed) the Paulomas, on earth the Kālakañjas; and in all these circumstances no hair of my body was hurt. And he who knows me (the Skt. commentary interprets: who creates me before his eyes, *sākṣāt kurvataḥ*), by no deeds of his of whatever nature will his future world (*loka-*; one might expect *loma-*"hair of his body") be hurt, not by theft, not by killing a brahman, not by killing his own mother or father; of him, even when he commits evil, the bloom (thus Cowell; text: *nīlam*; comm.: *kānti-*) will not depart from his face." The Skt. commentary adds that Indra is the knower of the Ātman; and because he possesses that insight, the ordinary ethical code does not apply to him. His insight was the result of his good karman. In the same way, the person who associates himself with this Indra and obtains insight into the nature of prāṇa and ātman stands above morality. We observe how the tradition of Indra's divine amoral behaviour has been adapted in this esoteric passage into the pattern of the emancipatory role of the yogin's course.

Still the meditation upon Indra's delusive powers may lead man also to more worldly ends, as is stated by ṢaḍvBr. 1, 2, 7-11: the priest who calls Indra during the Subrahmaṇyā litany with the names memorizing his various māyās or wondrous transformations, adding some formulas for driving away evil spirits, will procure to his sacrificer in an abundant manner the salutary forces of *brahman* and *śrī*. And in the next paragraph it is added that "this is the expiatory rite (*prāyaścitti-*) for all that is known and that is not known."

Our Vedic sources on the subject are too vague. But what must have been meant by the two text passages discussed above is that by a summing up of and meditation on the manifestations of Indra's māyā the worshipper or sacrificer obtains earthly welfare, atonement for evil, and even, if he has realized the faculty of mystical insight, the way to release from the round of births.

3. *Viṣṇu's māyā in the epic*

The considerable change in economical and social circumstances which took place between the periods of the early Veda and the epic is reflected by the emergence of other views of the world, other ideals, a changed mythology and other gods in the pantheon. We now turn especially to Viṣṇu who is in some respects Indra's successor in Indian religious history[34] and observe how this god applies his māyā or supranormal creative power. Already in the Vedas it is said that Viṣṇu by his mighty three steps kills his rivals.[35] In the epics the faculty of māyā is often ascribed to the Supreme God, be he Viṣṇu or another, and his unpredictable and seemingly irresponsible dealings with mankind.[36] We dwell here on a few instances in which the māyā of Viṣṇu/Kṛṣṇa is reflected upon in a characteristic manner. They belong to the best known passages from the Mahābhārata.

In Mbh. 3, 31, 19 the leader of the Pāṇḍavas, Yudhiṣṭhira,

has been beaten by Śakuni in the game of dice and in consequence thereof the Pāṇḍavas with their common wife Draupadī are driven out of the capital Hastināpura. This causes Draupadī to lament on God's unfair treatment of mankind as the cause of their precarious situation. The passage is worth to be looked at with some attention.[37] [3]

"My mind comes to an extreme state of bewilderment," Draupadī says, "and is distressed now that I have realized our sorrow and calamity of this size. Certain old sayings now come to my mind: the world stays in the power (*vaśe*) of the Lord, it has no power over itself. It is the Creator Who disposes happiness and sorrow, experiences which are hoped for or detested, to the creatures, pronouncing the bright things first. Just as a clever and experienced man keeps in motion the limbs of a wooden woman puppet [I follow the Southern recension], in the same way (God acts with) these creatures, O King. Like Space, the Lord pervades all beings and distributes here on earth the good and evil (experiences). This (world) without doubt is powerless, abiding in the power of the Lord, no master over itself nor over others, just like a bird bound to a thread. Like a jewel tied to a string, like a bull bound by a nose ring, (the world) follows the Creator's instructions; it is completely His, consigned to Him. Man is not even for a moment of time master over himself, like a tree torn loose from the bank and floating in the middle of the stream. These creatures are ignorant and without control over their own happiness or unhappiness; urged on by the Lord they reach heaven or hell. Just as some tips of grass are in the power of the overwhelming wind, so all creatures are in the power (*vaśe*) of the Creator, O Bhārata (28). No matter if the Lord binds them to noble or evil karman, penetrating the creatures He roams about without being observed. . . . Observe the power of His māyā, as it is wielded by the Lord: He causes living beings to kill living beings, having deluded them by His own māyā (31) . . . . (35) that Lord, the Spontaneously-Born One, the Primeval Grandfather, disguising Himself (*chadma kṛtvā*) harms the living beings, using them as His tools; this Lord, combining and separating, acting according to His own desire, plays as it were with His creatures just like a child with his toys. Not like a mother or a father, O King, does the Creator deal with His creatures; it seems as if He acts in a rage, just like all other human beings here on earth" ....When I observe how noble and righteous beings are in a shameful and wretched position, and how the rascals (*anārya*) are happy, my mind is disturbed...."

In this impressive lament Draupadī shows herself overwhelmed by man's powerlessness and helplessness before the irresponsible drive of the divine activity which seems to play a cruel play with mankind. It is true that the divinity addressed here is Brahmā, the Creator and Grandfather of the human race, but Yudhiṣṭhira in his answer in the next chapter (Mbh. 3, 32) clearly identifies this Creator with Kṛṣṇa/Nārāyaṇa Who is the All-god. The essence of Yudhiṣṭhira's pious pleading is that Draupadī by speaking thus has fallen into an irreligious (*nāstikya*) point of view. One should on the contrary always honour and adore the Lord Who opens the door to final release out of the evils of the world, says Yudhiṣṭhira. But Draupadī's words retain their force and are certainly not without parallels. Already in AV. 4, 16, 5 (a cursing stanza) it has been said that Varuṇa handles his creatures according to his will, like a dice player the dices.[38] Another instance is to be found in the drama Mṛcchakaṭika, where in the sixth act Vasantasenā says[39]: "Alas ! alas ! O Lord, Destroyer ! Thou playest with the fortunes of mankind which for Thee are equal to drops of water fallen from a lotus leaf" [4].

Viṣṇu's māyā is alluded to on several places in the Great Epic. For example, in 12, 325, 4 Viṣṇu is called among others by the name *mahāmāyādhara* "Bearer of supranormal Māyā" (compare PST. 21, 59 *māyātman*). In Mbh. 12, 290, 57 [5] it is stated by Bhīṣma that the world is to be compared to foam of the waters, enveloped as it is by Viṣṇu's hundreds of māyās. In the next lines the speaker dilates upon the pool of inertness (*tamas*) in which the quality of activity (*rajas*) has been immersed like a helpless (*avaśa-*) elephant sagged in the wet mud of a drinking pool. Only those who reflect (*sāṃkhyāḥ*) are able to cut these bonds by the sword of wisdom and the rod of asceticism (st. 60); the perfect munis cross the dreadful ocean of existence. After some intermediate stages they reach the Lord Nārāyaṇa who at last causes them to enter the Supreme Ātman (76).

The best known statement on Viṣṇu's māyā from the Mbh.

is without doubt BhGītā 7, 13-15 [6]: "By these three ways of existence which consist of the (three) basic qualities (guṇas) this whole world is deluded (*mohitam*); it does not recognize Me as being elevated above them and imperishable, for divine and difficult to overcome is this māyā of Mine which consists of these three qualities. But those who seek their refuge in Me alone will cross this māyā. The evildoers, the deluded (*mūḍhāḥ*), the despicable sort of men, do not seek their refuge in Me; their insight has been taken away by the māyā, so that they cling to a demoniac state of existence".

In this passage the māyā occurs as a deceptive power by means of which the Supreme Lord subdues those who do not resort to Him or worship Him as their God. Those who possess the insight realize that this māyā is no other thing than the three basic strands of the cosmic process. The evildoers, however, are caught by these three and deluded by them. This means that they have fallen into the state of demons, or, more exactly, counter-gods (Asuras) doomed to be tricked and subdued by God's power. The Vedic Asuras who were overpowered by Indra and the other gods have taken on human flesh and blood here as the sinners and heretics. The god who wields this māyā has some affinity with the god of the Old Testament who made the King of Egypt to harden his heart. No clear distinction is made between human responsibility and divine decree of destiny. The deluded are the same as the evildoers.

It is important to note in this connexion that by His māyā God as it were conceals Himself from ordinary creatures. Although we evade the question of etymology, one should point to one of the names by which Viṣṇu is known in Tamil literature: Māyōn "He who conceals Himself" (Tamil root *māy-* "to conceal").

In BhGītā 7, 25 Kṛṣṇa says that he is not revealed to everyone because he is veiled by his māyā which is a yoga, which means that it realizes itself by a methodical exertion from the side of God. In Mbh. 12, 323, 42 it is told how Viṣṇu appeared on a certain hour of worship, while the people present were unable to observe him "deluded by his māyā" (*vayaṃ tv enaṃ na paśyāmo mohitās tasya māyayā*; place discussed by Devanandan, p. 66). From later literature we cite KulaCT. 1, 18;

māyayācchādya cātmānam "having veiled Myself by māyā" (here the Great Goddess is the speaker); while Kabīr in one of his poems accuses Hari (Viṣṇu) of being a brigand who avoids being recognized hiding himself and terrorizing the innocent soul.

The māyā is a veil, a shroud, like the shroud in the temple by which the image of God is usually concealed from the eye of the spectators. Rāmānuja, on BhGītā 7, 14, mentions as the specific function of the māyā that it causes the real nature of the Lord to disappear (*asyāḥ kāryaṃ Bhagavatsvarūpatirodhānam*). Nīlakaṇṭha in his commentary on the same passage of the BhGītā calls the māyā a mirror created by phantasy in the Pure Intelligence (*cit*) in which no difference between God and soul exists. The false representations created by this mirror overpower or subjugate (*vaśīkṛtya*) the individual soul which in reality is no other thing than a reflection of that Pure Intelligence, and obscure that reflection.

It is remarkable how this idea of "subjugating" (*vaśīkaraṇa-*) is in the minds of the epic authors and the commentators when they come to reflect on God's māyā. God is sometimes called a *vaśin* "Possessor of subjugating power", perhaps for the first time in ŚvetUp. 6, 12: *eko vaśī niṣkriyāṇāṃ bahūnām* "the unique Possessor of the power which subjugates the many (souls) which are without activity". The Mbh. calls Hari a *vaśin* in 12, 326, 9. And the Balinese hymn called Vedasāra (Stuti & Stava No. 381) in its second stanza says the same: *vaśīkaro devo Viṣṇuḥ, sarvaśatrubhayaṃkaraḥ* "God Viṣṇu is a Subjugator Who inspires fear in all His enemies". Draupadī insisted that the entire world is in the Lord's power (see above), and the same is implied in Mbh. 8, 49, 17 where Kṛṣṇa pronounces his judgment on mankind:

Aniścayajño hi naraḥ kāryākāryaviniścaye|
avaśo muhyate pārtha yathā tvaṃ mūḍha eva tu||

"Man is incapable of any decision on the moment of decision between what should be done and what should not be done; devoid of disposing power, he is subjected to delusion, O Arjuna, just as you are deluded."

In Mbh. 13, 135, 135 it is again declared that "this world comprising all moving and unmoving creatures, including the gods, counter-gods, Gandharvas, Yakṣas, Serpents and Rākṣasas, is in the subjugating power of Kṛṣṇa"; and, in st. 140: "The unique Viṣṇu, the Supranormal Being, has penetrated the beings separately in different forms, the three worlds; and He, Whose Self is identical with the beings, enjoys them, the Enjoyer of all, the Imperishable One" [7].

In a more philosophical context the māyā itself is stated to be a subjugating force by Nīlakaṇṭha in his commentary on BhGītā 7, 14: "The mirror of māyā which has been conceived within the Pure Intelligence in which no separation between Soul and Lord exists— (this māyā), having subjugated the Soul the form of Which is a reflection of Intelligence proceeds obstructing the quality of Intelligence inherent in its reflectory nature" [8]. Another view is expressed in two stanzas quoted by Dhanapati in his commentary on the same passage of the BhGītā: "It is taught that Nature (*prakṛti*) which consists of the three strands of inertia, activity and lucidity is twofold (viz. pure and impure); it is further taught that out of the pure and impure aspects of its nature develop māyā and avidyā ("Ignorance"). The Lord, the Omniscient One, Whose reflection is the māyā, keeps Her (Nature) in subjection". The reader might remember the words of the ŚvetUp. 4, 9: "Out of it the Wielder of māyā creates this entire world; but by this same māyā the others are being captivated within it" [9]. Śaṅkara on BhGītā 9, 8, while paraphrasing the word avaṣṭabhya which denotes the activity by which God is said to influence Nature, again uses the term vaśīkṛtya "having subjugated". As an instance from the Purāṇas there is DevīBhPur. 6, 31, 46f.: "the whole world including gods, counter-gods and human beings is subjected to māyā; the embodied soul, being subjected to māyā, moves about in obedience to its subjugating power" [10]. This power of subjugation (*vaśīkaraṇam*) is also one of the most characteristic faculties of the earthly magician, as will appear below (see Chapter 6.5).

4. *Deluded by māyā*

Another faculty which is of a specifically magical character and which is constantly, almost invariably expressed side by side with the Lord's māyā is that of "delusive power". The AV. (3, 1, 5) invited Indra to delude the inimical army with the words *Indra senāṃ mohaya* and *Indraḥ senāṃ mohayatu* (st. 6);

while in AV. 6, 67 both Indra and Pūṣan were addressed for this end with an additional command to the army itself: *múhyantv adyámūḥ sénā amítrāṇām* "these armies of the enemies should at this moment become deluded (lose their senses)". This idea of causing others to lose their senses (*mohana-*) is applied in the epic and the Purāṇas on the speculative plane. Viṣṇu deludes (*mohayati*) mankind and mankind is being deluded (*mohita-*) by Him so that they are bereft of their senses (*mūḍha-*) and lose the way to final release out of sight. Nīlakaṇṭha on BhGītā 7, 15 paraphrases *mūḍhāḥ* with *ātmānātmavivekahīnāḥ* "being devoid of the insight into what is the Self and what is not the Self"; indeed the word *moha* "delusion" often occurs in philosophical texts as a synonym of *ajñāna* "ignorance", the fundamental cause of man's being bound to the karmic existence. This delusion is compared to the state of the credulous spectators at a performance of jugglery who with open mouth gaze at the creation of mystery without realizing the trick. Rāmānuja on BhGītā 7, 14 argues that also a magician is called *māyāvin* "possessor of māyā" because during a magical performance he creates the idea of reality with respect to something which is devoid of meaning; he does so by means of spells, herbs and other ingredients. Further on he adds: "this whole world, deluded by the māyā of the Lord, does not recognize the Lord as the embodiment of unceasing boundless joy" [11].

Some other statements on the delusive character of Viṣṇu's māyā are presented now. It would be easy to increase their number. A few cases were already mentioned in passing. Draupadī complains (Mbh. 3, 31, 31) that the Lord "deludes people by His 'māyā". According to BhGītā 7, 13 the world is deluded by the three guṇas. This state of affairs is due to God's māyā (7, 14). The evildoers are deluded; their insight is taken away by māyā (7, 15). Śaṅkara on BhGītā 7, 14 considers the māyā as the force which deludes all beings (*sarvabhūtamohinīm*). In Mbh. 12, 323, 42 those present declare that they are unable to behold Hari "being deluded by His māyā". In Mbh. 12, 47, 48 Viṣṇu is addressed with these words:

Yo mohayati bhūtāni snehарāgānubandhanaiḥ /
sargasya rakṣaṇārthāya tasmai mohātmane namaḥ //

"He who causes the beings to be deluded by the fettering

emotions of attachment and passion in order to preserve creation—to Him Whose Self is delusion, honour". Harivaṃśa (78, 32 Critical note line 12f.) says that on a certain time the karma of all souls will become manifest, and that the māyā which is difficult to see through even for the gods will disappear; the fact that this world is deluded is caused only by the karman [12].

Instances from other texts are abundant. The comparatively recent Kṛṣṇa Up. in stanza 12: *durbodhaṃ kuhakaṃ tasya māyayā mohitaṃ jagat* "difficult to realize are His tricky ways; by māyā is the world deluded". The Purāṇas are never tired of repeating the point over and again. MtPur. 47, 11 says with respect to Kṛṣṇa:

So 'vatīrṇo mahīṃ devaḥ praviṣṭo mānuṣīṃ tanum/
mohayan sarvabhūtāni yogātmā yogamāyayā//

"He, the God, has descended on earth and entered a human body, deluding all creatures; by the supranormal feat of His māyā, because His Self is supranormal activity". Here we again observe the close relation which sometimes exists between the words yoga and māyā. Gonda, 1970, p. 199, n. 120, who cites the passage, translates māyā with "his inscrutable creative power". It seems, however, that the idea of "creativity" is not exactly what is meant in a context like this. It is the incomprehensible faculty of fallacious shape-changing which causes mankind to lose its orientation which is glorified here as the guiding principle of divine behaviour.

From younger sources: BrVPur. Kṛṣṇajanmakhaṇḍa, 78, 19 asserts that man is "enveloped in all his works by passion, anger, greed and delusion, always being deluded by māyā, devoid of insight and weak" [13]. The same text, Gaṇapatikhaṇḍa, 7, 122 reports Pārvatī's words to Viṣṇu: "By Thy māyā I became the Māyā, and having deluded the Asuras in former times I killed them all...". In ch. 8 of the same khaṇḍa (st. 2), Pārvatī is allowed to obtain the sight of Kṛṣṇa's form which is the cause of delusion to all (*sarvamohanam*); this occurs in the cadre of her observance which was taken up in order to obtain a child. In BhPur. 8, 12, 21 Śiva beholds Viṣṇu in the guise of a woman who "deludes the world by her own māyā" (*vimohayantīṃ jagad ātmamāyayā*). And some lines further (st. 38) Viṣṇu, having resumed his own form, says to Śiva:

"Congratulations to Thee; Thou art again restored in Thy normal state of mind; because Thou hast been easily deluded by me in the guise of a woman, by the force of My māyā..." In stanza 43 Śiva then addresses the sages: "Have you beheld the māyā of the Unborn One, the Supreme Man, the most exalted Divinity? I, Who am the Bull of divine constituents, am being deluded by it, although independent of nature (? *vaśa-*); how much more others who are dependent !" The whole twelfth chapter bears the name Śaṅkaramāyāmohanam. The BhPur. constantly repeats the theme. In 8, 5, 30 Viṣṇu is praised "whose māyā nobody is able to overcome; (the māyā,) by which people is being deluded and does not know what is best". In 12, 10, 2:"by Whose māyā even the gods are deluded, and which is cleared up only by insight". In 3, 6, 39: "the māyā of the Lord, which deludes even other possessors of māyā"; and in 10, 23, 50 in honour of Kṛṣṇa: "Honour be to Thee, O Lord Kṛṣṇa of the razor-sharp insight; by Whose māyā our intelligence has been deluded, so that we wander on the byways of karman" [14].

The South Indian Vaikhānasa Āgama called Vimānārcanakalpa and ascribed to the sage Marīci in its concise discussion on the nature of existence (ch. 88, p. 505) argues: "this soul (? text: *dehaḥ*), having undergone birth and being fettered with the noose of family life, is deluded by the māyā of the Lord; and that is the reason that he commits all these sins of passion, anger, greed, delusion, pride, jealousy, and violence" [15]. The BNārPur. (36, 10) varies the same theme with: "They who, being deluded in their minds by His māyā, do not observe the Self although it is within their reach; these same people, when the māyā has gone away from them, observe His own form which is the Self of all" [16]. We do not give instances from literary sources and content ourselves with pointing to Kathās. 12, 25, 51 *māyājālaṃ vimohāya* "a net of māyā in order to cause delusion" and 12, 25, 64 *tanmāyāmohitaḥ* "being deluded by His māyā".

But also Śiva is the owner of a māyā and by it he created delusion according to LiPur. 2, 51, 10: *mohayāmāsa māyayā*. In ŚivaPur. (p. 180, st. 25) the māyā of Śiva is stated to be "difficult to be seen through for all embodied beings here on this earth, except for the devotee who has surrendered himself to God; the whole world is being deluded by it" [17]. Not insight but bhakti is here the quality which is able to lead man out of the māyā. The same force is ascribed to the Great Goddess in DevīBhPur. 6, 25, 24: "the māyā is strong, O brahman, and difficult to be left behind by those who have not developed themselves; it is formless and devoid of symbols; it deludes even those who possess insight"; and in 6, 26, 2: "in this round of births there is no embodied being free from delusion." Even all gods including Viṣṇu and the ancient sages are enveloped by it and wander about on the path of existence. A little further, 6, 28, 2 again repeats: "by māyā the entire world is deluded including moving and unmoving beings" [18]. A related text, the Tripurārahasya, Māheśvarakhaṇḍa, 9, 61, declares: *anādiśaktyā tava māyayā vai baddhā janāś cirakālād vimūḍhāḥ* "by Thy māyā which is the beginningless Energy mankind is bound and deluded from length of time". The same work, Jñānakhaṇḍa,[40] connects the māyā also with Śiva: "People continue to lament without any cause, being deluded by the māyā of Mahādeva". Māyā is like a snake created by magic; but this illusory power of the divine consciousness has no effects on that consciousness itself, just as a juggler is by no means deluded by his own tricks (idem, p. 117). One might compare BhPur. 12, 10, 30: "Not for so much; the experience of the Lord is not defiled by these activities which are only manifestations of His māyā; just like the tricks of a juggler (*māyin*)" [18a]. The image of the juggler has been alluded to above.

Even Buddhist texts apply the theme.. The KCT. (2,12) teaches that everybody experiences sorrow in all six states of his life, and that this whole world is deluded by māyā (*sakalajagad idaṃ mohitaṃ māyayā ca*). The MMD. (22,76) recognizes the māyā as the force which "always is the cause of the world's delusion" (*jagatsaṃmohinī sadā*). The famous Namdev says: "...there is scarcely one who understands Him, all being deluded by the variegated picture drawn by Māyā".[41]

As a special feature of God's māyā it is sometimes told that He assumes other forms in order to delude mankind by teaching false doctrines. The best known instance is ViPur 3, 18, 10ff., according to which Viṣṇu incarnated as the ascetic Māyāmoha and led the heretics astray. An interesting aspect is that Viṣṇu did this in order to come to the aid of the gods who had been defeated by the Asuras.[42] Against the Pāñcarātra school the argument was raised that God had taught its tenets for the delusion of the unbelievers.[43] The same assertion was also made with predilection against the unorthodox Tantric cults.[44]

These instances may suffice. It is clear that there is a very close connection between the māyā of God and the magical power of spreading delusion. It has been shown also that the māyā of this sort is not restricted to Viṣṇu: Śiva and Devī are also said to possess this power, although probably less frequently. In Mbh. 13, 17, 85 Śiva also is called Mahāmāya (Viṣṇu is called by this name in Mbh. 13, 135, 31). Thus the names of the gods may differ, but the way in which they wield their inscrutable powers is essentially the same. These powers appear to human experience as magical in nature. God is a magician. He plays with his subjects. They are brought to bewilderment; they are deprived of their senses and subjugated completely to His discretion. They wander helplessly about on the path of life, being driven out of their homes, as has been so beautifully stated by BhPur. 10, 23, 50 cited above.[45] But by the same powers they are being irresistibly attracted towards God as the Cowherdesses once were to Kṛṣṇa the divine Herdsman and their enchanting Lover; they all forgot their married state and hurried towards him. This is His magical power of attraction (*ākarṣaṇa-*), even recognized by the Balinese hymn (Stuti & Stava No. 540) in its stumbling Archipelago Sanskrit: *Nārāyaṇa kākarṣaṇam* "Nārāyaṇa is the force of attraction". This force is described simply but effectively in this passage from a tribal song of the Bhumij[46]:

"What to do and where to go ?
I can stay no more in my home.
Which magic has he played ?
I can stay no more in my home."

5. *Kṛṣṇa's fallaciousness*

The question may be asked which are Viṣṇu's motives for applying His delusive powers. It is a fortunate circumstance that He very often acts in this way in order to destroy enemies and demons who menace the human race. In this quality he is in the Veda the chief companion, later one of the chief successors of Indra. It is unnecessary to dwell upon this point here. The motivation of Viṣṇu's incarnation as Kṛṣṇa is twofold according to MtPur. 47,12: restoration of the dharma (*dharmasya saṃsthānam*) and destruction ofthe Asuras (*asurāṇāṃ praṇāśanam*). In the Mbh, Kṛṣṇa energetically supports the sake of the Five Pāṇḍavas. He slays a great number of Asuras. He is one of the chief driving forces behind their ultimate victory. With Arjuna he forms a famous pair of "Black and White". He has been considered to represent in particular Viṣṇu's nature of māyā; the Kṛṣṇa Up. (st. 11) calls him *māyāvigrahadhāraṇa* "bearing the bodily manifestation of the māyā".

But we may well ask who is this Kṛṣṇa. The fallacious, even treacherous sides of his character are too well known to be dilated upon here[47]. We shortly recall a few instances. He tricked the enemies in various ways such as confronting them with unnatural darkness (Mbh. 7, 121, 15ff.). He took away Rukmiṇī who was the betrothed of Śiśupāla(2, 42, 15ff.)[48]. He suggested to Droṇa that his son Aśvatthāman had been slain which was not true (7, 164, 101f.). He censured Yudhiṣṭhira for his generous behaviour towards Duryodhana (9, 32, 1ff.). It was Kṛṣṇa who advised Arjuna to take the opportunity and kill Karṇa while that hero was busy repairing the wheel of his war chariot, notwithstanding Karṇa's request to wait till he had finished the repair (8, 66, 60ff.). Again incited by Kṛṣṇa, Arjuna had already beforehand attacked Bhūriśravas from behind and cut off his arm (7, 117, 54ff.). Of course the opponents do not lag behind in practising evil methods; yet one necessarily feels sympathy for men like Bhīṣma, Droṇa and Karṇa who are fighters of pure and steady mind ; perhaps even for Duryodhana who is cruel and ill-tempered but also honestly courageous in battle. Contrary to the codes of martial behaviour he is killed after being struck on the thigh by Bhīma on Kṛṣṇa's advice (9, 57). In Bhāsa's one-act dramatic play Ūrubhaṅga "The Breaking of the thigh" the details are still more explicit: Kṛṣṇa had slapped his own thigh as a secret token for Bhīma when the latter came into conflict with Duryodhana (prose after st. 22). When Bhīma swung his mace for the decisive blow, Kṛṣṇa himself entered the weapon[49]. Duryodhana's reaction after he has been struck down is that he frankly admits Kṛṣṇa's divinity: "He, by whom Indra's celestial tree has been robbed together with that deity's bumptiousness; and who by His playfulness remained sleeping on the ocean for a thousand years of the gods; by Him, Hari, Who is loved by the world, I have been referred to the clutches of Death after He had entered the hard mace of Bhīma, because He prefers the fight with divine display of power" [19]. Yet on a former occasion the same Duryodhana, according to the Dūtavākya by the same author[50], had uncompromisingly and haughtily thrown all Kṛṣṇa's deceptive methods before his feet, when the latter entered Duryodhana's palace as an envoy. After Duryodhana refused to speak with him still further, Kṛṣṇa fell into vulgar abuses. Duryodhana ordered his brothers to kill the envoy who had exceeded all restrictions inherent in his function; and even after Kṛṣṇa had assumed his multiple divine form (*viśvarūpa*) Duryodhana asserted that he would kill him even if he used all his divine māyās (I, 40).

When Kṛṣṇa comes to speak on his insights respecting truth and untruth[51], he frankly confesses himself to a policy of pure-self-interest: in certain difficult circumstances untruthfulness is admissible. He brings this into practice e.g., in Mbh. 7, 164, 99 where he addresses Arjuna : "Thou shouldst save us from Droṇa : let untruth prevail over truth, for when speaking untruth in a matter of life and death one is not stained by one's untruthfulness" [20]. It is unnecessary to push the matter further; Kṛṣṇa's character and methods are too well known and in proving this we would only repeat other authors. This does not imply that one should adhere to the 19th century theory of a reorientation from the Kaurava to the Pāṇḍava side in the "prehistory" of the epic. The point is only that Kṛṣṇa, this trickster, is the Supreme God who is the ultimate refuge of all mankind. His position involves that he is elevated above all ethics of the ordinary kind. "Observe God's supreme nature and greatness, O Nārada; He is never stained by His deeds, be they good or evil" [21]. And the Purāṇa author (MtPur. 4, 6) applies this consideration to divine behaviour in general: "Because things which should be done or not be done do not entail their effects of happiness or sorrow for the gods, therefore it is not meet that man should deliberate on their actions".

Kāryākārye na devānāṃ śubhāśubhaphalaprade |
yasmāt tasmān na rājendra tadvicāro nṛṇāṃ śubhaḥ ||

Like Indra, Kṛṣṇa is a lover of married women. This side of his nature has been amply illuminated by the Purāṇas and later devotional literature. The *gopīs* or cowherdesses were already alluded to above (p. 25) ; they are married to human husbands but their heart is with Kṛṣṇa. At night they leave their home and go to Him. Do not their husbands have any notion of what is going on ? Certainly not, for Kṛṣṇa by his māyā creates pseudo-gopīs who spend the night with the deceived husbands. By this method, which is described only in comparatively late sources, Kṛṣṇa avoids the taint of adultery, be it in a rather circumstantial way : the real gopīs as a matter of fact are only his own (*svakīya-*), while the husbands content themselves with their magically created counterparts.[52]

It needs hardly be said that God Viṣṇu in His own form is irresistible for womankind. The Śivaite LiPur (1, 80, 19f.) describes how the ladies of heaven are exalted with joy when they observe Viṣṇu entering the celestial city, just as earthly women are often described to rejoice when their king enters the residence: "Then the women, having beheld Viṣṇu, with eyes moving to and fro out of passion, with hips broad, immediately set themselves to dancing, merrimaking and singing; and some of these women, when they saw Hari, sang with their faces gently smiling, their garments somewhat loosened with strings of gold falling loose" [22]. The ability of inspiring womankind with love seems to have been considered an essential feature of divine state. Let us add that the gods, especially Kṛṣṇa and Indra (see above p. 9) often apply this power in order to seduce the wives of the demons or counter-gods ; acts by which they weaken the latters' power[53]. In short, Indra and Viṣṇu may be unreliable, but after all they are on the side of mankind. Perhaps they are unreliable exactly because they are on this side. Thus the māyā can be a power which works for good.

6. *Viṣṇu in disguise*

In keeping with what has been said before about an important aspect of the word māyā in the Veda, it should be noted here that in epic and purāṇic Hinduism Viṣṇu's māyā often reveals itself by the creation of appearances in which this God presents himself in disguise. The first allusion to the assumption of another form by Viṣṇu seems to be RV. 7,100,6 : "what has been Thy motive, O Viṣṇu, when Thou proclaimedst : 'I am Śipiviṣṭa'? Do not conceal this assumed form from us, when Thou wart present in the conflict in another shape"[54] [23]. The ability to assume disguises has been considered to be a peculiarity of Viṣṇu's power from the earliest known source of Indian religion onwards. In a speculative context even the whole world may be recognized as this God in disguise, because by His māyā God, who is in reality One and Unique, appears as if He were manifold[55]. In the Mbh. (5, 109, 5 Crit. Note) Viṣṇu appears in the Northern region as "with thousand eyes, thousand legs, imperishable ; with thousand heads, full of lustre, and observed as manifold by His māyā" [24].

One of Viṣṇu's oldest manifestations in disguise seems to be the Dwarf, who is repeatedly alluded to in the Veda. By means of this māyā manifestation Viṣṇu was able to deceive the king of the demons, Bali the son of Virocana, who had obtained sway over the universe. The Dwarf induced Bali to grant to him as much ground as he could encompass by three steps. When this had been granted, Viṣṇu changed himself into cosmic size and by making three steps won the earth, atmosphere and heaven while Bali was relegated to the nether world[56]. According to AV. 10, 5, 25-36 these three steps can be repeated in the cadre of a ritual for destroying the enemy. The Ṛgvidhāna (1, 17, 4-6), commenting on RV. 1, 22, 17-21 records another interesting application of the Dwarf myth. Stating that Viṣṇu as Dwarf appeared on earth in the size of a thumb in order to kill demons, it suggests that during the funeral rite of *śrāddha* a brahman should put his thumb into the food (saying the Ṛgveda stanzas in question) in order to remove the demons who surround the ritual scene. Obviously the performer's thumb has been thought mystically to represent Viṣṇu in dwarfish manifestation, and the motif is, as always : fighting the enemies of mankind.

The tradition of the Viṣṇu of small size is further represented by his manifestations as a child. The best known is of course the child Kṛṣṇa who in a characteristic passage in Bhāsa's

Bālacarita "The Adventures of the Child (Kṛṣṇa)" is honoured by Nārada as "the Lord of the threefold space who has assumed the state of a babe by His māyā"[57]. The recently born Kṛṣṇa is brought by Devakī outside the house in her arms, and this is described as follows: "She, troubled by sorrow yet peaceful, the moon-faced one, carries in her arms the Teacher of the gods Who is the Cause of security to the worlds, Who effectuates the end of the demons, in Whose hand is the Disc, as if she carried the mountain Mandara". The comparison of the baby Kṛṣṇa with the immense mythical mountain Mandara by means of which in former times the gods churned the ocean enhances the mystery of God who has become child [25]. Like Simeon, Nārada honours the new-born God and he concludes with satisfaction : *hantaitad utpannaṃ kalahasya mūlam* "well, a source of strife has here arisen".

Another important manifestation of Viṣṇu as child is alluded to in Mbh. 12, 47, 38 : "He, Who sleeps as a child, having consumed all creatures and made the whole world into a flood, being Himself the only living being still existent; to Him Whose Self is māyā honour" [26]. At the end of the world (which means : in the period between the existence of two world aeons) Viṣṇu lives on the waters as a child; and this child contains the whole of existence within himself. This was revealed to the sage Mārkaṇḍeya who had obtained the boon of perpetuated existence during an immense period of time. The Mbh. (3,186,77ff.) introduces to us Mārkaṇḍeya swimming on the cosmical flood after the final deluge. When he becomes tired and does not find a place to rest he observes a fig tree (*nyagrodha*) raising out of the water, and on one of its branches a child resting, whose face is like that of the full moon. The sage wonders who this may be. The child who is Viṣṇu invites Mārkaṇḍeya to enter his mouth and rest inside his body as long as the sage may wish. "Then that child suddenly opened his mouth wide, and I, being no master over myself (*avaśa-*) was caused to enter into it by the action of destiny (*daivayogāt*) (st. 91). Then, having entered his belly without hesitation, O King, I saw the whole earth occupied by kingdoms and cities, and the Gaṅgā... (and other rivers)...all these rivers I saw, roaming about in the belly of that exalted One (96). Then I saw the ocean filled by shoals of sea monsters, the treasury of jewels, the gathering place of waters; and I saw Space, lighted by the Sun and Moon, flaming intensely by Its powers of heating which were equal to fire and sun; and I saw the earth, O king, adorned with nuggets. At that time brahmans were busy sacrificing by means of various kinds of sacrificial ceremonies; and the kṣatriyas were busy pleasing all the other ranks of society; the vaiśyas performed their ploughing activities in the required method, and those of the lowest ranks were content by serving the twice born in obedience" [27]. The sage also saw the mountains of Jambūdvīpa and all kinds of animals; the gods, demigods and demons, in short, all that is present in the world during its period of existence he saw in the belly of that divine Child (109). By this vision Mārkaṇḍeya is strengthened; he feels himself reborn and falls to the child's feet (120). He expresses his desire for a full explanation of the things he has seen and which are summarized by him with the word māyā : *jñātum icchāmi tvāṃ deva māyāṃ cemāṃ tavottamām* (122). In answer the Child Viṣṇu explains his cosmical functions and his identity with the other gods and all existence (ch. 187). He sets the wheel of time (*kālacakra-*) into motion (187, 34). He is present in everything, but is observed by nobody. All afflictions which were experienced by Mārkaṇḍeya are aimed in deepest sense at his own hail. (37)

The vision of Mārkaṇḍeya has been retold in the Purāṇas[58]. The essence remains the same: the child manifestation of Viṣṇu, resting on the primeval waters, contains in itself the whole of creation. The BhPur. (12, 10, 1) calls this manifestation a proof of "the power of purposeful application of māyā created by Nārāyaṇa" : *Nārāyaṇavinirmitaṃ vaibhavaṃ yogamāyāyāḥ.* The sage in devotion delivered himself to God and He, again by His māyā, entered the space of his heart (*tadguhākāśam*, 12, 10, 10). This is a hint to the psychological explanation of the vision: this manifestation of Viṣṇu in the waters is present in the very heart of him who by his insight and devotion has obtained communion with the Lord . As is cited by Nīlakaṇṭha in his commentary on Gaṇeśa Gītā 3, 6 [28] :

> "The past and the future, the moment as well as the aeon, that what is to come, be it near or removed; the coarse and the minute,

all these things are contained in the Self of Reflection;
behold, it is Māyā's unfolding !"[59]

Viṣṇu also manifests himself as an animal. Here again, the motivation for these exploits is chiefly the maintenance or the restoration of the dharma in the world. This salutary function of the animal appearances is much clearer for Viṣṇu than for Indra. Of Viṣṇu's ten classic Avatāras five are in animal form: the Fish, the Tortoise, the Boar, the Lion and the Horse[60]. Besides, there is the bird Garuḍa, the god's mount, who may also be considered as a manifestation of certain aspects of Viṣṇu's power. As a bull, Viṣṇu appears in MtPur. 136 where he drinks up a pond which had been created with magical art by Maya, the architect of the demons. Other theriomorphic appearances of Viṣṇu are the Swan, the Serpent (especially Śeṣa) and the Monkey[61].

About these animal manifestations, which will not be discussed further in these pages, the general remark may be added that they probably represent originally independently worshipped beings, seats of supernatural power, and that they were afterwards brought into connection or identified with Viṣṇu, because their nature was felt to be related to that of the latter god[62].

There are still other manifestations. In BhGītā 10, Kṛṣṇa describes himself as the most eminent of all that exists on earth. He is also present in seemingly lifeless objects, for example the śālagrāma stone. A peculiar tradition is that of Viṣṇu fulfilling the role of Śiva's arrow. According to the Mbh. (8, 24, 91) Śiva in his battle against Tripura makes use of an arrow consisting of Viṣṇu in combination with Agni and Soma:

Dṛṣṭvā tu taṃ rathaṃ divyaṃ kavacī sa śarāsanī |
bāṇam ādatta taṃ divyaṃ Somaviṣṇvagnisaṃbhavam ||

A similar tradition is preserved in AitBr. 1, 23 ff. but in another context[63]. In one of Śiva's "plays" performed at Madurai in South India Viṣṇu's manifestation Narasiṃha functioned as the arrow of Sundareśvara, the local Śiva incarnation (Dessigane, 1960, p. 35). The arrow is repeatedly presented in Sanskrit literature as a magical device. AV. 3, 25 deals with the arrow of Kāma aimed by the poet at his beloved's heart. KauśS. 35, 22-28 declares the application of the stanza to be that the performer of a rite should shoot an arrow on a designed figure on the ground (Jacques, p. 245 f.; cf. Renou, Anthologie sanskrite, p. 55). The five arrows of Kāma are a topic in court literature[64].

Coming now to Viṣṇu's human manifestations, we may pass in silence his classical anthropomorphic avatāras like Rāma and Kṛṣṇa because of their great celebrity. Some aspects of Kṛṣṇa, who is much more of a māyā manifestation than Rāma, were discussed above. Here we spend only some attention to the occasions on which the god assumed a momentarily changed form in order to influence some situation on earth. There was already occasion to refer to his appearance as a muni teaching false doctrines (p. 24). In the Ceylonese Buddhist historical poem the Mahāvaṃsa (7, 5ff.) he is entrusted under the name Uppalavaṇṇa with the guardianship of Laṅkā by Sakka (Indra) and incarnates himself as an ascetic, in which guise he is met by Prince Vijaya whom he protects against a dangerous Yakkhiṇī. [29]. The Purāṇas present other instances of a more capricious character. BrVPur. Gaṇapatikhaṇḍa (8, 19) relates how Viṣṇu in the guise of an old, emaciated brahman beggar called at the door of the place where Śiva and Pārvatī were engaged in amorous play and interrupted their intercourse by demanding food and protection [30].

In LiPur. (Uparibhāga, ch.5) he assumes the form of a beautiful young man in order to teach Nārada and Parvata a lesson. In stanzas 86 ff. it is described how these two devotees have decided to compete for the daughter of king Ambarīṣa, called Śrīmatī, on her svayaṃvara (a ceremony during which a princess chooses her own husband from the assembled suitors who usually are expected to be of royal rank). Viṣṇu by his māyā suddenly takes up his position between the two would-be aspirants. They are aware of the fact that this can be no other thing than somebody's māyā, and soon realize that the greatest possessor of māyā is their Lord, Janārdana Himself (108). As was to be expected, the girl chooses the deceitful god by hanging a wreath of flowers around him; and he takes her away with him. The two devotees declare themselves shocked by such behaviour of their God and become bhaktas of Śiva ! (156). "Anybody who listens to this tale", the Purāṇa author asserts, "will become pure of self, push off the māyā and reach Rudra's abode". Of course the author, who promulgates Śiva's greatness, tries to make some fun of Viṣṇu's activities; but this tale is in keeping with what other sources relate on the subject of this god's behaviour. In one of the Śiva legends of Madurai (Dessigane, 1960, p. 75) Mārkaṇḍeya mistrusts Viṣṇu during their conversation on the cosmical waters after the destruction of the world, just because of the god's deceiving his own devotees on the occasion related above.

A variant legend is found in Śiva Pur. (p. 184ff.). Nārada had become proud because of his sanctity and was in the assumption of having vanquished God Kāma. Conforming to Śiva's desire, Viṣṇu thereupon created (*cakāra*) a māyā, as he is the god experienced in māyā (st. 4 : *māyāviśārada-*). He made a town on the muni's path a hundred miles wide. The king of that town, called Śīlanidhi, desires to give his daughter Śrīmatī away by means of a svayaṃvara. He receives Nārada hospitably and asks him to foretell his daughter's future. Nārada broods on a means of obtaining her hand. He runs for his Master and begs him for the temporary possession of that God's beautiful appearance. This is granted, but in secret Viṣṇu provides Nārada with a monkey's face on the divine body[65]. Those present on the ceremony do not notice the monkey face except Śrīmatī herself and two of Rudra's servants who are among the assistants. Śrīmatī feels herself insulted by the sage's appearance and falls into a rage. At that moment Viṣṇu himself arrives in the shape of a king, invisible for all except for Śrīmatī who chooses him for her husband. Afterwards the two servants of Rudra inform Nārada of the real state of affairs; and the sage in his fury curses them to become Rākṣasas.[66]

There certainly existed a belief among the people of God's power over the minds of women. Cases are narrated of clever youths who take advantage of this belief by presenting themselves as Viṣṇu; for example a weaver in Pañcatantra 1, 5 (cf. Winternitz/Jhā, III, 1, p. 323); and the Brahman Lohajaṅgha in Kathās. 2, 4, 148ff. In both cases, the pseudo-Viṣṇu also terrifies the inimical army by appearing in the sky riding on "Garuḍa".

7. *The deceitful manifestations of Śiva*

As an interlude within the presentation of the various aspects of the māyā of Viṣṇu, it is illuminating to have a side-glance at similar characteristics of Śiva. Both Viṣṇu and Śiva can assume the character of mysterious wielders of power, incomprehensible to man, changing their form and intentions at will, holding creatures in their grip, even deluding and cheating them. It seems as if the idea of the divine in the Indian mind is unavoidably mixed up with irrationality, irresponsibility and malicious playfulness. We recall a few characteristic points. In the first place, it will become clear that Śiva, who acts out of supernatural power for his own ends, is also considered a source for those faculties by which man, if endowed with the right knowledge, is able to act supranormally himself.

A short look at the mythological inventory of the primitive peoples of Central India reveals that they sometimes deduce man's magical powers from a mythical first magician. This timeless figure, called Nanga Baiga by the Baiga (Hermanns, p. 303), is considered to be mystically present whenever his faculties are being executed on earth by present-day man. The Nanga Baiga was wedded with his own sister Nanga Baigin and was made by Bhagwan, the all-overseeing *deus otiosus*, to be henceforth the Lord of Animals, Paśupati, and at the same time a powerful magician and sacrificial priest. The Hinduizing traits in this myth of origin have identified the primeval magician with an important aspect of the Śiva of Hinduism. The same Hinduizing tendency is still more pronounced with the Gonds, where the first husband and wife are told to be Mahadeo (Mahādeva = Śiva) and Pārvatī. Although these identifications are due to the ever increasing influence of the "great tradition" of classical Hinduism, yet a basic similarity must be the necessary prerequisite which renders such an identification possible.

The Korkus believe that the powers of sorcery of the Parihar priests have been derived from Mahadeo (Hermanns, p. 85f.). When a Parihar is to treat a sick person, he begins by invoking this Mahadeo who is for the Korku the primeval magician and the tutelary spirit of the performers of magic of today (Hermanns, p. 107). It should be noted that among this people Mahadeo fulfils only this function and does not act as the creator and destroyer like the Śiva of classical Hinduism. During creation he only plays a secondary role as a kind of demiurge beside Bhagwan.

Leaving these data for what they are and coming now to Sanskrit literature, we notice that Rudra/Śiva from the Veda onwards has been conceived of as an uncanny figure, a dangerous being who wanders outside human habitations and is prayed to turn his back immediately after receiving his share which has been set apart for him by a perhaps trembling hand. It may be that of his names Rudra represents an Aryan tradition, as Hermanns (p. 109) asserts; the problem is not relevant here. What is relevant is that this god is repeatedly spoken of with respect and awe in Vedic literature and even identified with the Supreme Being in ŚvetUp. (ch. 3)[67].

The Śiva of classical Hinduism retains uncanny qualities similar to those of the Vedic Rudra. Besides, Śiva is considered a great yogin, wonderworker and magician. His appearance—untidy, the hair untrimmed, clad in tiger's skin, beating a drum, indeed recalls that of the magician (Hermanns, p. 187ff.). He haunts cemeteries. He intrudes while his presence is unwished for by other gods or humans. In the Mbh. there is the famous tale that he destroyed the sacrifice of the semi-divine ancestor Dakṣa because he had not been invited. The same epic gives the legend of Śiva as a child with five locks of hair seated on Pārvatī's lap (Mbh. 13, 145, 30); when Indra made ready for killing the child with his thunderbolt, Śiva paralyzed Indra's arm.

Moral considerations do not figure high in Śiva's psychology. It seems as if this god acts as a personal representation not only of man's dangerous surroundings, but also of the fearsome aspects of his(man's)own psychical possibilities and liabilities. The Southern Indian Āgamas of the Śivaite denomination contain references to the incorporation of fearsome psychic qualities in the figure of Śiva. The Ajitāgama (Kriyāpāda, 1, 13) asserts that among other qualities Śiva incorporates passion (*rāga-*) and hate (*dveṣa-*): *rāgadveṣaṃ ca jantūnām... sarvam etat sa eveśaḥ.* In 1,22 the continuity which connects this Śiva with the ancient tradition of the sages is emphasized : *catvāraś ca tathā Vedā rahasyena vadanti tam* "also the four Vedas mystically proclaim Him"; and in the following stanza Śiva is said to encompass all religious lore of all denominations: "also in the (tradition) of the Fearsome God, and in the other (traditions) like that of the Lord of Animals, and in the Viṣṇuite and Buddhist lore as well as in the worship of the deities of the regions. . all that is no other than He, the Ruler of the gods, the Eternal, called Śiva" [31].

It is often emphasized that this God's conduct runs counter to the usual codes of fashionable behaviour. A characteristic assertion occurs in Stuti & Stava (No. 471, Śivastava, st. 7) :

Abhakṣyabhakṣaṇaś caiva surāpānamadānvitaḥ /
yuvatīratisaṃyuktaḥ sandhyābhraṣṭas tu saṃyutaḥ //

"He consumes what is forbidden for consumption; He is intoxicated with the drinking of fermented liquors; He practises enjoyment of love with young women; He is in the habit of breaking His agreements" (the last quarter contains a corruption). All these deeds are unambiguously ascribed to Śiva in the following stanza (8): *etāni sarvakarmāṇi yaḥ karoti Mahāśivaḥ* "He Who performs all these deeds is the Great Śiva". And almost immediately afterwards, in stanza 10 of this hymn, follows the statement that "a person, whether he is impure or pure, even when he is involved in all kinds of actions (v.l. : desires), should meditate on God Īśāna (Śiva), and he becomes pure outwardly and inwardly" :

Aśucir vā śucir vāpi sarvakarmagato 'pi vā /
cintayed devam Īśānaṃ, sabāhyābhyantaraḥ śuciḥ //

This is only one example of a tradition known all over India where Śiva is adored. A beautiful summary of Śiva's abnormal or extra-human conduct is contained in Māṇikka Vāchakar's Hymn No. 12 (Pope, p. 159f.).

As is to be expected, Sanskrit literature contains also some references to Śiva's māyā. The famous place ŚvetUp. 4, 10 asserts that Nature is māyā and that the Lord is the Owner of māyā. In 3, 1, this text of Śivaite outlook uses the word *jālavān* "possessing net(s)" while giving a description of the mystical nature of Rudra Śiva. Carrying a net may be considered a symbolical expression for the activity of the divine magician who holds mankind in his grip by means of his incomprehensible māyā (see below Ch. 5). The commentary by Upaniṣad-Brahmayogin in this place of the ŚvetUp. explains *jāla* as "the Energy called Māyā, the characteristic activity of which is that it catches the fishes which are human souls".

That the Lord wields this net denotes that he presides over and enlivens this cosmical energy of Māyā (*tadadhiṣṭhātṛtvena tadvān Īśvaraḥ*). In this way he rules all by his ruling powers (Śvet-Up: *Īśanībhiḥ*, explained again by the commentator as *māyā-śaktibhiḥ*) [32].

Later Upaniṣads are more explicit about Śiva's māyā. The Śarabha Up (st. 31) states : "by the subjugating power of His māyā the gods are deluded with the conceptions of 'mine' etc.; it is impossible to proclaim even a minute particle of His greatness". Kaivalya Up. (st. 12; Śaiva Ups., p. 52); "He (the *Jīva* or human soul), his self being completely deluded by the māyā, descends to a body and performs all acts; by means of various enjoyments such as women, eating and drinking he attains satisfaction in the waking state" [33]. Pañcabrahma Up. 24 : "Being deluded by the māyā of the Gracious One the gods do not recognize the Great God, the Teacher of the world, the Cause of all causes" [34]. These places again adduce material for the frequent association of the force of māyā with the magical act of "delusion" (*moha*; see above p. 20f.). A characteristic of Śiva's māyā also is that he hides his real nature by it. It is often said of Śiva that he conceals his nature from human beings.[68] He is wont to have his superior play with other beings trodding about in darkness. His dance constitutes the three strands of creation (guṇas; Kālidāsa, Mālavikāgnimitra, 1,4). The world in its outward appearance is like a dream city created by a yogin of magic powers, as is expressed in the Śāntistava by Tyāgarāja (st. 31) : *māyikasya jagataḥ sthitiḥ. . . .svapna-kālanagarīva yoginaḥ.*

There are numerous legends, especially South Indian, in which Śiva is revealed as the divine Bewilderer and Deluder. Many of his famous sixty-four "sports" or "plays" in and around Madurai were aimed at the bewilderment of the devotees, in order to try them or to prove their wrong convictions; "and in several of these the God is represented in an exceedingly unfavourable light", as Pope (p. xxxvii) with Victorian authoritativeness assures us. Anything in life, especially what is unexpected, terrible, or incomprehensible can be the manifestation of that fearsome arbitrariness of the God Who plays havoc with human emotions. For example, any religious mendicant may be Śiva Himself. It is therefore advisable to treat such persons generously and hospitably, no matter what demands they may make on the host's endurance. Pope, i.c., refers to the tale how Śiva as a religious mendicant took to test a "lowly devotee", who, by the way, was a distinguished doctor, tender of horses and warrior. The mendicant demanded as the food destined for him the flesh of the devotee's only son. After this wish had been granted out of superior devotion, everything turned out to be a mirage, delusion, divine sport.

As an ascetic Śiva sometimes is said to have appeared in order to test the virtue of married women. In the thirty-second of the "sports" at Madurai he becomes a Kāpālika (skull-bearing Śivaite mendicant) for this end (Dessigane, 1960, p. 48). He appears before the wives of brahman sages and of course they cannot stand the test. They are cursed by their husbands to be reborn as merchants' daughters in the town of Madurai, where Śiva again comes in their way as a vendor of bracelets. The most famous instance of Śiva's seducing the wives of ascetics or sages is the Dāruvana legend which is related in LiPur I, 29-34, whereby his māyā the god caused them to fall into evil ways (LiPur I, 29, : *viparītāni petur Bhavamāyayā*) : the legend is also alluded to in inscriptions and in stotras[69]. Some literary references to the pranks and deceit wrought by Śiva are to be found in Gonda, 1970, p. 114f.

There can be no doubt that the character of the divine trickster belongs to Śiva as well as to Viṣṇu Kṛṣṇa; these traditions seem to represent a general conviction about the nature of divine power as manifested to man in the vicissitudes of his existence. But it is the greatness of these gods that they, besides enveloping the soul in a veil of incomprehensible mystery, by their grace grant the way towards release from the ocean of existence by means of unfailing devotion.

The similarity which exists between Viṣṇu and Śiva in certain traits of character is parallelled to a certain extent by recurrent statements of their mystical identity. That Śiva and Viṣṇu, often flanked by Brahmā as the third member of the Trimūrti, are in reality but one is perceived by the wise devotee who is gifted with insight by divine grace. Gonda (1970, p. 96 ; p. 198, n. 93 ; p. 202, n. 186) mentions several cases from the Purāṇas, to which may be added some places from the BNārPur. cited by Jacob on Skanda Up. 9 (Eleven Ath. Ups., p. 161). This late Purāṇa in 14, 213f. warns that the devotee who makes a difference between Hara (Śiva) and Viṣṇu is guilty of thousands of murders of brahmans and goes straightway to numberless hells. In 15, 74-76 Viṣṇu says: "worship the Gracious One (Śiva), who is a manifestation of Mine, with songs of praise as much as you can; He will convey to you all good things without any doubt. I Myself daily worship that Husband of Pārvatī ; therefore, pacify that Ruler with songs of praise, Who is worthy of praise and will grant happiness to you. That God, Who is without beginning or end, and who grants the fruition of all desires, when honoured by you, O King, will procure the best to you" [35].

DevīBhPur. (6, 18, 44f.) describes Viṣṇu as meditating on Śiva and Śiva on Viṣṇu. There is no difference between them. Viṣṇu even assures that his own devotees will go to hell when they hate Śiva. A late Upaniṣad, the Rudrahṛdaya Up. declares (st. 5): "They who honour Govinda, honour Śaṅkara ; they who worship Hari with devotion, worship Him Who carries the bull sign ; they who hate Him of the Deformed Eyes (Śiva), hate the Inciter of Mankind (Viṣṇu); they who do not recognize Rudra, do not know the Long-haired One". The text in st. 7 then alludes to the respective roles of the two gods in the cosmic process : "the seed comes from Rudra, and Janārdana is the womb of the seed". In other words, Śiva acts as the Father of creation, Viṣṇu as the Mother ; a doctrine which is found elsewhere and which might be compared to the legends of Viṣṇu incarnating as a woman and seducing Śiva (see below p. 42). A similar idea is expressed with the help of the image of the cosmic sacrifice in Stuti & Stava No. 636 ("Tribhuvana"; st. 2): *Naivedyaṃ Brahmā Viṣṇuś ca bhoktā devo Maheśvaraḥ* "Brahmā and Viṣṇu are the offered food of the sacrifice, Maheśvara is the divine Consumer".

The Skanda Up. (st. 9) declares on the identity of the two gods : "Just as Viṣṇu consists of Śiva, thus Śiva consists of Viṣṇu ; just as I do not perceive any difference, thus there may be wellbeing during my whole period of life ; just as there is no cleavage between Śiva and the Long-haired One, thus my body is proclaimed to be a seat of the divine ; that soul is the pure Śiva" [36]. In this Upaniṣad, the mystical insight of a religious adept is recorded, and its tone is therefore different from the passages in the Purāṇas on the same subject, which are of a more didactical or moralizing character. The devotee in this Upaniṣad claims the supranormal insight into the secret realities of the divine, together with impregnability during his existence on earth as a direct consequence of that insight ; and this is brought into effect by way of the parallellism which exists between the unity of the divine and the integrated state of the devotee's self.

The equally late Śarabha Up. (st. 24) connects the similarity between Viṣṇu and Śiva with their māyā : "The Māyā of me and of Viṣṇu, O pious one, is the cause of excessive delusion; but She, although difficult to cross, becomes easy to cross by means of the meditation on His (Viṣṇu's) lotus feet":

Atimohakarī māyā mama Viṣṇoś ca suvrata |
tasya pādāmbujadhyānād dustarā sutarā bhavet ||

8. *Mohinī*

Returning now to Viṣṇu we shall consider an important aspect of his māyā not yet taken into account : his manifestation as a woman. The loving and tender side of this god's character certainly was apt to evoke the idea of womanliness. In Mbh. 3, 187, 55, for example, Viṣṇu is called the Father and Mother of all. It is also in the Mbh. that we find the first occurrence of the legend of Viṣṇu's incarnation as a woman. The first book (Ādiparvan, ch. 16) relates how during the churning of the ocean the Water of life was obtained by the gods while the Asuras laid in wait. Stanzas 38-40 : "When the demons saw that most wonderful object, there arose among them a loud outcry for the Water of life, while they roared : 'This is mine !' Then the Lord Nārāyaṇa took on a delusive false appearance (*māyām āsthito mohinīm*). He assumed the wonderful form of a woman and betook himself to the demons. Then these, their minds deluded, gave that water of life to her, to that woman, all the Dānavas and Daityas, because they had lost their minds on her account" [37]. The episode is told very briefly indeed. The name of the woman is not mentioned. It is only said that this appearance was "delusive" (*mohinī*). Later tradition considered the word Mohinī to be the woman's proper name. Besides, the epic, as often, seems to put up two contrasting traditions; the next chapter implies that Viṣṇu obtained the Amṛta by force: "Then God Viṣṇu, the Heroic One, took that Water of life and snatched it from the kings of the demons, the Ruler, assisted by Nara" (1,17,2) "Then all the groups of the gods drank that Water of life, having obtained it from Viṣṇu during the confused struggle" (3) [38]. It is clear that Viṣṇu as Mohinī would not have needed Nara's help, while no allusion to his heroism would have been necessary. In our opinion, the version of ch. 17 is the oldest at this place. In some mss. of the Southern Recension a few lines have been inserted (after 16, 40) which render the controversy still more striking : "She, the māyā of Nārāyaṇa, bearing the jug (with the Amṛta)—while the Daityas together with the Dānavas were sitting down—gave the gods to drink, but not the demons; whereupon they wept". In ch. 17 (after 3) almost the same mss. add : "Hari had the gods drink the Water of life and at the same time kept the bowbearing (demons) far off by the strength of his arm and by his bow" [39].

Although the legend is thus alluded to rather vaguely and confusedly, the motif is clear: by deceiving the demons and snatching the Amṛta from them, Viṣṇu provides for the gods' ascendancy and, as a happy consequence, for the safety of the human race. The motif can indeed be compared with that of Vāc during the ritual Soma purchase in the Veda, as has been argued by Gonda, 1965, p. 68 f., to whom we refer for more particulars.

The Mohinī legend became popular and has been retold in several later sources.[70] The adventures of Viṣṇu/Mohinī have also increased in number among devotional circles of various regions in India. In his regrettably biased book "The land of the Liṅgam", Arthur Miles (p. 37) relates that Śiva was once persecuted by a giant. Viṣṇu changed himself into a young girl and distracted the giant's attention from Śiva who was hiding in a castor oil plantation. Stories of the female Viṣṇu in connection with Śiva seem to have been popular in the Indian South. The Bh-Pur. (a southern source) gives one of them in 8, 8, 41ff. and 8, 12, 12ff. After Viṣṇu had once deceived the demons by his māyā female form (*māyāyoṣidvapur Hariḥ*, 8, 9, 8)Śiva desired to behold that ravishing form of Viṣṇu for a second time. When the other agrees, Śiva loses his head and runs after the woman while his own wife, Umā, looks on (8, 12, 25). He is subjugated by Kāma (27 : *Kāmasya vaśaṃ nītaḥ*). His seed falls on the ground while he runs after her, and lo ! on all these places there originated holy places (*kṣetrāṇi*, 33) of silver and gold. Viṣṇu, however, is pleased and says (39) : "What man will free himself of attachment beside Thee and cross My māyā which creates manifold emotions, being difficult to overcome by those who have not subdued themselves ? This māyā, which consists of the guṇas, will not subject Thee"; and Viṣṇu promises that the Māyā will become the female half of Śiva in his manifestation of Ardhanārīśvara. In stanza 47 the reciter pays his honour to God : "He Who took on the deceitful manifestation of a young woman, deluding the demons, to Him I pay honour" [40].

The same legend is told with some variation in the South Indian Śākta text Tripurārahasya (Māhātmyakhaṇḍa, ch. 48). According to this source Śiva desired to behold Viṣṇu's Mohinī form again and expressed this wish to Viṣṇu. This god considered that Śiva at that time was an ascetic and that he himself would be liable to be killed by fire from Śiva's third eye just as had happened in former times to Kāma. In order to avoid this he worshipped Tripurā, the Great Goddess. Tripurā promised to him (22) : "no matter if you wish to assume a ravishing male or female form, you can have it. You will obtain half as much as my own beauty". Viṣṇu now presents himself before Śiva as Mohinī. Only by touching her Śiva has an emission of semen "just like a quite ordinary man" (51); which means that all the merits of his yoga were lost at one stroke. The morale of the passage is of course : with the help of Tripura everything is possible.

In still another version Śiva and Mohinī become the parents of the South Indian god Śāstar[71]. And Pope (p. lxii) tells the story of Patañjali from the Tamil Koyil Purāṇam : Śiva accompanied by the female Viṣṇu enters the wood Tāraka in order to visit some disobedient seers. Śiva acts as a religious mendicant, Viṣṇu as his wife. When the wives of the sages behold Śiva, they all fall in love with him, while at the same time their husbands desire Viṣṇu. A tumultuous scene follows. The seers go as far as performing a black magical sacrifice against Śiva by means of which they produce a tiger, a snake and a dwarf. When they realize that all their effort is in vain they submit themselves before the divine masters of trickiness.

The name of this very effective manifestation of Viṣṇu has found its way into human magic; with the Baiga of Central India *mohinī* is the word for "erotic magic" or "spell of erotic magic". It used to play an important role in the life of this people (Hermanns, p. 296 ff.).

The chief truth to be drawn from the various versions of the Mohinī motif is that God when disguised in female form is irresistible even for supranormal beings. The female Viṣṇu is the impersonation of the magically delusive nature of existence which fetters all beings to the rounds of births and deaths and the vicissitudes of life. But our interpretation must take another step. All human life is a play of the bewildering presentation by the Māyā. Earthly women are no other thing than an incarnation of the Disguised God. This is taught in the texts by means of the experience of that quarrelsome and conceited devotee of Viṣṇu, Nārada, when he questioned his Lord on the exact nature of māyā. The legend is told in the Śākta text DevīBhPur. (6, chs. 27-30) and is worth to be recounted here in some detail[72]. The context is that Nārada enlightens Vyāsa on that sage's question after the cause of the delusion because of which he wanders through the saṃsāra (6,25,61). Nārada explains that without delusion as the force which maintains life on earth nobody would be incarnated. Even the gods are enveloped by māyā (6, 26, 1ff.). Having narrated how by God's māyā he had been induced to woo a princess and punished for this by means of a curse of his fellow-devotee Parvata, Nārada proceeds (6, 27, 51) : "Once when I visited Viṣṇu and when we were walking in a sportive mood, God took fancy to change me into a woman. I became a king's daughter, being deluded by the strength of māyā". The tale is unfolded further in ch. 28 : "Hear from me, O best of the munis, the salutary legend; māyā's strength is difficult to realize even by munis who are excellent experts in yoga. The whole world including the moving as well as the unmoving beings, from Brahmā down to a blade of grass, is deluded by the māyā which is invincible and difficult to become conscious of" [41].

At a certain time Nārada entered Viṣṇu's palace while the Lord sat in the company of His consort Lakṣmī.

Immediately when she saw the sage entering, the goddess made for her inner apartments. Nārada, somewhat annoyed by this, questioned Viṣṇu about the reason for her behaviour : "I am no bonvivant, no rogue, but an ascetic who has subdued his senses, his wrath and all illusion (*jitamāyaḥ*, 6, 28, 11)".God answers that a man should never stay in the company of a woman married to another, because "māyā is very difficult to overcome, O wise one, even by yogins who have subdued their breath" (14). One should never say of oneself that one has conquered the māyā ; even Brahmā, Śiva and Viṣṇu himself are her subjects how much more earthly creatures ? Time (Kāla), Who is formless, assumes her form as His own (19); in her power live all souls. When Nārada asks for more particulars, God explains that the māyā is threefold, i.e. that she consists of the three guṇas, that she is the support of all; she is omniscient, invincible, assumes many forms and abides in the world pervading everything (24 : *sarvaṃ vyāpya sthitāṃ jagat*). "If you desire to behold the māyā, O Nārada, then ascend Garuḍa with me and accompany me on a journey". They then betake themselves to the neighbourhood of Kānyakubja, where Viṣṇu ordains Nārada to bathe himself in a lotus pool nearby. The place is adorned with many blooming lotuses of many colours, aquatic birds and swarms of humming bees, in short: a beautiful scenery. By means of his bath in this pool Nārada is suddenly changed into a woman.[73] When the transformation has occurred, Viṣṇu secretly takes his leave. Nārada, having assumed his ravishing form (47 : *mohinīrūpam*) is just coming out of the water when a young and handsome king by the name of Tālavṛnta observes her. He asks her after her identity and the woman, who has forgotten her former existence, can only say that she does not know her antecedents and has nobody to rely on (ch. 29, first stanzas). This opens the way for the king who, sick of love, marries her in due ceremony. She obtains the name Saubhāgyasundarī "the Beautiful of the happy family life". The king was so fond of her that he neglected the state affairs and she also was "subjugated by the emotions of amorous play" (29, 17 : *krīḍārasavaśīkṛtā*). She was completely absorbed in her small happy circle and had forgotten all about former wisdom and asceticism. She obtained twenty sons, and "I was again deluded by guarding them and fondling them with tenderness"

(29, 29 : *mohito'haṃ tadā teṣāṃ prītyā pālanalālane*). Still later the grandchildren added greatly to her delusion, and besides there arose within her a certain feeling of egotism (*ahaṃkāra*) by the thought : "I am the most fortunate of all women". "So was I", Nārada resumes, "being deluded by Kṛṣṇa". The vicissitudes of fortune, however, took a fatal direction. A fierce enemy declared war on the kingdom and in the ensuing battle just outside the walls of the capital all the woman's sons and grandsons were slaughtered. The king himself, a broken man, brought the news. The matron went to the battlefield herself and wept over the bodies of her dear ones. Then again Viṣṇu in the guise of a brahman came to her and said (51) : "Why dost Thou despair, O slender one ? Here the ramble of our life has been revealed; because husband, sons and home are no other thing than a cuckoo's cry caused by delusion" [42]. "Millions of mothers", the brahman continues, "lost their sons. Get up and cease weeping. Your sons have reached the other world. They will certainly not return by your crying. You had better go and bathe yourself in that beautiful place of holy water (*tīrtha*)". The woman obeyed and by the bath in that pool, which was the same as the preceding one, she became the man Nārada again. At that moment Nārada obtained the recognition (*pratyabhijñā*) : "I am Nārada, and being in the company of Hari I obtained the existence of a woman, being deluded by māyā (64 : *hariṇā saha strībhāvaṃ prāpto māyāvimohitaḥ*). The man is perplexed but a smiling Hari on the bank calls him : Please come out of that water, what are you doing there ?"

Of course it is true that the māyā which was explained to Nārada in such a lively form is not exactly Viṣṇu's but Devī's; but the fact remains that Viṣṇu is the god who communicates this mysterious force to his worshipper ; and he seems to have devised this ingenious method of instruction on his own accord.[74] There is one other thing : in this complicated legend a certain peculiar structure might be recognized. We shall revert to this below:—

Beside Viṣṇu's appearance as a woman there is the conception of the Māyā acting independently as a female being. A short mentioning of a few facts will suffice ; the subject is too comprehensive. The Gonds know a Māyā devi (Hermanns, p. 418f.), but she might have been borrowed from Hinduism.

In Sanskrit literature, Māyā is often identified with Prakṛti, primordial Nature, after ŚvetUp. 4, 10 : "One should know that Nature is a Māyā, and that the Great Lord is the Owner of the Māyā". The Māyā is also considered to be Viṣṇu's spouse, Śrī or Lakṣmī, especially in Pāñcarātra speculation, where the Māyāśakti is said to issue from Lakṣmī,[74] but also in some places in the Purāṇas (e.g. AgPur. 308; KūPur. 2, 20). In its first chapter (st. 34), the KūPur. presents Viṣṇu saying : "She is My Māyā, My Beloved, without limit; by Her this world is maintained. . .She brings forth the entire world, Nature which consists of the three basic qualities" [43]. According to BhPur. 3, 25 the Māyā is impregnated by God. There is also the doctrine that the Māyā is Sītā, the wife of Rāma. Devanandan on p. 169 refers to some passages in the work of Tulsī Dās on this point ; and one might compare KālPur. 62, 21ff. (Van Kooy, p. 108f.). Not only God's spouse, also God's mother may be referred to as Māyā. We only passingly refer to Buddha's mother whose name was Māyā. The rather recent Kṛṣṇa Up. (st. 7) considers Kṛṣṇa's mother Devakī as such : "Also the invincible Māyā of Viṣṇu, unconquered even by the Unborn One (Brahmā) in former times, is She, Devakī, the Sacred Wisdom Who is praised in song by the gods". The commentary adds that from Her originated the Brahman in the form of Kṛṣṇa [44].

The Great Goddess, Durgā, is repeatedly called by the name Māyā, for example by the Vaiṣṇava text BhPur. (2, 3, 3) : *devīṃ māyāṃ tu śrīkāmo* (*yajet*) "A person who desires welfare should worship the Goddess Māyā," and the commentator says that on this place Māyā=Durgā. MkPur. 81, 41f. (=Devīmāhātmya 1, 41f.) says : "One should not be astounded at this ; it is the yoga sleep of the Lord of the world, the Great Māyā of Hari ; by Her the world is brought to delusion. That venerable Goddess as Mahāmāyā attracts by force even the minds of the wise and hands them over to delusion" [45]. The DevīBhPur. as a matter of course speculates on the nature of the Goddess as Māyā or the Lady of Māyā. In 6, 31, 29 Vyāsa, after having heard of Nārada's adventures described above, instructs Janamejaya as follows : "just as some magician takes a wooden puppet into his hand and makes it dance according to his free wish because it is in his power (cf. what Draupadī says in the epic, see above p. 16), so the Māyā causes the entire world of moving and unmoving beings to dance; from Brahmā down to a blade of grass, including the gods, counter-gods and human beings, all who are provided with the five senses and obey their mind and thought. The basic qualities are the cause for this, O King" [46]. These basic qualities or guṇas, the text proceeds, in their turn have their origin in māyā. The māyā is subjected to the Goddess, Who is the Lady of the māyā (Māyeśvarī). The same DevīBh-Pur. (5, 33, 6ff.) seems to identify the Goddess with Māyā outright. King Suratha has been vanquished by his enemies and is brought to reflection on the nature of delusion in this world and within himself. He is instructed by Sumedhā that She Who is called Mahāmāyā holds all beings in direct dependence upon Her. She has created the world and this world now "abides in subjection to Her, being enclosed by the net of delusion": *tadvaśe vartate nūnaṃ mohajālena yantritam* (st. 13). Even the gods are in Her power because "they also wander about in this world in delusion, by the power of passion" : *te 'pi rāgavaśāl loke bhramanti parimohitāḥ* (st. 15). It is indeed remarkable how the expressions "subjugating power" (*vaśa-*) and "delusion" (*moha-*) sometimes accompanied by a form of the verbal root *bhram*—"to roam, wander", return again and again in the relevant passages, so that they seem to have become little more than commonplaces. It is not without reason that the poet in a meditation stanza on Durgā in the Āsurikalpa[75] honours her as "the Asura Lady Who subjugates the whole" : *Durgām..akhilavaśakarīm āsurīṃ tvāṃ namāmi.*

The Tantric texts are acquainted with the cult of Māyā Śakti, as is shown by Devanandan (p. 67ff.) ; this Śakti is the direct cause of the world of change and sorrow and is personalized in Durgā, Kālī or any other name which may be given to the Goddess. In one of the sacred texts of the Dharma Cult of West Bengal and Orissa it is stated that Mahāmāyā was produced from the left side of Lord Dharma. When she had grown up, Lord Dharma married her against her will[76]. In KulaCT. (3, 42) Mahālakṣmī is called Mahāmohā ; in his introduction to this text on p. 11 Avalon equates these names to Mahāmāyā.

It is quite imaginable that for those who are truly impressed by the transitory and pitiful state of existence the Goddess of Māyā assumes a terrible shape. The Purāṇas know Māyā as the Mother of Death (MkPur. 50, 30 ; ViPur. according to Devanandan). Ekanath, one of the poets of bhakti from the Maratha country, sees the Māyā as "the Great Enchantress" (Devanandan, p. 159). Also Kabīr is haunted by the vision of the Woman (Devanandan, p. 172, who rightly emphasizes the magical character of the bewilderment caused by Māyā). According to Kabīr, the three worlds are held by Her in subjection by means of Her magic spell. She is a huntress. She is a whore who shamelessly strips herself before anyone who happens to look on ; a love-sick princess who prosecutes the poor weaver Kabīr. But the poet has taken his refuge with Rāma; against Him She is powerless[77].

9. *The terrible Viṣṇu*

Like the Māyā Viṣṇu himself as the owner of the power of cosmic bewilderment sometimes manifests himself to human consciousness as a terrible god. The māyā is His bow; Kāla is His arrow which kills the beings (Kṛṣṇa Up. 25). Viṣṇu who is usually the friendly and compassionate Protector of His creatures, may in a few cases go as far as assuming the threatening traits of a demon. It was argued (above p. 2) that in the Veda there seems to exist no essential difference between the wondrous māyās wielded by the gods and those which are in the possession of the counter-gods or demons. Indra is considered a favourable god because he happens to fight on the side of man. Varuṇa's character as the supreme judge and sovereign ruler is still more ambivalent. That the same powers may seem divine or demoniac is functionally connected with the different roles played by them in the eternal struggle for the vital parts of the cosmical organism[78].

In post-Vedic times the Asuramāyā, the magically creative power of the enemies of the gods and the humans, has been partly inherited by Śiva and Viṣṇu and sometimes also by the other gods. BhGītā 9, 12 calls Nature "Āsurī" and "Mohinī". Śiva's terrible appearances are so frequently mentioned and so essential a part of his mythology that they need not be dilated upon here. The dreadful side of Viṣṇu is less frequent and, as a consequence, less known ; but occasional references in the texts bear testimony to the fear which still remained within the god's staunchest devotees. According to the Vaikhānasa text KJ (ch. 99 ; trsl. Goudriaan p. 298), if worship is omitted for some time in His temple, the Lord will take it ill ; the demons haunt the place and extensive ceremonies should be carefully performed in order to avert the god's wrath. In general, any omission in temple ritual will cause its evil results, if no corrective rites (*prāya-ścitta-*) of some kind are made. If the image is not constructed with the expenditure which suits the sacrificer's wealth and status, that person's death will follow (KJ, ch. 21, end). If the measurements are too small, the children will die (KJ, ch. 42).

The ambivalence of all the three chief gods : Brahmā, Śiva and Viṣṇu, is explained by Vyāsa in DevīBhPur. (6, 31, 33). Here again, the three guṇas are referred to as its cause. "These basic qualities are different in nature from each other. They have sprung from māyā. There are three of them, of different sort : pacified (*śānta*), horrible (*ghora*) and deluded (*mūḍha*) ; therefore, man is always constituted out of these. How would he be able to exist without them ?" As a piece of cloth (*paṭa*) cannot exist without the threads from which it has been woven, so both god and man are necessarily built up out of the three guṇas. The gods may be tender (*prītiyukta*—), resentful (*aprītiyuta*—) or despondent (*viṣādayukta*—; 37). This holds good for Brahmā and for Rudra, but also for Viṣṇu (41) : "Also Mādhava, when He is in His pacified state, tender and full of wisdom, will always in all respects be based upon the quality of Lucidity (*sattva*) ; but by a preponderance of Passion (*rajas*) He will become resentful and of a horrible appearance to all beings, because also Ramā's Lord is dependent upon the basic qualities" [47]. And the ViPur. (1, 2, 63) while arguing Viṣṇu's identity with the other gods of the Trimūrti, is even more radical : "When the quality of Darkness is preponderant within Him at the end of a world period, the Inciter of Mankind, assuming the form of Rudra, consumes all creatures in an extremely horrible manifestation, O Maitreya" :

Tamodrekī ca kalpānte Rudrarūpī Janārdanaḥ /
Maitreyākhilabhūtāni bhakṣayaty atidāruṇaḥ //

And in 1, 2, 7, this text described Viṣṇu as the god who "desires to swallow the All" (*Viṣṇuṃ grasiṣṇuṃ viśvasya*). Another source, while praising him as the Cosmical Being, locates Yama in his eyebrows and Kāla in his eyelashes ; these two gods of death and destruction thus are made into inherent parts on vital places of Viṣṇu's cosmical body (BhPur. 8, 5, 42: *bhruvor Yamaḥ pakṣmabhavas tu Kālaḥ*). When resentful, Viṣṇu wields his disc (*cakra*) as a terrible weapon, of which stories are told in the Purāṇas (e.g. BhPur. 9, 4, 48ff.). The fearsome manifestation of the Disc is described in PST. 22, 14ff. and other Tantras.

One of Viṣṇu's Avatāras is especially known as a fierce terrible figure ; Narasiṃha, the Man-lion who came out of the pillar and slew the demon Hiraṇyakaśipu. In the Nṛsiṃha-Uttaratāpanīya Up. the māyā is said to be Narasiṃha's creative power (Gonda, 1965, p. 170). The Narasiṃhāṣṭaka recorded in Bali (Stuti & Stava No. 100), unfortunately in a very defective form, describes Narasiṃha's cosmical body. In other Balinese Sanskrit fragments he appears as a protecting deity of the noblemen[79] (see also below.

The most famous description of the Terrible Viṣṇu is communicated in the BhGītā (ch. 11) by the messenger Sañjaya to King Dhṛtarāṣṭra : the vision which Kṛṣṇa granted to Arjuna when the latter asked him to show his divine secret form. It is not enough to casually declare that this vision symbolizes the Cosmic Fire (Inde Cl., I, p. 486). It stands in the Vedic tradition of the Primeval Puruṣa whom one might call with some anachronism the anthropomorphic representation of existence and also shows a connection with the revelation of the Child on the waters (above p. 30). In some earlier passages the BhGītā already laid stress on the māyā, that magical, supernatural and delusive power of God. A part of the relevant stanzas from ch. 11 are translated once more below, because they are indispensable in the present context (the translation is especially indebted to that by Edgerton).

(11, 7) "Behold, here in My body the whole world and everything which you desire to see is confined on one place, with its creatures moving and unmoving...you are unable to behold Me with this ordinary eye of yours; I give you a divine eye; behold My supreme and lordly mystic power. !" Kṛṣṇa now assumes his divine form and Arjuna bows his head in awe and praises God (11, 16ff.) :

"With manifold arms, bellies, faces and eyes
I behold Thee, Thy form without limit anywhere;
I do not discern an end, middle or origin
of Thee, Lord of all, Who appearest as the All !

I see Thy ornaments: the Diadem, Club and Disc;
Thou art a mass of fire, glowing everywhere.
Thou art hard to look at, no matter from which side,
Thou shinest like the flaming sun of immeasurable size.

Thou art the Eternal, supreme Goal of wisdom,
The ultimate Resort of the whole of existence;
Thou art standing forever as the guardian of dharma,
I experience Thee as the timeless Being.

I behold Thee as the Infinite of infinite heroism,
Whose arms are without limit, Whose eyes are the Sun and Moon,
Whose countenance flames like a fire blazing fiercely,
Who heats all this world by His fiery power.

Between heaven and earth this world is confined
and all this and the regions are pervaded by Thee alone.
When beholding this form of Thine, wondrous and overwhelming,
the threefold world is brought to confusion, O Great One !

For behold, into Thee all these throngs of gods enter;
some of them, full of fear, with folded hands praise Thee—
saying "hail be to Thee !" crowds of seers and perfect ones
exalt Thee by means of ingenious hymns of praise.

When seeing this huge form of Thine, O Great-armed One,
with many faces and eyes, many arms, thighs and feet,
with many bellies, and many mouths tusked and gaping,
these worlds are confused in the same way as I am.

Having seen Thee reaching to the sky, multicoloured,
opening Thy mouth wide and Thy large eyes flaming,
my self has fallen into a state of confusion
and I find no strength and no rest, O God Viṣṇu !

At the moment of seeing Thy mouths tusked and gaping
like the Fire at the end of the world fiercely burning,
I do not know where to go and how to reach any shelter;
be gracious, O Lord of the gods, Who stays within us !

Just as moths who enter the flaming fire
with still increasing speed fly towards their destruction,
in the same way towards their destruction these worlds
enter also Thy mouths with speed still increasing.

Thou lickest while devouring these worlds
on all sides with Thy flaming mouths;
with Thy fiery appearances Thou fillst the whole world
and Thy fearful rays burn it, O Viṣṇu !"

Arjuna trembling and stammering expresses his complete subjection to this God and his preparedness to obey His commands without question. Kṛṣṇa made clear (11, 32f.) that in his frightful appearance he is Time in its destructive aspect who will cause the world to end; all creatures will disappear as the course of nature.[80]

This passage from the BhGītā has set the pattern of similar descriptions of terrible gods or goddesses with cosmic symbolism. Another apocalyptic manifestation of Viṣṇu was experienced by Bhīṣma, a long hymn by whom on Viṣṇu's greatness is handed down in Mbh. 12, 47. In stanzas 37 and 38, the warrior-sage says [48]:

"He Who at the end of the thousand world-periods
(appearing as) the Fire with flaming rays
will absorb the creatures—
to Him in His horrible nature, honour !

To Him Who, having absorbed all creatures
and having made the world into one great deluge,
appears alone as a sleeping child,
to Him of the incomprehensible self (*māyātmane*), honour !"

The cosmical nature of this manifestation is accentuated in st. 44 :

"Whose mouth is Fire, Whose crest is Heaven,
Whose navel is Space, Whose feet the Earth;
Whose eye the Sun, Whose ears are the farthest ends—
to Him in His cosmical nature, honour !"

Of other descriptions of Viṣṇu as the cosmical being we mention BhPur. 12, 11, 6ff. "This is His form as the Puruṣa : His feet are the earth, His head is heaven, His navel is space; His eyes are the sun; the wind is in His nose, the regions are His ears. His genital organ is Prajāpati, death is His lower circulation of breath. The Protectors of the worlds are His arms; the moon His mind; Yama His eyebrows; His upper lip is shame, greed His lower lip; moonlight His teeth, error His smile. . . ." Among his ornaments, He bears His māyā which consists of the guṇas as His wreath of wild flowers. The weapons have also symbolic meanings (14) : the club is the element earth, the conch is water, the disc is fire; his sword is darkness, his bow is Time (*kāla*) and his quiver consists of karma, while the arrows are the senses [49]; and the description still goes on. We do not try to give here a systematic presentation of this Mahāpuruṣa tradition; but it may be emphasized that very often it is the force of Kāla, destructive time, that is equated with these cosmical manifestations of horrible form. Śiva in his fearsome aspect is called Kāla; Durgā appears as Kālī with hanging tongue and breasts, emaciated, swallowing human bodies (as in the Kālikāstotra, cf. Stuti & Stava No. 324, 12). According to DevīBhPur. 6, 28, 18f., the Māyā Herself appears as Kāla : "How would a man who consists of the three (guṇas) be able to vanquish that Māyā ? Because Kāla Itself is Her form, although It is devoid of form and creates Its own form (?); the embodied soul stays in Its power, no matter if it is wise, dull or mediocre"[50].

Demoniac figures can be described in a similar manner. The Balinese hymns to the King of the Demons (Stuti & Stava Nos. 133 and 136) say of Rāvaṇa that he is "very horrible, possessing the brilliance of a thousand solar rays, provided with six heads...he has huge eyes...he bears all kinds of weapons... he is seated on a big corpse, and he is adorned with a serpent as his sacred thread..." And : "he has ten heads, He is a great deity, inspiring terror with his thousand arms; he is horrible, bearing all kinds of weapons, while his row of teeth is equal in lustre to the moon" [51]. The cosmical nature of this Demon King is proved by stanza 3 of No. 133 :

Īśaḥ puruṣo vidyā ca kālo rāgo rajas tamaḥ /
sattvaṃ buddhir ahaṃkāro manaś caikādaśānanaḥ //

"The three realities; the Lord, soul and wisdom; time, passion, the three strands of activity, inertia and lucidity;

reflection, ego-consciousness and mind; these are His eleven faces".

By realizing the terrible and demoniac nature of existence man obtains for himself, seemingly contradictory to say, a high degree of safety and protection. Meditation on the Terrible God means identifying oneself with Him. In iconographical tradition, fear-inspiring figures of gods and demons often have a protecting function.[81] In the Mbh. (3, 186, 16), Mārkaṇḍeya declares : "Who knows this Puruṣa, even the gods do not know him". The Balinese Buddhastava (Stuti & Stava No. 528) which describes Buddha as the "subjugator of all creatures" (? *sarvabhāvavaśaṃkara*, st.2) with "flaming mouth" (*jvālāmukha*, 3); but this same "adept in yoga" (*mahāyogī*, 4) is pacified (*śāntika*,3) and liberates from all stains (? *sarvakleśavimuktanā*, 4).

There is another aspect of Viṣṇu's māyā nature which has not been discussed in these pages: his ability to assume different colours. This subject will be treated below (ch. 4). Instead, the next chapter further concentrates on the utility the māyā of the gods can have for mankind itself, especially for the religious adept who is able to say (GarPur. 194, 22) : "I include all the gods in myself; I am invulnerable to all creatures, because of my meditating on the God of gods, Viṣṇu of boundless fiery lustre".

Apradhṛṣyo'smi bhūtānāṃ sarvadevamayo hy aham /
smaraṇād devadevasya Viṣṇor amitatejasaḥ //

2. WORSHIP AS SĀDHANĀ

1. *Divine power and man*

At the beginning of this chapter it seems opportune to repeat some important trends of Indian religion and world view. They may shed a better light upon the chapters which are to follow while providing the link with what has been argued in the preceding pages.

1. A fundamental aspect of Indian thought is the conception of a basic, mystic unity between macrocosm and microcosm. The cosmic process is reflected in human existence. Speculations on the nature of things, the cosmos, and God find their parallel in speculations on the individual soul and personal life. The structure of creation is comparable to the structure of the human body. Man is the centre and a replica of the universe. This belief is illustrated clearly for the first time in the Upaniṣads, where speculations on the gods and the universe (*adhidaivatam*) are often followed and parallelled by those on the own self (*adhyātmam*)[1].

2. A concomitant belief is that cosmical and personal events not only resemble but also influence each other. Appearances in the sky, movements of animals, apparitions in dreams etc. have inevitable consequences for human life. Besides, the deeds of gods, heroes and progenitors of the human race performed in the beginning of times have set the example for present patterns of conduct and states of affairs on earth.[2] Myths and legends fulfil the task of keeping man informed of the divine prototypes of his actions.

3. A third important fact which should be restated here is that it is man's basic desire to emphasize, strengthen and, if necessary, to recreate this mystical connexion between his own existence and the cosmical process. His own actions should reflect their mythical prototypes performed by divine agents ; his individual soul should be a replica of the cosmical essence or the deity's secret nature. In the identification with the universal source of existence lies the individual's salvation. This desire is exemplified by the speculations on Brahman and Ātman in the Upani-

ṣads and later philosophical texts, but also in the numerous sources which treat on the worship of deities or the Supreme Deity. In short, and not without an element of generalization, one can say that the essence of worship of a personal god in Indian devotional literature consists of the desire after identification with this god. The supreme goal of the true bhakta or devotee in medieval Indian religious works is the attainment of *sārūpyam* "being of the same form" with God, a state which is reached through successive stages of increasing similarity with the deity's nature. When the texts describe the ritual of pūjā or ceremonial worship of a deity, it is sometimes expressly stated by them that the officiating priest should identify himself with God. "He should meditate on himself as being Hari" says the Vaikhānasa text Yajñādhikāra ascribed to Bhṛgu (32, 20 : *ātmānaṃ bhāvayed dHarim*)[3]. On Bali the same goal of identification with the divine, together with similar techniques of preparation, is shared by the Śaiva priests of the island (Hooykaas—esp. on p. 28f.; 36f.; 66-85). One of the Balinese stutis (Stuti & Stava, No. 145), between stanzas 9 and 10 in some mss contains the prescription : *Īḍe śarīrāntar Brahmamūrtim* "I Meditate on thy body as being a manifestation of Brahmā".

The Tantric ritual of nyāsa is one of the methods employed for this end. The divine presence is invoked into the individual body by means of the application thereon of sacred syllables which contain the supranormal as it were in a nutshell. When the worshipping priest has gone through the identificatory techniques at least a part of God's strength comes to him and by way of him God creates well-being for the people. But also each individual person may, at least theoretically, reach communion with the divine by means of certain procedures which have been elaborated in the Āgamas and Tantras of post-epic Hinduism. It is conceivable that such a communion or even identification will transmit to that individual some part, however small, of God's cosmic powers. Or stated differently : by identification of his own self with the universal harmony and unity, one may be able to appropriate something of the mystic power which is believed to permeate the universe. Similarly, the objectives which the gods attain by means of their supranormal faculties and the means by which they attain them are able to show the way to the worshipper or meditator to attain the same objectives by the same means, although on a small scale, in his personal or social existence on earth. And this is perhaps the point where we touch the way of thought called magic.

The essence of magic is a grasp for power. At its base lies the idea that the object or end desired becomes one with the individual who desires it; that it becomes in a certain way as it were absorbed within him.[4] In magic one strives after concrete, practical goals with the help of non-natural methods and powers. This is not to say that magic as such would be non-natural or abnormal. The recourse to such methods and powers is a function of the gap which exists between the realities of the natural environment and the sovereign motivating force: Desire. And the foremost bearers of supernatural powers are the gods.

In primitive cultures there is a widespread tradition that the gods or the spirits were the first and foremost possessors of magic. In olden times they transmitted its secrets to mankind, because mankind would be unable to live without its possession.[5] In general: the suprahuman powers which created man also presented him with the means and tools to make life on earth possible and enjoyable to him. Seen in this light religion is not so much a means of attaining release or of the thrusting to the heart of cosmic mysteries as rather a technique which helps man in keeping his ground in the needs and exigencies of daily life. Radin (p. 61) emphasizes that the chief drive for magical coercion of the supernatural lies in the existence of fundamental organic needs: hunger and the sex instinct. The oldest and most persistent rites of magic cluster round these two poles. Besides, it is essential that the performer of such rites should be protected from any danger which may befall him during his interference with the supernatural.

Also in India, the foremost function of both primitive and popular religion—that is, the religion of people who for various reasons live on the level of bare subsistence—is "not to interpret life, but to obtain those things which are accounted needful to its existence"[6]. When, for example, the Kanikkārs of Southern Kerala worshipped the moon on full moon day, they tried to obtain cure of whooping cough.[7] Toda prayers express the need for earthly things. They contain expressions like:

"may it be well...with the buffaloes and calves;...may there be no disease...no destroyer...no poisonous animals...no wild beasts...no fire...may rain fall...may clouds rise...may grass flourish...may water spring"[8].

When a "higher" form of religion, in casu Hinduism, takes its hold on the minds of the people, and they become acquainted with prescriptions and ideals of a more "ethical" character, nevertheless the old fundamental goals and needs persist and remain expressed time and again. And even in complex societies like the Hindu society of Ancient India with a highly spiritualized religious lore thought out and elaborated by a class of specialists like the Brāhmaṇas, the strive after daily well-being and material goods of the common people remained characterized up to a high degree by magic. Even the adoration of a Supreme Deity may be motivated for the greater part by economic factors and may function in a magical pattern of thought.[9]

While they deal with the worship of God, it is often claimed by the Hindu Sanskrit texts that the worshipper's exertions will have their results both for ultimate release from existence (*mukti*—) as for enjoyment of earthly objectives (*bhukti*—). Already in the Brāhmaṇas (e.g. ŚatBr. 13, 1, 3, 3 and 4) the hope is expressed that the sacrificer attains heaven, but that he also becomes "firmly based" (*pratiṣṭhita-*) in this world. In the Tantras the proclamation of bhukti as well as mukti sometimes becomes a standard phrase.[10] For the Purāṇas we refer to MtPur. 95, 35; KālPur. (van Kooy, p. 23). The same claim is made by the Vaikhānasas for their temple cult (KJ ch. 1; 105). Nor is this statement of the double-sided result of religion absent from the Buddhist tradition. In his Tattvasaṃgraha[11] the Mahāyāna author Śāntarakṣita says : "That by which earthly welfare is constituted as well as the supreme good, such is called "the Dharma" by all the learned" :

Yato'bhyudayaniṣpattir yato niḥśreyasasya ca |
sa dharma ucyate tādṛk sarvair eva vicakṣaṇaiḥ ||

By strengthening the suprahuman powers and by identifying oneself with them, the religious man obtains a fresh quantity of the sacred vigour which permeates the entire world of creation. This divine gift realizes itself for him in the sphere of his daily life and practical objectives—welfare and happiness, a good crop, absence of disease, absence of fear and danger, continuance of life, happiness in marriage and so on. And if this holds good for the worship of the "high deities" of the great tradition of Hinduism, how much more for those much smaller and closer divinities to which the ordinary village man was wont to address himself in his daily needs? The fundamental economic and psychological presuppositions lie at the root of their creation; and, as has been ably summarized by K. Das[12]: "The villagers never worship any God aimlessly".

When the worshipper strives for release from the rounds of births and deaths, his state of mind is apt to be called "pure" religion or philosophy. When he strives after earthly objectives, his religion is often considered to be of a "lower" character. When he considers the divine or demoniac powers, or even God's sovereign will-power as a tool set in motion by his "worship" for the attainment of such objectives, and operating automatically, his religion is said to be mixed up with magic. But it would create a false impression to try to separate these aspects of religious feeling. "Religion is replete with magic" (Radin, p. 61). Man is practical; he is fixed a great deal by his environment. He has concrete, often immediate, ends in view. The religious man, even the religious formulator, even the philosopher, may at the same time, consciously or unconsciously, be a magician. It may be true, as Heiler (p. 27) says, that the magician stands above his object and the religious man below it, but it should be added that the magician and the religious man can be one and the same person. And it seems better to refrain from the statement that the combination magic-religion would be secondary (Heiler, l.c.). It has indeed sometimes been said that "in the beginning there was magic" (cf. Radin, p. 60, 75). This should however, not lead us to distinguish between a "primitive" or "original" state in human development which would have been characterized exclusively by magic, and which would have been followed by a religious stage. Nor the reversal happens to be true.[13] Man as such seems to be capable for religious feelings and magical convictions at the same time. At least he appears to us to be so from those specimens of Sanskrit literature which were utilized for this study.

And, if magic is defined in a slightly different way, he still is so in our own times.

The man who practises magic may or may not need the aid of the gods for his rituals; it does not make an essential difference. The fact that a deity's or demon's power is utilized in ritual for human ends is encountered almost universally. Of course, magic is a law of nature effective in itself, but it can use with profit any additional power which might be adduced to its help. When it is practised in a primitive society, powerful spirits are often invoked and presented with sacrificial gifts before the ritual itself is executed.[14] In the Veda the hymns of a magical purport may or may not contain invocations to the gods (Malaviya). The god can be the guarantee that the man will obtain the things desired by him, and as the gods' methods are not basically influenced by "ethical" considerations, why should their human followers act otherwise?

But what is good and desirable for the one, may not be so for the other; it may straightway cause him harm. It is tragic that there is often no place under the sun for free and unbounded self-development of the individual and his neighbour (or between neighbouring communities). And magic, which had been originally intended by the gods or ancestors for the common good, is sometimes said to have been diverted by the evil-minded for selfish ends.[15] No wonder; all social life is beset with conflict. There is a suggestive word play in a Balinese Yamarājastava (Stuti & Stava, No. 815, 10): the word *nirāmaya* "unhurt, healthy", when read backwards, produces *Yamaraṇi*, the name of the fearsome Goddess of Death. It is highly significant that the primitive traditions sometimes record that the Creator (s) at the beginning of times were also the first teachers of kinds of destructive magic. They have some times been presented as the first evildoers or black magicians themselves.[16]

In the preceding chapter it was argued how the ancient Indians sometimes thought of their gods as possessors of mysterious, uncanny powers, which they did not hesitate to apply fallaciously. It seemed a matter of foremost importance for man to be on the right (that is: the winning) side in the face of such powers and their wielders. Only in that case could he hope to appropriate the faculties of divine sorcery for himself in order to ward off dangers and enemies of the most diverse kinds and to promote his own happiness. Consequently, besides *bhukti* and *mukti*, a third legitimate goal is expressed in the Sanskrit texts by the word *abhicāra*—"inimical action".[17] Incantations are sometimes recommended by a reference to their first use by some god in the cadre of a cosmical contest, as in the AgPur. (133, 31) in connection with a mantra belonging to Umā and destined for use against enemies: "in former times it has been carried in the hands and on other (places of the body) by Brahmā, Rudra, Indra and Viṣṇu; and during the terrible battle the gods were protected by the spell":

> *Hastādyair dhāritā pūrvaṃ Brahmarudrendraviṣṇubhiḥ |*
> *gurusaṅgrāmakāle tu vidyayā rakṣitāḥ surāḥ ||*

In Vedic as well as Tantric literature the intentions of the worshipper are sometimes expressed most unambiguously. One instance from the Bagalāmukhīrahasya (p. 124) which its author says to have quoted from the Rudrayāmalatantra :

> *Te sarve vilayaṃ yāntu ye māṃ hiṃsanti hiṃsakāḥ |*
> *mṛtyurogabhayakleśāḥ patantu ripumastake ||*

"may all these evildoers who cause harm to me go to their annihilation; death, illness, fear and affliction should fall upon my enemy's skull". In Balinese stutis the own protection is more than once proclaimed in one breath with the adversary's destruction, as in Stuti & Stava, No. 145, 2: *ātmarakṣam idaṃ stotraṃ sarvaśatruvināśanam* "this word of praise (to Brahmā) should serve for my own protection and for the destruction of all the enemies". It would of course be difficult to maintain that the trend of thought shortly delineated above has been extinguished by what we call modern civilization.[18]

2. *Appropriation of supranormal powers according to Sanskrit sources*

In Sanskrit literature a wealth of material exists to illustrate what has been said above. In the first place there is what one might call the "magical application of speculative ideas or religious truth". A prominent case : in the Veda, the word *brahman* denotes the fundamental supporting power of the universe. It reveals itself especially in the sacred formula as it is applied during the sacrificial ceremonies, but also in hymns and prayers, while it is embodied in the priest himself. Very often this brahman is felt to be a supernatural power loaded with magical effectivity.[19] There is a conviction that meditation on brahman cleans and purifies the subject or, for that matter, the object on which the subject in addition concentrates his thoughts; and anything which is pure is less liable to evil influence. In a certain set of sacrificial formulas recorded in the Baudhāyanagṛhyapariśiṣṭasūtra (2, 13) and elsewhere some articles of worship are said to be *pūtā brahmapavitreṇa* "purified by the Purifier which is Brahman". Evil karman does not attach itself to the wise man who knows the mystic truth of the Ātman (ChUp. 4, 14, 3). BhGītā 10, 12 says of Kṛṣṇa: *paraṃ brahma paraṃ dhāma pavitraṃ paramaṃ bhavān* "Thou art the supreme Brahman, the supreme Abode, the supreme Purifier". From Tantric literature: the Tantrasāra p. 73 cites the Viśuddheśvara Tantra which says: "the purification of the elements which exist in the shape of the body by means of their unification with the imperishable Brahman, this is taught to be the 'purification of the elements" [1].

It is also said sometimes that the brahman speculation can help the adept towards material prosperity. In the Upaniṣads such prosperity is more than once promised in unequivocal terms for those who have obtained insight into the secrets of the universe. For example, ChUp. 4, 5, 3: "He whom knowing him in this way, meditates on the fourfold fourth part of Brahman as luminous, becomes luminous in this world. He conquers luminous worlds...". In 4, 12, 2: "He who, knowing thus, meditates on this (*puruṣa*), drives away the evil craft, he possesses a world, he reaches his complete time of life, he lives long, his offspring does not dwindle away. We (thus say the sacrificial fires) support in this and yonder world him who knows and meditates thus". At the same time it is said of those who follow the path of brahman (4, 15, 6): "those who follow it do not return to this human vortex". In 5, 19, 2 the text promises for him who knows the Ātman in its totality: "he reaches satisfaction by offspring, cattle, food, lustre, lustre of the brahman class" [2]. This is the harvest of a cursory glance in the ChUp. only.

The power of brahman is applied not only for promoting

the good, but also for warding off the enemies. There are various instances in the AV. beside a few in the RV. In AV. 5, 20, 10 the effect of a wardrum is said to be sharpened by Brahman.[20] The Brahmaudana "sacrificial porridge of Brahman" can be directed against enemies (e.g., Kauś S. 49, 15ff.). In Ṛgvidh. 1, 15, 4f. the recitation of a mantra in inverted order is advised for the destruction of foes; its effectivity is ascribed to "the strength of brahman" (*etad vai brahmaṇo balam*, 1, 15, 5d). In Ṛgvidh. 2, 4, 4 another spell which destroyed the Vasiṣṭhas is called "a Brahman pronounced by Kuśika" (*brahmaitat Kuśikoditam*). AitBr. 8, 28 describes a ritual called *Brahmaṇaḥ parimaraḥ* "the killing around Brahman". Its essence consists in a meditation on the processes of nature in which five *devatāḥ* "forces of nature" in succession disappear around brahman which is Wind. The adept should realize this and connect this with his personal situation. When he observes, for example, the lightning disappearing into rain, he should meditate: *dviṣan me mriyatāṃ so 'ntardhīyatāṃ taṃ mā nirjñāsiṣuḥ* "my foe should die, he should disappear, people should not recognize him any more". The effect will follow suit. The performer should realize himself, however, that the forces of nature are always born again; he should therefore add some additional imprecations against the rebirth of his personal enemies, at the same time expressly allowing the lightning and the other forces to run their natural course. The *Brahmaṇaḥ parimaraḥ* is said to have been applied first by Maitreya Kausārava for king Sutvan Kairiśi; and indeed five inimical kings are said to have died around Sutvan while he himself reached *mahat* "a great position". An additional injunction is that one should never take a seat before the enemy does so, and never go to sleep before him.

In the Mbh. the Brahmāstra "missile of brahman" is known as a supernatural weapon of infallible effect. Later its deity is said to be the goddess Bagalāmukhī (see below Ch. 2.). The Siddhanāgārjunakakṣapuṭa (N), a textbook of magic, records a ceremony (p. 310) for obtaining such a Brahmāstra so that the client will be able to conquer all his enemies.

That the word brahman in the minds of the people often meant little more than "spell" or "sorcery" is proved by Mbh. 3, 63, 18 (Nala 14, 18) where *brahmavid* occurs in the meaning of "sorcerer". In the tale of Mandapāla at the end of the Ādiparvan (Mbh Book 1) the effect of the brahman said by the young bird sage Droṇa (st. 88ff) is twofold : the liberation of himself and his brothers from the fire, and the burning by that same fire of their enemies, the wild cats. The Dattātreya Tantra, another magical tract, according to its Benares edition (2, 4) allows killing by magic only for those who "with the eye of wisdom behold the Ātman which is Brahman (?) in its cosmic expansion" [3]. N 4, 26 (p. 287) applies the mantra *Oṃ ānanda brahmā svāhā* during ritual of the subjugation of a woman. This mantra is a corrupted form of one of the most famous maxims from the Upaniṣads : "Brahman is joy". Having looked at these data one better understands the words of Vāyu Pur 65, 27 : "The science of Brahman was provided with two heads and bodies; with terrible devices of witchcraft as well as with methods for warding off such evils" :

Brahmavedas tathā ghoraiḥ kṛtyāvidhibhir anvitaḥ |
pratyaṅgirasayogaiś ca dviśarīraśiro 'bhavat||

It is also understandable that the students of such science, and the philosophers or yogins who strive after mystical insights, have been often considered to possess magical powers. The sources on yoga often allude to the miraculous faculties (*siddhi*) to which the yogin gains access, although he is warned not to misuse them. The word yoga itself is sometimes used in a sense approaching to "magic". Stuti & Stava, No. 507 (Vīramantra), a prose spell, contains the words *sarvamantrān sarvayogān vihana vihana* "destroy all spells, all methods of magic". The magical tracts edited in the Indrajālavidyāsaṃgraha often conclude their descriptions by *siddhayoga udāhṛtaḥ* "thus an unfailing method has been expounded". In Kathās—12, 22, 25 the master sorcerer Mūladeva has at his disposal a yogagulikā "magic pill" by which he is able to change himself into an old brahman; by a second one a young man is reshaped into a beautiful girl [4]. This connotation of the word yoga cannot be separated from its general meaning of "a creative discipline of mind" by which one obtains supranormal power. The ŚatBr (11, 5, 7, 1) says that Veda study (*svādhyāya*) causes a person to be *yuktamanāḥ* "disciplined of mind", which also means "of powerful mind-force" (cf. Oldenberg, p. 149, n.2).

According to ŚvetUp 2,1 Savitar in olden times raised himself up from the earth by "disciplining his mind" (*yuñjānaḥ prathamaṃ manaḥ*); and in the next stanza the poet expresses his desire to imitate this divine example. The gods are indeed the foremost possessors of this enviable faculty. In Mbh 12, 47, 8 Viṣṇu is called *Yogeśvara* "Lord of yoga". The BhPur (10, 23, 48) overstates this with *Yogeśvareśvara* "Lord of the lords of yoga". Śiva is also a *yogeśvara* (Mbh 3, 80, 126) when he creates ten million examples of his own form (see above p. 4). In BhGītā 9. 5 Kṛṣṇa invites Arjuna to contemplate his "lordly yoga", *yogam aiśvaram*; in 7, 25 yoga serves to specify the word māyā in the compound *yogamāyā*. The two words yoga and māyā sometimes denote two sides of the same mysterious divine force. Zimmer (p. 62) remarks that the questions after the māyā and the divine magic called yoga amount to the same because what is called māyā from the side of the creatures who are enveloped by it is yoga for the God Who wields this māyā. The divine siddhis are exemplified in creation. God is "more minute than the minute, greater than the great" (TĀr 10, 10, 1).

The compound *yogamāyā* further occurs in the Purāṇas, as in BhPur 12, 10, 10, where Śiva by his *yogamāyā* enters into Mārkaṇḍeya's heart. According to the same text, 8, 5, 43, the guṇas which regulate karman have been fixed by the Lord's *yogamāyā*; in 3, 6, 35 the institution of the grades of society is said to spring from the power of this same *yogamāyā* (*yogamāyābalodayam*). A *yogin*, just like a *māyin*, can be a magician or wonderworker. SM (No. 93, p. 181) uses the word in this sense : *saptāhena tadā yogī labhet kanyāṃ svavāñchitām* "by a period of seven days the yogin will obtain the lady desired by him". For this text there seems to be no difference between the methodical psychic exertion by the aspirant for release from the karmic bond and the exertion performed by the adept in supranormal power for earthly objectives. They can be one and the same person. In popular usage, a yogin often is tantamount to a performer of magic (Jacques, p. 264) or a wandering beggar (K. Das, p. 110); these two varieties also might be embodied in the same man.

The power ascribed to such real or reputed possessors of religious wisdom in the popular mind often assumes the character of a magic force. Sāyaṇa in the beginning of his commentary on the BA Up says that by esoterical knowledge one is able to gain the same results as by the horse sacrifice.[21] The Śaṅkaradigvijaya, the legendary biography of the great philosopher Śaṅkara, reflects this when on the occasion of the victory of Śaṅkara over Maṇḍana in a philosophical dispute it states : *iti vaśīkṛtamaṇḍanapaṇḍitaḥ* "having thus subjugated the Pandit Maṇḍana", using the magical term *vaśīkṛta*—for the defeated opponent. The philosophers or founders of religions have often been believed to be possessors of magic powers also. In various texts of Buddhism the Buddha is represented as possessing powerful spells.[22] Likewise, in Jainism Pārśva and Mahāvīra have been thought to have pronounced magical formulas.[23] The Jātakas give evidence of the belief in the great magical effect of sanctity (Fick, p. 152). The famous Buddhist philosopher Nāgārjuna was believed to have been a great magician at the same time. It seems to be pretty certain now that there were at least two Nāgārjunas, the philosopher and the adept in Tantrism who lived centuries afterwards, but Joshi (p. 316) mentions the Tibetan traditions that the philosopher Nāgārjuna was also a *mahāsiddha* (Joshi : "great magician") who proclaimed *dhāraṇīs* and *sādhanas* : an expert in medicine, alchemic and divination. It does not matter for us here in the first place if this tradition was correct; the interesting fact to note is that such a tradition actually existed. Something similar has been said by Tāranātha about the later philosopher Vāgīśvarakīrti (Conze, p. 171). Śaṅkara whom we met already above is said to have laid the base of the wealth of the temple at Tirupati by designing there a *dhanākarṣaṇayantra*, a symbolic figure drawn on the ground or on some other object in order to attract money (Ramesan, p. 65; see also below—). The PST and other Tantras have been ascribed to the same Śaṅkara (Kane, 1962, p. 1105). These traditions testify to a without doubt frequent tendency of the popular mind, a tendency related to that almost universal belief that piety and religiosity result, or ought to result, in success in earthly matters. And who knows if there is not a germ of truth in the persistent tradition of philosophers and scholars with magical inclinations? In any case, those who devoted themselves to the divine were believed to be able to appropriate divine powers for themselves.

Besides, an appeal to a fundamental truth is said to ward

off evil and dangers. The ChUp describes how a man who has been accused of theft and subjected to an ordeal defends himself by solemnly declaring his innocence so that his hand is not burned by the heated axe (6, 16, 1). The place shows that truth could be thought of as a kind of armour able to protect him who appealed to it.[24] On a certain place in the Jaina canon Truth is praised as the source of all power (Jhavery, p. 274). In modern times this conviction was revived, of course in modified form, by Gandhi and his followers when they developed the satyāgraha pattern of social action.[25]

The same conviction that fundamental principles or supreme truths when appealed to will avert evil meets us in the Balinese Sanskrit hymns. In Stuti & Stava, No. 307 (Vīramantra) protection is requested among others against inimical spells and sorcery; the litany is concluded with the words *sarvasattva svāhā* "O Thou Who art all beings (or : Who art equal to all reality), hail!" The same expression occurs in No. 504 (Aṣṭamahābhaya Kliṅ). No. 336 (Bhairava-naramāṃsaśūnyastava) praises the Buddhist interpretation of reality as the Void, the supreme secret which devours all; the hymn is applied against poisoned food. The effectivity of this hymn is created by the mystical analogy between the all-devouring Void and the human performer who swallows all food unhurt. In No. 636 (Tribhuvana) a statement of the mystical nature of Brahmā and Viṣṇu as the cosmical food and Maheśvara as the cosmical consumer is followed immediately by a statement of rewards which promises the annihilation of disease, and victory, fame and success in all things, besides at the end communion with the Supreme Śiva [5].

3. *The sacred word*

A related phenomenon is the application of hymns or other utterances from the Veda for other ends than they were originally meant for. That the AV and its ritual companion the KauśS were usually meant to be applied in magical context is self-evident. But some of these AV hymns are identical with hymns in the RV and thus originally destined for invocation by the hotar priest. Besides, many of the RV hymns were also used out of their ritual context for goals such as promoting fertility, a long life, warding off or curing disease or doing harm to an enemy. A list of such usages exists as in the Ṛgvidhāna (see below, —ch. 5). The SVBr applies the stanza *Ud vayaṃ tamasaḥ pari* "Upwards from the darkness we...." (RV 1, 50, 10) in a ritual of defeating old age and death; and the same stanza in 2, 5, 3 for subjugation. Very powerful is the Gāyatrī (RV 3, 62, 10); Ṛgvidh, 2, 6—2, 12 is devoted to it. In the LiPur it forms the kernel of a *Vajreśvarī vidyā* (2, 51, 18) while it could also be assigned to the body in the form of a *kavaca* or magical armour (introduction to Gāyatrī Tantra by Pandit Tārakā Nātha Bhaṭṭācārya, p. 3). It is not different with the Sāmaveda. ChUp 2, 2 states the effects of a fivefold Sāman for obtaining rain. AitBr 3, 46 lays down the magical use of a part of the Vāmadevya sāman (the syllables *pu-ru-ṣaḥ*) for procuring *śānti*, which means freedom from evils and inimical magic. The JaimBr sometimes describes the sāmans as fearsome agents of destruction (thus in 1, 129; 1,152) sent away to the enemy like evil demons summoned by the singer. The SVBr contains directions for such applications of the sāmans.[26]

In general the sacred word is considered to bestow effects mysteriously created but at the same time very real and practical. In the West, the power of quotations from the Bible was widely recognized in the Middle Ages and afterwards.[27] Prayers often were and are used as means working automatically to acquire elementary needs. This is even the most basic form of a prayer.[28] Besides, the prayer and the sacred word in general are useful to ward off dangers and demons: they are products of the mind (*manas*) whose powerful, creative thinking (*manana*) results in a *mantra*. That is why Stuti & Stava, No. 362 ("Śivālayatattva") in stanza 36 promises: "by the mantra one obtains release, by the mantra one will gain prosperity; the mantra destroys the sorrows, it is a purifier destroying evil; even the man who commits evils in various ways, who (kills) even his own father and mother, his soul becomes purified by means of the mantra; it purifies all evil" [6] (the mantra in question is a short formula of praise directed to a manifestation of Śiva). The act of such "thinking" is praised in ST 3: "By thinking one saves (others) from evil, by thinking one reaches heaven; by thinking one reaches release, and one will realize the four ends of life" :

Mananāt pāpatas trāti mananāt svargam aśnute /
mananān mokṣam āpnoti caturvargamayo bhavet //

Among Indian primitive peoples, the solemn or sacred word is often believed necessarily to create its effect. Hermanns (p. 286) relates how a Baiga girl evoked a tiger against some enemies of hers only by saying: "the tiger should kill them". Hermanns proposes that the magical word is considered to be an imitation of the divine archetype: Bhagwan, the Creator and Supreme God, spoke only one word and created by that alone. He provided the primeval magician with the same powers. In Indian literature the cursing power of brahmans is a universal motif.

One of the most powerful kinds of sacred word is created by the recitation of a god's name. The name is intimately connected with its bearer and has the power to evoke, often even to compel that bearer. Its soul is identical with the bearer's soul. By muttering a god's name man is able as it were magically to attract that god to his presence and to force him to listen to the wishes pronounced to him.[29]

Thus the Kanikkār of Kerala used to mutter every morning the names of their important gods in order to ward off evil spirits (Iyer, p. 38f.). The name of the Buddha occurs as a wonder-working power among the Sinhalese of Ceylon.[30] In Northern India, Rāma's name written on the door of the lying-in chamber was thought to chase away evil spirits (O 'Malley, p. 134). Stuti & Stava, No. 229, Rāmakavaca, for the greater part identical with the Indian Rāmarakṣāstotra, honours Rāma with a number of epithets which taken together summarize his exploits told in the Rāmāyaṇa. The recitation of the hymn is advised for the lonely wayfarer (stanza 20 in the Indian version). It is significantly accompanied by a kavaca or "armour" during which the names of a god are invoked for protection on various parts of the body. A very fine example of a Viṣṇukavaca is to be found in GarPur 194. Pronouncing the names of Viṣṇu is considered by AgPur 270,15 to lead to the destruction of all evil occurrences : *acyutanāmakīrtanāt praṇāśayet tu trividhaṃ mamāśubham*). No wonder that the religious specialists tried to invent and to assemble as much names as possible which at the same time described some aspect of the divine nature and activity. The results are recorded in the Sahasranāmastotras "Hymns containing a thousand names" in the Mbh and later sources. The effects of some of the many names of Viṣṇu are specified in AgPur 284. For example, the name Dāmodara "With the band on his belly" frees from bondage; Puṣkarākṣa "The Lotus-eyed" drives away a disease of the eye (284, 9).

The mentioning of a god's names thus most often implies allusions to his exploits. By this method that god's powers are activated, and these powers may come to man's help and even enable him to perform miraculous deeds. A remarkable instance is furnished by Stuti & Stava, No. 97, called Vīramantra or Pañcarakṣākṣamā in the manuscripts. This hymn of praise to the Five Tathāgatas of Mahāyāna Buddhism occurs also in the Indian SM. It describes in obstruse style the mysterious and gracious nature of the Tathāgatas. One of the two Balinese manuscript sources says that recitation of the hymn procures wisdom (*prajā*, read *prajñā*), but it also suggests its application for the following ends : 1. Cure of poison. 2. Becoming dear to anybody (see also below,) 3. Defeating the enemies. 4. Release from calamities like those caused by planets. 5. In the next life, obtaining the faculty of remembering one's former births.

The Divine Name is also considered very powerful when it occurs in a short formula of praise accompanied by the word *namaḥ* "honour". For instance, the words *śrīgaṇeśāya namaḥ* "Honour to the Venerable Gaṇeśa" when painted on a wall were thought to contain the *śakti* of that deity (Abbott, p. 446). Another important mantra of this kind is the Śivaite Pañcākṣara, that is the five syllables *na-maḥ Śi-vā-ya* "honour to Śiva". Their recitation has been sometimes advised in order straightway to obtain release from saṃsāra (Pope, pl xxxix-xlii). They symbolize the Five Entities of Śaiva Siddhānta : Śiva, His Śakti, Āṇavamala "Primeval Stain", Māyā "Force of becoming", and Ātmā. At the same time it can represent man's religious development in a nutshell: Śi and Va are the "mystic action of Śiva's grace"; Na and Ma the "whirl of impurity", and between them there is Ya, the Soul. He who strives after release should take care to recite *Śi-vā-ya na-maḥ*, not *na-maḥ Śi-vā-ya*. According to the Gokarṇeśvaramānasikārādhanam, a praise of Śiva as Lord of the place of pilgrimage Gokarṇa, stanza 19 (Aithal, p. 163), these five syllables destroy the five major sins. A person with more carthly aims can apply them in the method advised bv LiPur 85, 113f. He should assign them to the fingers by the method of *nyāsa* while reciting them (*aṅgulijapa*, 109). When this is done with the right concentration of mind, the following results will appear; the thumb brings about release, the index destruction of enemies, the middle finger wealth, the fourth finger safety (*śānti*). In addition, the performer should note the direction faced by him. The east brings about power, the south black magic, the west wealth, the north safety. In Stuti & Stava, No. 450, Mahāmāyā (see below ch. 3), a spell consisting mainly of the words *Aghorebhyo namaḥ* "To the Non-terrible manifestations (of Śiva), honour" is applied together with meditation on Viṣṇu for the realization of five feats of magic.

4. *Some powerful words and syllables*

The word *namaḥ* may appear also alone with a special connotation, but most often in cooperation with a few other small words. When the Viṣṇuite brahman priest of South India in the cadre of his worship prepares himself for receiving the God in his body and mind, he performs among other rituals the *ṣaḍaṅganyāsa*. During this act he assigns higher power to six parts of his body and apparel. The act is accompanied by formulas which are concluded by six small words, the first of them being *namaḥ*. According to Rangachari (p. 134) the Śrīvaiṣṇava brahmans perform it in this way : the priest touches his heart while saying *jñānāya hṛdayāya namaḥ*; his head, saying *aiśvaryāya śirase svāhā*; his tuft of hair, saying *śaktyai śikhāyai vauṣaṭ*; his shoulders, saying *balāya kavacāya huṃ*; then "he takes round his head his right hand and slaps both the palms twice" saying *vīryāya astrāya phaṭ* ; and he touches his eyes with his right hand and says *tejase netrābhyāṃ vauṣaṭ*. In this way he appropriates the six divine qualities postulated by the Pāñcarātra school : wisdom, dominion, energy, strength, supranormal power of mind, and fiery energy.[31] Their rivals, the Vaikhānasa priests, omit these six qualities but say the same words at the end of their six formulas during Ṣaḍaṅganyāsa. An unedited treatise on Vaikhānasa daily worship, the Arcanāsārasaṃgraha, presents these six formulas as follows : 1. *Śrīṃ oṃ hṛdayāya namaḥ*. 2. ...*oṃ śirase svāhā*. 3. *Drāṃ oṃ śikhāyai vauṣaṭ*. 4. *Hrāṃ oṃ kavacāya huṃ*. 5. *Klīṃ oṃ netratrayāya vauṣaṭ*. 6. *Rāṃ oṃ astrāya phaṭ*. In Śivaite South Indian Āgamas and also in the Balinese Sūryasevanā, the six words *namaḥ, svāhā, vauṣaṭ (or vaṣaṭ) huṃ vauṣaṭ* and *phaṭ* are often replaced by six occurrences of the word *namaḥ*.[32] The six words just mentioned for the greater part have no meaning in ordinary Sanskrit, but apparently they were thought to be indispensible on this stage of the ritual because they contained an element of supernatural power. They constitute a good example of short, often apparently meaningless words which came to be considered as highly potent bearers of the supernatural and the magical. These six words are an inheritance from the Veda. Some of them, especially *svāhā* and *vauṣaṭ,* are often applied in the Vedic ritual as invervening exclamations. A few instances suffice to prove that they were believed to contain a mysterious power. In AitBr 2, 4 it is said of *svāhā* that its nature is *pratiṣṭhā* (*pratiṣṭhātmaka*) and that in this quality it provides the performer of the ritual or his sponsor with a firm base (*pratiṣṭhā*) in existence.[33] The word *vaṣaṭ* possesses a more malevolent power. AitBr 3, 6 argues that if one desires the death of his enemy he should exclaim *vaṣaṭ* while concentrating his thoughts upon him, because the sound *vaṣaṭ* is equal to the front of a thunderbolt (*vajrasya pratīkam*; presumably because both words *vaṣaṭ* and vajra begin with the syllable *va* ; Malaviya, p. 36). The same is implied in ŚatBr 1, 6, 3, 28 and again in GopBr 2, 3, 3 (Malaviya, p. 169). TS 3, 4, 8, 5 says :*yád vācáḥ krūrám tena vásaṭkaroti* "he pronounces vaṣaṭ with the evil force of Speech" (Caland—p. 161, n. 18).

Perhaps one should interpret in this light the passage from Stuti & Stava, No. 314, stanza 1: *śāntipuṣṭivaṣaṭkarma, kāryasiddhiś ca jāyate* "(by worship of the Guru's feet) the rituals of pacification, creation of welfare and black magic are realized, and also success in one's enterprises" (in Stuti & Stava, *vaṣaṭ* has been translated here with "offering"). The word *vaṣaṭ* would in that case have been meant as a synonym for abhicāra, which often occurs together with *śānti* and *puṣṭi* in a triad of human strivings in the theory of ritualism (see below, p.95).

The word *phaṭ* is loaded with magic. Originally it seems

to have been an onomatopoeic denoting a breaking or cracking sound. Kane, 1962 (p. 1037, n. 1) devotes some attention to this word. It occurs in the sense of "sound of breaking" in MS 7, 3 : *upari pruto bhaṅgena hato 'sau phaṭ* "N. N. is killed by the breaking caused by that which comes upon him from above : crack" (the place is also referred to by Malaviya, p. 95). KauśS 47, 17-22 also mentions *phaṭ* in a context of *abhicāra* (Henry, p. 224 ; read : 47, 21). In the Ṛgvidh, (3, 20, 1) it is pronounced during the breaking of an image of the performer's beloved. Gonda in his commentary on this place (p. 81) refers to BhPur 6, 8, 8 where Indra is said to have conquered his enemies by applying *phaṭ* after the formula *Oṃ Viṣṇave namaḥ* in the four quarters of the sky.

So much is clear that an enumeration of the six words in question in a fixed sequence evokes forces for good as well as for evil. Their tradition is maintained and elaborated in the Tantric tradition and the Purāṇas influenced by it. AgPur (125, 41 f.) records that saying *namaḥ* fits in with rites of pacication and conciliation; *vauṣaṭ* is correct during ceremonies for obtaining welfare, subjugation of others, and the like; *huṃ* is for liquidation of an enemy or for destruction of somebody's goodwill; *phaṭ* is for causing people to hate each other and for driving them from their homes; *vaṣaṭ* for a soma sacrifice and for "Dīpti and the like" (enumerating the eight śaktis of Sūrya, the first of who is Dīptā?) [7]. According to Kane, 1962 (p. 1111) the Jayākhyā Saṃhitā says that *svāhā* is for homa, *svadhā* for ancestor worship, *phaṭ* for destructive activities, *huṃ* for creating hatred, and *namaḥ* for release. The probably 15th-century compilation Mantramahodadhi (MMD) (24, 92ff.) divides all formulas into three groups : male, female and "eunuch". Those which end by *vaṣaṭ* and *phaṭ* are said to be male; those which end by *vauṣaṭ* and *svāhā* are female; those with *huṃ* and *namaḥ* are "eunuch". The male formulas are useful for subjugation, eradication and obstruction; the female ones bring about a quick success in destroying those of evil intentions: the eunuchs are applied in rites of destructive magic [8]. The doctrine of the "sex" of formulas is well known from other sources for instance the KJ. This text at the end of ch. 4 says that all formulas which end in *namaḥ* are female, while those in *svāhā* are male and all others neuter.

The same principle of the application of these six words for good as well as for evil ends is present in the Buddhist KCT (3, 80). Here the mantras which end by *svāhā* bring about welfare; those on *namaḥ* cause pacification; those on *vauṣaṭ* are useful for attracting someone towards oneself; on *vaṣaṭ* are for subjugation; those on *hum̥* for black magic; those on *phaṭ* for "piercing", that is: rendering immovable (on "piercing", see below,—ch. 6, 8) [9]. It is easily seen that, although in these different sources the principle of application is the same, the details differ widely.

The idea that short, unintelligible formulas or syllables may contain great power is widely diffused.[34] Their effect can be applied for the realization of material goals including sometimes evil designs but they can also serve as a guide for reaching the realization of infinite bliss and salvation. In Indian mantra lore they are called *bīja* "seed syllables" or "kernel syllables". They are taught to contain the essence or body of a divinity.[35] They are found already in Vedic literature. As is often the case, Tantrism did here little more than elaborate on ideas conceived by the Vedic sages.[36] Behind the mantra and bīja tradition lies the conviction that all phenomena in the universe are mystically connected while manifesting themselves in different categories of reality. Consequently the world of visible existence and its divine prototype must be parallelled by a range of audible manifestations materialized for our experience in a number of basic sounds or syllables (sounds and syllables are closely connected with each other in Indian linguistic speculation). As the universe is permeated by forces both good and evil, the world of sound and its symbols must be invested with the same forces.

The chief difference between the Vedic and the Tantric tradition seems to lie in the former's exclusive character, while Tantrism presents itself as accessible to people of all classes and descent. In Tantric texts some practices seem to have acclimatized which were the cultural property of castes or tribes of non-Aryan provenance. But one should be very careful in making statements like this. Nor is this to deny that the Vedic Aryans knew and practized magic. But the kinds of magic owned by different ethnic stocks or strata of society may have contained important differences. Rudrayāmala Tantra 17,

121ff. (Kane, 1962, p. 1034) asserts that the right sādhanas (meditations on deities in magical context) should be acquired from three sources; the regions of the Buddhists, the Atharvaveda and Mahācīna (Tibet and other Himalayan regions).

The most important and perhaps also the oldest of the bījas is of course the syllable *OM*. The speculation on this sacred sound begins in the Upaniṣads and continues into the Tantric texts. It is thought to represent the sound aspect of brahman. Its three components *A-u-m*—are equal to the Trimūrti : Brahmā, Viṣṇu and Śiva who are said to create, maintain and destroy the universe. According to the Śiva Pur, a text which deals profusely with the symbolism of *Oṃ*, the Three Deities just mentioned originated from these three components. In the same text (p. 841) *Oṃ* is divided into five components : the *A*, *u*, *m*, *nāda* and *bindu*. They possess as their presiding deities : Brahmā, Viṣṇu, Rudra, Maheśvara and Sadāśiva who together constitute a Śivaite pentad performing the Five Acts of Śiva (Śiva Pur, p. 761). At the same time these five components of Oṃ symbolize the Five Faces of Śiva : Sadyojāta, Vāmadeva, Aghora, Tatpuruṣa and Īśāna (Śiva Pur, p. 762). In Śaiva Siddhānta speculation, Oṃ contains the five entities: Śiva, his Śakti, the Primeval Stain (Āṇavamala), Māyā and the Soul (Pope, p. xl). Just like its philosophical counterpart Brahman, the syllable *Oṃ* has the power of protection. The GT (p.2) advises those who recite the Gāyatrī always to pronounce *Oṃ* at its beginning or end in order to drive off the evil (*praṇavaṃ prajaped dhīmān pāpoccāṭanakarmaṇi*). This is without doubt one of the reasons why the syllable *Oṃ* came to be repeated so frequently at the beginning or/and the end of all kinds of mantras.

We will not occupy ourselves with the numerous other bījas here. It is worth mentioning that *Oṃ* often occurs in combination with other syllables, thus helping to constitute a powerful sort of mantras. The Buddhist MMK (I,p.15), for instance, deals with the mantra *Oṃ āḥ huṃ*. This is the heart mantra of Yamāntaka Krodharāja, the "Lord of Anger". It accomplishes all things, such as pacification, welfare, destructive magic, miraculous powers like rendering oneself invisible. It has been taught by Mañjughoṣa (Mañjuśrī) and destroys all obstructions. In combination with the words

Namaḥ Śivāya (see above p.),*Oṃ* gives the *Ṣaḍakṣara* "mantra of six syllables" : *Oṃ namaḥ Śivāya.* It is praised by Stuti and Stava, No. 809: "The Ṣaḍakṣara is a great spell, secret and supremely effective; it is called the Body of Sadāśiva, and it destroys the greatest sins" :

Ṣaḍakṣaraṃ mahājapyaṃ guhyaṃ paramasādhakam /
Sadāśivāṅgam ity uktaṃ mahāpātakanāśanam //

One particular kind of mantra which deserves to receive some attention here is the *dhāraṇī.* As its name says, it is believed to "bear" or "contain" (root *dhṛ.*) some power—a meaning which does not differ much from that of brahman in "supporting and protecting force"[37]. The dhāraṇīs are found in Hinduism, Buddhism and Jainism, usually not in the earlier sources. In Hinduism they are considered to belong to the characteristics of Tantric influence. They are probably most frequent in Buddhist texts. A dhāraṇī most often consists of an introductory formula paying honour to some deity, followed by an invocation of some power which is requested to protect the speaker and to destroy all evils that beset him. Its most lively element is the use of a chain of imperatives, each usually repeated once, which should adduce strength to the spell. It is often not at all clear which power is invoked and ordered by means of these imperatives to assist the speaker. The dhāraṇī usually ends with a few of the potent words known in ritual, like *huṃ* or *svāhā,* Its translation is often extremely difficult.

From the mass of dhāraṇīs recorded in Buddhist literature, we present here as an instance the relatively simple one found in MMK III, p. 662[10]. The context is as follows : Indra had been defeated by the Asuras. In his distress he sought refuge with Kāśyapa, and this sage taught him the formula in question in order to activate the power of the Bodhisattva Mañjuśrī (the chief deity adored by the MMK). This is the spell : "Honour to all the Buddhas and Bodhisattvas, whose commands are irresistible. *Oṃ,* kill kill all dangers, conquer, uproot, terrify, crush, split, break, flame, flame ; *huṃ phaṭ svāhā*". It is to be noted that its introduction is of the same kind as those which are found at the beginning of the canonical sūtras. The formula had hardly been said or Mañjuśrī, the Kumāra, shook the earth, and besides the words of this mantra became presided over (*adhiṣṭhita*) by all the Buddhas. Indra, his eyes wide open in admiration, worshipped Mañjuśrī, learnt the mantra by heart, and advanced against the Asuras who made off in panic for the nether world. Thus Mañjuśrī, bodily present in his mantra, shaped the opportunity for Indra to create his "new order". Indra installed a picture of Mañjuśrī on his banner and from that time onwards the danger from the counter-gods had vanished.

An interesting context is also furnished by the dhāraṇī recorded by the MMK a few pages further (III, p. 666). Mañjuśrī there says to Buddha that in the future people will cease to maintain their faith in the word of the Buddha and by that reason will fall into a state of the utmost depression. It will be necessary then to provide for their help. The Buddha praises Mañjuśrī for his merciful character and teaches him a *vidyārāja* or "king of spells", a mantra of especially high potency, which will serve "for the profit, the good and the welfare of all beings and for showing compassion to the world" : *sarvasattvānām arthāya hitāya sukhāya lokānukampāyai*.... This mantra should be memorized particularly in the hour of death. Mañjuśrī is again its deity. Like the preceding one, the spell is introduced by a phrase borrowed from canonical scripture. It runs as follows : "Honour to all Tathāgatas the Qualified Ones, Who have become duly enlightened! *Oṃ*, O Thou Who possessest the form of a princely youth, Origin of all, come, come; *lahu lahu, bhrūṃ bhrūṃ*, O Conqueror of the conquerors; O Mañjuśriya, Whose glory is eminent, save me from all sorrows, *phaṭ*, pacify pacify; O Thou Who hast originated from the Water of life, destroy my evil, *svāhā* !" [11]. To the person who memorizes thus, the MMK says, Māra will not find an entrance. All his obstructions will disappear.

This dhāraṇī is somewhat more elaborated than the preceding one. At the same time it contains more obscure expressions, a feature which probably has been deliberately sought in order to enhance its magical potency. The language which is not understood by the hearer or speaker may be the language of the spirits, the demons or the gods themselves.[38]

As to the evolution of the Indian dhāraṇī, it can be said with safety that its antiquity must be considerable. Vedic literature contains passages which may have served as models for such formulas. One may compare RV 7, 104, 1 : "Indra and Soma, burn the evil demon, press down, throw down, O Bulls, those who rejoice in the darkness ! crush those who are devoid of sense, burn them down, kill, drive away, sharpen (Thyselves against) the devourers !" [12]. In later times the hearing of imperativesis said to be a good omen by KJ ch. 13 (trsl. p. 52) : "if he hears words like 'go, bring, take, speak, win, command, be gracious'. . . . he should announce highest welfare". It is understandable that imperatives, the most direct representation in language of the working of a person's will, are considered auspicious and magically potent.[39]

Another aspect of the dhāraṇī is that it may contain words or expressions used out of their original context, sometimes taken over without regard to their original meaning. It has been noted already how its introductory formula sometimes resembles those found in canonical sūtras. But also important doctrinal statements may be applied within a dhāraṇī. Although Bharati (p. 113) is too categorical in saying that the dhāraṇīs are originally "contractions of longer canonical passages", sometimes indeed they contain such contractions or deformations of important statements which presented some essence of the doctrine in a compact form. A good example has been furnished and amply discussed by Bernhard[40]. He showed that the words *īne mīne dapphe daḍapphe* which often occur, sometimes in a slightly modified form, in Buddhist magical formulas, are deformations of a compact summary of the Four Noble Truths of Buddhism in a Dravidian language. As Bernhard says (p. 167), the Four Noble Truths, when still understood to be meant by the above-mentioned mysterious four words, may have been applied by way of a *satyakriyā* "appeal to truth" (see above p. 67) Later they assumed the character of mere sacred syllables applicable for magical protection. Their chief function seems to have been the destruction of poison (Bernhard, p. 162). In HT (p. 2) the words *ili mili phuḥ phuḥ* which probably are a further corruption of the Four Noble Truths in Dravidian occur against snakes.

Besides the mysterious efficacy of sacred words, there are the sacred object and the sacred action as additional sources of power. The belief is common that the effect of liturgical performances will occur *ex opere operato*. Religious objects like reliquia or sacred ashes are widely venerated (Heiler, p. 295). As an instance from the Balinese Stutis we mention No. 121, entitled Bhasma Āgama-Tīrtha "The Holy Water tradition of the Ashes", the first śloka of which is: "The bath with ashes is the best purifier; Śiva in the nature of the ashes will protect; ashes are also a means of conquering threefold Space."

Bhasmasnānaṃ varaṃ tīrthaṃ pavitraṃ pāpanāśanam |
bhasmarūpaṃ Śivaṃ rakṣed bhasmaṃ trailokyasādhanam ||

In utterances like this the sacred object is considered an independent means of acquiring purification and even supreme wisdom. At the same time it remains a charm, a magically potent object which effects protection from danger and destroys inimical beings and powers. A magical performance, in order to be effective, needs not only effective words or formulas but also potent objects which serve as receptacles of the powers handled by man. In Sanskrit words, a magical sādhana, in order to reach *siddhi* "completion" should have not only *mantra* at its disposal, but also *yantra*. As a yantra any object may serve which is able to guide and strengthen the performer's meditation. By thus activating his spiritual powers such objects are the visible counterparts of the audible formula. In this way the three aspects of human action: thinking, speaking and acting, are mobilized together in order to reach the greatest possible effect.

5. *The aims of worship*

An appeal to the gods can be caused out of a pure religious feeling or be motivated by material needs or desires. The person who attempts to invoke a deity may strive after release from saṃsāra or after the completion of his mundane designs. Perhaps he strives after both at the same time. The same duality in the motives for the worship of the gods can be observed in the motivation for asceticism. The ascetic by his mortification obtains the mastery of supernatural faculties. His goal may be definitely to escape the world's plights and sorrow but he might also be motivated by the desire after other things like the execution of power over other beings, or the winning over of the beloved (as Pārvatī did when she desired to win Śiva) or the obtaining of a husband (as Draupadī did, Mbh 1,157, 6ff). In fact, in Ancient Indian literature this second motivation of the performance of austerities is extremely frequent. A standard pattern is that the gods out of their celestial dwellings observe somebody on earth who is engaged in rigorous asceticism. Without further deliberation they assume that this person does not strive after release but that he tries to coerce them, for instance by compelling them to grant him a boon of enormous size (as Bali did). The ascetic's coercive activity can even result in driving the gods away from their positions and occupying them himself (as Hiraṇyakaśipu did, Vi Pur 1,17, 2ff).

These two roads to power: asceticism and worship of the gods, can be combined. By a difficult, ascetic preparation one can compel some god to appear before oneself and comply to one's wishes. Such a procedure is called *sādhanā* or *sādhana* "realization" (of the deity concerned or of the desired result). It contains also the nuances of "evocation" and "propitiation".[41] The same word can be used for a course of action the goal of which is liberation from existence. Success in both types of *sādhanā* is called *siddhi*. A person who strives after siddhi and who is on his way to realize it, is called a *sādhaka*; those who have reached their goal are the *siddha*. In the remainder of this chapter we shall pay attention to a number of sādhanas.

In the Vedic religion, all kind of success was expected as a result of the sacrificial ceremonies. The various types of such ceremonies were each destined for the creation of their own specific results; thus the commentary on Pañcaviṃ a Br (6,3,2) says : *ukthyena paśukāmo yajeta* "he who strives after cattle should sacrifice by means of an *ukthya* ceremony". Of another kind are the prescriptions as found for instance in AitBr2,1 (Adhyāya 6) : for obtaining different results the *yūpa* should be made out of different kinds of wood. The sacrifice was thought to bring about its results without divine intervention.

In post-Vedic Hinduism, the worship of the gods by means of images occupies the chief place. In Sanskrit terms, *yajña* or *vedakriyā* was for the greater part superseded by *pūjā*. The sādhanas for material ends remained possible, however, this time by the manipulation of the pūjā ceremony and the image of the god concerned. This is not to say that the old methods disappeared: the sacrificial fire, for example, remained an essential part of the ritual procedure and even an important tool of magic (see below-ch.6.3). But the image of the gods developed into one of the most powerful kinds of *yantra* (see p. 80). Of course the most diverging objects can be utilized as such; often it will be a *maṇḍala* or sacred diagram, but also a pot filled with water, a plant, a part of an animal's body. When the ritual is accompanied by a prayer to a deity, which means that the deity is invoked as a strengthening force which comes to the performer's aid, the image itself takes the foremost role as a material source of power. Images of the gods were often thought to possess such a power of their own right. According to KJ ch. 53f. and other ritualist and iconographic sources, different kinds of images produce or are helpful to produce different kinds of results (*yoga*, *bhoga*, *abhicāra* and so on)[42]. The image of course need not be of stone nor even of any other material : it may exist merely in the performer's mind where it is created by him by way of creative meditation (*bhāvanā*) for his specific purpose. As we saw above, the gods are the possessors and the wielders of māyā, and the performer's identification with such a god by means of his compelling meditation will result in obtaining what he desires and subjugating whom he desires.

The pattern of image worship of magical character, performed for the realization of specific ends, is frequently represented from a variety of literary sources. The performer invokes the deity, sometimes after a long period of preparatory sacrifices, concentration of mind, or asceticism, and pronounces his desire to that deity. The god, who has been forced into a benevolent state of mind by the performer's exertions, manifests himself and allows the "worshipper" the gratification of his wish. The constant recitation of one or more mantras is of course necessary in order to secure success. An instance from popular legend : in connexion with the Viṣṇuite temple of Akiripalli near Vijayawada, Andhra Pradesh, it is told that a certain king named Śubhavrata meditated during a long period on Viṣṇu while performing rigorous asceticism. At last Viṣṇu appeared to him and granted him a boon. The king, who was a sincere *bhakta*, requested his God that He might deign to incarnate together with His spouse Lakṣmī in his own body. Besides, the same Śubhavrata also performed asceticism for

Śiva. That is the reason that both Śiva and Viṣṇu settled till the present time on the hill Śobhanādri[43].

These were acts performed by a pious man out of devotion. There are many others described which have been ventured upon for the realization of boons connected with earthly life. Famous is the penance dome for obtaining a child, usually a son. It is often described in literature, for instance in the tale of Sāvitrī (Mbh 3, 277) where King Aśvapati while employing the mantra Sāvitrī subjects himself to rigorous restrictions during eighteen years. After this period the goddess Sāvitrī, who is a personification of the mantra, manifests herself and announces to the king the future birth of a daughter who will bear the same name. Ceremonies of worship of a certain god during a certain period of time have been very frequently executed by women for the same end (the *vrata*). But other goals were not lacking. King Purūravas paid worship to Viṣṇu in order to obtain a large kingdom (MtPur 115, 12: *rājyakāmaḥ*). The Dattātreya Tantra (13,17) describes worship of the Śivaliṅga thrice a day accompanied by the presentation of gifts of frankincense in particular. The result is that a Yakṣiṇī appears and grants the boon of material wealth and a long life. Other religious ceremonies conducted for certain specific ends may be: ritual bathing, the organization of festivals, pilgrimages. The result of a festival is expected to be welfare for the ruler (who sponsors the festival and has it organized) as well as for his subjects, or, when it has been organized in time of crisis, the averting of danger (KJ, ch. 88, beginning, and ch. 90, conclusion).

In the Tantric "way of mantra", a *sādhana* proper, in order to be performed correctly, usually needs : a deity, a formula, a visible aid (*yantra*), and a human mediator (*guru*). The role of this human mediator is stressed much in the later texts. Besides, the MMD emphasizes the point that during such a ceremony one should never omit to feed the brahmans (24,131 : *sambhojyanānānnaiḥ*). The same text (25,49ff.) lays down that during expiation or comparatively innocent ceremonies of magic the brahmans should obtain one tenth of the sacrificial food; during more serious rites of sorcery, they should obtain one fifth, one third, or even as much as the amount sacrificed. In the last case a ceremony of magical killing is concerned.

For the performance of a Tantric sādhana a mantra suitable for the particular deity and purpose is necessary. This mantra in itself is usually not yet able to come into effect. It should be perfected (*sādhita-*) by a ritual of *puraścaraṇa*—"preliminary course" or *pūrvasevā* "preliminary worship", during which the mantra is recited for a certain great number of times together with certain offerings and other rituals.[44] During sādhana the performer concentrates his thoughts on the deity concerned, especially on the outward characteristics of its figure (*dhyāna-*); he conducts acts of worship, accompanied by the worship of attendant deities, invocation on a pedestal, offering of eatables and other attendances. This pūjā should by preference be done in the mind (*mānasī pūjā*). The help of a visible aid is facultative. The sādhana is always concluded by the statement of the rewards brought about by it (*phala-*).

As an instance may serve the sādhana of the monkey god Hanūmān described in MMD ch. 13. For the sake of convenience it is divided here into eight elements.

1. (stanzas 1-4). The *mantroddhāra*, the description of the mantra in the circumscriptive method characteristic for Tantric literature.
2. (5-7). Assignment on the body (*nyāsa-*) of the kernel syllables (*bīja*) which accompany the mantra and of the syllables of the mantra itself, which are 21 in number.
3. (stanza 8). Dhyāna of Hanūmān.
4. (stanza 9). Rules for the recitation (*japa-*) of the mantra for a great number of times, accompanied by oblations into a fire (*homa-*). The elements 2-4 together form the *puraścaraṇa*.
5. (10-12) : pūjā of Hanūmān after invocation on a pedestal (*pīṭha-*). The pedestal is considered to have the form of a lotus. On its filament the limbs of Hanūmān's body are worshipped; on its leaves, his other names, which are eight in number.
6. (12, 13). On the tips of the leaves, Hanūmān's attendants, the monkeys, led by Sugrīva. They are also eight in number; they are accompanied by the Lords of the regions (*dikpati-*).
7. The results. They comprise by far the greatest part of the passage (14-45). When the mantra has been perfected

in the way described above (*evaṃ siddhe manau*), the mantrin is able to realize all his wishes, both those of himself as those cherished by others. Then follows a discussion of the specific results; they can be brought about by such expedients as the use of different kinds of materials (see below—ch.6.3).

8. Stanzas 46ff. describe the *yantra* or mystical diagram of Hanūmān. The word yantra is used here in a narrower sense as above. In the present context it usually denotes a special kind of diagram destined for a specific purpose, often one of destructive magic.

A few points should be emphasized here. The acquisition of the result desired by means of manipulation of the supernatural demands a difficult and protracted course of preparation. This course can have the form of rigorous asceticism, as we saw in the instances mentioned a few pages before. But as a rule the preparatory measures consist of the performance of a great number of oblations into the fire, accompanied by recitation for an even greater number of times of the correct mantra. These recitations amount to thousands or even hundreds of thousands. The supernatural is not easy to coerce. In primitive societies it has often been stated that rigorous preparatory measures are necessary in order to reach contact with the world of the spirits[45]. Of course some restrictions or taboos should also be observed by the performer. Only thus will he be able to overcome the resistance offered by the world of the supernatural. This resistance may consist of dreadful appearances of ghosts or attempts at seduction by beautiful women (JT 17, 13ff.; PST 13, 38ff.; see also below).

The second thing to be stated will concern us in more detail in the following pages. A sādhana can be performed for the gratification of one's desire also when this implies the harming of others. In the Mbh it is described how Arjuna performed rigorous penance in order that Śiva might appear to him and present him with the Pāśupatāstra, a legendary weapon which would enable him to destroy all his enemies. His purpose was granted by Śiva, but not before that god had put Arjuna to test by appearing before him in the guise of a primitive mountaineer (Kirāta) and fighting with him. In general : the more serious and fearsome the goal which the performer has in mind, the more difficult and dangerous his preparation[46].

The appropriation of the divine power can be equally effective on the field of love. Viṣṇu is the foremost god who subjugates all womankind by his beauty (see above p.28). MtPur (70, 32ff.) gives the rules for courtezans who desire to be sure that their charming talents will be successful. They should worship Viṣṇu and meditate on his identity with Kāma the god of love. This is done by concentrating on each particular limb of Viṣṇu as being a limb of Kāma. His feet should be addressed with : "to Kāma (honour)" ; his legs with: "to Him Who creates bewilderment (*mohakāriṇe*)", and so on. After this the woman in question should invite a brahman who knows the dharma, worship him as the God of Love and surrender herself to him. After a year there is another ceremony during which the same brahman and his wife are adorned and worshipped as Kāma and his spouse and the courtezan pronounces among others thes ewords : "Just as I never observe any difference between Kāma and Keśava (Viṣṇu), in the same way all my desires should constantly come true, O Viṣṇu"... "Just as the Lotus Woman (Lakṣmī) never departs from Thy body, O Keśava, let in the same way my (body) be a part of Thy own body, O Lord" [13]. In former times this Veśyādharma (also called a vrata) had been told by Indra to the demons' wives with the injunction that they should behave themselves in the manner of public women to the sage Dālbhya (MtPur 70, 28; 70, 61).

Subjugation even of kings is also possible by way of a sādhana. Kane, 1962 (p. 1103) refers to the Śāradātilaka (10, 105ff.) where a certain mantra is enjoined to be repeated for 500.000 times, together with 50.000 outpourings of ghee while the goddess Devī should be worshipped. When these requests have been followed up correctly one gains everything desired up to the subjugation of kings. The same text (in 9, 103) describes a sādhana for gaining the control over women.

The recitation of hymns can be effective for similar ends. The authors of stotras usually do not omit to state at the end the rewards for saying or hearing their poem. The Varāhamukhīstava, also called Vārāhyanugrahāṣṭakam "Poem of eight stanzas to Vārāhī's grace" (Aithal, No. 18) records as its results among others: 1. *Tarati vipadaḥ* "one overcomes one's troubles". 2. Lordship over demons (bhūtas) and the roaming dead (pretas). 3. Eradication of enemies, brought about by devotion to Vārāhī (stanza 3). 4. Fluency of speech (stanzas 2 and 8). 5. Subjugation of the entire world (*vaśayati jagat sarvam*, stanza 2). It would be worthwhile to execute further research into the results stated by the devotional literature in Sanskrit.

As to harming the enemy, a festival may also be organized for that same result by a ruler. The Devīpurāṇa promises such rewards from the Durgotsava (Kane, 1958, p. 156, n. 399). For the Dasahra festival the Dharmasindhu enjoins worship of Aparājitā Devī for those kings who want to undertake a military expedition (Kane, o.c., p. 190). Besides, appeals to the gods by individuals with evil ends in view must have been done in practice. Some comparatively recent cases are recorded by Dare (p. 53; about the year 1930).

For such kind of ceremonies, it has been considered sometimes especially rewarding to associate oneself with power of darkness such as evil spirits or demons, or with those gods whose power was feared in a special degree. As a matter of fact, approaching and manipulating such dreaded powers was considered highly dangerous, the more so as the aims were often amoral. On the manipulation of demons we return presently. First we give an instance of worship of a much feared group of heavenly forces, the planets. The Mt Pur (93,140ff.) advises the worship of the nine planets for a person who has in mind to practise various kinds of destructive magic. The ceremony should be accompanied by an offering for ten thousand times by means of particular kinds of fire-wood, flowers and incense. There should be present three pots filled with the blood of recently killed crows; the performers should sacrifice with dishevelled hair while meditating on the enemy's misfortune (151). Muttering a certain sinister mantra, one should manufacture an image of the enemy and cut it into pieces with a knife. The pieces he should throw into the fire [14].

It should be added that performances of this kind need not to be restricted to the worship of fearsome forces. The MMD, for example, often prescribes the invocation of a usually benevolent deity for thoroughly honourable ends or for unspecified results like "all desires are fulfilled" or "any objective realized"; but immediately afterwards in the cadre of the same invocation it often adds special methods for those who follow the path of sorcery. For example, in 12, 139ff. : "when he thus constantly worships the Venerable Lady Sundarī together with her nine groups of surrounding deities, his senses subdued, he will obtain all desires. From here on the special methods will be explained which confer on the performer (*sādhaka-*) his particular wishes" [15]. These wishes appear to include: becoming equal to Rudra, obtaining lordship of speech, deluding the world, obtaining a kingdom. They belong to the range of divine powers appropriated by the ritual adept when he minutely follows the rules. The alternatives in the ritual which help to realize these objectives are in this case the sacrifice of certain specified kinds of flowers (see also below, ch. 6.3) We may surmise that the performer has been cautious and that he expected nothing more than that such oblations stimulated him in his strivings after the goal he had set himself.

Which are the results striven after by means of such kind of magical sādhanas? The texts themselves sometimes contain elaborate statements of such results. The MMD ch. 13 concludes the discussion of the pūjā to Hanūmān (see above) with such a list which is represented here in an abridged form.

1. A thousandfold offering with fruits of the *kadalī* (banana), *bījapūra*, and mango during which the brahmans are fed regularly, will result in the destruction of all danger for bhūtas, poison, thieves and so on.
2. A 108-fold recitation of the mantra destroys poison.
3. A 900-fold recitation performed at night during nine successive nights removes the danger from enemies and rulers.
4. In case of fever inflicted by sorcerers or demons, the mantra should be uttered above water or ashes while the patient is hit with it. After three days the fever will be gone.
5. (stanza 19). A sick person should consume a certain herb over which the mantra has been spoken; he will regain his health.
6. Ashes or water over which the mantra has been spoken, when smeared on the body, will render the person invulnerable in battle.

7. Festering wounds will dry up (?).

8. In case the danger from enemies is imminent, one should say the mantra during seven nights while burying a wooden peg together with ashes. The result will be that the enemies begin to quarrel under another (*vidveṣaṃ mitha āpannāḥ*) and make off.

9. (st. 24). A mixture of ashes, water and sandal is spoken over with the mantra. Such a mixture, when brought into contact with a certain person, for instance by being put into his food, will render that person a slave of the performer.

10. One should make a small image of Hanūmān, of approximately the size of a thumb, and endow it with "life" (*prāṇa-*). Such an image, when buried under one's door, will have the effect of warding off all calamities and dangers. Besides, one will become prosperous and obtain sons.

11. On a cemetery one should pierce an image of the enemy while muttering the mantra and the name of the victim, accompanied by the words *chinddhi* "cut through" and *bhinddhi* "split asunder" and *māraya* "kill". After that one should press the image together (it has been made of clay or similar material). This should be repeated during seven nights. The enemy will die.

12. A sacrifice performed in a sacrificial pit in the shape of a half moon, and by means of products associated with evil such as the wings of crows and sticks from the *śleṣmātaka* tree, is also very harmful towards an enemy. One should perform it with dishevelled hair during the night while facing the South, and repeat it 300 times. After that the enemy will die.

13. (st. 35). The mantra should be recited for 600 times at night on a cemetery. A *vetāla* (vampire, a demon which incarnates in the bodies of persons who have recently died) will appear and predict the future to the performer.

The list is continued still further, but the instances given above present a fair impression of the power of Hanūmān's mantra. We give a few other instances from the same MMD. Chapter 2 deals with the mantras of Gaṇeśa. The mantra of six syllables (*Vakratuṇḍāya huṃ*), when recited 12.000 times during half a year while the god is worshipped, will destroy poverty. When the performer recites the mantra 10.000 times while making 108 outpourings (of ghee ?) a day, he will become wealthy (*dhanasamṛddhimān*). A sacrifice repeated a thousand times a day with the aid of certain fragrant plants will result in the acquisition of a mass of wealth within a month. After a variation of the same rite he needs only a fortnight to become as wealthy as Kubera.

Another mantra of Gaṇeśa, comprising .. syllables, is also able to effect the acquisition of wealth (*nidhi-*). When a person desires to conquer or otherwise obtain a kingdom, he should say the mantra while worshipping an image of Ucchiṣṭa-Gaṇeśa of the size of a thumb and meditate on his own identity with the god. The kinds of clay of which such an image has been made are conducive to specified results. Potters' clay brings about the gain of a kingdom, while clay mixed with salt brings the enemies into confusion (*kṣobhayed arīn*). Clay from under a *nimba* tree destroys the enemies. The mantra can produce also victory in gambling or in a dispute. It is added that Kubera himself gained his position as Lord of Wealth by muttering exactly this mantra.

In ch. 18,169 the propitiation of Caṇḍī (a form of Durgā) is recommended when calamities beset the king, such as a famine, an earthquake, excessive rain or drought, or when inimical armies have approached. All these obstructions or their effects will disappear when the hundredfold method of Caṇḍī has been executed. Diseases are annihilated and enemies destroyed, and one becomes rich in wealth and sons (18,170f.) :

sarvavighnā vinaśyanti śatacaṇḍīvidhau kṛte /
rogāṇāṃ vairiṇāṃ nāśo dhanaputrasamṛddhayaḥ //

The worship of Svapnavārāhī is advised especially for the subjugation of all kinds of people and wild beasts (10,56). A colourful statement is made in 10,112 : when Vārāhī has been worshipped according to a certain method, during which she is accompanied by secondary figures, the effect will be that the whole throng of enemies is consumed by troops of supernatural "sorceresses" (*evaṃ kṛte vairivṛndaṃ bhakṣyate yoginīgaṇaiḥ*). In general we can say that in the description of the MMD any effect is attainable by the worship of any god. There is not much evidence of a specialization of the gods in a particular kind of effectivity.

The Buddhist MMK is much older than the MMD. It is usually considered to be one of the oldest Buddhist Tantras.

It mentions a great number of vidyās (spells) and concomitant ritual for very divergent aims. Some instances from the second chapter (p. 26-52) : On pp. 26-29 a number of vidyās is prescribed which will help destroy the enemies and inflict illnesses on them. All kinds of evil are warded off. On p. 30 the mantra *Oṃ riṭi svāhā* is said to destroy poison, while *Oṃ niṭi* wards off the planetary evils. *Oṃ niḥ* attracts Yakṣiṇīs, *Oṃ jñaiḥ* hits Ḍākinīs. The mantra *Oṃ varade svāhā* is conducive to prosperity (*śreyasātmaka-*); *Oṃ bhūri svāhā* removes fever; *Oṃ nu re svāhā* removes obstruction. On p. 31, *Oṃ vilokini svāhā* is said to procure the mastery of treasures. A certain long mantra opens the possibility to enter into the body of whatever other creature (*sarvasattvāveśinī*). The Mahāśvetavidyā, *Oṃ śvetaśrīvapuḥ svāhā*, effects marital happiness or the mastery over husband or wife. The Yoginīvidyā overcomes all evil beings. Its wording is as follows : "*Oṃ khikhirikhiri*, Thou Who art able to break (? in classical Sanskrit the word *bhaṅguri* would mean : fragile), all enemies immobilize, devour, delude, bring under Thy sway, *svāhā*" (*Oṃ khikhirikhiri bhaṅguri sarvaśatrūṃ stambhaya jambhaya mohaya vaśam ānaya svāhā*).

The words *Oṃ śrīḥ* are able to procure the command of a kingdom. On p. 32 a mantra is given for the warding off of enemies. On p. 33 a spell is said to attract material goods, while another one effects all results desired by man (*sarvamānuṣakaphala-*). The Kārttikeyamañjuśrīmantra, when accompanied by the worship of its deity, performs all works, terrifies all spirits, attracts, subjugates, causes to dry out, hits, in short effects anything which might be desired by the wielder of the spell (*yathepsitaṃ vā vidyādharasya tat sarvaṃ saṃpādayati*). It is clear that the constraining of demons and other supernatural beings occupies an important place in prescriptions of this kind. Great emphasis is also laid on the procuring of material gain and mastery over other beings, subjects in which all moderation seems to be lost out of the eye.

Another interesting spell (on p. 33 of the MMK) is the Mahābrahmamantra : *Oṃ brahma subrahma brahmavarcase śāntiṃ kuru svāhā* "Oṃ Brahman, Benevolent Brahman, procure pacification to him who possesses the lustre of brahman (or : for attaining the lustre of brahman), *svāhā*". It is important to note how this Buddhist text makes use of Hindu philosophical concepts (although not unknown in Buddhism) for the enrichment of its magical lore. The effects of the Mahābrahmamantra are that all spirits and especially Śītalā, the dreaded smallpox goddess, are pacified. A general state of safety (*svastyayana-*) occurs. Besides, this spell is also applicable in abhicāra (*abhicāreṣu sarveṣu athavo cedapa thyate*, ?), which reminds of the application of the Brahman concept in the Veda (see above p. 63).

A few other objectives mentioned in the MMK, chs. 2 and 3 : on p. 34, all spirits will be destroyed. Poison is antidoted by means of a Vainateya mantra, directed to Garuḍa the legendary enemy of snakes. On p. 39 destruction of all hindrance by spirits and all beings of evil intentions (*duṣṭacetasa-*) is obtained by means of the mantra and worship of Yamāntaka Krodharāja, the "King of Anger". In ch. 3 (p. 53) a maṇḍala together with a mantra of one syllable (*jaḥ*) is advised for those who desire sovereignty over a kingdom; material wealth (*bhoga-*); sons; elephants or horses; and for those who suffer of all kinds of ailments like snakebite, fever, possession by Rākṣasas or Piśācas and so on. All those people should be initiated into this maṇḍala on different places. On p. 54 special directions are given for those who desire the kinds of fame which are particular to a man or woman (*striyāḥ puruṣasya vā yaśo 'rthinām*) (the author probably means potency and fecundity), or for those who suffer of diseases of all sorts. At last there is a *phalaśruti* "statement of results" in general terms of a stylized and conventional kind : "One is released from all illness and obtains the things desired : he who has no son obtains a son; he who is poor (in marital happiness) will become happy; a beggar obtains material goods, only by looking to this maṇḍala; one will always obtain success of the kind desired, no matter which, (the kind desired) by a woman or man, or by (those who organize) the *śrāddha* ritual" [16].

In one of its later chapters (55; vol. III, p. 668ff.) the MMK gives prescriptions for those who wish to wield power over their fellow-beings, in the first place by binding their partners in love. Even the queen is subjugated by him who, while respecting the ritual prescriptions, hits the image of Mañjuśrī, which has been painted on a cloth, (*paṭa-*) on the forehead with white flowers for 8.000 times. He who desires to subjugate a brahman woman should sacrifice in front of that image on cloth 80.000 *bilva* flowers. The result of other manipulations with the same painted image is that one obtains wealth, becomes invisible, gains overlordship over all Siddhas, is able to procure food merely by meditating about it (*manasāhāram utpadyate*), or to live for 500 years. A person who desires to evoke all nāgas (serpent demons) and cause them to execute all his commands should lay down the painted image of Mañjuśrī on the bank of the Gaṅgā and build on it a dome (*caitya-*) of sand. He should have this accompanied by an offering of honey and milk, food appreciated by snakes. In order to attract the Yakṣas for similar ends, one should lay down the paṭa on the top of a mountain and offer to them *candasakalikā* (?) watered with sesamum oil. On p. 669 prescriptions are given by following which one will attract the Vidyādharas or the King of the Serpents. This personage will give to the performer a jewel and he will gain the status of a Vidyādhara for himself. On p. 678ff. rules are given for those who wish to become master over a village (*grāmasvāmin*), to carry off victory in a debate, to be invincible in battle, to pacify Mārī the goddess of pestilence, to be immune to pain, to live for ten thousand years, to have a safe delivery (*sukhaṃ prasavati*) or to deliver a son (p. 685), to become dear to all people (*sarvajanapriyo bhavati*, p. 686), and so on. For the last-mentioned end one should among others apply a mark of beauty to the forehead (*lalāṭe tilakaṃ kṛtvā*; see below—ch.6.5).

So far for the MMK. These instances show that nothing is impossible for the magician who knows and applies the rules and formulas in the right method. Another Buddhist Tantra of the Vajrayāna school is the Hevajra Tantra (HT). It contains a great deal of magic of the sort discussed from the preceding texts. A few instances of the results promised in ch. 2: the attraction of rain (*varṣāyana*, ?); the splitting of clouds (for the same purpose ?) during which the performer should seat himself on old or ragged garments on a cemetery (?, *śmaśāna-karpaṭa-*) while he mutters the mantra *Oṃ āryaśmaśānapriyāya hūṃ hūṃ hūṃ phaṭ svāhā*;the destruction of an inimical army by means of the "method of the cutting thunderbolt" (*vajrakartarividhi-*), during which a mantra should be recited 1.000.000 times, or 100.000 times after a preceding pūjā; inflicting fever on the enemy by means of the mantra *Oṃ Hevajra jvala śatrūn bhruṃ hūṃ hūṃ hūṃ phaṭ svāhā* "Oṃ Hevajra, burn burn the enemies..."; causing a victim to vomit alcoholics; subjugating a young woman, for which end one should clothe oneself in red and eat fruits of the *madanaphala* while he says the mantra *Oṃ hrīḥ amukī me vaśībhavatu svāhā*..."the lady N.N. should come under my power..." for 10.000 times; even for subjugating the sun and moon, which means to cause them to stand still, as appears from the mantra. The heroic dimension of this last feat is reflected by the prescription that the mantra in question should be recited 7.000.000 times[47].

The Balinese Sanskrit hymns edited in Stuti & Stava are often accompanied in the mss by prescriptions about how to apply them and which results to be expected from them (see in Stuti & Stava the rubrics called "Ritual Environment"). An anthology of some of these results : release for the deceased (046) or liberation for oneself (091,223); protection, very often in battle (passim); the subjugation (094, 097, 546) or destruction (094, 381 , 507 and others) of enemies ; rescue from planets (097, 507); protection against inimical spells (630); against disease (136, 157, 193, 369 and others); against epidemics (154, 369, 790, 851, 902); against calamities (202, 396, 450, 857); protection of the crops (302, 345, 369); against mice (378); obtaining rain (348); longevity (369); welfare of the house (733); purification (166, 286, 345); exorcism of demons (369, 414, 504, and passim ; see Appendix 4 to Stuti & Stava s.v. *bhūtas*); protection against or cure from poison (097, 336, 441, 507); becoming dear to others (097); control over others (325); obtaining a better memory (712). The list is not complete and one should bear in mind that there are many other hymns destined for the propitiation and praise of a god and nothing more.

The rituals prescribed in the Indian Tantric literature for the attaining of goals like the preceding often seem to be fantastic,sinister or even impracticable. When one remembers how Joshua in the Old Testament (Joshua 10, 12) called the sun and moon to a halt in order to influence the course of a battle, it is difficult to imagine how this same goal could be reached by someone who had first to recite a certain mantra for seven million times. It is even most surprising for a modern reader to find concrete ritual prescriptions for realizing this feat altogether. In some cases, especially in a yoga context, it seems better to assume that such powers have been stated only as functions of the evolved state of spiritual development won by the adept which he realizes only and merely by his meditation. The accompanying ritual would then only serve as an external aid to help him bring about this spiritual stage. Recitation of a high number of mantras during such ceremonies is certainly attainable with the help of a rosary (cf. Jacques, p. 259; and below ch. 6.3 C. for specific functions of the rosary). Besides, the fantastic and hyperbolical seems to be an essential prerequisite for the language of magic (see below, ch.5.6; for Iamblichus' exposition of this point, see de Jong, p. 149).

The effects kept in view by the performers can be summarized under three heads : those of pacification or warding off evil, disease or danger (*śānti*) ; those of promoting happiness or material wealth (*puṣṭi*) and those destined to harm others (*abhicāra*). This triad is often mentioned by the texts themselves. The author of the KJ in ch. 4 enumerates the objects connected with the rituals of *śānti*. Then in chs. 5-8 he makes a digression on the magical lotus fire, after which in ch. 9 he discusses the appeasement of evil forebodings, a subject which equally falls under the heading of śānti. Then in ch. 10 follows the enumeration of the objects which cause welfare (*puṣṭi*), and those which spread evil influence (*abhicāra*). The latter class is constituted by all objects and actions which run contrary to the usual prescriptions, such as an image not installed in the correct method, a fire kindled in a skull, fire-wood taken from trees of bad renown.

The MMK (I, p.123) distinguishes three kinds of logs of wood for sacrifice to Agni. They are applicable respectively in rituals of pacificatory, acquisitive and fearsome purpose (*tathā prayuktasya śāntikapauṣṭikaraudrakarmeṣu tridhā samidhakāṣṭhāni bhavanti*). The fire during these three kinds of ritual is characterized by three shades of colour: white, red and black or smoky (see below ch.4.2). We need not give other instances on this place. It might only be mentioned that the Śrīcakrasaṃbhāra Tantra[48] mentions four goals of the ritual : *śānti*, *puṣṭi*, *vaśīkaraṇa* and *māraṇa*, which the translator renders by "peaceful", "grand", "fascinating" and "destructive". We emphasize, however, that these three (or four) objectives cannot be sharply separated from each other: for instance, harming an enemy by destructive magic may be executed for the welfare and safety of the own community.

6. *The manipulation of supernatural beings*

The usual attitude to spirits or demons in India is to drive them away or at least to request them to leave. The request is most often accompanied by a small offering (*bali*) which is destined to propitiate the spirit. Of course there are many kinds of such beings. Some of them are extremely vague, others possess the dim outlines of an anthropomorphic figure or even the beginnings of a mythology. Some are rather innocuous; they may even consider the protection of the human community as their duty. Others are evil minded and specialize in wrongdoing, which ranges from petty teasing up to outright menace with disease and death. The demons in the stricter meaning of the term are always evilly minded[49].

It is, however, possible for an energetical person to manipulate them and utilize their powers for his own ends. The invocation of demons or spirits for such purposes is considered to be a powerful kind of sādhana. It usually takes the form of conjuring and compelling them. These practices are certainly old. The Jātakas allude to those who practise this art; they are called *bhūtavejja-* in Pali (Fick, p. 153). From classical Greek and Latin literature there are indications of the same practices having been performed. Plotinus (Enneads 4, 4, 43) mentions the liability of demons to be influenced by magic (de Jong, p. 129). In primitive societies the magician who has mastered one or more demons often occurs[50]. Such demons which often accompany and serve their masters are called the magicians' "familiars". The Indian aboriginals know them and their magicians employ them (Elwin, p. 64, 66). In Ceylon the conjuring up of demons was practised for various purposes; it was effected chiefly by the utterance of powerful spells by which the demons were considered to be irresistibly fascinated (Gooneratne).

The conjuring of the supernatural world sometimes goes even so far as insulting and menacing the spirit in question,

Dare (p. 127) refers to this practice as a current phenomenon among those who try to exercise their magic on the gods or godlings. The Kanikkārs of Kerala, while going out on a hunting expedition, first revere their Muthans or hunting deities; they add that, might there be no game, their conclusion will be that there are also no Muthans. This menace always procures its effect within a week (Iyer, p. 53). The Egyptian magical papyri contain many instances of menacing the god by the magician (de Jong, p. 147ff.). The reason may be that the magician who dares to menace the inhabitants of the spiritual worlds not only thereby gives a clear show of his own supernatural power, but also creates a mystic communion between himself and these spiritual beings. By such excessive statements he becomes one of the gods himself (see below, ch.5.6).

Among the primitive or semi-literate societies the magicians often execute pressure upon the spirits. In Malacca a sorcerer who invokes the help of Prophet Tap for his manipulations may say to him : "if you do not make N.N. sick or kill him, you will rebel against God !"[51]. The MMK (III, p. 565) in the cadre of the rules for the Yakṣiṇī Naṭikā considers the case that she does not arrive after the prescribed preparations have been made. In that situation the performer should mention the King of Anger in his formulas, and then she will come without any doubt (*krodharājasahitaṃ japed niyatam āgacchati*). SM No. 111 (Tārāsādhana) contains provisions for the case that the goddess refuses to release a person in prison. The performer carries on expressing his demand, and "there will be pain in the head, severe fever, an evil sharp pain (?), and she manifests herself to the performer, and on the seventh day necessarily sets (the prisoner or the performer) free" [17].

But on the other side, he who ventures upon the dangerous path of conjuring up the malicious powers of the unseen should realize himself that he plays with fire. The demons will stubbornly try to resist the call of the magician which threatens to subjugate them, and they will do this by all kinds of teasing or menacing. The performer should, however, not be impressed by all this and quietly stand his ground. As HT (p. 6) expresses it, "even if a demon in strength equal to Indra appears before him, he should certainly not fear him; he should wander around in the manner of a lion" :

Śakratulyo 'pi yo daityaḥ purato bhavati niścitam |
bhayaṃ tatra na kurvīta siṃharūpeṇa paryaṭet ||

Crooke (I, p. 262) makes mention of the particular dangers which await those who meet the Bhūt called Airi. Such a person runs the risk of being burnt by a flash of his eye or being devoured by his dogs. But if one comes through this, the Bhūt will show him the way to hidden treasures.

We now proceed to give some instances of the manipulation of some specific kinds of supernatural beings. Late Vedic texts give rules for such acts, for example Ṛgvidh, 4, 5 (the Night); SVBr 3, 7, 3 (Piśācas); 3, 7, 5 (Gandharvas and Apsarases). We concentrate on Tantric literature and come first to the Yakṣiṇīs. These are female spirits most often believed to inhabit trees or other representants of the vegetative world[52]. Their manipulation is often described. The most common motif for it is certainly the acquisition of wealth.

A few instances. MMD (ch. 7) describes the sādhana of Vaṭayakṣiṇī and other similar figures. Of the magical treatises edited in the Indra-jālavidyāsaṃgraha, K mentions the Yakṣiṇīsādhana on p. 122, N in ch. 14. D gives similar rules in ch. 12. According to this last text, the sādhana of Yakṣiṇīs will result in the gratification of all desires. In the version of the Indrajālavidyāsaṃgraha the author proceeds by describing the method for the Yakṣiṇī Dhanadātrī "Giver of money". The performer should climb an aśvattha tree, concentrate his mind and mutter the formula *Oṃ aiṃ klīṃ śrīṃ dhanaṃ kuru kuru svāhā* "*Oṃ*,. .procure money, *svāhā*". When he climbs a mango tree, he will obtain a son. In that case the mantra should be *Oṃ hrāṃ hrīṃ hrūṃ putraṃ kuru kuru svāhā*. The climbing of trees suggests the habit of Yakṣiṇīs who are sometimes depicted as leaning against a tree, as in the famous railings of the stūpa at Sāñchī. Other trees in the same way concede their particular results : climbing a *vaṭa* procures welfare (*śrī*); an *arka*, victory; sitting on the root of a *tulasī*, a kingdom (6 : *tulasīmūlam ārūḍho rājyam āpnoti*); on *kuśa* grass, success in enterprise; on *apāmārga*, success in disputes, and so on.

The same chapter (D 12, 13ff.; Benares ed. : 17, prose) describes the worship of the Yakṣiṇī Surasundarī. The performer should worship the Liṅga regularly thrice a day, presenting fragrances and muttering the mantra for three thousand times. This mantra runs : *Oṃ hrīṃ āgaccha āgaccha Surasundari svāhā* "*Oṃ hrīṃ*, come come, S., *svāhā*". After one month she arrives, and he should address her with these words : "O Goddess ! I am stricken by poverty, be the cause of its destruction". He should present her with arghya offerings and make a bow to her. Then she asks : "What do you want ?" and after hearing his wish, she is well pleased and grants to him wealth and a long life [18]. The simplicity of the description is indeed striking. Another Yakṣiṇī mentioned in this chapter is Amṛtā who hands out the Water of Life (st. 15). The mantra for her is *Oṃ klīṃ candrike haṃsaḥ oṃ klīṃ svāhā* (Ben. ed. *krīṃ klīṃ-svāhā*). In stanza 16 there is Karṇapiśācinī who grants the faculty of prediction. In st. 17, Haṃsī concedes freedom from obstruction. The Benares ed. in st. 18 mentions the worship of Manoharī and in the following stanzas that of Kāmavatī and Kāmeśvarī who both may become the sādhaka's wives.

MMK in its peculiar kind of Sanskrit gives an instance of the manipulation of a Yakṣiṇī in ch. 26 (II. 293). "The person who desires to attract a Yakṣiṇī should, uttering her name, worship for seven days with oblations of *aśoka* flowers. On the seventh day she comes and grants a boon; within a week she necessarily arrives (again), and (becomes) his mother, sister, or wife, just as his request is : but, if she does not come, her (his ?) head will split asunder" [19]. In the same way a *nāgī* or serpent woman is dealt with. She is worshipped with "serpent flowers", *nāgapuṣpa*. The threatenings uttered in connection with the Yakṣiṇī are repeated in slightly other form on p. 294, where the male god Vajrapāṇi is the object : "after seven nights without any doubt he concedes his presence; if he does not do so, he (or : the performer ?) will go to ruin" (*saptarātraṃ niyataṃ darśanaṃ dadāti* ; *atha na dadāti vinaśyati*). And further on, in connection with Maheśvara : "..if he does not concede his presence, his (or : the performer's ?) head will split asunder in twenty one parts" (*darśanaṃ dadāti* : *yadi na dadāti trisaptadhā mūrdhnā sphuṭati*). The purport of these remarks is as yet unclear to us.

Further on (III, p. 564ff.) the MMK describes the sādhana of a group of eight Yakṣiṇīs : Naṭikā, Naṭṭā, Bhaṭṭā, Revatī, Mekhalā, Sumekhalā, Ālokinī and Tamasundaryā. Naṭikā, the first of them, is worshipped with the mantra *Oṃ Naṭi Mahānaṭi āgaccha āgaccha divyarūpiṇi svāhā* "*Oṃ* Naṭī, Great Dancer, come come, O Thou of divine form, *svāhā*". This spell should be said 8.000 times. A figure of her should be drawn : she is sparkling black, richly decorated, and leans to a tree (*vṛkṣāśritā*). Her hair hangs loose, her eyes are red; she smiles a little, beckoning the sādhaka with her right hand while clutching with her left hand the branch of the tree. The recitation of the mantra should be accompanied by the same number of oblations by means of palāśa wood. This should be going on thrice a day during seven days. On the seventh day a rich offering (*udārabali-*) should be presented. The performer should wait till midnight. He should light the lamps with ghee and continue saying the mantra. At last she arrives in her usual form and says : "what can I do ?". The sādhaka answers : "be my wife". She concedes this and disappears; but from that moment onwards she is indeed the sādhaka's wife who procures to him all his desires and leads him to her palace. She even gives to him the *elixir vitae*, and he obtains a celestial form. In the case that she should not come on his command he introduces the King of Anger, as we saw above.

The second Yakṣiṇī, Naṭṭā, is treated similarly, only her mantra is as follows : *Oṃ Naṭṭe śuklāmbaramālyadhāriṇi maithunapriye svāhā* "Oṃ, Naṭṭā, who wearest a white garment and garland, Who art desirous of sexual intercourse, *svāhā*". Bhaṭṭā, the third one, is attracted by "*Oṃ* Bhaṭṭā, Thou Who observest, why dost Thou hesitate, come come, come here (2x), perform my work, *svāhā*" [20]. She also becomes the sādhaka's wife and grants to him all things he desires. He plays the game of love with her, and she renders him omniscient: *tayā sārdhaṃ krīḍati...sarvajñaṃ saṃpādayati*. Revatī is invoked in this way: "honour to all Yakṣiṇīs; Oṃ, Thou Red One, with shining red lustre, with red unguent, *svāhā*". Her further description : "Revatī is the most desirable of the Yakṣiṇīs; she is sportive and loves intercourse; her garment is reddish, her hair is black and somewhat undulating; this Yakṣī's limbs are all beautiful, she always delights in the enjoyments of love; she constantly grants enjoyment and wealth; one should characterize her as someone who grants boons" [21].

The next one, Mekhalā, is invoked by *Oṃ Mekhale mahā-*

yakṣiṇi mama kāryaṃ saṃpādaya svāhā "*Oṃ*, M., Great Yakṣiṇi, perform my work...". Sumekhalā is invoked by : *Oṃ Mekhale Sumekhale mahāyakṣiṇi sarvārthasādhani oṃ samayam anusmara svāhā* "*Oṃ*, ...Who realizest all objectives, *Oṃ*, remember our agreement, *svāhā*". Ālokinī has a short mantra: *Oṃ lokini lokavati svāhā*. The last of the eight is Tamasundaryā or Andhārasundarī (= Andhakārasundarī ?). Her mantra is *Oṃ ghuṇu guhyake ghuṇu ghuṇu guhye ehi ehi guhyake svāhā*. Her being addressed as a Guhyakā "secret being" gives her a special position among this group. The word *ghuṇu* might be a corruption of *ghūrṇaya* "cause to shake or tremble" which occurs in a mantra in AgPur 323,21. The mantra of Tamasundaryā should be said for 10.000 times during a full moon's night on a lonely secluded place, accompanied by worship. During one month the ritual should be maintained in this way: one should before going to sleep say the mantra 800 times over the right arm. Then she will arrive without any doubt in the next full moon's night. He should not speak when he beholds her, but make love to her, and repeat this for six months (*tūṣṇīṃbhāvena kāmayitavyā ṣaḍbhiḥ māsaiḥ*). From then onwards she will be mastered (*siddhā*). She becomes his wife and procures all his desires. These may be of the most extravagant character. For instance (p. 567) she can take him on her back and bring him to Mount Meru. At night she can lead him around the world. She enables him to kill an enemy even as remote as a hundred miles. There is, however, one important condition: the sādhaka is forbidden to desire any other woman. Henceforth he should completely commit himself to his supernatural spouse.

The MMK (III, 567ff.) then describes the mastering of another group, this time of seven Yakṣiṇīs. These are Andhāravāsinī, Guhavāsinī, Naravīrā, Kumārī, Madhuyakṣī or Vadhūyakṣī, Manojñā and Surasundarī. They roam about over the earth in the desire to do the good of creatures. They are beautiful and follow up all instructions. They have been revealed by the Bodhisattva (Mañjuśrī) in order to realize the enjoyment of creatures. The first of them, Andhāravāsinī, is the same as the last of the eight Yakṣiṇīs mentioned above. The second, Guhyavāsinī (the manuscript is not consistent in its spelling) is attracted by the mantra *Oṃ guhile guhamati Guhavāsi ānaya bhagavati mayāntikaṃ samayam anusmara svāhā* "*Oṃ* Secret

One, of secret intentions, Thou Who dwellst in secret, bring to my presence...., O Lady; remember the agreement, *svāhā*". She is said to live in a cave in Mount Meru. Her figure should be depicted on a cloth (*paṭa-*). Her colour is golden. She arrives after the necessary preparations by the performer and says : "My dear, what can I do ?" And he asks her to become his mother. Under no circumstances should he desire her as his wife. From that moment onwards she does everything for him just as a mother would do.

The third of the group of seven Yakṣiṇīs, Naravīrā, is invoked with a simple formula : *Oṃ Naravīre svāhā* (p. 568). She stands grasping an Aśoka tree with her hand. She is willing to become the performer's sister. Among her feats is the ability to attract women for her master. The fourth one Yakṣakumārikā (she has been announced previously by the text as Kumārī) is evoked with *Oṃ Yakṣakumārike svāhā.* She also grasps an Aśoka tree. She is Kubera's daughter. The sādhaka, after having succeeded in evoking her, gives her a choice: becoming his mother, sister or wife. As a mother she will procure him whatever he desires. As a sister she is able to bring a woman to him even from a distance of a hundred miles. As a wife she lives with him for a thousand years and realizes all his wishes. The fifth, Vadhūyakṣiṇī, is evoked by the short mantra *Oṃ niḥ.* She arrives and clutches her arms around the performer's neck. She becomes his dear wife. At night she comes to serve him, in the morrow she disappears again. And after each night she leaves a string of pearls and a thousand golden coins in the sādhaka's possession. He is warned, however, never to disclose anything of his adventures. He should, of course, cease to love any other woman, including even his own wife.

Manojñā, the sixth, is attracted by her mantra *Oṃ Manohare madonmādakari vicitrarūpiṇi maithunapriye svāhā* "*Oṃ* Charming One Who art a cause of exhilaration, Who appearest in manifold forms, Who desirest intercourse, *svāhā*". The essential lines of her worship (*upacāra-*) are : the sādhaka lays ready a garment for her, after which she arrives in the night without clothes and puts on the garment (p. 571). Then the sādhaka enjoys love with her as long as a lamp lighted by him keeps burning. When the lamp has gone out she disappears leaving the garment behind, but not without having put a piece of gold on it. At that same moment the sādhaka should try to take hold of her, by her finger, head, foot or some other part of her body. The ornament caught by him in the process is given to him by her. The sādhaka should not hesitate to spend the money obtained from her on the same day. This Yakṣiṇī may also become his wife. She can be invoked by another mantra : *Oṃ mahānagni nagnije svāhā* "*Oṃ* Great Prostitute, born from a prostitute,...", or : "...Naked One...". The seventh Yakṣiṇī, Surasundarī, has been met already above from the Dattātreya Tantra. She is invoked with *Oṃ Surasundari svāhā*, and executes the performer's wishes. According to N (p. 351), when duly worshipped, she daily makes a gift of a thousand *dīnāras*.

On p. 572, the MMK reiterates the theme in a passage of poetry. He who desires to have intercourse with supernatural women can evoke with his mantras all kinds of female demons and live with them in the nether world (*pātāla-*) for a complete world-period (*kalpa-*). Besides, when the future Buddha, Maitreya, will arrive on earth, he will hear the Noble Doctrine and be liberated from existence. The performer is even able to subjugate divine ladies (*surakanyāḥ*) by such methods. But henceforth he should not even touch earthly women. On p. 573, the same text describes the worship of the Yakṣiṇīs Padmoccā, Samodā, Ajitā and Jayā. The ceremonies are delineated according to the same pattern.

The successes the performer is able to win with these Yakṣiṇīs might be an expression of the siddhis he is considered inevitably to obtain in the course of visionary processes. Hallucinatory experiences are apt to occur after a difficult and prolonged course of physical and mental preparation or after huge exertions involving lack of sleep.

It is perhaps striking that experiences similar to those just described, viz. the appearance at first of demons evoking fear and afterwards of beautiful damsels offering their love, were part of the Buddha's "temptation by Māra"; and siddhis like these also occur to the yogins or Buddhist monks who strive after release by way of a course of introspective psychical exertion. A yogin might be able to make use of these siddhis if he chooses to do so; but he should abstain from them if he really clings to liberation from existence as his direct goal. Seen in this light, the MMK presents an aspect of genuine Buddhist tradition; but it deviates in this respect that the sway over the supernatural world seems to be considered by it as a goal in its own right.

From a theistic point of view it should moreover be noted that the meditation on the chief gods like Śiva and Viṣṇu also implies that the worshipper is confronted with a host of attendants and other secondary divinities. He should pay them honour before proceeding on his way, but as his goal is to identify himself with the god of his choice, it is imaginable that on a certain moment he will be able to rule over them.

7. *Sādhana of female deities*

Besides the Yakṣiṇīs there are other females whose services sometimes are less innocuous. Such a one is Pratyaṅgirā. Her name "Counter magic" implies a direct connexion with the Atharvavedic practice. In the Ṛgvidh. (4, 6, 4) the method of applying to Pratyaṅgirasa, a male figure, is advised in order to counteract evil rites performed by experts in the Atharvaveda (cf. Gonda, n. 4 on p. 105 of his translation). In more recent times Pratyaṅgirā seems to fulfil a similar function. She has been known and adored by the Jainas. Jhavery (p. 224) presents the first and 25th (last) stanza of a Pratyaṅgirāstotra written by Bālacandrasūri. The last stanza promises for the reciters of the hymn that Pratyaṅgirā, being satisfied, will procure all kind of welfare and destroy all distress. Another Jain doctor wrote a Pratyaṅgirākalpa, presumably in the thirteenth century. The Buddhist SM contains a sādhana of Mahāpratyaṅgirā (No. 202; vol. 2, p. 402). Among the characteristics of her figure are her blackness and her six arms.

Her sādhana is also discussed in MMD 9, 84ff. Her main function is that she destroys the magical creations of enemies (*parakṛtyāvimardinī*). She is evoked by means of the following mantra of 37 syllables in Sanskrit :

Oṃ hrīṃ hrāṃ Yāṃ kalpayanti no 'rayaḥ krūrāṃ kṛtyāṃ vadhūm / iva brahmaṇā apanirṇudmaḥ pratyak kartāram ṛcchatu hrīṃ oṃ //

"Oṃ *hrīṃ*, the magical form which our enemies create like a young woman, the horrible one, *hrāṃ*, we push it back by means of the brahman; it should return and hit its creator, *hrīṃ oṃ*". This spell is presupposed by Bṛhaddevatā 8, 45, which means that it is of considerable age. It may be assigned by the performer on fourteen places of his body in a method explained in the Sanskrit commentary to the MMD. Besides, it should be recited for 100.000 times while one meditates on the deity (MMD 9, 91). In this way the spell becomes "mastered", "effectuated" (*siddhamanu-*) For special objectives (*prayoga-*) it should still be recited for a hundred times. A bali to the spirits might for example be brought, while the following words are recited ten times into the directions of the compass : "The evil which exists to the East of mine, by cause of my evil deeds here on earth, Indra the King of the gods should break, anoint (?), stupefy, destroy, kill it; he should assign the Kali to it; for me it is well (*kṛta-*), for me it is beneficial (*śiva-*), for me there should be safety and welfare" [22]. In this way one should say the formula into the other directions also, except of course that he mentions the respective directions instead of the East, and that he replaces the name Indra by those of the other Lokapāla gods. We have here an instance of how old Vedic formulas continued to be in use as effective spells and destroyers of evil into the Tantric surroundings.

Another of these figures is Bagalāmukhī whose worship is presented by the same MMD in ch. 10. It seems that this is originally a deity with an animal face (=Chagalāmukhī, "The Goat-faced One" ?) and thus akin to such goddesses as Svapnavārāhī or to Ṣaṣṭhī who was originally cat-faced. The worship of such goddesses was prominent in the *vrata* religionof the regions of the lower Ganges and its Delta (S. K. Ray, p. 10-14). Bagalāmukhī is sometimes considered to be one of the ten Mahāvidyās or chief female manifestations of Śiva (Mon. Williams, Hinduism, p. 87). Her special function is the immobilization of the acts of an enemy (she is *śatrūṇāṃ stambhinī*). She is the deity of a shrine (*pīṭha*) at Datia near Gwalior. A treatise dedicated to her worship at this place written by the head of the pīṭha has been issued in 1965[53]. The author begins by asserting that Bagalāmukhī is able to grant the four aims of human existence (*caturvidhapuruṣārtha-*), and that her worship has been expounded already in a number of Tantric texts. He wants to give a summary of these traditions. The text most often cited by him is the Sāṃkhyāyanatantra, but he also presents portions from the MMD, Merutantra, Kuṇḍikātantra, AgPur etc.

The origin of the goddess is that during the Kṛtayuga she was seen emerging at midnight from a great yellow pool (*mahāpītahrada-*; yellow is her specific colour) in the form of her vidyā (mantra), the Brahmāstravidyā; this vidyā was able to immobilize the threefold world. Her glow was derived from Viṣṇu; among her names is Mahāmāyā (p. 25). The mantra runs: *Śrīvidye samaye maheśe Bagale*. The opportunity for the new goddess to assert herself came soon when Skanda found himself unable to overcome a Rākṣasa who possessed various forms of sorcery (*nānā-māyāvin*). Śiva was applied to for help, but soon he recognized that without a Brahmāstra they would be unable to destroy the enemy. Then he informed Skanda of the existence of Bagalā, "the *Brahmāstra-stambhinī-vidyā*, who immobilizes all māyā and mantra; also the lady Bagalā is able to call all activities to a halt". Besides, the vidyā was able to perform many other works which are passed over here in silence. It is important to note how there is scarcely made any difference in this fragment between the mantra and the goddess. Both are identical; the mantra is the sound manifestation of the body of that power which we call a goddess when representing it in an image in external material or in the mind.

Another powerful goddess of this kind is Svapnavārāhī ("The Swine Lady of Dreams") whose worship is discussed in MMD (10,35ff.) and SST (3,19,32-73). Her special ability is to bring others under her power (she is *vaśakāriṇī*). She is surrounded by a group of sixteen attendants (śaktis): Uccāṭanī "The Eradicating One", Śoṣaṇī "Who dries up", Māraṇī "Who liquidates", Bhīṣanī "Who terrifies", Trāsanī "Who evokes fear", Kampanī "Who causes to shudder", Ājñāvivartanī "Who causes others to follow up her commands"; the Ladies (īśvarī, īśī) accompanying these seven (Uccāṭanīśī etc.); Vastujāteśvarī "The Lady of the multiplicity of objects"; and Sarvasampādanīśvarī "The Lady of the procurement of all things". The author of MMD enjoins that also the Mothers and Bhairavas associated with this goddess should be worshipped, without, however, mentioning their names. The goddess should be regaled with coconut milk and water from bathing places. On an uncanny place one should fabricate a small image (*puttalī*) of the victim (*sādhya-*). One should prepare a yantra and write the goddess' mantra within it, provided with the victim's name in the accusative and the following words : "eradicate, dry out, liquidate, terrify, destroy (*nāśaya*; very probably a wrong reading for *trāsaya* "evoke fear"), cause the head to shake, cause (somebody, N.N.) to follow up my commands, procure that particular kind of substance, perform everything, *svāhā*". Each item of this list should be repeated once [23]. The reader notices that there is a particular śakti available ready to execute each of the performer's commands. One may choose the commands most fitting in one's particular circumstances.

Among other figures we only shortly notice on this place Jayā, one of the secondary deities accompanying Lakṣmī in the description of the LT. Her sādhana is described in LT 48 (Gupta, p. 317ff.). Above all she affords victory in battle, as her name implies[54].

The AgPur in chs. 123-149 gives a number of rituals destined for him who desires to obtain victory in battle and to get rid of an invading enemy by means of magical methods. This portion of the text is called *Yuddhajayārṇava* "Ocean of rituals granting victory in battle"; it includes the worship of several deities, mainly female, by methods similar to those described above. One of these is the terrible Trailokyavijayā. Her vidyā is contained in ch. 134[55]. We try to give a translation of this chapter :

"Īśvara said : I will expound the Trailokyavijayā Who crushes all charms (yantra). *Oṃ hūṃ kṣūṃ hrūṃ, Oṃ* honour, Lady of the tusks, of horrible countenance, of greatly fearsome appearance; *hili hili*, of red eyes, *kili kili* (Shastri's translation : "shriek and sound"), of terrible sound, *kulu*, *Oṃ*, of lightning tongue, *Oṃ*, Emaciated One, *kaṭa kaṭa*, Thou Whose ornament is (the snake) Gonasa, *cili cili*, Whose garland consists of corpses—put to flight ; *Oṃ*, greatly horrible One, Who art clad in a hide still moisty; yawn; *Oṃ*, dance; Thou Who bearest swords like ivy (?); Whose eyes are frowned, Whose countenance is marked by malicious looks, Whose limbs are smeared with fat and marrow, *kaha kaha* ("eat?" Shastri : "roar"); *Oṃ*, laugh laugh, rage rage; *Oṃ*, Thou of the colour of a black rain cloud, Who hast made Thyself an ornament out of a string of clouds, vibrate; *Oṃ*, Thou Whose body is bedecked by tingling bells; *Oṃ*, Thou Who art standing (or: seated) upon a lioness (*siṃsisthe*, read as *siṃhīsthe*), Whose colour is that of dawn; *Oṃ*, *hrāṃ hrīṃ hrūṃ*; Whose appearance is horrible; *hūṃ hrīṃ klīṃ Oṃ hrīṃ hūṃ*; *Oṃ*, attract; *Oṃ*, shatter; *Oṃ he haḥ khaḥ*, Wielder of the Thunderbolt, *hūṃ kṣūṃ kṣāṃ*, Whose appearance is angry, burn through, burn through; *Oṃ*, Thou who art terrible and frightening, break; *Oṃ*, Thou of impressive size, split; Oṃ, Thou of open mouth, *kiṭi kiṭi* ("cut"?); O Great Mother of the demons, Who wardest off all those of evil mind; O Jayā, *Oṃ*, Vijayā, *Oṃ*, Trailokyavijayā *huṃ phaṭ svāhā*".

The passage winds up : "During a magical act of securing victory one should sacrifice to her, who is dark blue of colour, who stands upon a corpse, who has twenty arms; and having practised the assignment of the mantra on five limbs of the body, one should sacrifice red flowers into the fire; in a battle the rout of the inimical army will come to pass after the recitation of Trailokyavijayā". The reader notices that here again the Sanskrit text scarcely differentiates between the mantra and its goddess.

After this comes another mantra which, strangely enough, is addressed to a male deity whose name is not mentioned : "*Oṃ*, Thou of manifold forms, stupefy stupefy; *oṃ*, delude ; *oṃ*, put all enemies to flight; *Oṃ*, attract Brahmā; *Oṃ*, attract Viṣṇu; *oṃ*, attract Maheśvara; *oṃ*, kick (*ṭālaya= tāḍaya*? Shastri: "make tremble") Indra; *Oṃ*, shake the mountains; *oṃ*, dry out the seven oceans; *oṃ*, split split; to Thou of manifold forms (Shastri : the god Bahurūpa), honour". The excessive demands made to this last deity again serve to emphasize the magician's participation in the cosmical powers which are able to mould or destroy according to their will. A last unclear stanza seems to imply that the performer should meditate on the enemy as being the serpent adorning the goddess' body.

The same passage directed to Trailokyavijayā has been preserved in corrupted form in Bali (Stuti & Stava, No. 325). The motives for ritual application of the fragment contained in the sole manuscript include individual protection (in battle);

regaining influence by a person (presumably a nobleman) who is "despised"; the exercise of control over another or even over the gods (for this last end, the fragment should be recited for a thousand times). It is unclear in how far this Trailokyavijayā is identical with the Mahāyāna goddess of that name alluded to in the Introduction to the Balinese version.

Of other such goddesses we mention the names Kubjikā and Tvaritā, discussed in AgPur 143 and 309-312 respectively. And of course there are the deities of Buddhist Tantrism described in the SM and other texts. One example from the HT 1, 11, end : Kurukullā, who is said to subjugate all beings. She is described as follows : "The goddess who was born from the syllable *hrīḥ*, red of colour, having four arms, having arrow and bow in her hands, bearing lotus and elephant hook ; by merely meditating on her one may bring the threefold world under one's power; by means of a hundred thousand fold (recitation of her mantra) the kings (are subjugated), by means of a number of ten thousand the subjects (*prajāloka-*); by means of ten million, cattle and Yakṣas; by means of 700.000, the Asuras; by means of 200.000 (?), the gods; by means of only a hundred, those who utter spells"[24]. Kurukullā seems to have been named after a mountain somewhere in the Himālayas[56]. Sādhanas of her occur in SM Nos. 171-190. No. 173 advises the use of the the mantra *Oṃ Kurukulle hrīḥ amukaṃ me vaśam ānaya hoḥ svāhā* "Oṃ, Kurukullā,...bring N.N. under my power...". After a correct performance the adept will then see his opponent lying terrified at his feet, completely subjugated by the goddess and her mantra. No. 174 promises that by a ten thousand fold recitation of the mantra all ordinary people will be subjugated; by reciting a million times, all sorcerers; by reciting a hundred thousand times, all kings. In Jainism Kurukullā has also been known as a protective deity of the Jain mantravādins. Jhavery (p. 217) records a contest between the Jain Devasūri and a certain yogin who had a number of poisonous snakes at his command. The creatures even managed to creep over some magical lines drawn by Devasūri and were about to attack him when the goddess in the form of a bird of prey intervened and picked up the snakes. The same Devasūri composed a hymn to Kurukullā by recitation of which one is protected against snakebite. A Kurukullāmantra against all kinds of dangers is handed down already in the Mahānisītha (Jhavery, p. 284). The mantra *Oṃ Kurukulle svāhā*, given against snakebite in GarPur 19, 14-15 according to Jhavery (p. 298) is however read in the edition of GarPur used by us as *Oṃ kuru Kunde svāhā*.

In this connexion attention may be drawn to the ceremonies discussed by KJ ch. 7 and 8. In ch. 7 there occurs a description of an extraordinary worship of Śrī, Viṣṇu's spouse, by someone who desires to obtain welfare (*śrī*) for himself. Such a person should bring a sacrifice into the lotus fire (*pauṇḍarikāgni-*), a particular kind of fire hearth fit for magical purposes. The author first distinguishes two kinds of *śrī*, "secular" and "spiritual". The "spiritual" *śrī* (*Brahmaśrī*) should be honoured in particular by Brahmans. He who feels himself inclined to approach the Secular Śrī can know himself to be backed by a word from the Veda "One should exert oneself in order to obtain prosperity" (quotation unidentified). The course of the worship of Secular Śrī in the lotus fire is as follows : one prepares a fireplace with 200 leaves and alight the fire, meanwhile observing the forebodings which manifest themselves in the fire's behaviour. He should offer oblations with the right hand only, lest the Yātudhānas should catch them. He should not speak in the meantime, lest the Asuras should master them. While performing his oblations, he should practise meditation on the figure of Śrī as the Goddess of Lotuses, glowing with beauty. After a hundred thousand fold oblation with lotuses accompanied by the recitation of the Śrīsūkta the Goddess will manifest herself and the performer may ask for the object desired, which Śrī is certain to grant him. "By mere meditation on this goddess, one will become wealthy, let alone by serving her", the author asserts.

A sādhana of Śrī is also described in AgPur 308. The worshipper should choose one particular part of a nine fold mantra and recite it 100.000 times or more, in preference in a temple of Śrī or Viṣṇu. The results, specified in accordance with the kind of offerings he chooses to bring, are welfare (*bhūti-*), wealth, the subjugation of kings, the destruction of the evil influence of planets, and so on. The instructions include a meditation on the Goddess' appearance and worship of her attendants. After stanza 16 the chapter proceeds with directions for the worship of Durgā. In the Kathās. (2, 2, 10) we come across a literary reference to the worship of Śrī for obtaining wealth, performed by a young Brahman, Kālanemi, at Pāṭaliputra: "Having observed that these others, householders, were rich, Kālanemi out of jealousy tried to master (*sādhayāmāsa*) Śrī, concentrating on his observance; and she, Śrī, being satisfied, appeared to him and spoke to him : ...". The goddess promises to Kālanemi future wealth. His son will even become a king; but he himself will die as a thief, because he made oblations into the fire with his mind obscured by impatience [25].

Having discussed the worship of Śrī, KJ in ch. 8 proceeds to describe the method for Sarasvatī for him who strives after wisdom. The performer should proceed as follows. He provides the fireplace of the lotus fire with 96 leaves, uses firesticks of *aśvattha* wood, and offers beforehand oblations to other gods, among whom is Viṣṇu. Then he should concentrate himself on Sarasvatī as the manifestation of wisdom (*vidyārūpām*, ms L) in the form of a beautiful lady adorned with jewels. He should offer the oblation to the goddess for 12.000 times during twelve nights. Then, characteristically, in the night of the thirteenth day a terrible figure manifests itself. The performer should not be shocked, even not when afterwards he observes another ghost of deformed figure. His steadfastness will at last be rewarded by the appearance of the Lady Herself. He should consider her as his mother and pay homage, after which the goddess grants him a boon. He should not express himself immediately, but first utter the mantra of Sarasvatī for 108 times and implore the goddess' grace. When these rules have been followed, the goddess will certainly comply with his desire for wisdom.

The worship of Sarasvatī has been described by the author of the KJ with somewhat more liveliness and detail than the propitiation of Śrī in the preceding chapter. It conforms in a remarkable way to the descriptions of the Yakṣiṇīsādhanas given by the MMK. The Vaikhānasa author judged it desirable to describe an example of such methods, but rather chose a higher Hindu goddess as the object of the ritual. Of course in confrontation with such a respectable personage the adept should be courteous and submissive—but the results of his "worship" are as certain as in the case of the Yakṣiṇīs.

Sarasvatī's worship is often described by other texts, for example the Devī BhPur (9, 4, 10) where the author states that any blockhead will become a wise man by it. In 9, 4, 30ff. this text describes the pūjā to Sarasvatī, and in the stanzas 73ff. of the same chapter her kavaca, which begins : "*Śrīṃ hrīṃ*, to Sarasvatī, *svāhā*; She should protect my head from all sides; to the Goddess of Speech, *svāhā*; She should further my crane constantly..." [26]. In stanza 89 come the results: after saying the kavaca for 500.000 times, it becomes "mastered" (*siddha-*). The performer becomes equal to Bṛhaspati, a great rhetor, a lord of poets, and able to be master of everything in the world—and in concrete this might mean that he is able to secure for himself a safe and lucrative position as a court poet[57].

Those goddesses who are said to be particularly able to "delude" the world may confer important magical powers to their worshippers. We saw that Durgā or Umā is worshipped also under the name Māyā (p. 47). The BhPur says that one who is desirous of prosperity (*śrī*) should worship Goddess Māyā and the commentator explains Māyā as Durgā. In AgPur (137, 15) the use of *mahāmāyāpaṭa* (cloth with a painting of Mahāmāyā on it?) is recommended in battle (on other Māyāsādhanas see below p. 129). A similar goddess, indeed only another manifestation of Durgā, is Gaurī Trailokyamohanī "Deluder of the Threefold World" described in MMD (9,30ff.). In stanza 36 she is invocated : "She Whose lotus feet are honoured by a throng of celestials; Whose lustre is that of dawn; Whose headdress is adorned by the waxing moon; Who delights in Her outfit of a red garment, red unguent and red flowers; Who bears an elephant goad and a noose. She should be gracious towards us" [27]. The goddess may be worshipped in this way : her mantra is recited for 10.000 times, while 1.000 oblations are made with rice boiled in milk and with ghee. The performer meditates on her as residing in a lotus. Her limbs are on the filament. The Mothers, Brāhmī etc., are on the leaves. Outside are the guardians of the regions and their weapons. When worshipped in this manner, the goddess will grant happiness and prosperity. He who sacrifices during three days with grains, sesamum, fruits, red lotuses, will be able within a month to subjugate all grades of society (39). An alternative is that one meditates on the goddess as abiding in a maṇḍala of the sun. In this case only 108 oblations are required for subjugation of the world. Afterwards follows a mantra of forty syllables in which the goddess is requested to subjugate all people for the worshipper (*mama vaśaṃ kuru kuru*, 42). The stanzas 50ff. advise to make a small image of a victim, infuse it with breath (*prāṇa-*) and bury it into the ground. In this case the victim will become the performer's slave.

As the last of this series of goddesses we mention Kālarātrī, a fearsome appearance of Durgā, whose method is described in MMD 18. The commentary begins by giving her mantra : "*Oṃ aiṃ hrīṃ klīṃ śrīṃ*, Kahneśvari, Thou Who charmest all people, Who stupefiest the mouths of all, Who subjugatest all kings, Who tramplest upon all evildoers, Who attractst all women and men,—destroy all fetters and bonds (?, *vandīśṛṅgalāḥ*), rout rout all enemies, crush crush all haters, stupefy stupefy everything, eradicate eradicate the haters with Thy delusive missile; subjugate subjugate everything, *svāhā*; grant grant everything, O Kālarātri, Lady of the throng of heavenly women, honour" [28]. The passage in the MMD text contains specialized procedures accompanied by their own mantras. Thus, for subjugation (*vaśīkaraṇa-*), the following spell is recommended : "*Oṃ aiṃ klīṃ hrīṃ śrīṃ glauṃ hsauḥ*, honour, O Kahneśvari, delude delude everything; O Black One of black colour, Who wearest a black garment; attract attract everybody; subjugate subjugate them quickly, *aiṃ hrīṃ klīṃ śrīṃ*" [29]. For immobilizing a victim (*stambhana*), one should pay worship with yellow objects such as gorocana and cows' urine. The yantra should be constructed upon a cloth dyed with turmeric. The mantra is : "*Oṃ hlāṃ hlīṃ hlūṃ*, Thou of charming eyes (or Kāmākṣi) and of elusive appearance (*māyārūpiṇī*), Who charmst all, immobilize immobilize, obstruct obstruct, delude delude; *klāṃ klīṃ klūṃ*, O Kāmākṣi, O Kahneśvari, *huṃ huṃ huṃ*"[30].

Stanzas 60ff. contain the directions for practising delusion (*mohana*, i.e. causing the victim to lose control over his senses); to this end the adept should act on a Sunday. He should mix up turmeric with mothermilk. With the product he should design a circular yantra. The accompanying mantra is relatively simple : "*Oṃ*, to *Kāma*, *klauṃ klīṃ*, to the Lovely One, *klīṃ*". By this method the adept will be able "to delude the entire world", provided that he keeps on for five days reciting the mantra, and that he manages to maintain an angry mind (he should be *kruddhamānasa-*). Other magical procedures follow: attraction (67ff.); eradication (79ff.; this should be done in an empty house on the fourteenth of the dark half of the month); sowing discord (86ff.; two planks to be buried near to an ant hill); and liquidation (93ff; cut off the head of a small image of the victim).

8. *Sādhana of male deities*

Besides Yakṣiṇīs, there are also their male counterparts, the Yakṣas, who are liable to be influenced by the human will. The attraction of Yakṣas is dealt with in MMK II, p. 293f. (ch. 26). The sādhaka's goal is a boon to be conferred on him. He should sacrifice during three months, after which the Yakṣas headed by their leader Kubera will appear. Henceforth they send one from their number each day to serve him. Such a yakṣa servant is ready to lead a woman to the sādhaka over a distance of a hundred miles (*yojanaśatād api striyam ānayati*). The sādhaka may climb on his back and go where he pleases. Yet it seems as if the Yakṣas, and in general all male gods, are not valued as highly by the magically-minded adept as the female supernatural beings. At least they do not seem to be manipulated as frequently in the texts.

One of these Yakṣas is Ghaṇṭākarṇa "Bell Ear" who is described in the AgPur (50, 41f.) with eighteen arms. He is invoked especially against diseases like smallpox and tumors and he has played a considerable role in popular religion (see Jhavery, p. 285). Kathās-9,6,94 summarily mentions a propitiation of the Yakṣa Sthūlaśiraḥ "Big Head" in order to force him to concede a certain demand of a king. The king is advised in the matter by his Chief Minister who declares: "There is a Yakṣa named S., and of him I know the propitiatory mantra, by which he (is forced to) give the requested boon":

Asti Sthūlaśirā nāma Yakṣas tasya ca vedmy aham/
mantram ārādhanaṃ yena varam iṣṭaṃ dadāti saḥ//

An interesting passage on the conjuring up of the King

of the Counter gods (Asurendra) is contained in the KCT (4, 159ff.). The adept is a Buddhist of the Kālacakra denomination who conducts his ritual in the course of his Bodhisattva vow. His goal is to win higher powers in order to help the world on its way towards spiritual illumination; his motivation is Compassion (166; *tasmāt sattvārthahetoḥ paramakaruṇayā sādhanīyo 'surendraḥ*). He begins by meditating upon an image of the Buddha in combination with the recitation of a mantra : *Oṃ hrīṃ hreṃ hūṃ phaṭ*. Mantra and image should be mastered (*siddha-*) first within the own mind (which means that the performer accumulates into himself the power of both), otherwise nothing will be achieved. A maṇḍala should now be drawn, and pūjā and oblations brought. The place fit for the ceremony is the cremation ground. After the preliminaries have been handled in the correct way, the King of the Counter-gods appears (163) : "When the oblations have been completed (he appears), flaming, his tongue and head quivering (? *laladaśirasinaḥ*), his tusks sharp, with three eyes; and by roaring and trampling the ground with his feet he tries to terrify the performer; having taken his stand within the fireplace he laughs: *kaha kaha*, and he dances, his body fear-inspiring; the mantrin who beholds him with fear will lose his mind and falls into Yama's stronghold (the abode of the dead) within a moment". But the sādhaka (164) "who strives after realization of the powers of his mantra on the cremation ground should not fear even the Asurendra; unshocked in his mind should he be when beholding him; in this way the Lord of Demons is mastered; when he has heard (the Demon) saying : 'I am mastered by thee, Heroic Man, speak what thou wilst, what can I do for thee now ?' the sādhaka should ask for the interest of others desired by him in his mind" [31]. In stanza 165, the nature of the sādhaka's noble request is expounded; it appears to lie in the field of magical properties and substances such as potent stuffs like the fruit Amṛta, (*go*)*rocana*, *añjana*, other kinds of ointments and especially the eight siddhis or supernatural performances which are believed to lie within the reach of the successful yogin; further, the feats of destructive magic such as causing other people to hate each other, driving them from their homes, finding treasures, immobilizing, attracting. After hearing the requests, the Demon says: "I shall comply with all that", and disappears. "Having mastered the Lord of the Demons", says st. 166, "the sādhaka is able to go where he pleases, within the nether world or through the air, up to the sphere of the most eminent gods, on top of the Meru, to the other side of the ocean; having ascended Him with a sword in his hand, he accomplishes the weal of the world during a dissolution of the earth" [32]. The KCT mentions the manipulation of other such demons more concisely in ch. 2, 154ff.

These remarkable stanzas are clearly the account of spiritual exercises of a visionary character, stylized by Buddhist Tantric tradition. The performer should realize that all terrible appearances evoked by him are the products of his own mind. Thus the function of this description is in the first place purely psychological, but on the other hand the adept is without doubt considered to become enabled to execute real feats of sorcery. It seems as if the emphasis on the uncanny powers of witchcraft has been encompassed here within the ideal of spiritual emancipation and made an expedient on the way to this very goal.

The MMK (ch. 2; vol. I, p. 29) deals with a related figure : the Six-headed King of Anger (Ṣaṇmukha Krodharāja). This demon is conjured up by the following mantra, which starts in the way usual in Buddhist Mahāyāna sūtras : "Honour to all Buddhas and Bodhisattvas, whose commands are irresistible. *Oṃ*, perform perform, do do my work; break break all obstructions; burn burn all obstructor(s) of the Vajra; O Thou Whose head...; Who causest life to end, Whose appearance is awesome and deformed ; digest digest all the evilly minded; O Thou Who causest even the life of the mighty Gaṇapati to end, bind bind all evil planets ; O Thou of the six heads ! Thou of the six arms ! Thou of the six feet ! Bring Rudra here ! Bring Viṣṇu here ! Bring here all the gods headed by Brahmā ! do not tarry, do not tarry; *jhal jhal* (=*jvala* ?), cause (them) to enter into the middle of the maṇḍala; remember the Agreement; *huṃ* (6x), *phaṭ phaṭ*, *svāhā*" [33]. This King of Anger is able to destroy all obstructions. It is understandable that this figure with his six faces is set to work against obstructions and obstructors, and even against Gaṇapati who in ordinary Hindu mythology is also the god who removes (but also causes) obstructions of all kinds. Moreover, the Vināyakas "Obstructors", a kind of secondary manifestations of Gaṇeśa, are said to be six in number; they are enumerated for example in Stuti & Stava, No. 519, 3.

When the mantra translated above has been recited, the author of the MMK asserts, all Bodhisattvas run away in panic. How much more the evilly minded who cause the obstructions ! Besides, one may recite this King of Anger's most intimate formula (*hṛdayamantra-*) : *Oṃ hrīḥ jñīḥ vikṛtānana huṃ sarvaśatrūn nāśaya stambhaya phaṭ phaṭ svāhā*"..."Thou of the deformed face...destroy, immobilize all enemies...". When the enemies hear this, they are all afflicted with the disease called *mahāśūla* in which one feels pierced by iron pins. There are still other mantras. At the end the Demon is sent away by means of a special mantra of dismissal which contains the words : "enter again into Thy abode".

There is a similarity between this Krodharāja and the Skanda who is conjured up in the same MMK (vol. I, p. 32); the text calls him Kumāra. This god who is famous from classical Hinduism is described by the text as six-headed, red of colour, and of a horrible countenance. He is equated with Aṅgāraka, the fiery red planet Mars. The sādhaka requests him to perform all kinds of work for him. Skanda is able to attract even Brahmā and the other gods, let alone a result desired by man. On the next page he appears to be an inferior manifestation of the chief deity of the MMK, the Bodhisattva Mañjuśrī, who is indeed often called Kumāra. Skanda Kumāra's mantra on this place is (the mantra of) Kārttikeya-mañjuśrī (Kārttikeya = Skanda). Like most mantras taught in the MMK it is very short; *Oṃ huṃ jaḥ*. Its special function is to attract all kinds of enjoyments (*bhogākarṣaṇatatparaḥ*). On p. 153 he is described as he appears against evil dreams: "The Great (personification) of Anger is constituted, with six arms and six faces; a great mantra of four syllables has been emitted from the mouth of Kumāra; it has a horrible appearance, awesome and horrible, originating from the Swine manifestation...hung about with the coils of snakes; with a sword in its hand...of great overwhelming power" [34].

Again: he drives away all obstructions and evil creatures. The mantra this time runs: "Hear, hear, O Great Anger! Six headed One ! Six footed One ! Slayer of all obstructions! *hūṃ hūṃ*, why dost Thou tarry, Obstructor ! Thou Who causest life to end ! destroy my evil dream ! leap over, leap over ! remember the agreement; *phaṭ*, *phaṭ*, *svāhā* !" [35]. Immediately after its recitation all obstructive ghosts and demons appear in terror and pay honour to the Lord Buddha Śākyamuni and to Mañjuśrī. On p. 154 the author intimates that this King of Anger on the sādhaka's request is ready to burn and dry out all evil beings, but not to kill them.

In chs. 50-52 of the MMK (vol. III), the six-headed demoniac figure is again conjured. He is called now Yamāntaka "Destroyer of Yama". His services are for example sought in ch. 51 against inimical kings. The King of Anger is also described in KCT 4, 134ff., where he assists in the mastering of demons and clouds. Sādhanas of Yamāri and Yamāntaka are further contained in SM Nos. 268-282 (a six-headed Black Yamāri in No. 274). With such six-headed figures one may compare the Bhūtarāja "King of the Demons" who is addressed in Stuti & Stava, No. 133 :

Bhūtarājā mahākrūraḥ sahasrakiraṇaprabhaḥ /
ṣaḍvaktrasaṃyutaś caiva sakaliṣyataśekharaḥ //

"The King of the Demons, very horrible, having the brilliance of a thousand solar rays, and provided with six heads; his crown is. . . ." (last quarter corrupt). In stanza 2 he appears to possess twelve arms and to ride upon a corpse. The two next stanzas, however, explain his symbolical nature: he possesses eleven (?) faces which consist of Śivaite philosophical concepts, and he seems to be identified with Śiva. Unfortunately the text is hazy and unclear (See also above, p.54).

Not only demigods and demons, but also the higher gods of Hinduism and Buddhism are liable to be manipulated by the adept's prowess. For example, the MMK describes a sādhana of the great Mañjuśrī himself (ch. 11; vol. I, p. 106ff.). The ritual should be accomplished at night, and preferably on top of a mountain. A mantra should be recited for 600,000 times. The sādhaka should take a meal of prescribed composition and guide his meditation by means of a painted cloth; he also performs 8,000 oblations. At midnight there will appear the demon Mahākṛṣṇameghavatamaṇḍalī "She of the circle of storms of great black clouds". This is a critical moment. The adept should not be frightened. He should not rise from his seat. He should merely protect himself by means of Mañjuśrī's most intimate mantra of eight syllables, and by "binding the mystical diagram" (*maṇḍalabandha*, ?). Then the demoness disappears, but the trial has not yet come to an end. A number of beautiful women appear, who declare to have been mastered by the performer. But he should present them with the usual gifts of hospitality combined with fragrant water and *jātī* flowers (white). This induces also these women to disappear. The sādhaka now takes up the paṭa, worships all the Buddhas and Bodhisattvas and betakes himself to another place suitable for the last stage of his sādhana. There he should remain during the night, making a sacrifice for 8,000 times of white flowers. He should continue in this way during twenty-one days. At last, at midnight, Mañjuśrī himself appears to him.

These preparations of the sādhaka, although not clear in all respects from the description given by the MMK, again remind in some aspects of the visions undergone by the Buddha himself during his meditation under the Bodhi tree. While the Buddha's goal was the obtaining of the spiritual illumination which leads to final emancipation, the aim set himself by the sādhaka of the MMK may be in essence the same, but it is expressed in quite other language: "He beholds the Venerable Mañjuśrī from eye to eye. He (Mañjuśrī) grants to him the boon chosen; the ability to fly through the air, or to disappear at will; the stages of the Bodhisattva and the state of an Individual Buddha (*pratyekabuddhatvam*); the state of being a learned monk, or the Fivefold Wisdom (possessed by the Five Buddhas); the gift of longevity ; the obtainment of a large kingdom or of exquisite enjoyment, or the gift of being the favourite of princes; or the gift of being allowed to wander together with the Venerable Mañjuśrī; in short, anything desired by him, all this He gives; or for what he asks, that he concedes. And all material goods he may gain ; and he is able to attract all powerful beings (in order to extract gifts from them); in short, anything mentioned by him, He will give. Also sins committed in former times are cleaned by Him; thus spoke the Venerable Lord Śākyamuni". In the text now follows another sādhana of Mañjuśrī with similar results. In ch. 26 (vol. II, p. 294), the author discusses the sādhana of Vajrapāṇi[58].

The forces of nature can also be conjured. MMK ch. 26 (vol. II, p. 298) describes how a performer who wants to try his art on the ocean should act: "Having laid down his painted cloth on the seashore, facing the West, he should kindle a fire by means of logs of *nāga* wood and bring an oblation of 100,000 *nāga* flowers to the ocean. Then the waves of the ocean will approach him, but the adept should not be frightened, if he desires to realize his objectives. When he persists in this way, the ocean will appear to him after some time in the guise of a brahman and say : 'What have I to do ?' The sādhaka should say : 'Be an addicted servant to me (*vaśyo me bhava*)'. After that the ocean will do anything desired by (the performer)" [36]. In this connection we can refer to a ceremony conducted near a river and aimed at the obtainment of wealth described in AVPar 36,26. In the description of the MMK the force of the procedure is enhanced because the methods have been adjusted to the power to be manipulated. The performer faces the West because this is the region dominated by the Lord of the Ocean, Varuṇa (and it seems to be implied that the ceremony should be conducted on the shore of the Western, i.e. Arabic, sea). He uses *nāga* logs and flowers because the Nāgas (Serpents) are inhabitants of the aquatic element. The sādhaka is aware of the harmony of the cosmos and handles it.

There are other rituals of this kind. The MMK and other texts sometimes allude to a peculiar kind of sādhana : embarking on a boat and seeking the large or drifting down a river. In RV 7, 88, a "mystical" hymn to Varuṇa, the poet describes in the third stanza his longings for union with his chosen deity by sailing with him in the same boat. Sailing over the water is described more than once as an image of mystical rapture or as the scene of spiritual revelation. According to the MtPur, Manu received his revelations from Viṣṇu as Fish while sailing on the ocean during the Primeval Flood[59]. A case of "water magic" from the Veda : the KauśS

(19,9; Caland, p. 48) assigns the hymn AV 2,24 to such an act. Caland (n. 7) explains that a performer should betake himself to the middle of the lake on a raft made of reed covered with clay. On this raft he should bring oblations of ghee. Unfortunately the allusions given by the text are vague.

As a short instance of the manipulation of one of the higher gods of Hinduism may serve the discussion of the "worship" of Gaṇeśa in the Varadapūrvatāpanī Up. (ed. in Jacob, p. 131). The god is installed on a pedestal, on the sides of which are invoked among others the Six Vināyakas. "He who by means of this (ritual) brings oblations of 100,000 sacrificial cakes on the fourth days of both halves of the month (the fourth day being sacred to Gaṇeśa), from that same moment onwards he will be Kubera, the Bestower of Wealth (by his riches). If he offers during three months a rice dish called *siddhaudana* into the fire, his mind concentrated, while in the same time sacrificing *pṛthuka* rice grains, he will become Vaiśravaṇa (Kubera) in own person" [37]. A sacrifice with *vibhītaka* flowers, brought by someone with evil intentions, will drive the enemy away; if products from poisonous trees are applied (Skt. commentary: from the *kāraskara*), the victim will be liquidated. Lotuses are apt to subjugate the object of the ritual. We had already an occasion to point to the results expected from the sādhana of Gaṇeśa in the MMD, ch. 2 (see above p.89). Another such ceremony can be found in PST 17.

Sanskrit literature often speaks of the fear of the gods, especially Indra their king, from other beings who by their austerities or other feats try to secure themselves a place among the gods or to push them from their throne. That Indra's feelings were not entirely without reason might be inferred from a passage like AgPur 302,3 where a sādhana of Indra is taught for the benefit of someone who desires to master also that deity. Stanzas 6ff. in the same chapter contain the method for subjugating Kāma, the god of love. The mantra is: "*Oṃ hrīṃ oṃ*, honour to Kāma who procures the good for all beings, who deludes all beings, who flames brightly; cause cause that the hearts of all people become directed towards myself, *oṃ*" [38]. The same chapter at the end gives rules for procuring the aid of Śiva Tryambaka for the protection of the cows. A sādhana of Śiva is included in the MMK (ch. 26; vol. II, p. 293). Śiva is approached in his Dakṣiṇāmūrti. Here also, a frightful experience awaits the performer; there occurs a sound calling out : *ha ha.* But if he stands it, Śiva is sure to appear prepared to meet the adept's wishes[61]. In the same way also Viṣṇu and Brahmā can be attracted, but only after the performer has carefully taken his measures in order to protect himself. On the sādhana of Viṣṇu more will be said in the next chapter.

3. MEDITATION ON VIṢṆU'S MĀYĀ

1. *Indian Viṣṇusādhanas*

The Kathās (2,4,127ff.) relates how the clever Brahman, Lohajaṅgha, tells King Vibhīṣaṇa a story that some time ago, being oppressed by poverty, he performed penance in a Viṣṇu temple by remaining for some time in front of the god without taking any food. Viṣṇu then came to him in a dream and instructed him to seek the company of Vibhīṣaṇa of Laṅkā, because that king would give money to him. Of course the author presents this tale as a phantasy invented by Lohajaṅgha in order to win Vibhīṣaṇa's favour ; but the hero of the tale expected to be believed on it, and thus it might have a base in historical performances of such procedures as alluded to above. And we indeed find descriptions of them in the texts of prescriptive character. For example, the Skt. commentary on the Nārāyaṇa Up (ed. Jacob, p. 64f.) cites a passage from the Nṛsiṃhapurāṇa, Nārāyaṇādhyāya, which gives the rules for a meditation on Viṣṇu with the help of the silent recitation (*japa*) of the mantra of eight syllables, the famous : *Oṃ namo Nārāyaṇāya.* The fragment begins by presenting the prospect of release (*mukti*) and eternal communion with Viṣṇu, which means Nirvāṇa. This final goal can however only be reached by reciting the formula for 800,000 times. As this number may deter most aspirants, but perhaps in the first place because many of them set upon the worship of Viṣṇu with other ideals in their minds, the text proceeds by summing up more practical aims to be achieved by a perhaps smaller amount of exercise : evil dreams, demons, thieves and disease are powerless against him who performs the japa of this formula. And the performer may also expect a long life, material wealth, sons, cattle, wisdom and renown. In short, such a person obtains the four ends of life : keeping up with tradition (*dharma*), the winning of the goods of the earth (*artha*), various kinds of enjoyment (*kāma*) and, if he gives proof of his desire for it by holding out long enough, final release (*mokṣa*) :

Āyuṣyaṃ dhanaputrāṃś ca paśūn vidyāṃ mahad yaśaḥ/
dharmārthakāmamokṣāṃś ca labhate ca japan naraḥ//

The *phalaśruti* further contains the assertion that also the seers of yore, the ancestors, the perfected (siddhas) and even the Asuras and Rākṣasas reached their highest perfection by means of this japa. It is said to be specially effective for someone who still carries on with it during the last moments of his life. Such a person immediately reaches Viṣṇu's Supreme Abode (*paramaṃ padam*)[1].

Of course the method for propitiating a god for the attainment of mundane designs is a feature wholly accepted and uniformly spread in Hindu religious literature. Some instances were discussed in the preceding chapter. The BhGītā (7.22) says : "The person who, animated by faith for (a particular deity), seeks to worship that (deity), obtains from him all his desires ; I Myself ordain them to be fulfilled". The Vaikhānasa text Atri-saṃhitā promises : *iṣṭān kāmān avāpnoti tadīyaṃ ca paraṃ padam* "one obtains the desire scherished, and also His (Viṣṇu's) Supreme Abode" (1, 28). From the passage from the Nṛsiṃhapurāṇa mentioned above it appears clearly that there is only a gradual difference between the various ends of life: what is good for the realisation of final release may also be useful while one still dwells in the earthly body, and thus why not make use of it ?

But this invocation of the god for the goal of mundane prosperity and safety implies also an effective protection from those who are intent upon destroying these aims. No wonder that Viṣṇu can also be worshipped by somebody who wants to overcome his nemies. The KJ (ch. 10; trsl. p.44) expresses this quite clearly : "The destination of a ruler is to win victory over his enemies. The method by which he is able to gain that victory over them, because he has worshipped the Lord beforehand, is called the 'magical' method (*abhicārika-*)". Then follows in that text a list of objects, creatures, images of the gods and other items which by some or another reason are of an uncanny character and as such may be of use for a person who desires to execute a ritual with the objective of harming an enemy (and not, as the translation of KJ says, which are liable to magic; *abhicārika* means "leading to [the execution of] magic" just as *śāntika*-means : "leading to safety" and *pauṣṭika*—"leading to prosperity"). Such unfavourable objects may be a piece of land (destined for the erection of a sanctuary) when unfavourable trees like the *nimba, arka* or *vibhītaka* grow on it; when the wrong kind of animals roam on it or when the wrong kind of birds sound their ominous voice over it; "if the colours red and black are too frequent in it" : (abhicārika is further) an image made of bricks or mud (and not of precious metal, as would befit a temporal ruler); an image not constructed according to the exact measurements prescribed in the iconographical canons of the *śilpaśāstras*; an image installed during the wrong time under evil constellations; a fire kindled in a skull or other unfavourable objects; an image of Viṣṇu if painted with unnatural colours like dark blue or green, or bereft of its spouse, Śrī ; in short, anything which is not done in accordance with the rules as presented by the ritual handbooks of the Vaikhānasas. We must however concede that this list of abhicārika objects in the KJ is theoretical in character, and that one of its functions is presumably to inform the rulers who intend to finance ritual practice what is expected of them and what not. Expected is a lavish spend in accordance with the priests' standards and methods; if this is not followed up, one falls into a category which one never had wished for.

The possibility of performing incorrect rituals with the aim of doing harm to the enemy again appears from KJ ch. 53, where the different kinds of Viṣṇu images are discussed ; but here also there is an atmosphere of theory. One of the images is the *viraha* type, a standing one which is not accompanied by the two spouses of the god, Śrī and Bhūmi, and also bereft of the usual attributes conch and disc. The Atri Saṃhitā discusses this image also (20, 17-18) [1]. This kind of image can perhaps be identified with the abhicārika image described by another and more famous Vaikhānasa Āgama, Marīci's Vimānārcanakalpa (ch. 19, p. 81ff.). Marīci distinguishes three types of abhicārika images : a standing, sitting and recumbent one. The standing one is furnished with two or four arms; its colour is grey, its lips dark, its face emaciated. It is characterized by the basic quality of inertia (*tamas*), whatever this may mean in practice; its eyes gaze upwards. Attendant figures are lacking, and the image is installed on a wrong place under an evil constellation. The sitting image has similar characteristics; it should face the direction of the sky in which the enemy is located (*śatru-diṅmukhe*). In the recumbent variety both Viṣṇu and the serpent Śeṣa on whom he rests should be furnished with evil characteristics.

It seems, however, that the theory of abhicārika images propounded in these works has been seldom or never put into practice. These books were meant to be guides for the temple cult organized and sponsored by a member of the ruling class ; in case of war there would be too little time to have such an image constructed and installed; and one would scarcely think about having constructed it beforehand, because such a dangerous object would act like a boomerang upon one's own position. Besides, a ruler would perhaps by preference leave such malicious tasks to specialists who handled their own deities—if he would resort to such practices at all. And as a rule destructive magic tends to be executed by individuals. In any case practically no Viṣṇu images of this type have been found[2], although one might consider Narasiṃha and Hayagrīva as abhicāra aspects of Viṣṇu[3]. But the goal of victory over enemies, held in view by rulers and their vassals, appears clearly from a few of the Balinese stutis. In Bali, Viṣṇu is the favourite deity of the nobility and its representants considered themselves Viṣṇuite as distinct from the *padanda* priests who are Śiva or Buddha worshippers. This state of affairs is reflected in Stuti & Stava, No. 384 (Janārdana mahāvīra) and No. 381 (Janārdana labhet kāryam)[4].

The Man-Lion incarnation of Viṣṇu (Narasiṃha) is further present in the Balinese stutis as a terrifying appearance on whom the warrior should concentrate before engaging in battle. Stuti No. 100, Narasiṃhāṣṭaka, contains expressions like *caṇḍadaṃṣṭro Yamābhaḥ* "with impetuous fangs, equal to Yama", *tīkṣṇadaṃṣṭrakarālam* "with wide open mouth and sharp fangs" or *bhīmāṭṭahāsam* "of the terrible roars of laughter"; but it winds up with *vidadhatu..śrīpāram* "should bestow on you the highest degree of prosperity", thus reminding the reader of the benedictory stanzas found often at the beginning of Sanskrit works. No. 842, Lokamantra, describes the Man-Lion in very defective Sanskrit as dark blue of colour, four-armed and three-headed, and provided with the weapons mace and disc. In the Sprinkling Formula at the end he is equated with Paśupati and the Fire of Dissolution ; the formula is concluded by the spell *Oṃ vaṣaṭ oṃ vaṣaṭ namaḥ svāhā* (see below ch.3.5). No.887 is borrowed from the Nṛsiṃha-pūrvatāpanīya Up; it is none other than the famous stanza of worship to Narasiṃha which begins with *Ugraṃ Viṣṇuṃ mahāvīram* "The fear inspiring Viṣṇu of mighty force". Some of the Balinese mss which contain it continue by suggesting a meditation on oneself as the Narasiṃha who slays the demon Hiraṇyakaśipu as in the famous legend of Prahlāda ; one should also meditate on eight supernatural weapons which surround one's body on all sides.

Indian texts also teach the efficacy of Narasiṃha. Although Tantric texts like the MMD are usually meant for individual worship and not for "social" performances done for the public sake as is for example the case with the Vaikhānasa pūjā, the MMD while discussing the mantras of Viṣṇu (ch. 14) also gives attention to a mantra and sādhana of Narasiṃha. The mantra may be *hrīṃ kṣrauṃ hrīṃ* or *Oṃ k rauṃ Oṃ*. Its syllables should be assigned to the canonical "six limbs" (*ṣaḍaṅgāni*). One is advised to meditate on Narasiṃha's appearance while performing a pūjā to him. The results are said to be manifold; the author summarizes them by saying : "why fall into prolixity ? The Man-Lion is able to grant all the results desired by man". In the stanzas 25ff. the text gives the sādhana of another manifestation of the same god called Bhītihārīṣṭasādhaka "Remover of fear and Realizer of the desire". The mantra in this case runs "*Oṃ śrīṃ hrīṃ*, be victorious ; to the Beloved of Lakṣmī, Whose mind is eternally filled with joy, of Whose body the (left) half is inhabited by Lakṣmī, *śrīṃ hrīṃ*, honour" [2]. In stanzas 48ff. follows the mantra for Abhayanṛsiṃha "The Man-Lion Who grants safety".

Nṛsiṃha (and Hayagrīva) are invested with such particular potency because they are theriomorphic manifestations. Together with Varāha, Viṣṇu's third incarnation, they form male counterparts of the animal-faced goddesses discussed shortly above (p.105ff). Viṣṇu's power of presenting himself as an animal was alluded to on p.32.

We now come to Viṣṇu's human manifestation of Kṛṣṇa (as to the other famous human appearance, Rāma, we only refer to Stuti & Stava, No. 229, Rāmakavaca). Kṛṣṇa's deeds and marvellous qualities were shortly dealt with in ch. 1 (p. 25). The MMD in the chapter 14 mentioned just above proceeds (51ff.) by presenting the rules for the Gopālamantras (the Formulas of the Cowherd). This means in the first place the formula of ten syllables : *Gopījanavallabhāya svāhā* "To the Beloved of the Cowherdesses, *svāhā*". From stanza 64 onwards the text enjoins special rules for various aims like the allegation of fever or hatred and the destruction of enemies ; for this last end one should meditate on oneself as being Kṛṣṇa who killed the tyrant Kaṃsa (*ātmānaṃ saṃsmaran Harim.... Kaṃsaripum*). One may also succeed in subjugating anybody whom one desires (72: *vaśam ety acirāt saputrapaśubāndhavaḥ*). Another effective method for subjugating others, this time probably in the first place in erotic matters, is to meditate on the Kṛṣṇa who as a cowherd sung his songs in the idyllic Vṛndāvan in the company of the Cowherdesses ; the performer should in that case make oblations with the magically highly effective *apāmārga* plant. If one meditates on Kṛṣṇa as being engaged in amorous sports (*rasakrīḍāgata-*) and at the same time sacrifices for 10,000 times and keeps on doing this during six months, one will obtain any girl one desires as a wife (*vāñchitāṃ kanyām udvahed bhaktitatparaḥ*). On the other hand, a woman who says the mantra a thousand times, meditating on Viṣṇu as being present in a *kadamba* flower, obtains the desired husband. He who sacrifices with products of the *bilva* (Lakṣmī's tree), honey and lotuses, becomes Lord of Lakṣmī, which probably means that he obtains material wealth. In stanza 77 the author again says that further discussion is unnecessary because Kṛṣṇa grants all its wishes to mankind.

Still another mantra of Kṛṣṇa is discussed in stanzas 77ff.: *klīṃ Hṛṣīkeśāya namaḥ*. A performer who makes oblations of *vijayā* "victory" flowers early in the morning, of course while reciting this mantra, will gain anything which he desires within a month. A woman who sacrifices 10,000 times with ghee will obtain mastery over her lover or husband (*bhojayet*:

she will cause him to enjoy her). A man who applies the mantra for similar ends is able to beguile a throng of lovely women (he becomes *kāminīvargamohaka*). Another mantra of sixteen syllables serves to beguile all people (*lokavimohana-*) : *Oṃ namo bhagavate Rukmiṇīlvallabhāya svāhā* "*Oṃ*, honour to the Lord, the beloved of Rukmiṇī, *svāhā*". A person who wants to put this mantra into effect should recite it a million times while making oblations of lotuses. Viṣṇu should be worshipped and the names of his manifestations invoked in the directions of the sky. Another mantra, *klīṃ Govallabhāya svāhā*, when brought to perfection, will enable the performer to become a "dwelling of prosperities" (*saṃpadām ālayaḥ*, 103). To achieve this end he should say the mantra 800,000 times and sacrifice for 8,000 times. The manifestations of Viṣṇu which are to be worshipped here beside the god are : Vāsudeva, Saṃkarṣaṇa, Pradyumna, Aniruddha, Rukmiṇī, Satyabhāmā, Lakṣmaṇā, Jāmbavatī; further the Guardians of the Regions and the Weapons personified (*āyudhāni*). The stanzas 104ff. give the rules of the short mantra *klīṃ Kṛṣṇa klīṃ*. The performer of this ritual should meditate on the naughty child Kṛṣṇa who steals the butter. One should recite the mantra 400,000 times, and sacrifice 40,000 times with bilvas. Viṣṇu and his manifestations and attendants are again worshipped and the god is this time humbly requested (st. 111) for the boon desired [3] :

> "O Son of Devakī, Govinda, Son of Vāsudeva, Lord of the world,
> give me a son, O Kṛṣṇa; I have taken my refuge unto Thee".

2. *Some sādhanas on divine Delusion and Māyā*

Viṣṇu's Māyā is often said to manifest itself by the delusion with which it envelops the world of creatures ; and Viṣṇu himself is often called the god who deludes (*mohayati*) that world (see above p.21). For the Indian worshipper this is an impressive, sometimes even sinister, aspect of Viṣṇu's supernatural faculties. Its appropriation by an act of sādhana is described by the AgPur (ch. 307); the same mantra can be found in PST (36,6ff.). The Lord of Fire who proclaims the Purāṇa announces that he will explain the mantra of

Viṣṇu Trailokyamohana "Who deludes the Threefold world" for the perfection (*siddhi*) of all the four stages of life. This elaborate mantra runs : "*Oṃ śrīṃ hrīṃ hrūṃ oṃ*, honour, the Most Perfect Person ; Thou Whose appearance is that of the Most Perfect Person ; Dwelling place of Lakṣmī, Shaker of the whole world, Tearer of the hearts of all womankind, Who causest the threefold world to lose its senses ; the minds of gods, men and womanfolk heat heat, light light, dry out dry out, kill kill, stupefy stupefy, mollify mollify, attract attract; O Thou of supreme loveliness, Who art the cause of all marital happiness, Bestower of desires, kill kill N. N. with Thy disc, with Thy mace, Thy sword; with all Thy arrows pierce pierce, with Thy noose bind bind (?, *haṭṭa*); with Thy hook hit hit (?, with the elephant hook, *aṅkuśa*, one usually forcibly attracts the victim); hurry hurry, why dost Thou not move; very quickly what is desired by me should become realized; *huṃ phaṭ namaḥ*"[4]. Another mantra follows immediately : "*Oṃ*, O Most Perfect Person, Who causest the threefold world to lose its senses; *huṃ phaṭ*, to the heart honour ; attract attract, O Thou of great strength, *huṃ phaṭ*, to the Missile : O Lord of the threefold world, the minds of all people kill kill, tear up tear up, bring bring under my power ; *huṃ phaṭ*, to the Eye; O Beguiler of the threefold cosmos, Who appearest as Hṛṣīkeśa, O Thou Who attractst the hearts of all women, come come, honour". This last formula seems to be corrupt and to be meant for directing the assignment of the force of Trailokyamohana to the Six Limbs. The performer, while reciting, should sprinkle the fire 50,000 times; then offer a sacrificial dish into the fire for a hundred times, and so on. In the course of the ritual a special *gāyatrī* stanza for Trailokyamohana is also said : *Trailokyamohanāya vidmahe, Smarāya dhīmahi, tan no Viṣṇuḥ pracodayāt* "we direct our intellect towards Tr., we meditate towards Smara (Kāma) ; let thus Viṣṇu impel us". The god himself should be meditated upon (st. 13ff.) as sitting on Garuḍa who stands upon a lotus; his limbs are those of a beautiful young man but his eyes flicker while being red with exhilaration; his behaviour is unsteady because he is possessed by Love; he smiles and is adorned by a celestial wreath, garment and unguents; he bears the five arrows (of Kāma) and is surrounded by celestial women. This appearance of Viṣṇu is clearly intended to be a manifestation identical with Kāma. AgPur gives as the result of such a worship a concise remark (23) that one obtains all desires; it further only mentions the goal of longevity (25). PST 36,56ff. gives more particulars. By worshipping the god only once one is promised to obtain Lakṣmī (a vague statement alluding to wealth or lustre); by sacrificing 8,000 times happiness in family life is the result ; other aims are the cure of disease, annihilation of sorrow, obtaining a woman, rendering princes one's slaves (becoming their favourite), forcing a thief to return the stolen property, and various others. It should be added that the Trailokyamohana discussed above is different from the figure described by T. G. Rao, I, 1, p. 257. There he is said to have sixteen arms, ride on Garuḍa, bear a great number of attributes and have two of his hands in the yogamudrā. He has four faces, respectively those of a man, of Narasiṃha, of Varāha and of Kapila[5].

Before concentrating on the meditation of Viṣṇu's Māyā, we shall first shortly consider a few other Māyāsādhanas, leaving aside those directed to a female Māyā representant. A Varadapūrvatāpanī Up, devoted to Gaṇeśa, contains the following passage on Gaṇeśa's māyā (ed. Jacob, p. 123ff.): "Of Him (Gaṇeśa) there are Six Limbs (*ṣaḍ-aṅgāni*): *Oṃ*, to the Heart, honour; to the Head, *svāhā*, to the Tuft, *vaṣaṭ*; to the Armour, *huṃ*; to the Three Eyes, *vauṣaṭ*; to the Missile, *phaṭ*; thus for the first time with the first (syllable), for the second time with the second...for the sixth time with the sixth; for each syllable there are on both sides the Māyā and the Lakṣmī"[5]. This obscure statement is elucidated by its Skt. commentary. It appears that rules are presented here for the recitation of a few words in pseudo-Vedic style *rāyaspoṣasya dātā ca* "The Bestower of wealth and welfare". Each of the eight syllables of this concise description of Gaṇeśa's foremost function is preceded by the Māyā (represented in Tantric lore by the syllable *īṃ*) and followed by Lakṣmī or Śrī (represented by the syllable *śrīṃ*). The result is as follows : *īṃ rāṃ śrīṃ īṃ yāṃ śrīṃ īṃ syoṃ* (read : *spoṃ*) *śrīṃ īṃ ṣaṃ śrīṃ īṃ syaṃ śrīṃ īṃ dāṃ śrīṃ īṃ tāṃ śrīṃ īṃ cāṃ śrīṃ hṛdayāya namaḥ.* The same is repeated for six times, each time followed by another part of the six limbs instead of the heart. The Up gives a further comment on the mystical implication of this practice: "for this Māyā of Vināyaka creates all this world, protects all this world and destroys all this world; therefore he who knows this Māyā as the Cosmical Energy, he conquers death, he overcomes evil, he attains extraordinary lustre (*śrī*); he becomes a skilled debater (*abhivādin*, explained by the commentary with *ābhimukhyena vadanaśīlaḥ*), a master in the Six Acts (*ṣaṭkarmasaṃsiddhaḥ*; see below ch. 6), and reaches Immortality". The fragment is practically identical with a passage from the Nṛsiṃhapūrvatāpanī Up (3,1) only with *vaināyakī* instead of *nārasiṃhī*; so that also Narasiṃha has been the object of the same meditation. Does not its statement of rewards remind one of what had been expressed long before in ṢaḍvBr 1, 2, 7-11? (see above p. 15).

An interesting description of a Buddhist male Mahāmāyā is found in the NiṣpY (p. 22). As the editor explains in p. 43 of the Introduction to that text, this is the name of a particular manifestation of the Vajrayāna deity Heruka. It has four faces and four arms, and is accompanied by its śakti Buddhaḍākinī. The editor mistakenly states that the deity's colour is "black or blue"; the text itself makes clear that this Māyā can assume four colours : *nīlapītaśvetaharitamūlasavyapaścimavāmacaturmukhaḥ* "He possesses four faces: the chief one, and (the others) directed towards the right, back and left; their colour is respectively dark blue, yellow, white and green". Then follows the description of the arms and their attributes, and that of the accompanying four goddesses called respectively Vajra-, Ratna-,Padma-and Viśva-ḍākinī (in the E., S., W., and N.). All of them possess four faces with four different colours. The front faces have the colours dark blue, yellow, white and green, in harmony with the colour of Mahāmāyā Heruka's faces in the four directions. The Buddha-ḍākinī, who resides in the Centre, has her front face red (and not white as the editor says on p.16). Each of these Ḍākinī belong to one of the Families (*kula-*) of the Dhyānibuddhas, while Mahāmāyā belongs to Akṣobhya's Family. The kernel mantras of the four Ḍākinis at the sides when combined together form the words *Oṃ svāhā*, written *Oṃ-svā-a-hā*.

Such a kind of multicoloured and multiform deity is not uncommon in the NiṣpY. On p. 26 of the text, there is for example a Saṃvaramaṇḍala, the deity of which also has four heads, while the colours are black, green, red and yellow. It appears, however, that there is only little affinity between the Buddhist Mahāmāyā discussed just above (or related figures) and the Viṣṇuite one which we shall deal with below.

We mention one other example of Buddhist provenance. There exists a tract devoted to the Bodhisattva Mañjuśrī, called *Mañjuśrījñānasattvasya paramārthā nāmasaṃgītiḥ* "Proclamation of supreme value regarding the names of Mañjuśrī the Personification of Wisdom"[7]. In 1, 28ff. it deals with the greatness of the syllable *a* from which the Buddha took his origin. In 30ff. this syllable is identified with the Families of the basic Vices: Passion (*rāga*), Hate (*dveṣa*), Delusion (*moha*), Anger (*krodha*) and Greed (*lobha*) which are presided over by the Five Tathāgatas. Then (32ff.) a number of epithets are added, all beginning with *mahā-*, and among them are Mahāmāyādhara "Bearer of mighty Illusory Power", Mahāmāyārthasādhaka "Realizer of the Meaning of mighty Illusory Power", Mahāmāyāratiḥ "Delighting in...." and Mahāmāyendrajālika "The Magician Who wields mighty Illusory power" (on the word *indrajāla*, see below p. ch,5.1.). After an elaborate string of other epithets, stanza 162 addresses the same entity as Māyājāla "Net of Māyā" and then in the second part of this stanza there is a fragment from the Five Pañcabrahmamantras (see below p. 156) : *namas te sarva sarvebhyaḥ* "Honour to Thee, All, to those who are the All". In the preceding stanza (161) there is a quotation from another of these Five mantras: *bhavodbhava* "Thou Who art born from existence" (?); the text reads: *abhavodbhava*, which is against the metre and the tradition). The Five Mantras are directed towards the Five Faces of Śiva, the Pañcamukha or Pañcabrahma, and their occurrence—or at least the occurrence of a few parts from them—is significant. It shows the tendency towards identification of similar concepts which had arisen in the same period within different religions. The related concept in this case is the fivefold representation of the Chief God in the Centre and in the four main directions accompanied by symbolic explanations—and also the Viṣṇuite Mahāmāyā of five aspects discussed presently is meditated upon with the help of a fragment from the same Pañcabrahmamantras, while it is characterized at the same time by its assuming different colours. Regarding this last feature we also refer to KCT 5,245, where Kālaçakra is called *viśvādivarṇam* "possessing a multiplicity of colours and also the other (colours separately)," while 5,248 sums up : *sitaharitamahāviśvavarṇaikavarṇaḥ* "having a white and a green colour, a multiplicity of colours and at the same time a unique colour". And stanza 247 promises that this God of manifold appearances will obtain the result of any act conceived by Him in his mind.

3. *Viṣṇu's Mahāmāyā in Bali*

Among the Sanskrit hymns and fragments handed down by the Brahman Śivaite and Buddhist priests of Bali, Indonesia, there is a curious fragment which deals with the Māyā as the Delusive Manifestation of Viṣṇu and its sādhana. In Stuti & Stava it has been edited and translated as No. 450 of the collection. The complete passage of 21 stanzas is present in only one ms, a relatively good one preserved in the Museum of Ethnography, Rotterdam. It describes the Pūjā Kṣatriya, the daily worship of the orthodox Viṣṇuite Balinese nobleman, of which the present fragment seems to constitute a facultative part. Another ms, now in the Leiden Oriental Collection, contains stanzas 1-17. Both these sources present also a paraphrase in Old Javanese which proved very helpful in determining and interpreting the Sanskrit text. The title of the fragment in these sources is *Mahāmāyā* "The Great Delusive (or: Illusory) Manifestation" (and under this name it will be henceforth referred to).

Besides, the stanzas 14-16 occur in at least five other Balinese mss and in S. Levi's publication "Sanskrit Texts from Bali" (Gaekwad Or. Ser. No. 68). These three stanzas are usually called by the name *Caturvarṇaprāyaścitta* "The appeasement by means of the four colours". As to the ritual application of the Mahāmạyā fragment, the Rotterdam ms states that it might be recited daily for the warding off of all disease and calamities. Although the text has been edited and discussed in Stuti & Stava it is necessary to deal with it again in the present context, and it seems desirable to do this in a detailed manner, because much can still be said on it while the treatment in Stuti & Stava was not completely satisfactory. The Mahāmāyā has not been handed down faultlessly, but its original wording and meaning is generally clear, not in the last place by the help of the paraphrases mentioned already above[8]. When restored, the Sanskrit appears to be generally correct and even of more than mediocre quality, although a few irregularities cannot be explained away. Without doubt its provenance is Indian; its style is better than that of the average Tantra or Āgama from the Indian "Middle Ages". Unfortunately we did not succeed in tracing it in its original environment.

MAHĀMĀYĀ

1. Māyātattvam idaṃ śāntaṃ pavitraṃ caiva durlabham /
yaḥ śrutvā cintavān vāpi sarvapāpāt pramucyate //
2. Devo Viṣṇur dvinetraś ca gadāśaṅkhāsicakrabhṛt /
caturbhujaś ca sauvarṇaḥ pīṭhāmburuhasaṃsthitaḥ //
3. Sarvāmaragaṇasevyaḥ sarvābharaṇabhūṣitaḥ /
Oṃkārajapane hīdaṃ sarvabhayanivāraṇam //
Oṃ oṃ Viṣṇave namaḥ svāhā
4. Yady ākarṣaṇakāryārthī śvetaṃ devaṃ vicintayet /
śvetavastraṃ sapuṣpādyaṃ vaṣaḍ aṃ vaṣaḍ ucyate //
Oṃ vaṣaṭ Aṃ vaṣaṭ namaḥ svāhā
5. Dvīpāntaragato bhūtvā dūrasthānanikālitaḥ /
saṃprāpto rājā dravyāṇi saṃdadyāt sādhake nataḥ //
6. Pravṛddhāmbhodasaṃbhūtajalasaṃpūritā sarit /
śāntajalā viniyāti pratilomaṃ ca kṛṣyate //
7. Vaśīkaraṇakārye ca raktaṃ devaṃ vicintayet /
raktavastraṃ sapuṣpādyaṃ vaṣaḍ ghoṃ vaṣaḍ ucyate /
Oṃ vaṣaṭ Ghoṃ vaṣaṭ namaḥ svāhā
8. Madavantaś ca kariṇaḥ pramattāḥ krūramānasāḥ /
ripavaś cāpy avijeyā vaśyante japakāraṇāt //
9. Mattamātaṅgagāminyaḥ pīnottuṅgapayodharāḥ /
candramāvadanākārā dāsībhūtā japen naraḥ //
10. Yadi stambhanakāryaṃ ca pītaṃ devaṃ vicintayet /
pītavastraṃ sapuṣpādyaṃ huṃ phaḍ reṃ huṃ phaḍ ucyate //
Oṃ huṃ phaṭ Reṃ huṃ phaṭ namaḥ svāhā
11. Sarpāḥ krūratarāḥ kruddhā bhramanto bhakṣyacintanāt /
stambhanāt sādhakendrāṇāṃ rudhyante śamitendriyāḥ //
12. Yady uccāṭanakāryārthī nīlaṃ devaṃ vicintayet /
nīlavastraṃ sapuṣpādyaṃ huṃ phaḍ bhyaḥ huṃ phaḍ ucyate //
Oṃ huṃ phaṭ Bhyaḥ huṃ phaṭ namaḥ svāhā
13. Kaṭhinātmātivipulāḥ sthāvarāḥ prāṇavarjitāḥ /
śailendrāś ca vinaśyanti kṣaṇaṃ sādhakalīlayā //
14. Prāyaścittakaro yogī caturvarṇaṃ vicintayet /
caturvastraṃ sapuṣpādyam aṃ ghoṃ reṃ bhyas tathottamam //
Oṃ Aṃ Ghoṃ Reṃ Bhyaḥ namaḥ svāhā

15. Ulkāpātasahasrāṇi nakṣatradhūmasaṃyutam /
grahayuddhaṃ śilāvarṣaṃ śamayet sādhakaḥ kṣamaḥ //
16. Śatasaṃvatsare vyādhisaṃghāghātāturo janaḥ /
ucchinnaś cet parikhinnaḥ prāyaścittāt sukhī bhavet //
17. Ity evaṃ devakarmāṇi nityakarma tataḥ śṛṇu /
trisandhyaṃ pūjyate Māyā vaśyate ca dine dine //
18. Dhyāyet sindhūrasadṛśaṃ vaśyakarmaṇi karmaṇi /
māraṇe kṛṣṇavarṇaṃ tu vidveṣaḥ śyāmarūpadhṛk //
Oṃ hroṃ vaṣaṭ namaḥ vaṣaṭ hroṃ oṃ /
Oṃ hroṃ huṃ namaḥ huṃ hroṃ oṃ //
19. Uccāṭane dhūmravarṇaṃ śvetaṃ caiva yaśo 'rthinaḥ /
mayūrakaṇṭhasadṛśaṃ stambhane 'bhinayet sadā //
Oṃ hroṃ huṃ namaḥ huṃ hroṃ oṃ
Oṃ hroṃ vaṣaṭ (namaḥ vaṣaṭ) hroṃ oṃ
huṃ
20. Oṃkāraṃ vinyasen mūrdhni aṃkāraṃ mukhamaṇḍale /
ghoṃkāraṃ hṛdaye sthāpyaṃ remkāraṃ yonike nyaset //
21. Bhyaḥkāraṃ pādayor nyasyaṃ muṣṭinā bāhyakaṃ nyaset /
evaṃ nyāsaḥ prayoktavyaḥ svaśarīre mahātmanā //
Oṃ vaṣat Oṃ vaṣaṭ namaḥ
Oṃ vaṣaṭ Aṃ vaṣaṭ namaḥ
Oṃ vaṣaṭ Ghoṃ vaṣaṭ namaḥ
Oṃ huṃ phaṭ Reṃ huṃ phaṭ namaḥ
Oṃ huṃ phaṭ Bhyaḥ huṃ phaṭ namaḥ

Iti sarvaprāyaścitta-

The Great Delusive Manifestation

(14-16) : *The Pacification with the Four Colours*

1. One who will have heard of or meditated upon
the nature of this Delusive Manifestation in pacified form
Which is a Purifier difficult to obtain,—
he is released from all evil.
2. The God (of your meditation be) Viṣṇu,
and He with two eyes, bearing
mace, conch, sword and disc; with four arms,
golden of colour, standing upon a lotus as pedestal.
3. He is to be honoured by all the hosts of the Immortals,
adorned with all kinds of ornaments;

in the case of a recitation in combination with the sound *Oṃ*
this (mantra) averts all danger.
(mantra)

4. If one needs an act of attraction,
one should meditate on the God as white;
with a white garment, and flowers (and other gifts) white;
one utters the words *vaṣaṭ aṃ vaṣaṭ*.
(mantra)
5. (Then) a king, even when he lives in another continent
and when he has been driven away to a remote place,
will appear on the scene and humbly present
his riches to the performer.
6. A river filled to the rim with water
which came from swollen rain clouds,
quietly streams forth with her water pacified
and is pulled into the opposite direction.
7. And in case of an act of subjugation,
one should meditate on the God as red,
with a red garment, and flowers and other (gifts) red;
one utters the words *vaṣaṭ ghoṃ vaṣaṭ*.
(mantra)
8. And (then) elephants in rut, excited and of a cruel mind,
and also unconquerable enemies
are subjugated by the recitation (of this spell).
9. (Damsels) with the gait of rutting elephants,
with breasts full and high,
with faces shaped like the moon,
become his servants if a man recites (the spell).
10. And if an act of immobilization has to be performed,
one should meditate on the God as yellow
with a yellow garment, and flowers and other (gifts)
yellow;
one utters the words *huṃ phaṭ reṃ huṃ phaṭ*.
(mantra)
11. (Then) serpents of a very ferocious nature, malicious,
roaming about in their desire for prey,
are restrained with their organs of sense brought to rest
by the immobilizing act of the lordly performers.
12. If one needs an act of eradication
one should meditate on the God as dark blue,

with a blue garment, and flowers and other (gifts) blue;
one utters the words *huṃ phaṭ bhyaḥ huṃ phaṭ.*
(mantra)

13. And mountains of hard material and enormous size,
immovable and devoid of life
are destroyed within a moment
by the performer's effortless activity.

14. A yogin who acts for pacification
should meditate on (Viṣṇu) as possessing four colours
with garments, flowers and other (gifts) of four (colours)
and says *aṃ ghoṃ reṃ bhyaḥ*; this is preferable.
(mantra)

15. (Thus) the able performer will appease
thousands of cases of falling meteors,
opposition of planets, and hailstones,
combined with the smoke of stars.

16. If a man suffers under the strokes of a multitude of diseases,
if he has been cut off (from life or health) or is exhausted;
he will become happy during a hundred years,
as a result of (this) pacification.

17. Such are the acts concerning the God,
now listen to the regular performance:
the Māyā is worshipped on the three crucial points of the day
and will be subjugated from day to day.

18. During each act of subjugation
one should meditate on (the God) as being like vermillion (in colour);
during an act of liquidation (He should be thought of as) black of colour;
when causing dissension, (He has) a green form.
(mantras)

19. During eradication one should imagine (the God) grey of colour;
and white in the case one desires fame;
and (coloured) like a peacock's throat
during an act of immobilization.
(mantras)

20. One should assign the syllable *oṃ* to the head,
the syllable *aṃ* to the circle of the face;

the syllable *ghoṃ* should be placed on the heart;
the syllable *reṃ* he should assign to the organ of generation.
21. The syllable *bhyaḥ* should be assigned to both feet;
with the first one should assign them from outside;
thus the assignment should be practised
on the body by an eminent person.
Thus the pacification of all things.

The first thing to say on this fragment is that it contains a description of another kind of magical sādhana. The powerful Delusive Manifestation of Viṣṇu is approached in the mind by an individual performer who seems to apply this meditation to the realization of various acts of magic. This Manifestation is called the Māyā, but the Māyā is not a female entity. It is the God Viṣṇu Who disguises Himself, Who assumes another appearance for the delusion of the world of creatures. The Māyā is constituted by Viṣṇu's multi-coloured manifestations, and the worshipper contemplates the figure of the God in these changing colours. Viṣṇu's ability to change his colour will be discussed again below (p 179). It is taught in the Mbh that he changes his colour in the four world periods, and as the ages of the world evolve along a deteriorating course, these coloured manifestations assume an increasingly malevolent character. The sequence of colours which occurs in the Mbh is maintained in the present fragment except for the occurrence of the multicoloured Viṣṇu in the stanzas 14-16.

The meditation is accompanied by the recitation of mantras, the essence of which are the words *Oṃ namo Viṣṇave* and *Oṃ Aghorebhyaḥ* "*Oṃ*, To the Reassuring Ones", the last one also distributed over different parts of the fragment. On these mantras, see below (p 154). Perhaps also a pūjā to the god is implied. The meditation on Viṣṇu's different colours, accompanied by the mantra and perhaps the pūjā, is sufficient for the worshipper to obtain the desired result. Viṣṇu retains his usual appearance. There are no fiery eyes, no frightful fangs. The image made up in the sādhaka's mind is not at all of the abhicāra type (see above p 125). It is a conventional kind of Viṣṇu image with two eyes and four arms, although these lack the lotus and hold four martial attributes[9]. It is adorned with a rich variety of ornaments and is honoured by gods and men.

The fragment deserves a more detailed discussion of its contents and implications. Hereafter, some notes follow on the contents. They are mainly philological and might be ignored by those not interested in the textual problems. After these, the following chapters will deal with a few more general topics, especially the role of the colours and the sort of magic alluded to.

4. *Some explicatory notes on the Mahāmāyā stanzas* [6]

Stanza 1. The Skt. text adopted is not quite clear and seems to be incorrect in the third quarter (*yaḥ śrutvā cintavān vāpi*). The idea of "hearing" beside "meditating upon" as a condition for success gives the impression of being a literary topic; it is expressed in Mbh 1, 56, 14:

Ya idaṃ śrāvayed vidvān yaś cedaṃ śṛṇuyān naraḥ |
te brahmaṇaḥ sthānam etya prāpnuyur devatulyatām ||

"He who will proclaim this (Mahābhārata), a wise man, and the man who will listen to it, both will reach the abode of Brahmā and gain a position equal to that of the gods". Of course, such a promise is more in its place in the epic destined to be recited and listened to than in a description of a sādhana for which meditation is the essential condition.

The first word in the text, Māyātattvam "The Nature of the Delusive Manifestation" is not unknown in the Āgama literature. It occurs in the ISP (3,1,84) and is paraphrased there with *indrajālabīja* "the kernel (lit. "seed") of magical creation". The words *pavitraṃ caiva durlabhaṃ* are again more or less topical. The Śvet Up (6, 21) already calls itself a *paramaṃ pavitram* "supreme Purifier".

A difficult point in this stanza is the word "pacified", a translation of Skt. *śāntam.* The two mss do not read *śāntam,* but *syatam.* This is impossible in correct Skt., although it exists in "Archipelago Skt." as a corruption of the optative *syāt* "let it be". But this would imply that the stanza has been written by someone who lacked a reasonable knowledge of Skt., an assumption which is contradicted by the whole fragment. It is better to assume a corruption in the tradition, and the emendation to *śāntam* seems the best one, the more so because it implies that the Māyā can also show its other side, becoming horrible (*ghora-*) to the worshipper's enemies. The term *śāntamāya*—occurs, e.g. in Kathās. (12, 25, 76).

Stanza 2 demands some comment. The chief problem is here that one of Viṣṇu's attributes, the sword, is due to an emendation of the text. The Stuti & Stava edition followed the reading of the mss : *gadāśaṅkhañ ca cakrabhṛt* "bearing his mace, conch and disc", which results in a quite incorrect Skt. and at first sight an irregular iconographical representation of the god. The correction of *śaṅkhañ ca* into *śaṅkhāsi* is certainly admissible in Balinese manuscript tradition (see Stuti & Stava, p. 7ff.). But the OJ paraphrase repeats the reading of the mss. And the unusual representation of Viṣṇu with only three attributes might be due to the particular magical character of the *dhyāna* in question. Besides, it is indeed not without parallels in literature. On at least three places, the Mbh describes Viṣṇu with just the same three attributes. In 3,187,38, during the description of Viṣṇu as the Child on the waters after the dissolution of the world (see above p. 30), the God says :

Ahaṃ Nārāyaṇo nāma śaṅkhacakragadādharaḥ /

"I am Nārāyaṇa by name, the Bearer of conch, disc and mace"; and he further explains to Mārkaṇḍeya that he remains asleep during a period of a thousand yugas embodying the all in himself before he wakes up for another creation. A second place from the Mbh is a stanza inserted after 12, 47, 51 in some mss of the Southern Recension. It deals with Kṛṣṇa :

Yo jāto Vasudevena Devakyāṃ Yadunandanaḥ /
śaṅkhacakragadāpāṇir Vāsudevātmane namaḥ //

"He who is born from Vasudeva and Devakī, the Pride of the Yadus, bearing the conch, disc and mace in His hands; to Him Who is 'The Son of Vasudeva', honour". The stanza occurs in the hymn sung by Bhīṣma (see above p. 53) and is therefore directed to Viṣṇu-Kṛṣṇa's awe-inspiring appearance. It would lay a welcome connexion with the Mahāmāyā fragment the more so as this appearance of Viṣṇu has been also addressed by Bhīṣma as *māyātman* (38) and as *mohātman* (48). It is tempting to cite also the next stanza in the same chapter (stanza 52) :

Pañcabhūtātmabhūtāya bhūtādinidhanātmane /
akrodhadrohamohāya tasmai śāntātmane namaḥ //

"To Him Who exists as the Self of the Five Elements (i.e. the world's material cause), Who embodies the origin and destruction of creatures, Who is free from rage, deception and delusion, and Whose Self is pacified, honour...!" One other example from the Mbh: stanza 5,48,23 mentions Kṛṣṇa as *śaṅkhacakragadāhastam*; he is flanked by Arjuna of the formidable bow taking up his weapons.

The three attributes again emerge in the Vāsudeva Up 2 (Jacob, p. 27) : *śaṅkhacakragadāpāṇe*, and in the Ātmabodha Up (Jacob, p. 77) : *Oṃ namo Nārāyaṇāya śaṅkhacakragadādharāya.* AgPur 308, 10 deals with a meditation on Viṣṇu's four emanations Vāsudeva, Saṃkarṣaṇa, Pradyumna and Aniruddha, *śaṅkhacakragadādharāḥ*, and characterized by the colours black, white, red and yellow respectively [7]. LT (10, 21ff.) again discusses the iconographical representations of these four Vyūhas of the Pāñcarātra tradition. They are provided with the six divine qualities (i.e. the first of them possess all six,-the other three each two; cf. Gupta,p. 55). In the realm of waking (*jāgratpāda-*) they possess four arms and are provided with all their attributes and ornaments. The first of these Vyūhas, Vāsudeva, holds the three attributes disc, conch and mace, and besides keeps his fourth hand in the pose of security (*abhayamudrā*). Three attributes are further described in connexion with Rāma by Bhāsa (Abhiṣekanāṭaka 4, 14) :

Mānuṣaṃ rūpam āsthāya cakraśārṅgagadādharaḥ /
svayaṃ kāraṇabhūtaḥ san kāryārthī samupāgataḥ //

"Having assumed a human form, bearing disc, bow and mace, he has come to us for the sake of his creation although being the Creator Himself".

The iconography of South East Asian Hinduism sometimes deviates from the Indian prescriptions. This is very often the case in the representations of Viṣṇu in Burma (N. R. Ray, p. 15-48). At Pagan a Viṣṇu image has been found, provided with ornaments, and bearing the attributes conch, disc and mace, while keeping the fourth hand in the pose of liberality (*varadamudrā*)[10]. We can also cite the Indonesian Śivaite mystical tract Kumāratattva (Balinese Kīrtya ms 2322), stanza 49 :

Svapnañ ca Viṣṇur ity uktaṃ divyarūpaś caturbhujaḥ /
śaṅkhacakraga(dā)hastaḥ khagendravaravāhanaḥ //

"Viṣṇu is told to incorporate the state of dreaming, divine of form, provided with four arms, bearing the conch, disc and mace in his hands, riding upon the foremost of royal birds".

This seems to be eloquent evidence, but it should be remarked that all these text-places mention the three attributes within one verse-quarter of a very formal character, while the sequence is always the same; conch, disc (or bow) and mace. The *gadā* never leads the series, as is the case in the Mahāmāyā fragment. Besides, there exist other representations of Viṣṇu with four attributes in which the sword is added to the aforementioned three. In ViPur 1, 4, 12 the Earth praises Viṣṇu in his Boar incarnation, describing him as *śaṅkhacakragadādhara*, but in the same chapter (stanza 31) the yogins address the same Varāha with these words :

Jayeśvarāṇāṃ parameśa Keśava prabho gadāśaṅkhadharāsicakradhṛk /
prasūtināśasthitihetur īśvaras tvam eva nānyat paramaṃ ca yat padam //

O Keśava, foremost Sovereign of the victorious rulers, O Lord bearing mace and conch and also sword and disc; Thou only art the Ruler, the Cause of creation, destruction and preservation, and nothing else exists as the Supreme Abode". No better proof could be given for the misleading formality of the compound *śaṅkhacakragadādhara*. And at the same time one observes that the sequence in which the four attributes are summed up in stanza 31 is exactly the same as in the Mahāmāyā fragment. It might be remarked also that the god who bears these four attributes is addressed as the cause of destruction as well as of creation and preservation. We further point to the MMK (vol. I, p. 44) which describes Viṣṇu in the cadre of the preparation of a maṇḍala as follows : "Viṣṇu holds the disc in his hand, possesses four arms, bears also the mace, conch and sword (*gadāśaṅkhāsi*, again the same sequence) in his hands, rides upon Garuḍa, and is adorned with all his ornaments" [8]. In South East Asian iconography, the Lotus as an attribute of Viṣṇu is often replaced by the Earth (K. Bhattacharya, p. 103f.), but in some cases by the sword.[11]

In the light of this evidence it seems preferable to choose the emendation of the text which implies the representation of Viṣṇu with four attributes including the sword. Philologically this is also the best solution because it constitutes a correct Skt. The reading of the mss leaves the text with a peculiar crux by breaking up a compound by means of the word *ca*. Such a thing would not be quite impossible in the worser kind of Āgamic Skt., but it would be below the stylistic standard of the present fragment.

We return to stanza 2. There is another point which needs comment : the word *sauvarṇaḥ* "golden". The Stuti & Stava, following the mss and the OJ paraphrase, reads *sarvajñaḥ*, but it is difficult to imagine what omniscience might mean in an iconographical context. Replacement by *sauvarṇaḥ* seemed to be the best solution, although it is certainly a far-reaching emendation. The representation of Viṣṇu with the colour of gold is indeed common in the tradition, and gold is the metal often associated with this god[12]. We have then to accept that Viṣṇu would be first described with a standard colour, while afterwards, when the sādhaka chooses to meditate on the god with a particular purpose the colour is changed. An additional argument may be that *sauvarṇaḥ* is stylistically preferable.

At last, the reading *pīṭhāmburuha* is an emendation of *pītāmburuha* "yellow lotus". The yellowness of the lotus does not seem to matter here (and it would be difficult to find a parallel for it), but its serving as a pedestal does. In its emended form the compound is of the identificatory *karmadhāraya* type.

Stanza 3. The third quarter is translated from an emendation of the text not yet represented in Stuti & Stava. There the text reads : *Oṃkāraṃ ca paṭhet siddham*, and the translation was: "one should recite the syllable *Oṃ* which is perfect". This is itself an interpretation of the evidence of the mss, one of which reads *capadhehiddhan* and the other *japadehindān*. It seems that the word *Japa* is present here in any case. As it is a very frequent feature in Balinese mss that *n* is changed into *d* or vice versa, the emendation into *Oṃkārajapane hīdam* seems to be perfectly admissible. Also *siddham* would be possible instead of *hīdam*, but it presupposes a change from *s* into *h* in the mss. The sense obtained in the present translation seems better to suit the context. Still another interpretation remains possible, based upon an emendation into *Oṃkārajapane siddhaḥ*, *sarvabhayanivāraṇaḥ* "He (Viṣṇu) is mastered (or : realized) in the course of the recitation of the syllable *Oṃ*, and He averts all danger".

Stanzas 1-3 taken together describe the preliminary meditation on (and worship of?) Viṣṇu (*puraścaraṇa*, see above p. 84) required for the adept before his rituals and the mantra employed by him can be able to effect their full result. It is accompanied by the (without doubt frequent) repetition of a general and basic mantra: "*Oṃ Oṃ* Honour to Viṣṇu, *svāhā*". In this mantra the twofold occurrence of *oṃ* is due to a change in the mss text which reads *oṃ uṃ*. The two syllables *oṃ* and *uṃ* are confounded very often in the mss and usually it is no easy venture to restore the correct state of things. In the present case the change was made with a view to stanza 20: *Oṃkāraṃ vinyasen mūrdhni*.

Stanza 4. The magical procedures begin with *ākarṣaṇa* "attraction", a famous aspect of supernatural power to which we will revert below (ch. 6.4). As attraction is most often relatively innocuous, it is accompanied here by a meditation of the white Viṣṇu, although the combination of attraction with the colour white is not the usual state of affairs. The first quarter of the śloka contains the change of *kāryāṇi* into *kāryārthī* in order to complete the grammatical structure; the same reading occurs also in Stuti & Stava in stanza 12. As to the "flowers" in the third quarter, it was assumed that they were meant as ingredients of worship, with the implication that an imaginary pūjā is also performed to the deity; but they might also be a part of the god's apparel. The Skt. is somewhat cryptic here; the mss give *sa*- "possessing" as the first element of the compound, but in other stanzas where this quarter recurs (7, 10, 12, 14) they read *ca* "and" as an independent word, which would create a difficulty in the Skt. On the mantra after stanza 4, see below (p. 154).

Stanza 5. The Skt. text is based to some extent upon emendation and interpretation. The first word, *dvīpāntara* "another continent" is pretty certain, although the most important ms reads *dvinara*. The OJ commentary explains it by saying *nusantara* "other islands" and mentions the land Kliṅ, (Java or India ?) as an example. In the second quarter *dūrasthāna* is an emendation for *dūrasthañ ca*. In the last quarter the optative *saṃdadyāt* corresponds to the absolutive *sandatvā* of the mss. As to *sādhake* : the mss say *sādhako*, but this is again corrected by the OJ paraphrase. This stanza implies that the worshipper's magic power acquired by his meditation is able to attract anybody from any place and to acquire all his possessions.

Stanza 6 promises the mastery of floods, or *banjirs* as they are called in Indonesia. For the magician it is not enough to evoke the rain in times of drought; he should also be able to control the phenomena of nature when they occur[13]. In a strict sense the stanza does not describe an act of attraction, but rather one of driving away. The Skt. as edited here is again partly based upon emendations. The first and second quarters were combined into one compound, which resulted in a better sense. The word *śānta* in the third pāda is read in the mss as *tyanta* (which in Archipelago Skt. is a form for *atyanta*). Another, less probable, possibility would be *tyakta*—"having lost (its water)". In the fourth pāda, *pratilomaṃ ca* corresponds with *tilomañ cati* in the sources. Thus we have to admit that those words which allude to the "pacification" or "drawing back" of the waters are only based upon hypothetical emendations. But the OJ commentary is on our side because it decidedly speaks of a returning of the water into its normal course from which it had flown over during the rainy season (*kāla niṅ rêṅrêṅ*).

Stanza 7. "Subjugation"; the magical standard term *vaśīkaraṇa* (see below ch.6.5). It has been argued (p. 19) how this power of bringing people under one's control (*vaśa*) was believed to be an important aspect of the Māyā wielded by Viṣṇu in Ancient Indian literature. The colour red is indeed often associated with this magical act.

Stanza-8. "Elephants"; it seems somewhat out of order that in this śloka two different objects, to wit the elephants and the enemies are dealt with, while usually in this fragment only one subject is treated in each stanza. Instead of the text of the first quarter which now contains the word *kariṇaḥ* "elephants", one could surmise a long adjective compound on *-kāriṇaḥ* "effecting....", which would then express a peculiarity of the enemies mentioned in the third quarter. The OJ paraphrase is against this: it actually mentions the elephants (*liman*). In the third quarter, the word "unconquerable" (*avijeyāḥ*) is based upon a change in the mss which read *anijñeyāḥ* "unknowable"; the emendation is backed by the OJ : *tan vnaṅ inalahakên* "who cannot be conquered".

Stanza 9. The subjugation of girls is a frequent feature in this sort of magic; it is often reckoned under the heading *ākarṣaṇa* (ch. 6.4.). Here also, the activities of Viṣṇu himself, particularly in his Kṛṣṇa *avatāra*, act as a prototype (p. 25). On the other hand, reducing other people to the state of servants or slaves is a characteristical accomplishment of "subjugation" (see ch. 6.5.). The stylistic standard of this stanza proves that the author must have had a sound experience in composing Skt. poetry. The OJ commentator on this stanza contents himself with a casual note that "also girls are subjugated by the sādhaka".

Stanza 10. "Immobilization" : the Skt. *stambhana* is again a standard term (see below ch. 6.6.). The colour yellow is characteristic for this act. Bagalāmukhī, the goddess who specializes in *stambhana*, prefers the same colour (p. 106).

Stanza 11. "Serpents" : the mss give *sarva* instead of *sarpa*, but the OJ commentator points to the correct reading (OJ *ula*). Here again, the Skt. is of literary quality. Alliteration is applied lavishly. In the last quarter, the reading *śamitendriyāḥ* remains closer to the mss (*samit*-and *sapit*-) than the interpretation *stambhitendriyāḥ* in Stuti & Stava. The OJ is vague on this place.

Stanza 11a. On this place, the OJ contains some words of mysterious provenance which describe another act of magic : "If black clouds completely darken the sky during the rainy season, they will certainly disappear by worshipping the yellow Māyā. Mantra :...." There is no Skt. stanza here. It might indeed have fallen out; the act of *stambhana* is described in only one stanza while two have been devoted to both *ākarṣaṇa* and *vaśikaraṇa*. In that case it would, however, still be difficult to account for the mentioning of a superfluous mantra in the last quarter by which the subtle balance of the mantric structure of the fragment would be thoroughly upset. The subject of this passage is again the control of tropical rain which might be of great use to an Indonesian magician another argument for its secondary nature.

Stanza 12. "Eradication", *uccāṭana*. On this feat of

magic, see ch.6.7. "Dark blue" : the Skt. *nila* indicates a very dark colour and sometimes seems to be used as an equivalent for "black". Stanza 19, however, prescribes grey for *uccāṭana*, and for this more parallels from Indian text can be adduced.

Stanza 13. "Of hard material"; emended text *kaṭhinātma*, backed by the OJ *pirakasa nikaṅ vukir* "no matter the hardness of a mountain". The mss read *kadina* instead of *kaṭhinā-*."By the effortless activity" : the reading *lilahā* of the mss (not commented upon by the paraphrase) has been emended into *līlayā*. This results in very good sense, because it implies a reference to the "playful" action of the divine example. The Indian religious texts often mention the *līlā* or cosmical play by which Viṣṇu or another Supreme God performs the acts of creation, maintenance and destruction of the cosmos. The example which is given in the present fragment of the act of *uccāṭana*—the splitting of rocks—seems to be unique in the Indian cultural area.

Stanza 14. "Pacification"; the Skt. term *prāyaścitta* has a ritual connotation. Usually it stands for the atonement to be performed for omissions and faults in the ritual, but here it is meant as a synonym for *śānti*, a word which in this context summarizes the magical acts of protection (see below ch. 6.9.) —"Yogin" : a striking use of this word as a synonym for sādhaka "performer", "adept" "practisant" of the Stanza 15. On these examples of omina, see below P.O. *magical ritual* (for the use of yogin as "magician", see p. 66).

Stanza 16. This difficult śloka has been emended with the help of the paraphrase, which is not always clear itself. The problems have been discussed shortly in Stuti & Stava (p. 280, n. 8). In the third quarter it seemed better to change the hypothetical rendering of Stuti & Stava: *ukṣaṇāc cet pariklinnaḥ* "when he has been wetted by sprinkling (?)". The only possible explanation in that case would be that a patient is sprinkled with a kind of Holy Water by the adept while he recites the mantra in question. There are indeed parallels for the term *(pari)klinna-* occurring in a context of Holy Water of ritual bathing. We mention two places from the Rāmāyaṇa (Bombay ed.) : 2, 63, 17 and 1, 48, 25; in this last case the sage Gautama is said to be *tīrthodakapariklinna-*. But the Holy Water is not alluded to in the text, nor in the OJ paraphrase.

By adopting *parikhinnaḥ* instead of *pariklinnaḥ*, we return to an old emendation by Lévi (p. 47); and *ucchinnaḥ* seems better to represent the OJ *alupa narakaharepnya vet nika sakitanya* "(if) a man has forgotten his former beauty by reason of his sickness". Yet we admit that the Stuti & Stava version is nearer to the reading of the best mss: *ukṣiṇayet pariklinnaḥ*. Another possibility would be *kṣīyate ca parikhinnaḥ* "if he dwindles away in exhaustion". So much is certain, that the stanza contains a praise of the adept's medical accomplishments.

Stanza 17 reflects the fragmentary nature of the text. In all probability it does not link up with the preceding passage. It would indeed better serve as an introduction to the next stanzas. It occurs in only three mss as against at least six sources for the stanzas 14-16; but on the other hand the following ślokas occur in only one source. The best hypothesis seems to be that here another passage on the worship of the Māyā, hailing from another Tantric text, has been attached to the preceding fragment. This hypothesis is corroborated by the fact that the contents of stanzas 18-21 deviate considerably from what has been stated by the stanzas 1-16 (see below). In stanza 17 it remains unclear what is being meant by "the acts concerning the God" as against the "regular performance" announced now. The differences which exist between the two fragments do not warrant such a strong distinction between "worship of God" and "regular worship". Both fragments deal with prescriptions for individual contemplation for particular ends. As long as we do not possess more particulars about the context, we cannot give a definite judgment on the point.

"Worshipped" : as we saw, the cadre is supposed to be a pūjā. Already in the Veda human beings can acquire Māyā by sacrificing (Devanandan, p. 21). "Is subjugated" : the Māyā is thought to be brought under the performer's power by his exertions. This is the normal course of events in a magical sādhana (ch. 2). Skt. *vaśyate* is, however, an emendation for *paśyate*, the reading of the mss and Stuti & Stava. The OJ commentator is silent here.

Stanza 18. "Causing dissension" : Skt. *vidveṣaḥ* is an emendation for *vaddhe śe*, Stuti & Stava *vadheśaḥ* "the Lord of killing". *Vidveṣaḥ* is certainly the correct reading; it is the standard term for a certain act of magic (see below ch. 6.8.).

—"Green" : *śyāma*, like *nīla*, denotes a very dark shade of colour. It cannot, however, stand for "black" here, because that colour is already a condition for *māraṇa*.

Stanza 19. "In the case one desires fame" (*yaśo'rthinaḥ*; the ms gives *yasotvinaḥ*) : the OJ paraphrase says : *yan makadon huripan ivvaṅ* "when he has the intention of reanimating a person". These are seemingly conflicting statements, but both can be reckoned under the heading of *śānti* (or *rāyaścitta*) as mentioned in stanza 14.

Stanza 20. In the last two ślokas the *nyāsa* of the syllables of the mantra is expounded. Here the syllables applied in the stanzas 1-16 occur again.—"Organ of generation"; the word *yoni*, said usually in connection with a female subject, here presumably serves as a general term.

Stanza 21. "With the fist" : the ms says *ustina*. Probably a second *m* has fallen out.—"From outside" (*bāhyakam*); there is also an "internal" *nyāsa* on the inner organs.

The differences between the contents of stanzas 1-16 and those of stanzas 18-21 may be resumed now :

a. In stanza 18, the magical acts of Liquidation (*māraṇa*) and Causing Dissension (*vidveṣa*) are mentioned, while they are absent in the first part. For *māraṇa*, see ch. 6.8.; it is indeed usually associated with a black colour. The omission of this act in 1-16 is perhaps not without reason. Buddhist and Jaina Tantras, even when they fully acknowledge the powers acquired by a sādhaka, often keep their ground in forbidding their adepts to make use of the power to kill; otherwise there would be a flagrant violation of the basic rule of non-violence (*ahiṃsā*) enjoined by these religions. For a few instances, see below (p. ch.6.8).

b. The colour which characterizes a eradication is said in 19 to be grey (*dhūmravarṇam*, lit. "smoke-coloured") and not dark blue as in 12. Grey would indeed be the colour expected in a text which conforms to the usual theory.

c. In stanza 19, the white Māyā is advised for meditation for someone who desires fame (an aim which is an aspect of *puṣṭi* "welfare" "acquisition", and this in its turn falls under *śānti*, although it is often mentioned as a separate heading; see p. 6.9). White is said to be the characteristic of attraction in stanza 4. Here again, it is the second part which conforms to the usual tradition.

d. The "colour of a peacock's throat" (a deep blue) is not the usual yellow which accompanies the act of immobilization (st. 10). In this isolated case, the first part reflects the tradition.

e. The mantras given by the OJ paraphrase after 18 and 19 deviate from those which belong to 1-16 and 20-21. They are characterized by the occurrence of the bīja (kernel syllable) *hroṃ*. Unfortunately they have not been preserved intact in the mss tradition.

f. Of the mantras prescribed after stanza 21, the first : *Oṃ vaṣaṭ Oṃ vaṣaṭ namaḥ*, is not found in the fragment 1-16. After stanza 3 another mantra occurs on its place.

g. The caption at the end is *iti sarvaprāyaścitta* "thus the pacification of all things", an expression which is not found in the title; but it indeed occurs in the OJ after stanza 16. This again suggests a different provenance for the two fragments.

The most impressive feature of the Mahāmāyā fragment is without doubt the application its author has made of the doctrine of the four colours assumed by Viṣṇu in the successive ages of the world. We refer to Ch. 4 below for a discussion of this topic in Skt. literature, in the course of which attention will be drawn to the uncanny, delusive side of Viṣṇu's coloured manifestation. The application of colours and of coloured images in magical ceremonies appears to have been a fairly frequent phenomenon in the texts. The Mahāmāyā fragment, however, handles the tradition in itṣ own way, as appears also from the meditation on the multicoloured Viṣṇu for the goal of protection (stanzas 14-16). Most often a white colour is advised for this end (as has been done indeed in stanza 19), while variegated or multicoloured manifestations are sometimes considered characteristic of the delusion or terror inflicted by the god in question (cf. BhGītā 11, 24 *anekavarṇam*). In the present meditation on the protective Mahāmāyā the point seems not to be its possessing four colours, but the harmony of these colours occurring together. Such a meditation is symbolical for and thus truly identical with the victory over the separate manifestations of existence, represented here by the fearsome appearances of Viṣṇu in the individual colours. Just as the god Viṣṇu was so often considered to be the source of the fundamental delusion which holds mankind under its sway (see p. 18), thus the spiritual adept is able by contemplating on this Viṣṇu to identify himself with one of His fearsome appearances and thus to assume the God's role.

This leads to the question which are the real aims which the worshipper or performer strives to attain. Does he really want only to practise ordinary magic, be it of the "white" or "black" variety? Such an assumption would be immediately contradicted by what is said in stanza 1 : *sarvapāpāt pramucyate* "one is released from all evils", a remark which on the contrary strongly suggests that we have to do here with an admittedly unconventional element of a course for liberation from *saṃsāra.* However it be, the procedures expounded and illustrated by examples in the present fragment are of a purely magical character. The Skt. words which hold a key position are *ākarṣaṇa* "attraction" (4), *vaśīkaraṇa* "subjugation" (7), *stambhana* "immobilization" (10), *uccāṭana* "eradication" (12) and *prāyaścitta* "pacification" (in this context; 14). Besides, the stanzas 18 and 19 contain the terms *māraṇa* "liquidation" and *vidveṣa* (*ṇa*) "creating dissension" while they circumscribe the aim of *prāyaścitta* or *śānti* with "desiring fame". These words are technical terms in the magical Tantras of India where they constitute the standard actions of magical prowess of an adept, the "Six Acts" (*ṣaṭ karmāṇi*; *ṣaṭkarman*). It has already been remarked that only the portion constituted by stanzas 18-21 presents these six in accordance with the regular tradition. The stanzas 1-16 mention only five of them. Moreover, the act of *ākarṣaṇa* does not belong to the Six in strict sense although it often occurs in the relevant lists. For a discussion of these acts of magic we refer to ch. 6.

It should be stated that the subject is treated by the poet in a very stylized manner. He has not tried to give a simple matter-of-fact description of the ritual or the meditation. This is again an indication that we do not have to do with a set of magical prescriptions pure and simple. The present function of the fragment as expressed in one of the mss: "to be performed daily for warding off all diseases and calamities" (Stuti & Stava, p. 275) probably reflects an adaptation to the needs and expectations of the owners who were members of the nobility. Perhaps we have to assume that these coloured images were originally meant to be the material tools (*yantra*) for the performer, even if (or: just because) they existed only in his own mind. In that case they fulfilled the same function as the demons mastered in the sādhanas described above (ch. 2.6). The accompanying mantras are as it were the magical arrows directed against the opponent. But while coercing the supernatural for the goal of exercizing destructive magic one incurs grave dangers, just like the Indra of yore during his amoral feats of valour (p. 12). In order to meet them the performer needs an act of śānti and he brings this about by contemplating the Viṣṇu who harmonizes within himself the diversity of colours. Thus he escapes the inexorable law of karman, and he becomes the like of Mārkaṇḍeya who witnessed the destruction of the universe, but who by a boon of the Lord was admitted to enter His body at the end of the four yugas (p. 30). The human sādhaka who by contemplating Viṣṇu's Māyā of colours also completed a symbolical course of yugas would be freed from death and destruction, although in the course of his spiritual development he had mastered just those powers which would enable him to inflict this same fate upon others.

5. *The Aghoramantra and its implications*

Some words should now be said on the mantric structure of the fragment, especially of the stanzas 1-16. They are accompanied by six mantras which are to conduct six different acts of meditation. The text edited above is misleading in that it suggests that these mantras form an inherent part of it. This is not exactly so. In their entirety they occur only in the OJ paraphrase on the stanzas concerned (3, 4, 7, 10, 12, 14); the stanzas themselves contain short references to them.

The first of these mantras (occurring after st. 3): *Oṃ oṃ* (or perhaps : *Oṃ uṃ*) *Viṣṇave namaḥ svāhā,* contains no peculiar features. The next four are all constructed on the same pattern; instead of the words *Oṃ Viṣṇave* they insert other groups of words of symmetric construction (on mantric symmetrism, see Bharati, p. 129). These inserted passages are respectively: *vaṣaṭ Aṃ vaṣaṭ vaṣaṭ*; *Ghoṃ vaṣat*; *huṃ phaṭ Reṃ huṃ phaṭ*; and *huṃ phaṭ Bhyaḥ huṃ phaṭ.* With the mantras thus built up one should compare the formula which is to accompany sprinkling during recitation of the hymn Stuti & Stava No. 842 : *Oṃ vaṣaṭ oṃ vaṣaṭ namaḥ svāhā*. This mantra is almost identical with the one given in our fragment after st. 4; and, significantly, the hymn No. 842, *Siṃhanāde vyāghram Caiva*, is addressed to Viṣṇu in his terrible aspect and destined to guide a concentration on a three-headed Viṣṇu emerging from the mouth of a tiger ! The our mantras from the present fragment contain the small words *vaṣaṭ* and *huṃ phaṭ*. The first word usually occurs in combination with relatively innocuous acts of magic (but there are exceptions), while the last two are incorporated in the mantras which accompany more dangerous performances; a state of affairs which is reflected in the fragment. Together with *namaḥ* and *svāhā* they occur in the list of the potent six words discussed above (ch. 2.4).

The central syllables of these four mantras, *Aṃ*, *Ghoṃ*, *Reṃ* and *Bhyaḥ*, occur together in the sixth mantra given after stanza 14 which belongs to the salutary act of *prāyaścitta*. This last mantra in a way summarizes and integrates the preceding ones. The syllables in question, when read together, form the word *Aghorebhyaḥ* "To the Reassuring Ones". This significant expression forms part of the famous Pañcabrahmamantras directed to Śiva's Five Faces (Stuti & Stava No. 360).

On these Five Faces, most often called Pañcamukha or Pañcabrahma, some comment is necessary in this context. As we shall see, the gods have sometimes been conceived of as a fivefold manifestation, and this may be expressed iconographically by means of five faces. This aspect of Śiva is very important and has repeatedly been discussed, recently by Gonda, 1970 (pp. 42-48). We intend here to give only a short characterization of them from the viewpoint of their multicolouredness.

The word *Aghorebhyaḥ* from the Mahāmāyā fragment is identical with the first word of the classical formula of Aghora, one of the Five Faces (the others are Īśāna, Tatpuruṣa, Vāmadeva and Sadyojāta). This mantra runs as follows (version of the MNUp) :

Aghorebhyo 'tha ghorebhyaḥ, ghoraghoratarebhyaś ca /
sarvataḥ sarvasarvebhyo namas te Rudra rūpebhyaḥ //

"To the Reassuring One Who are also awesome, Who are

even more awesome than the awesome, Who are all and complete in all respects honour to Thy manifestations, O Rudra! " The mantra is sometimes applied in magic, for example in K (p. 107) where the context is the "resurrection of the dead" (*mṛtasaṃjīvana-*), and in N (p. 310), where it is directed against enemies. The question is who are the forces addressed by the plural *Aghorebhyaḥ*. They must be manifestations of Rudra/Śiva, as is said in the mantra, and in our context it seems reasonable to assume that they stand for all Five Faces together. The mantra when applied in the Mahāmāyā fragment is cut into four syllables all accompanying a meditation on Viṣṇu in a particular colour, while the acts are concluded with saying the name Aghorebhyaḥ in full, the last procedure being apt to procure *śānti*. In this way there is a series of five acts accompanied by five methods of dealing with the mantra; if the five aspects of the divine had been located spatially, as is often the case, they would have been situated in the four main directions of the sky while the last and pacificatory manifestation would have been located in the Centre. The last act seems to be absolutely necessary in the Mahāmāyā description (it is indeed the one preserved in most sources); it is destined to round off and at the same time to pacify the magical procedures alluded to in the former acts. This is further in concord with the idea of the fifth number in the Centre as wielding sovereignty over the other four (below, p. 190).

It seems that also Śiva's Five Faces had the function to express the God's omnipresent manifestation as a divine Sovereign who reigns over all gods and other beings in the quarters of space and incorporates all aspects from benign to terrible. The Face which is known to particularly represent the terrible aspect is the Southern One, Aghora "the Non-terrible One" as he is called by euphemism (Gonda, 1970, p. 43). The LiPur (20, 50, 18 ff.) during the description of an *abhicāra* (black magical) ritual enjoins that one should meditate on oneself as Aghora; among other rituals one should also construct five sacrificial hearths and mutter the mantra to Aghora. But on the other hand, the same Southern Face is approached for protection in ŚvetUp 4, 21, while in more recent times there is a separate manifestation of Śiva as Divine Teacher called Dakṣiṇāmukha "the Face in the South". The word "euphemism" would thus not be a happy one in connection with Aghora, because it suggests that the thing or being designed by it is unable to change its malicious or evil character, while Śiva/Aghora can manifest his other side upon the devotees' plea. Calling such a power by its friendly name is the first step towards evoking its friendly manifestation. "O Rudra, Thy body which is wholesome (*śiva*), reassuring (*aghora*), not looking badly; with that body which is most pacifying, O Ruler of the Mountain, appear before us" [9] is a famous stanza from the Veda (Vājasaneyi Saṃhitā 16, 2; ŚvetUp 3, 5).

The five Pañcabrahmamantras alluded to above occur for the first time in TĀr-10, 43-47 (-MNUp. 7, 3-7). These five have remained in vogue in Śivaite worship. It seems that the ideas underlying them can for the greater part be recognized also in the ŚvetUp, although this text does not mention them as a body. Aghora is mentioned in ŚvetUp 3, 5; (Tat)puruṣa in 3, 8; Īśāna in 4, 11, while he is suggested by 3, 1 and 3, 2. Sadyojāta "the Recently-born One" is at least suggested by 4, 3, a passage which underlines the God's incomprehensible ability to manifest himself in the world in various shapes: "Thou art woman, Thou art man; Thou a boy, Thou a girl; Thou as the decrepit old man stumblest with the help of a stick; Thou art the recently born one, having faces on all sides"[10]. The stanza 4, 12 further contains the words *hiraṇyagarbhaṃ paśyata jāyamānam* "behold the Golden Germ being born". The Śivapūjāstava by Jñānaśiva (Aithal, No. 41), after describing the positions of the Five Faces in the five directions in st. 22, in the next stanza (23) speaks of their manifestations in human beings :

Īśatatpuruṣāghoravāmājavadanaṃ Śivam /
bālayauvanavṛddhastrīnarākāraṃ namāmy aham //

"I honour that Śiva whose Faces, Īśa, Tatpuruṣa, Aghora, Vāma(deva) and Aja (Sadyojāta) have the form of a child, a youth, an old man, a woman and a man".

The Five Faces are not the only representations of Rudra in the five directions. The TS (5, 5, 7, 1-3) honours Rudra with his bow in the S., the W., the N. and the Zenith in connection with four kinds of years; the Cāturmāsyas or quarterly sacrifices are also alluded to (Kane, 1958, p. 487). There are also Śiva's Five Mūrtis (manifestations) : Brahmā, Viṣṇu, Rudra, Maheśvara, Sadāśiva (Śiva Pur p. 927, 3). In Bali we have Īśvara (E.), Brahmā (S.), Mahādeva (W.), Viṣṇu (N.) and Śiva (C.) (Stuti & Stava, No. 369, and elsewhere). The worship of Sadāśiva with five faces existed in Medieval Bengal[14].

The Purāṇas give ample attention to the Five Faces Īśāna etc. An interesting discussion for our purpose is presented by the LiPur (vol. 1, chs. 11-15). This text describes how in former ages the Five Brahmās (= the Five Faces) appeared in answer to Brahmā's meditation as his sons. At first there appeared a youth in a white-red colour, accompanied and adored by four pupils clad in white. This was Sadyojāta (1, 11). The second to manifest himself was Vāmadeva who is, together with his pupils, characterized by a red colour (1,12, 10): *raktāmbaradharāḥ sarve raktamālyānulepanāḥ* "all wearing red garments and red garlands and unguent" as the time-honoured phrase runs. This occurred in the thirtieth *Kalpa* (world period), in which Brahmā himself is said to have been of a red colour (1,12, 1) [11]. In the next *kalpa* Brahmā was of a yellow colour and when he again desired to have a son there appeared to him a yellow manifestation, Tatpuruṣa, "wearing a yellow garment, his body anointed with yellow ointment, with a yellow garland and upper garment....with a sacred thread of golden colour, and a yellow headdress" (1, 13, 2f.) [12]. The following *kalpa*, called the Black (*asita*) witnessed the appearance of a black youth, who was Aghora, "of a black colour, very powerful, glowing with fiery energy, wearing a black garment and headdress, wearing a black sacred cord ; endowed with a black crown, and a black garland and black ointment" (1, 14, 4f.) [13.] This Aghora was also accompanied by four pupils in black.

At the end of this kalpa Brahmā, overwhelmed by the sight of this fourth manifestation, praised Śiva. The God became satisfied by this and declared that by means of this manifestation of Aghora He would remove all evils and sins, no matter how severe or serious. For example by muttering a formula for 100,000 times to the Reassuring Ones (*Aghorebhyaḥ*) even a killer of a brahman is released from his sin; *lakṣaṃ japtvā hy aghorebhyo brahmahā mucyate prabho* (1, 15, 6). It is possible that this stanza means that the formula to be muttered consists of the mere word *Aghorebhyaḥ* itself. In that case there would be a far-reaching agreement between the LiPur and the Mahāmāyā fragment which prescribes saying this same word as a supreme *prāyaścitta* (for *prāyaścitta* as pacification of evil deeds, see below. Recitation for 50,000 times, the LiPur proceeds, results in the pacification of all sins committed by speech; reciting half that amount destroys all sinful thoughts. But four times as much is required if the sin has been premeditated and eight times as much if it has been committed in anger (?). He who kills a kṣatriya (*vīraha-*) should recite for 100,000 times, and he who kills a brahman for ten million times. He who kills his mother should recite for a million times in order to reach purification. For all killers of cows or women, or for those who do not heed the good deeds done by others to them, a recitation of ten thousand times may suffice. The rewards stated look artificial and do not by any means deviate from similar descriptions in the Purāṇas; but it is interesting that the idea of pacification is worked out in such detail specially in connection with the figure of Aghora and his mantra which begins with the word *Aghorebhyaḥ*. The last stanza of this chapter (LiPur 1, 15, 31) states that "this is the secret doctrine of Lord Aghora ; by it a Twice-born will be continually victorious in order to purify all kinds of sin" :

Etad rahasyaṃ kathitam Aghoreśaprasaṅgataḥ /
tasmāj jayed dvijo nityaṃ sarvapāpaviśuddhaye //

At last (ch. 1, 16) the LiPur relates how the fifth and chief one of the Five Faces, Īśāna, made his appearance to Brahmā in the form of the Sarasvatī of variegated colour. "With great sound there appeared the Sarasvatī of variegated colour (*viśvarūpā*), wearing garland and garment, sacred thread and headdress of variegated colour; anointed with ointment of variegated colour, the Mother of all" (1, 16, 3f.) [14]. Īśāna himself is, however, characterized by the hue of pure crystal (1, 16, 4b). On the coloured Sarasvatī, see below (p. 201).

In its presentation of the appearance of the Five Faces with different colours in a given sequence, the LiPur on this place shows a remarkable similarity to the Mahāmāyā fragment. The sequence of colours in both texts is white—red—yellow—black—variegated (*viśva-*). Both texts lay special stress upon the word (or the formula) *Aghorebhyaḥ* as a magical device for destroying the consequences of evil, although they do this in different connexions : in the Māyā fragment the word *Aghorebhyaḥ* as a whole is prescribed during the meditation on the last and central manifestation, in the LiPur during the fourth and not the last one. In the Māyā fragment supranormal feats are further promised by a recitation of one of the syllables of the word in isolation. That Aghora's name came to be considered as able to represent the other faces of Śiva, can be explained best out of his special character as the Southern Face of terrible appearance; already in the Veda his is the most distinct individuality (Gonda, 1970, p. 43). Daniélou (p. 325) refers to a passage from the Mbh (Calc. ed. 13, 6384ff.) which locates the Five Faces in the quarters of the sky and also states that the Southern Face is terrible while the others bear benign expressions. The South is the dreaded region of the dead. Aghora's Māyā is emphasized in the Śivapūjāstava referred to above (Aithal, No. 41): he is called *bahurūpin* in stanza 28. Let us add that in Stuti & Stava, No. 362 (stanza 35) he is represented as the fourth manifestation of Śiva in the North, which means that in the Balinese Śivaite world view he occupies the same place as the black Viṣṇu. This feature renders the identity between Viṣṇu's and Śiva's coloured manifestations as the "Aghoras" in the Māyā fragment the more acceptable—and it is in complete accordance with the Indonesian tendency to coalescence of the two poles of Viṣṇuism and Śivaism in Hindu speculation.[15]

In most places, however, not Aghora but Īśāna occupies the central position. As an example we refer to the Pañcabrahma Up, a text which concentrates on the mystical equations around the Five Faces (Śaiva Ups., p. 79-86). It presents (5ff.) a fourfold system in which the Vedas, the Vedic fires and the Śivaite śaktis are introduced :

Sadyojāta—earth—Ṛgveda—Gārhapatya—yellow—*kriyāśakti*.
Aghora—water—Yajurveda— Dakṣiṇa — black — *icchāśakti*.
Vāmadeva—fire—Sāmaveda — Āhavanīya — White/dark—*śaktidvaya*.
Tatpuruṣa—air—Ath.veda—Fivefold Fire—red—*sarvaśakti*.

Īśāna—space—seems to escape all other characteristics. He is described by means of a number of general epithets which delineate his fundamental position. Among these are "pacified" (*śānta*), "superior to the pacified state" (*śāntyatīta-*) (20). Stanza 25 declares: "By Him everything obtains its lustre and in Him everything will disappear; that is Brahman, the Supreme, the Pacified; I Myself am that Brahman, the Supreme Abode". And 27 : "Knowing that these are Brahman's acts one reaches Īśāna; having caused this All, which is the Fivefold Brahman (= the Five Faces), to disappear within oneself, the wise should realize: 'I am He' and become immortal in Brahman" [15]. As we see, in this passage the Pañcabrahma speculation is applied in an Advaita context of Ātman-Brahman identification. The adept who by his spiritual exercise effects the unification of the fivefold function of the Five Faces into himself, obtains the position of the Supreme God Who is Brahman, and immortality; but not only that, he also wields His supernatural power or māyā, as appears from stanza 22: "Having performed the dissolution of the Five Brahmans into himself, (the adept) remains concentrated within himself, having dissolved all by his own māyā" :

Pañcabrahmopasaṃhāraṃ kṛtvā svātmani saṃsthitam /
svamāyāvaibhavāt sarvān saṃhṛtya svātmani sthitaḥ //

The Pañcabrahma Up also mentions (stanza 36ff.) the more immediate effects of worship of the Five Faces. They include the bestowal of all kinds of earthly and heavenly gifts on the worshipper : Sadyojāta grants the result of all desires; Aghora destroys the floods of sins, allays all evil and grants all kinds of dominion. Vāmadeva grants illumination and, besides, a happy family life on earth (*saubhāgya*) together with success bestowed on all actions. Tatpuruṣa heals all diseases and is the cause of creation, maintenance and destruction. Īśāna is the cause of all and will at the end of time again incorporate everything within himself. This description deviates from the usual meanings of the five functions of the Fivefold Śiva, which are : creation, maintenance, destruction or reabsorption, obscuration (of God's real nature), and divine Grace which is the cause of the souls' release. These functions are said to be executed by respectively Sadyojāta, Vāmadeva, Aghora, Tatpuruṣa and Īśāna (see Gonda, 1970, p. 47f., who cites other sources). As a matter of fact, however, also these classical five functions might in a sense be seen as magical acts, similar to those described in the Mahāmāyā fragment. Creation draws mankind into saṃsāra (*ākarṣaṇa*); Maintenance of the world causes people to be fascinated and subjugated by life's mirage (*vaśīkaraṇa*); Reabsorption (or, on the individual plane: death) snatches them away from their positions which they assumed to be safe (*uccāṭana*); Obscuration makes them to stay motionless in saṃsāra immobilizing them as it were (*stambhana*) by delusion; but Grace, by leading the way to final emancipation, affords the atonement for all evils committed (*prāyaścitta*).

4. BEWILDERING COLOURS

1. *A note on colour symbolism*

The Balinese Mahāmāyā fragment discussed in the preceding chapter lays great stress on the colours as magical operators. It describes a meditation of a Viṣṇu of changing colours to the aim of inflicting the results of various kinds of magical feats upon a victim. These feats always involve that the victim is psychologically affected, deluded or otherwise loses the normal use of his faculties of mind. Actually it is often said that the colours are directly connected with certain psychological or physical processes[1]. It seems, however, that only little has as yet been done in asserting the influence of colour symbolism in traditional lore. There are surprisingly little references to the subject in Smith Thompson's admittedly far from complete Motif Index of Folk-literature (vol. V,p. 552f.; 562). From Indian folklore some data are presented by Abbott (p. 276-283). The Indian mind loves colours, and the same holds good for the peoples living on the sidelines of the Indian cultural area, such as the Nāgas[2].

In this chapter we shall confine ourselves to a survey of some places from Ancient Indian Literature that give evidence of the power thought to be executed by the colours ; and in particular of the faculties of delusion, sometimes even of terror, considered to be inherent in their purposeful combination in ritual context.

At first we recall that Śvet Up. (4, 1) speaks of the God who "though being unique and colourless, appears manifold by the application (*yogāt*) of His cosmical energy, assuming manifold colours"; in the same stanza, this God is requested to provide the poet with "an auspicious resolve" (*buddhyā śubhayā*) [1]. Multicolouredness is seen here as characteristic of the evolved state of creation through divine agency, no matter if this state is in its last sense real or imaginary. And the multiform aspect of the divine is indeed ambivalent. In BhGītā 11, 24 one of the characteristics of Viṣṇu's fearsome cosmical manifestation (see above p. 51) is his assuming manifold colours (*anekavarṇam*). These are among the factors that rob

Arjuna of his peace of mind : "I find no stability nor equanimity" are his words in the same stanza. The Indian commentators tend to interpret the word *varṇa-* in this context in a wider sense of "distinction, situation". Śaṅkara, for example, paraphrases: *anekavarṇā bhayaṃkarā nānāsaṃsthānā yasmin* "in Whom there are various *varṇas*, that is terrifying different positions"[3]. Madhusūdana repeats this phrase. The Bhāṣyotkarṣadīpikā says *aneke nānā bhayaṅkarā varṇā yasmin tam* "in whom there are various, that means different sorts of, *varṇas* which evoke fear", without explaining the word varṇa further.

A combination of beautiful colours is further said to delude human beings. The magical deer described in Rām 3,41 which is no deer but a product of māyā, the demon Mārīca in disguise (see above p. 4), steals Sītā's heart ; its body is "brightened by various sorts of colours" (*nānāvarṇavicitrāṅga*, 3, 41, 13). Sītā desires to possess it and amuse herself with it (*krīḍārtham*, 3, 41, 9). There is no doubt here on the translation of varṇa as colour, and symbolically the wonderful stag might be seen as representing the Māyā which overawes and attracts mankind, creating in it the desire to amuse itself with Her.

The image of the delusive colours is found also in soteriological speculation. The twelfth book of the Mbh contains an interesting doctrine of the colours of the soul (12, 271, 33-55) which has been discussed by Bedekar (esp. on p. 335f.); we refer to his interpretation of the passage. Bedekar also points out that Bhīṣma in the preceding chapter (12, 270) argued that the soul by its own nature is spotless white but has been coloured by coming into contact with the products of karma, as the wind seems to assume a colour when polluted by various kinds of stuffs like red arsenic or black pigment. At the base of this process lies Ignorance (*ajñāna*) which is scarcely different from the Delusion (*moha*) caused by Māyā (see above p. 20). The colour assumed by the soul determines the state to be attained by it in a future birth (12, 271, 35); and this colour in its turn has been brought about by Kāla, the force of Time which is equal to the Terrible Viṣṇu (above p. 53). The essence of this fragment is that the colours are cosmical agents who influence the soul and create destinations. One needs not to be convinced by Bedekar's argument (p. 337) that this doctrine must be of Jaina origin in order to grasp the importance of the fragment in the present context[4].

Another instance. The Śivajñānabodham, a short but basic text of the Śaiva Siddhānta school of Śivaite philosophy (13th century A.D.) in stanza 8 introduces God speaking to the soul : "Brought up among savages, the five senses, thou hast lost consciousness", and the commentator adds : "These souls, confused by the five senses, do not know themselves, for the five senses reveal what they reveal like the colours in a crystal". The image is explained further : "Like the crystal which displays many colours, the soul assumes that its nature is displayed in the organs of sense. Then, perceiving that the false organs of sense, like the (crystal's) many colours, are different from it, it discerns the True and rejects the false as false...." (trsl. Gordon Matthews, Oxford 1948, p. 21). On stanza 9 the commentator remarks : "When the various colours which are non-real are perceived to be non-real, what thus arises is rightly understood to be Knowledge itself (*jñānasvarūpa* ; Matthews, o.c., p. 23). Here again, the image of multicolouredness characterizes the evolved and degraded state of creation and the fatal incarnation of the Pure Soul in the body of transmigration. Modern explainers continue to use the same image. Thus Paranjoti (p. 80) asserts that (in a certain state of the soul) "the various products of māyā....are here present in their rich variety. To the soul....these seem attractive.... it sees the world in false colours and leads a restless life in pursuit of the gaudy trifles....".

The doctrine of the colourlessness of the unevolved pure state of being has its counterpart in statements that Prakṛti, the unevolved material cause of the world, is white (which means : colourless). Thus ViDhPur (3, 48, 19) while commenting upon the symbolism of the Śiva Mahādeva image, remarks :

Jagato yad abhāvas tu Prakṛtiḥ sā prakīrtitā |
śuklā ca Prakṛtiḥ sarvā tena śuklo Maheśvaraḥ ||

"The state of non-existence of the world is taught to be Prakṛti; and Prakṛti in her completeness is white—therefore the Great

Lord is white". And the PST (1, 23) comes near to this when it states that the Prakṛti cannot be perceived by a differentiation of colours :

Na śvetaraktapītādivarṇair nirdhārya cocyate

"It is taught that (Prakṛti) cannot be ascertained by means of the colours like white, red, or yellow". Although white here plays the role of just an ordinary colour beside the others, the pattern is the same : Prakṛti is characterized by the absence of the delusive interplay of cosmical colours. In this connection it is understandable that colours sometimes play a role in yogic meditation. This is, for example, the case in the Yogāvacara manual of the Theravāda monks[5]. The Balinese stuti collection contains a description of involutive meditation on the Seven Selves (Stuti & Stava, No. 103; in reverse, evolutive order in No. 456) beginning with the Ātman (identified with god Brahmā) and ending with the Śūnyātman (identified with Paramaśiva). All of them except the last two are characterized by a certain colour. As they are also thought to be present in parts of the body from the navel upwards, there is some similarity to the Tantric practices, for example of meditation on the cakras (see, for example, Avalon, 1958, p. 28).

2. *The three colours*

From the Veda onwards there are descriptions involving the combination of three colours, usually white, red and black. The role of these three colours when occurring in combination has been dealt with by V. W. Turner in connection with their symbolical value in the cultural pattern of the Ndembu, an African tribe[6]. According to Turner, these colours belong to the earliest symbols of humanity and represent various products from the human body. Analogies to this physical experience are then found in society and cosmos, and this leads to colour systematization in these fields also. In this way the three colours would become a workable instrument for symbolizing a primordial classification of reality. Turner also refers to the ChUp. This text (6, 4, 1) presents the three colours as characteristics of the three basic constituents of nature: white of water, red of fire, black of food. All three can be present in all these three elements, so that in reality we obtain mixtures—but each colour dominates in its own province.

The same division into three colours is maintained in the doctrine of the three guṇas worked out in Sāṃkhya philosophy (Frauwallner, p. 306f.). A primordial state of Prakṛti (sometimes also called Māyā) is maintained by the equilibrium of these three guṇas (*sattva*—white; *rajas*—red; *tamas*—black ; on the guṇas, see also Eliade, p. 365f., with further literature). Śvet Up (4, 5) contains the image of the Goat (*aja*-. which can also be interpreted as "the Unborn One") of three colours, red, white, and black ; it gives birth to many children and is temporarily enjoyed by the He-goat, the Soul [2].

An interesting description of the three guṇas occurs in the Mbh (12,326,26) : "(The thinkers) declare that these are the guṇas: lucidity (*sattvam*), passion (*rajas*) and inertia (*tamas*, lit. : darkness). These are present in a quiet or a moving state in all bodies. The soul enjoys (experiences) these guṇas, but is not experienced by them. The soul is itself devoid of these guṇas, but it experiences them ; it creates them, being itself superior to them". The text then proceeds discussing the hierarchy of evolution, particularly the five elements. In stanza 54 the speaker, who is God Himself, declares: "Observe these three guṇas which are present in Me, but devoid of form". The Kṛṣṇa Up. st. 5 (ed. Jacob, p. 4) seems directly to continue the argument when it declares : "this is called My threefold Māyā, consisting of sattva, rajas and tamas; the element of sattva is declared to be present in Rudra, that of rajas in a devoted brahman, that of tamas in the party of the demons; thus the Māyā is explained to be threefold" [3]. Here the three basic strands with their three colours are interpreted as characteristics of the divine Māyā which deludes mankind; while the tripartite mystical nature of Reality is connected with the gods, the religious performers (and monopolists of religious literature), and the antagonists of both.

A similar statement is made in the DevīBhPur (6, 37, 48-50): the power of Māyā manifests itself in this way that the three guṇas are the cause of the embodiment of souls (*dehasaṃbhava*). The same text declared (6, 26, 2) that without delusion (*moha*) no soul would be embodied. It is also said (6,

31, 32) that the guṇas have their origin in Māyā (*māyāsamudbhavāḥ*). In their turn the guṇas are basic to the three cosmical energies, those of Wisdom (*jñānaśakti*), Action (*kriyāśakti*) and Matter (*dravyaśakti*). In BhPur (8, 5, 44) Viṣṇu is addressed with the words *guṇeṣu māyāraciteṣu vṛttibhir na sajjamānāya* "to (Thee) Who art unattached to the activities in the scope of the guṇas which are the product of Māyā".

Now this concept of the three guṇas of three colours can be shown to have been connected with rituals and their aims. A passage in the PST (6, 71ff.) deals with the distinction of the tongues of the ceremonial fire into three groups. Stanza 76 differentiates them according to aims. Oblation in the sāttvika group is advised during worship of the gods; the group belonging to rajas is connected with the rites motivated by a particular desire from the side of the sacrificer; the group characterized by tamas is destined for acts of evil intention:

Sāttvikā divyapūjāsu rājasyaḥ kāmyakarmasu |
tāmasyaḥ krūrakāryeṣu prayoktavyā vipaścitā ||

We now make a digression in order to include some instances of the powers with which the three colours were thought to be endowed also separately. Usually a white colour is considered to bring about all kinds of good influence, freedom from fear, and so on. The Vaikhānasa priest who laid himself to sleep in the temple precincts in order to have a dream of good omen had to clothe himself in a white garment (Atri Saṃhitā 13, 26). Śrī is clad in white (KJ 7). White flowers cause śānti (KJ 72). Kane, 1962 (p 1106) discusses a Mahāśveta (Great White) mantra directed to the Sun; it brings about any result desired. In some cases a white colour is associated with the foreboding of wealth or a magical rite to achieve this. The Mahāmāyā fragment connects white with the acquisition of wealth (see p. 138). This tradition has its roots in the Veda; the SVBr advises wearing white clothing and fasting during the bright half of the month for obtaining all kinds of desire. The commentary superficially specifies the aims with the word *rājādibhogān* (more probably : *rājyādibhogān* "enjoyment of a kingdom and other goods"). MtPur 93 describes the worship of the planets. Immediately after the remark in stanza 57 that this ritual is destined for the realization of all desires (*sarvakāmāptisiddhaye*), stanza 58 enjoins that the sacrificer should be clad in white and smeared with white unguents (*śuklāmbaradharaḥ śuklagandhānulepanaḥ*). MMK (vol. II, p. 538) advises to hit the images of a certain group of goddesses with *jātī* flowers (white) for a certain number of times, saying a certain mantra in the required state of mind : the result will be that the king becomes subjugated. The same act executed with buds of the *jātī* flower results in obtaining a beautiful princess with a rich dowry[4]. The ViDhPur (2, 176, 33) prescribes a white garment and wreath for a king in the course of a ritual aiming at victory in a military campaign. Instances of a belief in the effectiveness of the white colour can be traced from the modern folklore of the Indian subcontinent. Elwin (p. 65) relates how a witch predicted a man's future by sucking a little of his blood and mixing it up with milk. If the product was red, the man would die, if it was white, he would become wealthy. In Ceylonese folklore white clothes were prescribed for princes who set out on a hunting party ; in another folktale from Ceylon a prince who desires to win a lady has to procure a certain flower first. To this end he is endowed with a white garment by a local deity and thrice beaten with a white staff (Gooneratne, p. 47).

Black, on the contrary, is universally associated with the powers of evil, sometimes with death. It seems unnecessary here to expatiate upon this point[7]. More relevant in our context is that a combination of white and black is sometimes considered symbolical for a fundamental dualism. A peculiar case is constituted by the names of the two heroes of the Mahābhārata; Kṛṣṇa and Arjuna, who form a pair of mischievous, yet victorious "Black" and "White". The black Kṛṣṇa forms a similar pair with his brother Balarāma who is described as white in South India (Parpola, p. 16). Already in the RV, a distinction is expressed between the "black day" (the night) and the "white day" (Gonda, 1954, p. 159). White is associated with the RV, black with the SV in the symbolism of the Veda student's antelope skin seat (Gonda, 1960, p. 119, n. 19). The antelope skin also serves as a garment for god Brahmā according to ViDhPur (3, 46, 11b-12a), and its pattern of white—and—black is explained here as symbolical for the ambivalence of the aims of vedic sacrifice, "white" and "black" :

> *Yajñaṃ vitanvate santaḥ śuklāśuklena karmaṇā /*
> *śuklāśuklam ato jñeyaṃ vāsaḥ kṛṣṇājinaṃ Vibhoḥ //*

The Mbh in its Pauṣya section (1, 3) relates Uttaṅka's confrontation in the nether world with two women weaving white and black threads into a garment. His teacher explains to him afterwards that they represent the two gods Dhātar "Creator" and Vidhātar "Disposer" and that the threads are day and night. There is also a psychological variant of the image of "white" and "black". According to the VāyuPur Śiva's female aspect in the beginning of times divided itself into a white and a black half. From the first one sprung the mild Śaktis like Umā and Lakṣmī ; from the other one the fierce Śaktis such as Durgā and Kālī (Monier Williams, p. 86 f.). A "philosophical" application is presented by the ViDhPur (3, 47, 5) : Viṣṇu's garment, composed of white and black, represents Avidyā "Delusion"; the white threads symbolize Vidyā "Wisdom", the black ones Ajñāna "Ignorance", the two forces whose interplay is responsible for Avidyā according to this author. Still more interesting in the present context are those cases in which the two colours are associated with the two aspects of the mind : the "dark" one haunted by a propensity for evil, and the "bright" one which strives after light and virtue.

The third of the "three colours", red, is also connected with a rich folklore. Only a few aspects are shortly repeated here. Red is associated with fertility and reproduction, but also often considered to be dangerous. There is of course a connection between the red colour and blood. Christian tradition has tended to identify the wine of the Lord's Supper with it[8]. According to Elwin (p. 68ff.), the belief in the purifying and healing power of blood among the Maria tribe might even lead to murder. The same idea of the "power of blood" is present among the Hindus and Muslims of India (Elwin, l.c., who refers to Crooke, 1896 ed., II, p. 172 ff.). The drinking of blood can lead to supernatural power. Bhīma, the epic hero, did it; the Kāpālikas did it; O'Malley (p. 145) describes how some villagers drank the blood of victim animals[9]. This dangerous nature of the red colour is further exemplified by a Vedic rite called *śyenayāga-* "falcon sacrifice" (discussed by Kane, 1962, p. 1114, n. 1818). It is an abhicāra ritual (ĀpŚr 22, 4, 13ff. and 23; ṢaḍvBr 3, 8). The officiants don a red headdress and a red garment (*lohitoṣṇīṣā lohitavāsasaḥ*, ṢaḍvBr 3, 8, 22). The victim should also be red (*lohitaḥ paśuḥ*, 3, 8, 18). The meaning of the rite is that just as the falcon catches other birds, so the sacrificer catches his enemy. Red is applied in a rite of destructive magic also in MtPur (93, 150)[10]. The colour of blood is also often associated with dominion especially of the beloved. Mirabai sung : "Mira will be dyed with the dye of her own dear Hari" (Mirabai, Saint and Singer of India, London 1934, p. 33), and: "Beloved, I have dyed myself with the dye of Thy love" (o.c., p. 62). MtPur (93, 145) prescribes the sacrifice of *bilva* flowers and red lotuses in a rite of subjugation (for other examp les see below ch.6.5.)

Red and black are sometimes mentioned together as two ominous colours, as in KJ (ch. 10; trsl. Goudriaan, p. 44): a plot of land should be considered abhicārika when the colours red and black dominate in it (see also the trsl. , n. 6). Meyer (I, p. 61ff.) gives some further instances to which may be added the myth of the Baiga that the blood of the Primeval Being, Nanga Baiga, consisted of two colours; black from his right side and red from his left side. Whoever drank the black blood became a witch, while a man who drank the red blood became a *gunia*, white magician (Hermanns, p. 269f., who cites Elwin, The Baiga). AgPur (323, 3) addresses Kālī as the goddess who consumes flesh and blood and whose face is red-with-black (*māṃsaśoṇitabhojane raktakṛṣṇamukhi*); and she is ordered to subjugate other people for the reciter of the spell (*vaśam ānaya mānuṣān*). The KauśS (16, 20), commenting on AV 8, 8, 24, ordains that in the cadre of a rite against enemies a red branch should be wrapped up with two threads, a black and a red one (*nīlalohite sūtre*) and thrown away into a southern direction[11]. Red and black thus are seen to figure as complementary symbols of fierce supernatural effectiveness.

Now we return to the "three colours" occurring in combination. The ritual manipulation of a combination of three colours is attested already in JaimBr (1, 80f.; description of the ritual by Oertel, p. 190-192). The text deals with the legend of Svarbhānu, a demon who darkened the sun. The seer Atri succeeded in driving away the darkness in three parts. The first part became a black sheep, the second a grey sheep, the third a pale (*phalgunī*) sheep. And in his own circumstances the ritualist can master and manipulate these three sheep of darkness: "if one desires of somebody that he may suffer evil, one should throw a black (object) into that person's strainer; the person will suffer evil; but if one desires: 'let him be far nor near', one should throw a grey object into that person's strainer ; he will be far nor near; and if one desires of somebody: 'let him be better off and attain splendour', one should throw a pale object into his strainer, and the person will be better off" [5]. This is an early instance of that kind of theoretical colour differentiation of ritual aims which is so frequent in the later sources. A typical example occurs in the MMK (vol. I, p. 123ff.). This passage discusses the sacrifice of three logs of wood into the fire in the case of the three sorts of ritual : *śāntika*, *pauṣṭika*, and *raudrakarma*, which aim after pacification, welfare and evil effects. On p. 126 the text lays down that in these three sorts of ritual the fire should assume the three colours white (*śāntika-*), red (*pauṣṭika-*) and black or smoky (*pāyika-* ? ; text corrupt; perhaps read *upāyika-*"presenting a device" which would be an euphemism for *abhicārika*). In this way the "three colours" are combined with the three aims of sacrifice and worship : *śānti*, *puṣṭi* and *abhicāra* (see above, p. 95)— a significant elaboration of the "white-and-black" dualism discussed above.

The distinction of three colours in rituals is paralleled by the application of the same principle in iconography. The well-known tendency towards concretization has been operative also here. AgPur (ch. 137) describes a Mahāmārī (goddess of pestilence) with three faces in three colours; a black face to the East, a red and fearsome one to the South, and a white one to the West (st. 3-6). According to the KālPur (55, 24; van Kooy, p. 46) Mahāmāyā possesses three eyes of the colours red, white and black. Devī is meditated upon with three colours in vertical order in TSS 22, 70 for the destruction of evils. MNT (5, 55-60) enjoins a meditation on the Gāyatrī of the three colours during the morning, noon and evening. In morning she is a young girl of red colour; at noon she is a mature woman and black; in the evening she is old and white (according to Nowotny, p. 148, n. 188). The Śāṇḍilya Up distinguishes three forms of the three parts of the sound *Oṃ*. The *a* is represented by the goddess Gāyatrī who is red ; the *u* by Sāvitrī who is white; and the *m* by the black Sarasvatī (Nowotny, l. c.). The ascriptions of the colours to the three goddesses in these two sources is different, but the principle is the same. It is also this principle which ascribes the presidence over the three cosmical functions of creation, maintenance and destruction to the three members of the Trimūrti; Brahmā (red), Viṣṇu (white) and Rudra (black).

The doctrine of the three goddesses of the crucial points of the day is widely established in common Brahmanic ritual. There are interesting variants which contain a threefold meditation on a goddess in consonance with the three cosmical functions mentioned just above. T (p. 430) describes a threefold meditation on Ugratārā. In the variety of creation (*sṛṣṭi*) the goddess should be contemplated upon as possessing four faces and eight arms, endowed with a white garment, and riding upon a goose (*haṃsa*). The meditation of maintenance (*sthiti*) describes the goddess clad in red and standing upon a ship (leading over the ocean of saṃsāra). The destructive (*saṃhāra*) meditation creates the goddess in the mind as clad in black and provided with nine faces. MMD (5, 74ff.) deals with another meditation on three colours of Sarasvatī. "I proclaim her threefold meditation, in accordance with the three guṇas led by sattva; at first the meditation of creation; during this one should contemplate (on the goddess as) being clad in a white garment, standing upon a goose, being adorned with pearls, four-faced, and holding in her eight hands a *kuṇḍika*, a lotus, a noose, lance, rosary and garland of flowers, while showing the gestures of liberality and security, and standing upon ...(*śabdapayonidhau*)". The second meditation is as follows: one should concentrate upon her as wearing a red garment, seated upon a red throne adorned with gold, having one face, and her four arms characterized by respectively a rosary, a dish for drinking, and the gestures of security and liberality. She dwells in the White Continent. The meditation of destruction implies concentration on the goddess as wearing a black garment and standing upon a ship (in deviation of the description of T cited just above). Bones are her ornaments. She has nine faces and eighteen hands with predominatingly frightening attributes. She stands upon a red lotus. In this way the performer of the mantric method should meditate during rituals that are frightening (*krūra*) or auspicious (*saumya*) : "when the mantra has been made potent in this way, the performer will be like the Lord of Speech in the debate"[6]. The last sentence shows that the meditation on the threefold Sarasvatī is a part of the prescriptions about the manipulation of her mantra, and that this mantra should first be made operative by way of the preliminary worship. The real goal is the attainment of fluency of speech. We can compare this procedure to the meditaion on the bīja of Tripurā in three colours for three different kinds of results (JT ch. 19).

A Jain goddess of three colours, Ambikā, is described by Jhavery (p. 324f.). Her usual colour is that of gold (compare this with the basic colour of the Viṣṇu Mahāmāyā which seems to be also that of gold ; above p. 145). She may, however, be meditated upon as white, red or black (or dark blue) in the Sāttvika, Rājasa and Tāmasa varieties of meditation. Among the goals of Sāttvika meditation are peace and selfless devotion. Those of Rājasa kind are mundane in character, in general: prosperity or happiness. Tāmasa meditation is practised in order to harm an enemy. In the usual Sāttvika form the goddess is in a sitting posture and has two arms; her Rājasa form stands upright and has eight arms; her Tāmasa form is provided with a great number of arms—the exact number depends upon the object desired by the performer. There is indeed a striking similarity to the stanza Stuti & Stava, 483, 2, where Agni is presented as threefold, possessing three colours while he manifests himself respectively as Brahmā, Viṣṇu and Maheśvara; the effects of these manifestations are śāntika, pauṣṭika (or rakṣaṇa "protective") and abhicārika :

Trivarṇo bhagavān Agnir, Brahmā Viṣṇur Maheśvaraḥ /
śāntikaṃ pauṣṭikaṃ caiva rakṣaṇaṃ cābhicārikam //

The Ṣaṭkarmadīpikā varies on the same pattern when it associates in a certain context (stanza 34, p. 184) the colour white with Sāttvika meditation aiming at release from existence; the colours yellow, red and green with Rājasa meditation practised by those who strive after dominion; and black with Tāmasa meditation which should be directed against enemies and other kinds of evils.

These last instances clearly show how a meditation with the help of three colours can be conducive to the three chief objects of the ritual (at least in theory): pacification of evil, acquisition or happiness, and putting down all inimical forces. At the same time these three colours are associated with the cosmic processes of creation, preservation and destruction. In other words, a yogic performer's (or magician's) spiritual accomplishment is greatly enhanced when he is aware that his meditation or his ritual is based upon, symbolic of, and even identical with, the law of the cosmic cycle which realizes itself on the plane of the divine. At the same time we notice that within the three colour systems, at least one colour is usually associated with peaceful, salutary ends. But this is not necessarily so. The Stuti & Stava collection contains for example a set of three short hymns, each directed to a member of the Trimūrti (Nos. 151, 366, 534). Brahmā is described as four-faced and red, Īśvara as five-faced and white, and Viṣṇu as three-faced and black; but in all three cases the effect is the destruction of the enemy (*sarvaśatruvināśanam*).

The fact that especially goddesses of three colours are frequent may perhaps be connected with the relation of the three guṇas with the threefold Māyā, a principle which is worked out in the Āgamic tradition of the three Śaktis. In Western folklore we still have the figure of Snow White, the banished princess who died but was revived by a kiss of her prince; her cheeks were white, her lips red and her hair black.

3. *The four colours*

The number four is replete with symbolism. It is a "cosmic number", which means that it can serve to express the geographical and chronological dimensions of the traditional world view. "There are four directions of the sky", says the TB (3, 8, 5, 4) and he who is aware of this will have a firm base, which means: security, in these directions (*cátasro diśaḥ; dikṣv evá prátitiṣṭhati*). Four dishes containing a *brahmaudana* are offered to the four officiants who sit in the four directions during a certain phase of the Aśvamedha ritual (BaudhŚr 15,3)[12]. In the Veda there were further said to be four parts of the Primeval Being (RV10, 90, 2) only one of which was revealed to mankind. In more recent Hindu speculation there are four constituents of the basic syllable *Oṃ*; four states of consciousness; four stages in life; four grades of society. Even four magical glances are mentioned (HT 11). In this section a few instances are presented of the forces which were thought to reside in the combination of four colours in various circumstances, but particularly when applied to an image. These four colours usually are the "three colours" white, red and black, with yellow added to them. In the Mahāmāyā fragment, the yellow colour is connected with *stambhana*-"immobilizing" of an enemy, and in the magical tradition of the Tantras this is indeed the act most often associated with the colour of hate (see below ch.6.6. In folklore, yellow is renowned for its protective quality (Abbott, p. 282f.; Crooke, II, 28ff). Meditation on Tripurā's yellow bīja enables an adept to cure diseases (JT 19, 30ff.). Embracing a woman clad and adorned in yellow during one's dream is an auspicious omen (BrVPur, Kṛṣṇajanmakhaṇḍa, 77, 36).

The four colours are sometimes said to be characteristic of the Four Vedas. Association of the Vedas with colours is attested by ChUp 1, 7, 4 where the RV is equated with the white part of the eye and the SV with its dark part. The GT (p. 29) prescribes a meditation on the goddesses of the four Vedas with the aid of mantras. The SV is thought to be white, the RV red, the YV yellow (*gaura*) and the AV black, a colour which fits in very well with its contents of magic. Articles of worship can be also distinguished according to four colours. The Ajitāgama (22, 36-43; ed. Bhatt p. 271f.) admits four kinds of flowers: white, red, yellow and black. The priest who is about to pay worship with flowers should be familiar with this distinction and its symbolic value. The same division of flowers into four colours is given by KJ (ch. 72).

A very important application of the "four colours" which should be concisely dealt with here is that they are sometimes combined with the four grades of society. Indeed the Sanskrit word for "colour" and for "grade of society" is identical (*varṇa*-). It can be argued that the colour of people's skin has been an important factor, at least for the brahman theorists, but probably also in practice, in determining status in the Vedic cultural environment (as it sometimes still is in the India of today: Segal, p. 60). The Vedic Aryans despised the indigenous inhabitants of the subcontinent not in the last place because they were "blacks" (see e.g RV 9, 41, 1-2; 1, 101, 1; Sharma, 1958, p. 12). The dominating attitude of the Aryans against the non-Aryans must have been one of contempt mixed with fear (Jacques, p. 254); a situation apt to be enhanced by their association of black with evil and darkness. The contempt for the "black varṇa" is attested also by the Brahmanical lawbooks. The despised group in the meantime developed from "non-Aryans" into Śūdras (on this process, cf. Sharma, 1958). Black is the colour of the Śūdra according to AVPar 53, 4, 3 (Gonda, 1965, p. 419). The Baudhāyana Dharmasūtra says that a brahman who serves the "black varṇa" should perform ablutions (Ram Gopal, p. 128, n. 6); about the same is enjoined by Āpastamba Dharmasūtra 1, 9, 27, 10-11. An eloquent rule is laid down by the comparatively liberal Vasiṣṭha Dharmasūtra (18,18): *kṛṣṇavarṇā yā rāmā ramaṇāyaiva na dharmāya* "the woman of the black colour (grade) is for amusement only, not for the fulfilment of one's duty". In other words, a man of high grade may have intercourse with a woman of theb lack grade, but he can never beget a lawful son and heir with her. One is reminded here of Indra's adventure with the demoness Vilisteṅgā (above p. 12).

This is not the right place to take part in the discussion of the question if the word varṇa in this kind of context means in the first place "colour" or "grade of society". The second meaning was defended by Ram Gopal (p. 115). It is enough to emphasize here that social and also ethical values could be associated with colours. In early Buddhism the distinction noble-debased was sometimes still symbolized by the white-black pattern (DN I, p. 93; DN III, p. 82: *ariya versus kaṇha*). This pattern has been elaborated and harmonized with the later four grade pattern imposed upon contemporary society by the brahmanical social theorists. White became symbolical for the Brahmans, red for the Kṣatriyas, yellow for the Vaiśyas and black for the Śūdras. Damais (p. 77) mentions statements in the Bṛhatsaṃhitā to that extent. Even the ancestors are divided according to this pattern in GarPur (50, 36): "The (ancestors) of the Twice-born should be worshipped in the colour of a white lily or of the moon; those of the Kṣatriyas have the colour of the flaming sun; those of the Vaiśyas have the spotless hue of gold, and those of the Śūdra folk have a dark shade"[7]. And this same symbolism is applied in the ritual. Thus, the Ajitāgama (Kriyāpāda 4, 14) says that the liṅga of Śiva should have the four colours mentioned in the case of worship by each of the four grades of society (*śilā sitā raktanibhā ca pītā kṛṣṇā ca viprādiṣu yojanīyā*). The colours of these four grades are combined with the directions of the sky in BṛhSaṃh (3, 19, a.o.; Damais, p. 77) to this effect that the Brahman grade is located in the North, the Kṣatriya in the East, the Vaiśya in the South and the Śūdra in the West, so that we obtain the colours white, red, yellow and black in the four mentioned directions. Another application is set forth in AVPar (70a, 1 and 2);the colours of omina observed in the water apply to the four grades in the usual way: white ones to the Brahmans, red ones to Kṣatriyas, yellow ones to Vaiśyas, black ones to Śūdras [8]. In some cases the four grades simply lend their names to their respective colours without a differential application to them being intended; thus for example in T (p. 373), the earth on which the ritual firepit is to be constructed can be white, in that case she is *brāhmī*; or red (*kṣatriyā*), yellow (*vaiśyā*) or black (*śūdrā*). A similar distinction is made in ŚivaPur (p. 142, st. 7) concerning the mud used in a ceremony. The same four-colour distinction of articles of ritual is, however, sometimes made without reference to the four varṇas, as we saw above. But in any case we can say that the expression *caturvarṇa*—"the four colour system" can also mean "the four grade system" which stands for "orderly traditional society". This double meaning greatly enhances the symbolic value of the "four colours"; and it shows how colour distinction was one of the chief patterns by which the Hindu theorists shaped their cultural environment.

These same "four colours" are moreover often applied to gods and their images. This can be done in two methods: one god is thought of, like Viṣṇu, to manifest himself in four colours, or a combination of four gods with four different colours is thought to harmonize into a certain pattern, usually that of the four directions. It is here the place to first concentrate on Viṣṇu.

Viṣṇu's ability to assume different colours is an important aspect of his incomprehensible, fallacious māyā nature. Viṣṇu's Māyā appears in manifold forms. The Ambikāstuti by Hanūman (st. 6 ; Aithal, p. 62) says : "The multiform Energy of Indra and all the other gods, and of the Sun and other heavenly luminaries, which manifests itself, the Māyā of Viṣṇu I honour" :

Indrādisarvadevānāṃ sūryādijyotiṣām api /
yā śaktir dṛśyate citrā Viṣṇumāyā namāmi tām //

In Mbh 12, 326, Bhīṣma relates how Viṣṇu once enabled His privileged devotee Nārada to obtain a view of His omnifold manifestation. He appeared before the sage's eyes "for some part of a pure nature like the moon, for some part even more eminent than the moon ; for some part having the colour of fire, for another part appearing like a comet....". Other colours assumed by Viṣṇu in this passage are that of parrots' feathers, of crystal, black ointment, gold, shoots of coral, white, the colour of gold, cats' eye gem, black cats, eye gem, sapphire, peacock's neck (dark blue), and a string of pearls (st. 3-5). The next stanzas are also worth consideration : "The Eternal One contains these manifold colours in His form, the Illustrious One, furnished with a hundred heads and a thousand eyes, feet, bellies and arms, the Unlimited One; He emits the syllable *Oṃ* from His mouth together with its companion, the Sāvitrī; and from His other mouths He chanted the precious essence which issues from the Four Vedas: the Secret Wisdom (*āraṇyakam*) —He, the God, Hari, Nārāyaṇa, the Subjugating One"[9]. These last lines suggest that Viṣṇu when reciting the Veda is in the possession of four mouths—even of five when the syllable *Oṃ* is considered to issue from a central mouth[13]. In this appearance he is similar to Brahmā. The two gods in this case doubtless serve to embody the same concept : that of omnipotent wisdom directing itself towards (and at the same time encompassing) the whole of creation. Even Śiva possesses a similar four-faced manifestation: that of Tumburu, who according to a Cambodian inscription emits four Tantric texts of the Left Course from his four mouths[14]. This Tumburu is usually surrounded by four female companions led by Jayā;

and in the description devoted to them by the ViDhPur (3, 66, 10) these females are said to possess the four colours white, red, yellow and black; and the same is repeated with a small variation in the MMK (vol. II, p. 526ff.).

That Viṣṇu is fourfold is stated also by Mbh 12,47,17 : *caturbhiś caturātmānam*. Of special importance is the tradition referred to in the preceding chapter that this god assumes four different colours during the four successive periods of the world called yugas. This theory of the four world periods is permeated by a profound pessimism[15]. Creation is thought to be subjected to ever increasing decay. Dharma diminishes, ethical values will disappear. Time and fate inexorably follow their terrible course. Against this background Viṣṇu's manifestation in four different colours during these four yugas assumes a peculiarly uncanny character. The best known place on the subject from the Mbh is 3,148. The context is that Bhīma, who has obtained the privilege to converse with the monkey god Hanūman, requests him to manifest himself in the same immeasurable size in which he in former times jumped over the ocean and reached Laṅkā. Hanūman, who is an incarnation of Viṣṇu, laughs and explains to Bhīma that this is impossible because what was performed in a former age cannot be repeated in the present destructive Kali age (3,148, 6). Time cannot be revolted against (st. 8 : *kālo hi duratikramaḥ*). This answer arouses Bhīma's interest into the laws of the succession of times. He asks Hanūman to explain the subject to him, and this is conceded (st. 10-39). The four periods of time : Kṛta, Tretā, Dvāpara and Kali are treated in succession, and among other characteristics it is also explained that Viṣṇu in these four periods is characterized by the successive colours white, red, yellow and black (st. 16, 23, 26, 33). Besides, the four manifestations have different names, so that a scheme may be drawn up :

Yuga	Name of Viṣṇu	Colour
Kṛta	Nārāyaṇa	white
Tretā	Acyuta	red
Dvāpara	Viṣṇu	yellow
Kali	Keśava	black

Indeed, Viṣṇu appears in the Mbh as the black Kṛṣṇa who is nicknamed Keśava and, as we saw (p.25.f.), he has mischievous inclinations, while he is also a clever wielder of māyā. In another place in the Vanaparvan of the Mbh (3,187,31), Viṣṇu in his manifestation of the Child on the waters (above p.30) resumes for Mārkaṇḍeya his four colour appearance (with a change in the sequence of red and yellow):

Śvetaḥ kṛtayuge varṇaḥ pītas tretāyuge mama /
rakto dvāparam āsādya kṛṣṇaḥ kaliyuge tathā //

"White is my colour in the Kṛta yuga, yellow in the Tretāyuga; red after reaching the Dvāpara, and black in the Kaliyuga". And at the end of time He will appear as Kāla in exceedingly horrible form (*atidāruṇaḥ*) and destroy this whole world. This is His wielding the wheel of time (*kālacakra*, 34); but notwithstanding all this, God is the essence of all, and the ultimate source of joy of all beings (*sarvātmā sarvalokasukhāvahaḥ*, 33). He is the formless Brahman which pacifies all creatures (*brahmann aham arūpi vai śamanaṃ sarvabhūtānām*); and this whole process of creation and destruction is brought about by His own māyā (*ātmamāyayā*, 29) [10].

The doctrine of Viṣṇu's changing appearance during the four yugas has become classical in Hindu religious speculation. Bhāsa describes it in the opening stanza of his Bālacarita (ed. Devadhar, p. 511), where the Sūtradhāra (stage director) addresses his audience: "He Who in former times, during the Kṛtayuga, (appeared) with the colour of 'milk or a conch shell' (?, *śaṅkhakṣīra*), Nārāyaṇa by name ; and during the Tretā as Viṣṇu, of golden colour, in his ability to encompass the threefold world by three strides ; in the Dvāpara age as Rāma, of a colour dark like a blade of *dūrvā* grass, engaged in the killing of Rāvaṇa ; and in the Kaliyuga with the (black) hue of collyrium, Dāmodara (=Kṛṣṇa)—He should uninterruptedly protect you" [11]. The scheme implied in this stanza is strikingly at variance with the evidence of the Mbh. It is as follows :

Yuga	Name of Viṣṇu	Colour
Kṛta	Nārāyaṇa	white
Tretā	Viṣṇu (Trivikrama)	golden
Dvāpara	Rāma	dark (green)
Kali	Kṛṣṇa Dāmodara	black

The most important difference is that the colour red is lacking and its place taken by *śyāma* which is indeed the specific colour of Rāma. There is no fundamental difference between yellow and the colour of gold; they occur also on other places as synonyms. The Mbh and Bhāsa are in complete agreement in the first and last yuga only. The yellow Viṣṇu seems to have moved from the third to the second age (or the reverse).

The same four colour doctrine is repeated in the Purāṇas, e.g. the BhPur (10, 8, 13): "There were three colours of Him when He incarnated in three successive yugas: white, red and yellow, and nowadays he has assumed a black shape" [12]. The place is cited by Dasgupta (p. 357). BNārPur (38,13ff.) says the same, and the doctrine is also reproduced in LT 36, 62 (Gupta, p. 218, n. 2, who refers to Sāttvata Saṃhitā 5, 82-92). Rūpa Gosvāmin, the 16th century Vaiṣṇava mystic, also knew it (Dasgupta, p. 357). All these sources agree in mentioning the colour sequence white, red, yellow, and black for the four successive ages, thus following the doctrine of the Mbh (3, 148). Only Rūpa Gosvāmin ascribes a dark green (*śyāma-*) colour to the Dvāpara manifestation. But in general one can say that the tradition is a consistent one; and that our present evil age, of which the Purāṇas give such vivid and startling descriptions[16], is overshadowed by the black manifestation of the frightening Viṣṇu.

On this point we recall that the word varṇa may mean "grade of society" as well as "colour". As there are precisely four grades of society in Hindu theory, there is no doubt a connection between this concept and the idea of the four colours. Viṣṇu is called *varṇātman* "having the social grades as His self" in the Mbh (12, 47, 43) where Bhīṣma praises the god with these words: "To Him, Whose mouth is the support of Spiritual Force (the mythical principle sustaining the Brahman grade), Whose arms are the support of the principle of nobility, Whose belly and thighs in their completeness are the support of the productive grade, and Whose feet are the support of the labouring grade, to Him Whose self are the grades of society, honour !" [13]. Here, of course, the famous stanza from the Puruṣa hymn (RV 10, 90, 12) operates in the author's mind. The myth of the primeval anthropomorphic state of the universal commonwealth, out of whose body the four grades originated, was reshaped by the Brahmans in order to explain as a divine, universal law an institution of human theory which existed during a certain time. People are encompassed by this immovable frame; they have to live and work within it; it is part of the divine nature itself. Even the BhPur, which on some places does not withhold its criticism of the Brahmans, handles the myth (3, 6, 33-35) and adds: "These varṇas, in accordance with their own dharma, sacrifice to their authority (guru) Hari with reliance, in order to purify themselves, because they have been born (from Him), together with their means of subsistence; O ruler, such is the divine work of the Lord in His own form. Who would dare to infringe on it?—its origin is the force of His exertion of supernatural power (*yogamāyā*)" [14]. We also refer to Mārkaṇḍeya's vision in Mbh 3, 186 (see p. 30 above). In this way it is conceivable that Viṣṇu, the maintainer of society, is embodied in the earthly king whose destination is to rule his kingdom and preserve the existing state of affairs (see also below, ch.5.5.).

Another fourfold manifestation of Viṣṇu realizes itself in the category of space. In this form it is a leading principle in Pāñcarātra speculation. In this system God's four Vyūhas: Vāsudeva, Saṃkarṣaṇa, Pradyumna and Aniruddha, are associated with four colours. We only discuss here LT 10, 21ff.: Viṣṇu's four Vyūhas, provided with the six basic qualities, in the realm of waking (*jāgratpāde*) possess four arms and all kinds of ornaments and attributes. Of them Vāsudeva is white and wears a yellow garment. Saṃkarṣaṇa is red, his garment has the (yellow) colour of the flower of the flax plant. Pradyumna has the colour of gold or of a firefly and a red garment. He also bears a banner provided with a dolphin and as one of his attributes the bow and arrows—characteristics of the god of love. His wife is Māyāvatī (Zimmer, p. 384f.). At last, Aniruddha is black of colour and his garment is yellow. The LT (11, 41) further explains that these multi-coloured manifestations of the Lord appear for the sake of the bestowing of compassion and grace (*anukampa-*; *anugraha-*) (Gupta, p. 56, 61). The Vyūhas are usually located in the four main points of the compass beginning with the East, in the sequence in which they are mentioned above.

A fivefold manifestation of Viṣṇu is worshipped in the

equally South Indian Vaikhānasa tradition. Four of them are to be installed (or meditated upon) in the four points of the compass, and the fifth who is the base and origin of the four others has its place in the Centre. The Vaikhānasa ritual handbook KJ describes worship of this Pañcamūrti in ch. 77. The central form is called Viṣṇu; the four others are Puruṣa (E.), Satya (S.), Acyuta (W.) and Aniruddha (N). They possess the four qualities of dharma, jñāna, aiśvarya and vairāgya respectively. Their colours are: white for Puruṣa (garment presumably red), black for Satya (yellow garment), golden for Acyuta (with the light green colour of parrots' feathers), and sparkling like coral for Aniruddha (garment black). The central Viṣṇu should obtain a deep black colour (like a black cloud). The division of colours here is original, but the principle is the same. The texts add that the Four Manifestations (Puruṣa etc.) also stand for the four yugas, the four stages of life, the four grades of society and the four Vedas ; if duly worshipped, they are a cause of welfare to all.

The principle followed in these last-mentioned instances is that of four divine manifestations (or a fourfold manifestation of one divinity) in the category of space, which means the four main points of the compass. Each manifestation has its own colour, and the four colours are most often white, red, yellow and black. The idea expressed seems to be in the first place the divine victorious omnipresence. It is useful to note in this context that also the symbol of Viṣṇu's all-conquering sovereignty, the Disc (*cakra-*) has been described as having four colours. According to PST (22, 35) its central part should be yellow, the spokes vermillion, the intermediate space between the spokes dark, and the outer rim white. AgPur 306, 9 says the same, and although the place is corrupt, the wording is so similar that both texts must record a common tradition [15]. The colours located in the four points of the compass must have been felt as powerful magical operators. We cannot help recording a remarkable parallel from the Navaho Prostitution Way Chant Legend : two famous magicians from the past, when assailing another witch who had protected himself by guards in all the four directions, collected some hail of four colours: black, blue, yellow and white. The black hail they blew to the East, the blue to the S., the yellow to the W, and the white to the N.

These developed into four clouds which started hailing, so that the guards in all the four directions were scared away inside (Kluckhohn, p. 172). Although the principle of the colours of the four points of the compass is not present in the Mahāmāyā fragment discussed in the preceding chapter, it is so frequent in the minds of the formulators, Balinese as well as Indian, that one is tempted to assume that it has been understood and implied also by the author of that fragment.

Thus, the usual pattern is : four deities, four directions, four colours. The deities can however also be only surrounding figures of minor importance attending a central God. There was already an occasion to mention Tumburu's four companions Jayā etc., and we also refer to the AgPur (308, 6ff.) which enumerates four gatekeepers of Śrī Trailokyamohinī. Balākā stands in the E. and she holds a white lotus ; Vanamālinī in the S. holding a red lotus ; Vibhīṣikā in the W. with a white lotus ; and Śāṅkarī in the N. without a flower being mentioned for her. The ladies themselves are characterized by other colours: *śyāma*, white, green,. . . (we doubt the correctness of the text tradition). As to the four manifestations of a single deity: this idea is sometimes expressed in iconography by a figure with four faces (cf. Viṣṇu, Brahmā and Tumburu above). Another instance may be taken from the SM (No. 93, Vajratārāsādhana) which describes Tārā in the Centre of a maṇḍala of the Mothers, with eight arms and four faces embodying four articles of worship. The South is faced by Dhūpatārā who is black; the W. by a yellow Dīpatārā; the N. by a red Gandhatārā, and the E. by a white Puṣpatārā. By meditation on this deity the worshipper is able to effectuate his recitation of her mantra and to perform various feats of magic. A similar figure is Mahāpratisarā in her sādhana included in the SM as No. 194 (vol. II, p. 396). Her figure is yellow, but she possesses four faces the first (Eastern) one of which is yellow, the second white, the third dark blue and the fourth red [16]. PST (29, 60) describes a Tāraṇī (=Gāyatrī) of four faces which are white, yellow, black and red (*mandārāhvayarocanāñjanajavācchābhair mukhaiḥ*). In this tradition probably stands Stuti & Stava, No. 600, Śrīstava, when it describes Śrī as *caturvarṇā* "four-coloured" (st. 1) and as *caturvidhā* ("fourfold"? ; st. 3); she is praised as the "essence of wisdom and personal effectiveness" (*prajñāvīryasāra-*; in Stuti & Stava this is translated by "essential wisdom and heroism").

A Śivaite variant of this system which is very frequent in Bali and which might indeed be called a leading element in the traditional world view of the Balinese brahman priest is the following: the East is occupied by Īśvara who is white; the S. by the red Brahmā; the W. by the yellow Mahādeva; while the black Viṣṇu stands in the N.[17]. It is remarkable that this sequence of colours is again in agreement with the sequence of Viṣṇu's manifestations in the four yugas according to the Mbh. The system is amply represented in the Stuti & Stava collection, although there are exceptions like Stuti & Stava No. 372, Caturkumbha or Caturdevastava, where Brahmā surprisingly obtains a grey instead of a red colour in stanza 2. This might be due to a coalescence of Brahmā with Agni which is attested also elsewhere in Indonesian tradition[18]; the stanza in question mentions Svāhā, usually attached to Agni, as Brahmā's spouse.

The same principle of division of the cosmos into four colours is met with in the Atoni culture on the Eastern Indonesian island of Timor (Schulte Nordholt). After emphasizing the encompassing nature of the Atoni political system which is based on sacral relations of various kinds (p. 198), the author expounds the fundamental dualism which underlays it : male-female, right-left, heaven-earth, and so on. The male is also associated with the colours white and red, and the female with yellow and black. The colours are moreover associated with the same points of the compass as in Bali, while the sequence is clockwise from East to North (Schulte Nordholt, p. 202)[19]. In assessing the position of these Indonesian traditions against the Indian doctrine, it is advisable to follow Schulte Nordholt (p. 223) and Swellengrebel (p. 51) in their opinion that the Indonesian four-colour and four-direction system is pre-Hindu (or non-Hindu) in origin; but in any case knowledge of Indian religious and political speculation has served greatly to confirm the existing pattern.

It is now time to give some attention of the application of the four colour system in a context of Tantric magic. HT (2, 1) reserves the white colour for a ritual firepit during a ceremony of pacification, yellow for a rite of acquisition, red for subjugation and black for destruction[17]. This doctrine is indeed typical and may serve as an example for many other statements of this kind. For example, the SCT (p. 52ff. of the trsl.) prescribes meditation on some mantras of the Buddha for a performer who desires to accomplish the "four kinds of effects", no doubt as a proof of his spiritual development. During a *śānti* rite one should imagine the mantras "in a dazzling white string" (issuing from the own heart; one meditates on oneself as being the deity concerned); in the case of *puṣṭi* "acquisition", the mantras assume "a bright yellow colour"; during *vaśīkaraṇa* "subjugation" they are red and "linked together like a chain"; and for destruction (*māraṇa-*) the colour is black. Emphasis is laid on the need for supernatural brightness and intenseness of the respective colours. One observes that the allocation of the colours to the magical aims in the SCT is identical with that in the HT, although in one case they belong to the firepit and in the other text to the mantras.

JT 17, 83-87 is an interesting place because here the colours are combined with the acts of magic as well as with the directions of the sky. If the worshipper embarks upon worship of Śiva's spouse with particular desires, he should observe the following rules. In the case of *stambhana* "immobilization" he should sit down facing the East upon a yellow seat, worshipping with yellow materials; for subjugation, he should face the North and apply a red colour; sitting towards the West and applying sandal, he obtains the power to charm any woman he likes; facing the South and applying the black colour, he may rob an adversary of his memory (on the combination of magical acts with the directions of the sky, see also below ch.6.3, B4). KCT (4, 130) assigns the colours to magical acts in still another way: white is said to belong to *śānti* and *puṣṭi*; red to attraction and subjugation; yellow to immobilization and delusion; and black (*kaṣaṇaghananibha-*) to liquidation and eradication. In this case the colours are combined with the deity meditated upon by the sādhaka, while the whole process is said to work itself out in the mind:

Śvetaḥ śāntiṃ ca puṣṭiṃ svamanasi kurute rakta ākṛṣṭivaśyam /
pītaḥ stambhaṃ ca mohaṃ kaṣaṇaghananibho māraṇoccāṭanaṃ ca //

In stanza 156 of ch. 4 the KCT connects the acts with five

colours and in a slightly different way. A different pattern is also followed by N (p. 271): white is characteristic for *śānti* and *puṣṭi* and some other acts, red for *vaśya*, *stambhana*, *mohana* and *ākarṣaṇa*, yellow for eradication and the causing of dissension, and black for liquidation. It is clear that, although details may differ, there is a system in the association of colours with feats of magic in the Tantric texts. The most common are the combinations of red with subjugation and black with liquidation or other evil acts; but also the associations white *śānti* (in deviation from the Mahāmāyā fragment) and yellow—*stambhana* are fairly constant. In a few cases the yellow colour is combined with *puṣṭi* "acquisition".

Another instance of the meditation upon a god who assumes different colours for achieving the aims of magic is furnished by the AgPur (301, 15ff =TSS 25, 47 ff.) in connection with the Sun. There is no reference to a manifestation of this god in the categories of time and space (also in the Mahāmāyā fragment a direct allusion to the four colour appearance of Viṣṇu during the yugas was absent). "Having assigned the basic (mantra) from the head to the feet and having worshipped one's own limbs with the gestures in accordance with the assignment (of the syllables as elements of the divine presence in the own body), one should meditate upon oneself as being the Sun. His meditation should be on the red (Sun) during subjugation; on the yellow during immobilization (TSS reading); on the white during acquisition (*āpyāyana-*); on the black during the ritual for liquidation of an enemy, while one should inflict delusion with the colour of Indra's bow (blue). He who is constantly engaged in the practice of initiation (*abhiṣeka-*), silent recitation, contemplation, pūjā and fire sacrifice, becomes filled with fiery energy, invincible, illustrious, and will gain victory on sea or land" [18]. One observes that the AgPur usually contains ceremonial advice for earthly rulers and their purohitas; and this is especially to be noted because the ritual application of the Mahāmāyā fragment according to the Balinese manuscript is also the private worship of the aristocrat class (we shall return to this point in ch.5. 5. below).

The goddess Ugratārā whom we already met above also affords the different aims when meditated upon with the four colours (T, p. 426). "One should create her in the mind as red during subjugation ; one should meditate on her as golden of colour during immobilization; as grey during eradication, and as black during the ritual of liquidation" [19]. An application on a more restricted scale is found in the SM (No. 181; vol. II, p. 378) in connection with Kurukullā in a context of snake charming: a white meditation delivers of poison ; a yellow one effects immobilization of the snake; a red meditation causes the poison to coagulate or to be crushed; a green one brings about the patient's regeneration. The Kurukullāsādhana in which these prescriptions occur has been derived, according to the compiler of the SM, from a Māyājālamahāyogatantra. Another meditation on Kurukullā (SM No. 185) specifies as follows: by a white colour one destroys the poison, by a colour of crystal one obtains wisdom, by golden colour one subjugates, and by the red of a lotus one destroys (one's adversaries).

To conclude this section we give a Jain instance which is recorded by Jhavery in his Appendix 25. It consists of a Māyābījastotra "Hymn to the kernel syllable of the Māyā". This syllable is *hrīṃ* which is called Māyā also in Hindu Tantras (Bharati, p. 119). It can be meditated upon as possessing four colours (Jhavery on p. 336 abusively speaks of a Trivarṇadhyāna). As has been remarked by Jhavery, the stotra is corrupt, and we give only a tentative translation of the stanzas 4-7 : "He who is contemplating upon Thee as resembling a white ray of moonlight, comprising the threefold space—from that moment onwards wisdom, pacification and acquisition take their abode in him in a flawless shape. He who in his meditation beholds Thee as having the colour of the disc of the recently risen sun, illuminating by Thy net of rays the entire world (?), to him anything in this world will necessarily become subjugated. He who creates Thee as being on all sides of a dark yellow colour with a pleasant lustre equal to molten gold—in his house the Goddess of Fortune (Kamalā = Lakṣmī), although She is unstable, will always make merry with full delight. And he who observes Thee as black, equal to the colour of the mixture of lamp-black, or grey like the smoke of... (?, *cātuṣa-*) certainly, the throng of his enemies arrives instantly at its destruction like a mango tree hit by the gale"[20]. In this poetical passage the symbolic value of the colours in the standard magical acts performed by a yogin is again in general harmony with the instances cited above. White is combined with śānti and puṣṭi, red with subjugation, yellow again with puṣṭi (in this case not with immobilization), and black with destruction. It seems as if there has been a tradition generally known in Tantric lore of all three denominations Hinduism, Buddhism and Jainism about the magical effectiveness of these "four colours".

4. *The Five Colours*

The number five is generally believed to be very auspicious[20]. From the Veda onwards a fivefold order is considered to exist in nature. "This all, whatever there is, is fivefold" (BAUp 1,4,17 a.o.; cf. Gonda, 1970, p. 45 for other text places and more instances of quintuples in the Veda). By recognizing twice five elements in the recitals of the *hotar* and *udgātar* priests (respectively called *śastra* and *stotra*) one reaches the *virāj* (Sovereignty represented in the category of number) (AitBr, Pañcikā 3, 23, 4). The ChUp (2, 2-7) discusses the supranormal effects of recognizing a fivefold order in the phenomena of nature and daily life : one should meditate on a fivefold sāman as mystically present in the macrocosmic elements earth, fire, atmosphere, sun and heaven (2, 2); in the various phenomena of the weather (2, 3); in the waters (2, 4); in the seasons (2, 5); in the animal worlds (2, 6); in the vital breaths (2, 7). All these meditations are directed towards specified goals. Thus, he who meditates upon the fivefold sāman as present in the animal world, becomes rich in animals. The realization of the secret quintuple nature of life in this method becomes an important source of power.

The belief that "five" expresses sovereignty[21] is amply expressed by a number of allusions to conquest of the earth in all the five points of the compass (*digvijaya-*). In the RV Indra is requested to conquer the five regions of the earth for the worshipper (RV 10, 131, 1; Gonda, 1970, p. 158, n. 53). According to the AitBr (8, 14) Indra is anointed by the gods in the directions of the sky (this time numbering 6) as the divine king. From post-Vedic literature we mention here a remarkable passage in Mbh 1,55,28-30 where four of the five Pāṇḍavas are stated to have conquered the four directions, while Yudhiṣṭhira is intended to reside in the Centre as a universal ruler: "Bhīmasena conquered the Eastern direction in his mighty strength; the hero Arjuna the Northern one, and Nakula the West; the Southern direction has been conquered by Sahadeva, the slayer of the inimical heroes; in this way they brought this whole earth into their subjection (*vaśe*). The earth shone brightly by means of a sixfold sun : the bright Sūrya Himself, and the five Pāṇḍavas of unfailing courage, who are equal to the Sun themselves" [21]. The theoretical, almost liturgical nature of this passage is the more significant because it has no connection with the course of events in this part of the Mbh.

The idea of the sovereign ruler in the Centre who controls the four ends of the earth is often repeated in Skt. literature. It has been concisely expressed in a stanza of the Mbh. not far from the passage discussed just above (1,62,3ff.) where king Duḥṣyanta, the forebear of the Puru line, is said to have been "the protector of the whole earth with its four limits; he, the ruler of mankind, enjoyed the whole of the earth divided into four" and "all regions....inhabited by people of the four grades of society" [22]. It should be remarked that while the sovereign is as it were the fifth who resides in the Centre, the number four in such statements easily becomes connected with the subjects: there are four points of the compass ruled over, and they are inhabited by the four grades of society. On the divine plane this sovereignty is sometimes expressed by the fiveheadedness of gods. There is a legend that Brahmā originally possessed five heads, but that Śiva deprived him of his lordly power by cutting the central head off. Śiva, on the contrary, is conceived as five-headed in his manifestations as the Pañcabrahma and as Sadāśiva ; while as Tumburu he may be depicted as standing in the Centre and surrounded by his consorts Jayā, Vijayā, Jayantī and Aparājitā (ViDhPur vol. 3, ch. 66). In Pāñcarātra speculation the number of the four Vyūhas has been extended by adding a Viśākha Yūpa (a vague Vedic idea of the *axis mundi* abstracted from the real sacrificial post, *yūpa*) in the Centre[22]. Among the five-faced deities figures also Hanūman (in Maharashtra; Ghurye, p. 235) while the ŚvetUp (2, 16) speaks of the Ātman as the god in the own heart who faces all directions (*sarvatomukha-*). Gods are often invoked with five names symbolizing five aspects or manifestations. Jacob (p. 28) gives some instances for Kṛṣṇa; one of the sources even states that worship of the five Kṛṣṇas is sufficient to stop reincarnation. Five Kāmas are also known (JT 2,48) while the five gods Brahmā, Viṣṇu, Rudra, Īśvara and Sadāśiva serve as five Pretas "Corpses" in the mystical symbolism preached in JT 3, 11.

We now come to some instances of quintuples in connection with colours. The five colour system and its relation to the five points of the compass has been discussed also by Kirfel who refers to the existence of a similar system in Chinese speculation. As Kirfel's article was not accessible to us, we cannot go into further details here[23]. In the first place now Parpola's opinion may be mentioned that the colours of the chief five planets which are known from Sanskrit and Tamil sources (Mars—red; Mercury—green; Jupiter—golden or yellow; Venus—white; Saturn—black) were familiar already to the Indus people who were proto-Dravidians and who mentioned them in their seals[24]. As to the Veda and its literature, relevant places on the five colours and the points of the compass in which they have been located according to the ChUp and the BAUp have been given by Damais (p. 76). BAUp (4, 4,9) gives these colours as white (*śukla-*), dark blue or black (*nīla-*), brownish (*piṅgala-*), green (*harita-*) and red (*lohita-*). The ChUp (3, 1-5) distinguishes five forms (*rūpāṇi*) of the Sun, the colours of which are respectively red, white, black, deep black and "that what as it were throbs in the middle of the Sun" (*etad yad etad ādityasya madhye kṣobhata iva*). These colours, although five in number, are little more than a modification of the "three colours": white, red and black. A colour group of more identity also mentioned by Damais occurs in ChUp 8, 6,1. This group is identical with the one from BAUp, with the exception that yellow (*pīta-*) occurs instead of green, so that we have white, black, yellow, red and "brownish". Their function in this context is that they are the agents by which the arteries (*nāḍī*) of the heart and the sun are mystically connected with each other. At the end of his life the man who knows this correspondence is conveyed to heaven (a world beyond the sun) by means of these arteries which are indeed the sun's rays. The aim is thus clearly expressed here as in other places of the ChUp. Transferred into terms of later Hinduism, it would be stated thus that the performer of this meditation is able to reach release (*mukti*) by it. As we saw (p. 59) religion is thought to procure the means for release as well as enjoyment of mundane benefits; it all depends on the worshipper's personal disposition, although this disposition itself may have been shaped to a great extent by karmic law.

An important application of the five colour system is within the doctrine of the five elements. The Five Elements play an important role in mystic speculation. The Mbh (12, 326, 32) asserts :

Pṛthivī vāyur ākāśam āpo jyotiś ca pañcamam /
te sametā mahātmānaḥ śarīram iti saṃjñitam /

"The Earth, Wind, Space, Water and Light (Fire) as the fifth—these together are known to be the body of the Universal Soul". Like other notions of universal dimensions, the five Elements are ambivalent in nature (see above p.64) and that is the reason why one or more of them have been sometimes found applicable in magic rites of a "black" character (for some instances from the Veda, see Henry, p. 231; and Shende, p. 160, who relevates that in preparation to a ceremony of witchcraft one should perform a sacrifice to Fire, Wind, Sun, Moon and Waters according to the AV ritual). In Sāṃkhya speculation the Elements can be characterized by the three states of *śānta* "pacified" *ghora* "fearsome" and *mūḍha* "dull" due to the respective preponderance of the three guṇas of sattva, rajas and tamas (Frauwallner, p. 355), and the same doctrine is repeated in the ViPur (1,2,49)[25].

Now, according to Danièlou (p. 515) the Earth was connected with yellow, Water with white, Fire with red, Air or Wind with black, and Space again with white—which means the "four colours" with a double occurrence of one of them. There is, however, a tradition which connects them with the colours in a different way. On an 18th century painting from Nepal published by Mookerjee (plate 62) the Elements are represented by five pairs of hands beside each other, each holding up a cup of *amrta*. Their colours are white, yellow, red, green and blue. Midway between these two traditions is the doctrine of the KCT (5, 185) also represented by Damais (p.

85) which equates five metals with the five elements combined with jewels of their respective colours, as follows : [23]

Metal	Element	Colour
gold	earth	yellow
silver	water	white
red copper	fire	red
iron	air	black
lead	void (space)	green

It is interesting to combine this with a feature from the crypto-Buddhist Dharma cult practised in recent times in Bengal and Orissa. In this sect the use of five metals is prescribed for the worship of Lord Dharma on the five gates in the five directions. The metals are : gold in the West, silver in the South, copper in the East, red copper in the North, and diamond in the East. Metals have been associated with the planets in the various directions by Varāhamihira in his Yogayātrā (6,2-18; Damais, p. 78f.). It is significant that the five elements are also connected with Viṣṇu in the ritual of the Pañcamahābhūtavrata "Observation of the Five Elements". This implies that the worshipper should adore Viṣṇu in the form of the elements during a full year beginning on the fifth day of the bright half of Caitra (Febr.—March). The ritual is discussed by Kane, 1958, p. 337. By thus strengthening Viṣṇu in his completeness as the fivefold natural structure, also the most significant entity of the chronological pattern, the year, is constituted. It has been shown above that also Śiva in his Pañcabrahma aspect has been associated with the five elements, although the fifth and central manifestation, Īśāna, was not combined with a colour like the others (p. 159). Identification of the Five Deities of Balinese Śivaism: Brahmā, Viṣṇu, Mahādeva, Īśvara and Sadāśiva, with the five elements is implied by Stuti & Stava, No. 223 (Praṇavabheda), where these five gods are combined in stanzas 6 and 7 with the five components of the syllable *Oṃ* while the sprinkling formula which immediately follows mentions the Five Elements.

But the quintuple pattern also involves the human body itself. Eliade (p. 138) discusses a place from the Yogatattva Up, where a meditation is prescribed on the five elements as being present in the body with the five colours. The part from the feet to the knees represents the earth which is yellow and square of form; its syllable is *la*, its deity Brahmā. After a sufficient meditation on this aspect the yogin will be master over the earth and free from the danger of death. The part from the knees to the rectum represents the water, and meditation on it frees from the danger of drowning. The part from rectum to heart symbolizes fire and meditation on it is a safeguard against burning. The air is represented by the part from the heart to the brows, and space by the part of the head above the brows. Meditation on this last element enables the yogin to fly through the air. Such a practice is clearly related to the association of the cakras in the body with the elements taught by the Ṣaṭcakranirūpaṇa[26]. The lowest cakra, the Mūlādhāra, contains the maṇḍala of the Earth which is yellow; the white maṇḍala of Water is present in the Svādhiṣṭhāna cakra; the red one of Fire in the Maṇipūra; the grey one of Air in the Anāhata; and the white one of Space in the Viśuddha cakra.

The five colours feature also in a ritual context where they again seem to symbolize completeness. The Mahāvaṃsa (5,27) relates that for Aśoka's inauguration the gods procured garments in five colours (*pañcavaṇṇāni vatthāni*). A parallel for this is found in the Pañcamūrtivrata described by Kane, 1958, p. 337. This observance is to be maintained, like the Pañcamahābhūtavrata referred to just above, from the light half of the month Caitra onwards during a year on the fifth day of each light month half. Viṣṇu's attributes and the Earth are adored on these occasions, and at the year's end five garments in different colours are to be donated. The reward equals that of the Rājasūya, which means that it may be imagined in terms of unlimited political sovereignty.

The five colour pattern is further applied to the cow. It is stated that in ideal circumstances the Pañcagavya "Five products of the cow" should be prepared from five kinds of cows (Ajitāgama, Kriyāpāda, 22, 7; p. 266): urine from a reddish brown one (*kapilā*), faeces from a red one, fresh milk from a black one, curds from a white one, and ghee from a grey one. The reddish brown cow is also admitted as a source for all the elements of the pañcagavya. In a note the editor cites the Kāraṇāgama (1,35,35b-37a) which says that a black cow should procure the faeces, a dark blue one the urine, a reddish brown one the ghee, a white one the curds, and a red one the milk. The reader observes that even within two texts of the same Śiva Āgama tradition there is no unanimity on the subject; but what matters more is that the five colour system is consciously applied in both sources. Even the mythical "cows of abundance" (*kāmaduh-*) have been subjected to this system. According to the Bṛhajjābāla Up (1,10ff.) there are five of them in five colours, and they are at the same time associated with the Pañcabrahma and the five elements, while they produce five kinds of sacred ashes by means of their dung. The scheme is :

Cow	colour	element	Aspect of Śiva
Nandā	*kapila*	Earth	Sadyojāta
Bhadrā	black	Water	Vāmadeva
Surabhi	red	Fire	Aghora
Suśīlā	white	Air	Tatpuruṣa
Sumanā	*citra* (variegated)	Space	Īśāna

We note that *kapila* occupies the place of yellow in the most common variety of the five colour system, while *citra* which denotes a variegated mixture of colours now occurs on the crucial fifth place. That the combination of the colours with the elements and the Five Aspects of Śiva does not tally with preceding instances needs not to concern us much by now.

In some cases mention is made of the construction of maṇḍalas with the help of the five colours. The Śāradātilaka (3, 106-130; according to Kane, 1962, p. 1132 who mentions a few other instances) discusses the Sarvatobhadramaṇḍala (maṇḍala of the "good from every direction") which is to be prepared by means of powders of five colours, viz. yellow from turmeric, white from husked rice grains, red from the powder of the *kusumbha*, black from pulverized half-burnt cereals, and greenish from powder of the *bilva* leaf. The PST (5,63ff.) gives similar directions and also notes the locations of the colours within a maṇḍala. In the cadre of the Dīpāvali an earthly ruler might design a figure of Bali, the demon king, within a maṇḍala of five coloured powders (Bhaviṣyottara Pur 140, 47-73, according to Kane, 1958, p. 201). The MMK discusses a maṇḍala with five colours in vol. I, p. 39, which proves that the system was not unknown in Buddhist circles. It should be noted that the maṇḍalas, and especially the variety called *yantra* (those maṇḍalas which belong to a particular divine figure, such as the Śrīyantra, and prepared for a particular aim) were and are used for magical purposes, such as destruction of enemies or attraction of womankind (Kane, 1962, p. 1132).

This brings us to the magical application of the five colour pattern. A good example is afforded by the JT (20, 170) while dealing with the five arrows of Kāma : "A meditation on the white one is conducive to pacification; the yellow one causes immobilization; the red one is for subjugation and attraction, and for agitation (*kṣobhaṇa-*), while it calls hither the beloved one; and black is declared to be applicable during killing, and grey during eradication and the like"[24]. The colours are here differentiated over the various types of magical influence mentioned above ; and the system is remarkably akin to that of the Mahāmāyā fragment for the meditation on the different colours of Viṣṇu. The relation is especially explicit with the stanzas 18 and 19 of that fragment, where also grey is said to belong to eradication and white to pacification (and welfare); only the colour for immobilization differs. It has been observed (p. 86) that Viṣṇu may be worshipped in his aspect of Kāma ; many teachers have probably believed in their virtual identity.

Sanskrit texts occasionally contain meditations on other gods who assume five colours. One of the oldest instances is without doubt AVPar 50, 5, 4-6, where the observation of different colours in the moon is interpreted to imply an omen for corresponding classes of creatures, to wit the four grades of society and the animal world. A green colour of the moon leads to death in the animal world ; a black colour to death for the Śūdras; yellow spells death for the Vaiśyas and red for the Kṣatriyas; but, significantly, the (usual) white colour leads to *increase* of brahman (spiritual power) [25]. This passage thus contains the familiar association of the four colour system with the four grades of society extended by a fifth colour combined with the animal world ; the ascription of the "four colours" together with green as the fifth to the moon reminds us of the planetary role of these five colour shades noted above (p.192).

This first instance does not, like the following ones, concern a deity who assumes five colours at the same time as an inherent aspect of its personality. Possessing five colours seems to have been felt to be a symbol of the omnipotent, sovereign and all deluding power of a Supreme God. Manikka Vachakar (Tiruvachakam I, 50, 1; ed. Pope, p. 5, line 1), while meditating upon the great Śiva adored by him, exclaims: *niṛaṅgaḷor aindu-ḍaiyāy* "Thou hast the colours five!" (trsl. by Pope; these five colours seem to refer to the five senses as the all-deluding powers). Śiva is sometimes said to possess five heads of different colours. The MNT (14, 33) describes Sadāśiva as having his five heads in the colours grey, yellow, vermillion (*aruṇa-*), white and red[27]. The famous Pañcabrahma or Pañcamukha (Sadyojāta etc.) have more than once been described in five colours, for example in the LiPur (see above p. 158). The Śivapūjāstotra by Jñānaśiva (st. 21) also alludes to the colours of the Five Faces (Aithal, p. 265)[28]. And this peculiarity of the Five Faces again implies the division of the five colours over five points of the compass. Such a division has indeed been expressed in Stuti & Stava, No. 594, Rudrānalāgni "The Flaming Fire of Rudra"; perhaps the title should be emended into Rudrānanāgni "The Fire of Rudra's Faces" which would give better sense, the more so as Śiva in his Fire manifestation is described in the first quarter of the hymn as *pañcagrīva-*"five-necked". There are seven stanzas in incorrect Skt. which describe Rudra/Śiva's secret nature as a fivefold Fire located in the five regions and characterized by five colours. The division of these colours is the usual one in Bali: white in the East, red in the S., yellow in the W., and black in the N. For the Centre no colour is mentioned but we may expect a variegated colour (*viśva*; *pañcavarṇa*).

Another method to express a god's five-colouredness is to divide his body in five parts and ascribe the colours to them in a vertical sequence. Thus the PST (23, 18) describes the Varāha manifestation of Viṣṇu as "from the knees to the feet like glittering gold; equal to snow from the navel to the knees; from the neck to the navel in the glow of fire; then, from the head to the throat of a dark blue colour; and in the hue of Space from the crown to.... (*ākaṅkaralasat*)"[26]. Similar descriptions exist of Viṣṇu's mount and attendant Garuḍa; and this particular feature seems to have been associated even with Garuḍa in the first place. KJ (chs. 35 and 49) says that Garuḍa's body from feet to head consists of the five elements and, as we saw, these elements have been associated with colours[29]. The ascription of the five colours to the aquiline deity has been made explicit in the KCT (4,182), and here we meet also the variegated colour as the fifth: "Garuḍa by name, yellow from the feet up to the hips, and white like snow up to the line of the navel; red of colour up to the neck, and black like a raincloud up to the line of the brows ; and possessing all colours upwards from there; accompanied by the family of snakes, and sealed by means of the five elements (perhaps = accompanied by the gestures symbolic of the five elements and made by the worshipper)—when meditated upon (in this way) in combination with the gesture symbolic of him, he removes the poison of snakes and also demons, disease and other evils"[27]. The destruction of poison is generally the aim achieved by sādhanas of Garuḍa. This Garuḍa of five colours has also been known in Indonesia, because he is the addressee in a Balinese hymn called Bhairavastava (Stuti & Stava, No. 441). This hymn which is known to Buddhist priests describes Garuḍa as fearsome, with a sharp beak and red eyes and a massive neck, quick like the wind. The second stanza which has been imperfectly translated in Stuti & Stava (p. 270) ascribes a golden colour to the god's knee (which must mean: from the feet up to the knees). The navel (i.e.: the part from knees to navel) is said to be *acalākṛtiḥ*; this must be corrupt, and we expect a white colour. In any case Lévi in his "Sanskrit Texts from Bali" completely misunderstood the purport of the passage as is shown by his acceptance of the reading of one manuscript: *nārī caiva khagākṛtiḥ*. The stanza proceeds by ascribing the colour of the sun to the throat (i.e. : from navel to throat), and the hue of "divided" collyrium (deep black) to the head :

Jānuḥ kāñcanavarṇaś ca nābhiś caivācalākṛtiḥ |
kaṇṭhaś caivārkasannibho mūrdhā bhinnāñjanākṛtiḥ ||

The third and fourth stanzas to this hymn contain nothing else than an explanation of stanza 2 in clear and unambiguous language—a point missed in Stuti & Stava. The sprinkling formula added to the body of the hymn is corrupt, but it contained without any doubt beside a repetition of the four colours also a mentioning of four elements (wind and fire are actually mentioned). The fifth element and the fifth colour have not been preserved in this fragmentary piece but the aim of its recitation is again the destruction of poison, according to Juynboll (see Stuti & Stava, l.c.).

A Gaṇeśa of five colours has probably been expressed by means of five manifestations of that deity in an originally polychrome Vajradhātumaṇḍala handed down in Japanese esoterism. Lokesh Chandra, who discussed the five forms, could unfortunately mention only the colour of one of them, viz. Jaya or Jōbukuten in the North, who should be "of a pale flesh colour"[30]. Even the Buddha may be represented in five colours, as is the case on a Tibetan ṭanka (Eracle, p. 47), where the colours are white, green, blue, yellow and red while the Buddha is depicted preaching to the five kinds of creatures. It will be sufficient only to mention on this place the famous representation of the five Dhyānibuddhas with five colours in the points of the compass; "Stuti and Stava" contains an enumeration of them with their characteristics and colours in No. 477, Anaṅgavāyusūtra, edited earlier by F. D. K. Bosch. The Dhyānibuddha system has been dealt with repeatedly, for example by Dasgupta (p. 353) and by Damais (p. 85-88). It lies perhaps at the base of the tradition of the Dharma cult that Lord Dharma is surrounded in the directions of the sky by five Pandits whose colours are white, blue, red, yellow and green (their names are Setāi, Nīlāi, Kaṃsāi, Rāmāi and Goṃsāi). It is important in our context to note that each of these Pandits is also said to accompany the Lord in his (the Pandit's) respective colour in one of the five ages of the world (Dasgupta, p. 351, 349). As to the Five Buddhas, the conclusion lies near at hand that meditation on and identification with them must have been felt to yield magical powers to the aspirant ; but we could not find explicit information on this point in the texts studied by us. Yet on a stone inscription found in Sumatra (Damais, p. 93) the names of the Five Buddhas are mentioned and followed by *phaṭ*, that meaningful syllable discussed above (p. 73). The Hevajra Tantra connects yogins of the different colours with the Five Buddhas. "Any yogin who is black has Akṣobhya as his deity", and so on: white belongs to Vairocana, dark green to Amoghasiddhi, yellow (*piṅga-*) to Ratneśa, and red-with-white (*raktagaura-*) to Amitābha. In addition, the yogin who is white-and-pale (*śvetagaura*-) belongs to Vajrasattva's family, so that we have here strictly speaking a six-colour system. The Buddhist-Śivaite coalescence in Indonesia led to the identification of the Five Buddhas with the Five Manifestations of Śiva: Rudra, Brahmā, Mahādeva, Viṣṇu and Sadāśiva[31]. It is a consequence of the same tendency that in Stuti & Stava, No. 145 (Lokanātha) the Five Buddhas occur immediately after an enumeration of the Hindu Lokapālas.

But also in the worship of goddesses one comes across instances of the five colour system. In the hymn Stuti & Stava No. 800, Pañca-Sarasvatīmantra, the "Goddess of learning" is described in quite ungrammatical Skt. as wearing garments, bearing garlands and ointment, and loving flowers, of the five colours. These colours are, as might be expected in an Indonesian text, white, red, yellow, black and variegated (*viśva*-) ; the colours and their sequence conform to the Mahāmāyā fragment. Sarasvatī must have been thought of by the author of the "hymn" as able to manifest herself in the same way as Viṣṇu in five different colours in person (although this is not said explicitly; the colour system is limited to the goddess' apparel). Besides, this Pañcasarasvatīmantra has been applied, by means of small changes in its text, to other gods also: to the Five Tathāgatas (or Dhyānibuddhas ; No. 801); to the Four Lokapālas led by Indra (No. 802; the last stanza omitted); and to the four gods Brahmā, Viṣṇu, Īśvara and Rudra and their spouses (No. 803; here also, the last stanza has been omitted). The mentioning of the Lokapālas indicates an important fact : that here also the "four" are associated with the four directions of the sky, while the "fifth" is reserved for the central position of sovereignty. The division of the colours in combination with the strict systematism of the orientation pattern seems to be typical for Indonesia (see above, p. 186; on the importance of *viśva*-, *sarvavarṇa*-or *pañcavarṇa*-, see Damais, p. 90f. and 116f.). Further in No. 658 of the Stuti & Stava collection, Prajñāpāramitā in her Bharāli form seems to be connected with the five colours; at least, a hymn directed to her is followed by a prose "Sprinkling Formula" which mentions a fivefold Gaṅgā (symbol of the Water of Life, a pivotal aspect of Balinese religion) in the colours variegated, red, white, black and yellow, and connected with five syllables of her chief mantra: *Oṃ Diḥ Śrutivijña.* The meditation in question has been handed down also in SM as No. 156, where the mantra runs : *Oṃ Dhīḥ Śrutismṛtivijaye svāhā* "*Oṃ* Vision, O Goddess Who conquers Vedic and Post-vedic wisdom, *svāhā*". On the division of the colours over the separate syllables of a mantra , a feature which occurs also in the Mahāmāyā fragment, we shall return in short presently.

A study of goddess worship in the Tantras easily affords other examples of the five colour system. Two instances from the PST connected with Durgā will suffice. They are especially interesting because the colour pattern has here again been associated with the standard feats of magic. PST 35, 17 discusses the bījas of Śiva's spouse and their effectivity in combination with colours:

Bījāni raktāni tu vaśyakarmaṇy ambhodharābhāny abhicārakāle /
dhūmrāṇi vidveṣavidhau sahome pītāni saṃstambhavidhau smarec ca //

"One should meditate on the kernel syllables as red during the act of subjugation; as having the colour of a raincloud (black) at the time of an evil act; as grey during a ritual of creating dissension accompanied by a fire sacrifice; as yellow during the ritual of immobilization". Although only four colours have been mentioned, a fifth colour is clearly implied because grey never serves as a "fourth colour" and because śānti which is usually associated with white has not been mentioned. On another place (30, 54ff.) the PST gives a more detailed description of the effectiveness of the colours in this field. The alternatives this time concern the figure of the goddess herself; besides, changes in the sacrificed objects and the goddess' apparel help to bring about the different aims (the system will be discussed in detail in ch. 6.3.). " (Durgā,) when yellow and bearing the hilt of a sword and a mace in her hands, will cause immobilization by a methodical sacrifice by means of *pulaka* grains with buffalo ghee poured over them, and of *kodravaka* grains, while the fuel should consist of *vibhītaka* and *ariṣṭa* wood (trees of evil renown) ; Durgā will quickly effect subjugation when spotless white, when bearing the noose and elephant hook, being watered (? *saṃbhinnā*) by a rushing torrent of water; while a sacrifice is being performed with sweet stuffs by means of fuel from rotan; when red, and bearing noose and elephant hook, Durgā subjugates the world by a nocturnal sacrifice with flowers of the *agniśikha* and *kesara* watered with the sap of sandal;....and being more like vermillion, bearing the noose and elephant hook together with a trident and skull in her (four) hands, Durgā will effect attraction with the help of a small image (of the victim) made of salt and by means of a sacrifice wetted by the three sweet stuffs; by a meditation on a grey (Durgā) with club and trident in her hands, and in combination with a sacrifice of bones wetted with a sharp substance and of camphor in combination with the ghee of sheep covered with *nimba* leaves (*nimba* being believed to create dissension)—by this, dissension (is created);.... (another method with the grey Durgā)..; having the colour of fire and bearing arrow and trident in her hands, Durgā will cause delusion by means of a sacrifice of evil intention with intoxicating seeds (or: seeds of the *matta* plant) wetted with mustard oil, or with pepper mixed with (powder of) the *rājī* plant; being black and bearing trident and sword in her hands, Durgā will cause (the enemy's) death within a month by means of a sacrifice of exquisite fuel sticks which have been cut on a crucial (astrological) day of the enemy and which have been wetted with ghee from biting (plants)"..[28]. The passage proceeds with some other methods of liquidation to be effected by the black Durgā. Now descriptions like this are by no means uncommon in certain Tantras. The details, including the number of colours and their ascription to the magical acts, may vary more or less; the above passage contains six acts (seven, if one of the omitted stanzas is included) combined with the colours yellow, white, red, vermillion, grey, fiery and black. As vermillion and fiery may be considered as varieties of red, one may recognize a five colour system; but it is unnecessary to stick to this point because there are other passages which quite unambiguously deal with six, seven, or eight colours.

It is only left now to discuss an instance of the application of the five colour system to the syllables of a sacred formula. In the Mahāmāyā fragment the syllables of the word *Aghorebhyaḥ* were combined with a particular colour, and the word as a whole with a harmonious mixture of the same colours. A similar feature was alluded to in a hymn to Prajñāpāramitā discussed two pages above. And the same system has been applied to the formula *Namaḥ Śivāya* "Honour to Śiva" which has been made the object of a refined speculation in Śivaite schools. AgPur succinctly prescribes (304, 16): *kramāt kṛṣṇasitaśyāmarakta-pītā....mantrārṇāḥ* "the syllables of the mantra are respectively black, white, green, red and yellow"; besides, their figures should be meditated upon as staff-bearers (*daṇḍinaḥ*), while assignment should be made on the five fingers and five parts of the body. In the LiPur, a whole chapter (1,85) is devoted to the speculation on this Pañcākṣaramantra. The stanzas 48ff. characterize its five syllables in various ways, as follows:

Syllable	Colour	Region	Presiding deity	Sage
Na	yellow	E.	Indra	Gautama
ma(ḥ)	black	S.	Rudra	Atri
Śi	grey	W.	Viṣṇu	Viśvāmitra
vā	golden	N.	Brahmā	Aṅgiras
ya	red	Zenith	Skanda	Bharadvāja

In this system, the sages are those who are supposed to have "beheld" these syllables in primeval ages. The division of the colours over the syllables is completely different from that of the AgPur. A *nyāsa* is prescribed also here (54ff.), in three varieties: *utpatti* "origin" from head to feet and suitable for Brahmacārins (religious students); *sthiti* "maintenance" during which one starts from the heart, fitting for Gṛhasthas (householders); and *saṃhāra* "dissolution", done from the feet upwards; this last method is advised for Yatis (ascetic wanderers). The deviances of the present identifications from the usual ones in later Hindu speculation concerning colour, points of the compass, etc. are suggestive of a relatively early date of this system preserved in the LiPur. It is perhaps unnecessary to add that in Śaiva Siddhānta speculation the formula *Namaḥ Śivāya* can be applied as an effective means of realizing final emancipation (Pope, p. XXXIXff:, a translation of the relevant ninth chapter of Umāpati's "The Fruit of Divine Grace"). But the same mantra can be used for magical ends : the LiPur (1,85,113) describes how for this end the syllables should be assigned to the fingers. A pointing towards the E. means subjugation;

to the S. : destructive magic; to the W., acquisition of wealth; to the N., pacification :

> *Tat pūrvābhimukhaṃ vaśyaṃ dakṣiṇañ cābhicārikam /*
> *paścimaṃ dhanadaṃ vidyād uttaraṃ śāntikaṃ bhavet //*

5. *Six and more colours*

It should be remarked at the outset of this last section that the division of this chapter according to number systems necessarily contains an element of arbitrariness. In many cases there seems to be no fundamental difference between, say, magical prescriptions involving meditation on a deity or mantra in four, five or six colours; but on the other side the advantages of the followed system will have appeared, we trust, from the preceding pages. A threefold system centres round the conception of the three guṇas; the number four is mainly associated with the four varṇas and the orientation pattern of the four points of the compass; while the fifth number provides this pattern with a meaningful centre. When the number five is exceeded, a pattern becomes less easily recognizable. Still the number six might be connected with orientation by means of the four quarters, the zenith and the nadir. In the Siṅgālovādasutta (DN, No 31) the Buddha rebukes a person who worships the "six quarters". Moreover, the number six may contain an element of ill luck or uncanny power. It exceeds the auspicious number five by one. There are six Vināyakas; six organs of sense; six constituents of man's evil nature; and, above all in this context, six acts of magic. The preparation of six colours needed for the construction of a maṇḍala of Hevajra is a weird procedure according to the HT (1, 2). Black should be composed with the help of ashes from the place of cremation (*śmaśānāṅgāra-*) ; white by means of pulverized human bones (*narāsthicūrṇa-*) ; yellow by *haritālakta* (?) ; red by means of bricks from the cremation place; green by means of powder composed of *caurya* leaves and human bones ; and dark blue by means of a mixture of human bones and ashes of the cremation ground.

On other occasions we meet a description of a god in six colours. In LiPur (1,21,43f.) Śiva is addressed as follows:

Namo dhūmrāya śvetāya kṛṣṇāya lohitāya ca /
piśitāya piśaṅgāya pītāya ca niṣaṅgiṇe //

"Honour to the Grey One, the White One, the Black One, the Red One; the Adorned One (?) and the Tawny One; the Yellow One, Who bears the quiver". The KālPur (68,21ff. ; van Kooy, p. 167) contains a short description of a form of the goddess Kāmeśvarī with six heads facing six directions : white to the N. E., red to the E., yellow to the S., green to the W., black to the N. and variegated in the Centre. It may be argued that this is a five colour system with the auspicious N.E. direction added to it while usurping the white colour. Van Kooy, l.c., surmises that this six-headed form is based upon the five-headed śakti of Sadāśiva while the colours might have been directly or indirectly taken from the five heads of Śiva himself. In any case, deities of six colours are unfrequent. A description of an Ugratārā of this form is perhaps concealed in a citation from the Matsyasūkta contained in T (p. 380). The colours of the goddess are here combined with magical acts. The performer is enjoined to meditate on Ugratārā without particulars when he hopes to attain release; for pacification he should imagine her as being white like the full moon; and when duly worshipped in a grey colour within a maṇḍala of Wind the goddess without any doubt renders the enemies' army and mind senseless [29]. At this point unfortunately the citation breaks off.

The number six is also sometimes connected with the mystical side of the human psychic and physical system. There was already occasion to refer to the epic doctrine of six colours of the soul (Mbh 12, 271, 33-55 and the study made on this passage by Bedekar; see above, p. 164) The six colours have been combined in this fragment with the stages of spiritual development; an association which has been made also in Jainism (Bedekar, p. 336). The six colours of the soul are black, grey, dark blue, red, yellow and white—a sequence from dark to light which symbolizes the ascending course of man's eternal principle; at the same time we note that this sequence fairly accurately tallies with the colour sequence of the magical acts in the Mahāmāyā fragment and other texts on the standard acts of magic (of course into the opposite direction). Only red and yellow have changed position. Just as the colours in their mystical essence serve to characterize and influence man's soteriological course, in the same way they can lead the yogin who chooses to tread the path of magic towards obtaining power over other people's psychic and physical condition.

Another instance of this "psychological" approach is to be found in the KCT (2,29): "the conditions (*bhāva-*) enter the body like the experience of unity (*samarasa-*) the Space; and in the grip of these conditions the body should be understood by those who are experienced in yoga by means of the differences which are brought about by the basic strands of unevolved matter. These differences relate especially to the elements and the colours: the colours yellow, black, vermillion and white apply to earth, wind, fire and water respectively, while to (the elements) wisdom and space the colours dark blue and green apply; this is in accordance with the different conditions of the body"[30]. The reader is of course reminded of the familiar doctrine of the six cakras in the body on which we need not expatiate here.[32] The above fragment from the KCT is a good instance of the Tantric tendency to identify the human and the divine plane in psychology; very typical is also the doctrine expounded by the same text shortly before (2, 6) that Viṣṇu's ten Avatāras are realized in the human life from conception onwards.

The importance of the number seven needs not to be emphasized. There are some instances of colours having been associated with series of this number. The "seven planets" have their own colours. Mars is red, Mercury green, Jupiter yellow, Venus variegated, Saturn black, the Sun red and the Moon white according to Varāhamihira's Bṛhajjātaka (Kane, 1958, p. 573). The commentary on MMD 11, 48 records a meditation on a sevenfold Tripurasundarī Graharūpiṇī "in the Planet Manifestation" whose colours are those of the grahas (the details of the system differ). Stuti & Stava, No. 103, Saptoṃkāra, referred to above, describes seven kinds of Ātmans in ascending sequence which have the colours red, dark blue, white, yellow, equal to the Sun, spotless (*nirmala-*) and formless (*nirākṛti-*). Now there are places which connect seven acts of magic with colours. This is succinctly done by the Jayākhya Saṃhitā (14, 76-78) : "The mantra should be meditated upon as follows during recitation : in the case of pacification one should meditate on it as clear like crystal; as yellow during acquisition (*pauṣṭika-*); with the (deep red) colour of the *kiṃśuka* flower during subjugation; like the rock Nṛpa (?) during attraction; like lampblack during liquidation; like the feathers of the blue jay during the creation of dissension; and as grey during eradication. . . ."[31][33]. A different version of the same pattern is worked out in the PST (28,13), according to which the mantra of Ardhanārīśvara Śiva can be applied in different forms and different colours for different ends. The passage can best be rendered schematically :

First letter of mantra	Colour	Aim
ś (*śukla*)	white	*puṣṭi*, *śānti*
r (*rakta*)	red	*ākṛṣṭi*, *vaśya*
h	golden	*kṣobhaṇa* "agitation"
		saṃstobhana "paralyzing"
y (*samīra*)	grey	*mardana* "crushing"
		uccāṭana "eradication"
m	yellow	*stambhana*
—	spotless white	*mukti*
?	black	causing various diseases

It is clear that there is no difference in principle between passages like these and others which involve six, five, or perhaps four kinds of magic. The pivotal point is always the māyic effectivity of the colours.

A special case of a seven colour system is constituted by the Śaktis or tongues of the god of Fire. AgPur (304, 22) enjoins meditation on Agni's nine Śaktis in the form of flames; they are called respectively Śvetā "White", Raktā "Red", Sitā "White", Pītā "Yellow", Śyāmā "Green", Vahninibhā "Fiery" Asitā "Black", Kṛṣṇā "Black" and Aruṇā "Vermillion". Better known is the doctrine of Agni's Seven (or thrice seven) Tongues which also have female names (e.g. in MuUp 1,2,4 ; PST 6, 72 ; MMD 25, 47ff.; MMD 1, 133ff. ; Ajitāgama, Kriyāpāda, 21, 112f.; S 2, 17). The magical effectivity of these tongues is dealt with in LiPur (2, 25, 55ff.). They are also located in the directions of the sky. The central one is significantly called Bahurūpā "Multiform" and is characterized by a variety of colours. The others are also named after their colours. The second, Hiraṇyā "Golden" is located in the N. E. and affords wisdom. Kanakā "Golden" belongs to the E.; a specific effectivity is not mentioned for her. Raktā "Red" belongs to the S.E.; she is able to effect dissension and delusion (*vidveṣaṇa-mohana-*). Kṛṣṇā "Black" is located in the S.W. and causes death. Suprabhā "Bright" flames in the W. of the fire; she has the hue of a pearl and grants śānti and puṣṭi. The N. W. tongue, Atiraktā (text: *abhivyaktā*) eradicates the enemy. The central tongue, Bahurūpā, besides granting śānti and puṣṭi, is also conducive to mokṣa. One observes that Agni's mystical tongues can help a performer to all possible aims he may have set himself; and there is again no division in principle between mundane designs and the desire for release. It is even strongly suggested that the religious adept who masters the intricacies of the magical system is at the same time in a favourable position on the way to the final goal of emancipation.

It seems unnecessary to go into details here on the system of the eight colours in eight directions of the sky practised in Indonesia (we refer to Damais, p. 95ff.). The JT (17,83ff.) also contains a passage on destructive magic executed into the eight regions, but it mentions only four colours. In the next chapter (18) the JT discusses the effectivity of nine jewels. The "Nine Gods" are constituted in Indonesia by adding the God of the Centre to the group of eight alluded to above. A special case of an eight colour system is the speculation on the syllables of the Viṣṇuite mantra of eight syllables : *Oṃ namo Nārāyaṇāya.* Meditation on their different colours and other characteristics is prescribed in the "spurious" chapters 106 and 107 of the KJ, and also in PST (20, 49 ff.). Jacob (p. 61 and 64) records two further cases from the Mahākapila-pāñcarātra and the Nṛsiṃhapurāṇa.

This chapter may be wound up by once more calling attention to the integrative role of the harmonious combination of colours which sublimates the possible evil results of each colour operating separately. In the Mahāmāyā fragment this has been expressed by Caturvarṇam "The fourfold colour"; in other Indonesian patterns by Pañcavarṇa or Viśva (varṇa); in connection with Agni's Seven Tongues by Bahurūpā. In the orientation pattern its place is in the key position, the Centre (see also ch. 6.3) ; on the plane of supranormal effects it is conducive to *mukti* "final emancipation" or to *śānti* "pacification".

5. UNDER INDRA'S NET

5.1. *Indrajālam : a divine example for earthly magic*

In the Mahāmāyā fragment the subject is magic ; that is to say, a specialized and sophisticated form of magic with a long tradition behind it. In order to be able to effectively elucidate this particular aspect of the fragment, we shall have to cast a glance upon some features of this tradition at the hand of the Sanskrit sources. It is only natural to start with the Veda; but this does not of course mean that the Vedic texts themselves present the earliest stage of Indian magic or even of the varieties of magic which are of relevance here. With the Veda we only obtain for the first time the foothold of documentary evidence.

In the first chapter it has been shown how in the RV the god Indra had been conceived of as a great magician, at least a great possessor and wielder of māyā. By his application of this māyā the god was able to trick his enemies by their own weapons, for these enemies also were in the possession of this supranormal gift. But Indra's māyā proved to be victorious and this meant that human life and prosperity on earth could be continued. In this way Indra could even be invoked as a protector against inimical sorcery (AV 8, 4, 20-23). The methods by which the Slayer of Vṛtra achieved his goal were often not of what we would call a high moral standard; but an ethical outlook is entirely out of the question here. By his māyā Indra, conjuring up appearances, changing himself into all kinds of beings, human as well as animal, succeeded in murdering his enemies, seducing women, winning riches and glory—performances which were and are often attributed to accomplished magicians, and which they execute in behalf of themselves or of their clients. This does not imply that Indra should be considered merely a divine prototype of an earthly magician: his mythology is much too complicated for that. Nor is he the only god who possesses māyā and who applies it for aims salutary to man. Gods like Varuṇa or Soma also wield their māyā. It is only argued that the ways and methods by which Indra reached his goals are often of a character similar to those which have been applied by persons who specialized in securing human life and prosperity by penetrating into and making use of the mystical powers of nature. The supranormal powers displayed by the god for his ends were felt as exemplary for the human community and attainable for those who sought to imitate them. That is why the KauśS (47, 12-22) prescribes that the magician in the cadre of his *dīkṣā* should take a staff which symbolizes Indra's vajra (Gonda, 1965, p. 323). In RV 10, 166, 2 the poet unambiguously states that the achievements of Indra have been realized also by himself :

Ahám asmi sapatnahéndra ivā́riṣṭo ákṣataḥ
adhā́ḥ sapátnā me padór imé sárve abhiṣṭhitāḥ

"I am the killer of my rivals, unharmed, unhurt like Indra; all these rivals of mine have been placed under my feet". It is to the background of this line of thought that Indra's teaching to Pratardana from the KauśBUp might be studied (see above p.14). A hymn directed to Indra may even lack such references to the slaying of the enemies or the killing of rivals, and yet have been applied in such a context afterwards. Such a case is presented by Ṛgvidh 1, 18, 1 : "He who mutters after correct preparation the hymn by Hiraṇyastūpa (R V1, 32) praising the deeds of Indra restrains his enemies without effort" [1]. It was considered sufficient to set into motion (by praising) the enormous overwhelming force represented by the god in order to gain the upper hand over one's enemies—assuming, of course, that the person who performs the rite is qualified by birth and ritual purity and that he makes the right preparations. In the same way the GopBr (2, 1, 18) says that one who performs a certain ritual will become free from rivals (*apratiratha-*) just as Indra had conquered the Asuras and became free from rivals (Malaviya, p. 168). The imitation of Indra might also have been a governing motive for the Śyenayāga, an abhicāra rite discussed above. The executors act as "falcons", and also Indra has been likened to a falcon (the point is discussed by Eggeling, Vol. II, Introd. p. XIX). Further, the magician addresses his girdle in the AV (6,133) as the daughter of Faith who will bring to him Indra's wisdom and strength (Shende, p. 154).

Such instances might be added to. Their general pattern is that by associating oneself with Indra's mighty deeds the human performer becomes an imitator of the god, so to say his earthly manifestation which achieves the same ends on the mundane plane. While in this way he reaches the god's status, he reduces his adversaries to a low position from where they can only "croak upwards" to him "like frogs" (RV 10, 166, 5 *adhaspadā́n ma údvadata maṇḍū́kā udakā́diva*). The ŚatBr (4, 2,7,5 KSS ed.) says that just like Indra in mythical times conquered the Vṛtra, the great obstructor, and afterwards lived in safety, in the same way nowadays "when they praise by means of this pressurage at noon, then the dakṣiṇā cows are brought to a conquered, fearless and safe place; thus also he (the sacrificer) by means of these five spoonfuls (of soma) hurls a thunderbolt against his antagonist and his rival; having destroyed the Obstructor, the Evil One, he lives in a conquered, fearless and safe place...; therefore he takes these five spoonfuls"[2]. In short : god's victory lays the pattern for human victory. The same principle continues to underlie the royal ideology in Kāvya sources (for a few instances, see Gonda, 1970, p. 116 and n. 68).

In the Purāṇas the pattern is varied by the assertion that a certain spell or magical object has been applied by the gods beforehand and on that occasion proved its efficacy. In the AgPur (133,31) an incantation in the shape of an address to Umā, applicable against enemies, is recommended by the statement that the same spell had been borne on the wrist beforehand by Brahmā, Rudra, Indra and Viṣṇu so that the gods were protected by it in battle [3]. The Viṣṇupañjara, a prose stotra to Viṣṇu printed in the BSR (p. 77f.) and also present in the Balinese collection of stutis (Stuti & Stava, No. 787) has, according to its author, been inaugurated by Brahmā who communicated it to Śiva when the latter went out to destroy Tripura (*Tripuraṃ dahamānasya Harasya Brahmaṇoditam*; Indian version, st. 3a). Thus the divine use of spells before they were divulged on earth seems to be kind of a topic in Skt. religious literature.

The association of Indra with earthly magic appears from the very name given to the performance of occult feats by magicians in Skt. : *indrajālam* "Indra's net". Sometimes this word is used in a broad sense in which it can be more or less equated with the English "magic". On other places its use is restricted to the performance of spectacular feats like jugglery or the creation of phantasms. The word indrajāla seems to trace its origin from the AV (8, 8, 5-8) where it is used in a magical context. Stanza 8 runs:

Ayám̥ lokó jắlam āsīc Chakrásya maható mahắn /
ténāhám Indrajāléna amū́n támasābhī dadhāmi sárvān /

"this world was the net of the great Śakra (Indra), of mighty size; by means of this net of Indra I envelop those people all with darkness." The speaker first states the power wielded by the divine prototype on a mythical occasion and then adds his own pretensions, emphasizing that he himself applies the same means. These consist of a weapon of cosmical size, equal to the whole "world" (*loka-*), which means the sphere of activity of all the creatures in their earthly existence. The cosmical nature of this net has been expounded by the author beforehand in st. 5. The "net" itself was characterized there as the *antarikṣa-*, the intermediate space between heaven and earth, while the directions of the sky were the net's sticks (*daṇḍāḥ*) by means of which it was fastened into the earth. With this net Indra conquered all his enemies. In st. 6 the god is invited to apply it against the common foe ; in st. 7 Indra's victory is proclaimed. The broadness of vision applied in the cosmical equation is the most effective source of power employed by the reciter—it might be compared to the "mystical insights" recorded in the ChUp and their practical results (see above, p. 63). The hymn as a whole is intended for application in behalf of a tribal chief in time of war; KauśS includes the ritual connected with it within the "army rites" (16, 9-20) and among other things states that the footmarks of the inimical army should be strewn with symbolical objects, among others a net prepared from hemp. The next stanzas of the incantation clearly show the reciter's intentions: the enemy will be stricken with all kind of disease and calamity; the adversaries are bound with the bonds of death, and so on. In his last stanza (24) the poet concludes by saying that he spreads over his enemies a net of black-and-red colour : *nīlalohiténa amū́n abhyávatanomi*, which has also been interpreted as "by means of the Black-and-Red One (Śiva) I spread the net over them."

As a supernatural weapon the word *indrajāla* occurs in the Mbh, where it is applied by Arjuna (3, 14995 Cal. ed.).

5.2. *The net as a magical device in Sanskrit literary tradition*

In the preceding section the net used by Indra appeared to be a weapon supernaturally effective by means of which this god conquered his enemies, like a fowler catches the birds who unsuspectingly come under the net spread by him. The same motif occurs in AV 8, 4, 13, where the "net" is expressed by means of the word *prásiti*. "He kills the *rakṣas*, he kills the speaker of untruth ; both lie within the net of Indra" : *hánti rákṣo hánty ásad vádantam ubhā́v indrasya prásitau śayāte.* It is to be noted here that the subject who executes the act is not Indra but Soma, although this god also makes use of "Indra's net"—an indication that this expression was on the way to become a term for an act of magic in general without being confined to Indra any more. The idea of the "net" at the same time suggests the "noose" (*pāśa-*), the characteristic attribute of Varuṇa, who by means of this device catches those who transgress his ordinances like animals (Jacques, p. 266). AV 8, 8, the same hymn in which the simile of Indra's net is worked out, also speaks (st. 16) of the "nooses of death", *mṛtyupāśā ḥ*, by which the enemies are caught.

Like the noose, the net is apt to develop into a symbol of the divine superiority, the malicious infallibility by which its wielder is able to conquer and destroy those whom he chooses, no matter if the choice has been motivated by sheer malice, by the decree of fate, or by providence. This idea is expressed by the ŚvetUp (3, 1) : *ya eko jālavān īśata īśanībhiḥ* "He who, with His net, rules alone by means of His sovereign powers." This passage describes the greatness of the Rudra who is proclaimed to be the Supreme God and identical with the Ātman. Śaṅkara in his commentary on this place calls him the Paramātman and explains *jāla* by *māyā*, emphasizing the infallibility of this *māyā* by citing BhGītā 7, 14 : *mama māyā duratyayā* "My Māyā is impossible to overcome." According to the same commentator, this infallibility is the main identificatory factor between *jāla* and *māyā*: "the net is the māyā because of its being impossible to overcome" (*jālaṃ māyā duratyayatvāt*). Śaṅkara's conclusion is that the Wielder of the "net" is the same as the Possessor of the māyā (*jālavān māyāvīty arthaḥ*) Who is described as such in the same ŚvetUp (4, 10), and Who by His māyā keeps all others in check (ŚvetUp 4, 9) (for another commentator on ŚvetUp 3, 1, see above, p. 37). So the "net" is an image well fitted to illustrate the action of the divine Māyā. Indeed the terms Indrajāla and Māyā are sometimes used as synonyms. Ṛgvidh. (4, 23, 1) says : *Śāmbarīm Indrajālaṃ vā māyām etena vārayet* "one will restrain by this (stanza) the māyā called Śāmbarī and the māyā called Indrajāla." Indrajāla here appears as a subdivision of the general term māyā, but on other places the two terms are identified outright, as in the place already cited from the ISP (3,1,84; see above p.—141). The Śāntistava by Tyāgarāja, st. 22 (Aithal, p. 141) declares that he who has obtained the insight that all this existence is only a short-lived product of indrajāla reaches the supreme peace (*śānti*), which consists of the realization of the own identity with Śiva [4]. An elaborate stanza quoted in Böhtlingk, Indische Sprüche (St. Petersburg 1863), Nr. 2277, says of Śiva : ...*yanmāyā hi ruṇaddhi viśvam...jālavat* "Whose māyā restrains the all...like a net."

The identity of the Māyā with a net spread over mankind can also be expressed by means of a compound *māyājāla*—"the net which is māyā." This word does not occur in PD. The Kathās. (12, 25, 51) mentions a certain spell (*vidyā*) which creates "a net of māyā destined for delusion", *māyājālaṃ vimohāya*; and this "net" significantly appears to consist of the performer's transformation into another human being which undergoes a course of life without insight (the pattern has been discussed above, p.44f). The word *māyājāla* is again used in the same context in stanza 69 of the same chapter. It further occurs twice in an inscription from medieval Nepal the date of which is lost; it is preserved now in the Government Museum in Kathmandu (Regmi, p. 13). Stanza 4 of this inscription, addressed to Śiva, begins with *māyājālamada-* "the intoxication caused by the net which is *māyā*". The next stanza is directed to Durvāsas, the irascible sage, who is styled a *māyājālakalaṅka-mardaka* "Crusher of the stain caused by the net of māyā". In this function the sage is said to have abandoned his wrath (*krodhaṃ vihāya svakam*). The word *māyājāla* is also found in the Buddhist tract MPN (st. 162) among an extensive list of names of Mañjuśrī. SM (No. 181) mentions a Māyājāla-mahāyoga-tantra, a title which connects the net of the Māyā with the term *yoga* (cf. p.66). A variant of *māyājāla* is *māyāyantra-* "the device which is māyā" which occurs in GarPur (18, 1) : *Brahmadhyānaṃ pravakṣyāmi māyāyantrapramardakam* "I shall proclaim the meditation on Brahman, a meditation which crushes the apparatus of māyā." A further search would certainly result in more instances.

Beside the māyā, other notions of a similar character are sometimes considered to be "nets" and described by means of compounds. None of these compounds occurs in the PD. The term *moha* "delusion" which, as has been argued above (ch. 1.4), is very often associated with māyā, produces *mohajāla-* "the net of delusion" in the Vedānta philosopher Sureśvara's explanatory stanzas on Śaṅkara's commentary on the Taittirīya Up (2, 166; van Boetzelaer, p. 83). According to this stanza, the human mind is enveloped by this net and afterwards carried off by the hook of desire. The round of births, *saṃsāra*, is called a net in YogV (Nirvāṇaprakaraṇa, 1,20,23), where the crow sage Caṇḍa addresses his twenty-one sons: "Sons, have you by now found the way out of this net of saṃsāra which has been woven by means of the endless threads of the psychic strands ?" [5]. The term *Brahmajāla* occurs as the name of the famous first Sutta of the Pali Dīghanikāya. *Duḥkhajāla-* "the net of sorrow" is found in GarPur (223, 24) : *japed idaṃ santataduḥkhajālaṃ jahāti nīhāram ivāṃśumālī* "if one recites this (mantra of Narasiṃha) one leaves the net of constant sorrows like the sun the mist." SM (p. 4) contains *kleśaduḥkhajālān* "the nets of affliction and sorrow" which the Buddhas and Bodhisattvas are asked to disperse. The word *doṣajāla-* "net of faults" occurs in the same SM (No. 66, p. 133) in a description of Vajradharma who disperses this net (*Śrīvajradharmaṃ dhutadoṣajālam*) while he emits a "net of rays", *raśmijālam*, himself. The KulaCT (5, 48) says that the goddess Kulasundarī has been "woven by means of a net of all faults", *samastadoṣajālena grathitā Kulasundarī*. *Pāpajāla-* "net of evil" is found in SkPur (2, 26, 6) where it is argued by the sacred rivers of India that "all human beings, being beset by evil, exert themselves in bathing in our waters; having got rid of their nets of evil people have reached their goal and return home; but how will this net of evil (having attached itself) to us, be completely destroyed?" [6]. The JT (17, 14) states that "Nāga damsels coming from the nether world are intent upon agitating" the yogin; but "the sādhaka is not brought to delusion by the nets of their sidelong glances" (*kaṭākṣajālaiḥ*). [7]. A Tantra belonging to the "Right Course" (*dakṣiṇasrotas*) is called Yoginījālā, thus suggesting the overwhelming powers of the Yoginī(s) in question (Bagchi, p. 217). A mantra in the Siddhanāgārjunakakṣapuṭa (2, 17) speaks of a goddess Vajrajālinī "Foremost Possessor of the net" Who "subjugates all the world" (*sarvalokavaśaṅkarī*). It may be repeated that this list of occurrences of compounds featuring *jāla* is certainly not exhaustive; it might only serve as a sample.

Now the human magician by applying the magic called indrajāla in imitation of his divine forerunners spreads his net of māyā over those he has chosen to be the object of his manipulations. Just as the māyā seems in the first place to denote a creative power or faculty, by means of which its bearer is able to create as it were out of nothing (see above, p. 1) so the indrajāla often implies that the magician creates something before the eyes of the spectators which does not really exist, or rather which does exist only in the spectators' minds as a result of the fallacious powers of the *indrajālin*.[1] That the Buddha acted as an indrajālin—or was believed to have acted in that way, which makes no essential difference in this context—by his miraculous performance at Śrāvastī where he multiplied himself, has been noted by Jacques (p. 265). The Lalitavistara mentions a Bodhisattva called Indrajālin (PD, s.v.).

At this point a short excursus may be made into Classical Antiquity where this kind of illusory magic has also been practised. Origenes, the famous Church Father, cites his adversary Celsus, an Epicurean who lived in the second cy. A.D. and who polemized against the Christians, trying to show that the miracles which were performed by Jesus were also within the reach of pagan sorcerers. Celsus' argument is that even if it be true that Jesus in a miraculous way procured bread and fish for a multitude of five thousand (and the feat is reported only in the apostles' tales), the Egyptian magicians were able to create out of nothing sumptuous dinners, richly loaded tables with exquisite dishes, all non-existent but quite real to the minds of the public. "Should we have to call all these doctors the Sons of God?" Celsus exclaims.[2] Another treatise by a Christian author, presumably of the fifth cy. A.D., argues that this kind of magic was characteristic for the miracles wrought by demons, while those which come from God, for instance the miracles performed by Moses and Aaron, did result in a real change in the object in question (Pseudo-Justinus, Quaestiones ad Orthodoxos, 26; cited by de Jong, p. 153).

If one confines indrajāla to its stricter sense of creation of illusory appearances before the public, it is understandable that this activity was very apt to become an image for the great Illusion which holds ignorant mankind in its grasp according to the Advaita theorists. It is also significant that there seems to be no essential difference between *avidyā* "ignorance" and *moha* "delusion" as the factors which lead to this "human bondage." In Sureśvara's Taittirīyabhāṣyavārttika referred to above the words *avidyā* and *moha* seem to have been used indiscriminatingly. For instance, in 2,469f. ignorance is the all-encompassing cosmical power which holds mankind in the grip of fear; but in the next stanza (2,471) delusion is called the cause of this fear; the same in 2,473. And in the preceding stanza (2,468) the Lord Himself is said to be responsible for it (translation of this passage by van Boetzelaer, p. 133f.). *Moha* is paraphrased by *ajñāna* by the commentator (Sāyaṇa) on SVBr 1, 2, 7 and 3, 7, 1. Sureśvara in his work mentioned just above also says (2, 374) that "this daily manifestation of both name and form from Viṣṇu is the 'becoming' world, like the multiplicity (conjured up) by a magician" (translation by van Boetzelaer, p. 118) [8]. In the Dattātreya Tantra (11, 11), Nārāyaṇa is even requested by the poet to perform miraculous feats of Indrajāla. Viṣṇu as a magician is an image worked out by Kabīr in one of his poems : the conjurer Hari makes a show of his tricks and attracts spectators by beating his drum, inviting everybody into his tent. Nobody has seen through his trickery except Kabīr himself (Vaudeville, p. 109).

5.3. *Magic in the Veda*

It is impossible to present anything like a history of Vedic magic in the cadre of this study. Although the subject has been studied by various authors, a careful reappraisal of the material in the light of recent developments in the science of religion might result in an important monograph[3]. If the term "magic" is circumscribed by paraphrasing Webster (p. 55) with "the utilization of the supranormal power thought to be inherent in the universe for public or private ends", then it must be stated that the Veda is replete with it. The entire mechanism of Vedic sacrifice is destined for effectuating certain aims cherished by those by whom or for whom the sacrifice is performed; the aims are mentioned in the texts and their realization as an effect of the automatism of the ritual performed and the texts uttered is confidently stated. That all this is sometimes combined with the worship of lofty divine figures or even with passages which express flashes of mystical rapture—nobody will deny it. "Magic" and "religion" sometimes go inextricably together (the point was discussed above on p. 60). In the magical mantras themselves the gods' assistance is invoked (Malaviya on p. 34 and elsewhere distinguishes *abhicāra* and *prārthanā*, but this division cannot be strictly maintained).

The most important source for our knowledge of Vedic magic is of course the AV, supplemented by its ancillary texts, in the first place the KauśS and its commentaries. A brief survey of the aims expressed in some hymns from the first six books of the AV is given now (they are taken from the translation by Whitney/Lanman) in order to convey an impression of the subjects cherished most by the authors of these poems. These aims include in the first place victory over enemies (1, 19-21; 2, 19-23; 4,31 and 32 addressed to Fury; 4,40; 6, 65-67; 6,98 to Indra), but also the discovery of inimical sorcerers (1, 7 and 8 to Agni) or the counteracting of witchcraft (2,11) and curses (2, 7); cure of the possession by demons (2,9; 5,29); protection by worship of the deities of the quarters of the sky (1,31; 3,26 and 27); the destruction of snakebite (5, 13; 6, 12; 6,56) or of poison in general (4, 6 and 7 ; 6,100); getting rid of wild animals and thieves (4, 3) or of birds of ill omen (6, 27-29); success of the chief by means of an amulet (1,29); obtaining wealth (1,15) or success in trade (3,15); abundance of rain (4,15), winning the love of a woman or girl (1,34; 2,30; 3,25; 6, 8 and 9); precaution against premature birth (6, 17); victory in disputations (2, 27). The KauśS has done much to systematize this veritable spectrum (see the survey over KauśS 7-52 given by Caland, pp. 1-9). One might say that the contents of the AV are of a double nature: on the one side, the desire to avert dangers, to allay the fear of misfortunes of all kinds; on the other side, the effort to eliminate the enemy, or to gratify one's hate or passion. It would thus be too onesided a statement (although it may be true to a great extent) to say with Shende (p. 154) that the primary aim of all witchcraft is self-defence. It depends on one's angle of vision. There is certainly also a good deal of self-assertion in it, and this is reflected in a traditional twofold division of the AV. itself:

1. Those mantras which are intended for *śānti*, for the allaying of all sorts of dangers and evils; they are called *Pratyaṅgiramantrāḥ* or *Ātharvaṇaḥ.* Beside śānti, they aim at greater welfare (*puṣti-*) or extension of life (*āyuṣyam*).

2. Those mantras destined for abhicāra, which means: for harming others. They are called *Aṅgirāmantrāḥ* or *Āṅgirasaḥ.*[4]

The fundamental power (*brahman*) which penetrates existence is neutral in itself and can be utilized by qualified specialists for good as well as for evil ends (Shende, p. 153; see also above, p—62ff.).

The rituals which are presupposed by these hymns called mantras are expounded in the KauśS. From the technical side they can hardly be considered to form a separate class within the body of Vedic ritual tradition. As Shende (p. 162) remarks, there is no essential difference between the methods of a normal sacrifice and a sacrifice with abhicāra as its goal. The magician's initiation is also similar to the initiation of a priest (Shende, p. 154 ; on the initiation of magicians, see also Gonda, 1970, p. 322f.; Henry, p. 223f.). The difference lies in the first place in the performers' and the sponsors' intentions; but in this context it should also be emphasized that the KauśS most often presents rites of theoretically salutary character, such as defence against demons or diseases. General prescriptions for abhicāra rites are, however, included (47, 1-11; cf. Caland, p. 157, n.1).

Both the usual śrauta or gṛhya sacrifices and the "magical" ritual can be denoted in Skt. by means of words derived from the root *kṛ-*"to do, make". *Karma* "deed" can mean a sacrificial ritual of all kinds; the same holds good for *kriyā-Kṛtvan* "proficient in deeds", a characteristic of the Ārjīkas in the RV (9, 65, 23) seems to mean at the same time "proficient in witchcraft". *Kṛtāni* "things done" is used instead of "acts of sorcery" in SVBr (3, 5, 6-8) : *nainaṃ kṛtāṇi hiṃsanti tāny eva pratigacchanti* "things done do not hurt him, they just turn back." The commentator paraphrases with *parakṛtābhicārādiprayuktāni kṛtyā dīni* "devices such as kṛtyās which are employed in abhicāra rites or other means created by the enemy." This word *kṛtyā* "creation" has, as is well known, specialized in an abhicāra sense. It denotes a figure, usually female, created by the magician in order to inflict some evil upon a victim. AV 10, 1 has such a kṛtyā as its subject. The KauśS (ch. 39) discusses the removal of kṛtyās (*kṛtyāpratiharaṇa*; see Caland,p. 132ff. according to whom kṛtyā here means a bewitched doll which may for instance be buried near the enemy's house). The Ṛgvidh. (2, 9, 3) also mentions a kṛtyā which rises from the water and Gonda in his note on this place (p. 42) refers to Mbh 13, 93, where a certain Vṛṣādarbhi prepares a kṛtyā called a Yātudhānī. The kṛtyās have not become extinct in the Tantric texts. PST 30, 79 alludes to their destruction by means of a certain mantra (*japtvā mantram amuṃ ca rogasahitāḥ kṛtyā nikṛtyā kṛtāḥ*) and stanza 84 in the same chapter describes how a kṛtyā returns to its creator and destroys him : "The kṛtyā is destroyed by his (the performer's) gaze without fear (as well as) evil planets and the like; (or) a kṛtyā wrathfully turns back upon its creator and causes him to be lost body and soul"[9]. The Ṣaṭkarmadīpikā suggests a rite in which a kṛtyā is created by the performer himself and instructed to drink the blood of the enemy's heart (p. 191). This text even addresses the Kṛtyā at the outset as a kind of protective deity in stanza 2 (p. 179). "I bow before the Kṛtyā Who flames with rage, Who emits fire from Her mouth; Who burns creation and swallows the demon; Who utters terrible sounds and Who roars with hunger, the Terrible Kālī" :

Krodhāj jvalantīṃ jvalanaṃ vamantīm
sṛṣṭiṃ dahantīṃ ditijaṃ grasantīm
bhīmaṃ nadantīṃ praṇamāmi Kṛtyām
rorūyamānāṃ kṣudhayograkālīm

The magical tradition is continued in texts of the late Vedic age and in the Vedic "appendices". New rituals and new practices occur in all four Vedic specializations: the Ṛgveda Brahmans produced their Ṛgvidhāna; the Sāmavedins the Ṣaḍviṃśa and Sāmavidhāna Brāhmaṇas; the Atharvavedins the Atharvavedapariśiṣṭas. The Sāmavidhānabrāhmaṇa (SVBr) has been composed with the objective of providing the priests with the rules for the use of the sāmans, Vedic chants, in ritual ceremonies destined to procure all kinds of results. The performer has to prepare himself for these rituals just as in the case of a śrauta sacrifice, by fasting or doing other kind of penance. He should have obtained a thorough knowledge of the means to restore faults in the rituals performed (*prāyaś-citta-*). After communicating all these necessary preliminaries in Part 1, the text proceeds in Part 2 by discussing the *kāmyāni*, the rituals which procure the desired ends. In general these are related to the main concerns of life : obtaining a long span of life (*āyuṣyāni*), averting disease, protecting life and health of the children—always a precarious matter—, release from the grip of demons, protection against snakebite, procuring an abundant crop, obtaining a safe journey. In the confrontation with enemies the sāmans can also be very helpful: a group of them, when meditated upon, procures invulnerability for the weapons of the approaching foe (SVBr 2, 4, 4 on the Devavrata sāmans). A king and his purohita by the correct application of another series of sāmans can effect victory in battle (SVBr 3, 6). In the personal life also results can be obtained: SVBr 2, 5 and 2, 6 discuss the method of securing the friendliness and love of the members of one's household, the wife in the first place. This procedure is called *āvartanam* "turning (others) toward oneself", it procures *saubhāgyam* "domestic happiness". Such rituals, may, however, assume an aggressive character: in one of them the performer makes use of the notorious device of preparing—and then cutting into pieces—a small image of the person who is to be influenced by the ritual. After he has consumed the heart of the image himself (the image is made out of grains) the performer necessarily brings the victim under his power (2, 5, 5). Another ceremony (2, 6, 16) is still more dreadful: after a fast of three days the performer takes something from the ashes of a burnt corpse and after an animal sacrifice strews a part of it in the antagonist's house. The result is that the rival finds no rest and is forced to leave the neighbourhood. Among the other goals are: the obtainment of victory in disputation (2, 7); the obtainment of healthy sons (2, 8) and of wealth in various forms (3, 1-3); in connection with the latter the passage 3, 3, 7 gives rules for the widely diffused ceremony of securing safety for a recently built house (*vāstuśamanam*). Foretelling the future in various ways (3, 4); anointing a king (3, 5) and subjugating various supernatural beings (3, 7, 3f.) also belong to the practices knowledge of which is considered desirable by the author of the SVBr for those brahmans of his school who are ready to offer their services—without doubt for a good price to the public. By "public" one should in the first place understand the king or the nobleman (see below). The Ṛgvidhāna has been written with a similar purpose, but its arrangement is different: the order of the RV is systematically followed and the author presents his notes on the various applications of the Ṛgvedic hymns in due sequence. This may be due to the author's more recent date. In his Latin introduction the German editor of this text distinguishes four kinds of ritual (*karma*): *kāma*, destined for accomplishing various desires; *śānti*, for averting misfortune; *abhicāra*, for inflicting misfortune or subjugating other people; and *gṛhya*, domestic rites, for instance those concerning marriage and death. The editor systematically notes instances of each of these four sorts of ritual from the contents of the Ṛgvidh. This distinction implies that all kāma and abhicāra rituals would be executed for the public benefit by specialists, which may not always have been the case although it certainly holds good for the great majority of such ceremonies. The distinction into four tends to obscure the real state of affairs when the kāmas or desires are separated in this way from the performance of śānti or abhicāra; all these actions are based upon particular mundane motivations and might as such be said to belong to the sphere of "desire". Strictly speaking of course, all (Vedic) ritual is done out of a motivation to promote human aims. This is also what Manu says (Manusmṛti 2, 4): "Here on this earth there is no (ritual)action whatsoever performed by somebody without a purpose; anything which is performed is performed by the urge of desire."

Akāmasya kriyā kācid dṛśyate neha karhicit /
yad yad dhi kurute kiṃcit tat tat kāmasya ceṣṭitam //

The Ṛgvidh. itself also summarizes all motivation for its rituals under the head of "utterance of desire" (*āśāsyam*, 1, 1, 6): "The utterance of desire has been told in former times to be fourfold: longevity, a heavenly status, wealth, and sons; (but) other desires have been pointed out in hundreds by the sages in their hymns, together with deities (presiding over them)":

Āyuḥ svargo draviṇaṃ sūnavaś ca
caturvidhaṃ. proktam āśāsyam agre /
anye kāmāḥ śataśaḥ saṃpradiṣṭāḥ
saṃstuvadbhir ṛṣibhir devatāś ca //

The reader observes that among the mundane designs also obtaining a place in heaven is mentioned. In the view of these authors, religion and the tools afforded by it express the care for the present life as well as the hereafter. Besides, very frequently in the Brāhmaṇas the gods are stated to have reached heaven by means of a certain new device in the śrauta ritual and the same result is on such occasions usually promised to the sacrificer. The integration of all objectives is seen even clearer in the SVBr (3, 7, 1). There immediately after some instructions destined for the liquidation of an enemy another sāman is taught by means of which the performer is freed from ignorance or delusion (*moha*; the text says *amuhyan* "being free from delusion") in his future births; a wording which suggests that the subject tries to eventually reach the final emancipation from the round of births. The sāman in question is SV 1,421,1-RV 5, 79, 1 : *mahé no adyá bodhaya* "for greatness awake us today." But immediately after this lofty goal the SVBr teaches how to obtain supremacy over the element of fire, and how to cause demons to appear who will execute one's wishes. It thus appears that the same people who might be expected to have the final emancipation within their reach, or in any case who possess some knowledge of the path which leads towards it, are at the same time able to handle the means of procuring various effects in the mundane sphere by methods which we would call magical; and by such methods they hold their own in the world or even more than that. Among these effects the Ṛgvidh. (1, 2,5) mentions *vidveṣaṇa* "causing people to hate each other"; *saṃvanana* 'procuring somebody's friendly disposition'; *viṣaghna* "(means for) destroying poison"; and *roganāśana* 'destruction of illness." Other objectives from the Ṛgvidh. have been rubricated by Meyer (Introd. to his ed., p. XIIff.). It may be useful to give one instance of the way in which the Vedic hymns are handled; RV 1,1 *Agním īle puróhitam* "I praise Agni, Who is placed at the head" can be applied in a rite procuring wealth (Ṛgvidh. 1,13,5); it contains in stanza 3 the words *Agnínā rayím aśnavat póṣam evá divédive* "by Agni one will obtain richness and welfare day after day"; in stanza 1 Agni is called *hótāraṃ ratnadhā́tamam* "invoking priest most able to bestow riches." In other cases the connection of the contents of the recited hymn with the aim of the ritual as taught by the Ṛgvidh. is less evident. The Savitṛ (RV 3, 62, 10), believed to be a particularly powerful mantra, is able to procure a great diversity of results : averting evil, procuring wealth and cattle, and welfare ; but also, when said in an inverted order, the destruction of the enemy (Ṛgvidh. 1,15,4; trsl. Gonda, p. 20).

It might be emphasized that the Ṛgvidh. also stresses the importance of the preparation of the performer by means of austerities, asceticism, study of sacred texts and preliminary ceremonies as well as internal preparation consisting of restriction of the organs of sense and the emotions (Ṛgvidh. 1,2f.). The same point is relevated by Hillebrandt (p . 173) who refers to ĀpŚr 15, 19, 8. It is true that the RV hymns are all directed to gods, but these gods are not worshipped in the Ṛgvidh. as almighty powers who graciously grant the worshipper's desires as an answer to his humble prayers. The man who utters the stanzas after the correct preparations have been made and who sticks to the correct details of the ritual can be confident that he by these means wins a position of power. For him the gods are no more than auxiliaries who help to procure what he wants on his behest. By the right application the mantras inevitably lead to success (Ṛgvidh. 1, 2, 1 ; 1, 2, 5 and 1,3, 1 ; cf. Gonda, Introd., p. 3).

The AVPar is completely permeated with similar considerations. This text contains a great number of alternatives taught on details of the ritual for those who strive after some particular goal. Besides, it discusses a number of ceremonies of a predominantly magical character. We mention ch. 35, Āsurīkalpa, which "contains the ritual for various magical practices with the black mustard plant" (Bolling/von Negelein, ed. of AVPar, p. 215). The chapter is preceded by a few prose mantras which invite the *āsurī* plant to kill, burn, or subjugate the enemy or the woman desired by the speaker. A variant on stanza 4 says that this plant "destroys the enemies' objectives and causes the spells of the good people to bear fruit" (*hanti kāryaṃ ca śatrūṇāṃ sādhūnāṃ mantrasādhanam*). The next stanzas contain directions for the subjugation of members of all the four grades of society. Among others those results are stated that an enemy is afflicted with epilepsy (*apasmārī*, 35,1,10) or madness (*hāsyaśīlo 'bhijāyate*, explained by the commentary as *sa unmatto bhavati*; 35,1,13) from which the victim may, however, be released again (st.14; *tasya mokṣo vidhīyate*); further, the hypnotizing of others so that they become one's slaves (35,2,3); the realizing of domestic happiness (35,2,4) ; changing water into milk (35,2,6) and so on. Dominion and fertility are realized by him in whose home the *āsurī* resides (35,2,11; *nānaiśvaryaṃ nāprajatvaṃ yasya devy āsurī gṛhe*), thus the author concludes his chapter. The next chapter (36), called Ucchuṣmakalpa, invokes the Ucchuṣmas, manifestations of Rudra, by means of a series of mantras uttered for similar objectives. The performer should take care to prepare himself by a rite of self-protection during which mantras are said into the six directions (the four quarters, the centre and the zenith), invoking the respective presiding deities with their weapons. This is followed in the text by short prose spells styled *hṛdaya*—"heart formula", *kavaca*—"armour" and *astra*—"missile" in the vogue of the Tantric texts —but the kavaca does not at all correspond to the type known from later sources. The description of the rites themselves (in 36, 2 ff.) includes some picturesque ceremonies which should not be missing from a history of magical practices. The aims expressed are of the familiar kind : subjugation of people of the four grades, winning a lady, causing disease, separating a victim from his family or destroying that family (*kulotsāda-*, var. *kuloccheda*; 36,8,5). Ch. 36, 9 contains a few dhāraṇīs and an interesting series of names of Rudra manifestations. The chapter winds up (in 36,30) with a few general remarks, among which features the prescription that during an abhicāra rite one should meditate, contrary to the usual ritual practice, on the deity as turning his back to the performer.

5.4. *Some notes on magic in post-Vedic sources*

It has often been said that in such texts as discussed in the preceding section a number of non-Aryan or non-Vedic practices have been admitted into the sacred literature of the brahmans and sometimes been assimilated to their convictions. This may be true, just as it is true that already in the RV the poets express their contempt for the godless magicians, wicked people who did not shrink from causing the death of man and beast. Vasiṣṭha even emphatically and solemnly declared that he was no magician (*yātudhāna-*) himself (Kane, 1962, p. 1035). On the other hand, one may have one's doubts as to the difference in motivation between the Aryan and the non-Aryan or the Vedic and the non-Vedic religious specialists. Many hymns of the AV are also destined for the destruction of enemies; it is inadmissible that all evil practice be ascribed to non-Aryan influence. It seems that both parties had the same intentions and strived after similar goals: welfare for themselves or their sponsors, and the putting down of the enemies or of the rivals in the own camp. In the minds of the contemporaries it all just depended on the performer's provenance: was he one of the own community or not?[6] This mentality is reflected by the attitude assumed on the subject of māyā. Māyā has been thought of perhaps in the first place as being the characteristic of the demons' way of dealing with others. But since māyā is a force neutral by itself, it may as well, if need be, be applied by the gods and their human followers against their adversaries—and the adversaries of the human performers are of course considered to associate themselves with the demons (on māyā, see above ch. 1.1; on the attitude to māyā in the epic outlook, see Hopkins, p. 312f.).

It would even be a hazardous venture to try to distinguish Aryan and non-Aryan matter at all. Not all beliefs and practices of the Aryans are reflected in the Veda; and the Veda may already contain elements borrowed from the tradition of the indigenous inhabitants of India. Besides, it is possible that Aryans and non-Aryans in some cases tried to realize the same ends with similar means. One had thus rather speak of a Hinduization or perhaps Indianization which realized itself in the course of the centuries after the period of the Vedic Saṃhitā literature. This process resulted in the viewpoints and practices laid down in the Purāṇas and the Tantras. But it has been argued more than once that even the Tantras which represent the complete Hinduization of the subject-matter yet often declare themselves to continue and to culminate the revelations given by the AV.[7] Also according to Jain authorities Tantrism developed from the AV (Jhavery, p. 95, who cites passages to this extent from the Sūtrakṛtāṅga Ṭīkā by Śilāṅka). On the other hand, the Jainas trace the origin of their Mantravāda—science of spells—back to their legendary founder Pārśvanātha who is reputed to have flourished 250 years before Mahāvīra (Jhavery, p. 147ff.). The SST refers to three cradles of Tantric lore: the regions of the Buddhists, Tibet (Mahācīna), and the AV (Jhavery, p. 57 citing Avalon, 1952; on Mahācīna, see Bharati, p. 58ff). Vajrayāna Buddhism is reputed to have fused together the best traditions from Hinduism as well as Buddhism (B. Bhattacharya, p. XXXVI). In this way the Tantras themselves point to the Vedic and non-Vedic origins of their wisdom as being inextricably interwoven. And it is indeed certain that many Tantric practices and beliefs are in reality little more than adaptations, restatements or amplifications of subject-matter already found in the Vedic corpus (Gonda, 1963, p. 29f.). This presupposes that the promulgators of Tantric doctrine at least partly came forth from the same schools or communities which in earlier periods helped to produce the Vedic literature, in the first place the AV. It is handed down that the Bhairavas who propagated Yāmala Tantrism were in part Atharvan Brahmans.[8] And what can be said of Tantric doctrine in general, should also be said of what we would call practices of magic. In practice brahmans until recently sometimes served as professional exorcizers specializing on Tantric magic (Crooke, p. 149). There is less innovation here, let alone revolution, than one would at first sight suppose when comparing the chief characteristics of Vedic and Tantric tradition.

Professional magicians are often traceable in post-Vedic literature. There are numerous allusions to people who claimed supernatural powers by their application of spells and secret rituals; and in some cases they seem to have played an important role in the society of their days. Eliade (p. 143) translates

Āp(Dh) Sūtra (2,9,23,6-8) which mentions people who are able to realize all their wishes by merely concentrating their minds; they can cause rain to fall on earth, gaze into a far distance or move as fast as they wish. Of course these allusions to siddhis (supranormal powers) acquired by yogins are quite numerous. What specially interests us here is that such siddhis or other miraculous powers were often used (or only claimed) by persons who wished to make a living out of them. The Jātakas describe brahmans who act as sorcerers; they believe in the magical effects of their asceticism and make use of various spells; they can create a rain of precious stones, they know the languages of animals, they understand the science of conjuring demons and spirits (*bhūtavijjā*) and they ward off diseases and snakebite; they possess spells by means of which the earth can be conquered (Fick, p. 151ff.). The science of *bhūtavijjā* occurs also in DN 1, Brahmajālasutta, where it features in a long list of undesirable occupations which constitute the "net of Brahmā". A general term in this Sutta for such occupations is *tiracchāna-vijjā* "animal wisdom" (Hillebrandt, p. 168, who also records other places from Pali literature). In the Tevijja Sutta the Buddha strongly condemns brahmans who make their living by sorcery (Jacques, p. 275).

The Jaina canon often refers to the use of vidyās and mantras (for the data we are indebted to Jhavery). Ascetics were believed to possess miraculous powers by means of which they even, if irritated, might burn their victim to ashes—a belief also amply illustrated in Hindu literature. The same people were reputed to possess spells and charms by which they could wield all kind of supernatural influence over others.[9] A certain text (Praśnavyākaraṇa 1,1,17) even contains references to yantras or diagrams loaded with power which are constructed for driving away an opponent (Jhavery, p. 274). Other places refer to the subjugation, stupefaction or rendering senseless of enemies by magical means. The Āvaśyaka Niryukti (vs. 927) mentions eleven kinds of Siddhas "Perfected" among whom are the Vidyāsiddhas, Mantrasiddhas and Yogasiddhas. A Yogasiddha, to take an example, is acquainted with various mixtures of powders which he applies in his ritual. A Jaina Sādhu is warned not to use all this kind of practices except in cases of dire need, and even then only for themselves, not for the benefit of others (Jhavery, p. 279; this author systematically collected references of this kind in the Jaina Canon, on p. 271-287).

The Purāṇas abound in descriptions of magical practices. There are complete chapters devoted to them, especially in the Agni and Garuḍa Purāṇas, but also in the MtPur (93), LiPur (2,50) and others. The rites dealt with by the Purāṇic authors, however, are usually destined to be executed in the political or social sphere: hail of the own community, elimination of political antagonists, etc. Their performers would not by preference be called yogins. They are to be sought among the priestly functionaries at courts or other professional ritualists. But it is difficult to decide which people were the "priests" or the "magicians" or the "yogins". Perhaps such labels could have often been applied to one and the same person. It is also impossible to distinguish sociologically between those who conducted the Vedic rituals from those who practised all kinds of other ceremonies for securing their own or their clients' interests. For the client, the method by which his aim is realized was the concern of the religious specialist, no matter if he was a guru, yogin or purohita ; his own concern was only that the effects were obtained. The religious specialist was expected perhaps to have various expedients at his disposal. The same goal might, for example, be striven after by way of similar ritual ingredients and procedure, but in one case with Vedic mantras and on another occasion with meditation on a Hindu deity and its bīja (AgPur 260, 24 describes a common ritual for "becoming dear to others" with the recitation of a Vedic passage). In the cultural environment presupposed by some Purāṇas the teacher of bhakti may have even been the same as the practiser of the Six Acts of magic : in the GarPur, ch. 104 on the latter subject is immediately followed by ch. 105 : Nārāyaṇabhakti. For the layman those who taught the road to salvation by means of philosophy or mysticism seem to have sometimes been scarcely distinguishable from great wonderworkers (see also above, p. 66F). In Tribal India of recent times terms for "holy man" are sometimes also applied to "wizards" or "magicians". Professional teachers of the magic art are apt to be called guru (Crooke, I, p. 147). It must be conceded that there is often a difference between a purely religious functionary and a "spirit-doctor".[10] With the Korku of Central India any Bhūmaka (sacrificial priest), should, however, be at the same time a proficient Parihar (magician) ; only then will he be admitted to the function of village priest (Hermanns, p. 84).[11]

Thus in Ancient Indian literature as well as in the Tribal India of the present century we meet the religious specialist—in former times called guru, ācārya or purohita, or in some cases yogin—who combines into himself the knowledge of various expedients for procuring the welfare of the clients as individuals or of the community as a whole. These expedients include: praising the gods and praying to them; performing the fire-sacrifice, if one was qualified for it ; curing the sick ; driving out demons, and so on. Such a person was sometimes expected to be a sacrificial priest, political adviser, religious teacher and magician at the same time. It would not be opportune to try to consider this state of affairs as a characteristic of Aryan society, however much similarity these functionaries may have had with their counterparts among other nations speaking Indo-European languages, like the Druids in the Celtic regions. One should rather look for the reasons of the Indian situation in the social and economic structure of Ancient India itself. The brahman or religious specialist who for his subsistence often had to rely on the patronage of his clients had to assert his indispensability by offering that what people expected most of him: ceremonies securing safety and welfare as well as victory over enemies. Starving brahmans like Ajīgarta who would go to the length of selling their own son to be the victim in a human sacrifice (AitBr 7, 15) would certainly not object mixing their Vedic tradition with more popular devices. The brahman, in order to increase his indispensability, tended to emphasize the dangers by which human life was beset on all sides—a tendency very much alive in religious specialists from the primitive situation onwards, as has been demonstrated so brilliantly by Radin (*passim*; cf. p.17, 22, 24, 142). The greater the risks and dangers, the greater the need of those who knew the methods for averting and counteracting them; the more expensive also the ceremonies and the more intricated the spells and ritual details necessary to evoke the salutary powers. In this way the religious specialists made their services highly esteemed and their persons dreaded.[12] They capitalized on the innate feelings of fear for natural danger and suspicion of strange elements.[13]

The religious specialist also tended to emphasize his own particular power of inflicting damage on those who counteracted or neglected him in any way. Already the RV (10,117,6) calls off evil over the niggard who declines to give the brahman his due. AV 5,18,9 asserts that the brahmans pursue those who offend them with their *tapas* and their *manyu* "Fury" and pierce these offenders from a distance (Oldenberg, p. 146). Their curse is a missile conceived in the mind (Mbh 8,66,41; inserted stanzas 1123 and 1124; cf. Hopkins, p. 313). It is true that the practice of magic is frowned upon by Manu and other Dharma authorities, but the penances inflicted for it are comparatively light (Jacques, p. 273f.) and these authors perhaps deal with it as a possible source of danger for the rulers themselves and the stability of society; or they may envisage practisers among the common people who try to make a living by their arts without being sanctioned by public authority. They certainly did not mean to include those who practised for the weal of the community or who defended the interests of the brahman grade of society.[14] And the Manusmṛti itself argues (11, 31-34) that the brahman, who has no means to defend himself beside his knowledge of sacred texts, may use them as a weapon. In case of need, Manu emphasizes, the brahman should chastise evildoers by means of his personal potency (*vīryam*) which is stronger than the *vīryam* of the king (11,32); the next stanza states more precisely that one "should not hesitate to make use of the spells of the Atharvaveda, for Speech is the brahman's weapon, and by it the twice-born should kill his enemies. While the kṣatriya overcomes his difficulties by the valour of his arms and the vaiśya and śūdra by means of money, the brahman should (obtain this end) by recitation (of mantras) combined with libation (into the fire)" [10]. The importance of this passage has been duly understood by other theorists. Ṛgvidh. 1,2,3 is identical with Manu 11,34 while Ṣaṭkarmadīpikā 1, 5 copies Manu 11, 32. Of Western authors on the subject of Ancient Indian magic, Henry (p. 220) and Jacques (p. 273f.) devoted attention to it. An idea which is particularly insisted upon by Manu in these stanzas is that of *vīrya-*; this denotes the brahman's special store of supranormal power by which he performs miraculous deeds effecting welfare or destruction just as he chooses. The Mbh (1,71,9) calls Kāvya a possessor of *vīrya*-because he knows the *saṃjīvinīvidyā*, the ability to restore a dead person to life (cf. below,—ch 6.8). A person in the possession of such *vīrya*-is a *vīra*-, like Vasiṣṭha according to Mbh 1,224,28. It is significant that also those who were initiated in Left hand Tantric esoterism were called *vīra*-.[15]

As has been argued above, the brahmans emphasized their supernatural abilities in order to enhance the importance of their services to potential clients. Among these figure in the first place the kings and nobles and this implies that the magical rites advocated in the texts have very often been meant to be applied in the political sphere. The magician who acted for the ruler enabled that ruler by means of his functionary to execute supernatural functions in ruling his subjects and eliminating his enemies. This point deserves some attention.

5.5. *Application of māyā in politics*

It has been argued by earlier writers that there are connections between the figure of the ruler and the cosmical functions executed by Viṣṇu (Gonda, 1954, p. 164ff.). The BhPur adores Viṣṇu as the Protector of the varṇa system and ascribes its origin to an act of this god's māyā (see above, p—183). The SkPur (7, 1, 9, 38) also addresses Viṣṇu as *caturvarṇyasya prabhavaś caturvarṇyasya rakṣitā* "origin and protector of the four varṇa system" (Awasthi, p. 279). And, like the religious specialist, also the political ruler should imitate his divine example. In a Vedic environment this was Indra in the first place, but later Indra's role was largely taken over by Viṣṇu. Yet the Indra ideology left its traces. Indra kept his position, at least in theory, as "king of the gods", and in literary convention earthly rulers continued to be very frequently compared to him. The Mbh (1,57) relates the career of King Uparicara, alias Vasu, who acted as an earthly ruler on principles communicated to him by Indra himself. By conforming to such principles the king, so to say, performed an "Indravrata" (term by the present author) and this of course implies that he would, like Indra in days of yore, spare no efforts to smite those who stood against him without scruples (on Indra's unscrupulousness, see above p—13). And it did not matter if the king adhered to a "Viṣṇuvrata" instead.

With this in mind it will not surprise us to read in the MtPur (222, 2f.) that indrajāla or māyā is a necessary component of *rājanīti,* the science of politics. In most cases the magical methods and aims propounded in the Purāṇas will have been destined for application by the ruler (by means of his ritual functionary). In the ViDhPur, second khaṇḍa, which treats in detail the rights and duties of the king (*rāja-dharma-*) there is also a list of magical practices to be realized with the help of the recitation of the *mahāvyāhṛti* mantra (ViDh-Pur 2, 125, 1-14). The passage also occurs in the AgPur (260, 1-14) ; in both cases it falls under the heading of Yajur-vidhānam "The method of (magical application of) Yajurveda mantras." The mere fact that Yajurvidhānam has been put to the service of the king in the first place suggests that this will also have been the case with the Sāma-and Ṛgvidhānam discussed above. According to the last-mentioned passage the aims cherished by a sacrificer who embarks upon the *mahāvyā, hṛti* method include *śānti,* the winning of cattle, food or gold-attaining of the mastery over a village (for a local grandee), recovery from illness, killing of enemies or creating dissension between them, obtaining a son, driving the enemy from his home. The use of magic against political enemies is of course amply testified, beginning with the AV. The SVBr devotes at least one chapter (3, 6) to the subject, immediately after its treatment of the anointing ceremony of the king (*abhiṣecanam*). The mantras to be said on the occasion of that ceremony already contain a refrain *nainaṃ kṛtāni hiṃsanti tāny eva pratigacchanti* "things done do not harm him (the new king), they just return (to their deviser)", and the Skt commentary, to avoid all doubts, intimates, as we saw, that "things done" refers to *para-kṛtābhicārādiprayuktāni kṛtyādīni* "devices employed in black magic or other evil practices done by the adversaries, such as Kṛtyās." This shows how māyic performances distinctly operated in the consciousness of the rulers and their ideologues, the court priests. And the answer against possible attacks with the aid of such performances lies ready in SVBr 3, 6. The armament race (if we may use this gross anachronism) fought on the mantric plane entailed a challenge to the ingenuity of the ritual specialist, and without doubt an important, although risky, road to prestige.

An important passage on the subject is GautDh 2,2,17. It gives a short survey of magical practices serviceable to a ruler (the chapter 2, 2 deals with *rājadharma*). "In the central fire of the residence", the author lays down, "one should perform rites destined for welfare, viz. *śānti*, creating an auspicious day, a safe course, longevity, good auspices; as well as those rites which pertain to the creation of dissension, to winning over (a rival), to destructive magic, or to the ruin of the enemy" (11). Here the author makes a clear distinction between rites promoting the good of the own party, and those aiming at the harm of others. The Skt. commentary Mitākṣarā gives useful information on the nature of the rituals alluded to. What interests us here in the first place is that it explains "the creation of dissension" (*vidveṣaṇaṃ*) as *yenāsya śatruḥ prakṛtīnāṃ vidveṣyo bhavati*" (a rite) by which one's enemy becomes hated among his subjects." Divide and rule ! "Winning over" (*saṃvananam*) is a rite *yenāsya śatravo vaśyāḥ praṇipatanti* "by which one's enemies are subjugated and fall to one's feet" (this is perhaps a somewhat too radical interpretation by our commentator). "Destructive magic" is straightway commented upon as a device *yenāsya śatravo mriyante* "by which one's enemies are liquidated". The "ruin of the enemy" means *ṛddher abhāvaḥ... yenāsya śatravo vigataiśvaryā bhavanti* "the absence of prosperity... (a rite) by which the enemies are bereft of their sovereignty."

The rite of *śānti* "pacification" mentioned also in the above passage comprises a great variety of ceremonies executed very frequently in behalf of the ruler and his kingdom. That the execution of śānti rites is in the first place the king's concern is argued by BṛhSaṃh 45, 3 ; *nṛpaḥ śāntiṃ rāṣṭre prayuñjīta* "the king should perform a śānti rite in his kingdom." The context here is the warding off of the effects of evil omina (*utpāta-*, *nimitta*), but these are interconnected with the political realities.[16] The ViDhPur (2, 159,47) praises another kind of śānti rite (the *nīrājana-*) as "leading to wealth and fame, and to the destruction of the enemy; bringing about happiness, unsurpassable; to be performed with the utmost exertion by rulers for the sake of the kingdom, O Scion of the Bhṛgu race":

Dhanyā yaśasyā ripunāśanī ca
sukhāvahā śāntir anuttamā ca
kāryā nṛpai rāṣṭravivṛddhihetoḥ
sarvaprayatnena Bhṛgupravīra

In this stanza the accomplishment of śānti is associated also with the destruction of the enemy. We shall have occasion below (ch.6.9.) to return to the subject of the relation between śānti and abhicāra. As to the political application of abhicāra, we can once again refer to the KJ (ch. 10 trsl. p. 44) which asserts that the method by which a king is able to vanquish his foes is called the *abhicārika* method. The use of magical means in political strife can be attested from historical sources also. The Yaudheyas who began to extend their power in the course of the 2nd century A.D. in the N.W. of India seem to have designed themselves as "bearers of the mantra of victory" (*jayamantradharāḥ*) according to a clay seal found near Ludhiana (Majumdar,/Altekar, p. 30). We may assume that other dynasties will have made use of similar devices. Many of such mantras, combined with appeals to the gods, are found in the Purāṇas, especially in AgPur chs. 123-149, a section called Yuddhajayārṇava "Ocean of Victory in Battle". The same section includes other methods such as determining the enemy's unfavourable days by astrology. The Kathās. (9,6,94) refers to the sādhana of a Yakṣa in case of danger of war. Magic can also be employed by those who are sceptics themselves as a means of psychological warfare. As is well known, Kauṭilya's Arthaśāstra in ch. 14 discusses such methods as "Secret means to injure an enemy"; they look rather artificial. Also the ViDhPur (2,148 and 149) advises to try performances of indrajāla in an inimical country. In ch. 148 such feats, which include the artificial creation of omina, are summarized by the word *māyā*: in the next chapter by *indrajāla* or *māyājāla* (the latter term refers to the creation out of nothing of a complete army). But one should not overstress the importance of such devices; both the chapters 148 and 149 in ViDhPur 2 are very short and without doubt their function was meant to be marginal.[17] But less spectacular rites will have been practised frequently at courts and we find allusions to them also in Tantric texts. The MMK (III, p. 551ff.) describes a Yamāntakapaṭa which can be applied against the ruler's enemies.

The PST (24, 36) refers to magic executed by a specialist for a king who desires to overrun another country : *atha pararāṣṭra-jayeccho rājñaḥ kuryāt....* We can safely assume that also the Six Acts (see ch. 6) will have often been applied at courts, for the benefit of the rulers, and in their service. S (p. 188) warns that a sādhaka who embarks upon an abhicāra rite on a remote place should make sure that he is protected by a company of soldiers, lest "another king, having been informed of the situation by means of spies, would kill him" : *na cec cānyaḥ kṣitipatiś cārair jñātvā nihanty amum.* The passage suggests that the king himself is the sādhaka in this case. It may be remarked that the ritual environment of the Mahāmāyā fragment which ascribes its recitation to the Balinese nobleman himself "for warding off all diseases and calamities" (see above, p—153) may have its roots in an Indian custom. But in general, especially in the older period, the ruler will have left these matters to one or more religious specialists employed by him.

Such a specialist from the Vedic period onwards usually served as *purohita* or "court priest". Of course the purohita's functions were many-sided (see also above, p—231) but here we are interested only in his performance of magical rites.[18] He has his mythical counterparts; in the Mbh (1,71,5ff.) we are informed of the rivalry which existed between the two purohitas of the gods and the counter-gods, Bṛhaspati and Śukra. The background is the eternal strife between these two classes of divine beings—the mythical forerunner of all political clashes on earth. The Mitākṣarā commentary on the passage of the GautDh (2, 2, 17) discussed just above, after explaining the meaning of the rituals commended, deals with the question who is supposed to execute them : "Who (should perform these rites) ? The king. He becomes equal to an executor by the mere fact that he sponsors (the ceremony) by means of procuring the materials and other (facilities)". This wording implies that not the king, but the *purohita* is the actual performer of the ceremonies. A little before, the Sūtra (in 2,2,12) enjoined that the king should appoint a brahman as purohita, and perform the rituals according to that functionary's directions (*brāhmaṇaṃ ca purodadhīta...tatprasūtaḥ* (comm. : *tadanujñātaḥ*) *karmāṇi kurvīta*). The commentary on 2,2,17 records the opinion of another authority that "the purohita should perform the rites which lead to welfare himself, but leave the execution of the other rites (i.e. the abhicāra rites) to others" [12]. But in SVBr 3, 6 the purohita is clearly meant to execute the ritual directed against the enemies himself. The purohita is also the one who applied his force of brahman by saying the "political hymns" from the AV; compendia like the AVPar were destined for use by him. And the brahman might use his spiritual force also against the king, for example to force him into benevolent attitude which would induce him to take the brahman into his service or otherwise pay him favours (cf. AVPar 36, 26). There are several allusions to *rājavaśīkaraṇa* "subjugation of the king" in Tantric sources (see below,—ch.6.5.) and it is also in this light that one may perhaps interpret the fifth stanza of the Mahāmāyā fragment (above, p—146f.).

In any case a considerable number of brahmans must have found employment at the courts as performers of magic, in their quality of purohita or otherwise. Fick (p. 156) concludes from allusions in the Jātaka tales that brahmans who occupied themselves with such rites were for the greater part active at the royal court, and Jhavery (p. 232) argues that in the Middle Ages persons who were reputed to be able to perform such prodigies might reckon to be favourably received by the king. Such doctors even sometimes competed with each other in the royal presence. It is not necessary to pursue the subject further. The point is often only vaguely alluded to, as in LiPur 2,50,17 : *ātmano 'rtham nṛpasya vā* "for his own sake or for the king." LT (49, 42) says that one should always perform indrajāla practices "in the presence of royalty" (Gupta, p. 324). Magicians who visit the court to this end are sometimes mentioned in literature, for example Rājaśekhara's Karpūramañjarī (1,21ff.), Budhasvāmin's Bṛhatkathāślokasaṃgraha (19, 2ff.; the king's brother) or the YogV (Utpattiprakaraṇa, ch. 104, 26ff.).[19]

There is another aspect of political magic the importance of which is still more difficult to assess but which should be at least shortly mentioned here: its role in the relation between a ruler and his subjects. Malaviya (p. 47f.) calls attention to a place in the AitBr (3,19; adhyāya 13) which describes a supernatural device to be employed by the hotar priest in the course of his recitation in order to ensure for his employer, a member of the kṣatriya grade of society, that he will be able to vanquish the vaiśyas. To this end the hotar should interrupt the hymn recited by him by three intercalatory passages called nivids. As the hymn (*sūkta-*) symbolizes the vaiśya grade and the nivids the kṣatra, in this way the vaiśya grade is pierced and vanquished by the kṣatra grade. ŚatBr 6,4,4,13 mentions as the secret meaning of a certain ceremonial detail that the two lower grades of society are enclosed for subjection by the two upper grades, the brahmans and kṣatriyas.[20]

But the Janus face of the magical science can show also its other side. The passage from the AitBr referred to just above contains an additional regulation in which, by changing a detail in the recitation, the opposite effect is reached that the kṣatriya grade is pierced by the vaiśya grade. The Veda contains other references to abhicāra devices which may work themselves out against the employer if he for some reason incurred the wrath of the officiating priests. An instance from the Purāṇas is ViDhPur 2,125,8 (=AgPur 260,8), where it is suggested that a brahman may "make an image of the king consisting entirely of rice, and sacrifice it into the fire in a thousand portions; (in this way the king) will come under the power of his subjects":

Sarvavrīhimayīṃ kṛtvā rājñaḥ pratikṛtiṃ dvijaḥ
sahasraśas tu juhuyāt prajāvaśagato bhavet

We are left entirely in the dark as to who these "subjects" may be. Most probably the king in question is a political enemy and the ceremony in that case would be destined to evoke a revolt in his country. Only very seldom do we come across an allusion in a post-Vedic text to application of magic against the own king. The LiPur (2,50,48) gives a negative indication by warning that abhicāra rites may never be executed against the ruler of the own country ; a fool who would try to do this would destroy himself in the first place and his whole family also [13]. Statements like these suggest that as a rule the Hindu rulers managed to keep effective control of those who conducted the ceremonies for them. On the other side, there exists inscriptional evidence from the Indonesian empire of Śrīvijaya that persons who rebelled against the king tried to employ magic as a means of overthrowing him (see below,—ch.6.5.). The frequent allusions to persons who "desire a kingdom" (*rājyakāmāḥ*) in magical passages or in statements of rewards might perhaps have been meant to include similar cases. Exiled princes who had recourse to guerrilla tactics might have been in special need of some supernatural aid. The term *rājyakāma-* will presumably have in the first place been meant for those who could claim a legal right to succession. This is clearly the case in MMK I, p. 49 which ordains initiation in a "great maṇḍala" for "a prince of the blood (lit.: son of the king) anointed on the head" or the son of a kṣatriya (i.e. one of princely blood), or any other person who desires great status or a kingdom" [14]. The MMK contains a number of other rites destined for one who strives after royal dignity (e.g. I, p. 129ff.; II, p. 284ff.). In vol. I (p. 51) such a person is addressed during the Jayavijayābhiṣeka "Anointing to victory and conquest" with the words "Unassailable for all creatures, inconquerable for all beings, obtain Thou according to Thy wish the conquering force of all (Thy) mantras" (or, perhaps better: "...the ability to conquer all inimical mantras") [15]. The MMK, being a Buddhist text, basically conforms to the samc social pattern as some Purāṇas : it is destined as a handbook and guide for those who want to be of use to the ruler with a set of still more forceful rites annex background ideology. In the Middle Ages Hinduism, Buddhism, Jainism and Islam all vied with each other in producing wonder workers at the courts who all presented their own version of supernatural means. And if on some occasion another dynasty secured a throne (or an old one regained its position), there would be a specialist who provided the new king with a fresh cult (as an instance we mention the Devarāja cult in Cambodja installed by Hiraṇyadāma and Śivakaivalya for Jayavarman II) and thus sanction his position.[21] In cases like these great renown might await the ritual specialist; but he should always be a man of high intelligence and gifted by a strong driving force and belief in himself. Just like the king, he should always emphasize that his powers were serviceable to the good of the people. As we saw above, Vasiṣṭha (in RV 7, 104) already maintained that he was no black magician. In the Tantras expressions like *jagato hitāya* "for the good of the world" (e.g. PST 9, 43) are often found. For the Buddhist doctors, securing the hail of all beings was an integral part of their doctrinal equipment.[22] Of course, a reason for such statements in the Tantric texts may also be that their authors wanted to defend themselves against possible social disapproval.

5.6. *The magician's self-confidence*

In this section we shall examine the psychological basis which enabled the ritual specialist who claimed the possession of māyic powers to substantiate his claim. When reading the Mahāmāyā fragment (above, ch. 3.3.) one is struck by the tone of superior self-confidence, one might say even arrogance in modern eyes with which the poet expressed himself. In stanza 5, the ritual of attraction is said to result in the king arriving from afar and personally presenting his wealth to the performer of the rite; in the following stanzas he claims that fierce enemies are subjugated (8), beautiful ladies become his servants (9), mountains of enormous size are destroyed without effort (13), and thousands of evil omina of the most cruel kind are suppressed (15). Such utterances of seemingly arrogant self-confidence are rather common in texts of magic. In the course of time they must have become a convention—but a necessary one; without these assertions of the performer's power the rite would apparently lose much of its force. We can safely assume that such statements are motivated partly by the sheer want to advertize one's supernatural abilities as well as possible.[23] But the subject would not be exhausted by merely making this point.

An important feature in such expressions of confidence is that the goal strived after is stated by an author as having become reality in advance. The KauśS (20, 16) records that in the cadre of a fertility ritual during ploughing the owner of the soil should take up a handful from the ploughed field and upon a ritual question by his wife answer to her that he just took up welfare, vegetative power, offspring, cattle and food (cf. Caland, p. 53, n. 8, who refers to parallels). We find the same principle *mutatis mutandis* in AV 8, 8, 8, where the poet asserts that by means of the "net of Indra" he already catches all his enemies (Jacques, p. 249, wrongly refers to 8, 8, 4). In 8, 8, 10 the enemies are said to have been bound by the bonds of death. "Arrogance" shines us in the face when we read AV 4,36,9 : "those who excite my wrath with their talk of gibberish, like mosquitos an elephant; I consider them troublesome, just like small bats for a man" (16) (cf. Shende, p. 160). We find other examples in AV 3,2,2 *Agnir....amūmuhat* "Agni.... brought to delusion" and AV 4,36 in which the speaker boasts that the Piśācas flee from him like dogs from a lion. The infallibility of the procedure resorted to is often stated with emphasis. In AitBr 8, 28, the discussion on the ritual called "the Killer around Brahman" (*Brahmaṇaḥ parimaraḥ*) ends with the assertion that "even if the enemy possesses a head of stone, one still smites him quickly" (*api ha yady asyāśmamūrdhā dviṣan bhavati kṣipraṃ haivainaṃ stṛṇute*).

Post-Vedic texts, Hindu as well as Buddhist, retain this characteristic emphasis on the infallible results of the magical act. Statements like SM vol.I, p. 13 : *vīryānurūpaṃ karmānurūpaṃ cāvaśyam eva sidhyati* "in accordance with one's supranormal power and with the ritual performed, (the rite) necessarily succeeds" are quite common. One instance from the MMK (vol. II, p. 540); after a rite of love magic, "from that moment the woman comes, burned up (by love), even from a distance of a hundred yojanas" (*tatkṣaṇād dahyamānā strī āgacchati yojanaśatād api*). Hindu Tantras also abound in such remarks. Sometimes the authors seem to vie with each other in expressing themselves as strongly as possible—a counterpart to similar conventions in Kāvya literature. Remaining in the field of love magic, we may quote JT 187, 6 which asserts that "the hearts of all women become deluded by the spell, and their minds become devoted to the performer by merely obtaining the sight of him" :

Vidyāvimūḍhahṛdayāḥ sādhakanyastamānasāḥ
taddarśanena deveśi jāyante sarvayoṣitaḥ

The poet expresses himself even more elaborately in JT 17,29 ff. Another very eloquent passage is PST 9,23-27 which in all possible ways tries to describe the overwhelming emotion created within the victims : "Young women from the classes of the gods, demons, perfects, yakṣas, vidyādharas, gandharvas, serpents and heavenly singers, submit to a wink of his eyes (st. 27); by the urge of their passion they have allowed their ornaments to go out of order, and the mass of their hair to be deprived of the headdress of fine cloth; their limbs waver with the wavering caused by their unbearable feelings of love, and quiver with scorching pain; their thighs breasts and shoulders are hung about with the pearls of drops of sweat produced by their formidable inner heat; their bodies are pressed by the jars of their high and well-developed breasts which rise massively from the creeper-like slenderness of their limbs set with erect-standing hairs; the kicks of their feet are unstable because their lotus feet tremble, exhausted with the exhaustion following the overall tremor caused by the load of their longing ; they have been cleft asunder by the direct hits of the arrows of the God of love; their figures are submerged in the ocean of passion; their lower lips undulate because of the depths of their sighs; their eyes are afflicted by the full load of their tears ; with both arms they offer the gesture of submission (*añjali-*) against their foreheads; their eyes are like those of young deer ; they are intent upon accomplishing all things desired" [17]. It might be objected that the author's intentions may be different here from those expressed in, say, the AV, because they are embedded within a context of Tantric mysticism; but this does not seem to make any difference to the point discussed on these pages. In our view the self-confidence of this Tantric performer, deliberately strengthened by means of the literary prolixity as an additional device, can be legitimately placed in the same perspective as that of the Vedic practiser.

One could quote many instances from the magical tracts. In the Ṣaṭkarmadīpikā (S) its author, when discussing rites which accomplish śānti, says on p. 200 (he cites the Sanatkumārasaṃhitā) : "one should assign the threefold mantra on one's crest, forehead and heart; and health for all creatures spontaneously arrives at his wish" [18]. Very frequently a certain mantra is recommended by saying that the mere knowledge of it is able to afford the possessor all kinds of results, as in S, p. 201 : *yena vijñānamātreṇa jāyante sarvasiddhayaḥ*. The same text states on p. 234 that a goddess (accidentally called Mahāmāyā) "grants her results to the sādhaka; by merely meditating on her (he) might immediately immobilize the threefold world" [19]. Frequent are also statements like that of the Siddhanāgārjunakakṣapuṭa (N), 2,12 *vaśaṃ nayati rājānam anyalokeṣu kā kathā* "one subjugates even a king, let alone other people"; or of the PST (24, 39) : *sendrasurāsurarakṣoyakṣān api jayati kā kathā manuje* "one vanquishes even the gods, Indra included, the counter-gods, the rākṣasas and the yakṣas, let alone a human being." Evidently we are here on the same ground as in the Mahāmāyā fragment.

It is unnecessary to present further instances from these texts. One could find them almost on every page. Although being thus a quite conventional element of these authors' style and method of presentation, yet they are never entirely meaningless. They serve to express that an attitude of self-assurance should be a second nature to the magical performer, no matter if he is an ordinary magician or a Tantric adept who strives after perfection by unconventional methods.[24] Moreover, in this case also there is a structural likeness between the attitudes of magicians and priests. Both are naturally inclined to present their rituals and the mysteries they possess as effectively as possible. This might be shown also by means of a phenomenon which is in our opinion closely related to the present subject: the very frequent occurrence of the word *sarva-* "all", "complete in descriptions of the value of the ceremonies presented or in the statements of the rewards that await the sponsors.

Some examples of expressions with *sarva* from the MMK: in vol. I, ch. 2, p. 26, a mantra is said to be *sarvadurgatinivāraṇaṃ sarvaśāntikaraṃ sarvakarmakaraṃ kṣemaṃ nirvāṇaprāpaṇam* "averting all evil course, producing complete pacification, realizing all activity, effectuating tranquillity and the gain of Nirvāṇa." On p. 29, the bīja *hūṃ* when said to the accompaniment of the Mahāśūlamudrā is described as *sarvakarmakaraḥ sarvānarthanivāraṇaṃ sarvabhūtavaśaṅkaraḥ* "performing all activities, averting all poverty, subjugating all creatures." On p. 153, in the description of Mahākrodha, a mantra deity of terrible figure and a swine's head, the following expressions occur : *sarvavighnavināśārtham... nirghṛṇaḥ sarvavighneṣu..sarvavighnopahārikaḥ... sādhakaḥ sarvamantrāṇām* "in order to destroy all obstructions.... relentless to all obstructions ..the remover of all obstructions.. the master of all mantras..". In Vol. II, p. 322, the mantra *Oṃ vākyeda namaḥ* is advertized as follows : "unconquerable by all creatures; anointed by the whole world;[25] impregnable for all creatures; purifying the road of existence; causing the dharmas of the Buddhas to be attained ; averting all depravities ; rejoiced in by all the Buddhas; realizing all welfare; most exalted among all mantras in the teachings of Mañjuśrī"[20].

In the AgPur (302, 6), in a chapter dealing with incantation, Kāma is addressed with the following mantra: "*Oṃ hrīṃ, oṃ* honour to Kāma the Benevolent One for all mankind, the Deluder of all mankind, the Flaming One; render render the hearts of all mankind devoted to my Self, *oṃ*" [21]. The text then continues saying that by muttering this mantra (while performing the correct ceremony) a performer will subjugate "the entire world" (*sakalaṃ jagat*). In SST 1, 12, 7 the person who is in the possession of the Tārāyoga, a procedure styled, in the usual phrase of this author, "secret and most secret", is a "lord of all, and omnipresent; accomplished in all mantras; a knower of the meaning of all Tantras; accomplished in all Tantras" [22]. He who performs this yoga in the correct method should not maintain any doubts that he will reach perfection by it (st. 9). The Pañcabrahma Up. among other things describes the mystical natures of the four Vedas and their effects. The Ṛgveda "grants the result of all desires", *sarvābhīṣṭaphalapradam* (st. 6); the Yajurveda "destroys the floods of all sins", *sarvāghaughavināśanam* (8); it "allays all evil appearances" and "grants the result consisting in all dominion" (*sarvaduṣṭapraśamanaṃ sarvaiśvaryaphalapradam*, 9). The Sāmaveda "offers all domestic happiness for man; it grants the results of all activities" *sarvasaubhāgyadaṃ nṛṇāṃ sarvakarmaphalapradam* (13). The Atharvaveda among other proficiencies "is the medicine for all sorrow and illness "while it "bears all potencies" (*sarvādhivyādhibheṣajam....sarvaśaktidhṛk*, 17).

Thus it appears that the inclusion of epithets beginning with *sarva* is a convention in the laudatory passages of the texts which describe mantras and their use, or which praise magically powerful gods and entities. To such passages attach themselves the more simple kind of hymns to the gods. The Balinese priests who from the Middle Ages onwards were closed off from the Sanskrit tradition of India nevertheless (or perhaps: in consequence thereof) made lavish use of this phenomenon in the more recent hymns of their own making. In the Introduction to Stuti & Stava (p. 12) it has been noted as one of the chief characteristics of Archipelago Sanskrit—that is, the Sanskrit of the hymns composed by the priests without possessing a knowledge of Sanskrit grammatical construction--that "there is a striking frequency of pādas beginning with the word *sarva*-". Epithets like *sarvapāpavināśanam* "destroying all evil", *sarva*-

duṣṭanivāraṇam"averting all depravity", or *sarvajagatpratiṣṭhānam* "supporting the entire world" are of frequent occurrence. The hymn No. 040, directed to the Element of Space (Ākāśa) considered identical with Śiva, is a good example of this kind of poetry in pseudo-Sanskrit. In its sixteen stanzas the epithets beginning with *sarva* occur not less than sixteen times. In No. 148, Dvijendrastava, directed to Brahmā and consisting of eleven stanzas, such expressions recur ten times. No. 642, Śambhustava, addressed to the god of the North-East in the Balinese Śivaite pantheon, in its seven stanzas contains eight expressions beginning with *sarva-*. No doubt this kind of literature would be tedious to read for those who consider themselves secularized and rationally thinking people; but they were without doubt regarded as very effective by their authors and reciters in the course of the ritual.

Such expressions of confidence are thus common to both priests and magicians. It may be propounded that for the magician his characteristic utterances of "arrogance" should be interpreted as the counterpart of the idea of *śraddhā* "confidence" which for Hindu theorists writing in Sanskrit is a necessary preparatory stage for anyone who desires to engage upon a ritual act or a course of yoga.[26] Gonda, Savayajñas (p. 286) circumscribes *śraddhā* as "an active and confirmative attitude towards religious acts including the confidence in their transcendental effects." He refers to the Sanskrit commentator Devala who paraphrases *śraddhā* with *pratyayo dharmakāryeṣu* "confidence in the (effectiveness of) the works of dharma" and who adds that for a person who lacks this confidence there is no motivation to enter upon these activities. This same attitude of confidence is, however, postulated by the author of the Ṛgvidh. (1,1,4) as a condition for the success of the magical rites described by him. "The ancient sages obtained insight in...ritual activities granting various results and connected with pacification of evil and promotion of welfare; and also in the perfections based upon asceticism ; (all this is within the reach) of him who performs the rites with a confident mind" [23].

The importance of self-confidence for him who strives after the realization of supernatural acts has been duly stressed by Jhavery (p. 12f). This author distinguishes the following principal conditions as a "triple key" for "Attainment" (doubt less his translation of the word *siddhi*); 1. An intense desire for the goal strived after; 2. An earnest and confident expectation that it will come to pass; 3. The persistent concentration of the will towards it. On p. 16 he considers Desire and Will as the two poles in the performer's mind which cause his "mentative energy" to succeed. They enable him to execute acts of magic which are white as well as black. Webster (p. 79ff.) discusses the importance of "imperative willing" as a condition for success in magic in primitive societies. Such will-power, when combined with an intense concentration of the mind upon the result wished for, creates "the faith that moves mountains" (Webster). The mere act of such "thinking" can sometimes suffice to create all kinds of afflictions for a victim, even his death.[27]

When one realizes that the state of the performer's mind (*manas*) is thus of paramount importance during the execution of a ritual, no matter if this ritual is in our eyes "magical" or not in its objective and method, it is easier to understand that remarkable stanza 5 of the hymn Stuti & Stava No. 330 called Saṃkṣiptapūjā "Concise worship". This śloka, which has apparently no direct connexion with the preceding part of the hymn, states that "Mind is the perfume, Mind is the flower (variant; the unhusked grain, *akṣatam*), Mind is the incense, Mind is the ritual act; one should offer the pure organ of thought which consists of Mind to Thee, Great Lord":

Mano gandhaṃ manaḥ puṣpaṃ mano dhūpaṃ manaḥ kriyā
śuddhacittaṃ manomayaṃ dadyāt tvayi mahāprabho

The fact that this stanza occurs in a context of pūjā, worship to a deity, not in the least invalidates the hypothesis that "mind" is considered here an important source of power able to effect the same results, or even more, as external ritual. It is scarcely necessary to repeat that Tantric and other texts often attach great value to the execution of "mental worship" (*mānasapūjā*) which is sometimes said far to exceed in effectivity the external worship with lamps, flowers, grains and other articles. The subject still awaits an independent study.[28] Here again, we observe a certain parallelism between the spheres of the "priest" and of the "magician".

But there is more. The magician acts as god. He enfolds a creation of his own. He might indeed boast of changing a rope into a snake.[29] He displays his powers, and as it were plays with objects and creatures; his is a "playful" existence (cf. PST 18,53 *krīḍed devavan mānuṣeṣu*). In the Mahāmāyā fragment (stanza 13) the sādhaka's activity is also described as a play (*sādhakalīlayā*). This word *līlā* is also typical of the divine activity by which the entire creation is made to appear, continue and be destroyed again at the end. The magician's magic is divine in origin; his actions are divine actions. His rage is like God's rage, and by it he can deal with his subjects just as God was accused by Draupadī in the Epic to deal with His creatures (above, p.—16). In a certain way the three main aspects of ritual activity—respectively resulting in pacification (*śānti*), acquisition (*puṣṭi*) and affliction (by *abhicāra*) can be compared to the three main characteristics of divine activity in the world: creation, preservation and destruction. By means of śānti one creates the presuppositions for a safe existence in this world; puṣṭi secures all kinds of material prosperity implying avoidance of stagnation; abhicāra is the road to destruction inflicted upon the adversary.

In this way also the magician should assume a cosmical, at least a divine, consciousness. He rides out against the enemy in a divine chariot (AV 8, 8,22). He identifies himself with the Goddess and robs the enemies of their insight (PST 14, 79 : *ātmānam Āryāṃ pratipadya ..muṣṇāti ca bodham eṣām*). Just like a priest may meditate in the cadre of a pūjā on the disc and conch of Viṣṇu as being in his own hands (KJ ch. 69 ; trsl. p. 199f.), a magician who performs "attraction" may imagine himself as bearing the suitable divine attributes, noose and elephant-hook (N, p. 296). While executing his ritual he may become Narasiṃha (PST 24, 28) or Kālī (SST 3, 15,63) or Śiva (SST 3, 18, 21). In the last cases the identification with the divine even has become a characteristic of the Tantric adept's entire existence. Such a status involves that the adept assumes the divine way of life, a privilege expressed sometimes in the SM, e.g. in No. 98: "after identification with the Lady, one may act as one pleases" (p. 206 *bhagavatyahaṃkāreṇa yatheṣṭaṃ vihared iti*); or in No. 134; *devatāyogena vihartavyam* "one should behave oneself according to the divine code", or "one should live in communion with the deity." SM, No. 139 contains the words *tadyogenaiva yathāsukhaṃ viharet* "by communion with Him one may live as one pleases." In No. 209—

and on other places—there is a variation on this motif : *kṣaṇena prāpyate bodhiḥ kiṃ punar anyāḥ siddhayaḥ* "within a moment spiritual illumination is reached, let alone the other accomplishments." Other texts contain similar expressions. We have already referred to PST 18,53 *krīḍed devavan mānuṣeṣu.* (p. 420) says. . *etāṃ vidyāṃ japed yadi/sarvasiddhiparipräptir devavad vihared bhuvi* "if one recites this formula, one obtains all accomplishments and abides on earth like a god." Other places, instead of "abiding" or "dwelling" emphasize the adept's freedom of movement while he lives like a god : he becomes a *kāmacārin* (GarPur 180,/1 *kāmavad vicaren mahīm*; 194, 21f.; already Ṛgvidh. 3,41,5 *siddho vāpi caren mahīm*).[30] As to the magician, it is true that he sometimes draws his self-confidence from an association with the demons (e.g. AV 7,38, 2); and the chief characteristic of the demoniac being is just its relentless conceit, its overstressed self-confidence (Zimmer, p. 154). On other cases the Tantric performer tries to master them and to make them his "familiars". Such a course of action may lead him straightway to fabulous mundane accomplishments. But even then he needs not to have given up his hope for release. He combines within himself both the magician and the mystic. He claims divine status and impregnability. This conviction has been expressed by a poet in a stanza of Indian provenance included in Stuti & Stava (No. 676, 17) :

Ahaṃ Śivamayo bhūtvā vicarāmi mahītale
Haradeva cara kṣipraṃ śatrūn hatvā samatsarān

"Having become identical with Śiva, I roam about over this world; God Hara, quickly proceed killing my foes and those who envy me."

6. THE SIX ACTS

6.1. *Introductory remarks*

In the present chapter we shall try to deal in some detail with a comparatively neglected part of Tantric achievement. In the above discussion of the Mahāmāyā fragment it has been said that this fragment contains some Skt. terms which denote standard acts of magic, included in what are commonly called the Six Acts (above, p. 153). The first and most important part of the fragment (st. 1-17) contains five of these terms: *ākarṣaṇa-* "attraction", *vaśikaraṇa-* "subjugation", *stambhana-* "immobilization", *uccāṭana-* "eradication" and *prāyaścitta-* "pacification". The only element of the usual group of six omitted in these lines is *māraṇa-* "liquidation". In the closing stanzas (18-21) all the Six Acts occur: *vaśyakarman, māraṇam,* and *vidveṣaḥ* in 18 (if the text has been emended correctly); *uccāṭanam, stambhanam* and *ākarṣaṇam* or *śāntiḥ* (text: *yaśo'rthinaḥ*) in 19. It seems that the authors of both parts of the Mahāmāyā fragment were acquainted with the theory of the Six Acts, but that the poet of the first part deliberately omitted the most far-reaching of them, *māraṇa* - a practice which has its parallels (see below, ch.6.8.). In the following pages we shall try to comment on these terms, first by concentrating upon the Six Acts as a group and afterwards by studying each of them separately, at the same time paying attention to minor varieties. In keeping with the nature of this book, the emphasis will also in this chapter be on aims rather than on methods.

The term. Something may be said first on the Skt. expression *ṣaṭ karmāṇi* "Six Acts" (condensed hereafter into Ṣaṭkarman). In the preceding chapter it has been argued that the root *kṛ-* "to do, make" and its derivations are polyvalent. They can denote all kind of ritual actions including those which we would call magical. The word karman conforms to this tendency. It denotes a "ritual work" but also a "magical act". In its broadest sense it encompasses all human activity conceived as a natural force which shapes man's present life and future destiny. Besides, human deeds can be seen as a replica on a minor scale of divine work performed by the gods. Without divine activity life on earth would be unable to maintain itself (BhGītā 3, 22-24). But this same cosmic action which permeates the world and human life is the cause of the cosmic delusion which holds all creatures within its grip. The Harivaṃśa (78,32 Critical Note line 12; text, see Skt. note 12 on ch.1) says that on the destined time the karman of all becomes visible, and ascribes this to the *māyā* which is incomprehensible even to the gods. Moreover, the karman is said to be the cause for the delusion of the world.

Also the magician in his small perspective treads the track of this cosmic karman. For example, just as according to the description of the Mbh (12,271,33ff.) this karman works by means of Time in distributing states of existence characterized by colours, so in the Mahāmāyā fragment the practiser (*sādhaka*) acts by means of the Māyā and her colours in conferring the state desired by him upon the victim. The ambivalent sense contained in the idea of karman is reflected by the different meanings which are possible for the term *ṣaṭ karmāṇi*. The PD gives the following three meanings under the heading *ṣaṭkarman*:

1. The six occupations permitted for a brahman: studying and teaching sacred literature (*adhyayanam, adhyāpanam*); sacrificing for himself or for others (*yajanam, yājanam*); presenting or receiving gifts (*dānam, pratigrahaḥ*).

2. The Six Acts of magic discussed here, for which PD refers to the dictionary Śabdakalpadruma.

3. The six methods of purification in Yoga: *dhautī, vastī, netī, trāṭakam, naulikam, kapālabhātī* (cf. Woodroffe, p.127).

It should be noted in addition that the six Indriyas or sense organs are all said to possess their own activity (*karman*), for instance in the KCT (2,83). And it may be useful to add that there are six chief sinful acts (Woodroffe, p.141). On the other side it must be remarked that the "magical acts" do not necessarily group themselves into six. In Ceylon, for instance, there is a group of eight (Gooneratne). The Six Acts are sometimes described within the cadre of a wider spectrum of siddhis or ritual aims (e.g., in SST 2,34,17).

Place in the ritual. It has been remarked above (p.95) that all karman in the ritual sense was divided into three kinds: *śānti-* "pacification", puṣṭi- "welfare" or "acquisition", and *abhicāra-* "harming others." This perspective is broad enough to comprise all ritual activity, black magic included, within its scope. Another subdivision of the ritual popular in the texts is that of *nitya-* "regular", *naimittika-*"occasional" (ceremonies performed on the occasion of certain occurrences, usually a calamity or evil omen), and *kāmya-*"facultative", that is: rituals performed by or on behalf of someone who cherishes a certain objective. Within this distinction the Six Acts fall under *kāmya-*, because they are never seen as obligatory but always executed for the realization of certain aims cherished by an individual or a community.[1] The specialist who has been initiated into the correct mantras and the right method of adoring and applying them, obtains control over the powers which are able to grant him these objectives. It is unclear in how far the authors pay lip-service to orthodoxy when they warn their readers that kāmya rituals do not lead their performers to salvation after death. Thus, it is remarked in T (p. 354) that "there is no other world (as a recompense) for those who execute kāmya rituals; their result merely consists of the success of their particular ritual and nothing else, for there is never a twofold result of a single method; therefore . . . one should worship a deity without cherishing desire" [1]. Similar remarks are made by the author of the MMD (25, 74ff.) : Vedic sacrifice and pure devotion is to be preferred above the performance of kāmya ritual. The latter is the characteristic business of those who are still bound to the objects of the senses. The result obtained by them does not exceed the particular function of the ritual performed (*tāvanmātra-*). Those who worship God without desire will see all their wishes come true. A wise man should strive after knowledge of the Ātman (81). It is none other than the Supreme Ātman, the Lord, Who, manifesting Himself in the guise of various deities, grants to mankind the fulfilment of its desires (102). Pious utterances like these, however, do not keep the authors from setting forth the details of the magical science in all prolixity.

An act of magic is often performed in the course of a greater ritual; it is then constituted by way of some modification of or addition to a certain phase in that ritual, most often near to the end. The mechanism is indicated in its main outline by passages like Mt Pur 93,140: "acts like subjugation or incantation, and also like eradication and so on; such facultative acts can be performed after one has gone through the ritual of sacrifice to the Nine Planets" [2]. In section 6.3. we shall revert to these significant changes in the details of the ritual.

The nature of the Six Acts

The chief feature which distinguishes the Six Acts from what is usually understood by the term magic is that they are a theoretical body of doctrine found in Tantric literature and in monographs on the subject strongly influenced by that literature. This doctrine is the result of deliberate choices made by the authors from a rich variety of magical traditions with their aims as handed down in older texts and doubtless also in oral lore. This eclectic character of the Ṣaṭkarman theory also appears from the mutual differences between the descriptions devoted to this theory. It is not entirely clear which were the motives that led to the incorporation of the Six Acts (and other elements of the magical science) into Tantric books. The reason may partly be that those who sought their individual salvation by means of the methods described in the Tantras at the same time were active as magicians and performers of supranormal feats. On the other hand, the way in which some authors describe the subject creates the impression that they deal with it as an object of meditation only without real performance of the Acts being intended. A good instance is furnished by the Mahāmāyā fragment, and a similar position is suggested by KCT (4,129) and SST (2,15, 12ff.). In the latter place, knowledge of some of the Six Acts as well as the possession of *jñāna* and *vijñāna* are said to be prerequisites for an adept in the *kula* practices. In cases like these, the concentration on feats of magic is probably meant to constitute a necessary stage in the yogin's path towards ultimate release by personal accomplishment. One of the germs of such a theory may be the Prajñāpāramitā view that the salutary activity of a Bodhisattva is nothing else than an act of *indrajāla* (Conze, p. 166f.). Within the same sphere lies the doctrine of purification by a full realization of the nature of evil.[2] In any case a description of the Ṣaṭkarman theory can be presented without the question of the real or imaginary execution of the Acts being decided upon.

In the sections 6.4-6.9 we shall try to discuss the contents, limits and, above all, the objectives of the *ṣaṭ karmāṇi* in the relevant texts. A closer study soon reveals that it is extremely difficult to limit them off against each other. Sometimes two or three of the Acts overlap to a considerable degree. Some aims, for instance the conquering of enemies, are discussed by different texts under different headings. In our treatment the Indian way of presenting the subject-matter will be followed in principle, although sometimes rationalized by creating compartments which do not exist in the texts themselves. The sequence in which the Acts will be handled is not the classical one, but has been inspired by the Mahāmāyā fragment. It will be clear that the systematization of the science of magic into the mould of the Six Acts does not render justice to the bewildering diversity of the subject ; but it would be difficult to devise a pattern which does. In this study the construction of such a pattern is not attempted. It will only be attempted to give an impression what the texts themselves understand by the technical terms they use. It will also be tried, by including some other instances from Skt. literature, to sketch the practice of the feats in question outside the specialized Ṣaṭkarman environment.

Another warning is neccssary from the outset : this study is on aims, not on methods. We do not intend to give a systematic description of the procedures. This would have been impossible for the present author on account of his mere ignorance of the details of Indian herb lore and other practical features of the system. Besides, the indications in the texts are not always as detailed and unequivocal as one might wish. This means that we will restrict ourselves in the sections mentioned to circumscribe the terminology ; to give instances from literature ; and to discuss the objectives. Only occasionally a method will be described by way of illustration. It will also appear that the Ṣaṭkarman system is not merely a group of "cruel acts", six or more particular feats of magic, but that it comprises the whole range of human effort and objectives as reflected in the ritual. This will also be illustrated from the section 6.3 where instances will be discussed of the occupation of complete sets of alternatives by the system, like in Nos. A 3 A 4 B 4 C 3 and so on.

The sources. The discussion of Ṣaṭkarman is one of the seven characteristics of the Āgamic tradition according to the Vārāhī Tantra (quoted by Jhavery, p.51) : "creation and dissolution of the world, the worship of the gods, the mastering of them all and the preliminary worship, the mastery of the Six Acts, and the fourfold practice of meditation; the wise teach that the Āgama possesses these seven characteristics" [3]. The Six Acts are indeed often dealt with or alluded to by the Tantric texts. It is necessary here succinctly to enumerate the main sources utilized for the following pages.

Buddhist (for particulars we refer to the Bibliography): MMK, esp. ch. 55 (vol.III, p.668-721); GST (incidentally); HT; KCT; SM.

Jaina: BPK, esp. ch. 3.

Hindu Purāṇas and Tantras: AgPur; MtPur (esp. ch.93); JT; PST; SST.

Tantric compilations: MMD (esp. ch. 25); T (a seventeenth-century compilation from Mithilā by Narasiṃha; p.352ff.); BMR; TSS (a work hailing from Kerala and compiled by the 16th century scholar Nārāyaṇa. It appears that the relevant chapters in the AgPur are for the greater part no more than a condensation of the subject-matter found in the TSS).

Very important for our purpose are a number of magical tracts which have been edited together in a volume called Indrajālavidyāsaṃgraha "Compendium of the Magical Science" (ed. J. Vidyasagar's Sons, Calcutta 1915). A few of them may be of a quite recent date, although one has been ascribed to the great Siddha Nāgārjuna who lived in or about the seventh century A.D. Their names are as follows:

1. Indrajālaśāstram or Indrajālam, Siddhikhaṇḍam (Is). This small opening work seems entirely to consist of quotations from other sources; in its present awkward form its consultation seems useless. On p.12 it contains the colophon *iti Kālanāthaviracite Indrajāle prathamo' dhyāyaḥ* : on p.13 a colophon runs *iti Indrajālatantre tṛtīya upadeśaḥ*; the tract ends on p.21 with *iti Śivoktam Indrajālam*.

2. Kāmaratnam by Nāgabhaṭṭa (K). It occupies pages 22-131 in the Indrajālavidyāsaṃgraha. Presumably this work hails from Assam; an Assamese version has been edited by Pandit Hemchandra Goswami Tattvabhusan, Shillong 1928 (KA). In his Preface the editor mentions an edition of the Sanskrit Kāmaratna by B.M. Bose, Calcutta, Bengali Era 1319. We were unable to consult it. About the Assamese Kāmaratna

its editor informs us (Preface, p.III) that it was in the possession of the Na-Gosain family in the North of Gauhati. This family traditionally produced the gurus of the Assamese rājās. The book had always been kept in secrecy; only one ms. of it existed. Its age was estimated by the editor to be at least 300 years.

3. Dattātreya Tantram (D), comprising pages 132-179 in the Indrajālavidyāsaṃgraha. This text may be the oldest of the collection; it appears to be the least systematized. It has been edited also by B.M. Pandey, Benares Saṁvat 2019 (Chr. era, 1962-63). The work is anonymous.

4. Ṣaṭkarmadīpikā (S) (pp.179-264). The author calls himself Śrīkṛṣṇavidyāvāgīśabhaṭṭācārya in stanza 1. The work is a systematical compilation probably of rather recent date. The author usually takes care to mention his sources.

5. Siddhanāgārjunakakṣapuṭam (N) (pp.264-390). This is the largest text of the collection. It contains a wealth of information especially on illusionism, mastery of divine beings and other siddhis.

While making use of these works it is necessary to keep in mind that their editions in the Indrajālavidyāsaṃgraha are far from perfect: uncritical, without adequate numbering of stanzas, without introductory comment by the editors, and without any warning that on some places the material is incomplete, perhaps because of deliberate omission by the editors. Incompleteness of D, for instance, immediately appears from a comparison with the Benares edition of this text. We are fully aware that on all these points we were scarcely or not at all able to improve upon the Vidyasagar edition. Besides, the position of these tracts in relation to their Tantric sources and to each other remains unclear. Usually we could not trace the quotations given by the texts with or without mention of their sources. It also appears that the tracts of the collection often have considerable passages in common (this is especially the case between K and N, where K is in our opinion probably the borrower).

It thus appears that we have in the main relied upon Hindu compilations and monographs on the subject, which in general tend to be of a comparatively recent date. Other Tantras not consulted might contain much additional material. Many of them certainly discuss the subject. For instance, D (1,4) refers in general to the Āgamas, the Purāṇas and even the Veda; in the next stanza (1,5) it mentions by name the Uḍḍīśa, Merutantra, Kālacaṇḍeśvara (Ben.ed. Kālīcaṇḍīśvara), Rādhātantra, Tārātantra, Amṛteśvaratantra. S (1,3) refers as sources to the following Tantras : Unmattabhairavī, Pheṭkārī, Ḍāmara, Mālinī, Kālottara, Siddhayogīśvarī, Yoginījāla, and Saṃvara. On other pages, this text also quotes the Viśuddheśvara (191), Śāradā (tilaka) (195), Tantrarāja (202), Vārāhī (215,218) and other Tantras ; besides, the "Ātharvaṇa" (201,226). N(p. 265) mentions a great number of sources: Śāmbhava, Yāmalaśāstra, Maula, Kauleya, Ḍāmara, Svacchanda, Kākula (?) Śauca, Rājatantra (=Tantrarāja ?), Mṛteśvara (=Amṛteśvara?), Uḍḍīśa, Vātula, Ucchiṣṭa, Siddhīśavara, Kiṅkinī, Meru, Kālacaṇḍeśvara, Śākinī, Ḍākinī, Raudra, Śālya, Haramekhalaka, Gāruḍa and other Tantras; and also to Ātharvaṇamahāveda as well as to the opinions of the Cārvākas and what has been handed down by mouth (*vaktrād vaktreṇa yac chrutam*). In all these sources we may expect to find particulars about Ṣaṭkarman also. In addition, Kane, 1962 (p.1051) in his discussion of Ṣaṭkarman refers to Vaiṣṇava Tantras like the Gautamīya; and on p.1070 to the Śāradātilaka (23,122ff.)[3]. T again mentions the Pheṭkāriṇī Tantra. The Tantrasāra has been quoted by us only once on the authority of Goldstücker; the Siddhikhaṇḍa by Pārvatīputra Nityanātha on that of Weber. In the Buddhist tradition there are many Vajrayāna works not consulted or inaccessible (cf. the list compiled by B. Bhattacharya in the Introduction to SM, p. LXXXIX-CXXII). Jhavery (p.290f.) mentions a number of other Jain Mantrakalpas beside the BPK. This rapid survey suffices to demonstrate that the sources are rich and varied and that the following discussion is necessarily incomplete. Besides, it runs the risk of telescoping or otherwise misrepresenting the facts. Needless to say for anyone who is acquainted with the nature of Indian literary tradition that to aim at the presentation of anything like a survey of historical development is a very dangerous thing; in general, we have refrained from trying to do this.

6.2. *Classification of the Six Acts*

In trying to classify the terms which commonly denote the Six Acts we have distinguished four types of lists. By "list" is understood an enumeration of names of six or more magical actions which may or may not have been labelled by the term Ṣaṭkarman (or *ṣaṭ karmāṇi*). This distinction into types has not been made in order to assess their historical sequence, nor even for tracing some structural differences, but only for convenience in ordering the mass of material and for the sake of showing the floating character of the tradition.

For reasons of space the technical terms for those magical actions which usually or often come under the head of *ṣaṭkarman* have sometimes been rendered in the following pages by means of a number code :

Term in Sanskrit	Translation	Number
śāntiḥ	Pacification	1
vaśīkaraṇam	Subjugation	2
stambhanam	Immobilization	3
vidveṣaṇam	Causing dissension	4
uccāṭanam	Eradication	5
māraṇam	Liquidation	6
mohanam	Delusion	7
ākarṣaṇam	Attraction	8
puṣṭiḥ	Acquisition	9

There are other terms also, but their occurrence is much less frequent. The nine terms given above have sometimes been circumscribed in the texts by variant formations or synonyms. For these the reader is referred to the treatment of the act concerned.

Type 1 is the most easily recognizable. It consists of a standard list of the Six Acts in a fixed sequence. Some instances :

1.1. PD quotes from the Śabdakalpadruma, a Skt dictionary which in its turn refers to the Śāradātilaka (Jacques, p.266), presumably the passage 13,122ff. referred to also by Kane, 1962, p.1070. This list of what PD calls the "Sechs Zauberkunste" (Six Magical Arts) is as follows:

1. *śānti*. 2. *vaśya*. 3. *stambhana*. 4. (*vi*) *dveṣa*. 5. *uccāṭana*. 6. *māraṇa*.

1.2. Another representant of this type hails from the

Bengal Viśvakośa, a dictionary quoted by B. Bhattacharya p. LXXXVIf. He lists the following terms : 1. *śānti*. 2. *vaśikaraṇa*. 3. *stambhana*. 4. *vidveṣaṇa*. 5. *uccāṭana*. 6. *māraṇa*. He calls them the "six rites" and further on, incorrectly, the "six cruel rites of Tantrism."

1.3.K (p. 22) cites the following stanza in which the same acts are given in the same sequence (1-2-3-4-5-6) :

Śāntivaśyastambhanāni dveṣaṇoccāṭanaṃ tathā
māraṇāntāni śaṃsanti ṣaṭ karmāṇi manīṣiṇaḥ

1.4. S (p. 179, st. 5) cites a nearly identical śloka:

Śāntivaśyastambhanāni vidveṣoccāṭane tathā
māraṇāntāni śaṃsanti ṣaṭ karmāṇi manīṣiṇaḥ

1.5. T (st. 10)declaring to cite the Pheṭkāriṇītantra gives a śloka almost identical with the one contained in K and S.

1.6. The MMD begins its chapter 25 with this śloka:

Karmāṇi ṣaḍ atho vakṣye siddhidāni prayogataḥ
śāntir vaśyaṃ stambhanaṃ ca dveṣam uccāṭamāraṇe

"I shall now expound the Six Rites which grant perfection (if executed) by the right method : pacification, (bringing to) subjection, and immobilization; (causing) dissension, (and) eradication together with liquidation."

1.7. The SST (1,8,105) contains a stanza which enumerates the same acts, but in a somewhat different sequence (1-3-2-6-5-4) :

Śāntistambhau vaśīkāro māraṇoccāṭane tathā
dveṣaṇaṃ ceti deveśi ṣaṭkarmāṇi yathākramāt

As in the preceding instance, *māraṇa* and *uccāṭana* have been combined here into a dual compound.

These sources of the first type represent the Hindu Tantric doctrine of the Six Acts in a "classic" form. They are in fact almost the only sources which mention the term *ṣaṭ karmāṇi*. The following types enumerate the acts (sometimes six of them, sometimes more) usually without labelling them by a general term.

Type 2. Its general characteristics are that the term *śānti* (1) is lacking, so that the rites assume a more "cruel" appearance. We might have added a subdivision into three, if this would not have involved too much casuistry : a. *Śānti* is replaced by *mohana* (7); b. *Śānti* is replaced by *ākarṣaṇa* (8); c. Both *mohana* and *ākarṣaṇa* occur, and another term is left out or not.

2.1. The Tantrasāra (according to Goldstücker, s.v. *abhicāra*, quoted by Hillebrandt, p. 177, n. 1) gives: *māraṇa* (6), *mohana* (7), *stambhana* (3), *vidveṣaṇa* (4), *uccāṭana* (5), *vaśīkaraṇa* (2). Goldstücker called them the "Sechs Zwecke der Beschwörung" (The Six Goals of Incantation).

2.2. SST (1,8,104) gives the following stanza as the second of three opinions on the subject; it contains the sequence 2-3-7-6-5-4 and is ascribed to the authority of "Virāj":

Vaśyastambhanasammohā māraṇoccāṭanaṃ tathā
vidveṣaṇaṃ ca deveśi ṣaṭ karmāṇi Virāṅmate

2.3. *Ākarṣaṇa* instead of *mohana* is added in the stanza which precedes in the SST the one cited just above (1,8,103). The sequence this time is 2-8-3-4-5-6 and the doctrine is ascribed to Virūpākṣa:

Vaśyākarṣastambhanaṃ ca vidveṣoccāṭanaṃ tathā
māraṇaṃ caiva deveśi Virūpākṣasya sammatam

We notice that this stanza has some similarity to the ones given under the numbers 1.3. and 1.4. The third opinion referred to by the SST in the same passage has been quoted in 1.7.

2.4. D 1,15 (Ben.ed.; 1,14 in the Vidyasagar ed.) comprises within one half-śloka: *māraṇaṃ mohanaṃ stambhaḥ vidveṣoccāṭanaṃ vaśam* (6-7-3-4-5-2, just as in 2.1.) But the list does not stop here. Other activities are mentioned in a long series: *ākarṣaṇam* (8), *indrajālam*, *yakṣiṇī* (*sādhanam*) "gaining control over Yakṣiṇīs", *rasāyanam* "preparation of elixir", *kālajñānam* "knowledge of the hour of one's death", *anāhāram* "causing a shortage of food", *sāhāram* "creating an abundance of food", *nidhidarśanam* "finding a treasure", *bandhyāputravatīyogam* "the method of causing a barren woman to have a son", *mṛtavatsāsutajīvanam* "bringing back to life the son of a woman whose child has died", *vājīkaraṇavidyā* "means of stimulating passion", *bhūtagrahanivāraṇam* "averting evil influences of demons and planets", *siṃhavyāghrabhaya* (*nivāraṇam*) "averting the danger from lions and tigers", *sarpavṛścikānāṃ bhaya* (*nivāraṇam*) "averting the danger from snakes and scorpions." Here one obtains an impression of the manifold powers of the practisers.

2.5. Pārvatīputra Nityanātha in his Siddhikhaṇḍa (referred to by Weber, p. 1184) gives the list in another sequence : *vaśya* (2), *ākarṣaṇa* (8), *stambhana* (3), *mohana* (7), *māraṇa* (6), *uccāṭana* (5) and *vidveṣaṇa* (4). It thus amounts to seven items. The Siddhikhaṇḍa further adds the accomplishments of *vyādhikaraṇam* "causing illness"; *vehākaraṇam* (?); *kautukakaraṇam* "performing awesome feats", "jugglery"; *yakṣiṇīsādhanam*; *añjanasādhanam* "mastery over supernatural ointments"; and *mṛtasañjivanī* "reviving the dead".

2.6. The introductory verse to KA gives the terms in the sequence 2-8-4-3-6-1-9, adding-*ādi* "etcetera". *Uccāṭana* has been left out, but this act is mentioned immediately afterwards translated by "excitation) : a clear proof that one should not attach too much importance to stray verses enumerating a number of the Six Acts without being complete.

Under *Type* 3 we have listed some enumerations from Buddhist texts and a few others similar to them. The term Ṣaṭkarman is lacking. *Śānti* and *vidveṣaṇa* are not always mentioned, but *mohana* and *ākarṣaṇa* are always included and often also *puṣṭi* (9) comes in. In some cases there is a group of eight instead of six.

3.1. SM, No 221 (Jvālāmukhīsādhana) lists the following : *mohana, stambhana, vidveṣa, uccāṭana, vaśya, ākarṣaṇa* (thus: 7-3-4-5-2-8), and adds *jambha* "devouring (?)" and *kutūhala* "(feats of) awe".

3.2. The same text, (Raktayamārisādhana) gives : *śānti, puṣṭi, ākṛṣṭi, moha, vaśya, stambha* (1-9-8-7-2-3), and continues with *preraṇa* "expulsion", *nigraha* "coercion" and *uccāṭana*.

3.3. KCT 4,130 (referred to above, p.187 presents a list of eight and characterizes them in pairs by way of colours : *śānti* and *puṣṭi* (white); *ākṛṣṭi* and *vaśya* (red); *stambha* and *moha* (yellow); *māraṇa* and *uccāṭana* (black) (1 and 9; 8 and 2; 3 and 7; 6 and 5). This classification reminds of the presentation found in the Mahāmāyā fragment. The sequence of the colours is the same; there are differences in the number and arrangement of the acts.

3.4. In the poetical style of the KCT some variant lists

are presented which are not important from a viewpoint of classification but which are repeated here for the sake of their intrinsic interest. At first, 4,137 gives: *stambha, śānti, vaśya, paradhanaharaṇa* "taking the money of others" (=*ākarṣaṇa*), *māraṇa, uccāṭana* (3-1-2-8-6-5).

3.5. KCT 4,139: *śānti, puṣṭi, vidveṣa, uccāṭana, vaśyādi, kīlana* "piercing", *māraṇa, jīvana* (1-9-4-5-2-. . .-6- . . .).

3.6. KCT 4,143ff. : *śānti, vaśya, uccāṭana, vidveṣaṇa, stambhana, mohana, māraṇa* (1-2-5-4-3-7-6). This is the reversed sequence of type 2.1, with only *śānti* added.

3.7. KCT 4,156 again adds colours, but in another sequence: *śānti* and *puṣṭi* (white); *vaśya* and *ākṛṣṭi* (red); *vidveṣa* and *uccāṭana* (black); *stambha* and *kīlanādi* (yellow) (1-9-2-8-4-5-3-. . .).

3.8. KCT 4,189 mentions *stambha, ākṛṣṭi, moha, balakaraṇa* (=*vaśīkaraṇa*), *śāntika, uccāṭana* (3-8-7-2-1-5).

3.9. PST 28,13, although Hindu, can best be classified with the Buddhist sources. It also combines pairs with colours, but with some originality : *pauṣṭika* and *śamana* (white); *kṛṣṭi* and *vaśya* (red); *kṣobha* "agitation" and *saṃstobhana* "paralyzing"? (golden); *mardana* "crushing" and *uccāṭana* (grey); *stambhana* (yellow) and *mukti* "release" (*vimala* "spotless"). The next stanza adds a circumscription of *vyādhi-karaṇa* "making sick".

3.10. In N (p. 265) there is again no question of a list of six items (but the term Ṣaṭkarman is implied on p. 270 in the expression *karma-ṣaṭkānurūpiṇī*). The rites mentioned are *vaśyam, ākarśaṇam, stambhanam, mohanam, uccāṭamāraṇam* (2-8; 3-7; 5-6); *vidveṣavyādhikaraṇam*; *paśunāśanam* "destruction of cattle"; *śasyanāśanam* "d. of the crop"; *arthanāśanam* "d. of possessions"; *kautukam*; *indrajālam*; *yakṣiṇīsādhanam*; *ceṭakam* (?); *añjanam*; *adṛśyam* "becoming invisible"; *pādukāgatiḥ* "flying through the air by means of miraculous shoes"; *guṭikā* "magical bowl"; *khecaratvam* "flying through the air"; *mṛtasañjīvanam*, and so on (-*ādi*).

3.11. The Eight Acts known in Ceylon according to Gooneratne are *mohana, stambana, uccāṭana, ākarṣaṇa, vidveṣaṇa, māraṇa, tambanaya* and *paysana*. Their contents deviate from those current in the texts.

Type 4 is constituted by the Jaina BPK. The term

Ṣaṭkarman is not mentioned; instead, there is a tendency toward a group of eight. Mohana is lacking, but Ākarṣaṇa is always present. Māraṇa is usually circumscribed by *niṣedha* "the forbidden act", a change due to the importance attached in Jainism to Ahiṃsā.

4.1. BPK 3,1 : *śānti, dveṣa, vaśīkṛta, bandha, -stryākṛṣṭi* "attraction of women", *saṃstambha* (1-4-2-. . .8-3).

4.2. BPK 3,5 : *vaśya, ākṛṣṭi, stambhana, niṣedha, vidveṣa, cālana* (perhaps = *uccāṭana*), *śāntika, puṣṭi* (2-8-3-6-4-5-1-9). This list is almost identical with 3.3; only *niṣedha* is included instead of *mohana*, and the sequence of the items is different. There is also a similarity to 3.7 (here *niṣedha* instead of *kīlanādi*).

4.3. BPK 3,8 : *ākṛṣṭi, vaśya, śāntika, vidveṣaṇa, rodha* (=*stambhana*), *vadha* (8-2-1-4-3-6). Here the act of "liquidation" is not circumscribed by an euphemism. The passage enumerates alternatives of magical acts to be effected with the help of a certain series of mudrās.

4.4. BPK 3,9 : *ākarṣaṇa, vaśya, śāntipuṣṭi, vidveṣoccāṭana, stambhana, niṣedha* (8-2-1-9-4-5-3-6). The passage mentions the various postures and colours which help to produce the magical alternatives; the combinations are made explicit only in the commentary. *Śānti* and *puṣṭi* are combined with the same posture and colour, and this is also the case with *vidveṣaṇa* and *uccāṭana*. This suggests that also 8-2 and 3-6 may go into a pair. Similar pairs may be recognized in 4.2 and 4.3.

From Types 3 and 4 one might conclude that in Buddhist and Jaina traditions there circulated a list of eight acts going together in four pairs. Usually 8 goes with 2, 7 or 6 with 3, 5 with 6 or 4, and 9 with 1.

4.5. A non-Jaina example of a list of eight items is found in BMR, p. 2. The list is designated in the previous śloka by the term Ṣaṭkarman, but seems to consist only in a casual summing up of the various practices which can be realized by the power of Bagalāmukhī. They are : *stambhana, vaśya, śānti, mohana, ākarṣaṇa, vidveṣoccāṭana, māraṇa*. Two other items : *bhrāntiḥ* "causing to wander" and *udvegakaraṇam* "causing excitement" bring the number to ten.

In older texts, but also in comparatively recent ones, the reader often comes across statements of magical actions which might be called incomplete in the light of the preceding material. In younger sources they may be no more than short indications without any intention to give something as a "list"; or their motivation may lie in the authors' wish to refer to what they considered to be the most important items. In older sources, however, such enumerations may reflect an older stage in the theory of magic, during which systematization was absent, some terms not yet in vogue and other terms still alive which later went into abeyance. A characteristic of such older enumerations is that *abhicāra* "destructive magic" is often mentioned as a separate item. Speaking boldly, one can also reduce these older statements to the classic threefold ritual aim of *śānti*, *puṣṭi* and *abhicāra*, and in this way the Ṣaṭkarman tradition might be interpreted as another separate branch of the Vedic Kalpa tree. We shall give a few examples of the older "lists". Numbers are given to them only for the sake of easy reference; they do not suggest that we have always to do here with varieties of a theory of "Six Acts".

5.1. In the Ṛgvidh., terms denoting acts of magic are spread through the whole work. There seems to be no trace of systematization. Here follows a sample : in 1,2,5 we have *vidveṣaṇam*, *saṃvananam* "winning friendship", *viṣaghna*-"destroying poison", *roganāśanam* "annihilation of disease". In 1,15,7: *pīḍanam* "tormenting" and *uccāṭanam*. In 1,17,4: *bādhayet* "one will obstruct". In 1,17,5 : *vadha*- "killing". In 2,10,5 : *vidveṣaṃ janayet* "one will create dissension"; in 2,17,2 ; *cyāvanam* "causing to fall". The third chapter mentions *vaśaṃ netum* "to bring under one's power" (3,16,4); *śāntyarthāya sukhāya ca* "for the sake of pacification and happiness" (3,17,1) ; *vaśaṃ nayati* "one brings. . . under one's power" (3,18,4); *abhicaret* "one will succeed in practising destructive magic" (3,18,3) ; *saṃvananam*, "winning (a woman's heart)" (3,19,3). The last item is repeated in 3,21,3 and its complement, *puṃsāṃ saṃvananam*, is added. It is clear that here sometimes the same terms appear as in the Tantric compilations, but without any attempt at systematization and side by side with other expressions which are found only seldom or not at all in younger texts. Of the Six Acts which constitute Type 1 only *stambhana* is, however, not represented.

5.2. The SVBr evidently represents a still older stage. Here the technical terms are almost absent, although often the same kinds of actions and aims are described. The passage 2,5,1ff. discusses *āvartanam* "turning hither", an equivalent of the later term *vaśīkaraṇam* by means of which Sāyaṇa paraphrases it. Another commentator, Bharatasvāmin, circumscribes with *abhimukhapravarttanaṃ samīpanayanam ity arthaḥ*, a phrase which is equivalent to the act denoted by the later term *ākarṣaṇa*. As a result of a certain action 2,5,4 states *guṇībhavati*, explained by Sāyaṇa as *vaśyo bhavati*. The following expressions also occur: *subhago bhavati* "one obtains domestic happiness" (2,6,1); *vaśyā bhavanti* (2,6,13); and *naikagrāme vasati* "(the victim) is unable to stay in a certain village" a result which typically belongs to the act of *uccāṭana* (2,6,16). Sometimes a term characteristic for the Veda is included, like *yaśasvī bhavati* "one becomes famous" (2,6, 17), or *brahmavarcasvī bhavati* "one becomes rich in spiritual splendour" (2,7,2). Such terms occur also in the Ṛgvidhāna and they continue to be occasionally expressed in the later sources. A few more examples of aims from the SVBr: *śrutanigadādī bhavati* "one becomes proficient in the recitation of the Scriptures" (2,7,4); *dhanyo bhavati* "one becomes rich" (3,1,2); *daivān poṣān puṣyati* "one fares well by examples of divine welfare" (3,3,4). In 3,6,12, a method for killing a personal enemy is described without any technical term for "liquidation" being used. In short, this text is a good instance of a state of preservation of Vedic traditions combined with the emergence of new ideas and restatements of older practices within the minds of the same persons, in this case Sāmaveda brahmans. The Ṛgvidh. presents almost the same picture in a further stage of development for the Ṛgveda brahmans.

5.3. GautDh 2,2,17, a passage quoted earlier (p. 236) in connection with a question after the performer's identity, mentions the following series: *śānti*, *puṇyāha*, *svastyayana*, *āyuṣman* (=*āyuṣyam*), *maṅgala*, *vidveṣaṇa*, *saṃvanana*, *abhicāra* and *dviṣadvyṛddhi*.

5.4-6. Presumably a younger stage is represented by the AVPar, although here (as elsewhere, for that matter) we have to reckon with interpolations in the composite text. The Word Index to the edition by Bolling and Von Negelein mentions of the Ṣaṭkarman terms *uccāṭana* (21,3,2; 26,4,1; 26,5,3; we add *uccāṭakarman*, 36,4,2); *vaśīkaraṇa* (35,1,6; 36,5,1 and 3); *vaśya* (25,1,11); *vaśa* (five times); *vidveṣa* (21,3,2; 64,4,9; 64,5,5);

stambhana (26,5,4); *stambhanī* (36,1,4). *Ākarṣaṇa* does not occur in the Index. *Śāntika* and *abhicāra* are mentioned in a passage (21,3,1) which enumerates in the same way as younger texts do the different kinds of materials needed for the performance of the various magical rites.

5.4. In the passage just mentioned (AVPar 21,3,1) the magical acts are enumerated: *śāntika*, *abhicāra*, *uccāṭana*, *vaśya-karman*, *vidveṣa*, *pauṣṭika*, *vijayāvaha* "invoking victory", *amṛtādi* "rites for defying death, and so on". The list is already akin to Tantric examples.

5.5. A similar list occurs in AVPar 25,1,9ff. (variations in the construction of the fireplace): *vijayāvaha*, *sarvaśāntikara*, *śāntika*, *pauṣṭika*, *abhicāra*, *vaśyādi*, *māraṇādi*, and *vidveṣa*. Another similar list occurs in 26,3,2ff. (measurements of the fuel sticks).

5.6. In 26,5,1ff. (different kinds of wood for the fuel sticks) occur the terms *puṣṭikāma*—"one who strives after welfare", *śāntikarman*, *vittārthī* "one who desires wealth", *rājyadhīḥ* "one who concentrates upon (obtaining) a kingdom", *śrīkāma-*,*vidveṣa*, *maraṇa* (not *māraṇa*), *uccāṭana*, *stambhana*, *vijaya*, *saubhāgya* and *āyuṣkāma*—"one who desires longevity."

5.7. We continue with some instances of "incomplete lists" from the Purāṇas. MtPur (93,140ff.) mentions the following acts to be realized in the cadre of worship of the planets : *vaśya*, *abhicārādi*, *uccāṭanādi*; and again (st. 149) : *vidveṣaṇa* and *abhicāra*. These aims are summarized under the heading of *kṣudra*—"insignificant" or "vile". After these the author records *ṣāntika*—in st. 155 (the passage has been discussed by Kane, 1962, p.1114).

5.8. AgPur 306,1ff. mentions *stambha*, *vidveṣaṇa*, *uccāṭa*, *utsāda* "overturning" or "causing destruction", *bhrama* "causing to wander", *māraṇa*, *vyādhi*. Here also, the term *kṣudram* is used for the group as a whole. An almost identical stanza occurs in TSS—17,1.

5.9. AgPur 315,1 announces the discussion of *stambhana*, *mohana*, *vaśya*, *vidveṣa-uccāṭana*, *viṣa* "poison", *vyādhi*, *aroga* "(restoring) health", *mārana* and *śamana* (=*śānti*). This list contains the acts 3-7-2-4-5 and 6 interspersed with a few others.

5.10. AgPur 260 (instructions for the use of the Mahāvyāhṛti formula) mixes up Vedic aims and Saṭkarman performance: *śāntikāma-*, *pāpāpanutti* "removal of evil", *paśūkāma-* "desiring cattle", *kanakaṃ bahu* "a large amount of gold", *kanyākāma-*

"desiring a girl (for wife)", *grāmārthī* "desiring (mastery over) a village", *vaśyakarman*, *śatrūṇāṃ vadhakāmyayā* "out of desire to liquidate the enemies", *vyādhivināśinī* "destroying disease", *brahmavarcasakāma-*, *vidveṣaṇa*, *medhāvī jāyate* "one becomes wise", *uccāṭanam*, and others. In general, the AgPur betrays a fair knowledge of magical theories and practice in a number of chapters, and more than once mentions a number of actions without intending to be complete.

5.11. LiPur 2,52,2f. enumerates some possibilities realized with the help of the Sāvitrī : *vaśya*, *ākarṣaṇa*, *vidveṣaṇa*, *uccāṭana*, *stambhana*, *mohana* (text : *mocana*) (2-8-4-5-3-7), and further *tāḍana* "kicking", *utsādana*, *chedam* "cutting", *māraṇa*, *pratibandhanam* "checking", *senāstambhana* [4].

5.12. It might be useful to refer also in this connection to the probably earliest Buddhist Tantra, the GST, which in the cadre of its unconventional theory of spiritual emancipation (ch.9, p.35) expresses the characteristic abilities of the five Kulas "Families". In the Family of Hate (*dveṣa*) presided upon by Akṣobhya one is able to kill all beings, *sarvasattvaṃ vighātayet*; in the Family of Delusion (*moha*; Vairocana) there is *haraṇaṃ sarvadravyāṇām* ("taking away all possessions", cf. *ākarṣaṇa*); in the Family of Passion (*rāga*; Amitābha) one will enjoy all women, (*sarvayoṣitaḥ*) *upabhuñjayet* (cf. *vaśīkaraṇa*); in the Family of the Thunderbolt (*vajra*) one may utter lies, while in the last Family, Samayakula, one "obtains wisdom by practising harsh talk and the like" (*pāruṣyavacanādyaiḥ sevayan jñānam āpnuyāt*). These acts, the opposites of the traditional Buddhist virtues, contain a certain likeness to the system of the Six Acts, although the passage can hardly be referred to as one of its sources.

5.13. The HT (ch.2) presents a list which is already very akin to the Six Acts; *stambhana*, *vaśya*, *vidveṣaṇa*, *abhicāruka*, *ākarṣaṇa* and *māraṇa*. A change of *abhicāruka* into *uccāṭana* would produce the items of Type 2: 3-2-4-5-8-6.

5.14. The probably much later SM gives some casual lists on p. 368f. We mention only these as instances. Many more similar passages could be probably found in the SM itself as well as in related texts. On the mentioned pages one first reads twice a series of *śāntika*, *puṣṭika*, *vaśya*, *māraṇa*. A third time *ākṛṣṭi* is inserted before *māraṇa*. A fourth time we find *śāntika*, *pauṣṭika*, *abhicāra* and *vaśya*. A fifth time this same list is extended by *ākṛṣṭi*; and afterwards there is a version in which *śāntika* and *pauṣṭika* are followed by *abhicārakarmāṇi sarvāṇi* "all acts of destructive magic."

A few examples of casual listings in Hindu Tantras:

5.15. The SST (1,6,2) gives *vaśya*, *stambhana*, *ākarṣaṇa* and *trailokyavaśyatā* "(the power of) having the threefold space subjugated"; the list is continued with a great number of siddhis.

5.16. SST 3,15, 18ff. enumerates the results of worship with flowers, they include *śāntikarman*, *vaśya*, *vāgvibhūti* "power of speech", *stambhana*, *mohana*, *māraṇa*, *ripūccāṭa* "eradication of the foe", *dhanāgamaḥ* "acquisition of wealth", and so on. 3,18, 14ff., in connexion with a similar subject, mentions *mantrasiddhi*, *vaśa*, *nāginīsiddhi* "mastery over a Nāga woman", *nidhana* "(finding) a treasure", *kavitā* "being a poet", *jaya* "victory", *kāminīṃ labhet* "one obtains the lady desired", and so on.

5.17. The JT (17,83-87) circumscribes the acts of *stambhana*, *vaśīkaraṇa*, *ākṛṣṭi* and *māraṇa* in association with the four quarters of the sky.

5.18. The PST (in 24,33) mentions in passing *vaśya*, *ākṛṣṭi*, *dveṣaṇa*, *moha*, *uccāṭa* and others (*-ādika*). *Māraṇa* is discussed—not without reservations—in the preceding stanza (6-2-8-4-7-5).

5.19. The SCT (p. 52) prescribes four colours for the mantras for the acts of *śānti*, *puṣṭi*, *vaśīkaraṇa* and *māraṇa*, which the editor calls "the four kinds of acts" (p. 66).

In referring to passages like these, one should not forget that the time-honoured aims of the Veda are still expressed in the Tantras also, as in the PTS (13, 45ff.) : *śrī*, *samṛddhi*, *āyuḥ*, *ṛddhi*, *puṣṭi*, *mahodaya*, *putrāpti* "obtaining a son", *sarvopadravaśānti* "pacification (on the occasion) of all kinds of calamities." Besides, short allusions like those mentioned above may have been motivated by the intention to pick up the most important aims which serve as pivots of the magical science. T (p. 370) records a variant of the division of ritual aims into *śānti*, *puṣṭi* and *abhicāra* by announcing *śānti*, *vaśya* and *abhicāra* in this role. On p. 372, the text accounts for this classification by saying that "attraction is done in the method of subjugation, and rites with a good purpose in the method of pacification; evil acts are to be done like liquidation (here probably a synonym of destructive magic); thus the ritual should be always localized by the adepts" :

ākarṣaṇaṃ vaśyavat syāt śubhaṃ śāntivad īritam
ugraṃ māraṇavaj jñeyaṃ karma sarvatra sādhakaiḥ

Two features which sometimes occur in Ṣaṭkarman descriptions should be shortly dealt with now. These are the combination of these rites with the directions of the sky, and their being presided over by goddesses. Execution of power into the directions of the compass is found already in the AV hymns (e.g., 3,26; 3,27; 4,40). The fear for dangers attacking the centre in which the person or community in question ritually resides induces the practiser to counteract them by magical rites which relegate these dangers to the regions from where they launch their attack. This same principle is continued unceasingly in Indian religious literature; and it is abundantly represented in the Balinese digbandhas (see Stuti and Stava, p. 17,579). For the Tantras we refer to JT 17,83-87 which effectively combines the desire to execute power into the directions with the application of some of the Saṭkarman acts; it is structurally related to the Mahāmāyā fragment [5]. The worship of Śivā, "Mrs. Śiva" is said in stanza 81 to destroy all sins; within a month the performer is freed from all evil committed in seven previous births (83). Worshipping towards the E. is connected with *stambhana*, towards the N. with *vaśīkaraṇa*, towards the W. with conquerring women (*dāsīm iva vaśaṃ nayet* "one will bring her under his power like a female slave", cf. the Mahāmāyā fragment, st. 9), and towards the S. with loss of memory for the enemy (see also above, p.269). The worship can also be conducted into the intermediate directions; in that case it will result in stupefaction, mutual dissension among the enemies, disease and eradication respectively (st. 89 a : *stambhavidveṣaṇavyādhiśatrūccāṭakaraṃ bhavet*). There is also a likeness between this passage and that from the GST cited above (No. 5.12) which connects the five cardinal vices with the five "Families". It is well known that the "Families" and their presiding Tathāgatas are localized in the four main directions and the Centre.

A related meditation (combined with colours) is described in SM, No. 97 (p. 197f.) as to be realized within the performer's own body. Ten female deities are worshipped symbolizing the ten stages of perfection. Among them are four Doorkeepers, called Aṅkuśī (white, in the E.). Pāśī (yellow, in the S.), Sphoṭā (red, in the W.), and Ghaṇṭā (red, in the N.). All these names can be preceded by *vajra-*. When afterwards the practiser of the meditation should cause the goddesses created by him to enter the "Diagram of the Truce" (*samayamaṇḍalam*), he does so for Aṅkuśī by means of the formula *Oṃ Vajrāṅkuśi ākarṣaya jaḥ*; for Pāśī with *Oṃ Vajrapāśi praveśaya huṃ*; for Sphoṭā with *Oṃ Vajrasphoṭa bandhaya vaṃ*; and for Ghaṇṭā with *Oṃ Vajra* (*ghaṇṭa*; text *-veśa*) *vaśīkuru hoḥ*. Thus at least three of the standard magical actions were associated by these Buddhist authors of the GST and SM No. 97 with the meditative practice of the vices; and from the SM it also appears that they could be associated with female deities. Goddesses of fearsome figure which symbolize magical actions occur also elsewhere in the directions of the compass as attendants of a central God; for instance, in N (p. 316) there are Jambhā "Devourer", Stambhā "Immobilizer", Sammohā "Deluder" and Śoṣā "Desiccator" around Vīrabhadra; and in the BPK (10,42ff.) the sixteenth Jaina Arhat, Śānti (!) is surrounded in the four intermediate directions by Jambhā, Mohā, Stambhā and Stambhinī.

In the SM No. 97, and in No. 110 (p. 229) there are also goddesses mentioned as incorporations of six Vices. Their presence should be assigned to the seats of the sense organs (p. 229): Mohavajrā on the eyes, Dveṣavajrā on the ears, Īrṣyavajrā on the nose, Rāgavajrā on the mouth, Mātsaryavajrā—she removes all afflictions and obscurity, *sarvakleśatamo 'pahām*—on the skin and Nairātmayoginī (connected with the mind as the sixth organ of sense) in the *āyatanas* "supports" of these sense-organs. These six "women" (*yoṣitaḥ*) all possess two arms and a single face and they should be meditated upon as bearing the practiser's skull in their hand. On p. 231 they are honoured and invoked for protection:

dveṣavajri namas tubhyaṃ mohavajri namo'stu te
mātsaryavajri māṃ trāhi rāgavajri prayaccha me (?)
mahāmātre (v.l.*-māne*) *maherṣyeti sarvavajri prasīda me*

The occurrence of Six Women in these texts is no exception. SM, No. 250 (vol. 2, p. 488) mentions six Yoginīs or Sorceresses who originate from a spell of six syllables—and, by the way, also six Cakravartins or Universal Monarchs, on p. 489—; and SM, No. 251 calls the god Saṃvara the "Lord of the Six Goddesses" (*ṣaḍdevatīnāthaḥ*). HT 5 also speaks of six women: the Mother, the Sister, the Dancer, the Washerwoman, the Casteless woman (Caṇḍālī) and the Brahman Woman. All of them are in reality identical with Prajñā, the Buddhist goddess of Wisdom and Mother of all Buddhas. The same chapter mentions the goddesses of the five "Families" and they are for the greater part identical with the above list of six: Ḍombī, the Dancer, the Washerwoman, the Brahman Woman and the Caṇḍālī. So the "Six" seem to be an extension of the "Five". The KCT (3,125) advises meditation on the following six women: the Mother, the Sister, the Daughter, the Sister's Daughter, the Wife and the Yoginī, in the course of a left-handed sādhanā.

In the light of this evidence it can be expected that six women are also described sometimes as presiding deities of the Six Acts, and this is indeed the case in Śāradātilaka 23, 122ff. (according to Kane, 1962, p. 1070). Their names are Ratī, Vāṇī, Ramā, Jyeṣṭhā, Durgā and Kālī. The same doctrine is echoed in S (1,10), MMD (25, 6) and T (p. 366; ascribed to the Kulaprakāśatantra). The HT (ch. 2, last stanza) already expresses the same principle by means of a group of seven goddesses with different names:

vajrā gaurī ca vārī ca vajraḍākī nairātmikā
bhūcarī-khecarī-yogāt stambhanādi kared vratī

It is not impossible that this doctrine of Six or Seven Women (goddesses or other females) presiding over the Six Acts or over the group of Six Vices arose under the influence of a remarkable tradition found until recently among aboriginal peoples of India, that in the beginning of time there were six or seven witches or female magicians (Hermanns, p.264). Gooneratne relates a legend about the origin of witchcraft in Ceylon: in former times there was a prince who had to choose his wife from among the seven daughters of the king of Ayodhyāpura. Six of them were specialized in the black arts while the seventh was an expert in counteracting all these sorts of witchcraft.

When this daughter was taken by the prince as his wife, the other six revenged themselves by assembling all their magical powers in a pumpkin and sent this pumpkin to Ceylon where its contents spread themselves over the island and are present there up till now. When there is really a connection between these old popular traditions and the Tantric groups of goddesses discussed—we only refer in passing to the "Seven Mothers" who do not seem to be directly connected with witchcraft—, we have here another instance of the appearance of non-Sanskritic material in Sanskrit literature. This symptom may be called a function of the gradual process of "Sanskritization" (Gonda, 1963, p.7,10 and 11).

6.3. *Alternatives in Ṣaṭkarman rituals*

The magical rituals described in the sources mentioned above are sometimes preceded by a set of general prescriptions the chief function of which is to equip the performer with the modifications required for the particular objectives he wishes to attain. This whole complex of alternatives is based upon the assumption that the intricacies of the ritual reflect, influence and even help to produce the realities which correspond to them. The power of the magician is awakened effectively only by his realization of this law of interdependence of the elements of the universe which hands over to him the keys of the machinery he prepares himself to tend (see also above, p. 56). A similar principle is also expressed by P. Bhaṭṭācārya in his Introduction to the Tārābhaktisudhārṇava (p.21); "... since every individual being or object in the universe is a manifestation of the one and the same Creative Energy, whatever somebody does or attempts to do, causes a tension in the creative atmosphere; and certain forces which are favourably affected favour the completion of the work...(and vice versa)... some writers on Oriental Philosophy claim to have discovered many of these forces...".

The alternatives apply to a variety of circumstances under which the ritual should be executed: the exact time, the correct astrological mansion, the method of tending the sacrificial fire, the materials offered, the accompanying gestures, the shape of the mantras recited, and so on. Any particular action requires the application of its concomitant rules. The performer's scrupulous adherence to them is his guarantee that he is actually on the right track, that he tunes into the correct wave-length of the mystical force of the universe. To be true, there are circumstances in which one may neglect them, as when S (st. 30) asserts that in a situation of dire necessity one needs not to abide the exact time required for a ceremony. There may also be cases of exceptional efficacy of the mantra or the material. Thus, for instance, D (st. 12, p.133) contains the sweeping statement that the mantras and herbs taught by the author are sufficient to bring about the result even without adherence to the rules about the correct days or constellations, the right method of worship, recitation or sacrifice. And probably many of these rules will have fallen into oblivion or even have never been observed at all in the popular tradition.

The system of correlation between the ritual and the desired reality which we find here does not seem to be essentially different from that which lies at the base of the Vedic ritual prescriptions. Vedic ritual even sometimes refers to the same kind of alternatives aiming at different results desired by the sacrificer (*yajamāna*) and brought about by the priest. One may point to the *kāmyeṣṭi-*, "non-bloody sacrifices performed for a certain objective" which consist of varieties of the full-moon and new-moon śrauta sacrifices. But they do not constitute a close parallel to the Ṣaṭkarman alternatives because they are independent items not connected by sets of corresponding changes in the ritual.[4]

What can best be compared to the later practice are usually short remarks made in the course of a ritual prescription. For instance, AitBr (Pañcikā 2, 1; Adhyāya 6) declares that for the realization of different objectives the *yūpa* (sacrificial pole symbolizing the *axis mundi*) should be made of different kinds of wood. When the Śrautasūtras describe the Agnihotra—the oblation to be made twice a day by the Aryan householder—they usually insert a few of such alternatives (these are discussed by Dumont). KātyŚr 4, 15, 21-26 (Dumont, p.5-7) gives these rules: "he who desires heaven performs the oblation with a rice-dish; or the same, if he desires cattle; one who desires to obtain (leadership in) a village should bring an oblation with a mess of barley; if one desires strength, with rice grains; if one desires strength of Indra (alertness of body and mind), with curds; if one desires fiery lustre, with ghee"—[6]. The ĀpŚr (6, 15, 1) gives the same set of rules (cf. Dumont, p.40), but restricts the oblation with the rice dish to the result of obtaining cattle; in 6,4,11 the author of the Sūtra had advised this oblation for someone whose cattle had been attacked by Rudra. The oblation of rice grains is said to produce *ojas* "overpowering strength", but *balam* "strength" according to "some authorities" (*ity eke*); we saw that this was also Kātyāyana's opinion. Āpastamba further adds that one may sacrifice a rice porridge (*odana-*) for obtaining food; a portion of flesh for obtaining renown; and soma sap for obtaining spiritual lustre. HirŚr (3, 7, 114) as usually stands close to ĀpŚr but prescribes the oblation of flesh for obtaining valour (*vīryam*; Dumont, p.90). Alternatives are also presented for the moment of sacrifice of the materials into the fire. For instance, a ruler who desires to extort as much as possible from his subjects for his own consumption should have the oblation performed into the fire immediately after kindling it when the flame has not yet grown to its usual proportion; if he wants to do so without destroying his subjects, the oblation should be made while the fire sends out frequent beams; when it flames at its highest, one should sacrifice for lustre and renown; when the fire begins to subside, for the obtaining of material goods from the subjects by friendly means; and when only the charcoals are still glowing, for obtaining spiritual lustre (KātyŚr 4, 15, 16-20; 27 adds that one may continue this kind of sacrifice for a year; Dumont p. 5-7). It may be remarked that these alternatives cover the whole existence of the sacrificial fire at the ceremony; in other words, the client is implicitly expected to have one of the mentioned objectives in mind when he launches the ceremony. ĀpŚr (6,10,3b) also presents alternatives on this matter but deviates in detail: the fire should produce only smoke during an oblation for acquiring power in the village; it should flame up for obtaining spiritual lustre; an oblation into the charcoals produces fiery lustre. These differences suggest a comparatively late development of prescriptions of this kind. The objectives stated in the Vedic texts—cattle, lustre, strength, food, ascendancy in the community, longevity —may differ at first sight from those of the Ṣaṭkarman rituals, but this difference is more apparent than real. The terminology differs but the objectives remain centred around the own ascendancy and welfare and the putting down of rivals; and—for a ruler—the exploitation of the subjects. There is one particular kind of prescription met more than once in the Veda which does not seem to occur in the later sources; this is the *abhicāra* which the priest may apply in order to bring harm to his own client, as we find it for example in Hir Śr 3, 7, 82 (Dumont, p. 101): "when he (the priest) desires of somebody (a client): may his power diminish, may he change for the worse, then he should bring a greater oblation in the first phase and a smaller one afterwards." This difference between earlier and later sources may reflect a change in social circumstances such as a less independent position of the brahman performers at royal courts or a closer understanding between the two uppermost grades of society.

We now come to the alternatives presented by the sources on what we call Ṣaṭkarman rituals. The reader can develop a keen sense of casuistry even from the simplified excerpts given on the following pages. The regulations usually refer to:

A. Time (choice of right asterism, day and hour).
B. Place and orientation.
C. Recitation (way of speaking, use of mantras, rosary).
D. Gestures and meditation.
E. Sacrifice (form of the fire, substances sacrificed).
F. Some other subjects (behaviour of performer; materials). These groups are each subdivided below into subgroups indicated by numbers (A, 1 etc.). In the schematic representations, use is again made of the number code for the Six Acts (see above, —p.259) which is repeated here in short:

1	Śānti	6	Māraṇa
2	Vaśīkaraṇa	7	Mohana
3	Stambhana	8	Ākarṣaṇa
4	Vidveṣaṇa	9	Puṣṭi
5	Uccāṭana		

A 1. The most general prescriptions on the right time for the performance of a ritual are those concerning the twenty-seven lunar constellations (*nakṣatrāṇi*)). The JT (20,163) allocates each rite to a nakṣatra: Ākarṣaṇa to Kṛttikā, Māraṇa to

Bharaṇī, Vaśa and Uccāṭana to Svātī, Stambhana to Jyeṣṭhā, Vidveṣaṇa to Śatatārā (=Śatabhiṣaj) and Śānti to Abhijit. These simple prescriptions leave however a great number of nakṣatras open; probably they have been meant only as suggestions for the best occasion on which to perform the rituals. In any case, all nakṣatras figure in the list found in K (st. 12-15, p. 23) and in the almost identical stanzas 22-26 of S (p. 182). There, each act is assigned to more than one nakṣatra, for example Stambhana to Jyeṣṭhā, Uttarāṣāḍhā, Anurādhā and Rohiṇī; Mohana to Uttarapadā, Śatabhiṣaj and three others; Vidveṣaṇa to Svātī and some others; Uccāṭana to Bharaṇī and some others. From a comparison with the data given by JT it appears that there is no conformity at all between the sources on this subject.

A 2. The rules on nakṣatras tend to be accompanied by those on *yoga* or *maṇḍala*—astrological combinations of planets. K and S (l.c.) distinguish those of Mahendra, Varuṇa, Agni and Vāyu (the last one fittingly prescribed for driving away a person, Uccāṭana). Observations regarding the signs of the zodiac (*rāśi*) are recorded in T (p. 365; from the Pheṭkāriṇī Tantra).

A 3. Rules on *tithi* (the days in the month) are generally combined with those on *vāra* (the day of the week, denoted by the planet which presides over it). The JT (20,165) only gives the planets of the days: the (day of) the Moon for attraction, Mars for liquidation, Mercury for... (*adhanam*); Jupiter for acquisition, Venus for the realization of all objectives; the Sun for all kind of respectable desires (*śubhāni*). K (st. 7ff.; p. 22) divides the acts over the days of the month as follows (without specifying the month-half): for subjugation, the seventh; for attraction, the third or thirteenth; for eradication, the second and sixth; for immobilization, the fourteenth, fourth or first; for delusion, the eighth or ninth; for liquidation, the eleventh or twelfth; for pacification, the fifteenth or the full moon day.

More complicated is the system presented by S (st. 15ff., p. 181), MMD (25,10-15) and T (ch. 10, p. 352). Except for a few different readings, S and T give the same stanzas; T refers to the Pheṭkāriṇī Tantra as their source. N (p. 269) gives the material in a slightly different manner and incompletely (this may be the editor's fault). The ślokas are not always clear as to which particular days are to be combined with the rites and we may have misunderstood them on some points.

Śānti	—second, third, fifth or seventh (in the light half of the month), on the days of Mercury and Jupiter (S adds: Venus and the Moon)
Puṣṭi (not in MMD)	—fourth, sixth to ninth and thirteenth (S adds the tenth); days of Jupiter and the Moon
Vaśīkaraṇa (MMD only)	—fourth, sixth, ninth and thirteenth; days of Jupiter and the Moon; this means that MMD gives for subjugation almost the same rules as S and T for acquisition (Puṣṭi)
Ākarṣaṇa (not in MMD)	—tenth and eleventh (N: eighth to eleventh); days of the Sun and Venus
Vidveṣaṇa	—MMD : eighth to eleventh; days of Saturn and Venus. S and T : new and full moon day; first and ninth; days of Saturn and the Sun. N : full moon, first, eighth and ninth
Uccāṭana	—eighth and fourteenth of the dark half (S adds the sixth); day of Saturn. These dates are also suitable for Citāsādhana, part of Vīrācāra (T, Introd., p. 20)
Māraṇa	—The same days, or new moon day (MMD omits the fourteenth); days of Saturn and Mars. Li Pur (2,50,36): the fourteenth of the black half
Stambhana	—Fifth, tenth or full moon day; days of Mercury and the Moon

In general, S (st. 21) advises to undertake favourable rites during the rise of a favourable planet, and terrible rites during the rise of the others (variant of this stanza in T, l.c.) For liquidation, a Sunday falling on the fourth. ninth or fourteenth and a yoga conferring death (*mṛtyuyogaḥ*) are especially recommended.

It is to be noted that the above listing of tithi and vāra

encompasses all the days, in any case of the light half of the month, and all days of the week.

A 4. An important regulation is the one concerning the divisions of the day. The Ṛgvidh. knows the principle that different moments of the day are suited for different kinds of rites. In 1,19,5-1, 20,1 (in reality one śloka clumsily cut up by the traditional method of numbering) it says regarding the recitation of a RV stanza (1,50,13b):

udayaty āyur akṣayyaṃ tejo madhyaṃdine japan
astaṃ vrajati sūrye tu dviṣantaṃ pratibādhate

"while the sun rises, (the result will be) indestructible longevity; fiery energy, if one recites at noon; and (if one recites) while the sun is setting, one oppresses one's enemy." This doctrine which appears here in a simple form has been eagerly worked out in the Tantric sources. Moreover, the period of twenty-four hours is dealt with by these texts as a replica of the year: it is regularly divided into the traditional six seasons. Usually the texts declare that six parts of the day are to be called the "seasons", as in S (st. 12, p. 181): *ṛtavaḥ syur vasantādyā ahorātre dinedine* "in any period of day and night there should be the seasons spring etc." The same line is found in T (p. 364), while K (st. 4, p. 22) and MMD (25,7) say the same in other words. The wording of N (p. 269) seems to imply that the rites should be really performed in the different seasons of the year, and within these seasons on the corresponding parts of the day, for example in the first line : *udayād yāmaparyantaṃ hemante pauṣṭike japet* "from sunrise for three hours one should recite in winter in the act of acquisition." But it is possible to interpret N in the same way as the other sources as pertaining only to a division of a period of twenty-four hours.

The directions for this sixfold division of the day are worded differently: S (st. 12, p. 181), T (p. 364) and MMD (25,8) give each "season" a time of ten *ghaṭikās*; K (st. 1) speaks of *daṇḍas* for them, N (p. 269) mentions six *yamas* or periods of three hours, while S (st. 13. p. 181) and K (st. 4, p. 22) divide day and night into six parts corresponding with the yamas in this way (the lines are identical in both sources): "The morning is spring, noon is called summer, the afternoon is the rains, the dewy season is known to be in the evening; autumn falls on midnight, while winter is in the period of sunrise" [7]. This very apt division of the day into seasons contains one change in the normal sequence: autumn and dewy season have changed place, probably because midnight with its clear star-spangled skies better conforms to autumn which is often praised for its clearness, while the "dewy season" may be aptly compared to the evening.

The sources give different ways of assigning the Six Acts to these seasons of the day. They are presented below in a slightly simplified scheme. Five variants (denoted by Roman capitals) may be distinguished. Eleven sources were made use of: BPK 3,6; JT 20,166; K p.22, st. 2; KA, introductory stanza; MMD 25, 8; N p. 269 (2x: N-1 and N-2); S p. 181, st. 14 (S-1); S p. 182, st. 27 (S-2); T p. 365 (2x: T-1 and T-2). For the acts themselves, use is made of the number code.

Part of day (season)	MMD S-1 T-1	BPK JT N-2	N-1	K KA	S-2 T-2
Morning (spring)	2	2	8	2,8	2
Noon (summer)	4	4	4	4	4,5
Afternoon (rains)	5	5	5	3	1,9
Evening (dewy s.)	3	6	6	6	6
Midnight (autumn)	6	1	1	1	3
Dawn (winter)	1	9	9	9	8
	I	II	III	IV	V

A few remarks explaining the simplification of the scheme are necessary. All five variants I—V are represented by identical or almost identical ślokas. This was the main reason to present N-1 as a separate item (III) in the list, although it is practically identical with II in contents (2, Vaśikaraṇa and 8, Ākarṣaṇa, being sometimes inter-changeable). N-2 and S-2 are both incomplete; their last line which contains two of the six seasons has been omitted in the edition. In the case of S-2 one can safely assume that this last line is identical with that of T-2, but this is not the case for N-2 and JT because N-2 in its first line gives a variant listing 9 (*puṣṭi*) together with 2 (*vaśya*) in the morning. KA, although being listed together with K, records 5 (*ucc.*) instead of 9 in dawn. In

BPK the details of the identifications are given by a commentary, while N-2 omits them altogether. T-2 ascribes list V to the Pheṭkāriṇī Tantra.

B 1. After the category of time, that of place is expected to be an important determinant for the execution of the rites. There are however, surprisingly few indications made about the locations most suited to the performance of the acts. Such indications are known to the Veda, e.g. LāṭyŚr 3.5,20ff.: *chadiṣi varṣakāmo, goṣṭhe paśukāmaḥ, sabhāyāṃ yaśaskāmaḥ, śmaśāne 'bhicaran* "under a cover (one should sacrifice), if one desires rain, in a cowpen when desiring cattle, in the council hall when desiring fame, on a cremation ground when doing black magic" (Hillebrandt, p. 174; he also refers to KauśS 48, 17 and KātyŚr 18, v. 147). The LiPur (2,50,15f.) in a chapter which deals with magical means of chastising evildoers advises a cremation ground (*pretasthānam*) or temple of the Mother Goddess (*mātṛsthānam*) as the scene for the ritual; the performer should, by the way, be proficient in the Veda and its auxiliary disciplines (*vedavedāṅga-pāragaḥ*). Only three of the Tantric sources utilized for this study seem to give directions on the subject, and at that incomplete T (p. 367) states that subjugation should be practised in a temple, pacification at home, and terrible rites on a cremation ground; or all rites may be done in a temple. N (p. 270) is somewhat more detailed. Subjugation is preferably practised in a temple of Śiva or his spouse; for attraction no special location is necessary; for causing dissension one can best choose a cremation ground; eradication is done upon a sinister place, for example a deserted temple; while liquidation is also performed upon a cremation ground or a place sacred to Kālī under additional circumstances which remind of the *śavasādhanā* (obtaining perfection by riding a corpse): *...pretam āruhya mantravit*

> *dakṣiṇābhimukho bhūtvā dantaiḥ sampīḍya cādharam*
> *ripuṃ smṛtvā japaṃ kurvan saptarātreṇa mārayet*

"the expert of mantras should seat himself upon a corpse with his face into a southern direction, bite his lower lips with his teeth (in rage) and recite the mantra, meditating upon the enemy; by a period of seven days one will cause him to die."

B 2. More is said on the kinds of hide on which the practiser of the ritual is supposed to seat himself. In the Vedic ceremonies the usual prescription is the hide of a black antelope (*kṛṣṇājinam*). In Ṣaṭkarman theory, the different animal hides are probably considered to bring the performer into immediate touch with the particular powers which were supposed to be manifested in these animals. To take an example, JT (20,168f.) says the following: "During immobilization, the hides of elephants (are prescribed as seats), and that of a buffalo during liquidation; the hide of a deer during eradication, and that of a goat on the occasion of a rite of subjugation. For causing dissension, that of a jackal is prescribed, and the hide of a cow for pacification; for the sake of obtaining various perfections and welfare, the hide of a tiger is laid down" [8]. Below, the lists given by five authorities are presented. They differ considerably between each other. Only MMD and T are in accordance on all points, but they give different ślokas. The data in S are incomplete; the gaps have been filled up from the BMR (p. 11) which declares to quote S.

Number code of ritual act	MMD (25,16) T (p. 367)	JT (20,168)	S(p.187, st. 50 and p. 234)	N(p.270)
1	cow	cow	(deer)	tiger
2	rhinoceros	goat	sheep	tiger
3	elephant	elephant	(cow)	—
4	jackal	jackal	horse	—
5	sheep	deer	camel	buffalo
6	buffalo	buffalo	buffalo	human hair
8	—	—	tiger	tiger
9	—	—	—	tiger
Mokṣa	—	—	elephant	tiger

Besides, JT says that a tiger skin is competent to effectuate all results, and S says nearly the same for a red cloth (*raktakambala*). One observes that the tiger skin is also greatly favoured by N. It would be cumbersome to give the Skt. names of the animals because they are often denoted by way of synonyms (e.g., *jambuka*, *pheru*, *śṛgāla* for the jackal). One observes that MMD and T (as well as JT in this case) remain true to the summing up of the Six Acts given by them beforehand; they only mention Nos. 1-6 (Type 1, above p.259). Sometimes an explanation can be attempted for the prescription of the hide of a particular animal. The cow, most pure of all animals, is naturally suited for a rite of Śānti—although the sinister thing is that the use of a cow's hide may presuppose a cow's slaughter. The elephant, most massive of animals, is suited for immobilization; the jackal for causing dissension. The buffalo is widely known in the Indian subcontinent as a symbol of death.[6]

A different treatment of the subject is contained in the SST (2,71). This chapter treats of the seats of the initiated (*dīkṣāsana-*). It mentions three categories of seats: those of metal, those of wood, and those connected with animals. The last category seems to imply a seat only in the shape of the animal in question. (2,71,1). The Ṣaṭkarman terms occupy only a minor position among the aims expressed. Thus, a horse is associated with the obtaining of one's wishes (*vāñchitāptiḥ*); a goose, tiger or elephant with similar vague categories: a serpent or hare with the destruction of an enemy; a lion with obtaining a kingdom; a falcon (*śyena-*) with eradication; a crane with immobilization. As to the metals, *loha* copper leads to liquidation, *tāmra* copper to Śānti, silver to temporal rule, gold to obtaining all wishes, and so on. Similar results are to be expected from seats of wood. It needs not to be assumed that the choice of these materials is a kind of automaton necessarily bringing about in the view of these authors the results mentioned for them; it is implied, however that a practiser who has a certain objective in mind should carefully choose from the expedients at his disposal those which are in keeping with the mainstream of his will so that they will be able to reinforce this stream in their turn.

B 3. As to the postures to be taken by the performer when he sits down, the situation in the texts is comparable to that with regard to the seats themselves. Only MMD and T are in complete agreement without using the same wording. Other sources sometimes differ considerably, but in one case all are in accordance: the Cock's Posture (*kukkuṭāsana*) belongs to the rite of causing dissension. The Padma or Lotus posture is preferred for Śānti and Puṣṭi. For the other correspondences the scheme may suffice:

Number of ritual act	code MMD (25,15) T(p.366)	BPK 3,9	S(p.187, st. 49)	N (p.270)
1	Padma	Paṅkaja (=Padma)	Svastika	Svastika
2	Svastika	Svastika	Bhadra	—
3	Vikaṭa	Kuliśa	Vikaṭa	—
4	Kukkuṭa	Kukkuṭa	Kukkuṭa	Kukkuṭa
5	Vajra	Kukkuṭa	Ardha-svastika	Ardhasv.
6	Bhadra (ka)	Uccabhadra	Ardhasthāpana, Pārṣṇika	Ardhotthāna
8	—	Daṇḍa	Svastika	Pārṣṇika
9	—	Paṅkaja	Svastika, Padma	Paṅkaja

Of these sources, T adds the details as to how each posture is constituted. BPK again gives the postures without assigning them to a particular act; these data are supplied by the Skt. commentary. Postures of the body are an important feature of the yoga system. By assuming one of them, the performer of a Ṣaṭkarman act sets himself upon his own path of yoga.

B 4. A very important point to be considered is the direction of the sky to be faced during the ritual. By turning his face towards a certain region the performer announces his intention to contact the forces that live in that same region and that influence from there the course of things in the Centre, that is: the scene of habitation and activity of the subject. All the forces of good and evil are represented in the compass, and all directions of the compass are present in the orientation system advised by the texts on Ṣaṭkarman; another sign that the whole range of human activity, for good as well as for evil, is comprised by these rituals.[7] As there are, strictly speaking, only Six Acts and eight (chief and intermediary) directions of the sky, it is understandable that a systematical text like MMD only fills in six of these eight directions; but some others try to occupy all eight of them. An example (S, p. 183, st.31 = T, p.365) : "In Indra ('s region) there is immobilization; eradication in Agni (the S.E.); all kind of witchcraft in Yama's region; in the Demon, causing dissension; pacification in the regions of Varuṇa and Vāyu (prob. corrupt) ; in the part of the Wind Gods (the N.W.), destruction of the family; in the Yakṣa (Kubera; the N.), strife and separation" [9]. There is considerable difference of opinion between the authorities also in this point, but the tendency towards a general pattern is recognizable. No.1, Śānti, most often wavers between the N. and N.E., but in two of the sources it is located in the W. Vaśīkaraṇa (2) often belongs to the N., Stambhana (3) is generally placed in the E. (presumably because Indra, the lord of that region, rides an elephant which is, as we saw, associated with this feat). Vidveṣaṇa (4) belongs to the S.W. and Māraṇa (6) to the S. For Uccāṭana (5) the sources are divided between the N.W. (the region of the God of the Wind) and the S.E. We can say that the general Hindu pattern of the division of the compass between good and evil forces has been roughly followed. The picture is, however, further complicated not only by the inclusion of Ākarṣaṇa (8), Puṣṭi (9) and Mohana (7), but also by the appearance of still other rituals and aims like *dāhakarman* "burning", *kulotsāda* "destruction of the family", *āyuṣya* "longevity", *sarvasiddhi* "general perfection" and *kalahavigrahau* "strife and separation". It should be noted also that, while the sources usually describe the region of the sky the performer should face (cf. MMD 25, 10; BPK 3,5; N), at least the JT (20, 161ff.) seems to have in mind the direction in which the firepit (*kuṇḍam*) should lie. Probably the one implies the other, although S (p.193) for a few cases gives special directions for the location of the firepit (for instance, to the N.W. for Ākarṣaṇa, Vidveṣaṇa and Uccāṭana).

Our sources are; BPK 3,5; JT 20,161ff.; K p. 23, st. 11; MMD 25, 9f.; N p. 272; S p. 181, st. 11 (S-1); S p.183, st. 31 (S-2); S p. 193, unnumbered stanza (S-3) ; S p. 193, st. 13 (S-4) ; T p. 365 (= S-2). The following scheme makes use of the number code for the Acts.

Source	E.	S.E.	S.	S.W.	W.	N.W	N.	N.E.
MMD	3	6	—	4	—	5	2	1
S-1	3	6	—	4	—	—	2	1

JT	(3)	*dāha-karman*	6	4	2	5	1	*sarva-siddhi*
S-2=T	3	5	6	4	1	*kulot-sāda*	*kalaha, vigraha*	(1)
S-3	1,9,3	5	6	4	—	2	1,9,8	—
N	—	5	6	4	—	2,9	8	—
K	3	4	—	—	7	5	(2)	—
BPK	3	4	8	9	1	5 (*calana*)	2	6
S-4	2	—	6	—	*dhana*	—	1,9, *āyuṣya*	—

Some further notes on this scheme:

1. JT says that Stambhana should be done in the *vāruṇī diś*, which means the W. But this is highly improbable, as the same source also places Vaśya (2) in the W. We took liberty to put Stambhana (3) in the E., its usual position, also for the JT.

2. S-2 and T give Śānti (1) two positions: both agree about the W., while the second position is in the N. (some) in T and in the N.W. (*vāyu*) in S. We took liberty to replace this second occurrence of Śānti to the N.E.

3. Māraṇa is circumscribed by the broader term *abhicārika* or *sarvābhicārika* in S-2/T and in S-4; by *niṣedha* in BPK.

4. In S-2/T, all other rites are relegated to "the position of Brahman" (*brahmaṇaḥ pade*), explained by the Skt. commentary to be the N.E. The term may point to a firepit in the Centre, the usual "position of Brahman" in orientation.

5. Two of the three lines found in K on the subject are also present in S (p. 182, st. 22).

6. Vaśīkaraṇa is mentioned in K without a corresponding region; it has been placed here in the N., its most probable position.

It is unnecessary to proceed always in the same detailed manner with the further intricacies of the theory of Tantric magic. They might provide the material for a thoroughly specialized study. As we saw, the general lines along which these classifications were made, are, beside the categories of time and place, the rules on meditation and recitation, the sacrifice into the fire and a number of diverse topics concerning the practiser's behaviour and apparel.

C. The performance of recitation (*japaḥ*) in magic pemands a sound knowledge of the rules of mantras and their application (*mantravādaḥ*). Mantras (formulas or spells) are supranormal devices with their own specialized powers, and identified with deities. They should be dealt with very carefully.

C 1. One should realize that the application of a mantra varies in accordance with its sex. A mantra can be male, female or neuter. The sex is usually, but not always, determined by the mantra's last word; thus, a mantra ending on the neuter word *namaḥ* "honour" is also considered neuter.[8]

C 2. The voice in which the spell is uttered is also important: the utterance may be done aloud, in a whispering tone, or in the mind. About the relative precedence of these alternatives the AgPur in its chapter on mantra traditions (293) has to say (st. 28) that an inaudible, whispering recitation is ten times preferable to japa done aloud; while japa done merely with the tongue is a hundred times as good, and mental recitation even a thousand times as preferable. It is in keeping with this set of relative valuation when N (p. 271) prescribes mental recitation for Śānti, Puṣṭi and final release; silent recitation for the "intermediate" actions of subjugation and attraction, and japa done aloud for all evil acts [10]. For other instances, the reader is referred to S (p. 193) and T (p. 370).

C 3. The mantras are determined up to a high degree by their closing words such as *namaḥ* and *svāhā*. The authoritative MMD (25,32; followed also in S, p. 198, st. 22) prescribes six of these words for the Six Acts, constituting six "classes" (*jātayaḥ*): *namaḥ* for Śānti, *svāhā* for Vaśīkaraṇa, *vaṣaṭ* for Stambhana, *vauṣaṭ* for Vidveṣaṇa, *huṃ* for Uccāṭana, and *phaṭ* for Māraṇa. One observes that these are the six words discussed above in connection with *pūjā* and other ritual (p.72). Other, older texts give other prescriptions. Thus, *svāhā* is mentioned for Śānti by BPK; for Puṣṭi by KCT; while the Mahāmāyā fragment opens and closes the syllable of its mantra Aghorebhyaḥ by *vaṣaṭ* and *huṃ phaṭ* only, ending besides by *namaḥ svāhā*. As peculiar features may be mentioned the association of *svadhā* with Puṣṭi by S and BPK, and of *namaḥ* with Māraṇa by SST (2,18,94). Needless to say that here, as elsewhere, the authorities often differ in their opinions although there is a general pattern of conformity (*phaṭ* is, for example, always prescribed for evil rites).

The simplified scheme given below is made up from the following sources: BPK 3,10; S p. 186, st. 45 (S-1) = T p. 369f.; S, l.c. (S-2)-T p. 370; S p. 198, st. 22 (S-3); MMD 25,32; KCT 3,80; AgPur 125, 41f. The scheme is simplified in this way that two statements given by S on p. 186 have been left out and that all references to rites other than the Six Acts (denoted by the number code) have also been left out.

Jāti	BPK	S-1 T-1	S-2 T-2	S-3	MMD	KCT	AgPur
namaḥ			1	1	1	1	1
svāhā	1	1	2,8	2	2	9	
vaṣaṭ	2	2		3	3	2	
huṃ	4	4	6	5	5	6	6
vauṣaṭ	8	8	7,9,4,5	4	4	8	9,2
phaṭ	5	5,6		6	6		4,5
svadhā	9	9					
ghe ghe	6,3						

C 4. It is important to know the method of inserting the name of the *sādhya*, the "victim" or "patient" of the ritual within the mantra. The name should in any case be mentioned because it is a manifestation of the sādhya's self. By enveloping the sādhya's name within the syllables of the mantra the practiser thus envelopes the sādhya himself. There are six methods of inserting the name, each helping to effectuate one of the Six Acts. According to the MMD (25,18) they are: *granthanam* (usually *grathanam*) for Śānti; *vidarbhaḥ* for Vaśīkaraṇa; *sampuṭaḥ* for Stambhana; *rodhanam* for Vidveṣa; *yogaḥ* for Uccāṭana and *pallavaḥ* for Māraṇa. Bhaṭṭacharya (Introd. to SM, vol. 2, p. LXXXVII) gives the same division but other sources may deviate. The alternatives are very simple; for instance, Grathana "knotting" consists in alternating the syllables of the name with those of the spell; Vidarbha is the same, but with two syllables of the spell for one of the name; Yoga is uttering the name before the spell while Pallava means the opposite (MMD 25, 19ff.; some other sources are BPK 3,1; T p. 369; S p. 185,39f.). The practice has its forerunners in Vedic literature. In the AitBr (12,8,9) the "cutting away" of the *nivid*—a stanza inserted in the hymn of praise—from the rest of the hymn by means of the syllables *somsavom* is said to be equal to the cutting away of the sacrificer—the ruler—from his subjects, because the *nivid* is the sacrificer and the hymn denotes the subjects (cf. also Hillebrandt, p. 102).

C 5. The correct recitation should be accompanied by regulation of the breath in various ways effectuating the Ṣaṭ-karman divisions. On this subject there seems to be the authority of the MMD (25,33f.) only.

C 6. The next regulations concern the handling of the rosary (*akṣa-mālā*). It is important to know the use of the correct fingers when revolving the rosary during recitation.[9]

C 7. The composition of the rosary itself should be also carefully arranged—its thread and the number and material of the beads (*maṇi-*) strung on it; thus, in order to drive the enemy from his home (Uccāṭana) MMD prescribes the use of the teeth of a corpse as beads, T the teeth of a horse. The system given by S (p.192) is: beads of corals or vajra for Vaśya and Puṣṭi; those made from the tusks of rutting elephants for Ākarṣaṇa; horse's teeth strung on a thread made of the victim's hair for Vidveṣa and Uccāṭana; and beads made from the teeth of a corpse or an ass for Māraṇa. The passage proceeds with other materials for different aims. In some cases the sources prescribe that for Māraṇa the string should be made from human sinews. In general we must say that here also the particulars differ considerably.[10] The SST (2,56,2) differentiates the beads according to the grades of society the performer belongs to.

D 1. About the *mudrāḥ*, gestures to be made in the different rites, there is complete agreement between MMD (25,26f.), S (p. 188, st. 51) and T (p. 367). The last two of these sources give identical ślokas. The lotus gesture (*padmamudrā*) is prescribed for Śānti; the noose (*pāśa-*) for Vaśīkaraṇa; the club (*gadā*) for stambhana, the mace (*musala-*) for Vidveṣaṇa; the axe (*kuliśa-*) for Uccāṭana; and the sword (*khaḍga-,asi-*) for Māraṇa. In this way each act is associated with a gesture considered symbolical of it. The BPK (3,8) among others adds the elephant hook (*aṅkuśam*) for Ākarṣaṇa. It should be noted that these mudrās cannot be separated from their material counterparts, the attributes carried by the images of deities or evoked together with the deities themselves in the mind of the adept who meditates on them. By making the gestures, say of pāśa and aṅkuśa, one assigns into oneself the divine powers of attraction and subjugation which so often appear together in the deities worshipped (the attributes pāśa and aṅkuśa often form a pair in opposite hands of the images of deities).

D 2. Besides these "emblematic" gestures, there is another group of three called *homamudrāḥ* "sacrificial gestures", destined to accompany the oblation into the fire. They are the representations of female animals: the antelope (*mṛgī*), the goose (*haṃsī*) and the swine (*śūkarī*). The Rudrayāmala Tantra (quoted by T, p. 374) prescribes Mṛgī for rites of Śānti, Haṃsī for those of Puṣṭi and Śūkarī for those of Abhicāra (see also S, p. 197f.; MMD 25,27-29 with differences).

D 3-5. It is of course important that the officiant exercises the right kind of meditation (*dhyānam*). Dhyāna is the execution of imaginative will-power which, if done correctly and consistently, is able to move mountains. Dhyāna regulations fall into three categories: those concerning the deity, the state of the own mind, and the victim.

D 3. The deity should for instance be meditated upon in the right colour and the right outward appearance, and wearing the right attributes (S, p. 188, 191; MMD 25,6; elsewhere). The point needs no further elaboration here.

D 4. As to the state of the own mind, one may refer to SM, No. 181, in which it is laid down that the performer of a Śānti rite should have a pacified mind; when he tries to promote welfare, he concentrates his thought upon welfare; while trying to subjugate, his mind should be in a state of intense desire, and when he executes the Māraṇa rite, his mind should be cloudy and disturbed:

śāntike śāntacittena puṣṭike puṣṭicetasā /
vaśye cotkaṇṭhacittena udvignena tu māraṇe //

Others say that the mind during Māraṇa or other evil rites should be full of anger; this anger should manifest itself also outwardly, for instance by biting the lips (*sandaṣṭoṣṭhapuṭaḥ*, S p. 188, st. 52). The LiPur (2,50,32) points out that during Abhicāra the practiser should be "senseless by rage" (*krodhamūrchitaḥ*).[11]

D 5. The victim or patient of a rite should also be meditated upon as being in a state answering the rite in question. There are general rules like that of S (p. 184, st. 33) that one should imagine the victim as standing during Māraṇa, sleeping during Uccāṭana and seated during other rites. Other prescriptions enter more into details. S p. 188, st. 52 says that the victim of a rite of Ākarṣaṇa should be thought of as being caught and dragged along like a fish by fish hooks; during Vidveṣaṇa one imagines the victim as being scolded by other people; during Uccāṭana he should be thought of as pursued by the people with sticks out of the village like a thief. Sometimes the texts engage in picturesque elaborations of this kind (thus in KCT 4, 144ff.; SM, No. 60,62,92 a.o.).

E. The fire sacrifice (*homaḥ*), that time-honoured method in vogue from the earliest Indian religious texts onwards, retains its full importance in the ritual of magic, at least in its Sanskritized shape. The fire is a supernatural force able to protect and destroy whom it wishes. By laying out the fire and worshipping it in the right method a practiser may be able to obtain all his desires (cf. the rules for the Lotus Fire in KJ ch. 5-8). But the performer of a magical fire sacrifice should first ascertain himself of the fulfilling of some conditions.

E 1. He should, for example, lay out the required form of the firepit. The firepit may have different shapes dependent on the kind of act practised. The different forms of the fire obtain already in Vedic tradition where we have the different shapes of the three fires Āhavanīya (square, destined for oblations to the gods), Gārhapatya (round, destined for cooking the oblations) and Anvâhārya (in the shape of a crescent; it is destined to ward off the evils from the South). The system presented by the AVPar (25,1,8) is preponderantly in Ṣaṭkarman style and sets the tune for Tantric schemes of the same kind. There is, however, not so much systematization on this subject as in some other cases. The MMD, for instance, omits it, while other sources are meagre on this point. Below, we give a simplified scheme for which the sources were the following: AVPar (25,1,8ff.); JT (20,159); SM (No. 181, p. 368); N (p.272); T (p. 3 3 .

Form of Kuṇḍa	AVPar	JT	SM	N	T
Square	1, *vijaya*	1			*sarva*
Circular	9	5	1	2,9	1
Crescent	2	2	2		*śubham*
Triangular	*abhicāra*	8		2,9	destruction of enemies
Sexagonal	6	3,6			*cheda*, 6
Octogonal	4				cure of disease
Lotus	1, *sarva*	various results			rain
Fish				5	
Vajra				6	
Wind-form (?)			9		
Space-form (?)			6		

Besides, other stray prescriptions are found on other places. Thus, Mt Pur (93,142) suggests a triangular form for Vidveṣaṇa and Abhicāra in the cadre of worship to the planets; and a round form for Va´ya and Uccāṭana on the same occasion. S p. 189, st. 2 strikingly deviates by advising a crescent form for Māraṇa. HT (2,1) prescribes a round form for Śānti, square for Puṣṭi and a triangle for Māraṇa.

E 2. One should also know the tongues of the fire and their positions, colours and functions (S p. 195f.; MMD 25, 47ff.; T p. 373f.).

E 3. One should choose different kinds of fuel (*samidh*) in accordance with the rite. Similar prescriptions are given already by the AVPar (26,3,2ff.). The Ṛgvidh (1,15,6) refers to fuel sticks which cause disturbance. The MMD system is as follows (25,37ff.); Dūrvā for Śānti; Dāḍima for Vaśya; Rājataru for Stambhana (also in JT 20,171); Dhattūra for Vidveṣa; Cūta for Uccāṭana; and Khadira for Māraṇa. Besides, these fuel sticks should be watered with specific kinds of ghee or oil (for other instances, see MMD 24, 125ff.; PST 14, 37ff.; PST 27,25ff.; JT 20,171ff.; T p. 377; ViDhPur 2,125, 1ff. = AgPur 260, 1ff.).

E 4. The most important regulations for Homa are of course those concerning the nature of the substances sacrificed.

They are of the following kinds: 1. Fruits including grains. 2. Flowers. 3. Sprinkled products. 4. Other substances. The texts devote much attention to the subject and many, many plants and other products find their place in the system. "Plants are like humans" (Kluckhohn, p. 185). The traditions about their applications often go back to the Veda. Their name may be an important factor in determining their ritual function, as when the plant *putrañjīva* is prescribed in a sacrifice for someone who desires healthy sons (*putra*; SST 3,19,57 a.o.) Lājās, parched grains used in marriage ceremonies, are prescribed for someone who tries to secure himself a bride by magical means (e.g., in PST 24,55), and so on. There are exceptional cases as when JT ch. 18 describes an elaborate system of pūjā (here included under homa) by means of flowers of gold combined with jewels. We give no further instances; a reliable treatment of the subject of materials for sacrifice would require an intimate knowledge of Indian plants and plant lore which the present writer lacks.[12] Suffice it to say that the whole Indian kingdom of vegetation seems to be represented in the Ṣaṭkarman system.

F. There are minor rules concerning the performer's apparel and the requisites used by him. We shall content ourselves with a succinct survey.

F 1. The method of wearing the sacred cord (*yajñopavītam*). This subject is dealt with by T (p. 366). For Stambhana and Vidveṣa, the cord may be prepared out of the intestines of cats and cocks; for Uccāṭana, cranes will do; for Māraṇa, owls.

F 2. One should restrict oneself to particular kinds of food (HT 2,10; T, p. 366).

F 3. In case the performer makes use of some ingredients, like dolls (*puttalikā*), he should be aware of certain rules about them, for example the kind of material they should be made of. Already in the SVBr (2,5,1), in the cadre of Vaśīkaraṇa, different materials are prescribed in accordance with the grade of society the victim belongs to. MMD ch. 2 specifies the sorts of clay of which a thumb-sized image of Ucchiṣṭa-Gaṇeśa should be made. S (p. 190), quoting "Āṅgirasa", differentiates the metals to be used for a ritual pot : a golden one filled with the nine kinds of jewels brings about Śānti; a pot made of *loha* should be used for Abhicāra, one of brass for Mohana, one of clay for Uccāṭana; or a pot made of red copper may hold good for all acts.

F 4. If the performer designs a Yantra (symbolical picture) in which the spell is inscribed (a very popular practice), the form and materials for it may be subjected to certain regulations (T, p. 365).

F 5. The ceremonial designs (*maṇḍala*) used are associated with the Five Elements. S (1,29) and MMD (25, 24) agree in combining Śānti with the maṇḍala of Water, Vaśya with Fire, Stambhana with Earth, Vidveṣa with Space, Uccāṭana with Wind and Māraṇa again with Fire. S also connects Māraṇa with Earth. KCT (4, 156) gives a slightly different scheme.

F 6. In general the performer should in all phases of the ritual give attention to the corresponding colours (see above, ch. 4). The general tendency is to combine white with Śānti, red with Vaśīkaraṇa, yellow with Stambhana, grey with Vidveṣaṇa and/or Uccāṭana and black with Māraṇa. Ākarṣaṇa may be associated with pink or red; in the Mahāmāyā fragment it is connected with white, while Śānti is reached by a meditation on an image of manifold colours. SST (2,18,96f.) combines white (flowers) with the attainment of eloquence (some sources : S 1,32; MMD 25,6; N p. 271; T p. 365f.; BPK 3,9).

F 7. At the end of the rite, the person for whose benefit it has been done should not forget the ritual gift (*dakṣiṇā*) by which he counterbalances the performer's services. MMD 25, 49ff., the only authority on the subject in the passages studied by us, specifies that, the more evil the rite, the higher should be the *dakṣiṇā*. The brahmans who serve at the ceremony should be without blemish and their food absolutely pure.

6.4. *Attraction*

Its nature. Although attraction by supranormal force does not feature in the list of Six Acts discussed above (p.259) as Type I, it is one of the best known and most widely performed acts of magic. The Skt. term *ākarṣaṇam* "drawing towards oneself" denotes any performance of the activity expressed by the compounded root *ā-kṛṣ-* "to draw towards oneself". As a technical term Ākarṣaṇa does not appear in the Vedic texts.

In the Epics and Purāṇas it may occur (e.g., MtPur 2,18) but probably usually without being a regular term for a specified magical action. In Tantric literature, the word is very frequent; it is often replaced by its synonym *ākṛṣṭiḥ*. By way of exception also *karṣaṇam* serves as an equivalent of *ākarṣaṇam* (SST 3,16,26).

The aims of magical attraction vary greatly. The objects of the act can be all those beings or things whose possession or neighbourhood are considered desirable, such as gods, women or material wealth. MtPur 93, 74 and 75 in one breath demands of the gods the obtainment of a wife and of jewels. The pattern of one type of sorcery being destined to bring about the possession of all kind of objects has its parallels in traditional societies dependent upon agriculture also outside India.[13] Attraction is usually brought about by a magician by means of the traditional methods of saying a spell, drawing a figure, or administering drugs sometimes mixed up with a fragment of the victim's possessions (in erotic magic). But there may be people who are able to accomplish their objective by the supranormal power of their thinking alone.[14] Ancient Indian literature procures many instances of holy men or gods who were able to draw the objects they needed towards themselves by merely meditating on them (*smṛtamātreṇa*). These powers can also be considered to fall under the category of Ākarṣaṇa although they do not imply a magical ritual. Viṣṇu summons his cakra in this way against the Asuras in the Mbh (1,17,20). He does the same with Garuḍa in the Devī BhPur (6,28,27). In the Kathās. (12,25, 35f.), a yogin summons a Yakṣiṇī by merely thinking about her. In Bhāsa's Karṇabhāra the hero Karṇa obtains from Indra an unfailing weapon by the hands of a celestial envoy who announces: *yadā smarasi tadā labhasva* "if you ever think of it, you will obtain it." In the MtPur (2,18), Manu is said to draw all beings towards himself by means of his yogic powers when the great flood has come; and the root *ā-kṛṣ-*is used to denote this feat:

bhūtān sarvān samākṛṣya yogenāropya dharmavit "having attracted all beings and caused them to go on board by means of his yoga, the pious one...". In mythology, God remains, however, the foremost wielder of Ākarṣaṇa. Kṣṛṇa attracts the gopīs by his youthful beauty and playfulness (cf. above, p.25). The Gar Pur (198,8) makes mention of a secondary divinity, attendant of Jvālāmukhī, who is called Ākarṣaṇī after this particular power which is her speciality. The same text a few chapters earlier (194,13) calls upon Viṣṇu to attract all the speaker's sin towards himself out of that speaker's body (*Viṣṇuḥ sadā cākarṣatu kilbiṣaṃ mama vigrahāt*). God's power of attraction will become also active during the end of the world: Hari then will draw towards himself the vital airs from the bodies of the creatures (MtPur 166,5 : *prāṇāpānasamānādyān vāyūn ākarṣate Hariḥ*). Attraction, like all acts of māyā, is a neutral force. Manu in primeval times made use of it for the immediate hail of beings; but, as often, it may fall into the wrong hands and be applied for selfish ends like enriching oneself at the cost of others. In a broad sense attraction may be stated to comprise even those devices by which a worshipper draws the deity adored towards the place of worship. As such may be reckoned the uttering of mantras, the recitation of hymns, and the meditation on the divine figure in accordance with a standard description (*dhyānam*). In all these cases the performer may have been thought to wield a supranormal power by which he is able to coerce his divine "victim".

In the Mahāmāyā fragment Ākarṣaṇa is exemplified by two types: the obtainment of wealth from a king and the containment of floods. These acts have their parallel in Indian literature, but remarkably enough they do not feature in the passages on Ākarṣaṇa of the Ṣaṭkarman monographs. Only S (p.249) mentions a method for attracting kings without stating the acquisition of wealth from them—although this has probably been understood, because for which other aim should a brahman or other religious specialist seek the king's company? In general, these monographs pay due attention to Ākarṣaṇa. K (p.33) restricts itself to a discussion of the attraction of a woman and then introduces other subjects, which do not belong to Ākarṣaṇa properly speaking. D (p.147, Benares ed. ch. 10) begins by announcing that the method for Ākarṣaṇa will be taught by which one is able to attract a king, his subjects, in short : all people. Anybody whose name is inscribed in the middle of a certain spell in a yantra will arrive quickly, even when he lives a hundred miles away. A preoccupation with women appears when the text adds that even Urvaśī would be attracted in this way. The mantra in this case is as follows (Benares ed.) : *Oṃ namo Ādirūpāya amukasyākarṣaṇaṃ kuru kuru svāhā* "*Oṃ*, honour to the Primeval Manifestation, effect the attraction of N.N., *svāhā*". Then follows another method by means of the goddess Tvaritā and her mantra. S (p.249, ch.7 : Ākarṣaṇa) deals chiefly with the attraction of women, among others by means of mantras of Tripurā and Kamalākṣī. The text refers to the Tripurātantra and Bhūtaḍāmaratantra. The chapter also contains a passage on Vidveṣaṇa. N (ch.6, p.296) also focuses upon the attraction of women, this time by means of a mantra of Raktacāmuṇḍā. In another method men and cattle may figure as victims.

Objects of Ākarṣaṇa : the gods. We now proceed by differentiating the beings and objects which may be affected by Ākarṣaṇa. Gods and other suprahuman beings may serve as such in the first place. The presence of the god worshipped is absolutely necessary for the efficacy of any ritual ceremony. In order to ensure this presence various methods already referred to above are employed. Of course the most respectable way is humbly to implore the god to bestow the grace of his attention to the gift destined for him and in answer to this gift to further the needs which motivated it. But other methods are also practised which can hardly be described under the term "worship". A few examples from Buddhist texts will elucidate this. GST (p.55,1f.) in its typical obscure style mentions the attraction of the Buddhas (*buddhākarṣaṇam*) by the sādhaka, whose attributes are the vajra, meditation on the personalized mantra, and the elephant hook (*aṅkuśam*) constituted by the performer's body, speech and mind (*kāyavākcitta-*). This vajrākarṣaṇa is followed by a *samayākarṣaṇa*—"attraction by means of the Agreement"· the word samaya, a catchword of this text, denotes the nature of the close connection between the adept and the supernatural forces with its consequences for the behaviour of both parties. The MMK (I, ch. 11, p. 106f.) alludes to the attraction of supranormal beings (*ākarṣaṇaṃ ca mahāsattvānāṃ ca karoti*). The same text, vol. III, ch.52 (p.575) declares that all gods can be coerced by means of mantras: "all of them, being attracted in consequence of the Agreement, are brought to this place by the power of Yamāntaka the king of Anger (a mantra considered identical with this fearsome figure), devoured by Him and placed into an agreement as obedient servants to Mañjughoṣa" [11]. The performer is advised to make a small image of the god to be coerced and to recite the King of Anger until the image begins to tremble, totter or sweat. This is the sign that the god has arrived in own person and that he will comply with any wish uttered by the performer. HT (ch. 4, *devatābhiṣekaḥ*) describes how the sādhaka has himself anointed by all the Tathāgatas whom he has drawn towards himself by means of a black ray in the shape of an elephant hook coming out of his own heart. The SM (No.35, p.80) prescribes meditation on the Sun with above it a red syllable *hrīḥ* emitting rays which draw hither the Tathāgata Amitābha. Such practices can be compared with the various forms of Yakṣiṇīsādhana (above, p. 98) by which the performer attracts a Yakṣiṇī and compels her to serve him. According to the SST (1,1,50ff.) Ākarṣaṇa is a particular insight (*ākarṣaṇabuddhiḥ*) obtained by Kāla as a gift from his female counterpart Kālī; by applying it he is able to realize that goddess' nature.

The Balinese collection of hymns contains an example of the power of attraction (Stuti and Stava, No. 402, p.252). When the Kṣatriya feels himself in a difficult position (in battle?), he may try to strengthen himself by means of a prose formula (a*vidyādharaḥ*) which seems to be addressed (the Skt text is unclear) to a mantra—or female deity representing a mantra—possessing various powers of attraction. By this formula the reciter draws towards himself the energies of Viṣṇu, of Garuḍa, and of Viṣṇu's weapons: the club Kaumodakī, the sword Nandaka and the conch Pāñcajanya. This procedure should be accompanied by nyāsa on certain parts of the body. The acts of attraction are invoked by the word *ākarṣaṇa-*: *Viṣṇuśaktyākarṣaṇe*, and so on. By thus drawing divine power into his body the nobleman can feel duly protected.

In methods like these man can attract gods and divine power, but the reverse is also true. Instances of divine attraction have been mentioned above. Demons have also this power like Kali the demon of dice who miraculously attracts Nala in the Mbh, Book 3 (Nala 10,26; *ākṛṣyamāṇaḥ Kalinā sauhārdenāvakṛṣyate*).

Attraction of human beings is sometimes effected by meditation on, which generally means identification with, divine beings invested with this particular power. Such a figure is Kālarātrī who "possesses the power of drawing towards herself all men and women", *sarvastrīpuruṣākarṣiṇi*, according to the mantra of Kālarātrī quoted in the commentary on MMD ch. 18. The SM (No. 115, p. 243) describes a design on cloth representing Tārā with four arms and in the colours red, dark green, black and white. In her hands she bears the attributes noose (*pāśa-*), sword (*khaḍga-*), lotus (*utpala-*) and elephant hook (*aṅkuśa-*) by means of which she attracts the beings (*ākarṣayanti*). She attracts them from even more than a hundred thousand miles (*yojanaśatasahasrād apy ākarṣayati*); but a necesssary condition is that her mantra should also be recited a hundred thousand times. A mystical attraction of all creatures by a Bodhisattva is described by the KCT (3, 199): "having attracted by means of his vajra elephant hook of Wisdom all beings which exist in the commonwealth of creatures in the threefold state of existence, motivated by supreme compassion, he should have them anointed by the Buddhas within the Maṇḍala (in his mind) by means of the vajra Water of Life which has the form of the spotless Moon; and after they have thus obtained the path of the Wielder of the Vajra, they should be sent back to their respective places, their sins melted away..." [12]. A great master in the art of Ākarṣaṇa is met with in the person of the Buddhist monk Nanda whose existence is predicted by the Buddha in the MMK (ch. 53, Vol. III, p. 617ff.). He is introduced as *mantrārthayuktātmā* "disciplined in the secret meaning of spells", *tantrajña*—"knower of Tantric lore", *bahuśruta*—"very learned". This holy man will possess a wonderful pot procured by a spell revealed by a Yakṣa (*yakṣamantrapracodita-*), the contents of which are continually being replenished. At a certain time this pot will be stolen, and the monk, enraged, will summon all beings "from Brahmā down to the tufts of grass" (*ā brahmastambaparyantam*, a standard phrase). By thus concentrating upon their quick attraction (*kṣiprākarṣaṇatatparaḥ*) he feels certain to have summoned also the thief. The text describes the effects of his power: "within a moment, having merely been thought upon (*smṛtamātreṇa*), by a mere uttering of the syllable *huṃ*, he would be able to summon (all beings) led by Brahmā on earth; attracted were all the gods, beginning with Brahmā and including Indra; they were afflicted, emitting cries of despair, shouting horribly"[13]. They arrive and bow humbly saying "what have we to do, why have we been summoned ?" The matter is investigated by the monk and the offenders turn out to be Pretas who live in a perpetual state of hunger. The saint in his mercy allows them to keep the pot in their possession. We have here an instance of attraction of all beings, gods and humans alike. This feat is aften alluded to by "attraction of the threefold inhabited world" (*trailokyākarṣaṇam*). We find such allusions for instance in the AgPur (312, 8) and the SST. This last text in 1, 14 describes a *trailokyākarṣaṇī siddhiḥ* connected with the goddess Madhumatī. It results especially in the attraction of Bhairavas, Vetālas, Kinnaras and Devas (st. 13ff.). The mantra itself contains the expression *sthāvarajaṅgamākarṣaṇī* "attracting all beings endowed with or deprived from locomotion". Other places in the SST are 3, 3, 92 (*ākarṣaṇaṃ trilokānām*) and 3, 14, 61-66 (*sarvākarṣaṇam* by means of a "doll method").

Among the beings liable to be the object of the attraction figure also kings (D, ch. 10; S, ch. 7, p. 250) and animals. The economic basis of the attraction of animals is evident in societies which are to a high degree dependent upon hunting game.[15] but scarcely less so when cattle forms one of the main sources of subsistence and wealth. In the Vedic environment this is illustrated by the sacrifices executed for the benefit of those who desire the increase of their livestock (*paśukāma-*). In later texts the procurement of animals plays only an insignificant role in the list of objectives. "Cattle" (*paśuḥ*) occurs only occasionally among the desired goods. But attraction of animals may occur in quite another context, as when in the Kathās. (2, 3, 4) king Udayana by his power of playing the *viṇā* entices the wild elephants of the jungle:

Tattantrikalanirhrādamohamantravaśikṛtān
ānināya ca saṃyamya sadā mattān vanadvipān

"He always (by his play) tamed and drew towards himself the wild rutting elephants who became subjugated by the delusive spells of the melodious cascades of his lute".

Attraction of women. The bulk of the space occupied by the treatment of Ākarṣaṇa in the relevant texts is devoted to women. These by nature feeble and unsteady beings-- as is often stated in Sanskrit literature —are particularly liable to become the object of the performer's prowess. The attraction of a woman, and of the object of a man's love in particular, is a frequent phenomenon in all cultures[16]. The subject could here be profitably combined with a discussion of erotic magic in general in the Indian cultural environment, but this would require too large a digression. Suffice it to say that also in the Indian view love means that the mind is attracted towards the beloved (Kathās. 2, 5, 71 : *tadguṇākṛṣṭacittatvāt*).

The AV which contains a number of love spells[17] describes in 3, 25, 4 the psychic condition of the girl magically attracted :

śucā viddhā vyoṣayā śuṣkāsyā abhisarpa mā
mṛdur nimanyuḥ kevali priyavādiny anuvratā

"betake thyself to me, pierced by scorching sorrow, thy mouth dried up; meek, devoid of anger, exclusively devoted to me, speaking amiably, loyal". The plastic description of the victim's situation without doubt has been meant to greatly enhance the force of the powerful word and accompanying act. The SVBr (2, 6, 8ff.) discusses methods to ensure a woman's love and suggests to sacrifice some dust from her footsteps to secure her coming. The mantras to be said are taken from the Sāmaveda, like Grāmageyagāna 1, 1, 1, 2 : *Agna āyāhi vitaye* "O Agni come to our feast". The ceremony should be continued until the victim arrives. The aim of "winning the beloved maiden" is often alluded to. We quote the AVPar (36, 6, 1 : *kanyākāmaḥ*) and the SST (3, 15, 22: *kāminiṃ vāñchitāṃ labhet*; 3, 18, 19: *kāminiṃ labhet*; 3, 18, 21: *kanyakāptiḥ*). With the mere motif of showing his power the attraction is performed by a magician (*indrajālikaḥ*) in the first act of Rājaśekhara's Prakrit drama Karpūramañjarī. The woman evoked is the heroine after whom the play has been named; she appears out of nothing before the king who immediately falls in love with her. The successful performer is a Tantric priest called Bhairavānanda who boasts of his ability to bring even the moon down on earth and to stop the course of the sun; he also declares himself ready to bring hither the wives of gods and spirits.[13]

The Ṣaṭkarman monographs give some details on the ritual procedures by which one attracts a woman. Their efficacy is advertized by statements concerning the distance bridged: "she comes from a hundred miles away"; the high quality of the woman concerned: "even a princess, a Nāga girl or a divine maiden"; and the psychic situation into which she is brought: "with signs of sorrow; tormented by the God of Love". These texts expatiate more on the practical method (especially the preparation of herb mixtures) than on the accompanying psychical activity of the performer. The mantra is always mentioned together with its deity. One mantra can be utilized in combination with more than one method. An instance of a prescription (N 6, 3): "One should design a yantra (containing the victim's name and the mantra in question) upon a red cloth by means of red lac and red saffron powder. That yantra should be worshipped and buried at the foot of a tree; during three weeks one should constantly water it at day-break with water mixed up with rice grains; and one will (by this rite) attract a woman from afar even if she had been bound with fetters". The goddess in question is Raktacāmuṇḍā, and her mantra runs: "*turu turu*, attract N. N., *hrīṃ svāhā*". It should be recited ten thousand times before becoming effective.[14] AgPur 323, 15 f. contains another mantra directed to Cāmuṇḍā to the same effect.

Other interesting instances are afforded by the Tantras; they devote more attention to the accompanying meditation. In some cases they even seem to present mere meditation exercises. For instance, JT 17, 20ff., while discussing the powers of the Śrīvidyā, says that this mantra, when written in a yantra in a certain method and said three hundred thousand times (accompanied by the right meditation on a beautiful image of Śrī) will enable the performer to attract a princess of a beauty never seen and scarcely heard of before. Devoid of fear or shame she approaches him, being deluded by the spell (*mantramūḍhā*). Stanza 28 promises to the performer after a similar ceremony even a Yakṣiṇī, a Nāga maiden, an Apsaras, a Deva girl, or the enemy's wife. Their condition is described poetically: "torment caused by the God of Love has arisen in them;

their buttocks tremble, their minds are pierced by Kāma's arrows, their eyes waver; all this because of the meditation (by the performer) on the Great Goddess personifying Love"[15]. A similar description occurs in the stanzas 43f., 58, 61 and 86. Other passages may be found in the Śāradātilaka (according to Ewing, p. 66) and the PST (9, 23 and 24; 13, 83; ch. 18, Kāma meditation; 28, 16; 32, 19; 32, 28). It should of course be emphasized again that the goal of these authors—emancipation of the adept by unconventional methods—is widely different from that of the Ṣaṭkarman monographs which is pure magic to be practised by means of spells, decoctions and herbs.

Another interesting instance from the SM: in No. 59, p. 123, this text describes a meditation by the performer on himself as "Lord Mañjuśrī as the vajra God of Love" (Vajrānaṅgamañjuśrībhaṭṭāraka). He is of a yellow colour, and has three eyes and six arms. His hairs are plaited locks. He looks like a boy of sixteen years, lovely in all respects. In his right hand he holds sword, arrow and mirror; in the left ones, a blue lily[19] and an Aśoka branch. This god is identical with the God of Love and should be meditated upon as such (*madanaprayogeṇa bhāvayet*).

The method of attraction concentrated upon is as follows: "with the arrow one pierces the victim's breast; with the Aśoka one hits her on the heart; with the sword one frightens her, after which one keeps the mirror in front of her; with the lotus one binds her feet and draws her towards himself despite her distress; her hair hangs loose. At the same time one utters a mantra: *Oṃ* Mañjughoṣa, attract N. N., *hrīḥ jaḥ*"[16]. The KCT (5, 43ff.) describes Ākarṣaṇa in the cadre of a Kaula ceremony. The adept meditates on and worships a mantra of Kālī—which also means: upon the goddess herself—and this causes the goddess to attract for him a maiden from the world of the gods or the Nāgas. Somewhat further (5,74f.) the author says that any woman whose name has been inscribed by the adept within the yantra worshipped by him will arrive, tormented by love, upon the place where he conduces his ritual. This woman should be given wine and meat and serve as his partner in the ceremony. A perhaps related meditation is described in Stuti & Stava, No. 073, 10-12, where on the occasion of worship of Smara, the God of Love, the performer should think on himself as being surrounded by various erotic sentiments and constituents of beauty in the eight directions; here the result is not Ākarṣaṇa but "extreme beauty, a shapely form ....a youthful age" and so on.

In the Mahâmâyâ fragment (Stuti & Stava No. 450, st.9) occurs a description of beautiful damsels in the cadre of Vaśīkaraṇa, not of Ākarṣaṇa. This brings us to the fact that the attraction, especially that of women, is very often closely combined with their subjugation. This can be observed already in the stanza from the AV quoted a few pages above (3, 25, 4f.); in stanza 6 of the same hymn the poet utters the wish that the lady may come under his power (*máma...váśe*). Vaśīkaraṇa and Ākarṣaṇa form a unity also in a comparatively early text like the MMK (for instance, vol.II, p. 531 : *dāsabhūtaṃ samāyātam*; p. 538). The same may be noted for SM No. 178 and preceding numbers. Negatively this is implied by the assertion of JT 17, 14 that the true sādhaka will not be deluded by the apparition of such beautiful women. A mantra recorded in the MMD (18, 43 f.) says : *sarvān ākarṣaya ākarṣaya śighra(ṃ) vaśaṃ kuru kuru* "attract attract all, bring bring them quickly under my power". Meditation on Tārā with four arms and four colours who attracts all beings leads to the result that one subjugates anybody one wishes: *yam icchati taṃ vaśam ānayati*. Cases like these imply that during the discussion of Vaśīkaraṇa we shall have succinctly to return to the manipulation of women. It may be only noted here that a rite of Ākarṣaṇa can theoretically be practised by a woman against a man. A Jaina text, Vyavahāra Bhāṣya (6, 148), makes mention of such cases performed against ascetics, and of the counter-measures advised which of course consist of certain spells (Jhavery, p. 281).

The attraction of material goods can also be traced in literature from the Veda onwards. The AV (1, 15) prays for "confluence of wealth" while in AV 3, 15 a poet tries to secure success in trade. Successful gambling may also be the subject. The TS (2, 3, 2) mentions the procurement of gold. The TBr (1, 1, 2, 3-4) suggests that someone who desires gifts from others should lay out the fire during the constellation Pūrvaphalgunī because Aryaman is its deity, and he is known as the bestower of wealth (Malaviya, p. 78). A rain of jewels is evoked according to the Vedabbha Jātaka (Jātakas, ed. Fausbôll, I, p. 253; Fick p.151 ff.). The economic aspect of the attraction of wealth in the texts concerns the brahmans as a class; for their livelihood they were dependent on their lay sponsors and the assumption lies near at hand that they have often tried to secure their position by influencing their clients by supranormal methods. We find already in the RV a poem in which its author threatens with evil consequences the man who withholds from the religious man what is due to him (RV 10, 117). The emphasis on rich gifts and dakṣiṇās in literature stands in the same tradition. But of course this focusing upon the brahmans does not exclude other people as possible executors of rites concerning the attraction of wealth, gold, jewels, clothings or food.

Of the Vedic ritual guides the SVBr (3, 1 and 2) procures methods for obtaining various kinds of wealth. Gold is promised in 3, 1, 2 (sacrifice of *bilva* leaves) when the ritual is successful; when it is not, silver will be obtained in any case. 3, 3, 3 promises a bucket of gold. Ṛgvidh 4, 10 offers a method for obtaining with the help of the recitation of RV 10, 141 the wealth of another person, presumably a personal enemy. Besides, the man is said to be completely destroyed. KauśS 19, 7 (trsl. Caland, p. 48) gives another method for the man who wants to become the owner of another's possessions. To that end one should consume a rice dish composed from ingredients taken from the victim's house; or, if this turns out to be impossible, he should make use of fresh cowdung from that homestead [20]. Methods for procuring gold are also given in AVPar 35, 2, 6 and 36, 21, 1; in the last case again with the help of the Bilva and by a sacrifice on the eighth or fourteenth day of the dark half of the month.

In a mythical setting the Mbh relates the attraction by the sage Uśanas of the possessions of Kubera the god of wealth (Mbh 12, 290, 12; acc. to Eliade, p. 159). A ritual counterpart in Buddhist literature is SM is No. 296 where Jambhala, Kubera's Buddhist colleague, is said to procure an endless stream of wealth as a result of a certain ritual. No. 293 promises the same, and besides any other thing desired like honour, sons, a kingdom, and after death the removal of all sorrow of existence. Here one comes upon the usual categories mentioned in the statements of rewards which figure so abundantly in this kind of texts. In N (p. 349, 3) a Yakṣiṇī is the victim of a performer's power of attraction.

Sometimes a god is not coerced but invoked and more or less humbly prayed to. It is difficult to draw a line between acts of magic and prayers with material intentions. The MtPur (93, 75) again tends towards coercion when its author simply declares: "just as all the gods are firmly established in (the possession of) all kinds of treasure, thus the gods should bestow upon me a gift of jewels" (17) (the word *ratna*—used in the text may have here a wider meaning of "precious object", "treasure").

Rich people or institutions are liable to be considered as having been performers or sponsors of this kind of magic. Thus the legend runs that the reason for the gorgeous wealth of the temple of Viṣṇu Veṅkaṭeśvara at Tirupati is that the famous philosopher Śaṅkara in days of yore established there a magical figure attracting money (*Dhanākarṣaṇayantra*) (Ramesan, p. 65). Jhavery (p. 226) relates a legend of Dharmaghoṣa Sūri: by reciting a certain hymn this Jain saint made the sea to offer jewels to a Jain temple on the shore. Obtaining jewels from the sea is advocated in N (p. 352, st. 17) where a mantra is given which addresses the Ocean as Rudra. In an interesting passage the PST (36, 60f.) mentions as a result of a rite that a thief will bring back the money stolen by him from the performer "bowing humbly and trying to pacify his wrath with presents". To this end a performer should sacrifice during three months with 108 sticks from a *bodhi* tree wet with sesamum oil while muttering the Gāyatrī of Viṣṇu Trailokyamohana. Attraction of wealth for the royal treasury is alluded to in LT 49, 24 (Gupta, p. 323). The SST (1, 14, 33ff.; 1, 15, 27f.) extols the result of Ākarṣaṇa done with the mantra of Madhumatī out of all proportions: one attracts goods (*vastūni*) from the ocean, the Meru, the ends of the earth, the nether world, Indra's heaven, Laṅkā and so on. It is of course also imaginable that such magic may be directed against the rich and powerful (cf. Kluckhohn, p. 141). This is exemplified by the statement of the Mahāmāyā fragment (Stuti & Stava, No. 450, st. 5): "a king, even when he lives in another continent...will humbly present his riches to the performer". It proved very difficult to find a good parallel for this highly stylized statement in Indian Sanskrit literature. Yet we might point to the AVPar (36, 26) which describes a rite as follows: "After a hundredthousandfold recitation (of a spell to Rudra) one goes to a river which runs to the sea and (constructs) on a platform of sand a liṅga and its base of the same material; one procures eight hundred red lotuses and performs Pūjā in the right method by them; standing up to the navel in the water one should further recitate the matutinal hymn; then the prince who rules the province will (come and) bow to him and give to him a hundred dīnāras and cows in full confidence, saying "care for me" [18]. The editors, Bolling and Von Negelein (p. 223) add the remark that the aim of the rite is "to force a neighboring king to seek the priestly services of the performer".

A related form of magic which is, however, usually not treated as a type of Ākarṣaṇa in the texts is the method for *finding a hidden treasure* (*nidhidarśanam, nidhānalābhaḥ*, etc.). It is alluded to by the Mbh (14, 65, 1ff.; Arbman, p. 215) and by the SVBr (3, 7, 7 and 8). The AVPar mentions it in 35, 2, 4 (*nidhānaṃ paśyate mahat*), and the SST in 3, 19, 55. We will not go into details here and only mention that N (p. 356 ff., ch. 15; Añjanam "Ointment") repeatedly deals with it, for example on p. 363, where the recitation of the Six Limbs Mantra is prescribed. "At midnight one should rise, and muttering the mantra for 1001 times (worship the goddess), and after a month the goddess certainly causes one to find a treasure" [19]. On the next page there is a meditation on fearsome figures to the same end. K (p. 100) also makes mention of "ointments causing treasures to become visible" (*nidhidarśakam añjanam*). MMK repeatedly refers to the subject, e.g. in Vol. II, p. 299; vol. III, p. 671.

The *attraction of food* is also exemplified in the texts. As the first allusion to it we shall have to consider the famous "Udgītha of the Dogs" in ChUp 1, 12. The AVPar (36, 15) speaks of a feat of multiplying a store of food fourfold. From the Tantras we mention the PST (32, 51) which discusses a spell procuring food (*annapradāyako mantraḥ*). In the SST, twenty ślokas (3, 20, 33-35) are devoted to the subject by means of the worship of Pathiṣad Rudra who is associated with the Goddess Abundant in Food (Annapūrṇā). Stanza 51 says that "a man who is devoid of food on a journey and is vexed by hunger should recite the mantra in question for 1008 times, and he immediately obtains delicious food which suffices even for a company of a hundred brahmans"[20]

Attraction of water. The second instance of attraction given in the Mahāmāyā fragment (Stuti & Stava, No. 450, st.6) runs: "a river filled with water from swollen rain clouds quietly streams forth with her water pacified and is pulled into the opposite direction" (*pratilomaṃ ca kṛṣyate*). The passage is thus more concerned with a "drawing backwards" of water than with a "drawing hither", more with *pratikarṣaṇam* than with *ākarṣaṇam*. Control and manipulation of water in the form of rain and floods is in any case frequently mentioned in the sources. Excessive drought as well as too abundant rainfall belongs to the phenomena of South Asian climate, sometimes with dreadful consequences. The recourse to magical practices performed on water will thus have often been motivated by dire necessity. The subject of rain-making is not discussed further here, although it is often alluded to in the texts. A few times there is also made mention of devices to cause the rain to cease (*anāvṛṣṭiḥ*), as in PST 17, 30 (a rite connected with Gaṇeśa) with the help of an oblation of salt. For increase of rain one should offer stalks of reed (the same methods are advocated in S, p. 195). An insertion in the paraphrase in Old Javanese to the Mahāmāyā fragment after stanza 11 speaks of the destruction of rain clouds in the sky by means of worshipping the yellow Māyā (see above, p.148). Crooke (I, p. 76-78) also mentions methods for averting rain (see also ch. 6. 6 and 6. 7).

It remains to pay some attention to the manipulation of rivers. In literature this feat is repeatedly spoken of. The AitBr (Adhyāya 8, Pañcikā 2,3) relates how Kavaṣa Ailūṣa drew the river Sarasvatī towards him when he desired to perform the Aponaptrīya ceremony. A different type occurs in ViPur 5, 25 where Balarāma is requested to forcibly draw towards himself by means of his ploughshare the river Yamunā—strictly speaking, no action of magic but of mere force applied on the mythical scale. The SST (1, 14, 34) contains directions for a rite by which one attracts a river without delay (*nadīm samākarṣati tatkṣaṇāt*).

A variety of this type is the splitting asunder of a sea or a river in order to render free passage to the performer.[21] RV 3, 33 contains a dispute between Viśvāmitra and the rivers Vipāś and Śutudrī which results in a passage created by these rivers for the army of the Bharatas. As a matter of fact the sage did not coerce the rivers but only persuaded them to comply with his wish. Also out of free will the Yamunā divided herself and granted a passage to the fleeing Vasudeva with the baby Kṛṣṇa in his arms (Bhāsa, Bālacarita, 1, 18 and prose; ed. Devadhar, p. 516). An action of pure magic is, however, recorded by Jhavery (p. 279): Piṇḍaniryukti 494-500 and the Sanskrit commentary to this text mention as an illustration of magic powers that the Jain sage Ārya Samitasūri "through mixture of magical powders divided the waters of the river Benā and crossed over to the opposite bank". One of the legends of Kāñcipuram (Dessigane, 1964, p. 23) tells us that Viṣṇu himself once stopped the flow of a river by adoring the Śivaliṅga.

The Mahāmāyā fragment speaks of obstructing the water's course and sending it into another direction. This reminds of two interesting passages from the KauśS. In 40, 1-9 this text mentions a method for changing the water's course. For this end one should lie down on the place menaced by the water and hit at it with the hand or the staff[22]. At the same time one should recite AV 3, 13 and a sacrifice to Varuṇa should be made (cf. Arbman, p. 139, n.1). Caland (p. 137, n. 4) very aptly refers to the tale contained in Mbh 1, 3 of Pāñcālya Āruṇi, the Brāhmaṇic student who tried to stop a breach in the dyke of a rice field by laying himself in it (Cf. Sāyaṇa on KauśS 40, 10: *nadīpraveśamārge śayita*). The promising pupil thus not only gave an example of uncompromising self-sacrifice at the guru's behest, but must also have known something of contemporary practices of magic.

In KauśS 38, 7 (Caland, p. 129) the subject is the stopping of rain. One peculiarity of the passage which leads to an association with the Mahāmāyā fragment is the expression *pratilomakarṣitaḥ* (Mahāmāyā fragment: *pratilomaṃ ca kṛṣyate.*) Caland in n. 7 gives due attention to this phrase and admits not to know its exact meaning[23]. In the Mahāmāyā fragment the "being drawn backwards" is said of the result of the magical act revealing itself in the backward course of the water. The use of the same expression in both passages might be sheer coincidence, but it is possible that a tradition is reflected here of *pratilomakarṣaṇam* "drawing into the opposite direction". In that case the text in the KauśS (cf. n.23) would have presumably been misunderstood by a scribe.

6.5. *Subjugation*

The Sanskrit terminology. The act of attraction, however powerful, if applied to persons is usually not performed for its own sake. As a matter of course, the victim will be expected not only to appear on the scene but to submit himself to the performer's will still further. In this way, subjugation may be considered a logical complement of attraction. We have seen above that attraction and subjugation indeed often join each other in the texts.

The Sanskrit term for subjugation is *vaśīkaraṇam*, to be explained as "reducing (someone) to the state of being under one's *vaśaḥ*, "power of command or control", "dominance". A comparison with other derivatives constructed in the same way, like *andhīkaraṇam* "making blind" suggests that the word *vaśīkaraṇam* stands for *vaśyīkaraṇam* "causing (somebody) to come under one's power of control", as such derivatives by means of *-ī* are usually formed from adjectives. Because the existence of this class of derivatives presupposes a similarly derived verb, *vaśīkaraṇam* suggests *vaśīkaroti* "to bring under one's power", a word which indeed sometimes occurs in the texts. The Purāṇas and Tantras also apply forms of a verb *vaśati*, like *vaśet* in the third person singular optative (e.g., GarPur 178, 19; TSS 22, 8). Beside compounds with *vaśī-*, there also occur those with *vaśa-*, *vaśaṃ-*, or *vaśya-*. The preponderance of the term Vaśīkaraṇa over its synonyms dates only from Tantric sources, although there also other similar forms remain in use, such as the simple *vaśyam* (lit. : "the state of being under dominance", but often used as a synonym of "dominance").

The word *vaśaḥ* occurs already in this sense in the Vedic Saṃhitās, cf. AV 9, 10, 24 *tásya bhūtáṃ bhávyaṃ váśe sá me bhūtáṃ bhávyaṃ váśe kṛṇotu*" all that has become and will be is under his power; he (the Virāṭ or Cosmical Being) should bring all that has become and will be under my power" (cf. Gonda, 1965, p. 196); or AV 3, 8, 6 *máma váśeṣu hṛdayāṇi vaḥ kṛṇomi* "I bring your hearts under my controlling powers". In the same collection (3, 25, 6) a poet bids that Mitra and Varuṇa should bring a lady under his power: *mámaivá kṛṇutaṃ váśe.* This use of *vaśaḥ* continues in later literature. Man can, however, also be himself under the dominance of his own emotions, especially of rage (instances in ViPur 1, 17, 18; GarPur 196, 10). Vaśa is sometimes used irregularly as a synonym of *vaśya*—"being under one's dominance", as in AVPar 35, 1, 9 *ā saptāhāt sarva ete āsurihomatō vaśāḥ* "after a period of seven days all of them will come under one's power as an effect of the sacrifice with the Āsurī plant"; another instance in the same text, 35, 2, 9; in 35, 1, 8, *vaśin* is used in the same sense (*strī vaśinī*), while it commonly means "powerful" (as in GarPur 196, 16). Thus it appears that the terminology in the older as well as in the more recent sources is far from precise.

In a social sense the noun *vaśaḥ* denotes the status and power by which a person is able to dominate his fellow-men. In this sense it forms a comparative *vaśīyas*—and in this way polarizes with *pāpīyas*; thus, "being relatively powerful" becomes an opposite of "being of comparatively low status"[24]. In a speculative context, *vaśaḥ* and its cognates express the dominion exercised by God in and over this world. ŚvetUp (6, 12) calls Śiva the "unique Controller over the many inactive ones" (i.e. the souls, according to Śaṅkara). By executing this power, God performs an act of Vaśīkaraṇa on the world and its creatures (see above p.19). These creatures may indeed feel, like Draupadī, that they are subject to the manipulations of a higher power. This power is sometimes designated as "fate", as in Kathās. (2, 5, 37) : *Devīyaṃ kāraṇavaśād avatīrṇā kṣitau* "this queen has been reborn in a lower state on earth by the subjugating power of fate". Sometimes God is said to exercise his *vaśa* on Nature (Prakṛti, the primordial material cause of the world); thus, a stanza quoted by the commentator Dhanapati in his Bhāṣyotkarṣadīpikā on BhGītā 7,14 runs: "the omniscient Lord Whose reflection is Māyā holds Her (Nature) in subjection; but the others are kept in subjugation by Ignorance by reason of her manifold appearances" [21]. The passage reminds of ŚvetUp 4, 9—(See above, p.20) On another place the state to which creation is reduced by God's subduing activity is compared to a kind of hypnotic sleep: "the whole fourfold mass of creatures from the grass up to Brahmā, the whole world of moving and unmoving beings is reduced to sleep by Thy Māyā" [22]. One can also meet the names of female divine powers as personifications of subjugation. Vaśinī "Lady of subjugation" together with Ugrā "Terrible One" form two aspects of the Dīkṣā according to TBr 2, 7, 17 (Gonda, 1965, p. 344). Ājñāvivartinī "She who forces (others) to follow up Her commands" and Ājñāvivartinīśvarī "The Sovereign Lady who forces.." are two Śaktis of Svapnavārāhī (MMD 10, 35ff.). Vaśavartinī "causing (others) to be subjugated" is said of the gift of poetry (*kavitā*) in SST 3. 16. 23.

Needless to say that this sovereign control over other beings must be a necessary goal also for the magician who by nature of his position strives after the execution of divine powers. The particular power of subjugation may even be regarded as his chief aspiration; it includes all specialized applications of magical prowess. Vaśīkaraṇa thus becomes the embodiment and prerequisite of anything which comes under the heading of Ṣaṭkarman.

The term *vaśīkaraṇam* is circumscribed shortly in a few of the concerned monographs. S (1, 7) defines it with the words *vaśyaṃ janānāṃ sarveṣāṃ vidheyatvam udīritam* subjugation is said to be the state in which all people may be manipulated" (the shortened form vaśyam is used here for denoting the state caused by the act of vaśīkaraṇam). MMD (25, 2) is still more laconic: *vaśyaṃ vacanakāritvam*"subjugation is the state in which one cannot do otherwise (a nuance included in the use of the suffix -*in*) than executing (the performer's) orders". The SST (1, 8, 108) divides the act of *vaśīkāraḥ* into three stages: 1. Prīti "winning sympathy"; 2. Mohana "delusion" and 3. Vaśīkāra proper. The text further intimates that the rite should best be executed during the downward course of Saturn at an ancient place of Śivaite worship containing an isolated liṅga. B. Bhattacharya (p. LXXXVI) circumscribes Vaśīkaraṇa as follows: "...gives the performer the power to bewitch all other men and women or even animals and gods, and get work done by them". Again in the SST (3, 3, 292) Vaśya is mentioned in one breath with Ājñāsiddhi "the supranormal attainment of (enforcing) one's command".

Vaśīkaraṇa often seems to imply the reduction of other beings to a state of complete and helpless obedience or dependence, like the position of a slave. The word "slave" is indeed used by the Mahāmāyā fragment in connection with this action *dāsibhūtā*); the term *dāsa* is found sometimes also in the Tantras and monographs (thus, *dāśatā* in SST 2, 18, 122). In this way one can even subjugate gods and the powers of nature and cause them to remain active only by one's own will—a power sometimes claimed also by magicians in other countries.[25] It is instructive to recur for a moment to the religious context and observe that in the face of the sovereign subjugating power of the Lord it is the task of the bhakta, devoted follower of God as he is, to wholly submit to His will, which means to willingly assume the state of being subjugated by Him. The ideal bhakta denotes himself as God's slave[26]; and it is a striking fact that the essence of devotion is sometimes described to be doing work for the Lord not only by means of ritual acts at home and in the temple, but also on a psychical level by devoting all actions, even the most trivial ones, to the Lord by means of a systematical mystical transmutation. Thus we read in BhGītā 9, 27: "anything which you do, which you eat, offer or give, and any act of asceticism performed by you, O Son of Kuntī, you should perform that as an offering unto Me" :

Yat karoṣi yad aśnāsi yaj juhoṣi dadāsi yat
yat tapasyasi Kaunteya tat kuruṣva madarpaṇam[27].

The sources for the feat of subjugation in literature are manifold. They begin with the RV (10, 85; 10, 145; 10, 159; 10, 162; 10, 183) and include the AV (passim) and the YV (e.g., TS 2, 3, 9, 1; MS 2, 3, 2; TBr 2, 3, 10; ŚatBr 14, 9, 4) according to Malaviya (p. 20). The SVBr (2, 5, 3; see also Malaviya, p. 142) describes subjugation with the help of images of the victim. The mantras prescribed for the occasion include the famous *úd vayáṃ támasas pári* (RV 1, 50, 10) "We have gone out of the darkness beholding a light supreme—God Sūrya among the gods". The Ṛgvidh. includes numerous passages on subjugation, as well as the AVPar (e.g. 35, 1, 2). In the Jaina Vipākaśruta (quoted by Jhavery, p. 274) a certain Priyasena is brought to the fore "who would control the king, lords and others by employing Vidyās and magical powders for fascination or being invisible or charming, controlling or making others subservient. This does not require further comment". Subjugation occurs often in the Purāṇas (such as MtPur 93, 145ff.; GarPur ch. 178ff.) and is mentioned by the Kathās.

in 2, 4, 64. The relevant passages in the Tantras are very numerous. We refer to the MMK (ch. 25, Vol. II, p. 287) where all kinds of beings are said to be subjugated by means of offerings of various objects and kinds of grains; the same text (Vol. III, p. 668ff.); HT (1, 54) in connection with the goddess Kurukullā; SM (passim; in No. 171 and 190 also with Kurukullā); JT (ch. 17) with a Śrīcakra belonging to the Mantra of Sixteen Syllables; KVT (ch. 15) among others with a mantra in Chittagong Bengali; and PST (7, 65; 9, 23-27; 32; 34, 13ff.). Of the Ṣaṭkarman monographs, D discusses the subject in chs. 7-9; S in ch. 4 (p. 227-232); N in chs. 2-5 (p. 274-295) and K on p. 25ff. A limited survey of some of the older sources will be sufficient to present an idea of the content of the act of "subjugation" and the rituals usually associated with it.

In some of these sources sometimes other Sanskrit terms for subjugation are in vogue. SVBr (2, 5) speaks of an act of *āvartanam* "causing somebody to direct himself towards the performer". Āvartana can have women as well as men as its object. The Sanskrit commentary of Sāyaṇa (ed. B.R. Sharma, Tirupati 1964) paraphrases by *kuṭumbādināṃ vaśikaraṇam* "the subjugation of family members in the first place, but also of others". Another commentator, Bharatasvâmin, explains by *abhimukhapravartanaṃ samipanayanam* "causing somebody to direct himself towards (the performer), that is bringing him into (the performer's) presence", a paraphrase which treats Āvartana almost as a synonym of Ākarṣaṇa and which seems to be too narrow in the context of the next paragraph of the text. The ceremony implies a vrata, religious observance, to be begun in the month Śrāvaṇa (2, 5, 2). A clay image of the victim should be made with its face into an eastern direction in the forenoon, towards the South in the middle of the day, towards the West in the afternoon and towards the North at night. The performer should stand on the region of its heart and utter a mantra from the Sāmaveda, differentiated according to the victim's grade of society. One may also use different materials for the image in accordance with the same criterion, and put them into the fire while bringing oblations of ghee with a sacrificial ladle made from Udumbara fig wood. The result will be that the victim comes under the performer's influence (*guṇi hāsya bhavati*; Bharatasvâmin paraphrases *guṇi* with *vaśyaḥ*).

Another method (2, 5, 5) is executed with the help of an image made with rice grains broken by the nails; the grains are made to exude liquor by heating. The limbs of the image are cut off one by one with a knife and sacrificed into the fire with the appropriate mantras. The remainder, that is: the region of the heart (comm.) he consumes himself; the author warns that in case of neglect of this stipulation the performer will die himself (*itarathābhāve mriyate*); at least this is the way Sāyaṇa interprets the passage. Bharatasvāmin here again has another interpretation; *sādhyasya vyāpattiḥ syāt*, "the death of the victim will come along" and this is not what was implied by the performer. A similar rite is described in the Ṛgvidh. (3, 19, 3—3, 20, 3). It is clear that this rite of subjugation closely resembles a cruel act of magic: the victim is symbolically deprived of his or her limbs and trampled upon the heart. But at the same time one should be aware that similar sacrifices of the limbs of a victim in image shape are sometimes performed without any evil intention.

In the SVBr (2, 6)a number of rites are described which in later sources would certainly be included under Vaśīkaraṇa but which are introduced in this text by the words "From here on, (the treatment) of those (rites destined for) happiness in human relations" (*athātaḥ saubhāgyānām*). The word *saubhāgyam* (it also occurs in AVPar 26, 5, 4) regularly applies to happiness within the small circle of immediate family relations, especially between husband and wife. A person who enjoys *saubhāgya* is called *subhaga-* "fortunate". Sāyaṇa on this place defines *saubhāgyam* as "the state of being loved dearly by wife and other (members of the family)" : *suṣṭhu yoṣidādibhir bhajanīyatvam.* The state of being *subhaga*—is held out as a result in 2, 6, 2-5 and is followed up in 2, 6, 6 by *sarvajanasya priyo bhavati* "one becomes dear to everybody". In 2, 6, 7 the result is plainly that "she loves him": *yāṃ kāmayet tāṃ śrāvayet. kāmayate hainam.* In 2, 6, 8 another method is prescribed in case a woman does not comply, *yāsya na guṇī syāt.* The performer should offer water to her and recite the mantra *Indro viśvasya* (SV, Grāmageyagāna, 12, 1, 456, 1-2); or he should sacrifice the dust of her footstep into the fire while saying another formula from the SV. In 2, 6, 13 the result of a similar rite is stated to be *vaśyā bhavanti* "they become subjugated".

An important conclusion from these details from the SVBr is that the action of "subjugation" often applies to situations within the domestic environment. The "victim" in many cases appears to be somebody within the family or household, frequently even the wife or husband. The recourse to magic seems to have often served as a panacea during the existence of domestic tension.

The Ṛgvidh. repeatedly discusses rites of *saṃvananam* "winning over" (3, 15, 2; 3, 19, 3; 3, 20, 5; 3, 21, 4); the same term occurs in GautDh 2, 2, 17, while Ṛgvidh. 3, 20, 4 mentions *guṇikaraṇam* as a synonym of *vaśikaraṇam*[29]. The same text (2, 10, 4) promises that anything will come under the power (*vaśibhavet*) of one who sacrifices a mixture of salt and honey while reciting the *gāyatri*. The domestic character of many of these rites again appears from 3, 14, 7 ff. where the result of the *saṃvanana* ceremony turns out to be the removal of illicit lovers (*sapatnān pratibādhate*, 3, 15, 1). The mantras prescribed on this occasion are RV 10, 83 and 84, styled *sapatnaghne* "the two killers of rivals". The PST (36, 3) still contains the term *vaśyasaṃvananam*. The Pali Canon contains an allusion to an *āvartani māyā* (Pali *āvaṭṭani māyā*) "device of winning other people's allegiance". According to the Aṅguttara Nikāya, 2, 190 ff., the Buddha was reported to be a magician (*māyāvin*) who made use of such a device in order to cause adherents ofother doctrines to become his own pupils. The Buddha, however, proved that his device consisted of no other thing than rationally arguing that people should get rid of evil influences and develop the good. A similar report about the Buddha is recorded in the MajN 1, 375.

In the Jaina Canon various terms are used for rites of subjugation, such as *āhevaṇa* "attracting people" and *abhiyogya* "making one subservient" (so Jhavery, p. 274). The AVPar on some places mentions *vaśikaraṇa* (35, 1, 6; 36, 5, 1 and 3; *vaśya* in 25, 1, 11; besides, 5x *vaśa*).

Some resources. In the case of Vaśīkaraṇa, it is worthwhile to devote some attention to the attributes, symbols or ingredients deemed helpful for this particular end. The SM (No. 71, p. 144) summarizes some of them in verse :

vajracakratriśūlaśaramudgarapāśāṅkuśādini
añjanapādalepatilakavaśikaraṇadravyāṇi (*sādhaniyāni*)

"(one should master) the following (attributes and) ingredients of subjugation: the vajra, disc, trident, arrows, hammer, noose, elephant hook, ointment, paste to be smeared on the feet, and painted spot on the forehead". Most of these are the attributes familiar to us from images of the gods, where they symbolize some aspect of the particular god's subjugating power. When performing subjugation himself, a man should meditate on himself as bearing one or more of these attributes. Two of them, noose and elephant hook, have been met already as characteristic attributes of Attraction; a reflection of the tendency to make Attraction a facultative introductory stage to Subjugation. In SM, p. 181 (No. 93, Vajratārāsādhana) the Goddess Tārā is designed by the worshipper as two-armed and bearing the elephant hook and a noose made of lotuses (aṅkuśotpalapāśahastāṃ vilikhya). These attributes are used by the goddess in this way: with the noose she binds the victim's neck and with the hook she pierces his (her) feet and in this way draws him (her) towards the performer who is free to deal with him (her) according to his will as a slave.

The three last items from the above list (SM No. 71): ointment, foot paste, and painted spot are of a different character. They are generally applied cosmetics but at the same time often considered to be powerful devices of magic. The Ṣaṭkarman monographs mention them frequently. Ointment (*añjanam*) is a product of collyrium or other materials applied to the eyelids[30]. It is mentioned in the AVPar (35, 2, 2). Of places from the Ṣaṭkarman monographs we mention N 2, 30 (p. 278) = K p. 26, 8. A man who smears his eyes with the root of the white Aparājitā plant picked during a lunar eclipse, while saying a certain mantra, will subjugate the threefold world :

Śvetāparājitāmūlaṃ candragraste samuddhṛtam
añjitākṣo naras tena vaśīkuryāj jagattrayam

K (p. 27, 9) mentions as the result of the application of another mixture to the eyes that the performer will become "dear to anybody whom he merely casts his glance on" :

Priyo bhavati sarveṣāṃ dṛṣṭimātraṃ na saṃśayaḥ

Añjana can be used also by a woman to subjugate her favourite or her husband (GarPur 178, 14). Against this background we can perhaps better understand the caution of the author of the Manusmṛti who warns (4, 44) that a brahman should not observe his wife applying (or having applied) añjana to her eyes. The glance of a person of more than ordinary power is a matter of great consequence, but merely beholding such a person can also be dangerous. "Those by whom he (the performer) is seen and those whom he beholds will become subjugated" (*dṛṣṭo yair yān vātha sa paśyati te vaśyāḥ syuḥ*, TSS 27, 57); and the GarPur (194, 23) records the following incantation: "he who beholds me with his eyes and whom I behold with my eye—of all evil and depraved persons Viṣṇu obstructs the eye-sight" [23].

For the Buddhist Tantrics, ointment of eyes and feet (*añjanam, pādalepaḥ*), which means of course the correct use of these ingredients for magical purposes, forms two of the eight great performances or mahāsiddhis (B. Bhattacharya, p. LXXXV). Añjana in this connection seems to be reserved for the power to miraculously observe objects hidden from the human eye such as buried treasures; pādalepa is applied with the result of being able to move about at will, for instance by flying through the air. SM (No. 115, p. 243), however, mentions an unguent of saffron (*gorocanā*) applied to the eyes as a means to attract the king's friendly attention; when the accompanying mantra has been muttered a hundred thousand times, all beings come under one's spell (*vaśyā bhavanti*). The MMK (II, p. 538) again mentions the powerful glance of the eyes: anyone who is looked at by the performer becomes his slave. The statement occurs within a context of the mutual relation between husband and wife. The same text (II, 540) promises as a result of a certain other kind of añjana that the performer's favourite woman will come towards him, burnt by passion (*madanāgninā dahyamānā strī āgacchati*). There is also evidence of the application of añjana with the aim of becoming invisible (GarPur 178, 9).

The *tilakam*, the famous "mark of beauty" on the forehead of Hindu women, is also very often alluded to in the texts as a device of magic, especially of subjugation. In such a context it would be applied by men as well as by women. The MtPur (62, 6) advises its use for obtaining domestic happiness, health and attractiveness for women (*lalitāupriyatvam*). The AgPur (123, 29 ff.) states that a tilaka prepared with (*go*) *rocanā*, red sandal and other materials results in subjugation; "even the gods with Indra at their head would come under its spell, let alone tiny human beings" (*sendrāḥ surā vaśaṃ yānti kiṃ punaḥ kṣudramānuṣāḥ*). The GarPur (185, 9) gives a similar receipt (thin leaf of Manaḥśilā stone, Gorocanā and saffron) for a tilaka which overpowers all women. Another tilaka made up with the Sahadevī, Bhṛṅgarāja, and white Aparājitā plants results in the subjection of the threefold world (GarPur 185, 10). A woman who looks at a man with on her forehead a tilaka composed of Gorocanā, red mineral and blood, will certainly cast him under her spell (185, 12). The same result is reached with another mixture according to AgPur 323, 13. The KālPur (60, 15 ff.; van Kooy, p. 92) mentions a *sarvavaśya-mantra* accompanying a tilaka. The SM in No. 235 records a tilaka which forces people to offer gifts to the wandering mendicant (B. Bhattacharya, p. LXXXIV). N p. 277 (a shortened version in K p. 26) gives several receipts for tilaka, all of them applicable in Subjugation. For example, the root of white Guñjā when applied in this way is able to subjugate men and women alike (2, 35), of course with the help of an appropriate mantra. The TSS also mentions the "tilaka act" (*tilakakriyā*, cf. 27, 13; 27, 59). These instances may suffice to show the popularity of this device in rites of subjugation.

Sometimes mention is made of smearing the body with unguents (*anulepanam, lepaḥ*). The magicians of Cambodia knew of "mysterious unguents" which they called *thnam léap* (< *lepa*) and which were usually applied for arousing love in the "victim" (Leclère, p. 132 f.). The SVBr (2, 6, 11) already prescribes an anulepana composed of the outer skin of a cow's embryo and other ingredients. One who smeared himself with this mixture would be able to create love in any woman touched by him (*tenānulipto yāṃ yām upaspṛśate sā sainaṃ kāmayate*). But this is restricted in the following paragraph (2, 6, 12): one should approach only a woman one is legally entitled to (*gamyā*) and never without having bathed beforehand. Another unguent described in 2, 6, 13 is composed of a flowering lotus and a quantity of panic seed. All kinds of women become subjected to the performer if he in addition recites a stanza from the SV (Grāmageyagāna 1, 3, 26, 1). The AVPar mentions an unguent of the feet in the same context. Passing to Tantric literature, the PST (7, 67) advises beauty mark and unguent as follows: "one who would daily smear himself with it, eat something of it, also apply a tilaka with it, and throw it on his head—he will be continually free from calamities, epilepsy, demons, unexpected death, evil planets and poison, and he is loved by his subjects (or : his children)" [24]. The TSS makes mention of unguents in many instances, using such terms as *lepa* (31, 67 and 71), *vilepa* (31, 66), *vilepana* (31, 74) and *ālepa* (31, 68), in all the mentioned cases applicable against enemies. Smearing with ashes (*bhasmalepa*) is advised in 27, 61 for subjugation with the accompaniment of a mantra which addresses a goddess "who charms the eye and mind" or "of the charming eyes" (*nayanamanoharī*). On another place (28, 39) the TSS ordains smearing over the whole body (*sarvagātrāṇi lepayet*). To give one instance out of the many cases provided by the Ṣaṭkarman monographs: N (2, 36) again prescribes the root of Guñjā mixed up with white sandal as an unguent. Instead of the sandal, honey is also possible.

A device of touching simplicity is the presentation of a mere flower, preferably a red one, to the "victim". The red flower on its own accord possesses the power of influencing a person's mind. The presentation of such a flower is a sign of one's sympathy and love, but at the same time it means setting in motion the subjugating power of the flower, enhanced by its colour (see above, p. 163), by a deliberate act of the will.[31] A woman may become subjugated by him who presents a flower to her, saying a certain mantra (TSS 22, 72). N 2, 39 (p. 280) discusses the application of the mantra *Oṃ kāmini mādhavi namaḥ* "*Oṃ*, Thou Lovely One, Honey-sweet One, honour". It may be recited a hundred times over a flower; the flower should be given to some man who then comes under the performing lady's power within seven days, provided she also during this time eats seven morsels of each of her meals inscribed with his name. According to N 2, 43 another mantra directed to Rudra (25) should be said seven times over a red oleander before presenting this flower to the "victim" with the desired effect. In the GarPur (178, 11) such a flower is applied for causing the donee's mind to wander (*bhrāmayet*). K (p. 25, 2) ordains for subjugation the presentation of a flower over which a mantra to Cāmuṇḍā has been recited (for fourteen times, according to KA mantra 11). In S (p. 228, line 7 and p. 230, 8) success is obtained by presenting a thousand red flowers over which a mantra has been said ten thousand times.

There are other methods and substances applied in Vaśīkaraṇa, but omitted from the present description, such as the presentation of betel (GarPur 178, 2; 178, 15); the sacrifice into the fire of various sweets (MtPur 93, 145; SM p. 181 for *kanyāsiddhi*); adding something to somebody's food (D 8, 2; TSṢ 28, 31ff.); or eating something inscribed with the victim's name. Fumigation with incense is mentioned as a method in TSS 28, 45.

The victims. These can be the same as the objects of Attraction. The Mahāmāyā fragment mentions as the objects of its subjugation rite: ladies, elephants and inimical kings. The JT (ch. 17) mentions all kinds of victims including kings, enemies, gods, women, "all beings" and "the world". The Ṣaṭkarman monographs mostly aim at the subjugation of "all people", kings, women and men (this last item usually means: husbands); such is the sequence given by N, followed by K, which summarizes its treatment. Attention is paid below to the "victims" in almost the same sequence as has been used in the discussion of Ākarṣaṇa: 1. Gods. 2. Kings and enemies. 3. All beings or the world. 4. Women or men. 5. Animals.

The subjugation of *gods* is mentioned surprisingly seldom in the texts although it is certainly often understood, for instance when "all beings" or the "threefold world" are said to be affected by the power of subjugation. Most often the gods seem to function in the recommendation of the supranormal efficacy of the device in question, such as AgPur 123, 31 referred to above: "all the gods including Indra come under his power, let alone tiny human beings". JT (18, 11 and 12) mentions both the gods and the demons among a great variety of other victims. The SST (3. 18, 14) specifies that Kālikā is subjugated by a sādhana of Mitā, one of the Nityā goddesses, with the help of betel. Despite the lack of prominence of the gods as victims of Vaśīkaraṇa, it seems that in practice they have often been subjected to it. The frequent manipulation of all kinds of supernatural beings referred to in Ch. 2, often directed to the aim of having the victim's characteristic activity at one's disposal, can be denoted with profit as varieties of Vaśīkaraṇa. A good instance from literature is furnished by the Kathās.,—12, 25 (Vetālapañc. 18), 35ff. A Yogin enters an abandoned temple of Śiva and evokes a "Spell Which realizes all desires" (*iṣṭasaṃpādini vidyā*) the presiding goddess of which appears by his mere concentrating his thoughts upon her, and says to him: "what can I do?" In other words, she is reduced by the Yogin to the state of a maidservant—a characteristic feature of subjugation. But not only these divine or semi-divine beings of a comparatively low status can be subjected to the performer's will. Is not in many cases the way in which the gods are approached by prayer, sacrifice or other rituals considered by the worshipper to be a certain means to success, which means to virtually forcing the deity to do what is asked of him: confer boons, grant material goods, work about health or cure, and so on? Is not almost any hymn directed to the great gods of Hinduism accompanied by a frank statement of the rewards which are said to be infallibly the result for him who recites the hymn with the right intention and concentration of mind? (see above p. 60) In a broad sense, all these aspects of widely spread methods of approaching the divine might be seen as variants of a different kind of this fundamental act of subjugation.

Kings as the objects of subjugation are frequently mentioned. The AVPar speaks of them in this context in 35, 1, 6 (*vaśīkurvaṃś ca bhūpatīn*). From the Tantras we mention JT 17, 8 (*rājā*); 17, 26 (*dhanāḍhyo bhūpatiḥ*) and 17, 52 (*rājendra*); PST 36, 60; TSS 22, 42: 27, 25. Of the Purāṇas, AgPur mentions subjugation of a king in 260, 8; 308, 4 (in one breath with *vṛddhi* "economic growth" and *śrī* "lustre" to be expected by the performer); 315, 9; the GarPur in 185, 3. In this last case, an oblation made for 108 times of black sesamum seeds sprinkled with ghee while a mantra to Gaṇapati is pronounced suffices to reduce a king to subservience within three days. Of the monographs, D (9, 4-16) gives similar recipes, this time accompanied by the mantra *Oṃ namo Bhāskarāya trilokātmane amukamahīpatiṃ me vaśīkuru svāhā* "*Oṃ*, honour to the Sun, the Self of the threefold world, subjugate for me the king N.N.". S (p. 228, 3) advises a mantra to Caṇḍālī for subjugating kings within a week. N (3, 3-12) discusses the Caṇḍamantra and its usefulness for this particular act. In 3, 2, this text gives another mantra, this time to the Disc Sudarśana, the result of which is stated somewhat differently to be that "one becomes honoured at the royal gate", *rājyadvāre bhavet pūjyaḥ*. It might be that this wording is applicable to the brahman who desires to use the mantra in his own interest. A religious man who wants to "subjugate a king" will mean by this phrase that he is received honourably by the ruler and his court and applied to for advice or for other services for which he will be liberally rewarded. The phrase "honoured at the royal gate" may, however, also allude to a successful pleading of one's case in court. Another instance in the GarPur (178, 6): "By spreading an incense consisting of a mixture of aloe, bdellium, blue lotuses and molasses, one becomes beloved at the royal gate" [26]. It is well known how at least some of the religious men depended upon royal favour for obtaining a livelihood.[32]

Another possible context of "subjugation of a king" is an action by the subjects or by inimical pretendents against the ruling prince. The ViDhPur (2, 125, 8) seems to allude to such a situation (see above, p. 240). An interesting case is furnished by an inscription in Old Malay found at Telaga Batu (South Sumatra, Indonesia).[33] This inscription, by far the longest known to us from the reign of Śrīvijaya, and dating probably from "the two last decades of the seventh century A.D." (De Casparis) contains a lengthy imprecation against the enemies of the state and the king. Line 12 alludes to conspirators who would make use of Tantric rites (among others the Śrīyantra). The next line (13) then refers to rites "used by the rebels to bring others into their power by bereaving them of their common sense" (de Casparis, p. 30). The terms mentioned here are *makagila* (line 8) and *makalaṅit*, both meaning "to make crazy", and *vaśikaraṇa*. That there is no question here of an abstract use of these expressions but of real magical ceremonies, is proved by a reference made by the king to certain methods used by the rebels such as designing or painting an image of him (*rūpiṇanku*) and application of ashes (*bhasma*), wizards (?; text: *vaidi*, which may mean *vaidika* or *vaidya*, or perhaps *vidyā*) and spells (*mantra*); or the last words should be combined to mean "vèdic mantras" [27]. De Casparis surmises (p. 30f.) that the king was about to go upon an expedition (this is hinted at in the text) and wished to secure the situation in his capital by means of the imprecation; or it may be that the expedition was directed against the rebels themselves. In any case such rites as referred to here must in the eyes of the contemporary ruler have meant "a real menace to the state" (de Casparis). As with the act of Ākarṣaṇa, it is a matter of probability that persons of high status and wealth such as kings have often figured as the victims of rites of subjugation.

One could indeed imagine that the rebels of Śrīvijaya had made use of a ritual like that described in SM No. 37: Raktalokeśvarasādhana. Its essence is that the performer should meditate upon himself as the red Avalokiteśvara, provided with red garment and garland, with four arms bearing noose, elephant hook, bow and arrows, standing under a flowering Aśoka tree and producing an overwhelming emotion of desire. The fact that this kind of meditation seems to be applicable in the first place to subjugation in the field of erotics does not detract from its usefulness in politics: in SM No. 178 a seemingly erotic meditation is said also to have its effect on functionaries of the royal court (*āmātya*), on subjects of the king and on the king himself. The rite of the Red Lokeśvara further requires an oblation of salt for 108 times, and the recitation of the mantra *Oṃ ciṭi cinaṭi vikloli* (2x) *amukaṃ sadhanaparivāraṃ me vaśam ānaya svāhā*". . bring N. N. under my power together with his possessions and his retinue." After three weeks a "great person" (*mahāpuruṣa*) will be subjugated. It is advised that an image of the victim should be made with bees' wax mixed with salt. The image should be four aṅgulas high. It should be heated thrice a day within a heap of charcoal resulting from the burning of Khadira wood. Smoke should be avoided. The person whose name is uttered within the mantra for the required number will be subjugated. It may be added that Hindu tradition knows similar methods of subjugation of rulers. AgPur 260, 8 suggests that "one should make an image of the king consisting completely of rice grains and make an oblation of it by means of a thousand pieces; and the king will come under one's power":

Sarvavrīhimayīṃ kṛtvā rājñaḥ pratikṛtiṃ dvija /
sahasraśas tu juhuyād rājā vaśagato' bhavet //

Political enemies. If the person in whose behalf the rite is executed is a king himself, the royal victim of such a rite usually will be a political enemy; and the intricacies of magical subjection of inimical kings are a necessary part of the intellectual equipment of the *purohita*. The subjugation of enemies is an element, sometimes even a synonym, of the victory over them leading to their destruction. The "destruction of the enemy" (*śatrunāśanam*) with the help of supranormal arts is as a matter of course often referred to; it can combine within itself aspects of the acts of Vaśīkaraṇa, Stambhana, Mohana, Vidveṣaṇa, Uccāṭana and Māraṇa. Consequently, it might be discussed in connection with each of these items separately. It might be also added that some sources allude to *jayaḥ* "victory" outside the cadre of the Six Acts in the context of the results of worship of a god or similar meritorious activities (e.g., LT 48, 20ff.; 48, 32ff.; 49, 43ff.). In the TSS the word *jayaḥ* has a twofold meaning: victory in battle or in debate. The former is promised more than once in ch. 22 (on Durgā) as the result of "blessing" the weapons with a certain mantra; but the latter is also implied in 22, 13 *yuddhe ca vyavahārādau jayen mantraṃ japen naraḥ* "a man will be victorious in battle and in legal processes and the like when he recites this mantra". The same text in 30, 45 : *saṅgrāmavyavahārayoḥ sa (mantro) jayakṛt.*

We shall now concentrate on a few instances of the act of Vaśīkaraṇa performed upon an enemy (or inimical army). The Mahāmāyā fragment, stanza 8, speaks of "unconquerable enemies" who are subjugated by a meditation on the red manifestation of Viṣṇu. In MtPur 93,148 a method is given which necessarily results, according to the author, in the subjugation of all inimical armies: *avaśyāni vaśīkuryāt sarvaśatrubalāny api.* The ceremony forms part of a sacrifice to the Nine Heavenly Bodies; the result is reached by making a special oblation of Bilva and lotus flowers while the mantra "Friendly should be to us the waters and the herbs" (*sumitriyā na āpa*, TS 1, 4, 45, 2 etc.) is recited. The sacrificer should wear a white garment and white flowers and honour the officiating brahmans with sacred cords embroidered with gold, besides giving to them garments of high quality, white cows and golden objects. By this method one will subjugate all armies and transform enemies into political friends, because "this sacrifice destroys evil." [28]

The JT (18, 15) mentions the subjugation of "those who have

a feud" (*vairiṇaḥ*). GarPur 185,4 gives as the result of a certain rite that the performer or sponsor will be "invincible in battle while all (enemies) have come to serve him" (*aparājitaḥ syād yuddhe ca sarve tañ ca siṣevire*). In court literature there are many allusions to the majestic power of a king by means of descriptions of the state of subservience into which he has reduced his enemies; these enemies are sometimes styled the king's "slaves". The "Ritual Environments" and statements of rewards of the Balinese hymns edited in Stuti & Stava often mention the aim of invincibility in battle.

The predominantly "white" character of the rite is stressed also by references to the subjugation of "villains" (*duṣṭa-*), e.g. in N (2, 38, on p. 279); in N p. 283 a passage of eight stanzas is entitled "Method of taming the villains" (*duṣṭadamanaprayoga*). The beings affected by these rites are specified as thieves, wild elephants and again, significantly, political enemies. Subjugation of a murderer by means of a stanza from the YV is discussed in AgPur 260,77. The methods are sometimes differentiated according to the social grade the victim belongs to (three cases from the TSS: 24, 28f.; 24,38; 27,16ff.)

The texts often express the conviction that a certain method is able to subjugate *all people*, everything which exists on earth, or the threefold cosmos (*trailokyam*). In a different context the ŚvetUp already stated that the perfect soul "is master over the whole world" (*vaśī sarvasya lokasya*). JT ch. 17 promises the subjugation of "everybody" (*sakalajana*, st. 49), "all grades of society (78), "the whole world" (*sarvaloka-*,85), "everything" (90), and the "threefold cosmos" (52,64). A Varāhamukhīstava (Aithal, p. 96f., No. 18) says in its stanza 2 that the worship of Goddess Varāhīmukhī will result among more in the subjugation of the whole world (*vaśayati jagat sarvam*). According to the PST (7,62) "he subjugates the entire threefold world" (*tribhuvanam akhilaṃ vaśīkurute*; another place in 9,28). The Ṣaṭkarman monographs often contain similar statements, thus in N (2, 47): "one subjugates the beings of heaven, earth and nether world" (*khaṃbhūpātālabhūtāni*); S, p. 228, st. 4: "all beings" (*sarvajantu*). D, ch.7 is called Sarvajanavaśīkaraṇam, and its first stanza in the Benares edition begins by stating that the methods advised by it will result in the subjugation of "men and women in general" (*narā nāryaś ca sarvaśaḥ*). Sometimes these rites make use of the services of a god called for the occasion "He who subjects the threefold cosmos"; thus, in D (ch.7, p. 144) : *Nārāyaṇa sarvalokavaśaṅkara*; in SM, No. 35 (Vol. I, p. 80) : *Trailokyavaśaṃkara-Lokeśvara.* Of course such statements of a vague and all-encompassing character should be read in connexion with the magical context and the importance of stressing the general validity of the method (cf. above, ch. 5.6).

A special case is formed by the claim that certain mantras and ritual will effect the veneration or the friendship of all people. The TSS (27, 57) promises that a successful performer, when betaking himself to the assembly hall, will be constantly honoured there (*sabhāṃ gacchet tadātmā pūjyate sadā*). PST 13, 38 claims that various kinds of people will regularly pay honour to such a person (*kurvanti sadā namaskriyām asmai*). More frequent are the passages which refer to the friendship or sympathy the performer wins from the people. In AtiBr 9, 20 (Malaviya, p. 45) the daily recitation of the Viśvāmitra Sūkta by the Maitrāvaruṇa priest is said to have this effect. N (2, 6) promises as the result that one will be "dear to all people" (*sarvalokapriya-*). SVBr (2, 6, 6) says : *sarvajanasya priyo bhavati.* We have here to do with a forcible change of the victim's mind worked about by the performer in order to have his wishes fulfilled or his popularity increased. The same effect can be reached, as we saw, by looking upon a person with one's eyes painted by collyrium—thus in a way hypnotising the victim. Other instances of "becoming dear" are AgPur 260, 24 (*janasya priyatām iyāt*; with the help of a Vedic mantra); AgPur 302, 6=TSS 27, 51 (in a mantra to Kāma: *sarvajanahṛdayaṃ mamātmagataṃ kuru*); AgPur 309, 14 (*janavallabhaḥ*; not in the parallel version TSS 22, 65); PST 7, 67 (*priyate ca prajābhiḥ*); PST 24, 22 (*nṛṇāṃ priyaś ca bhūyāt*); PST 24, 54. TSS 27, 60. In PST 18, 52-54 the same thing (*sarvalokapriyaḥ syāt*) appears to be used in a context of begging one's food along the houses; an interesting passage. Success on one's begging round is also expressed by TSS 20, 34 (*bhikṣor annaṃ ca sidhyati*). A variant of "being dear to people" is "the conciliation of someone who is enraged" (*kupitasya prasādanam*, TSS 23, 31); TSS 24, 35; "this method destroys the wrath of someone who is wrathful" (*vidhir ayam hanti ruṣṭasya roṣam*). Another term which sometimes occurs in such a context is *rañjanam* "pleasing" (PST 9, 30; 9, 38); it may have an erotic connotation, as in TSS 27, 69.

Stuti & Stava, No. 097 (p. 71) declares the state of "being dear to all people" to be one of the results of the recitation of the Akṣamā Pañca-rakṣa, the Balinese version of a hymn to the Five Tathāgatas which also occurs in SM (vol.I, p. 15); it begins with: *Asamācalāḥ samatasāradharmiṇaḥ*. For this particular end the hymn should be said above a quantity of "oil which is afterwards smeared on the head or throat"; then the performer "becomes dear to anybody who beholds him". The hymn should be repeated twenty-one times. In our opinion, this is a good instance of the preservation in Bali of ritual application of an Indian stotra in a magical context. At the same time we observe that the complex of subjugation, besides vanquishing an enemy, may also include placating him by appeasing his mind—in the latter case by means of the recitation of a hymn of philosophical character which describes the infinite greatness and compassionate nature of the Tathāgatas. But the same hymn is applicable, according to the Balinese sources, also for other cases like imploring the gods' forbearance during the ritual; destruction of sin; preparation of potent water which is able to destroy poison; defeat of the enemy; rescuing a person from the dangerous influence of planets. SM (p. 16) promises as a result of the same hymn abundant siddhi and the outcome of all desires such as a long life, wisdom or strength.

Women. Subjugation of women and unmarried girls is, like their attraction, a practice often referred to. A woman is liable to be subjugated by the mere experience of the gift of love, as appears from Kathās. 2,4, 89: "she (Rūpaṇikā), being subjugated by the consummate happiness of love afforded by this Lohajaṅgha, was convinced that no other result of her birth could exist."[29]. In Kathās. 2, 4, 134, Vibhīṣaṇa presents Lohajaṅgha with a magic bird which will bring him back to Mathurā as a "vehicle to subjugation" (*vaśikārāya vāhanam*). The GarPur (178, 18) states that "embraces and the like cause the subjection of women and girls" (*āliṅganādyā nāriṇāṃ kumāriṇāṃ vaśikarāḥ*). Instances of the subjugation of a woman by magical means are afforded by the AVPar in 35, 1, 8; 36, 2, 6; 36, 3, 2; 36, 6, 1 (in the last case for someone who desires to win a bride). In ch. 41, the GarPur relates the method to obtain a wo man by the recitation of a mantra which contains the name of a Gandharva : "*Oṃ*, the Gandharva called Viśvāvasu is the Lord of ladies; I obtain thee; after (Viśvāvasu ?) has created a lady; to him, Viśvāvasu, *svāhā*" [30]. The same mantra occurs thrice in slightly different form in the Ṣaṭkarman monographs, viz. in N, 4, 48; K, p. 32; Is, p. 12. According to N, the mantra should accompany a mere gift of water to the beloved, repeated seven times, and within a month she will be his bride decked beautifully:

Pānīyasyāñjalin sapta dattvā vidyām imāṃ japet |
sālaṅkārāṃ naraḥ kanyāṃ labhate māsamātrataḥ ||

The subjugation of women proper is discussed by N in ch. 4 (p. 284 ff.) and by D in ch. 8. In the second stanza of ch. 4, N even boasts the subjugation of other people's wives (*sadyo vaśyāḥ parastriyaḥ*). The efficacy of the rite is sometimes expressed by stating that even heavenly or legendary damsels such as Apsaras will be mastered by the procedure advised; N. 4, 5: *vaśīkuryāt Tilottamām*; TSS 27, 83 : *Rambhāpi vaśagā bhavet*; D, ch. 8, 1 : *yadi sākṣād Arundhatī*. In the last case the recipe consists of the flower of a black Dhustūra (Benares version: Dhattūra), leaf and root of a kind of ivy, pounded together with camphor and saffron in equal amounts; the materials should have been collected on a Sunday. A tilaka prepared with this mixture will prove successful. No mantra seems to be connected with this rite, or it would have to be the mantra given at the end of the chapter: *Oṃ namaḥ Kāmākhyādevi, amukiṃ me vaśaṃ kuru kuru svāhā* (Benares ed. *Kāmākṣyai devyai*). The effect is sometimes described with lively imagination: *śmaśāne roditi sadā bālā dattoktabhojanā* "when a lady has got (the mixture described in a previous stanza) in her food, she will always stay on the cremation ground weeping (out of love even after the performer's death)" (N, 4, 9). Almost the same stanza is found in D as 8, 2 (p. 144).

An interesting case is N 4, 26 (p. 287). The performer should obtain the left eye of a lizard (*kṛkalāsaḥ*), mix it with honey and sesamum oil, and prepare an ointment with it. A woman looked at by him with eyes thus made up will be out of her senses and immediately subjugated: *yāṃ paśyati naro mattā vāmā sā tatkṣaṇād vaśā*. The mantra employed here contains the famous Vedānta slogan "Brahman is bliss": *Oṃ ānanda Brahmā* (sic) *svāhā, Oṃ hrīṃ klīṃ plāṃ Kāli kapāli svāhā.* Other deities addressed in mantras in this context in N are Kāma (st. 28), Raktacāmuṇḍā (st. 34, p. 288) and again Viśvāvasu. Stanzas 36 and 39 give other instances of hypnotizing by means of certain eye ointments.

Other texts of a more sophisticated character may prescribe a mental act of subjugation by means of the meditation on a certain deity in a more elaborated form. A hymn to Devī as Mahāṣoḍaśī (Mahāṣoḍaśīvarṇaratnāvalīstotra, Aithal, p. 86) in stanza 13 describes Devī as the nectar contained in the ocean of the syllable *hrīṃ.* Daily meditation on her will result in the subjugation of women dear to the gods; they will be "tormented by the fever of the Bodiless One" (the God of love): *anaṅgajvaraklāntāḥ.* Such a meditation can be compared to the prescription by the Mahāmāyā fragment (st. 9) of concentration of the mind on the red Viṣṇu with the result that beautiful ladies will become the performer's servants (*dāsi*).[34] Elaborate descriptions of meditations for subjugation are found in the SM, in the cadre of the Bodhisattva course (for instance in No. 60, 62, 75, 92, 171-190). No 92, Vaśyādhikāratārāsādhanam, is conceived as follows: "Meditate upon a blue lotus born from the syllable *Tāṃ* (which represents the name of the goddess Tārā), and provided in the middle with this same syllable *Tām.* Then concentrate your mind upon the Venerable Goddess Tārā as developing out of that lotus, dark green (*śyāma*) of colour, sitting in the "favourable" posture, bearing a blue lotus in her left hand, and with her right hand making the gesture of granting a boon, and bearing Amoghasiddhi in her crown. The performer should unify her with his nature-of-intelligence (*jñāna-sattva-*). He should recite in the number mentioned before, and provided with the name of the "victim", the mantra *Oṃ Tāre tuttāre ture amukam amukiṃ vā vaśam ānaya svāhā.* Because the usual attributes of arrows etc. are absent, he should bind the victim's neck with the blue lotus and place her (him) under his power by filling her (his) body with bundles of beams of red colour which are emitted from his own body" [31].

In practice, the rite of subjugation has been often meant to be applied by a husband against his wife or the reversal. This aspect of Vaśīkaraṇa has been observed above (p. 316) in connexion with the Vedic sources. Other instances of acts of magic executed by married people against each other might be given.[35] RV 10, 159, ascribed to Śacī Paulomī, identified with Indra's wife, refers to a devoted wife who has vanquished her rivals and made her husband subject to her (*aháṃ pátim abhyasākṣi*). She has performed a sacrifice by which Indra has become successful and famous. From now on, her husband will live in accordance with her intentions (2: *máméd ánu krátuṃ pátiḥ....upácaret*). She describes herself as "possessing formidable power" (*ugrā*) and "in the possession of victory" (*sehānā*). The AitBr (3, 24) advises to recite a certain passage in a whispering tone in order to secure that the wife will henceforward refrain from contradicting her husband by making her *aprativādinīm* (Malaviya, p. 45).

Coming to the younger sources, we first observe that GarPur (178, 12) describes an unguent which causes the wife not to desire another man. A few stanzas below (178, 19) there is a mantra of the following wording : "*Oṃ*, *hrīṃ*, Goddess Gaurī, grant me marital happiness, sons and the ability to subjugate; O Goddess Lakṣmī, grant me complete marital happiness, and delusion of the threefold world" [32]. The *saubhāgyam* afforded by a magical ritual executed by the wife is often circumscribed by the phrase that "the husband will be a slave" (*patir dāso bhaviṣyati*; GarPur 178, 22; passim in the Ṣaṭkarman monographs); meant is in the first place the ability and willingness to sexual intercourse. The monographs contain chapters on this "marital subjugation": D ch. 9 (Puruṣavaśīkaraṇam); N p. 290 ff. (Drâvaṇam); p. 293 ff. (Pativaśyam); K p. 32f. (Pativaśīkaraṇam); p. 44 ff. (Rañjanam). These passages include recipes and prescriptions on various kinds of ointments and aphrodisiacs destined to increase the appetite for love and to fight impotence. The same kind of contents are found in GarPur 185. The result of such a method of subjugating the wife has been poetically described in PST 18, 33 in this way, that "if one thus enjoys love with one's own partner, she will be shocked by the arrows of the God of Seduction and remain attached to one like one's shadow even in a following existence":

Nijāṃ priyāṃ bhajed evaṃ sā māraśaravihvalā |
chāyevānugatā tasya bhaved api bhavāntare ||

We mention in passing that there are allusions to an act of subjugation executed by religious teachers against their pupils. It has been remarked already above (p. 316) that the Buddha was accused of a similar trick. An instance from the Jaina canon is given by Jhavery, p. 276: "invocation of a deity through Vidyā for the inducement of faith in a pupil..." One might be reminded of the fact that in initiation ritual there are traces of parallellism with the marriage ceremony (van den Berg. p. 27, 38).

Animals. The Mahāmāyā fragment in stanza 8 refers to the subjugation of "elephants in rut, excited and cruel". When there is a question of animals to be tamed and brought under power, the elephant will be the most impressive object on which a performer's abilities can manifest themselves. The miraculous deed of the Buddha who is said to have tamed the elephant Nālāgiri by his universal kindness (Thomas, p. 133f.) can be repeated by the recitation of mantras and the performance of supranormal art. The MMD (10, 56), mentions among other results of the worship of Svapnavārāhī the subjugation of men, women, kings, kings' favourites, lions, elephants and other terrible wild animals. JT says (17, 53): "kings, steeds, snakes, cruel elephants excited by rut, tigers and aggressive lions become subjected by him" [33]. N discusses some instances of the subjugation of animals, chiefly elephants, on p. 284. Thus, in st.4: *mahāhastī vaśo bhavet*; 5: *gajā yānti dūrato natasaṃmukhāḥ* (i.e., "attraction" in the first place"); 6: *dūre gacchanti kuñjarāḥ*; 7: *duṣṭadantibhayaṃ na syāt.* In stanza 8 it is said that the root of a white Aparājitā held in the hand during a certain ritual keeps off the elephants; the root of a white Bṛhatī destroys the danger from tigers. The subjects of *gajanivāraṇam* "warding off elephants" and *vyāghranivāraṇam* "warding off tigers" are discussed by K under the heading of Vaśīkaraṇam (p. 37). Here also the result may be described in a vague manner: "the danger for tigers or lions is removed" so that a maximum of practical situations is covered. It should be noted that "elephants" in many cases would prove to be military elephants operating in an inimical army (PST 14, 53). In the twenty-second of the sixty-four "plays" performed by Śiva at Madurai, such an elephant who leads the army of the enemies (the Coḷas) has been created by the Jainas by means of black magic. It is killed by Sundareśvara (a local form of Śiva) with Narasiṃha as his arrow (Dessigane, 1960, p. 36). Bringing animals to life out of images made of clay is discussed in the MMK (Vol. II, p. 299; ch. 26).

The taming of wild animals can also be considered as a kind of subjugation. T (p. 418), referring to the Brahmasaṃhitā on p. 415, mentions a procedure which consists of muttering a certain mantra into an animal's ear after which it becomes subjected to the performer's will. The mantra is said to be "delightful to princes" (*rājaputrapriyaṃkaraḥ*), the expected owners of the elephants in question. A similar method is described in TSS 30, 11. Such mantras serve as the animals' "secrets" known only to the owner and enabling the owner to get everything done for him which the animal is able to. We shall return succinctly to the warding off of animals in the next section.

6.6. *Immobilization*

The term Stambhana. The preceding two acts were intended to induce a victim to a certain activity—to attract him or to cause him to serve the performer. This leads one to expect that the magician should also be able to cause the activities of his object to stop—in short, the power of immobilization, or *stambhaṇam* as it is called in Sanskrit. In some cases, the term "paralyzation" might serve as a translation , but this has the disadvantage of implying too strong a "physical" or even "medical" sense. The act of Stambhana affects not only the body, but at the same time also the mind of the victim who is reduced to an overall state of immobility. Besides, it can be applied— just like Ākarṣaṇa and Vaśīkaraṇa—to inanimate victims like the powers of nature.

The power of immobilization is exemplified on many places in Sanskrit literature[36]. It is treated at some length in the Ṣaṭkarman monographs : N ch.7 and 8 (p. 298 ff.); D ch.4 (p. 135-140); S ch. 5 (p. 232 ff.); ch. 6 (p. 242-246); K ch. 4 (p. 37-41). Besides, there are many details on the subject in the BMR, and one may also compare TSS 17, 1-8.

The word *stambhanam* is derived from the root *stabh*—. The meanings of this root and its derivations are characterized by a certain ambivalence. On the one side it may mean (and does mean most often in the Veda) "to fix, consolidate, prop, confirm"; on the other side it can stand for "to make rigid, to stiffen"[37]. In the RV, *stabh*—seems to occur twenty-seven times as "to fix, prop". Sixteen times the subject is Indra; in eleven of these sixteen occurrences the word *divám* "the sky" is the object (Tripathi, p. 16f.). These are references to Indra's creative act of propping up the sky and rendering life on earth a possibility. After the RV this deed has been ascribed to Viṣṇu only, for instance in TĀr 1, 8, 2 (Tripathi, l.c.). The power by which Indra performs this feat is just *māyā*, as may appear from RV, 2, 17, 5 *ástabhnān māyáyā dyām avasrásaḥ* "by his supranormal creative power, (Indra) supported the sky (and in this way guarded it) from collapse". After the Veda this meaning of *stabh*—is also found. In the BhGītā (10, 42) God asserts *viṣṭabhyāham idaṃ kṛtsnaṃ ekāṁśena sthito jagat* "I remain supporting this entire world with one fraction of Myself". In his commentary on this place, Śaṅkara circumscribes *viṣṭabhya* with *viśeṣataḥ stambhanaṃ dṛdhaṃ kṛtvā* "having made (this world) eminently fixed, that means solid", thus using *stambhanam* as an adjective.

In post-Vedic texts the causative *stambhayati* tends to replace the Vedic *stabhnāti*. *Stambhayati* became the usual verbal counterpart to the substantives *stambhanam* and *stambhaḥ*. An example from the MMK (Vol. II, p. 538): *parabalaṃ dṛṣṭvā stambhayati* "as soon as the inimical army is within his sight, he immobilizes it". In the SM (No. 85), among an extensive list of the results of a certain Sādhanā occurs the expression *gatiṃ stambhayet* "one obstructs the moving power (of a victim)". Three imperatives loaded with power: *jambhayatu* "he should swallow", *stambhayatu* "he should immobilize", *mohayatu* "he should delude" occur in the PST, 34, 62, where these instructions are imparted to each of the eight Lokapālas or Guardians of the horizontal space.

As to the substantives *stambhaḥ* and *stambhanam*, they are characterized by the same dichotomy of meaning as their verbal counterparts. PD (VII, 1255) gives for *stambhaḥ* these four meanings: 1. Pillar (in this meaning, *stambha-* is a variant of the more usual *stamba-*). 2. Confirmation, support, strengthening, e.g. the strengthening of a seed, *bījastambhaḥ*. 3. Making rigid, rendering cohesive (or the state created by such an action); in this meaning, the water serves as the foremost object, as appears from an instance taken from the Rājataraṅgiṇī 3, 69: *stambhaṃ nīyata ambho mayāmbudheḥ* "the water of the ocean is brought by me to immobility". Other shades of this third meaning of *stambhaḥ* are motionlessness (Unbeweglichkeit), stiffening of the body or the limbs; paralyzation. A synonym for this meaning is *jaḍībhāvaḥ* "the state of rigidity". The Sāhityadarpaṇa is quoted for a paraphrase of stambha as a state of the mind appearing as "the obstruction of all mobility caused by fear excitement or disease": *stambhaś ceṣṭāpratighāto bhayaharṣāmayādibhiḥ.* Among other texts referred to figure the Mālatīmādhava by Bhavabhūti and the medical work of Suśruta. 4. A fourth sense of stambha is mentioned by PD as "Hemmung, Bannung (durch Zaubermittel)" ("obstruction, banishment by magical means"). The dictionary refers to some text places which make mention of certain types of stambha. This fourth meaning is evidently the same as the magical act of immobilization described in these pages. We also note that *apastambhaḥ* "obstruction" (PD: "Verschliessung") occurs as a magical act in JaimBr 1, 325.

The word Stambhana (PD VII, 1256) is not only used for "obstruction, paralyzation, stupefaction" ("das Hemmen, Lähmen, Festbannen"), but can also mean in positive sense "strengthening", as in the expressions *vīryastambhanam*, *cittastambhanam.* Stambhana can have a medical connotation: the PD refers to some places in Suśruta. Besides, the term occurs as one of the five arrows of Kāma (PD), while Stambhanī "Immobilizing One" is mentioned as one of Kāma's Śaktis in PST 18,6. The AVPar mentions Stambhanī, Jambhanī and Mohanī as epithets of Lady Śivā (36, 1, 4).[38]

As a technical term of magic Stambhana seems to occur from the AVPar onwards. This means that, as far as we can trace, it is not one of the oldest specimens of the terminology of Indian miracle-working. Sometimes the reader meets variations, usually *stambhaḥ.* This word occurs for instance in the BrVPur, Kṛṣṇajanmakhaṇḍa, 78, 32 ff., in a list of siddhis "perfections". Among the perfections mentioned there occur a few kinds of immobilization: those of fire (*vahnistambha*), of water (*jalastambha*), of wind (*vāyustambha*) and of weaknesses of the human body like hunger, thirst and sleep (*kṣut*, *pipāsā*, *nidrā*).

The BJUp, one of the younger Upaniṣads, mentions (8, 3) stambhana of fire and other powers as some of the supranormal results which can be obtained by him who studies the Upaniṣad; the objects are fire, wind, sun, moon, water, the gods, the planets, and poison. The Bagalāmukhīstotra included in S (p. 241) promises for its reciters and for those who wear it as an amulet on their body the power to immobilize kings, steeds, elephants blind with rut, snakes, lions and human enemies, beside the steady presence of the Goddess of Wealth—a good illustration of the wide range of objects to which the power of immobilization can be applied [34]. The Mahāmāyā fragment in stanza 11 restricts itself to stating the immobilization of snakes—but there is some evidence that on this place one stanza has fallen out (see above, p. 148; Stuti & Stava, p. 277, n. 12).

Just like the preceding acts of Ākarṣaṇa and Vaśīkaraṇa, the performance of Stambhana is ambivalent, which means that it can be executed for good as well as for evil ends. It would be incorrect to classify the acts of immobilization without more under the heading of "black magic", as will be evident from the following pages. But it remains true that with them one approaches the darker side of the magical science. TSS 17, 1 (= AgPur 306, 1) classifies Stambhana together with some other acts as Kṣudra "base performances":

Stambho vidveṣaṇoccāṭāv utsādo bhramamāraṇe |
vyādhiś ceti smṛtaṃ kṣudraṃ tanmokṣaś cātra kathyate ||

"Immobilization, causing dissension, eradication, putting to flight, causing to wander, liquidation and causing illness are known as the base performances; the remedies against them will be told below". It is significant that the remedies following in the chapter in question imply the invocation of awesome deities with fear-inspiring mantras. While mentioning spells destined for immobilization and the correct procedure for handling them (*stambhanavidyā*), the texts sometimes admit that they can be active also in causing evil results. Thus the vidyā of Bagalāmukhī is also fit for Vidveṣaṇa, Uccāṭana, Vaśya, Saṃmohana, even for Śānti (BMR, p. 3).

As synonyms for Stambhana there occur, beside Stambha mentioned above, *bandhanam* "binding" (S 44, p. 186 = T p. 369) and *rodhanam* "obstruction" (cf. Mahāmāyā fragment, st. 11: *sarpāḥ..rudhyante*). The term *rodhana* occurs as a synonym for Stambhana in the definitions given by a few texts. S (1, 8) circumscribes Stambhana with *pravṛttirodhaḥ sarveṣām* "obstruction of the activities of all beings (one desires)". MMD (25, 2f.) gives a similar definition: *stambho vrttinirodhanam* "immobilization is the obstruction of activity". It is remarkable how these definitions remind of the characterization of the nature of yoga in Patañjali's Yogasūtras (1, 2): *cittavṛttinirodhaḥ* "obstruction of the activities of the mind". Indeed the performance of yoga might be understood as an act of immobilization executed outside the magical context. B. Bhattacharya (p. LXXXVIf.) circumscribes the results of Stambhana with "..power is conferred on the worshipper for stopping all actions of others, and even when a cause is operating, to stop its effect". This formulation correctly stresses the fact that Stambhana can be applied against inanimate as well as animate "victims". Besides, Stambhana implies the idea of "banishing" as is stated in the paragraph on this word in PD.

Instances from literary sources. Skt. literature provides the reader with frequent instances of the act of immobilization. According to Sāyaṇa on ṚV 3, 53, 15, obstruction of the voice (*vākstambhanam*) was applied by Śakti the son of Vasiṣṭha to Viśvāmitra, the eternal rival of his father (Malaviya, p. 33). From the epic tale of Nala (Mbh., Book 3) we learn that the serpent king Karkoṭaka had in former times been cursed by Nārada with the words *tiṣṭha tvaṃ sthāvara iva* "remain motionless" (Nala 14, 6) until Nala would arrive and release him from his plight. Strictly speaking, this is a curse and no act of magic, but this is only a minor difference within the range of application of supranormal powers. The stopping of the movements of others by means of a mantra is accomplished by Āstīka according to Mbh 1, 53. The act is directed against the officiants functioning at Janamejaya's serpent sacrifice; its result is salutary, because Takṣaka, the king of snakes, is caused by the mantra to stay hanging in the air at the very moment of his falling into the fire by the power of the priests' prayers. Kṛṣṇa paralyzed Indra when that god was about to hurl the vajra (Mbh. 13, 149, acc. to Soerensen, p. 420). Śiva, seated on Pārvatī's lap as a child with five locks of hair, paralyzed Indra's arm when he tried to kill him with the vajra (Mbh. 13, 161 or 162 acc. to Soerensen). Indra is again the victim in a mythological tale recorded by the MtPur (47, 96). The mother of the priest of the Asuras, Kāvya or Bṛhaspati, acted as the refuge of the Asuras who had sought her help in her son's absence against an unlawful attack by the gods. She paralyzed Indra: "having collected all her requisites she bewitched Indra at that time; the goddess who was rich in ascetic power and who commanded powerful magic, paralyzed him":

Saṃbhṛtya sarvasaṃbhārān Indraṃ sābhyacarat tadā /
tastambha devī balavadyogayuktā tapodhanā //

Tripurā, a manifestation of Durgā, performs the same feat, again with Indra as the victim, by a mere smile according to the TripR (Māhātmyakhaṇḍa, 9, 21 and 22). In stanza 66 of the same chapter Indra alludes to this incident and recognizes that this act of Stambhana was no other thing than a proof of the Goddess' *anugraha* "mercy"—a contention due to the Śākta character of the text. A kind of Stambhana performed upon water is effected by Rāvaṇa by his mere appearance: the river Godāvarī out of fear for the demon king slackened her course (Rāmāyaṇa 3, 44, 7).

Thus it appears that the power to perform Stambhana forms part of the equipment of gods, counter-gods, demons and powerful human beings. But "Immobilization" may also be understood to be an aspect of the Māyā of the Supreme God by which He holds all humanity in check together with the rest of creation. The ŚvetUp (4, 9) teaches: "..the Wielder of Māyā creates this all; and within that (creation), any other (i.e.: anyone who fails to realize his fundamental identity with the divine Magician) lives obstructed by His Māyā" : *Māyī sṛjate viśvam etat / tasmiṃś cānyo māyayā saṃniruddhaḥ.* As we saw, the act of *rodhanam* "obstruction" sometimes occurs as a synonym —perhaps a little weaker—for Stambhana. The Divine Lord performs His immobilizing act against the victim which is creation, so that it will stay deprived of the motion towards salutary insight. As Śaṅkara explains in his commentary on ŚvetUp 4,9: *saṃniruddaḥ saṃbaddha avidyāvaśagaḥ* "obstructed means bound, i.e. being under the subjugating power of Ignorance".

Colour and deities of Stambhana. We return to Stambhana as an act of miracle-working. In the regular list of the Six Acts it occupies the third place. In the realm of colours it is intimately connected with yellow, the third of the Four Colours (see above, p. 176). The Mahāmāyā fragment combines it with yellow, and so does JT 17, 83f.: worship of the Ṣoḍaśavidyā with yellow ingredients after designing it upon a yellow place will result in the immobilization of all verbal opponents: *stambhayet sarvavādinaḥ*. Bagalāmukhī, the immobilizing goddess, should also be worshipped with yellow materials and adorned with yellow ornaments (S 5, 5, p. 235). MMD 10, 107 prescribes a worship of Vārāhī with yellow materials and accompanying recitation with a rosary strewn over with Haridrā (turmeric powder), a yellow stuff, when the worship is done for Stambhana. Many other places could be referred to (e.g., TSS 17, 6; 23, 3); the colour symbolism of Stambhana is fairly constant in the sources.

A god who "specializes" in Stambhana is Haridrāgaṇapati "the Gaṇeśa of turmeric" who is mentioned with his mantra in S (p. 243f.)—but meditation on him may also result in Ākarṣaṇa, S p. 244, 4. His mantra is as follows: *Oṃ huṃ gaṃ glauṃ Haridrāgaṇapataye varavarada sarvajanahṛdayaṃ stambhaya stambhaya svāhā*..to H., O foremost Granter of boons, immobilize immobilize the hearts of all people. . . .". The meditation stanza which follows refers to this god as "provided with an elephant face, three-eyed, illustriously adorned by his garment ointment, garland and ornaments, all of a yellow colour; showing the hand poses of noose and elephant hook, ferocity and axe, security and liberality (in his six hands); the supreme Lord of the gods" [35]. After a minute description of the particulars of his worship and the preparation of an appropriate yantra, the results are stated on p. 246. After a worship in this method lasting a period which ranges from one day to a week, one will be able to immobilize all beings: *stambhayet sakalān lokān*. This general statement is, however, further specified in the next stanzas. In the case of a ritual of attraction, the same Gaṇeśa is to be worshipped with red flowers. The same mantra may be applied, but instead of *stambhaya*, the performer should say twice *ākarṣaya* "attract". For attracting women one should take care to worship with white Arka leaves. A rite of Stambhana with the help of a mantra of Kukṣigaṇapati is mentioned in TSS 17, 6 (cf. the commentary).

Another deity specially associated with Stambhana is the Lady with the Goat's Head, Bagalāmukhī, who has repeatedly been alluded to above (see especially on p. 105). She dwells in the North of the Vindhyas near Datia, M.P., at the Pītāmbarapīṭha "Residence of (the Goddess) with the Yellow Garment". One of the guardians of this sacred place, called Śrī-Svāmin, composed the BMR, a work which comprises the particulars on this goddess' mythology and worship, for the greater part compiled from older sources such as the Sāṃkhyāyana-, Meru-, Rudrayāmala-, Kundikā- and Bagalāmukhītantra, and also from the Ṣaṭkarmadīpikā, the fifth chapter of which is devoted to Bagalāmukhī. She is able to immobilize the threefold cosmos (*trailokyastambhinī*); her fiery energy originates from Viṣṇu. This *vidyā* has the power of obstructing all activities (*pravṛttinirodhinī vidyā*). The enumeration of the mere name of Bagalā for a certain high number immediately suffices to work all kinds of miraculous effects without preparatory acts like nyāsa being accomplished—a statement ascribed on p. 4 to the AgPur. Meditation on her should be done as follows (p. 5): "One should concentrate one's thoughts on Bagalāmukhī who is able to immobilize the three worlds; she stands upon a golden pedestal, is three-eyed, with a brilliant yellow garment; her limbs emit the lustre of gold, her headdress contains the crescent, she wears a garland made of beautiful (yellow) Campaka flowers; in her hands she bears the hammer, noose, thunderbolt and tongue; her body is decked with ornaments."[36] After meditation a yantra should be constructed and worship performed to herself and her accompanying manifestations (śaktis) seated upon a lotus designed with eight leaves. On sixteen points of the compass her sixteen śaktis are located. Among them occur names like Stambhanī "Immobilizer", Jṛmbhiṇī "Swallower", Mohinī "Deluder", Vaśyā "Subjugating One", Kālākarṣiṇī "She Who attracts Kāla", Bhrāmikā "She Who causes to wander", Mandagamanā "She Whose course is slow". The worshipper should also dress himself in a yellow garment and put on a yellow garland. Another meditation stanza on this goddess, this time with two arms, is found in S (p. 239): "I meditate upon the Goddess Who is seated upon a throne which is fastened upon a platform of pearls within a temple consisting of jewels in the middle of the ocean of nectar (a favourite location of Devī); Her colour is yellow; Her body is adorned with a yellow garment, ornaments, and garland ; She bears a hammer and the tongue of the enemy."[37] Her bearing a tongue is without doubt symbolical of her capacity to obstruct the speech of an adversary in dispute on behalf of her worshippers.

The result of such a worship is stated eloquently by S in the Bagalāmukhīstotra on p. 240; "A disputant becomes mute, a lord of the earth is reduced to starvation, the fire becomes cool; the irate become quiet, evil people become good people, the quick runner becomes crippled ; the conceited become dwarfish, the omniscient become stupid, being affected by the spells of him who masters Thy spells; O Illustrious eternal Lady Bagalāmukhī, to Thee honour day after day, O Beauteous One". And the next stanza: "Immobilizing the evil-minded, pacifying formidable obstructions, dispelling poverty, performing stupefaction of the rulers of the earth, attracting the minds of the buckeyed (ladies), being the foremost abode of domestic happiness and (an ocean) full of Water-of-life of Thy compassion, and killing my foes, O mother, in this way Thy form should appear before my eyes !" And the prayer is continued with increasing effect: "O Mother, break the voice of my opponents, pin down their tongue, seal their speech, quickly destroy their intelligence, obstruct their evil course; pulverize my enemies, O Goddess, with Thy mace of sharp edge, O pale yellow One, clad with the yellow garment ; O Bagalā, daily remove the wave of obstruction in my behalf, O Thou Whose eyes are full of compassion !"[38].

Application of Stambhana to human beings. We now proceed to discuss some instances of immobilization seen from the viewpoint of the objects affected by them. All kinds of beings and powers may serve as victims. We consider them in this sequence: 1. Human beings and their faculties. 2. Enemies (strictly speaking, a subgroup of (1). 3. *Animals*, and 4. Gods and powers of nature.

As to human objects, D (p. 139, st.3) expressly refers to the act of *manuṣyastambhanam* "immobilization of human beings". The rite is directed against a man and its essence consists in taking the undergarment of a menstruating woman, designing the victim's portrait on it, and throwing it into a pot. K (p. 40) in a prose fragment describes a rite which is able to accomplish the immobilization of all those who are of evil mind. The victim's name should be written with Gorocanā (yellow orpiment) and (or ?) Ālaktaka (red lac) and (or ?) Kuṅkuma (saffron) upon a plate and this object thrown into the water. Another method is to fill the plate with ashes from the cremation ground and bury it on that place—both methods probably implying a symbolical death of the victim.

All kinds of human beings can be affected by the worship of the yellow Gaṇeśa already referred to (S, p. 246). One may for example direct the rite against armies, towns and villages, opponents in dispute, thieves or women.

In some cases the result of the immobilization rite is specified. Thus a term like *āsanastambhanam* means that the victim is clustered to his seat. D (p. 135 f.) describes how the magician who desires to accomplish this should throw down a certain mixture in front of the victim's seat, uttering the mantra *Oṃ namo Digambarāya amukasyāsanastambhanaṃ kuru kuru svāhā* "O Thou Whose cloak is the air, perform the immobilization of N.N. (so that he remains clustered) to his seat..." (version of the Benares ed., 4, 15). Another instance is to be found in N 7, 3. Here again, something is thrown in front of the victim's seat[39].

Another variety is called *gatistambhanam* "immobilization of the victim's faculty of walking". For this end N (7, 2) prescribes to write the victim's name on a piece of copper and bind it to a stone. The AgPur has a case of Gatistambhana in 312, 2 and the TSS in 17, 6 (*gamanast.*). While being on a ship in the open sea, a performer can effect *naukāstambhanam* "immobilization of a vessel" by throwing a wedge into the vessel's hold. The idea is ascribed to the hero of rogues, Mūladeva (D, p. 139, 6; Benares ed., 4, 50).

Immobilization is a power which in the first place affects the object's psychical faculties. This is in accordance with a general trait of the Six Acts. "Immobilizing the will", *buddhistambhanam*, is explicitly mentioned in D p. 136 (Benares ed., 4, 18f.). To this end a certain mixture is prepared and added to the victim's betel. The next śloka mentions a tilaka in the same context; and the same expedient is prescribed in K, p. 40. The mantra on that place (=N 7, 14, p. 300) mentions Viśvāmitra, the famous ṛṣi-magician: *Oṃ namo bhagavate Viśvāmitrāya namaḥ sarvamukhibhyāṃ Viśvāmitrāya Viśvāmitroddāpayati śaktyā āgacchatu.* The mantra is untranslatable (and probably corrupt) but its meaning is probably that some spirit is enjoined to come to the performer's aid on Viśvāmitra's behest. In N 7,13 immobilization of the will is directed against enemies: *sarvaśatrūṇāṃ buddhistambhakaraṃ bhavet.* The PD further mentions "immobilization of the mind" (*manaḥstambhaḥ*) and "imm. of the heart" (*hṛdaḥ stambhaḥ*), referring to the Pañcatantra 4, 57 and 8,18 respectively. It may be remarked that immobilization of the mind or the will is very similar to the act of delusion (*mohana*) to which we will briefly refer later on.

A very frequent miraculous feat of the same kind is *vākstambhanam* or *mukhastambhanam*, "immobilization of speech". This important and dreaded magical procedure is chiefly directed against the opponent in a disputation or a juridical process. It has been known outside India (de Jong, p. 36: in Greece). The mutual jealousy between two religious specialists or between factions among them is a well-known feature of Indian cultural history. For instance, Ṛgvidh. 2, 4, 2-4 alludes to a feud between the Viśvāmitras and the Vasiṣṭhas which is also known from other sources. Besides, disputations between two opponents were frequent, especially in later times (B. Bhattacharya, p. LXXXIV, 10). AV 2, 27 is destined to obtain a victory in disputation; rules for the same goal are contained in KauśS 38, 17-21 (process); 23-25 (disputation); 41, 10-13; 38, 27-30 is destined for success in the gambling-hall. SVBr (2, 7, 12f.) focuses on the same subject with *kathāsu śreyān bhavati* "one becomes the most proficient in discussions" (for this meaning of *kathā*, cf. Bodewitz p. 75, n.2) *uttaravādi bhavati* "one obtains the best result in disputations". Other allusions are found in BhārGṛh 2, 25; ĀpGṛh 22, 19 —23, 1. References to such practices are also found in the Pāli canon (Brahmajāla Sutta, DN 1, 1, 21ff.), and in the Jain Mantra tradition (Jhavery, p. 226). Jhavery relates how the Jaina doctor Dharmaghoṣa Sūri (13th century ?) was once affected by inimical female magicians with an "obstruction in his throat" so that he could not speak. But the holy man hit back hard: his opponents were "paralyzed and stuck to the ground". The Buddhist SM (No. 85, No. 151, a.o.)

also refers to the subjection of opponents in dispute. No. 151 ascribes this feat to the power of Prajñāpāramitā, the Buddhist counterpart of Sarasvatī. The Hindu JT says (17, 84) : *stambhayet sarvavādinaḥ* "one will immobilize all disputators". To this end Durgā should be worshipped upon a yellow pedestal; the worshipper sits down facing an eastern direction and makes use of yellow materials. AgniPur 315, 1ff. contains a peculiar rite of Mukhastambhana in which use is made of a tortoise and other materials; in AgPur 323, 11f. the same result is obtained with an incense.

The Ṣaṭkarman monographs contain various devices for silencing an opponent. N 7, 7 enjoins meditation on the letter *a* of the Devanāgarī alphabet as a serpent coiled up in the victim's ear. N 3, 3 (p. 283) and K (p. 37) describe the result as the opponent's becoming mute : *paravādi bhaven mūkaḥ*. N adds *athavā yāti digantaram* "or he goes to another place", which is properly speaking the result of an eradication rite. S ch. 5 (p. 246) advises to place a Gaṇeśa image upon the scene of a process; the victory will be certain. In D (p. 171 f.) victory in a disputation is discussed outside the cadre of immobilization. Rituals with the aim of winning a process are frequently mentioned, e.g. in AVPar 36, 23; AgPur 260, 64 (with a Vedic mantra as a spell), and GarPur 178, 13. The practice has continued until recent times. Wirz, p.229, figure 25 shows and discusses a yantra in use in Ceylon to obtain luck in a process (*nāduyantra*). The mantra which should be said at the time is *Oṃ Sri Muniya* (=Buddha), *jaya Muniya*, *jāya pilla* (Wirz: "Sieg auf der Stelle"). *Muniya ē svāhā*. It should be repeated 108 times.

Among other bodily functions liable to be immobilized are hunger and thirst (*kṣutpipāsāstambhanam*), evidently a rite with a positive aim, and sleep (*nidrāstambhanam*). D p. 139, 5 (Benares ed., 4, 48) advises to obtain the latter result by smearing eyes or nose with the root of the Bṛhatī plant and with honey. The idea has been launched by Mūladeva.

Another frequent kind of Stambhana is *garbhastambhanam* "stopping the embryo". Under this name one might classify some rites of positive as well as negative character. Definitely positive when in AV 6, 17 the power of Satya "Truth" is appealed to in order to help avoiding premature birth (Malaviya, p.

157). In the same way the TSS (23, 13) praises a certain method as *putradaṃ garbharakṣākṛt* "securing the birth of a son and guarding the embryo". The same text (29, 33) has a remedy for a lady *garbho na tiṣṭhed yasyāḥ* "whose unborn child does not remain in its place"; in 30, 1 a certain mixture is destined to "strengthen the womb of kine", *gavām udarabṛṃhaṇam.* In the negative sense, AV 7, 35 aims at stopping an embryo so that an inimical woman becomes sterile (Malaviya, l.c.); cf. also ViPur 4, 3, 15 which records the stopping of a rival wife's embryo by means of a potion (*gara*). Rites for avoiding birth are further mentioned in texts of diverse kind like the BAUp, the Brahmajālasutta (DN 1, 1, 21f.) and the BMR. In the Ṣaṭkarman monographs the aim of such a procedure is usually to become able—or to enable a client—to enjoy the company of a woman without running any risks: D p. 139 (Benares ed., 4, 51-53;) K p. 41, according to which some ingredient is to be bound to the hip after which one may have intercourse with one's beloved without danger of conception: *ramet kāntāṃ na garbhaṃ dhārayet kvacit.* The idea is ascribed to Nāgārjuna ! A variety of the same is *Śukrastambhanam* "stopping the semen". Practices of this kind may be the reason that in Sinhalese magic the word Stambhana became a term for "unlawful sexual practices" (Gooneratne).

The counterpart of Garbhastambhana, called *garbhasrāvaṇam* or *prajananam* "causing an easy birth", "causing a child to be born" is represented with high frequency and needs no elaboration here. We refer to ṚV 5, 78; KauśS 33, 1-20; Ṛgvidh. 1,23,3; 2,17,1; AgPur 302,22 = TSS 29,39 (*prasūte pramadā sukham*). For the Baiga tribe the first executor of this rite was the primeval magician Nanda Baiga who thereby stopped the obstructive powers of the witch Samduria (Elwin, The Baiga, quoted by Hermanns, p. 294).

Immobilizing the enemy is a variety of the manifold practices adopted in order to win a battle or in another way overcome the political or personal antagonist. We only discuss here a few references to immobilization proper. Webster (p. 94) notes a practice from New Britain where the Sulkas are said to call their enemies "rotten tree trunks" in order to slow off their motions (he refers to R. Parkinson, Dreissig Jahre in der Sudsee, Stuttgart 1907, p. 198). In the Indian cultural environment,

Mbh. 13, 1186 refers to *camūstambhanam* "immobilizing an army", and 15,227 to *śatrūṇāṃ stambhanam* "imm. the enemies" (both places according to PD). The AgPur (125, 47-51) discusses rites directed against enemies and their weapons: *stambhayec chatrum ātmanaḥ*; *stambhayec chastrajālakam*. A mantra directed to Bhairava is added : *Oṃ*, honour to the Great Fearsome One, of dreadful form with misfigured tusks, of red eyes, the Bearer of trident and sword (v. l., club), *vauṣaṭ*."[39] In order to "bind" an enemy (*bandhatvaṃ jāyate riboḥ*) a ritual is described in stanzas 49-51. The performer should sacrifice during the night a portion of human flesh mixed with blood and poison. He should be naked and his hair dishevelled. He should face the South, the region of the dead. The enemy's name should be uttered for 108 times and this mantra said: "*Oṃ*, honour to the Lady Kaumārī, dally (2x), cause to dally (2x), Lady of the Bell, kill kill N. N. by force, honour be to Thee, Lady Spell, *svāhā*"[40]. The use of the word "kill" *māraya*, is characteristic for the lack of compartmentalization between the Six Acts. The rite in question could perhaps be better classified with Māraṇa. Of course a performer himself will not mind the exact classification of the procedure as long as it is easy to find in his book and as long as he is assured, or is able to assure others, that it works allright. The same holds good for the spell presented next in AgPur 125, 51f., a long litany directed to Hanuman the monkey god, said to result in the enemies' being broken: *bhaṅgam āyānti śatravaḥ*. While the mantra is said, Hanuman's image painted upon cloth should be shown to the enemy. The mantra in translation is : "*Oṃ*, Thou of the vajra body, of the snout like the thunderbolt, Pale red One, of wide open mouth, of hairs erect, of great strength, of red mouth, of lightning tongue, mighty fearful One, of fierce tusks; devour, O Thou of the wide open mouth, of the mighty bold stroke, Constructer of the bridge towards the Lord of Laṅkā, Bearer of the rock, Who traversest space (?, *gaganavara*), come come, Lord of the great strength and valour, Bhairava issues his command (to Thee), come come, mighty fearful One, with Thy long tail envelope envelope N. N., devour devour, bury bury him, ...*hrūṃ phaṭ*".[41].

Of the Tantras we refer to MMK II, p. 538 and PST 14, 46 (in both cases, immobilization of an army), and to TSS 17, 3; 17,6; 17,8 (here, as often, the term *sainyastambhanam*);

23, 3. TSS 23, 5 refers to the breaking up of an immobilization which has been brought about by the enemy. Among the monographs, D (p. 136 f.; cf. also K, p. 38f.) lays down that for immobilizing inimical weapons one should bear something in the mouth or upon the head, or bind something to the wrist, and invoke Kumbhakarṇa. On p. 137f. (Benares ed., 4, 36f.), D enjoins, for immobilizing the leader of the inimical army, to bury a Śvetaguñjā plant upon a cremation place and lay a stone over it; and to worship the Mothers together with the eight Yoginīs, Gaṇeśa, Vaṭuka and Kṣetrapāla. The mantra, however, is directed to Kālarātri. N (p. 301 f.) refers to various expedients of immobilizing an army, an enemy or inimical weapons : *śatrustambhakaraṃ raṇe* (7, 19); *raṇeṣu stambhakṛd ripoḥ* (20);*vārayaty eva śastrasaṅgham* "one wards off a multitude of weapons' (21); *śastrair yāvajjivaṃ na bādhyate* "as long as one lives one will not be harassed by weapons any more" (22). The eighth chapter in N is even called Sainyastambhana "Imm. of armies", although it also includes other rites, especially of the Māraṇa class. On page 310, the same text concentrates upon the method to become a "hero" (*viraḥ*) by obtaining a Brahmāstra (see above, p. 106). Thereto the goddess Brāhmī, one of the Seven Mothers, should be invoked. Her colleagues follow suit, each of them presenting an appropriate weapon to the performer. The worshipper even obtains a divine cart from Brāhmī by ascending which he can freely roam over the earth. S ch. 5 discusses immobilization of the enemy in connection with the praise of Bagalāmukhī (see above).

Beside enemies, there are other beings of evil intentions whose actions have to be stopped. The AV mentions in this connection tigers, thieves, snakes, sorcerers and "wolves". N 7, 15 (p. 300; =K p. 41) refers to the immobilization of thieves, *caurāṇāṃ gatistambhanam,* by wearing stones (K: nooses) around the hip or the wrist. Another place is TSS 30, 21 (*corastambhaḥ*).

Immobilization of animals is repeatedly referred to by a general term like *paśustambhanam* (SM No. 93; S p. 241 and 246; N 7, 4=K p. 40). D p. 138 f. (Benares ed., 4, 43f.) specifies: "imm. of kine, buffaloes and so on"; the author advises the use of such objects as camel bones for this end. Usually, however, the victims of this rite are the wild animals who form a danger for human life such as lions (*siṃhastambhanam,* S p. 241, 246), tigers (AV 4, 3, 4; JT 17, 46; T p. 418) or rutting elephants (*mattebha*, TSS 23, 4). With respect to tigers there is an interesting passage in Bodding, p. 100: for a lonely wayfarer in the forest the Santals advise a mantra which is destined to charm all the limbs which an appearing tiger might move. The term used in the mantra for "to charm" really means "to bind" (*bandhe*). When an able person has pronounced this spell, "the tiger will sit quiet without moving". The driving away of a tiger by means of a mantra was once assisted by Elwin (Elwin, The Baiga, 1939, p. 351f.; quoted by Hermanns, p. 288).

The immobilization of snakes as a rite is very seldom mentioned in the texts, but there are many descriptions of ceremonies to ward them off, chase them away or destroy them. Brahmans as snake charmers (*ahiguṇṭhika*) are mentioned in the Jātakas (Fick, p. 154). Rites against snakes are found also in KauśS 50, 17 ff.; JT 17, 53; HT 2 (a snake chased away with the mantra *ili mili phuḥ phuḥ* see above, p. 79); SM No. 117-122; 181; S p. 241; TSS 23, 8. The best reference to the immobilization of snakes remains the eleventh stanza of the Mahāmāyā fragment (see above, p. 136). This short passage on snakes would not be complete without a reference to the many devices which existed against poison both coming from snakes and from other sources.[40] The BJUp (8, 3) contains the term *viṣastambhanam*. It may be mentioned in passing that also brahmans are able to send poisonous snakes to a victim, as appears from the tale of King Parīkṣit who was bitten by the snake Takṣaka as the result of a curse spoken by the young brahman Śṛṅgin (Mbh. 1, 36). Vedic mantra literature contains some hymns directed against snake poison.[41] The most effective rites against poison invoke the mythical bird Garuḍa, the enemy of snakes. A meditation on Garuḍa for this end is alluded to in the Śiva-jñāna bodham (trsl. Matthews, p. 23f.); such a meditation is described in the MMK, ch. 41; KCT 4,182 (a Garuḍa of five colours); MMD 14, 117ff. The whole Garuḍa Up (ed. Jacob, p. 83-88) is "simply a charm for the prevention of snakebite" (Jacob, Preface, p. 9); it contains among other things a meditation by the performer on himself as a Garuḍa of five colours with snakes serving as his necklace, sacred cord and belly string. A description of the fearsome manifestation of Garuḍa is contained in Stuti & Stava as No. 441, Bhairavastava. There is even a tradition that Garuḍa once rescued Kṛṣṇa, who had been bitten by the snake Kāli(ya), by sprinkling him with Amṛta (Song of the Snake-Charmer, translated from the Oriya in: K. Das, p. 169).

The magician's claims also pertain to the *immobilization of deities and powers of nature.* He may even boast to stupefy the whole cosmos: JT 18, 17 (*trailokyam*); S p.246 (*trailokyaṃ sacarācaram*). "All the gods" are the object in the BJUp, 8, 3. The same claims are made for the powers of attraction and subjugation, as indeed for the other specimens of the Six Acts also. Of course such statements are usually vague, standardized and theoretical and therefore of relatively small interest.

The immobilization of water (*jalastambhanam*) has some affinity to the act of attraction performed upon this element, discussed above on p.308. As we saw, the Rājataraṅgiṇī refers to a Stambhana of the ocean. Jalastambhana is further mentioned in the BrVPur (Kṛṣṇajanmakhaṇḍa 78, 32ff.), in the Pañcatantra (2, 3, 78 according to PD), in TSS 19, 20 (with a mantra of Vāyu) and in S p. 246. In N (p. 306, st. 3) this act is applied against a storm on the sea—a famous and very useful miracle—and stanza 5 on the same page contains a device for becoming able to walk upon the water. The next stanza refers to the use of miraculous shoes (*pādukā*) with the same effect. An astonishing miracle is presented in stanza 8: a pot filled with water is split while its contents remain standing in the same form; a mantra to Rudra should be uttered in the process. The last-mentioned feats are to be characterized as kinds of "show" (*kautuka*), artful performances of jugglers by which they seek to impress the public (N contains many of such devices).

Fire can also be the object (*agni-*, *vahnistambhanam*), for example in BJUp and BrVPur on the places mentioned above. The AgPur (306, 18) alludes to the immobilization of water as well as of fire. In TSS 19, 20 the feat is accomplished with the help of a mantra to Varuṇa. D p. 135, 1-8 also discusses the subject. A prominent method is to anoint the body with a certain mixture, often including the fat of a frog. After such preparations one is able to consume everything, even to keep a hot ball of iron in the mouth (a typical feat of kautuka). In K (p. 39f.) a few Mothers are invoked in the course of the process, among others Mahiṣavāhinī "She Who rides the buffalo", perhaps because of the buffalo's connection with mud and water. N p. 302 ff. handles the same subject; stanza 7,32 again advises to smear the body with the fat of a frog, together with that of an owl and a ram. The frog, an aquatic animal and a symbol of recurring rain, is constantly made use of in magical rites against fire. N. 7, 38 describes the result of such a rite as *bhramed aṅgāra-parvate* "one will be able to walk upon a heap of charcoal"; an allusion to the popular practice of fire-walking[42]. A mantra prescribed in N 7, 40 worships the power of the Water-of-Life and at the same time mentions the twin chief yogic arteries of the body, *iḍā* and *piṅgalā*: *Oṃ amṛtāya iḍa* (sic)*-piṅgale svāhā*. In stanza 43 a mantra is said to stop the burning of the house: *vahniḥ śāmyati raudro 'pi dahyamāne gṛhe sati*. Its wording is: "*Oṃ*, in the region to the North of the Himālayas there lives a flesh-eating demon by name of Mārīca; with his urine and faeces I immobilize the fire" [42]. Among other results of the application of devices against fire are the remaining intact of objects thrown into the fire (N 7, 46-50), or the not becoming cooked of heated food (N 7, 51f.). The mantra belonging to the latter passage is *Oṃ namo Mahāmāye vahniṃ rakṣa svāhā* "O Great Goddess Māyā, keep guard on the fire, *svāhā*".

The forces of the wind may be immobilized according to the places mentioned above from the BrVPur and the BJUp, (*vāyustambhanam*) and the SST (3, 3, 293). *Meghastambhanam* "immobilization of clouds" is discussed in D p. 139, 4 (Benares ed., 4, 46) with the peculiar device of placing two bricks into the ashes of the cremation ground; also in N. p. 314 (clouds and lightning); S p. 246 (rain); TSS 17, 6 (rain). The subjection of clouds and rain is of course of great importance for assuring a good crop; it has been dealt with also above (p. 308). The acts of immobilizing the sun (*āditya*), the moon (*soma*) and the planets (*graha*) are mentioned shortly in the BJUp (8, 3).

Release. As a counterpart to immobilization we succinctly mention here the frequently recurring subject of *bandha-vimokṣaṇam* "bringing about release from bonds or from prison by supernatural means"; a result passionately longed for by a great number of people in the course of the centuries. According to the SST (3, 2, 68) Kālī is the goddess who presides over release as well as immobilization (she is *bandhavimocanī* and *stambhaneśī*). Udayana worships Īśvara, the Supreme God, as the one who keeps the world as a prisoner when not being duly pacified; but out of satisfaction he releases mankind (Chemparathy, p. 156).

The theme occurs in Vedic texts like KauśS (52, 3-4) and Ṛgvidh. (1, 17, 9); in the latter source the result is obtained by the recitation of one or more of the hymns ṚV 1,24-30 which had been revealed to Śunaḥśepa when he had been bound to the sacrificial pole. The Kathās. 2, 4, 63 refers to *yogān nigaḍabhañjanān* "devices which cause fetters to break"[43] Of the ritual sources, SM mentions this result after a few sādhanās like Nos. 93 and 111. In the latter case it is enjoined that the Vidyā (spell) in question should be recited a thousand or eight hundred times daily by a prisoner, after which its goddess, Tārā, will release him from his bonds. In MMD 13, 37-39 the feat is ascribed to Hanuman, whose image should be painted surrounded by his written mantra. The performer, who in this case acts for a client, should write the name of the person who is to be released and twice add the word vimocaya *release* to it. Then the words should be wiped out with the left hand and written anew. This should be repeated for 108 times, after which the prisoner is released without delay. In Stuti & Stava No. 504, Aṣṭamahābhaya Kliṅ, release is one of the results demanded in the course of that *dhāraṇi* (p. 310f.): *ayobandhanamadhyagato vā...pramucyatām* "when being enclosed by iron bonds...he should be released".

6.7. *Eradication*

"Mountains of hard material and enormous size,
immovable and devoid of life,
are destroyed within a moment
by the performer's effortless activity".

By such words the Mahāmāyā fragment (st. 13) describes the effect of the act of *uccāṭanam* "eradication". Under this name goes what is without doubt one of the most spectacular feats of the magic art. Although it can certainly be performed with a view to accomplish a "positive" (i.e. socially beneficial) result, it definitely belongs to the sphere of "black magic". Curiously enough, for the pulverization of rocks described poetically in the stanza cited above no parallel has been met by us in the Indian sources under the term Uccāṭana—although there are instances of this feat known from Skt. literature; it is described as a magical feat in the LT, ch. 49 (Gupta, p. 324). The splitting of rocks has been described as a very positive activity symbolizing the creation of the material basis for human life and culture. The god Skanda splitted the mountain Krauñca. Balabhadra pierced the mountains around Kashmir Valley with his ploughshare ; the water which filled up the Valley as a lake was thus removed and this enabled Viṣṇu to detect the demon Jalodbhava who hid himself in it and to kill him. By these acts of the divine heroes the Valley became habitable.[44]

The terminology. It is not easy exactly to define what the authorities understood under the term *uccāṭanam.* In general we can say that the most prominent idea is that of "driving the victim away, uprooting him, depriving him of his position". S (1, 9) paraphrases Uccāṭana by *svadeśāder bhraṃśanam* "causing (the victim) to fall away from his dwelling-place or other (positions)". The MMD (25, 3) says *uccāṭaḥ sthānataś cyutiḥ* "falling down from one's position is called Ucc.". "Destruction of one's position" (*sthānanāśaḥ*) is also mentioned as a result of a certain spell in the LiPur (2, 50, 45). TSSC 17, 1 prefers to give a narrower circumscription of the term with *deśād deśāntara-preraṇam* "driving forth (the victim) from the place where he lives to another place." The PST (24, 29) gives a good description of such an effect:

> *Yāñ ca diśaṃ prati manunākṣipto' sau tāṃ diśaṃ prayāty acirāt |*
> *putrakalatradhanādiṃs tyaktvā na punar nivṛttaye sahasā ||*

"The direction into which he (the victim) has been thrown by the mantra, into that direction he departs without delay; by the power (of the spell) he leaves behind his wife and sons and his possessions, never to return". It is indeed a dreadful power that is able to produce such a terrible result.

In the most popular classification of the Six Acts (Type I), Uccāṭana occupies the fifth place, between Vidveṣaṇa and Māraṇa. Often it forms a pair with Vidveṣaṇa, sometimes with Māraṇa (in MMD ch. 20 and elsewhere). B. Bhattacharya's definition (Introd. to SM Vol. 2, p. LXXXVI) comes very close to the characterization of this act given above: "The fifth...

gives the performer special power to make his enemy flee from the country with all attendant disgrace"; but he adds that it has also been applied "in destroying the dwelling houses of enemies". An important other aspect is added by Panchanana Bhattacharya in his Introduction to the Tārābhaktisudhārṇava (p. 21), where this author defines Uccāṭana as "bringing about a mental disorder in a person". Although onesided, this definition justly emphasizes the psychological component in the act, by which the victim is affected mentally and brought to such a state of perplexity that he is forced to leave his home and his position. Both the material and the psychological effects seem to be essential in Uccāṭana as well as in the other constituents of the Six Acts.

In the light of this evidence the words by which the PD characterizes the act of Uccāṭana are somewhat meagre:' 'Das-aus-dem-Wege-Räumen eines Gegners" ("the expulsion of an opponent"), for which this dictionary refers to the Prabodhacandrodaya by Kṛṣṇamiśra, 61, 16; but of course the compilers of PD had no access to the Tantric literature of magic. On the same place PD adds the information (referring to the Kathās) that Uccāṭana is also the name of one of the five arrows of the God of love. We know that the five arrows of Kāma bear the names of five acts of magic.

Beside the word Uccāṭana, variant forms from the same root occur: Ṛgvidh. 2, 10, 5 uses *pracāṭayet*; the preverb *pra* in its connotation of "removing" even seems better to suit the case than the usual *ut-*. The preverb has been omitted in PST 30, 78 *cāṭanāya* "for eradication (or expulsion)". The question of the etymology of these words is a difficult one. They have obviously been derived from a causative verb *cāṭayati* which is based upon the root *caṭ-*. *Cāṭayati* has been paraphrased in the Dhātupāṭha as "to break" or "to kill"[45]; *caṭati* obtains various explanations, but never that of "to break" or "to be killed"; *caṭita-*, however, means "broken" or "fallen", and on one place (in the Jaina work Siṃhāsanadvātriṃśikā): "gone or driven anywhere" (MW, p. 382). Besides, there is the equally obscure root *cat-*, one of the many verbal roots which mean "to go" according to the Nighaṇṭu; but its causative *cātayati* occurs at least in the ṚV and the AV as "to cause to hide", "to frighten away" (MW, p. 383). *Cattá-*, the verbal adjective from this root, likewise restricted to the Veda, means "hidden, disappeared". All these forms may have their origin in Prakritisms derived f om an original root *cṛt-*, paraphrased by such different words as "to tie" (Dhātupāṭha) or "to hurt, kill" (Bhaṭṭikāvya 13, 20, according to MW, p. 401). On two places the TSSC (17, 32 and 17, 57) associates the metre *nicṛt* with spells of Uccāṭana and Māraṇa. Mayrhofer (I, p. 398) hesitatingly connects *cṛtati* with *kṛṇatti* "to spin" without referring to a meaning "hurt, kill". One might as well postulate a connection with *kṛntati* "to cut, destroy". With respect to *caṭati* and *cāṭayati* Mayrhofer (I, p. 370) admits that they have not been satisfactorily explained. His dictionary lacks an entry on *uccāṭanam.*

A synonym *cālanam* "causing to flee", an etymological connection of which with *uccāṭanam* would be difficult to explain, occurs in the BPK (3, 5) and in the SM (No. 181, vol. 2, p. 371). PST 35, 22 asserts that a good performer by executing a certain ceremony "will even cause mountains and forests to move; how much more those who possess souls (animate beings)?" (*girikānanādin pracālayet kiṃ punar ātmayuktān*). The term *preraṇam* "expulsion" which was met above in a definition of Uccāṭana seems to denote a separate act in SM No. 270 (vol. 2, p. 532); the LT (45, 83) mentions Preraṇī as one of Māyā's attendants, together with Mohinī, Bhrāmaṇī and Durgā (Gupta, p. 307). *Cyāvanam* "causing to fall" was met with by us only in Ṛgvidh. 2, 17, 2. *Pātanam* "idem" occurs beside *māraṇam* in AgPur 125, 1.

Another problem which arises in connection with Uccāṭana is its relation to *utsādanam*, a term which occurs sometimes to denote a similar, but presumably not identical, action. Besides "rubbing, anointing" (Pali *ucchādanam* in this sense) it can mean in the Veda "putting away or aside; suspending, interrupting, omitting" and in Epic sources "destroying, overturning" (MW). *Utsīdati* means already in the TS: "to fall into ruin, be destroyed"; *utsādayati*, besides "to rub, chafe" has generally the meaning of "to annihilate, destroy". There is a rather unclear *utsādya* in KauśS. 38, 5, the object of which is a storm which is evidently stilled. Caland (p. 128) translates "nachdem er entfernt hat" ("after having removed") but in note 4 on the same page he considers the possibility of a wrong reading. The reading is without doubt correct and the reference is to a magical act of *utsādanam*; not, as the commentator

Dārila surmised, to the removal of the roof of the house by the performer. Utsādana appears a few times in the AgPur. In 146, 1 the Mothers in Space (Ākāśamātṛs) are praised as "realizing all kinds of acts like the subjugation, destruction (*uts.*) and uprooting of all creatures", *sarvasattvavaśikaraṇotsādanonmūlanasamastakarmapravṛttānām.* Here *unmūlanam* "uprooting", otherwise quite infrequent, occurs side by side with *utsādanam.* In 306, 4 a certain powder thrown into a victim's house or upon his head will cause *utsādaḥ* (cf. TSS 17, 71 f.). In 137, 12 and 13, Uccāṭana and Utsādana are mentioned as two different acts beside each other: "by means of a sacrifice mixed with the blood of an ass one will eradicate the enemy (*uccāṭayet*); by means of a sacrifice to which the blood of a crow has been added, there occurs the destruction of the foe (*utsādanam*)" [43]. The spell to be used in the context is the Mahāmārīvidyā, given in 137, 1, which contains twice the word *utsādaya* "destroy". *Utsādaya* is also the demand uttered to the demon Gṛdhrakarṇī in TSS 17, 49. In AgPur 138, 2 and 3 Uccāṭana and Utsādana again occur as different actions. Uccāṭa is realized by means of the method of recitation called Pallava, while the Yoga method (see above, p. 288) should be applied in a case of *kulotsādaḥ* "destruction of the family". It is clear that both actions have been primarily directed against a victim's family life. In TSS 17, 1 (=AgPur 306, 1) one meets Utsāda and Uccāṭa beside each other in an enumeration of the acts which should be characterized as *kṣudram* "vile" (see above p. 267). The TSSC on this place explains both words; Uccāṭa, as we saw, with *deśād deśāntarapreraṇam,* and Utsāda with *punarāvṛttivarjito vināśaḥ* "a destruction which excludes the victim's returning again". In 17,28 the TSS discusses a certain method which causes *grahotsādanam* "destruction of evil planets" (perhaps a wrong reading for *gṛhotsādanam* "destruction of a house") effected when a certain mixture of ashes is laid in front of a door; the same mixture, if laid upon the victim's head, causes *vidveṣoccāṭane.* The two terms have also been regularly confounded with each other: in TSS 17, 57 occurs *ripor utsādanam,* which is repeated in the commentary as *ripor uccāṭanam*; note 6 to that commentary again writes *ripor utsādanam* and explains : *ripur unmattaḥ* "the enemy is deprived of his senses". In TSS 17, 70 *ripor uccāṭanam* is printed in the text; in 17, 72 (=AgPur 306, 4): *utsādanaṃ ripoḥ.* These instances give an idea of the confused state of affairs in such treatises themselves.

Another semi-synonym is *bhramaḥ* "wandering", "causing to wander". The AgPur (308, 17 = TSS 22, 1) mentions a Durgāhṛdayamantra which contains the demand *bhrāmaya* "cause to wander" directed to Durgā in her ferocious manifestation of Mahiṣamardinī. K, p. 80, speaks of *śatrubhrāmaṇam* "causing the enemy to err around"; BMR, p. 2, mentions *bhrāntiḥ* "wandering" as a result of the Brahmāstravidyā. As a synonym of *bhramati* the verb *aṭati* "to wander" occurs in PST 30, 60. To this important aspect of "wandering" as a result of "eradication" we shall return presently.

Varieties of eradication. The translation "eradication" for the word Uccāṭana has been chosen as a convenient term reasonably able to cover the shades of meaning included in the Skt. term. A few of these still have to be considered shortly. In the first place the application of the act against an enemy or an inimical army which is forced to flee or to roam about. AgPur 125, 3 refers to such an act performed immediately before a battle (*uccāṭayed raṇādau tu*). There are various allusions in the TSS, for instance 17, 22 *vairiṇaḥ senā sā bhītā pratigacchati* "the army of the enemy returns in panic"; 17, 23 senā *nāyāti tatpathā* "an army cannot proceed along that way" (a result akin to Stambhana); 17, 74 *uccāṭayanti ripusainyam* "they wipe out the inimical army"; other instances in 17, 36, 22, 9; 23, 4f.; in 17, 30: *bhrāmyate ripuḥ*, with the help of a mantra directed to Rudra which contains among others the demand *bhrāmaya*. An act of *senāpalāyanam* "driving off an army" is mentioned by D (4, 40 ff., Benares ed.) within the cadre of Stambhana. Uccāṭana may also in other ways be applied for the protection of a performer or his sponsor. In D (6, 1; Benares ed. 2; = N p. 316, 2) the remark is made that this rite should be used primarily by those whose property or wife has been stolen; the eradication is then a just retribution directed against the depraved (*duṣṭadaṇḍaḥ*; this word not in the Benares ed.). The variant version in N adds as a further reason that the enemy in question may have caused a person to "lose face" (*mānaṃ vā khaṇḍitaṃ yena*)[46]. The TSS 17, 40 mentions keeping off the rain within its discussion of Uccāṭana rites.

Another important aspect lies in the first place on the psychical plane; it is characterized in BMR, p. 2, as *udvegakaraṇam* "causing mental upheaval". Actions of this character are sometimes mentioned elsewhere. Thus, Wirz alludes to "Irrsinn", "mental disorder" caused by a kind of Kodivina (witchcraft) in Ceylon; the Sumatran inscription quoted above (p.323) contains *makagila* "to make crazy".[47] N (p. 316, st. 1) discusses *unmādakāraṇam* in an Uccāṭana context; K (p. 80) has *unmattīkaraṇam*. According to Jhavery (p. 274) the Jaina canon contains the act of *āvindhanam* "making one possessed". There are many instances in the AVPar, from which we refer to 35, 1, 13: the enemy becomes *hāsyaśilaḥ* "addicted to laughing", paraphrased by the Skt. commentary as *sa unmatto bhavati*. Other terms used by the AVPar are *udvejayati* (of a girl; 36, 6, 3), āveśayati (36, 12 a.o.) *unmattatā* (36, 28, a, o.). In the TSSC, *unmādaḥ* occurs twice as a textual variant of *utsādaḥ*; *unmādaya* "make crazy" is one of the demands uttered to Gṛdhrakarṇī in the mantra TSS 17, 46. In TSS 22, 63 (= AgPur 309, 12) the result of a sacrifice to Tvaritā with gambling nuts is said to be *unmattatā śatroḥ* PST 30, 72 alludes to the enemy's leaving his body (?, *deha*), "being possessed by delusion", *āviṣṭamohaḥ*. According to T (p. 380, professing to quote the Matsyasūkta) worship of a grey Ugratārā within a maṇḍala of Vāyu enables one to disturb the enemies' army force as well as their senses: *unmādayati śatrūṇāṃ balaṃ buddhiṃ na saṃśayaḥ*.

A relatively mild form of mental disorder, an inability to sleep (it seems to be never associated with Uccāṭana) is told about in AVPar 7, 1: "In former times Indra was unable to sleep as an effect of the potent herbs applied by the domestic priest of the demons with the help of spells, silent recitation and sacrifice" [44]. In this plight Bṛhaspati found out for him the Ārātrika ceremony—the modern Āratī—the essence of which consists of thrice moving a lamp round the god. According to ṚV 8, 47, 17 *duṣvapnyam* "bad sleep" has been sent to Trita Āptya (Hillebrandt, p. 179). Evil dreams may have been caused by magic and can be remedied for (PST 24, 23). The stimulation of sleep is also known. A hymn from the AV is destined to cause the parents of the beloved to be fast asleep while the lover pays his visit. ṚV 7, 55, 1 can be applied for bringing evil beings to sleep (Ṛgvidh. 2, 26, 5). Nidrākaraṇam is also mentioned in TSS 30, 43 and 44 (in the latter case connected with *bhramaḥ*).

Uprooting as a divine act. When the magician proceeds by Uccāṭana to deprive a victim of his home and security, his action may be viewed in a certain sense (i.e. intentionally or unintentionally) as a reflection of a cosmical act performed by the Māyā—or Ignorance—upon creatures. Such is at least the point of view of the BhPur. which repeatedly uses the word *bhrama* "wandering, roaming" to denote man's plight on earth as a consequence of his delusion. The best instance is the beautiful stanza quoted above (p. 23): people wander about on the ways of karman with their minds deluded by God's Māyā. Another place is BhPur 12, 10, 27 "he, having been caused to wander about for a long time by Viṣṇu's Māyā and being heavily tormented ..", *sa ciraṃ māyayā Viṣṇor bhrāmitaḥ karṣito bhṛṣam.* BhPur 3, 2, 10 says: *devasya māyayā spṛṣṭā...bhrāmyate dhīḥ* "the mental faculties, touched by the Māyā of God, err about". The same text, 12, 11, 8, identifies this wandering with Viṣṇu's eternal mysterious smile : *smayo bhramaḥ.*

The same motif is met with in the DevīBhPur. The stanzas 3, 53, 10ff. contain the argument that all creatures are subjected to the power of Devī Mahāmāyā . In st. 13 this situation is characterized as "being enveloped by the net of delusion", *mohajālena yantrita*— (for the image of the net, see above, ch. 5.2). In st. 15 the author concludes: *te 'pi rāgavaśāl loke bhramanti parimohitāḥ* "they also wander about in this world, being completely deluded by the subjugating power of passion". ViPur (1, 4, 40) strongly condemns the philosophical materialists who consider the world as material of nature (*arthasvarūpa*); such people "wander about on the ocean of delusion", *bhrāmyante mohasamplave.* The Trailokyamohana mantra which addresses Viṣṇu in his aspect of the universal Deluder contains the demand *bhrāmaya* (AgPur 307, 1; PST 36, 6). In the Tantras this image is maintained; KulT (2, 96f.) describes Śiva saying to his spouse during one of their speculative discourses: *bhrāmitā hi mayā devi paśavaḥ śāstrakoṭiṣu* "O Goddess, all people of vegetative nature have been caused by me to wander through millions of false teachings". And he adds that all these teachings have been proclaimed by himself in disguise *mohanāya durātmanām* "in order to delude those who are of evil mind" (Kane, 1962, 975). The

SST says (in 3,2,25) : *ajñānavaśato devi bhramanti hi itas tataḥ* "by the subjugating power of Ignorance, O Goddess, they wander about hither and thither". Bhrāmaṇī is an attendant of Māyā according to LT 45, 83. These few examples were taken at random without being the result of a systematical search. Yet they clearly demonstrate how the idea of *bhrama* is connected for these authors with God's fallacious and inscrutable dealings with mankind by the force of his Māyā, the paramount cause of human delusion. The whole earthly existence, the round of rebirths, is a continuous ramble undergone by those who have been driven from their spiritual home by divine magic.

Eradication in the Veda. Coming now to the enumeration of some instances of Uccāṭana as a deliberate act of magic, we should first note that similar rites or actions are often described in the Veda without the term Uccāṭana being applied to it. ṚV 10, 145 deals with the removal of a *sapatni* "rival" by a married woman. The lady enjoins a certain herb to "blow away my rival" after which she asserts: *párām evá parāvátam sapátnīṃ gamayāmasi* """we cause the rival to go towards the farthest distance". AitBr 2,32 mentions the possibility that the officiating Hotar priest takes away the "root" of the client and his sacrifice. To that end he should omit the Śaṃsana which is considered the root of the sacrifice (Malaviya, p. 47). Related actions are depriving a client of his base (making him *anāyatanavān* or *apratiṣṭhita*). Positive applications are also found, like the one in Kauśītaki-Brāhmaṇa 3, 2 (Malaviya, p. 60): by a threefold pronunciation of the syllable *hiṃ* (the vajra is threefold) the yajamāna removes all enemies and rivals out of this world.

A more homely instance, closer to what is usually understood as Uccāṭana is afforded by SVBr 2, 6, 16 (Hillebrandt, p. 176: 2, 6, 14; Malaviya, p. 142). On the fourteenth day of the dark half of the month (an extremely inauspicious moment), after a fast of three nights, the performer takes action. He collects charcoal from a funeral pyre and sacrifices it into a fire fed by wood of the Bādhaka "obstructive" tree as fuel together with a fish and a Kṛkara (kind of partridge). The scene is a crossroads (*catuṣpatha*). Two passages from the SV are recited which describe Agni's greatness; they accompany the sacrifice of the two animals. The remains he should collect and mix with Haritāla powder and the blood from the heart of a cow and on the first suitable occasion throw this mixture—under the recitation of another sāman—on the victim's bed and in his house. The result will be that the victim is doomed to flee and to find rest in none of the villages (*naikagrāme vasati*). The Skt. commentary calls this procedure an instance of Uccāṭana "in order to eradicate the rival from his position and dwelling place". The words *naikagrāme vasati* are paraphrased with *kiṃtu sthānabhraṣṭo bhūtvā deśāntaraṃ prāpnotity arthaḥ* "on the contrary, the meaning is that (the victim) becomes fallen from his position and dwelling place and seeks his refuge in another country". The JaimBr (1,325) contains a reference to *nirbādham* "driving out" (Caland, Das JaimBr. in Auswahl, ad loc.: "Hinausdrängung") effected by the priest while he pronounces the syllable *hiṃ* in a particular sāman, by mentally driving out the opponent into a certain region desired by the performer: *sāmno hiṃkriyamāṇa etāṃ diśaṃ yaṃ dviṣyāt taṃ manasā nirbādheta*; *tata eva sa parābhavati.* In the cadre of the Śyenayāga "Falcon ceremony" the ṢaḍvBr (3, 8, 14) advises the application of the powerful sāmans Bṛhat and Rathantara together with another sāman, the Plava, during the afternoon pressure in a soma rite: "By the Bṛhat and the Rathantara he removes him from these worlds; by the Plava (lit.: "Floating") he causes him to drift away; (the victim) goes to the farthest distance, he loses his base" [45]. The Ṛgvidh. (1, 15, 7) introduces the term Uccāṭana, together with *piḍanam* "oppression":

Ya icchet piḍanaṃ śatror api voccāṭanaṃ punaḥ /
pacchaḥ saṃpīdayec chatrūn varṇaśaś ca pramāpayet //

"He who desires to oppress his enemy or to eradicate him,—with (the recitation of the Sāvitrī stanza by) quarters he is able to press down his enemies; and with (the Sāvitrī recited by) syllables he annihilates him". Thus, "eradication" is considered here to be virtually identical with "annihilation"; there is no further indication of what the author exactly meant by these words. In 2, 10, 5 the Ṛgvidh uses *pracāṭayet* "one will drive forth"; the intention is clear because the word *deśāt* "out of the region or the place of living" has been added. The method again consists in reciting the Sāvitrī—here called Gāyatrī—, this time with the injunction to use oil from the Vibhītaka nuts. In his translation Gonda (p. 43) refers to a place from the AVPar (36, 5, 3, read 26, 5, 3) where the Vibhītaka comes in again in a context of Uccāṭana together with other trees of evil repute like the Kakubha, the Kaṭabha or the Kauvirāla. In AVPar 26, 4, 1 and 21, 3, 2 Uccāṭana recurs during the discussion of the different characteristics of the firewood and the Sruva. 36, 4, 2 mentions Uccāṭakarman with the help of the Kukusa and Tumbara plants.

Uccāṭana in post-Vedic sources. From Purāṇa literature the AgPur and GarPur, as is usual when the subject is magic, give the best information. AgPur 260, 13f., in a chapter which enumerates the magical applications of passages from the Yajurveda, lays down that a peg of eleven fingers' length made of copper or of Acacia wood should be buried in the enemy's home while the formula *dviṣato vadho'si* "thou art the hater's death" (VS 1, 28) is being recited. "This act will result in the eradication of enemies"[46]. AgPur 315, 11 for the same end advises to throw the head of a serpent into the enemy's house. Such actions are typical of what is generally understood by the younger sources as Uccāṭana. According to AgPur 313, 14 the same goal is reached with the help of a black thread (*nilasūtra*). In 125, 8 the same Purāṇa mentions some goddesses standing in a diagram of Fire (*tejocakram*) and causing eradication; their names are Saumyā, Bhīṣaṇī, Jayā and Vijayā. In the weird passage GarPur 177, 69 ff. some devices for Uccāṭana are explained; the ingredients chiefly consist of ashes, blood or faeces of such animals as owls, crows and mice ; they are to be thrown into or hidden in the enemy's house or strewn upon his head. In one case (st. 72) the result is that the victim is "eaten by flocks of crows" (*khādyate kākavṛndaiḥ*), in another (st. 73) that he is destroyed outright.

The Buddhist sources also know the secrets of eradication: MMK (II, ch. 27, p. 307) without mentioning the term Uccāṭana discusses the power of the mantra *muṃ*. A performer who applies this mantra should work himself up to a state of rage, go to an evil place or a place visited by outcastes... (a part of the passage, which is in abominable Skt., is not clear to me); the result is that the inhabitant of the house affected by the magic departs to another region, becomes totally upset, or flees away in the night; or his family will be "split". The victim, who seems to be the adherent of another deity (*anyadevatābhaktam*) may, however, be restored into his former position by libations during a whole year of 8000 or 80000 portions of fresh milk [47]. On another place (vol. I, p. 33f.) the MMK discusses what might be considered a special kind of Uccāṭana: the universal practice of driving out demons. The deity invoked in the accompanying spell is no less a figure than the god Viṣṇu (properly speaking: Śiva appearing as Viṣṇu) who is set to work by the command of the Bodhisattva Mañjuśrī. After a customary invocation of all the Buddhas, the mantra is intimated : "*Oṃ*, Thou Who ridest upon Garuḍa ! Who bearest the Disk in Thy hand ! Four-armed One ! *huṃ huṃ,* remember the Agreement ! The Bodhisattva issues the command, *svāhā* !" The effect is proclaimed (p. 34): "having been commanded by Mañjughoṣa, Śiva quickly fulfills the desire : in the form of Viṣṇu he causes the evil spirits to flee from mankind" [48]. The text adds that the Triśikhā mudrā should be shown during the ceremony. There is also an allusion to numerous other such expedients taught in the Vaiṣṇava Tantra tradition (*ya eva vaiṣṇave tantre kathitāḥ kalpavistarāḥ*); also these have in reality been revealed by Mañjughoṣa. The connection of Uccāṭana with the exorcizing of spirits is confirmed by Sinhalese magical tradition where *otchatana* has exactly this meaning (Gooneratne).

Driving out enemies or evil persons is of course mentioned on many other places like PST 30, 81 (*drāvayed arīn* ; GT, p. 8 *vāyubījaṃ japed vidvān pāpoccāṭanakarmaṇi* "during the act of eradicating evil people (or: of evil?) one should mutter the syllable of Vāyu (*va*)". A connection of Uccāṭana with Wind is found also in ŚārTil 7, 54 ff. according to which the effect is reached by burying a diagram of Wind (Vāyuyantra) near the door of a victim's house. When the victim does not leave, he will die (Ewing, p. 67). Other instances of Uccāṭana from the Tantras are JT 17, 77; 17, 90 ; PST 14, 44; 24, 29; 30, 78; almost a whole chapter in TSS 17, 18-74; SM No. 85 and 93. The methods applied do not differ much from what has been described above from the Purāṇas. The favourite device is, as we saw, to throw or bury something in the enemy's house : TSS 17, 24 (object laid down): 17,25 (object buried); 17, 73 (the object buried is a triangular peg inscribed with a mantra and the victim's name in the Vidarbha method) ; ViDhPur 2, 125, 13 (object buried).

Deities of Uccāṭana. The PST (30, 78) describes a meditation upon a certain goddess (Bhagavatī "the Lady", presumably Durgā) who should be created in the mind seated upon a lion and running speedily while the victim runs after her. This meditation and the accompanying ritual results in *cāṭanam.* In 14, 44 this text describes the same result as "being hated by the people he (departs) from the country and wanders about towards other regions: *sa tu vidviṣṭo lokair deśād deśāntaraṃ paribhramati,* thus connecting Uccāṭana with Vidveṣaṇa in the process. A mantra of Tārā applied in SM, No. 93 for Uccāṭana is : *Oṃ Tāre tuttāre ture cala pracala śighragāmini Devadattam uccāṭaya huṃ huṃ phaṭ* "*Oṃ*, Tārā,...move, move forward, O thou Whose course is quick, eradicate N.N.,..". MMD 18, 79ff. invokes Kālarātrī in the following way: in a deserted temple (*āgāra*) the performer during the fourteenth night of the dark half of the month sits down in the "cock posture" (Kukkuṭāsana, see above p. 283). He should face the South, the region of Yama, and his hair is dishevelled. He wears a garment of dark blue (*nila*) colour (in the Mahāmāyā fragment also, this colour is associated with Uccāṭana). Moving a cord made of Muñja grass and provided with knots he should recite the mantra *Oṃ blūṃ slūṃ mlūṃ kṣlūṃ Kālarātri Mahādhvāṅkṣi* ("Great Crow Lady"; the crow plays a preeminent role in this kind of rites) *amukam āśūccāṭaya uccāṭaya chindhi chindhi bhindhi svāhā* ("...quickly eradicate N.N., split him, break him") *hauṃ Kāmākṣi kroṃ.* A goddess who specializes in this matter, Dhūmāvatī "Smoky One", is described in the SST (2, 28). During her worship the adept should imagine the world as well as the mantra of the goddess to be grey of colour; he should blacken his teeth, wear black clothes, and observe certain regulations such as subduing his senses, eating little, and sleeping on the ground. He should "transform his own mind into a crow" (*svacittaṃ kākavat kṛtvā,* st. 7) and this is the "crow procedure" (*kākakramaḥ,* l.c.) by which one will eradicate the world (i.e., any victim one likes). The same Tantra (3, 21, 51 ff.) introduces Dhūmāvatī again and mentions her mantra. The goddess rides upon a crow (56); she is tormented by hunger and thirst and sick with fear (*kṣuttṛṣārtā bhayāturā*, 57). She is also mentioned by TSS 17, 56 where a similar, but different mantra is given. A performer should burn a crow in a fire of cremation and, saying the mantra, strew the ash in the enemy's house into the eight directions. Shortly before (17, 45-47) the TSS discusses the worship of Gṛdhrakarṇī, a kind of Kṛtyā with a deformed face, hanging breasts and protruding belly. She is invited by the performer to kill the enemy and drink his blood.

A grey goddess Dhavalamukhī with a crow's beak (Kākatuṇḍī) is addressed in an Uccāṭana spell in S ch.8, p. 253. She is described as "grey of colour, three-eyed, moon-crested, lean, and bearing in her hands a rosary of bones, a knife, and a lotus; with deformed eyes, dreadful fangs and an enormous belly reminding of the nether world" [49]. Other deities addressed in this chapter are a Rudra with a wide open mouth provided with fangs and a Kālāgnirudra "of the apocalyptical fire". The chapters on Uccāṭana in D, in N (p. 316-321) and K (77f.) present the same kind of rites as discussed above; they often contain identical or nearly identical stanzas. N addresses amongst others Rudra in some fearful manifestations like Uḍḍāmareśvara and Mahākāla; in a mantra on p. 321 this text has Kālarātrī set to work on the command of Maheśvara. N also contains a few directions for restoring the victim into his former state by making him *sukhi* "happy" again.

6.8. *Other destructive rites*

Sorcery. The concept of sorcery, under which we understand magical rites executed by professional or amateur performers with the intention of doing harm to others[48], is perhaps the best term by which to translate the Skt. word *abhicāraḥ*. The latter term, as well as the word "sorcery" can also be used for those cases in which the destructive ritual aims at the welfare or the protection of a community and thus are not socially disapproved. In the Skt. texts, Abhicāra is the most general of the terms which denote destructive magic. It occurs from the Veda onwards and remains in use in the Tantras, although it did not fit in with the set of specialized terms of the Ṣaṭkarman tradition which are the product of a more developed theorizing in the field. Abhicāra finds its place in the classical division of the aim of all ritual into three: Śānti, Puṣṭi and Abhicāra (see above, p. 95). It serves as the counterpart of Śānti and Puṣṭi together[49]. About the range of the term the younger sources widely differ. KA 5 assumes that Abhicāra includes Ākarṣaṇa, Vidveṣaṇa, Uccāṭana and Māraṇa; but the Skt. commentary on GautDh 2, 2, 17 equated it with Māraṇa only: *abhicārasaṃyuktaṁ yenāsya śatravo mriyante* "connected with Abhicāra is that act by means of which the performer's enemies die". The Sūtra on this place immediately after Abhicāra adds *dviṣadvyṛddhi-* "adversity of the foe", paraphrased by the commentary with *ṛddher abhāvaḥ* "absence of prosperity", while it adds *yenāsya śatravo vigataiśvaryā bhavanti* "by which one's enemies will be deprived of their leading position". On his own accord the commentator adds *uccāṭanādini* "acts of eradication and the like", and he emphasizes that the king should take the initiative for such ceremonies (see above, p. 236). In other words, the GautDhS recognizes the full right of rulers to resort to acts of sorcery when the interest of the state demands it. The king has the rites performed by his *purohita* "court priest" and himself only provides the required means and funds. A close connection between Abhicāra and the killing of enemies seems to appear also from TSS 25, 49 and its version in the AgPur (301, 16): where the TSS reads *abhicāravidhau*, the latter text has *ripughātavidhau* "during the practice of killing the enemy", although it should be noted also that no less than five manuscripts of the Purāṇa have the reading *vidyutpātavidhau* "during the practice to be followed in the case of a stroke of lightning". A term which expresses the same idea is *sarvaśatrunibarhaṇam* "destroying all enemies" (SST 3, 14, 54); *śatrunigrahaḥ* "coercion of the enemy" occurs in the SST (3, 21) and the LiPur (2, 50, 1); for other instances of *nigrahaḥ* "coercion", see below. *Kṣudram* or *kṣudrāṇi* "vile acts" is also found as a semi-synonym of Abhicāra; the SST (1, 6, 113) equates *kṣudrāṇi* with *krūrakarmāṇi* "terrifying acts" (for *kṣudra*, see also above, p. 267).

The Skt. terminology on the subject is rich. Of the Abhicāra terms discussed in the following survey, only Vidveṣaṇa "causing dissension" and Māraṇa "liquidation" commonly form part of the Six Acts; but the others are sometimes included in their scope. The less frequent of them seem to have been in vogue only as varieties of supranormal effects without having denoted an independent class of rites.

Creating dissension. This is a widely practised form of magic[50]. The term *vidveṣaṇam* (we find sometimes *vidveṣaḥ* or *dveṣaḥ*) is derived from the root *dviṣ-*"to hate" and is one of the oldest specimens of the Ṣaṭkarman terminology. S (1,8) defines Vidveṣaṇa as *snigdhānāṃ dveṣajananam* "creating dissension between two persons who are attached to each other". MMD (25, 3) says the same : *dveṣo 'prītiḥ prītimatoḥ* "(creating) hate is (the creation of) hate between two who love each other". Vidveṣaṇa is sometimes circumscribed by *prītināśanam* "destruction of sympathy". TSSC (17, 1) paraphrases with *snigdhānāṃ parasparakalahaḥ* "mutual strife between two who were attached to each other". The commentator upon the GautDh (2, 2, 17) mentioned shortly above interprets in the political sphere with *yenāsya śatruḥ prakṛtīnāṃ vidveṣyo bhavati* "by means of which one's enemy becomes hated by his own subjects". B, Bhattacharya (p. LXXXVI) again considers the personal sphere: "the fourth (of the Six Acts) gives the power to separate two friends, relatives, lovers...and so forth". From the above definitions it becomes clear that Vidveṣaṇa is in the first place a method by which the magician is able to create dissension between two who up till then were wont to love each other or to sympathize with each other; and very often the two concerned will be members of the same household, especially husband and wife. In that case an act of Vidveṣaṇa can become a tool for those who have or desire an extra-marital relation (the same is argued by Webster, p. 349). In politics it appears to be a pure representant of "divide and rule". But no matter in which situation it is applied, it is a psychological act which affects the state of the victims' minds in the first place; its special characteristic is that the victims are always more than one—two individuals, an individual and a group, or two groups (for instance, two parties within an army).

As one of the Six Acts, Vidveṣaṇa possesses a certain status in theory, but it is comparatively seldom discussed in the texts otherwise than as a mere item in enumerations of magical arts. It is never subdivided like Vaśikaraṇa or Stambhana. In literature similar actions are very little spoken of, although there are of course figures who are told to have a predilection for creating quarrels; thus, Nārada is called *kalahapriya-* "a lover of strife". The fear of mutual dissension as one of the chief imperfections which attach themselves to the round of births inflicted by the Supreme Power is illustrated by the opening words of the ŚvetUp: *mā vidviṣāvahai* "may we two not become hateful to each other". In the AV divine existence implies the absence of dissension, as appears from the spell AV 3, 30, 4: "By which the gods do not withdraw, and do not come to hate each other, that word of power we create in your house; concord between human beings" [50] (Shende, p. 205). AV 1, 28, 4 operates against the Yātudhānīs, female demons or sorceresses. "Instead of killing others, they are asked to kill each other" or to pull each other's hair (Shende, p. 169). Vidveṣaṇa and Māraṇa are combined in AV 8, 8, 21d: *mithó vighnānā úpa yantu mṛtyúm* "may they incur death by mutual killing". Creating dissension is discussed by KauśS 36, 38 by means of the spell AV 7, 113.

In the AVPar Vidveṣaṇa occurs thrice (21, 3, 2; 64, 4, 9; 64, 5, 5); besides, the demand *pradviṣa* "make hateful" is uttered to Rudra in 36, 9, 3. The Ṛgvidh. (2, 10, 5) advises to accomplish a Vidveṣaṇa rite by saying the Gāyatrī during a sacrifice of leaves of the Nimba, a tree of evil repute. In MtPur 93, 149ff., Vidveṣaṇa and Māraṇa are dealt with as two similar acts. AgPur 260, 11 in its chapter on Yajurvidhāna prescribes to sacrifice during a lunar eclipse the feathers of a crow and an owl together with ghee from a reddish brown cow under the recitation of the Mahāvyāhṛti. The same text (315, 9) advises to throw a mixture of ingredients including menstruation blood upon a bed and other places in the victims' house. The accompanying mantra is directed to Kālī. Similar methods are prescribed by GarPur in 177, 74 with the result: *tayor madhye mahāvairaṃ bhavet* "between these two there will be a big feud" and in 178, 4 : *tatra vai kalaho bhavet* "there will be strife on that place". In the last case the mantra employed is simply *Oṃ Hariḥ Hariḥ svāhā*. The TSS (23, 18) specifies in one case that the hate will occur between a father and his children: *virodhaḥ syāt tadaṅgajaiḥ*. The TSS discusses some rites of causing dissension in 17, 9-18. The first of these is of special interest because it is based upon a spell which has been handed down also on Bali (Stuti & Stava, No. 941, Eka-Yamarājastava). The spell, which is an untranslatable word-play, is given in TSSC on TSS 17, 9 as follows:

Yamarājasadomeyayamedoruṇayodaya
yadayonirayakṣeya yakṣeyaś ca nirāmaya

which is practically identical with the stanza edited as Stuti & Stava No. 941, 1 (the version of the TSS itself deviates, curiously enough, in the first quarter). The stanza addresses King Yama and ends with *nirāmaya* "sound and safe", perhaps in order to ensure the performer's safety. The TSSC gives directions for writing the spell on a Yantra which should be buried on a cremation ground after having been carried between the future victims. An image of Yama with the same spell inscribed within a Yantra in front of his belly exists in Bali[51]. The TSSC calls this device a Yamarājacakra "Diagram of King Yama". Another Yamamantra is given in TSS 17, 13-15. The next stanzas (17, 16-18a) are connected with the invocation of a female deity called Vidveṣiṇī who specializes in the field. She is called upon to create such dissension as exists between crows and owls. According to stanza 48 of the same chapter, also Gṛdhrakarṇī may bring about this result. According to stanza 75, mutual hate between two persons is effected inter alia by burying two objects inscribed with the names on opposite sides of a river.

Of the Ṣaṭkarman monographs, N discusses the subject in ch. 11 (p. 325f.). The first stanza ordains the sacrifice of the feathers of a crow and an owl and promises as the result: *ubhayor naśyati prītiḥ Kurupāṇḍavayor yathā* "the sympathy between the two victims disappears like that between the Kauravas and the Pāṇḍavas". A prerequisite is that the names of the victims should be uttered during the sacrifice. Other effects of the acts described in these pages of N are *tadgṛhe kalahaḥ sadā* "constant strife in their house" (2): hate between a father and his son (4); hate between brothers (5); the two latter results are reached by means of a certain incense with which the house is fumigated. In stanza 6 the result is that a woman will become irresistibly tempted to desert her husband; in 10 a man who has anointed his eyes with a certain mixture will be able to cause the persons looked at by him to hate each other : *añjitākṣo naraḥ paśyed vidviṣanti parasparam.* Stanza 11 invokes a terrifying goddess Mahākapālinī for the same end; stanza 13 invokes Gaurī (the mantra is corrupt). D (ch. 5, p. 140) mentions the creation of dissension between man and woman (wife) and between a king and his chief adviser. The chapter comprises one and a half pages of the usual kind of recipes. A mantra is directed to Viṣṇu Nārāyaṇa, but according to the more probable version of the Benares edition (5, 14) it addresses Nārada, the foremost creator of quarrels: *Oṃ namo Nāradāya, amukasyāmukena saha vidveṣaṃ kuru kuru svāhā.* S succinctly discusses mantras which cause dissension on p. 251 f. The general motif is that hate will arise between two persons whose names have been inscribed upon two separate yantras. One of the mantras is directed to Bhairava, another to Kalī: both of there deities are said to dwell on cremation grounds. A meditation on Kālī of the colour of sapphire (*indranīla*) is added.

Vidveṣaṇa is mentioned a few times in the PST. In 13, 48 it is, as in the Ṛgvidh., associated with the Nimba tree. In 14, 84 a certain sacrifice with an accompanying mantra of Durgā Vindhyavāsinī is said to result after a week in dissension and separation of two people who used to like each other : *divasaiḥ saptabhir iṣṭau dviṣṭau mitho viyoginau bhavataḥ.* In 30, 59 Vidveṣaṇa is effected by meditation upon Tāraṇī Gāyatrī with a grey colour and bearing the club and trident, accompanied by a sacrifice of bones sprinkled with acid substances, leaves of the cotton plant and the Nimba, and clarified butter from sheep milk. In the SST the creation of dissension is mentioned a few times in 3, 14, 53 ff. The objects are the enemy (twice) and the threefold world (*trailokyam*). The deity is Virodhinī. The MMD (13, 21 ff.) gives rules for Vidveṣaṇa in the cadre of the sādhana of Hanuman.[52] The vidyā of Hanuman should be recited for seven nights while a peg (an object suitable for the act) is buried together with ashes. It is especially directed against military enemies who begin to quarrel with each other before taking to their heels. In 18, 86 ff. the MMD presents a method with the aid of a mantra of Kālarātrī the central part of which consists of the demand *amukam amukaṃ śighraṃ vidveṣaya* (2x) *rodhaya* (2x) *bhañjaya* (2x) "quickly make N. N. and N. N. hateful to each other, obstruct them, break them". Two boards inscribed with the names should be buried near an anthill.

Wirz (p. 212, 217, 245) repeatedly speaks of magical devices which were current among the Sinhalese to create dissension between the members of a household.

Delusion. An act of *mohanam* "delusion" is repeatedly

referred to, although in most cases it does not belong to the "Six Acts". In a general sense it can be considered a replica of the divine influence which causes man's mind to be enveloped in spiritual darkness and inertia. However, in the context of magic, the meaning is more restricted. Mohana then most often seems to denote that power by which one is able to cause the victim to lose the normal control of his senses or even to faint; the same result is expressed in the AVPar (36, 8, 4) with *niḥsaṃjñatā*. In the younger sources, Mohana seems to have been most often applied in an erotic context. In the sense of "fainting", *moha* seems to occur in Bhāsa's Abhiṣekanāṭaka (2, 18; ed. C. R. Devadhar, p. 335), where Rāvaṇa mocks: "The gods, Indra included, and the demons have been broken by me in battle; really I am fainting today by these three syllables uttered by Sītā !"[51].

A great divine agent of delusion is Viṣṇu who bewilders mankind in various ways (see above,p.21), especially in his female manifestation as Mohinī and his male aspect of Trailokyamohana "Deluder of the threefold cosmos." Besides, Mohanī is the first of Kāma's śaktis (PST 18, 6) while Mohā is one of the fearsome ladies who surround the Five Lords of Jain Mantravāda (BPK 10, 42ff. in Jhavery's edition). The beauty of earthly women is also able to delude mankind.[53]

As an act of magic, Mohana appears in the Veda. According to KauśS 14 the hymns of AV 3, 1 and 2 are *mohana-* "causing delusion" (PD 5, p. 922). AV 3,1,1 prays that Agni delude the inimical army: *sá sénāṃ mohayatu páreṣām*; and in stanza 5 the same demand is directed to Indra: *Índra sénāṃ mohayāmítrāṇām*, immediately followed by a summons to destroy this enemy. In stanza 6 Indra is called upon to delude the army, the Maruts to kill it, Agni to take its eyes out, so that it will return crushed. AV 3, 2, 1-3 again call upon Agni and Indra who this time should delude the enemies' minds: *Agníḥ...sá cittā́ni mohayatu páreṣām...Índra cittā́ni moháyann arvā́ṅ ā́kūtyā cara*. The result is that all deliberations that were in the enemies' hearts are destroyed (st. 4). The gods should seize the enemies, pierce their hearts with darkness and burn them by sorrows (st. 5). The next and last stanza again prays that darkness may fill the enemies' minds so that "the one of them will be unable to recognize the other." The reader observes how the ideas of *moha* and *tamas* "darkness" are already interconnected in so early a specimen of Indian literature. In AV 8, 8, 9 moha is laid upon the enemy together with such qualities as *śrama* "fatigue" and *tandrī* "sloth". In AV 6, 67, 1 the gods who should delude (*muhyantu*) the inimical army are Indra and Pūṣan; as a consequence that army will be *mūḍha-* (2). The SVBr (3,7,1) presents a method to ward off moha in the sense of "spiritual delusion or ignorance." To this end one should regularly recite the SV passage *mahe no adya bodhaya* "awaken me today to greatness" (Grāmageyagāna 11, 8, 421, 1) and remember it at the time of one' s death. In his future births such a person will not be liable to delusion: *amuhyant sarvāṇy ājanitrāṇi parikrāmati*. In the Ṛgvidh. (1, 31, 5) the subject is *taskaramohanam* "depriving a thief of his senses" by means of the hymns beginning with *kanikradat* "crying repeatedly" (RV 2, 42 and 43; Gonda's translation of the Ṛgvidh., p. 36).

We now turn to some instances of Mohana as a magical act in post-Vedic ritual literature. Most often these are mere occurrences of the word without further description. AgPur 140, 10 mentions a *tilakaṃ lokamohanam* "a spot of beauty which deludes the people", a phrase which recurs elsewhere. The same text, 315, 8, promises the delusion of the world (*mohayej jagat*), again with the aid of a tilaka. In such cases Mohana seems to represent an aspect of the act of Vaśīkaraṇa, and *mohayej jagat* almost a synonym of *vaśayej jagat*. One might compare also N (4, 39) *añjitākṣo naro ramāṃ dṛṣṭvā mohayati dhruvam* "a man who has his eyes daubed (with a certain mixture) is without doubt able to delude a woman after he has looked at her". N on p. 293 speaks of Mohana at the time of sexual intercourse. In AgPur 323, 3-4 a certain mantra to Kālī which contains the words *vaśam ānaya mānuṣān* "bring human people under my power" is said to produce, besides Vaśīkaraṇa, the results of *antardhānam* "disappearing", *mohanam* and *jṛmbhaṇam* "devouring or stupefying". The mantra "subjugates the enemies and deludes their insight" (4b) : *vaśaṃ nayati śatrūṇāṃ* (?, perhaps read *vaśānayani śatrūṇāṃ*) *śatrubuddhipramohinī*. JT 18, 12 also connects Mohana and Vaśīkaraṇa; by a certain ritual "after twenty-one nights one will delude this world; gods and demons without any doubt come under his power"; but in 18, 26 Mohana of the world is described as a positive counterpart to the destruction of all evil actions committed by the performer [52]. In PST 18, 15 Mohana in combination with Vaśīkaraṇa is described as the result of a mantra and yantra of Kāma. In 18, 28 *mohana-* as an adjective is the quality of the successful performer who is able to steal the hearts of all women: *vanitājanahṛdayamohano bhavati.* The MMD (18, 60 ff.) describes Mohana by means of meditation on Kālarātrī with the mantra *Oṃ Kāmāya klauṃ klīṃ kāminyai klīm.* The proceedings are that one should on a Sunday mix turmeric with mothermilk and design a yantra with it, details of which are given. The performer should be in an enraged state of mind and recite the mantra for five successive days. Then he will "delude anything that exists", *mohayed akhilaṃ viśvam.*

Mohana continues also to be applied against enemies. The PST (30, 61) describes such a case (*ahitān vimohayet*) with the help of meditation on a Durgā of the colour of fire. The TSS in 31, 61 enjoins to bear some stuff on the head so that one will protect oneself and delude the enemy, *...mastake dhṛtam ātmānaṃ rakṣec chatruṃ ca mohayet.* In 31, 64 two plants are mentioned called *saṃmohinī* and *rājamohinī* (*saṃmohinī* also in 31, 73) the Malayalam equivalents for which are given in the TSSC, *ad locum.* Mohana executed by the king against the subjects may have been alluded to by the SST (1, 9, 95) : *trailokyavaśakāritvaṃ lokasammohanam.* In 3, 19, 1ff. this text deals with the Tiraskaraṇikā vidyā "spell which causes to disappear" which is said to be a powerful agent of delusion (*mahāmohanakāriṇīm*). By means of this spell one can temporarily eliminate other people's senses, so that one remains unnoticed. The deity of the spell is demanded to cause the faculties of eye, ear, tongue and nose of the victims to disappear : *cakṣuḥ śrotraṃ jihvāṃ ghrāṇaṃ tiraskaraṇaṃ kuru kuru ṭha ṭha svāhā.* According to SST 3, 16, 24, Mohana is effected by means of the worship of Dīptā, one of the Tantric Nityā goddesses, with liquor.

Among those who serve as the victims of Mohana, K (p. 42) mentions "royal families" (*rājakula*), "rulers' families" (*īśvarakula*), "bad people" (*duṣṭajana*) and "enemies". N discusses Mohana together with Uccāṭana in ch. 9 (p. 314 ff.). In many of the recipes the preparation of an incense (*dhūpa*) is the most important device. St. 5 on p. 315 circumscribes the effect with *svasthasyāveśakārakaḥ* "causing frenzy within a sensible person", thus reminding of an aspect of Uccāṭana discussed above (p. 357)[54]. The same is found in stanza 10 with *mohāveśakaro nṛṇām*. A mantra on p. 316 addresses Jambhā "Devourer", Stambhā "Immobilizer," Sammohā "Deluder" and Śoṣā "Desiccator"; they receive their commands from Bhairava and (who is ?) Vīrabhadra[55]. The magician has the power to cause the victim to return to his normal state of mind: *svastho bhaven naraḥ* (9): *mohāt suṣṭho bhaviṣyati* (13). D treats Mohana in ch. 2 (Benares ed. : ch. 3), which consists of 15 ślokas (21 in the Benares ed.) of the usual recipes. The Sunday is again mentioned as the most suitable day. The results are usually described in very vague terms such as *mohayet sakalaṃ jagat.* There is no separate chapter on Mohana in S.

Agitation. This act, *kṣobhaṇam* in Skt., is another instance of psychological magic parallel to *mohanam.* It plays a minor role and never obtains a separate treatment in the monographs. It should be noted, however, that the act of Kṣobhaṇa is one of the constituents of divine creation. The ViPur (1, 2, 29-31) says: "Hari, having entered primordial Matter and Spirit by His own sovereign will, when the time of creation had come caused them by agitation to produce the symptoms of decay and vanishing"...."He , the Supreme Spirit, is Himself the Agitator and the Agitated...."[53]. Kṣobhaṇa, like Mohana, often appears to be an aspect of Vaśīkaraṇa in its erotic sense. Kṣobhaṇī is one of Kāma's śaktis (PST 18, 6); Kāma is the god who agitates the senses of all creatures: *indriyakṣobhajanakaḥ sarveṣām* (MtPur 4, 14). Kṣobhaṇa is also the name of one of Kāma's five arrows (MW, p. 331).

The word *kṣobhaṇam* occurs in the RV, where (in 10, 103) Indra is called a *ksóbhaṇaś carṣaṇīnām* "agitator of mankind". In AV 8, 8, 1 this disturbing power of Indra is invoked when the god in his quality of *mánthitā* "churner", "disturber" is called upon to disturb (*manthatu*) the enemy so that "we will be able to slay the inimical armies", *yáthā hánāma sénā amítrāṇām.* Here "disturbing" is considered a preparatory act to "killing". Kṣobhaṇa as an equivalent of Mohana on the field of love is implied in MtPur 61,23f. Viṣṇu by his stern asceticism became a menace to the other gods' position and Indra sent Mādhava and Anaṅga, two manifestations of Kāma, accompanied by a throng of celestial damsels, to agitate his senses. When

Viṣṇu proved unable to be agitated (*vadā na...Hariḥ...praticukṣubhe*) the gods and damsels fell into despair. Viṣṇu in his turn now produced from his thigh the nymph Urvaśī "a woman able to delude all people in the threefold cosmos" in order to "agitate their minds" (st. 24):

Saṃkṣobhāya tatas teṣāṃ svorudeśān Narāgrajaḥ |
nārīm utpādayāmāsa trailokyajanamohinīm ||

As a magical act "agitation" occurs in JT 17. As its objects are mentioned women (17, 55); towns (17, 65) and the earth (17, 80). In 20, 170 meditation on a goddess of a red colour is said to be conducive to subjugation and attraction, to agitation and to causing the beloved to approach : *vaśyākarṣaṇayo raktaṃ kṣobhaṇārthaṃ priyāvaham.* AgPur 309, 14 (=TSS 22, 65) speaks of *purakṣobhaḥ* "shaking the stronghold" which presumably means "agitating the senses" (the same in TSS 24, 31). Some Śaktis called Drāviṇī "Mollifier", Āhlādakāriṇī "Gladdener" and Kṣobhaṇī "Agitator" figure in AgPur 313, 24 (=TSS 27, 27). The PST in 28, 13 associates methods of agitation and paralyzation (*kṣobhasaṃstobhanavidhiṣu*). With the aid of the goddess Nityaklinnā one will be able to "agitate the whole world", *kṣobhayet so 'khilaṃ jagat* (TSS 27, 47). In N 2, 1 (=K p. 25, 3), *kṣobhayate lokān* again occurs in a context of Vaśīkaraṇa. A mantra following in N on the same page addresses the Lady and begins with *Oṃ aiṃ puraṃ kṣobhaya Bhagavati...*[56]. In 2, 44 N contains a mantra addressed to a "Lord of beings" whose aid is invoked in subjugating a king and agitating other people : *Oṃ namo Bhūtanāthāya yaṃ* (?) *bhūpālaṃ vaśaṃ kuru kuru bhuvanakṣobhaka sarvalokān kṣobhaya kṣobhaya....*

Piercing. The word *kīlanam*, derived from *kīlaḥ* "pointed stick", "peg", occurs a few times as a magical act. It is not easy to define its exact meaning. In D (6, 13 Benares ed.) a *kīla* is made of human bone and buried at the door of a house in order to effect Uccāṭana, and nearly the same method is prescribed in N p. 317, 6 (K p. 78, 2); this time the *kīla* is made of owl bone. In TSS 17, 27, Utsāda is effected by means of a triangular peg made of Nimba wood (other cases of the use of a *kīla* in AVPar 36, 16; GarPur 20, 6). Kīlanam seems to be effective especially against opponents in a dispute. The BMR

(p. 20) records in a mantra the words *jihvāṃ kīlaya* "pierce the tongue". On p. 23 this text contains a Kīlakastotra which is directed against such opponents according to its sixth stanza: *sa bhavati parameśo vādināṃ agragaṇyaḥ* "he (the reciter) becomes a supreme ruler and leader of the disputants". S (p. 241) in another stotra to Bagalāmukhī invites this goddess to "break the mouth of my opponents, pierce their nimble tongue": *mātar bhañjaya me vipakṣavadanaṃ jihvāñ calāṃ kīlaya.* The SM (No. 85) mentions among the results of a sādhana that the mouth of the opponent in a dispute is pierced: *prativādimukhaṃ kīlitaṃ bhavati.* A performer will be able to "pierce feet", which means that he immobilizes a person's faculty of walking (*pādau kīlayet, gatiṃ stambhayet*), and to do the same to a heart, which means that he immobilizes a person's wrath (*hṛdayaṃ kīlayet, roṣaṃ stambhayati*). The text further describes that one can in the cadre of this sādhana destroy a victim's limbs by writing his name with a peg made from the shin bone of a man or made of copper and pierce the particular limb: *mānuṣajaṅghāsthikīlakena lohakīlakena vā nāma gṛhitvā yāny aṅgāni kīlayet tāni tasya naśyanti.*[57] In the GarPur (38, 5) Durgā is demanded among other horrible deeds to "pierce with a piercer" (*kīlakena kīlaya*); in the version of this long prose mantra which occurs in the AgPur as ch. 135 we read also *daṃṣṭrayā kīlaya* "pierce with Thy tusk". In the KCT (4, 139) Kīlana is executed with the help of demonesses, Āsurīs. The SST (3, 2,58ff.) while discussing the difference between *śāpoddhāraḥ* "release from a curse" and *utkīlanam* "unfastening, release from piercing or pinning down" argues that *kīlanam* implies that the victim is unable to move: *kīlane tu mahādevi na gatāgatam īritam* (st. 59). In connection with immobilization of enemies, Kīlana occurs in N (p. 299, ch 7, 8); *jāyate vairiṇāṃ stambho durgāgre kīlitaṃ dhruvam* (?). In erotics, Kīlana is an effect of the five arrows of Kāma in Bhavabhūti's Mālatīmādhava (p. 118) *sā naś cetasi kīliteva viśikhaiś cetobhuvaḥ pañcabhiḥ* "she (Mālatī) has been as it were fastened (pinned down) in my mind by the five arrows of the Mind-born One". The Skt. Commentary says on *kīliteva*: *yathā dārudvayam ayaḥśalākaviddhaṃ kīlitam* "binned down, just as two pieces of wood have been pierced by an iron nail...."

There is also a term *chedanam* "cutting" which occurs in T (p. 373) side by side with Māraṇa. *Gatiṃ chedaya* "obstruct the faculty of walking" is demanded of Rudra in TSS 13, 6.

Oppression, pīḍanam, is an effect aimed at in Ṛgvidh. 1, 15,7. The victim is the "enemy" and the act is mentioned in one breath with Uccāṭana. In later texts, *pīḍanam* plays no role. It is mentioned in an extensive list of magical faculties in the MMK (III, p. 514) in combination with *bhartsanam* "scolding". It might be added that one can also be *pīḍita-* "tormented" or "pressed hard" by an ascetic's curse (Padma Pur. 3, 5, 164, according to Kulke, p. 62; the victim is Śiva himself). Pīḍana is also one of the Mantrasaṃskāras (N p. 273).

Coercion. Skt. *nigrahaḥ,* seems to be a general term for the reduction to harmlessness of enemies and rivals. It is mentioned in SM (Vol. II, p. 531f.) in a list of the Six Acts (see above, p. 262), perhaps as an euphemism for Māraṇa. The TSS (23, 23), however, associates it with Vaśīkaraṇa. Nigraha of the evildoers is discussed in the chapter LiPur 2, 50 by means of an elaborate abhicāra ritual which makes use of the Aghoramantra; the enemy is destroyed or deprived of his position (st. 45); the coercion rite is characterized in the next chapter (st. 1) as "horrible in shape" (*ghorarūpa*). In SM, No. 151, *nigrahaḥ sarvavādinām* "coercion of all opponents in dispute" is promised as a result of a meditation on Prajñāpāramitā. In SST 3, 21 the coercion of enemies (*śatrunigraha*) with the aid of a manifestation of Bhadrakālī turns out to be tantamount to Māraṇa.

Checking. Bandhanam or *pratibandhanam* is in some cases met with as a semi-synonym for various other acts. In the BPK (3, 1) *bandhaḥ* figures between Vaśīkaraṇa and Stryākṛṣṭi "attraction of women" (see type 4.1 quoted above, p. 264). A repeated demand *bandha* "bind, check" is found in the mantra of Śrī Trailokyamohanī in AgPur 308, 2 (= TSS 21, 1) and elsewhere. In such cases, *bandhanam* has an erotic context. But in TSS 17, 41 *hṛdayaṃ bandha* "bind the heart" is uttered in a spell during a rite of Uccāṭana; and LiPur 2, 52, 3 mentions *pratibandhanam* immediately after Cheda and Māraṇa. In st. 12 of the same chapter *bandhanam* occurs as a variety of immobilization; but Māraṇa and Uccāṭana are mentioned in the preceding śloka.

Intimidation is the word which most correctly translates *trāsanam,* a term abstracted by us from the recurrent demands made to deities or spirits that they should inspire a victim with fear. As an instance we refer to the Trailokyamohanamantra in the version of TSS 20, 1: *surāsuramanujasundarimanāṃsi tāpaya dīpaya śoṣaya māraya stambhaya trāsaya bhrāmaya drāvaya ākarṣaya* "the minds of gods, counter-gods, men, fair ones, scorch, set on fire, dry out, kill, immobilize, intimidate, cause to wander, mollify, attract...." The Sudarśanamantra (TSS 20, 25) contains the words *bhūtāni trāsaya* "inspire the beings with fear"; the Viṣṇuhṛdayamantra (TSS 20, 35) : *bhīṣaya huṃ trāsaya huṃ* "intimidate, inspire with fear...". In the SST (2, 56, 12) it is promised that Devī will intimidate and destroy the enemies (*ripūn... trāsayen nāśayed devī*). An interesting case is furnished by SST 3, 19, 56 in the context of the worship of Svapnavārāhī; when duly worshipped with the entrails of cats, this goddess will intimidate anyone who tries to prosecute the performer in court: *mārjārāntraiḥ kṛto homas trāsayet sādhakārthinam.* The synonym *bhīṣaṇam* is found as the name of a magical act in SST 2, 56, 6, to be furthered by the use of a rosary with the beads made of the fruit of the Marīca shrub. Bhīṣaṇā is the name of a Yoginī who attends Kālī (KālPur 63, 96f.); Bhīṣaṇī is a Śakti of Svapnavārāhī (MMD 10,35ff.).

Kicking. Tāḍanam is met with in LiPur 2, 52, 2 and 10 after Uccāṭana, Stambhana and Mohana (the version *mocanam* in st. 2 is probably corrupt); this act is furthered by a sacrifice of the blood of an ass, an elephant and a camel in due order (st. 10). It remains unclear what result is thought to be attained by such an act; this can hardly be "kicking" in its literal sense. We found no parallels for *tāḍanam* as a separate act, although it should not be overlooked that kicking an image or other objects is sometimes said to have supranormal results in a positive (kicking of trees by young ladies as a fertility "symbol"; and cf. LT 48; Gupta , p. 324) as well as a negative sense (for instance, kicking the painted image of a political enemy on the head, LiPur 2, 50, 47). In the AgPur version of the Trailokyamohanamantra (AgPur 307, 1) one finds the demand *aṅkuśena tāḍaya* "kick with the elephant hook" (instead of "to kick", the meaning is here rather "to chastise"); the same expression in GarPur 29, 2. The TSS version (20, 1) reads *śūlena tāḍaya* "prick with the lance". Tāḍana is also an element in the Mantrasaṃskāra (Stuti & Stava, p. 209).

Crushing. In one place the term *mardanam* was met by

us as denoting a magical act; in the PST (28, 13) meditation on a grey Ardhanārīśvara is said to promote the acts of Mardana and Uccāṭana. Mantras containing the demand *marda*, *mardaya* or *pramardaya* "crush" occur more than once, for example in TSS 17, 32; 19, 20 (to Vāyu); 20, 35 (in the Viṣṇuhṛdayamantra). It seems that "crushing" has been especially associated with a political enemy (cf. the recurrent expression *arimardana* "crusher of thy foes").

"Devouring". The word *jambhanam* or its variant *jṛmbhanam* is often difficult to translate. According to MW, *jambhanam* in the Veda means most often "crushing, destroying", while Jambhā, Jambhī and Jambhaka are the names of demons; in the latter case also of "evil spirits residing in magical weapons". Of Rudra it is said in the TS (4, 5, 1, 6) that he is engaged in "crushing" or "devouring" (*jambháyant*) serpents and Yātudhānīs; Keith's translation "confounding" (trsl. of TS, II, p. 354) is probably too weak. The demand *jambhaya* is uttered to a deity in the MMK (ch. 2, p. 31; see above, p. 91). In the AgPur (323, 4), *jṛmbhaṇa* occurs as a separate act beside Vaśīkaraṇa, Antardhāna and Mohana; another instance is SM vol. II, p. 434. Jambhā is the name of a fearsome Śakti in N p. 316; Jambhanī occurs in GarPur 41, 3, SM p. 221 (name of Vajravārāhī Jvālāmukhī) and elsewhere; Jṛmbhaṇī is the name of a spell according to Jhavery, p. 262; Jṛmbhiṇī plays the role of a Śakti in GarPur 198, 10 (of Jvālāmukhī) and BMR p.5 (of Bagalāmukhī).

Desiccation. The term *śoṣaṇam*, denoting a magical act of drying out a victim, is only very seldom met with. There is a case in the MMK, ch. 47 (Goudriaan, p. 78). It is implied in the LT, ch. 49 (Gupta, p. 324) where a performer is credited with the ability of causing a tree to lose its sap. The demand "dry out", "desiccate" is, however, found various times. It is uttered to Gṛdhrakarṇī (TSS 17, 46 mantra) and to Trailokyamohana (AgPur 307, 1; TSS 20, 1; a.o.; cf. above s.v. Intimidation). In TSS 18, 62 the imperative *pratiśuṣyatu* is included in a pseudo-Vedic cursing stanza (called *vidyudṛc*, but not found in Bloomfield's Concordance) which according to the TSSC, *ad locum*, runs as follows:

Yathā vidyuddhato vṛkṣa ā mūlāt pratiśuṣyati /
evaṃ sa pratiśuṣyatu yo me pāpaṃ cikīrṣati //

"Just as a tree hit by lightning dries up with the roots included, thus should dry up anyone who desires to inflict evil upon me." The context is the worship of the Missile of Aghora. The names of Śoṣaṇī and Śoṣā occur as Śaktis; the former in connection with Svapnavārāhī (MMD 10, 35ff.), the latter in the same circumstances as Jambhā (N. p. 316; cf. Goudriaan, p. 92, n. 78).

Various teasings. These need not detain us long here, although some of the Ṣaṭkarman monographs devote considerable space to them. The AVPar contains such procedures as *pākaṃ surāpākam* "causing a cooked drink to change into liquor" (36, 14); rendering somebody poor (*nirdhanatāṃ vrajet*, 36, 16); causing somebody's house to burn down (36, 29). In post-Vedic sources they may come under the headings of Kautuka "show" or even Vinoda "pleasant pastime". Thus in TSS ch. 19 (Vinodapaṭala) an inventive would-be performer could find rules for actions like making somebody impotent, blind or deaf, conjure away his possessions, create plagues of mice or snakes, or change milk into blood. An example from the monographs: K (p. 83ff.) deals with Aśvamāraṇa "killing (a victim's) horses" (also in D p. 156), Sasyanāśana "destroying his crops", and such vexations as *rajakasya vastranāśanam* "destruction of a washerman's clothes" or *dhīvarasya matsyanāśanam* "causing a fisherman's fishes to disappear."

Making sick (*vyādhikaraṇam*). This relatively innocuous variant of Māraṇa is practised by a magician in order to make a show of his power or to force the victim to yield to some demand. We do not deem a discussion of the text-places necessary in this context and refer to AgPur 315, 12; TSS 17, 54; PST 30, 75-77; N p. 327ff. (with a heading *vyādhijananam* "creating illness"). The disease seems to have especially operated as a fever (cf. AVPar 36, 8, 1; 36, 10, 2; TSSC on TSS 17, 1; TSS 17, 65). A magician who makes his victim sick of course implicitly threatens to liquidate him[58].

Liquidation. The most fearsome of the Six Acts, *māraṇam* (S, p. 190: "an act greater than *māraṇam* does not exist"), is also in a sense the least interesting. Its aim is always the same: the enemy, personal or political, should be caused to die. In S 1, 9 this act is defined as *prāṇināṃ prāṇaharaṇam* "taking the life of living beings." MMD 25, 3 says the same : *māraṇaṃ prāṇa-*

haraṇam, while TSSC on TSS 17, 1 simply declares *maraṇakāri yat karma tat* "it is that act which causes death". B. Bhattacharya (p. LXXXVI) says: "the sixth (of the Six Acts)...consists in killing enemies by means of apparently harmless practices". Synonyms for Māraṇa may occur, especially in the older texts, e.g. AVPar 26, 5, 2 *maraṇam*; Ṛgvidh. 1, 17, 5 *vadhaḥ* (cf. RV 7, 104, 16c (*Índras táṃ hantu mahatá vadhéna*). In later texts euphemisms occur (*niṣedha*, *nigraha*).

During the performance of this cruel act the magician should be in the right state of mind. He should for example bite his lips in rage (*sandaṣṭoṣṭhapuṭaḥ*, S p. 188; *dantaiḥ saṃpīḍya cādharam*, N p. 270). He should act on a cremation ground, sitting on a corpse, or in a sanctuary of Kālī (N, l.c.). Māraṇa is associated with a black colour (Mahāmāyā fragment, st. 18). The awful implications of this act are the reason that sometimes the texts reveal a hesitation on the side of the Sanskritized performers to engage themselves in it. Māraṇa does not occur in the main part of the Mahāmāyā fragment, where the black colour has been reserved for Uccāṭana. The PST (24, 32) condemns it as "forbidden" (*aśasta-*). One who has committed it should purify himself by a 10,000-fold recitation of a certain mantra. The Viṣṇusmṛti (5, 191) classifies one who "kills another by Atharvavedic art" (*ātharvaṇena hantāram*) under the seven kinds of murderers who are to be executed by a king. A performer who nevertheless engages on Māraṇa, especially a ruler who has this done in time of war, should carefully take his precautions, as is prescribed in T, p. 353 (from the Brahmayāmala Tantra): one should in any case refrain from directing it against brahmans and other respectable persons and only choose as victims the evildoers such as violators of women or enemies of the state[59]. One should take measures to protect other people from one's wrath; never should one perform liquidation in order to gratify one's greed or fear. Māraṇa should always be accompanied by rites aimed at protecting one's self and followed by expiation [54]. Elsewhere (on p. 354), quoting "another Tantra", T advises to draw the enemy's horoscope at the outset. If this appears to be favourable, one should abstain from such an act altogether. A statement of principle is made by S (p. 191): "In a case where there is no other means of checking the danger from enemies, (only) then one should have such rites as Māraṇa performed, because there is no other recourse left"[55]. The Jaina Mantravādins, compelled by their ideology of Ahiṃsā, forbid Māraṇa altogether and in their classifications are wont to replace it by Niṣedha "the forbidden act" (Jhavery, passim). The HT (ch. 11) argues: "having realized the four kinds of mystical sight, a wise man should rescue the living beings; but in this connection (the passage speaks of the various sorts of supranormal powers) the power of killing should not be applied, because this would mean a complete break of the Agreement"[56].

The above considerations are sufficient to prove that Māraṇa should never be applied at random by a magician, but only in cases where the victim's death is considered politically or socially necessary. This means that we should translate by "execution" or "liquidation", not by the mere word "killing". It is, however, open to question if these reservations were always observed, as there have no doubt been persons who did not hesitate to attack the lives of their personal enemies or who committed such rites for a client for rich rewards. Māraṇa rites have been performed in India up till recent times. In Kerala it was known as a ceremony during which a figure of the enemy was made and buried in the ground on a place where he was expected to pass by (Fawcett, according to Thurston, p. 247). The Korku knew the practice of piercing a doll representing the victim[60]. Dare (p. 50ff.) mentions a case of Māraṇa with the aid of a deity summoned up by the performer. We abstain from giving more instances from the many cases of so-called "witchcraft murders" in recent times in India[61].

For a correct understanding of the procedure of execution by magic it should be borne in mind that this act is not a mere inflicting of physical death on a person by setting in motion a deadly automaton. There is also a psychological side to the matter: the aim is so adversely to affect the victim's mind and will that his faculty for facing life is completely broken. It is the culmination of the faculties of psychological subjugation wielded by the adept of the Six Acts. It has been actually observed how the victim of magical execution can become so terrified and convinced of his approaching end that he becomes sick and withers away without other people being able to help him, so that the psychical breakdown results in physical ruin also.[62]

In the Veda, liquidation by supranormal power is alluded to in RV 1, 80, 7b *yád dha tyā̃ṃ māyínaṃ mṛgáṃ tám u tváṃ māyáyāvadhīḥ* "when Thou hast killed that animal wielder of māyā with Thy own māyā" (the god addressed is Indra). A brahman was considered to be able to liquidate a person by his wrath according to the Mbh 1, 67, 5, where a stanza inserted in three manuscripts of the Southern recension says : *manyunā ghnanti te śatrūn vajreṇendra ivāsurān* "by their wrath they kill your enemies like Indra the counter-gods by his Vajra." The stories of sages who burn their adversaries with a fiery look from their eyes are famous and need not to be repeated here; they do not fall under what we understand to be "magic". Another method which they may resort to is related in the Cidambaramāhātmya in connection with the Dāruvana legend: when Śiva as a Kāpālika begging monk tried to seduce their wives, the enraged Ṛṣis created a tiger from an Abhicāra fire (Kulke, p. 12).

We now give a choice of instances of the act of liquidation taken from Sanskrit texts. AV 6, 133, 3 contains the sacrifice of a person to the God of Death by a magician (Shende, p. 154). By a certain method of singing during a Vedic sacrifice the officiant can execute the enemy (e.g. the *Jamadagneḥ saptahā*, JaimBr 1, 152). Methods of Māraṇa are presented by the Ṛgvidh. (2, 3, 5-- 2, 4, 3) with the recitation of the RV passage 3, 53, 21-24 (stanza 21d: *yám u dviṣmás tám u prāṇó jahātu* "whom we hate him the life breath should leave"), and 3, 17, 5 ff. SVBr 3, 6, 12 describes the method of creating a man with a lance in his hand out of the sacrificial site. For this end one should fast three nights and perform the rite on the fourteenth of the dark half of the month. Charcoal should be taken from a burnt corpse, firesticks from a Bādhaka tree; the scene is a crossroads. The ladle should be from Vibhītaka wood, the thousand oblations consist of mustard oil. The mantra is taken from the SV. When the man with the lance stands before the performer, the latter should command: "Kill N.N."; "and he kills him"[57]. This is an early instance of how the border between the products of concentrated meditation and reality seems to fade away for an adept performer.

The MtPur (93, 149) gives a colourful method of Māraṇa in the cadre of the worship of the Nine Planets (the text speaks of Abhicāra). The brahmans (*viprāḥ*) should perform a sacrifice in a triangular fireplace. Their clothing and apparel should be red. Among the requisites are three dishes filled with the blood of a young crow and firewood mixed with eagles' bones. The performers should wear their hair loose and should meditate the evil for the enemy. They should then with a knife over which a certain mantra has been recited cut through an image of the victim and sacrifice the pieces of the image into the fire. Continues the author: such practices may have their results on a purely mundane sphere, they can never add to a performer's religious emancipation; therefore one who desires his own spiritual well-being should afterwards conduct a pacificatory ceremony [58]. The pierced doll method is advised in AgPur 260, 8 during the discussion of the effects of the Mahāvyāhṛti mantra. The same text (306, 3 = TSS 17, 31) describes the piercing of an image's throat or heart with golden needles, by which the enemy will die (*mriyate ripuḥ*). There are other Māraṇa rites in this text (e.g., in 125, 49ff.; 315, 11); the TSS describes some in 17, 32ff. Sometimes the rule is added that the performers of the rite should face the South, the region of Yama (AgPur 125, 50; JT 17, 74; on the latter place a yantra inscribed with the victim's name is sacrificed). Similar rites are found in LiPur 2, 50, 28ff. (an image of the victim is buried); PST 14, 47f. (deity Kātyāyanī; the victim dies within two weeks; pierced doll method); PST 14, 51 (the same; the victims die immediately); PST 14, 80 (deity Vindhyavāsinī); PST 30, 62f. (Tāraṇī of black colour); 30, 73 and 34, 13 (pierced doll method). PST 22, 50 gives a meditation on Viṣṇu's four-coloured disc Sudarśana in a fiery form standing above the victim's head; as a consequence thereof this victim within a week is attacked by a scorching fever and within a month he departs to the spirits' abode. The MMD in a chapter discussing the effects of meditation on Kālarātrī (18, 93ff.) gives this spell for Māraṇa: *Oṃ mrā mrūṃ Mṛtiśvari kṛṅkṛtye amukaṃ śighra(ṃ) māraya u kroṃ.* The officiant should be dressed in dark blue (*nila*) and cut off the head of a doll image of the enemy which he sacrifices into the fire.

Rites of liquidation are discussed in detail by the monographs S (ch. 9. p. 255ff.) and N (ch. 10, p. 321-325; ch. 8, p. 307ff. in case of a battle). In various cases N gives a method for causing the languishing victim to recover, for example by digging up a buried root. Stanza 18 on p. 325 promises the enemy's death within a week, even if he be a Mahāsura. S (p. 191) discusses some general rules for Māraṇa. A performer will use *paridhi* sticks of Vibhītaka wood; he sacrifices the paws of crows and owls anointed with Nimba resin; he adds to the mantra in question for 108 times the words *dārayainaṃ śoṣayainaṃ mārayainam* "cleave him, parch him, liquidate him". After the sacrifice one should worship the Kṛtyā (see above, p. 222) who has arisen for him and command her to drink the blood from the enemy's heart. One should guard the fire for nine days. Then one should realize: "(the enemy) is dead now", *mṛtas tiṣṭhati*. On that same moment the enemy dies.

Resuscitation. A consequent magician who practises liquidation should also claim the ability to restore a victim to life when the necessary rites are executed correctly up to the most meticulous details. Like an ambivalent god who strikes but also cures and protects, the human wonderworker should be always able to undo his own proceedings before it is too late—and the affected should know this in order that he may recover. But the power of resuscitation (in Skt. often called *saṃjīvinīvidyā*) is also an independent feat which can be practised by persons who never have anything to do with acts of destruction and only serve as physicians. In both qualities, resuscitation strictly speaking forms part of Śānti (see the next section). The performers of the second kind also derive their powers from the gods. There is a tradition that Durgā revived Lakṣmī's son Kāma[63]. In the Nāgānanda by Harṣa the hero of the play, Jīmūtavāhana, on his mother's prayer is restored to life by Gaurī who sprinkles the Water-of-life over him; and the same is accomplished by Garuḍa for the Nāgas (Winternitz/Jhā, III, 1, p. 257). The science of rendering people immortal by means of potent herbs has been studied by Brahmā, Rudra and Indra (AgPur 141, 1). It is a matter of understanding that the gods who possess the gift of immortality and the Water-of-life also have the ability to execute the power of reviving.

The same ability is sometimes declared to be within the reach of powerful human beings, especially the semi-divine Ṛṣis. In the tale of Pauṣya (Mbh. 1, 3) the sage Kāśyapa revives a tree which had been burnt just before by the Nāga king Takṣaka (the power of reviving trees is attributed to an adept by the

LT, 49, 43-53; Gupta, p. 324). According to the Bṛhaddevatā, 84-90, the stanzas RV 10, 57-60 were revealed to the three brothers of King Subandhu who had been rendered lifeless (*mūrchita-*) by sorcery (Malaviya, p. 29, n.4). The JaimBr (3, 72-74) discusses the Traiśoka melody of Vedic liturgy, and in connection therewith tells the story of Kaṇva who married a daughter of the Asuras and his sons Triśoka and Nābhāka. The Asuras had enclosed Kaṇva within a big stone, but his two sons with the help of Vedic hymns freed him. When he was still lifeless, Nābhāka brought him to life again by touching him with the words *o yi jīva*; he became alive but was still enveloped in darkness. By saying *o yi diva*; this was also remedied, and even the entrance to heaven was procured for him by the words *o yi divam.* The Mbh. (1, 71, 7ff.) relates how the counter-gods who were killed by the gods in battle were resuscitated by their domestic priest Kāvya Uśanas by means of his magic power (*vidyābalāśrayāt*). Kāvya's deadly antagonist, Bṛhaspati, had to look on while his rival executed a feat he was unable to emulate because he did not know that power of revival : *na hi veda sa tāṃ vidyāṃ yāṃ Kāvyo veda vīryavān, saṃjīvanim* (st. 9). The gods thereupon sent Kaca, Bṛhaspati's eldest son, to Kāvya in order to study this science. After 500 years the Asuras killed Kaca while he herded the cattle. Śukra (=Kāvya) thereupon applied his *saṃjīvanī vidyā* while he called Kaca by the simple words *ayam ehi* "come here". After some other critical events the vidyā was obtained by Kaca who delivered it to the gods. The last of the Sixty-four Sports of Śiva at Madurai contains the story of the Śaivite saint Jñānasambandha who by a mere gracious look revived a young man who had been bitten by a snake (Dessigane, 1960, p. 110). The Kathās.. (12, 9, 21; Vetālapañcaviṃśatikā 2, 21) records how a mother threw her naughty little boy into the flaming herd and how the child was revived again by the father by means of a few mantras taken from a book in his possession. A guest in the house looks on in astonishment; at night he steals the book and runs away in order to revive his own beloved. The same text in 12, 16, 29ff. relates of a brahman who claims the possession of the power of resuscitation. He is, however, judged unfavourably by the king Trivikramasena (st. 37): "As to that third brahman, what is (my daughter's) concern with this degraded person, a magician who has fallen from his legal occupation but supposes himself to be a master-mind?"

Yo 'pi vipras tṛtīyo 'tra tenāpi patitena kim /
svakarmapracyutenendrajālinā vīramāninā //

From Indonesia we record the case of the sage Tumburu who revived his own son Kapuluṅan with holy water; the same feat is told of Nārada in the story of Pakaṅ Raras[64].

Sporadically we come across signs of a ritual of resuscitation having been actually performed. AV 5, 30 addresses somebody who is on the verge of dying as a consequence of sorcery. He is recalled as it were from death with the words *ánuhūtaḥ púnar éhi* "being recalled, come back" (Shende, p. 156f.). A Saṃjīvanayantra is given in TSS 13, 55.

In AgPur 285, a series of recipes is announced by Dhanvantari the god of medicine as bringing about restoration to life. In practice their function is the curing of disease, as stanza 1 itself says: "Now I shall again proclaim effective supranormal devices which cause the restoration of life, divine, formerly told by Ātreya, which crush all disease" [59]. The same text in 323, 17 gives a mantra which is able to "conquer death": oblations of honey accompanied by the mantra *Oṃ kṣuṃ saḥ vaṣaṭ* will have the desired effect. It seems as if often the "reviving the dead" or "conquering of death" is a method of advertizing potent herbs or other devices for curing the sick. The same can probably be said of the "Worship for conquering death" or "Worship of the Conqueror of Death" (Mṛtyuñjayapūjā) which is directed to the Śiva manifestation of Tryambaka and sometimes occurs in the texts (e.g., GarPur ch. 18; LiPur 2, ch. 53; PST 27, 31ff.; S. p. 223). Kane, 1962, p. 814 holds that Mṛtyuñjayapūjā is performed against premature death. The mantra in Tryambaka worship is the Vedic stanza *Tryambakaṃ yajāmahe* (RV 7, 59, 12): "We worship Tryambaka the Fragrant One, Who furthers welfare, and Who may deliver me from the state of death like a cucumber from its string" [60].

S discusses the Sañjīvinīvidyā on p. 203 as a form of Śānti, as appears clearly from this mantra: *Oṃ namo bhagavati Mṛtasañjīvani, amukasya śāntiṃ kuru kuru svāhā*; a meditation on this goddess follows. N treats the subject in ch. 19 (p. 379 ff. :

Mṛtasañjīvinīvidyā), K on p. 106. D (ch. 19) in 12 stanzas specializes on the method of resuscitating a woman's still-born son (*Mṛtavatsāsutajīvanaprakāraḥ*).

6.9. *Pacification.*

The nature of Śānti in the Ṣatkarman context. The last of the Six Acts in the order adopted here—but the first of them in the most common list—, the act of *śāntiḥ* or pacification, is the completion as well as the counterbalance of the other five. No study of Tantric magic is complete without the mastery of Śānti. In the following pages it has not been the intention to give a complete survey of the many shades of meaning implied by the word Śānti and the manifold acts and ceremonies which go under this name. This would require a monograph of its own and detailed study in the field has already been made by others (Hoens; Kane, 1962, p. 719-814; Kane quotes primary sources, generally post-Vedic, on p. 734f.). We do not even try here to give a balanced treatment of the concerned rituals as they obtain in Tantric literature. It is only endeavoured to mention a few aspects of this important part of Hindu religiosity which may be considered characteristic in connection with the Six Acts; but it may be emphasized at the outset that the character of Śānti as one of the Six Acts usually does not differ much from what goes under that name in the sources of ordinary Hindu ritual.

In the Ṣaṭkarman monographs Śānti, although being the first of the Six Acts, is not treated with special attention. The only source from the Indrajālavidyāsaṃgraha which devotes a longer section to it is S (ch. 3, p. 198-227); and this portion consists—as usual in S—of excerpts from other Tantric texts, in the first place the Śāntikalpa from the Sanatkumārasaṃhitā (p. 198-201), followed by fragments from "Ātharvaṇa", "Tantra" and "Purāṇa" traditions. The TSS deals with the subject in ch. 18 (18, 1-18 has a shorter version in AgPur 306, 5-17). This comparative neglect of systematic treatment of Śānti may be due to a looser connection of Śānti with the stock of popular non-Sanskritic magic which must have influenced Ṣaṭkarman theories and practice; but such a hypothesis should be handled with the utmost reservation, because rituals of pacification and recovery form the ubiquitous substance of the ritual supply of the performer of white magic. Many of the Śānti rites advocated in Tantric and non-Tantric brāhmaṇic texts certainly have ultimately been derived from non-brāhmaṇical sources, however much they may have been systematized and elaborated upon.

The word Śānti in the Veda most often indicates the state of being appeased or freed from evil, conform to a frequent resultative shade of meaning of the Vedic nouns on *-ti*. But Śānti can also in a few cases denote the state in which the evil powers themselves abide when conjured, and in a few more cases it can stand for the means of appeasing or the appeasing ceremony itself (Hoens, p. 182f. gives a survey of the meanings of Śānti and other derivatives from the root *śam-* in the Veda). In this last sense the term Śānti is usually known in post-Vedic Hinduism, and the same can be said of the Ṣaṭkarman ritual, where Śānti denotes the "act" of pacification. We choose this English rendering instead of "appeasement", because as a more general term it seems to us to sufficiently encompass the state of peace and freedom and its manifold implications denoted by the Skt. term. While appeasement restricts itself to the act of appeasing the powers that make for evil by nullifying their effects, pacification implies the creation of peace in its dynamic aspect: the stimulation of the powers which work for the good of the individual and of society. This seems also to be implied by the sources when they discuss acts of Śānti, although, it is true, it does not appear from their definitions. But often the efficacy of a rite to afford good results is praised together with its first object of appeasing evil; as an instance we quote MtPur 70, 62: *sarvapāpapraśamanam anantaphaladāyakam*. Kane, 1962, p. 719, when dealing with the general character of Śānti, paraphrases with: "propitiatory rites for averting a deity's wrath, a calamity or an unlucky event", thus departing from the meaning of Śānti as "appeasing ceremony". The evils against which Śānti serves as a remedy are divided by Kane into three groups: evil forebodings of omina when the evil itself has not yet arrived; the unexpected evil itself which should be undone; and ever-recurring inevitable evils like impurity caused by contact with death. In short, Śānti serves as a means of defence against all kind of fateful events. This is expressed clearly by the passage MtPur 93, 81 quoted by Kane (p. 752, n. 1207): "just as an armour is a means of defence against the strokes of arrows so the pacification is a means of defence against the blows of fate" [61].

The definitions of Śānti in the Ṣaṭkarman texts are, as usual, very short. S 1, 7: *rogakṛtyāgrahādīnāṃ nirāsaḥ* "the removal of disease, spirits of revenge, evil influence of planets and so on"; MMD 25,2 is even shorter with *śānti rogādināśanam* "pacification is the destruction of disease and other (evils)". It is therefore interesting to see how disease in both cases occupies the first place—the white magician's first preoccupation is medicine—, and how one of them also mentions the spirits of revenge created by sorcerers, thus expressing the general popular belief in black magic as an important source of disease and other evils. B. Bhattacharya (p. LXXXVI) also describes Śānti as the ceremony destined to destroy diseases or evil luminaries. but he adds among the evils those caused by the bad actions committed by the performer himself in previous births. This aspect of Śānti—undoing the consequences of the own deeds—is especially important in the Ṣaṭkarman context as we shall see presently.

Kane (p. 756f.) further quotes a more elaborate definition of Śānti from the Śāntimayūkha by Nīlakaṇṭha, a monograph on the subject from the seventeenth century, the essence of which is that Śānti may be used for the removal of all that is undesirable, especially those evils which are not known and which form a menace to life on earth; a further prerequisite is that the act itself should not aim at evil consequences for others. This definition, however, comes from a specialist in the field and is too technical for our purpose. Śānti in the texts which form the object of the present study also embraces defence against evils the causes of which are known (e.g. deeds from former births or evil committed shortly ago), while it may also be destined to procure an easier way to release of the spirit beside happiness in the present world. As to the avoidance of evil consequences for others, Tantric Śānti does not commit itself to such considerations, at least not in theory.

With respect to the aims held in view by the magician who wants to perform a Śānti ceremony, the short circumscriptions given above are typically inadequate. These aims are manifold. A good instance of the results to be expected from Śānti is furnished by the LiPur (2, 52, 13): "By means of (an oblation with) ghee there will be perfection of all things: by means of milk one is purified from sin; by means of sesamum there is destruction of disease; by means of a lotus one will obtain wealth":

Ghṛtena sarvasiddhiḥ syāt payasāghād viśudhyate |
tilena roganāśaś ca kamalena dhanaṃ labhet ||

In our opinion, the four aims mentioned give an idea of the intermingling of positive and negative values associated in the minds of the believers with the term Śānti. One might find the same association of "purification from sin" and "advancement of good things" in the statements of rewards attached to literary works, like in the case of Bhavabhūti's Uttararāmacarita (7, 20): *pāpebhyaś ca punāti vardhayati ca śreyāṃsi seyaṃ kathā* (see Gonda, 1970, p. 116). The following passage from the KCT (3, 203; one out of many of this kind) expresses the feats and values of Śānti in the negative: "Enemies, lions and powerful elephants, the yellow ones and the serpent rulers; thieves and bonds of captivity; a stormy sea, imps who bring with them the fear of death, illness, manifestations of Indra's power (excessive rain); poverty, separation from the wife, danger from enraged kings, the stroke of lightning, loss of possessions—all of these do not leave the man who is not pacified (has no Śānti performed for him), even when he meditates the feet of the Yoginīs" [62]. This statement, while being in the negative, implies that a successful Śānti act brings about very positive results: the counterparts of all the evils mentioned as staying with one who has not performed such an act. The conclusion must be that Śānti is a comprehensive idea, perhaps even as comprehensive as all the other magical acts together, including those of Abhicāra (as far as they are directed against evil people, which is of course always the case; cf. LiPur 2,50,6). The only restriction pertaining to Śānti is probably that it should not require another act of appeasement in its turn, otherwise one would enter upon a vicious circle; this means that such an act can hardly be directed against the person of an enemy, but should rather concentrate on the danger resulting from inimical conduct.

Synonyms of Śānti. Of the synonyms we first mention in

passing the word *rakṣā* "protection" which sometimes in the Tantras occurs in that function. PST 28, 24 ff. for example discusses a Rakṣāyantra, while the same text in 30, 83 provides *rakṣā* for a client (*sādhya*). Obviously rakṣā refers to protection of the own person in a sense more restricted than Śānti which aims at a general pacification. In S (p. 192), *rakṣā* occurs as one of the specifications of Śānti : *uttaraṃ śāntikaṃ bhavet, āyuṣyarakṣāṃ* (read : *āyuṣyaṃ rakṣāṃ*) *śāntiñ ca puṣṭiṃ vāpi kariṣyanti* "(recitation of mantras while facing) the North leads to pacification; in that case one will procure longevity, protection and pacification (in a restricted sense: perhaps appeasement of omina), or welfare." On the other hand, *rakṣā* may appear out of the Śānti context in the meaning of : preliminary rites to be performed by a magician on his own person (*ātmarakṣā*) before he embarks upon a rite of coercing the spirits or of sorcery. Without such a preliminary protection no performance of Abhicāra is possible (see above, p. 380).

Beside Śānti, there are the verbal derivations from the root *śam-* "to pacify". In the Veda we have *śāmyati* "to come to appeasement" and especially *śamayati* "to appease" "to conjure", beside the verbal adjective *śānta-* "appeased" (Hoens, p. 177f.). For *śamayati*, Hoens records various synonyms: *saṃdadhāti, saṃtanoti, akrūraṃ karoti* (against pain or fever) and *prīṇāti, mitraṃ karoti* (against wrath). Most of them have become obsolete in the Tantric texts, but *śamayati* remains in general use. For *śānta* there are in the Veda the synonyms *prīta* or *aghora*, while for Śānti in the dative there sometimes occurs *ahiṃsāyai* "for avoiding harm"; in another case *pratitiṣṭhyai* "for having a firm base"; against flaws in the ritual: *kḷptyai* "for making into order". Further synonyms of Śānti in the Veda are *kṣemaḥ, abhayam, śam* or *śivam*. For Śānti as "means of appeasing", there are various occurrences of *bheṣajam* "remedy", "medicine" as a synonym (everything in Hoens, pp. 178ff.). It seems that the Tantric vocabulary on pacification is less varied than the Vedic one. But there is one word not mentioned by Hoens as a synonym of Śānti which deserves special attention: *prāyaścittam* "reparation", "expiation". This word is used instead of Śānti in the Mahāmāyā fragment (st. 14: *prāyaścittakaro yogī*; the stanzas 14-16 are styled in the manuscripts Caturvarṇaprāyaścitta). Prāyaścitta is a Vedic term, and it seems that some instances can be adduced from the Veda to illustrate not only its affinity, which is self-evident, but also its virtual identity with Śânti in some cases. Hoens (p. 175) quotes a passage from the GopBr (1, 5,24 : 138) : *prāyaścittair bheṣajaiḥ saṃstuvanto 'tharvāṇo 'ṅgirasaś ca śāntāḥ* "The Atharvans and Aṅgirases, praising with words of expiation and words of remedy, become pacified (i.e. have pacification realized upon them)". Kane (p. 727) quotes AitBr 32, 4 which first states a question as to the nature of the expiation (*prāyaścitti*) in the case of overflowing of the heated Agnihotra oblation, and the answer is that one should pour water in that case "for pacification" (*śāntyai*), "for indeed the waters imply pacification" (*śāntir vā āpaḥ*). In his comments Kane notes the identity of Śânti and Prāyaścitti in this passage, but it does not have his special attention, although on p. 736 he discusses KauśS 13, where at the end a number of Śântis against supernatural (*adbhuta*) occurrences are summarized with *prāyaścitta*.

In the Śântimayūkha of Nīlakaṇṭha mentioned above, Śânti and Prāyaścitta are distinguished. According to this authority, Prāyaścitta implies care for the hereafter as well as for the present existence, while Śânti restricts itself to the present life. But this text, as we saw, is late and specialized. In general, "pacification" and "expiation" may be considered in non-technical texts to stand for two aspects of the same phenomenon: the endeavour to procure security from all kinds of dangers by ritual (or meditation, in some cases in the Tantra). The shade of meaning comported by "expiation" in that case tends to be: the atonement for one's own misdeeds, ethical as well as ritual. Of course, Prāyaścitta is often a pure ritual action destined to make good some omission in the ceremony. For example, in ṢaḍvBr 4, 1, 7: when the clarified butter flows over, the Yajamāna runs the risk of dying. In order to procure Prāyaścitta for this occurrence, the Yajamāna should hand over a certain gift to the officiating priest (Malaviya, p. 135). But in cases like SVBr 1, 8, 7-8, "expiation" can hardly be distinguished from "pacification" Kane, p. 733, comments on this passage with: "several *prāyaścittas* (really *śāntis*) on the happening of various incidents" (the words between brackets are Kane's). An interesting case is ṢaḍvBr 1, 2, 12 discussed already in ch. 1, p.15 After an enumeration of all Indra's māyās by means of which the sacrificer obtains a rich quantity of brahman and śrī, the author concludes his argument by saying that for all that is known and not known this is the *prāyaścitti* "expiatory rite".

It seems that often Śānti is the more general term when compared with Prāyaścitta; but, as we saw, both terms may occur as pure synonyms. In its turn, Śānti is sometimes used in a narrower sense which is usually reserved for Prāyaścitta: the atonement or expiation for the own misdeeds, ritual and ethical. A case of ritual wrongdoing the atonement for which leads to Śānti is quoted by Kane (p. 721; TS 6, 1, 7, 7-8): the pronunciation of a formula which contains the name Rudra should be followed up by another formula containing the name Mitra, "for Śānti", in order to undo the evil (*krūra-*) effect of mentioning Rudra's name. But also a magician who inflicts evil on a victim may on a certain moment feel the desire to revoke his magic or to undo its effects, especially when the victim has complied with his or his client's demands, or has been sufficiently intimidated in his opinion. Thus in the AVPar there are various places on which Śānti is advised as the revocation of acts of sorcery (e.g., in 35, 1, 12; 35, 1, 14, where the author uses the term *mokṣaḥ* "release"; 36, 10, 3; 36, 16, 2; 36, 28). Besides, the performer of destructive magic needs atonement for his own sin—that means, for his own magic performed recently or immediately before, not, or rather not merely, for actions done in his former life. The appeasement for the own magic has been discussed above in connection with Māraṇa (p. 380); we also refer to Malaviya (p. 23): *prāyaścittakṛtyāny aśubhānāṃ karmaṇāṃ duṣṭaphalānāṃ duḥsvapnādinañ ca śamanārthaṃ kriyante, ataḥ śāntir eva teṣāṃ mūlam* "the actions of Prāyaścitta are performed in order to pacify the bad results of evil deeds, such as bad dreams; and therefore pacification forms also their base." Śānti as a general appeasement or pacification of the own sins occurs in PST 7, 64 : *lakṣaṃ tilair vā juhuyād aghānāṃ śāntyai*; cf. JT 17, 81ff. (worship of Śiva's spouse with fragrant flowers) ; JT 18, 16 and 21 (in the places from JT the word Śānti is not mentioned but implied in my opinion).

There are various prescriptions in N for the revocation of magic. They do not contain the term Śānti, but most often describe the victim as *svastha-* "healthy" or *sukhī* "happy" : p. 314, 9 : *svastho bhaven naraḥ*; 316, 13 : *mohāt suṣṭho bhaviṣyati*; 318, 17: *snānād gokṣirataḥ sukhī* "he will become happy after a washing with cows' milk" (after Uccāṭana); 322, 9: *nikhanen mriyate śatrus tasyotpāṭe sukhaṃ bhavet* "when he buries it, the enemy dies; when he digs it up, there will be happiness"; 323, 15: *sukhī bhavet*; some cases in the chapter on Vyādhijanana (p. 327 ff.). It is possible that also in the Mahāmāyā fragment the Prāyaścitta given in st. 14 implies atonement for the destructive acts which were described in the preceding stanzas, especially because also here (st. 16) the poet promises that a person will become "happy by reason of the Prāyaścitta" (*prāyaścittāt sukhī bhavet*).

This discussion on the nature of Prāyaścitta in connection with the execution of destructive magic leads us to a more general consideration of the relation between *Śānti and Abhicāra.* As Malaviya (p. 23) emphasizes, there is already in Vedic magic no essential difference between these two ideas. There is only a difference of emphasis: Śānti means procuring the own security and welfare by magical means, without considering (or: while avoiding) possible detriment to others; Abhicāra is, in Malaviya's words, *ātmanaḥ śreyo aparasya hāniḥ* "the good for oneself; downfall for the other", and thus leads to the same goal of happiness and security for the performer, but with the emphasis on thwarting the other who blocks his way. Malaviya refers to the foremost goal of Vedic man : *yogakṣemaḥ*, which means: *alabdhasya lābhaḥ, labdhasya parirakṣaṇam* "acquisition of what has not been acquired, and protection of what has been acquired". These processes are complementary; the first of them might become realized by Abhicāra, the second by Śānti. *Yogakṣema* still occurs in the MMD, ch. 22; and it might be recalled that *yoga* in later times sometimes serves as an equivalent for "magic" (see above, p.66).

One might also say, as Malaviya, *l.c.*, does, that *abhicārakarmāṇy apa śatrūn daityāṃś ca śamayanti, yena na syād dhānir aśubho vā puruṣasya* "the acts of magic directed against an adversary are destined to pacify the danger resulting from that adversary, who may be a human enemy or a demon, so that there will be henceforth no downfall or calamity for man" (as we say :

"pacifying" a district by rooting out resistance). This she declares to be the reason that in her study on "Śānti and Puṣṭi", she also discusses Abhicāramantras; and, in our opinion, this is done from a correct insight into the human motivation for embarking upon acts of magic. For the Vedic observer, man's faculties may be sharpened into weapons which he recklessly wields to attain his objectives; but at the same time his desire is for peace to be procured by means of the same faculties: "those five senses, accompanied by the mind as the sixth, which have been sharpened in my heart by means of the brahman power, and by means of which the terrible has been created—by means of these same there should appear pacification for us" (AV 19, 9, 5, quoted also by Kane, p. 720) [63]. An association of the ideas of "pacification" and "destruction" appears also after the Veda in passages like ViDhPur 3, 48, 17 *trailokya-śamanaḥ krodhaḥ* "(Śiva's) wrath which pacifies the threefold world"; and the same text, 3, 50, 10 *duṣṭasaṃśamanaḥ krodhaḥ* "(Indra's) wrath which allays the evil-minded."

In post-Vedic ritualism we read of the ceremony of Vijayadaśamī on which kings were to perform Śānti on the tenth day of the light half of the month Āśvina; this went together with rites aiming at the victory over the enemies (Kane, 1958, p. 190ff.). On these occasions there was a honouring of the Śamī tree or of branches of that tree; the Śamī, because its name was associated with Śānti (in the Veda it served as a means for procuring Śānti: Hoens, p. 184). The MtPur in the introduction to its detailed discussion of the Navagrahaśānti (93, 2) remarks that this Śānti may also be performed in the case that someone desires to execute Abhicāra (cf. Kane, 1962, p. 749; the passage is similar to Yājñavalkya Smṛti 1, 294):

śrīkāmaḥ śāntikāmo vā grahayajñaṃ samācaret /
vṛddhyāyuḥpuṣṭikāmo vā tathaivābhicaran punaḥ //

"Sacrifice to the Planets should be taken up by someone who desires to attain lustre or pacification, or by someone who longs after expansion, longevity or prosperity; or also by someone who has his recourse to sorcery." That this last remark is no loose theoretization appears from the stanzas 140ff. of the same chapter where destructive magic is dealt with. The connection of Śānti with attack by and destruction of an enemy appears further from MtPur 228, 4f.: "One who desires to conquer others and one who longs after welfare,...and also who is attacked by others; also if one suspects sorcery, and during the destruction of the enemy, and when a great danger occurs, the type of Śānti called Secure (*abhayā*) is recommended" [64]. According to ViDhPur 2, 159, 47, Śānti to be performed by temporal rulers is "procuring wealth and fame, destroying enemies, conducive to happiness and insurpassable; it should be executed by rulers for the sake of the increase of the kingdom with all possible effort" [65]. The BṛhSaṃh (44, 21) expresses itself in the same spirit when it lays down that "having performed Śānti for the increase of the kingdom, a twice-born should further, with thc aid of mantras of Abhicāra, pierce with a lance the (image of) the enemy made of clay as a representative of the enemy himself":

> *Śāntiṃ rāṣṭravivṛddhyai kṛtvā bhūyo 'bhicārakair mantraiḥ |*
> *mṛṇmayam ariṃ vibhindyāc chūlenārehsthale vipraḥ ||*

The connection of Śānti and Abhicāra is preserved in the younger ritual monographs: according to Kane (1962, p. 735), the Kṛtyakalpataru in its volume on rites of pacification and prosperity (Śāntikapauṣṭikakāṇḍa) also contains a discussion of Abhicāra. The practisers of rites of pacification and destructive magic must have often been the same persons, ritual specialists (in the service of powerful laymen) who found the details of such performances conveniently together in their handbooks; and from this situation it is not a large step to the position of the magician who specializes in the Six Acts which include also Śānti. This is not to say that the Ṣaṭkarman monographs do not accord a much more prominent place to the rites of Abhicāra or Vaśīkaraṇa, but it would not be correct to assume watertight compartments between "white" ritualists and "black" magicians in Ancient Hindu culture[65].

A few instances of the proximity of Śānti and Abhicāra to each other in Tantrism may be adduced from the PST. Many passages in this text mention these two faculties in one breath as results attainable by ritual and meditation. In 9, 34, the author asserts: *sakalopadravaśāntyai jvarāpamṛtyupraṇodanāya vaśī* "one becomes able to subjugate for the pacification of all kinds of calamities, and for the removal of fever and untimely death." In st. 39ff. this is repeated in more detail: 39 speaks of Śānti of omina; 40 of subjugation; 41, idem. In 24, 27f. of the same text, a passage on Śānti is immediately followed by a meditation on the enemy as if he were the demon king Hiraṇyakaśipu who is being struck down and devoured by Narasiṃha (= the performer). The principle is put somewhat more cautiously in a preceding stanza, 24, 22; "in case of a terrible outbreak of calamities, this sacrificial ceremony serves for a pacification of evil for the people; and also any other wish desired by him in his mind, all that he obtains; moreover, he becomes a favourite of the people" [66]. PST 23, 30ff. describes a worship of Varāha in five colours which results in welfare, victory as well as Śānti. The earth is freed of rivals and prosperity (*puṣṭi*) is obtained. PST 30, 79 contains a ritual directed against disease and spirits of vengeance (*kṛtyāḥ*) which may serve at the same time for the fulfilment of all desires and the dislocation of the enemies [81]. The list could be continued. Two other instances from the SST: in 1, 12, 16 this text recommends a device "which creates protection for the realm and the destruction of inimical realms"; besides, it helps to accomplish the Six Acts: *rājyarakṣaṇayogaṃ ca...pararājyavināśakam...ṣaṭkarmasādhanam...*According to SST 3, 14, 57f., worship of Virodhinī leads to the infliction of fever on the enemy as well as to the protection of the own person from the sorcery devised by others: *...śatrur jvarayuto bhavet, parābhicāranāśārthaṃ svarakṣārthaṃ yathāvidhi.* In texts like these, Śānti, Vaśīkaraṇa, as well as Abhicāra, are only aspects of the supernatural proficiency of the successful performer. In the mythological sphere the same idea may be expressed by the convention of worshipping a protecting god, as an image of external material or created in the mind, surrounded by dreadful females who embody the destructive aspects of that god's power[66]. The sādhaka is the foremost receptacle of that power of Māyā by which he influences the own life and that of others for good or for evil. And it might be added that both Śānti and Abhicāra basically imply the combat against inimical power. The performer may act for his own sake or for the weal of the community; in both cases he strikes at the opponent, be he real or imaginary, a person or a force, human or suprahuman.

Pacifying meditation. In the Tantras the results desired are brought about by various means which are all considered sources of power and therefore should accompany and strengthen each other during the same ritual. Very important among these is the meditation (*dhyāna*), i.e. the creation of a mental world in which the situation aimed at is realized in a forceful way. The meditation creates the deity concerned sometimes in combination with the victim of the ritual. Some examples have been discussed above in connection with other acts. There are also specific Śānti meditations. We refer at first to S which (p. 199ff.) contains meditations on Viṣṇu for pacification, accompanied by regulations for his worship. Here we are on the border between magic and religion—if such a border is ever to be demarcated sharply. The aims for which this meditation may be applied are: cure of the diseased, birth of a son, cure of obsession by evil planets, and the realization of various desires including final release. The passage has been taken from the Sanatkumārasaṃhitā. Viṣṇu should be meditated upon as follows: "bearing disc and conch, with four arms, wearing the diadem, provided with all his emblems, standing upon Garuḍa; honoured by all the lords of the sages headed by Sanaka, accompanied by Śrī and Bhūmi, his spouses, with the lustre of the rising sun, standing upon a maṇḍala of the sun which rises at dawn; intent upon the preservation of the whole world, without limit, eternal, showing the gestures of security and liberality, of friendly appearance"[67]. Also the minor gods which surround Viṣṇu have a pacificatory effect. TSS 18, 13 (=AgPur 306, 14) records the mantra *Namo Viṣṇugaṇebhyaḥ* (AgPur-*janebhyaḥ*) *sarvaśāntikarebhyo baliṃ gṛhṇantu śāntaye namaḥ* "Honour to Viṣṇu's folks who procure pacification in all respects, they should accept the tribute of rice, for pacification, honour." In 18, 1ff. (= AgPur 306, 5ff.) the TSS specially deals with Sudarśana, Viṣṇu's fiery disc. When meditated upon in a terrible form, provided with tusks and arms and a variety of weapons, while pervading the cosmos, it removes for the worshipper all base things done towards him and the evil influence of planets, and it will enable him to accomplish all results (st. 1: *kṣudragrahahṛt sarvasādhakam*). Ch. 18 of the TSS also contains the discussion of an Aghorāstramantra, which runs as follows: *hrīṃ sphura prasphura ghora ghoratara tanurūpa caṭa pracaṭa kaha vama bandha ghātaya huṃ phaṭ svāhā* "*Hrīṃ*, shake, shake violently, horrible One, intensely horrible One, of lean body, drive, drive away, eat (?), vomit, bind, strike,..." (st. 57). This mantra destroys all calamities, sorcery, evil planets, and disease. One might especially apply it in a bathing ceremony with the aid of ten pitchers filled with fragrant water, in order to reach pacification for sorcery, demons and so on (*kṣudrabhūtādiśāntaye*, st. 58). The deity to be meditated upon is the Rudra Aghora, the charactersitics of whose figure are described by the TSSC, *ad locum*.

Another instance has been taken from the SM (vol. 2, p. 532); it forms a part of the Rakta-Yamārisādhana (No. 270). This terrifying god of Tantric Buddhism usually assumes a red colour, as his name says, but this colour can be varied in accordance with the aims with which he is approached in meditation. In a Śānti context the god appears as white: "During a Śānti act there is protection by means of yellow pigment (?). On a piece of white cloth or on a piece of cleaned bark of the young birch one should design two ritual figures (*cakra* = *maṇḍala*), surround them with specimens of the word *namaḥ* "honour", place it within a platter which does not contain impure substances, putting it in a mixture of ghee and honey, wrap it up with a white thread and worship it on the three crucial points of the day with white flowers. One should meditate on the manifestation of the white Yamāntaka (= Yamāri) facing the East. Having observed the victim as sitting to the East thereof upon a maṇḍala of the moon, (the god) anoints him with white flowers which have been filled with the Water-of-life obtained from the moon. One should mutter the formula *Oṃ hrīḥ strīḥ*, O Thou of deformed face, perform pacification for N. N., honour, *svāhā*"[68]. Besides the method for pacification, there is one for welfare or acquisition (Pauṣṭikavidhi) characterized by the colour yellow; but its description starts with the information that it can be applied for Śānti as well as for Puṣṭi. The god this time faces the North. These methods are followed by one destined for subjugation in which the god is red and the victim is meditated upon as trembling and falling to the god's feet.

It its chapter on pacification, S contains some other instances of this kind of meditation. On p. 202 it records a pacification of fever taken from the Tantrarāja Tantra in which the victim should again be imagined as being anointed with Water-of-life from a vessel by the god Tumburu, a manifestation of Śiva (cf. Goudriaan, *Ibid.*). Tumburu should be worshipped in this context with white Dūrvā flowers which are considered particularly apt to promote longevity, presumably because of the association of Dūrvā) with *dūra-* "long"; the ceremony is declared to be conducive to welfare as well as to pacification. As one observes from the above instances, the Water-of-life (*amṛtam*) plays an important part in such meditations of Śānti. The person whose well-being the performer tries to further, is created in the mind as being showered with amṛta. Belief in amṛta as a pacifying power is a continuing element in Ancient Indian religion. It is expressed in ṚV 10, 9, where the Waters are addressed, especially in stanza 4 : *śáṃ no devī́r abhíṣṭaye* "the Waters, the goddesses, should stream towards us for hail"[67].

Objects of pacification. The appearances or persons against which a pacification is deemed necessary do not differ substantially in the texts of magic from those in other ritualist or dharma sources, Vedic and post-Vedic. It might be noted that in the Veda the Śānti is often connected by a grammatical construction with the persons or beings on whose behalf the ceremony is performed, like *śāntir gavām* "pacification for the benefit of kine" (against disease; AVPar 36, 2, 5), while in the younger sources the object of Śānti usually is the inimical power or being. Śānti is sought against a wide variety of powers and circumstances—against anything which may cause the fears and suspicions of the individual or the people. It cannot but strike the reader how often the object which needs to be pacified is expressed in vague terms: "evil", "calamity", "demons", "sorcery", and so on. On the one hand this reflects the vague feelings of fear which generally obtain in individual and social life of former as well as modern man; while on the other hand the exact cause of some disaster which really occurred was very often unknown. Śānti may refer to real occurrences—epidemics, war, sudden death—or only to those which threaten to happen or which are to be expected from evil forebodings. Besides, there is a positive aspect of Śānti, as we saw above: the securing of relative prosperity, generally covered by the term Puṣṭi (see below).

Taking now a short glance over the various objects of pacification expressed in the texts, the first thing to be considered is that sometimes the object feared is inimical sorcery, in most cases not specified further. As needs not to be emphasized, the fear of magic is indeed a current factor in traditional societies. We refer to one recent instance told by Ishwaran (p. 106f.): a cow produced blood instead of milk. A neighbour of the owner had shortly before observed a certain person collect the dung of that cow; and that person was suspected of having performed the magic. The sorcerer may be known or not; a protective ceremony will have often been felt to be necessary. The AV contains some passages aimed at counteracting sorcery (e.g., 2, 11). A Śānti in case of suspicion of sorcery (*abhicāraśaṅkāyām*) is ordained in MtPur 228, 4 quoted above. The TSS in 18, 50 describes a meditation on the Krodhāgnirudra who "removes all sorcery" (*sarvābhicārahṛt*). This chapter often contains references to *kṣudram* "vile deeds", probably to be explained by "evil magic". One can almost say that the author(s) is (are) haunted by this idea. A short sample :18,1 *kṣudragrahahṛt*; 18, 16 : *kṣudragrahāpahaḥ*; 18, 41f. *kṣudrādihṛt*; 18, 58 : *kṣudrabhūtādiśāntaye*; 18, 64 : *kṣudraṃ vinaśyet*. That magic is probably meant can be concluded from 18, 59f. where a ceremony is advised *kṣudraśāntaye* "for the pacification of evil deeds", while the TSSC, commenting on this passage, prescribes the recitation of the mantras *Yāṃ kalpayanti*...and *Yathā vidyut*..., both evidently directed against inimical magicians.

A few examples from the Tantras. JT 17, 68 says *bhayaṃ na vidyate devi paramantrābhicārajam* "there is no fear...from sorcery inflicted by the spells of others." In the same chapter, st. 87, the worship of a certain black maṇḍala with a sorcerer's name inscribed in it will be sufficient for destroying the sorcerer's spells (*cakraṃ kṛṣṇaṃ yadārcayet, yasya nāmāṅkitaṃ tasya mantrahāniḥ prajāyate*). In this last case, the identity of the sorcerer is at least known. PST 24, 27 : *mantrauṣadhābhicārikakṛtān vikārān ayaṃ manuḥ śamayet* "this mantra will pacify the evil consequences produced by acts of sorcery, by means of spells and potent herbs." Abhicāra is also mentioned in this context in PST 24, 56 and 27, 48 (*ghoratare 'bhicāre*). The same text, 30, 79, speaks of the Vedic concept of the *kṛtyā*, a female evil spirit evoked by the sorcerer and sent to the victim. The *kṛtyāḥ* are said to be accompanied by diseases (*rogasahitāḥ*). On this point not so much seems to have changed since the days of the AV (see above, p. 219). The SST (3, 14, 58) advises to use a certain method *parābhicāranāśārthaṃ svarakṣārthaṃ yathāvidhi* "destined for the destruction of the sorcery committed by others, and for the sufficient protection of oneself."

Vague circumscriptions of that against which Śānti is sought occur in the AV, e.g. in 19. 9, 14 *tā́bhiḥ śā́ntibhiḥ sarvaśāntibhiḥ śamayāmy aháṃ yád ihá ghoráṃ yád ihá krūráṃ yád ihá pāpám* "by these means of pacification which pacify the whole I pacify anything which is terrible, which is cruel and which is evil in our surroundings". The same vagueness is continued in terms like *duḥkhaśāntiḥ* "pacification of sorrow" (PST 9, 37); in PST 30, 79 the sorrows are brought about by different kinds of demons and by enemies: *tāṃs tān bhūtapiśācavairivihitān duḥkhān asau nāśayet.* There is also *drohaśāntiḥ* "pac. of injury or damage", or perhaps: "pac. of deceit", especially promised in the TSS. We mention TSS 18, 27 (*drohaśāntaye*); 18, 35 (*drohahṛd bhuvi*); 20, 44 where the *drohaḥ* appears to be directed especially against the crops (TSSC : *ukteṣu yogeṣu kṣetradrohaśāntikareṣu*; read also *kṣetradroha-* instead of *kṣatradroha-* in TSS 18, 26); the crops to be protected against *droha-* are also mentioned in 18, 39f. : *sasyādike...govarāhamṛgādibhyaḥ...droho na jāyate* "no damage to the crops is inflicted by kine, swine, deer and other such animals." We have also *vighnaśāntiḥ* "pac. of obstructions" which occurs in SM, No. 181 (vol. 2, p. 367). Man is indeed "afflicted by all kinds of obstructions" (*sarvavighnair upadrutaḥ*, PST 36, 4); with the term *upadruta-* one can compare the various passages in the PST which mention *upadravaśāntiḥ* "pac. of calamities" (e.g., 13, 49; 24, 22; 30, 87 *naśyanty upadravāḥ*; 14, 36 has *vipad* as a synonym). Other instances are to be found in the TSS, like *vipadaḥ* (18, 4); a method is *āpadbhayāpaham* (23, 37); the Śūlinīvidyā is *sarvopadravanāśini* (22, 11); a mantra of Narasiṃha is *sakalāpannivāraṇaḥ* "driving away all calamity" (18, 49; the version in AgPur 306, 18 has *sakalāghanivāraṇaḥ*). *Bhayaḥ* "fear" or "danger" is pacified according to PST 28, 24 ff. (a protective yantra against all sorts of disease and danger) and 30, 84 (*bhītiḥ*). MtPur 228, 5 prescribes the Abhayā "Secure" Śānti in the case that a terrible danger might arise. MtPur 70, 62 mentions pacification of "evil" with the term *sarvapāpapraśamanam*; TSS 25, 58 refers to the "destruction of stains" (*malakṣayaḥ*).

A circumstance in which a man felt a special need for a ceremony which would guarantee him security from danger, was the undertaking of a journey. We find various instances of it in the Veda, where Pūṣan acts as a protective god in such a circumstance[68]. In the TS (3, 4, 10, 3) the verb *śamayati* occurs in connection with a journey of the sacrificer: when the latter would depart from home without having sacrificed to Vāstoṣpati, the lord of the homestead, Rudra would kill him on the way; for Vāstoṣpati is Rudra; therefore one should perform a sacrifice for Vāstoṣpati, and thus he pacifies him by allotting his share to him (*bhāgadhéyenaivái̇nam śamayati, nártim árchati*). Other places from the Veda are AV 3, 17; KauśS 18, 27-31; 24, 11-17; 50, 1-11; and cf. the Ṛgvidh., 1, 18, 4. The Tantras contain promises of security against danger during a journey at sea; thus KCT 3, 203 mentions a storm in a list of evils that are eliminated.

An almost ubiquitous phenomenon is the Śānti directed against disease of all kinds. The instances are so numerous from the ṚV onwards that we feel entitled to pass them here in silence, leaving them for a special study[69]. A few Tantric examples: JT 17, 59f. (in one breath with *sapatnāḥ*, rivals); TSS 15 (*āmayadhvaṃsapaṭala*); 18, 41; 20, 39; SST 3, 15, 23 (advocating suitable herbs at the same time); PST 14, 36; 24, 27; 27, 48; 27, 29; 30, 79. S p. 199f. advocates a meditation on Viṣṇu against illness (discussed above, p.398). On p. 209, S presents a still other device, this time taken from "Hārīta" against fever caused by the influence of evil asterisms (*nakṣatra-doṣāj jvaraśāntiḥ*). On p. 213 there is a *dhāraṇi* from the same source for the same end. We emphasize that also the Mahāmāyā fragment, st. 16, promises for the yogin the annihilation of all disease and continuance of life (see above, p.139).

The pacification of evil omina is another very extensive subject on which only a few words are spent here. There are a great number of evil forebodings classified according to certain standards. One group is constituted by those which occur in the sky (*divya-*) and the most important of these are caused by the influence of the planets (*grahāḥ*). *Grahaśānti* is treated by Kane (p. 736); the PST mentions it in 14, 36; 27, 26f.; 30, 84.;

D, ch. 26, is called *Bhūtagrahanivāraṇam* "Driving away demons and evil planets." Graha and Bhūta are often mentioned as causes of disease; TSS has methods against Grahas in ch. 13 (*Grahadhvaṃsapaṭala*); some methods are effective against "vile deeds" (*kṣudra*) and Grahas at the same time (e.g., 18, 1; 18, 16; 18, 20). TSS 23, 6 gives the impression that there is little difference between Grahas and demons: "Grahas and the like run away, shouting with fear, leaving their victim alone" (*prayānti hitvā taṃ grastam ārtanādā grahādayaḥ*). To return to the Śānti of omina, KCT 2, 107ff. states that this feat can be realized by the adept performer (*siddhayogin*), a statement which can be compared to stanza 15 of the Mahāmāyā fragment. There the yogin who performs Prāyaścitta is said to be ablc to pacify thousands of certain kinds of evil omina, doubtlessly meant as examples in order to illustrate the performer's competence in the field. These examples are Ulkāpāta, Śilāvarṣa, Nakṣatradhūma and Grahayuddha. Ulkāpāta refers to the "falling of meteors" which is often mentioned in the texts as a very dangerous phenomenon. In AV 19, 9, 9, we read *nákṣatram ulkā́bhihataṃ śám astu naḥ* "the fact that an asterism has been hit by a meteor should be pacified for us." The characteristics of Ulkāpāta as an omen are discussed in the AVPar, ch. 58b (cf. the book by Kohlbrugge)[70]. Śilāvarṣa "rain of stones" refers to hail; it was often endeavoured to conjure the detrimental effects of hailstones on the crops[71]. For Nakṣatradhūma "smoke on asterisms" we found no exact parallel. Varāhamihira (in BṛhSaṃh 45, 83) mentions *rajodhūmaḥ* "smoke of the space" (cf. Kane, 1962, p. 768). Grahayuddha "fight of planets" refers to the opposition of planets. Kane (1958, p. 587) presents the doctrine of Garga, repeated in the Adbhutasāgara, that Grahayuddha is the case when of two planets the one somewhat obscures the other or covers it, or with its light drives away the light of the other, or takes up a position immediately to the left of the other. There are tables which teach which planets are friendly or inimical to each other on certain points of time (Kane, 1958, p. 586). The AVPar treats Grahayuddha in ch. 51.

Other objects for which Śānti may be sought are evil dreams (for instances in the Veda, cf. Kane, 1962, p. 728f.; see also 774f.) which are mentioned in PST 24, 23; wild animals, for which we refer to AVPar 36, 27: KCT 3, 203: PST 14, 36 (snake); 24, 24; D. ch. 28: *siṃhādibhayanāśanam*); this aspect of Śānti overlaps the acts of immobilization against wild animals discussed above (p. 347). Śānti of inimical behaviour in politics and of inimical weapons is the subject in AVPar 35, 2,10 (*rājābhayam*); 36, 24 (*raṇe...na jīyate*); MtPur 228, 5; PST 27, 29; SST 3, 14, 59 (*śatrunivāraṇam*). Of course the disposing of the danger from enemies by magical means is a subject which also overlaps other parts of the Ṣaṭkarman theory (see above, p. 325). Śānti is even possible against *moha*, the basic delusion which binds man to the round of births. It is mentioned in PST 27, 48 in a context of disease created by sorcery, and perhaps the word moha here only refers to—"attacks of fainting". (cf. Mohana, above p. 370). S (p. 200), however, mentions *mokṣa* among the results of the meditation on the healing Viṣṇu; in TSS 20, 41, *mukti* (=*mokṣa*) occurs among Puṣṭi aims. It seems that for a magician ultimate release could fall, at least in theory, within the range of Śānti.

Acquisition. Śānti is not only a passive defence against inimical powers, it also implies the very positive aspect of obtaining the better side of life: welfare, prosperity, happiness. This is what is called in the texts *puṣṭiḥ* "acquisition", literally: "a well-nourished condition" (in this more restricted sense called *śarīrapuṣṭiḥ* in TSSC 30, 29). Puṣṭi is often combined with Śānti in the basic threefold classification of ritual aims (see above, p. 95), and already in the ṚV (1, 114, 1b) *śam* and *puṣṭaṃ* occur in combination with each other (quoted by Kane, 1962, p. 719; see also Hoens, p. 179). S (st. 16) paraphrases Puṣṭi as *dhanajanādīnāṃ vardhanam* "increase in such values as wealth and people". A good idea of the range of this term is procured by AgPur 309, 13 (=TSS 22, 63f.) where oblations with different kinds of flowers or fruits are said to result in *dhanadhānnyāptiḥ* "gain of money and natural wealth", *tuṣṭiḥ* "satisfaction, *mahāpuṣṭiḥ* "great welfare" and *mahodayaḥ* "great rise in status" (this last term also in SST 3, 16, 25); and the list is continued by other objectives like *āyuḥ* "longevity", *lakṣmī* and *śrī* "welfare" or "lustre" and *dhana*. In the TSS, 18, 17ff., we find a list consisting of *brahmaśrī* "spiritual lustre", *āyuḥ*, *śrī*, *putrāḥ* "sons", *gosiddhiḥ* "success in cattle-breeding", *medhā* "wisdom" and *yakṣī* "mastery of a (wealth-spending) Yakṣiṇī"; TSS 18, 48: the results of a method applied with the mantra of eight syllables to Vāsudeva are that evil deeds (*kṣudra*), adversity and guilt are destroyed while protection, longevity, welfare and victory are obtained; it is further advised for the cure of cattle, children, pregnant women, and those stricken by evil planets [69]; in 23, 12 a method is called *āyuṣyaṃ pāvanaṃ puṣṭilakṣmisaubhāgya-vaśyakṛt* "leading to longevity and purification, and conducive to acquisition, welfare, domestic happiness and subjugation of others"; it further removes the danger from thieves, dangerous animals and water, promotes the birth of sons and protects the unborn child, and, again, destroys evil planets, disease, and vile deeds. In TSS 27, 9f. the results are that the performer will be able to memorize all sacred books, be healthy, live long and without fear for thieves, tigers, snakes and so on. Anything which is desirable occurs amongst the things to be acquired; in the words of the Lakṣmī Tantra: "he becomes dauntless on this earth, has good luck and a long life; beyond death he attains happiness" (LT 49, 53; trsl. by Gupta, p. 325).

As synonyms of Puṣṭi one might further mention *sakalā-bhyudayaḥ* "increase in all things" (PST 7, 66; cf. 7, 67; 23, 35); *samṛddhiḥ* "welfare" (PST 14, 38; Śānti and Samṛddhi combin-ed; PST 24, 53 *dhanadhānyasamṛddhagehaḥ* "his house is opulent in money and natural wealth"); *vṛddhiḥ sampadām* "increase of good things" (PST 32, 15); *āpyāyanam* "growth", "becoming fat" (PST 22, 53; S 44, p. 186); TSS 25, 48 = AgPur 301, 16).

Some values which sometimes serve as the motivation for acts of magic can best be considered as aspects of Puṣṭi. To these belongs the protection of the property. In TSS 18, 37 a device is called *gehagrāmādirakṣitā* "protector of the house, the village and so on" (as to the fields, cf. Drohaśānti above). Often remedies are sought against theft: TSS 23, 13 *cora... bhayāpaham* "removing the danger from thieves"; 30, 18 *coras tan na viśed gṛham* "a thief will not enter that house", a result effected with the aid of a meditation of Helakī. TSS 30, 17 contains a method for finding out a thief afterwards: *steye... coranāma na dahyate* "in case of theft...the thief's name is not burnt". A method for protecting merchandise is discussed in TSS 30, 35. The AgPur (302, end) contains a mantra destin-ed for securing the protection of cows which runs as follows: "*Oṃ*, honour to the Venerable Tryambaka; pacify pacify,....,

..., split split....O Thou (female deity) Who appearest as a cow, Who wieldest the disc, *huṃ phaṭ*; in this village perform perform protection and pacification of the cowshed". A śloka follows which mentions Ghaṇṭākarṇa the "forceful man with a great army and great power" as the destroyer of Mārī (goddess of pestilence); he is further addressed as a lord of the earth for protection. These ślokas are styled "protecting the cattle" [70]. A pacification of cattle (*śāntir gavām*) occurs also in AVPar 36, 2, 5. The Tantras occasionally mention protection of property in general terms, for instance when PST 32, 22 promises security from thieves, demons or serpents.

Acquisition of property or food (or destruction of poverty) is offered various times in the TSS; thus in 20, 37 (recitation of the Viṣṇuhṛdaya mantra combined with a sacrifice of Bilvas) *tatkule na daridraḥ syāt* "no beggar will there be in his family"; 26, 31 *taṃ muñcati daridratā* "poverty leaves him" (worship of Maṇibhadra); 26, 35ff. (Jambhala/Maṇibhadra); 30, 36 (Annapūrṇā; food); 30, 37 (Maṇibhadra). Debts are to vanish by the power of the Jyeṣṭhāmantra (30, 36). Increase in land (*bhūvṛddhiḥ*) is realized by the Bhūhṛdayamantra directed to Goddess Earth (20, 45). In 30, 33 a method turns out to be directed against mice and other harmful animals which consume fruits and crops. A special aim is the finding back of lost property for which a method is offered in the HT (*naṣṭadravyānveṣaṇam*, ch. 2) by means of conjuring spirits who point out the thief (cf. Webster, p. 293); in TSS 30, 48 it is promised that anything lost, including a woman, a man and a cow, will be won back.

Another important aim connected with Puṣṭi and mentioned already above is *āyuḥ* "longevity", which means the guarantee of a continuation of life, if possible up to the traditional ideal limit of a hundred years. In the Veda the AitBr (13, 10) contains a stanza on Śānti for securing the long life of the sacrificer (Kane, 1962, p. 721 f.; for longevity, see also p. 737; 757f.). The "hundred years" still occur in the AgPur (313, 18). And PST 27, 48 says : *tanoti śāntiṃ na cireṇa homaḥ sañjivanaṃ cābdaśatapramāṇam* "such an oblation secures pacification within a short time, and continuation of life up till the limit of a hundred years". The same text, without using the term Śānti, promises in 26, 73: *dhanavibhavayaśaḥśrisaṃpadā dirghajivi* "one will be in the possession of longevity combined with wealth, status, fame, lustre and welfare". Instances from the TSS are 27, 9 (*ciraṃ jīvet*); 20, 38 (sudden death is avoided); and 17, 78, where one who desires longevity is advised regularly to guard the tree which agrees with his horoscope (*nakṣatrataru*).[72]

Another ideal is the obtaining of wisdom or intellect. Pāṇini the famous grammarian realized this aim by austerities and worship of Śiva according to the Kathās. (1, 4, 20ff.); originally he is said to have been a student of very mediocre intelligence. We find various places which contain advices for acquiring strength of intelligence or memory by magical means. Among these are AVPar 36, 18 (for one's son); 36, 24, 2 AgPur 309, 15 (omniscience); SVBr 7, 4 (being able to recitc the Scriptures); T, p. 383; PST 9, 29 (one becomes "an abode of Sarasvatī"); 24, 41; SST 3, 21, 27 (knowledge of threefold time); 3, 21, 35 (eloquence); TSS 25, 85 (for a good memory; worship Vyāsa); 26, 55 (idem; worship Vāmana); 27, 9ff. (knowing all Scriptures; being wise and eloquent). A variety is stated in SST 2, 56, 8: *gurur bhavet* "one will become a guru". Social status is implied in passages like TSS 20, 41 (*suyaśaḥ*) or TSS 21, 33 (mastery in a village). Regaining the lost position of a ruler is the subject in TSS 26, 13: *tenābhiṣecayed rājyabhraṣṭaṃ tat so 'cirāl labhet* "with this one should anoint (a ruler) who has lost his kingdom, and he will regain it soon."

A goal mentioned shortly here is the gift of obtaining children, for which we refer to AgPur 323,14; SST 3, 19, 57; TSS 20, 41; 27, 22f.; 29, 22ff. A variety is called *Bandhyāputravatikaraṇam* (D ch. 18) "causing a barren woman to bear a son".

This rapid survey of the aims for which rituals of Śānti and Puṣṭi have been commonly executed shows that these aims cover a field almost as broad as the totality of human striving. We saw that Śānti-Puṣṭi in some cases overlaps other aspects of the Six Acts; Śānti is sufficient in itself to secure goals which have also been sought for by means of other expedients which were at the disposal of the specialists. Besides, because these objectives are usually common to all human endeavour, it is reasonable to expect their occurrence also among the results obtained by the "higher" religious activities such as worshipping or praising a deity (see also above, p.59f.). That this is indeed the case can be amply demonstrated by the numerous *phalaśruti-* "statements of rewards" attached to literary works and especially to the stotras or hymns to the gods. As an example we quote the praise of the results of a stotra to Śiva sung by Bāṇāsura (to be found in the BrVPur, Brahmakhaṇḍa, 19, 67ff.) [71]:

"That man who recites with devotion this stotra which procures good results, he without any doubt obtains the results of bathing in all holy watering places; one who lacks a son obtains a son, if he listens to it for one year...(worshipping Śiva)...; he who is in an advanced state of leprosy or who suffers from acute attacks of gouts will be certainly released from his illness if he listens to it during a year...; the man who is bound in prison will obtain security: having heard this stotra during a month he is certainly released from his bondage. Someone who has lost his kingdom will recover it...who has lost his money will regain it....he who is consumed by tuberculosis...is certainly released from his illness by the grace of the Gracious God; for one who constantly listens to this lord of hymns with devotion, nothing is beyond his reach in the threefold world...; never will he be parted from his dear ones...and he obtains unshakable paramount sovereignty without any doubt; he who listens to it during one month concentratedly and devotedly—one who lacks a wife obtains a wife who is gentle, faithful and desirable; and a great blockhead of dull intelligence who listens to it during one month obtains intelligence and wisdom by the mere teaching of his teacher; he who suffers because of his evil deeds and who is poor will certainly obtain wealth after listening a month to it by the grace of the Gracious God; having enjoyed happiness in this world and procured for himself unique fame as well as religious merit of various kinds, one will in the end reach the Abode of Śiva...".

The divine nature of Śānti. All ritual has its counterpart in mythology and its basic motivation in a certain evaluation of reality. It is not different with the idea of Śānti. The ritual way open to man for the pacification of his own or his client's environment also opens for him the prospect of an earthly parallel of the characteristics of divine existence. The state of being *śānta-*, pacified, which means free from all defects and dangers, can even be compared to the realization of ultimate release. The state of Śānti (or the absence of such a state) can be recognized also in the dealings of God with the world. In the first place there are two poles of divine bearing which may be called *śānta* "pacified" and *ghora* "terrible". Seen from this angle, *śānta* thus becomes a synonym of *aghora* (cf. Hoens, p. 180 and the mantra of the Mahāmāyā fragment); instead of *ghora*, we also find *ugra* as the counterpart of *śānta* (e.g. in the KālPur; van Kooy, p. 32f.). In his terrible manifestation God produces evils which torment mankind, as is implied in the BhPur (3,2,15):

Svaśāntarūpeṣv itaraiḥ svarūpair
abhyardyamāneṣv anukampitātmā |
parāvareśo mahadaṃśayukto
hy ajo 'pi jāto Bhagavān yathāgniḥ ||

"when His own pacific manifestations are being tormented by other manifestations of Himself, the Lord of far and near out of His compassionate nature, though unborn, incarnates Himself with a mighty part of His essence, just as a fire (kindled from another fire)."

The divine state of Śānti is characterized further by a synonym *ātmarata-* "taking pleasure in the Self", "absorbed in the Self". God needs no others beside Him; His own existence is sufficient, because He embodies the whole of existence. The Śivapūjāstava, st. 18 (Aithal, p. 265) describes Sadāśiva as *śānta*; in the Śivagaurī-stotra by Jñānaśiva, st. 12 (Aithal, p. 261), Dattātreya is called *śānta* and *ātmamāyārata* "taking pleasure in His own Māyā". The term *śāntamāya* can also occur (e.g. in Kathās. 12, 25, 76). The author of the GarPur (195, 3) addresses Vāsudeva as *ātmarāma* and *śānta*, and free from the erroneous insight of duality: *ātmarāmāya śāntāya nivṛtadvaitadṛṣṭaye.* Yet this God incorporates all manifestations: *tvaṃ rūpāṇi casa rvāṇi.*

It appears that the *śānta* or pacified state can also mean the unevolved state in which God is sufficient to Himself (cf. LT 18, 19; Gupta, p. 99) and needs not to obscure His being by the acts of His power of evolution, māyā or śakti. His māyā can be pacified, as can be His śakti; in the BhPur we read: *namo 'stu tasmai upaśāntaśaktaye* "honour be to Him Whose dynamic force has become pacified". In the imagery of mythology, this relation of God, Who is śānta, and the terrible aspects of

His śakti can be represented, as we saw above, by the figure of a god (or sage) in the Centre, surrounded by ferocious females in the directions of the sky.

This aspect of Śānti as the absence of evolution, which means of transformation of perfection into imperfection is also expressed by the relation of the terms *śānta* and *mūḍha*, "pacified and "deluded". The Trimūrti, the threefold manifestation of the unique God as the Creator, Maintainer and Dissolver of the universe, has been characterized in the DevīBhPur by the three states of being *śānta*, *ghora* and *mūḍha* (see above, p.50f.). On the plane of human existence there are the *śāntāḥ* mentioned in MuUp 1, 2, 11 as the counterpart of the *mūḍhāḥ* in 1, 2, 7 and 8. *Mūḍha* means: under the sway of *moha*, the cosmic delusion the cause of which is the divine Māyā (see p. 20f.) and Śānti implies the absence of such māyā. A way to reach this state is yoga, which is apt to clean, literally "pacify" human affliction or soilure (*kleśapraśamāyālam*, ViPur 6, 6, 49), it leads to the state of ultimate release, described in the ViPur (6, 6, 21) as follows:

Mohaśrame śamaṃ yāte svasthāntaḥkaraṇaḥ pumān |
ananyātiśayābādhaṃ paraṃ nirvāṇam ṛcchati ||

"When the fatigue of delusion has come to rest, man, being of sound self, reaches the supreme state of peace which is not oppressed by the superiority of something else". On the other side, for those who are deluded, there is no Prāyaścitta, as was emphasized by Yudhiṣṭhira (see above, p. 17). Life is magic; the glamour of the world is a product of Indrajāla (*jāgati hendrajālaśrī*, YogV, Utpattiprakaraṇa, 104, 1).[73]

The essence of the experience which brings about spiritual Śānti is, in simple words, the realization of the unity behind the manifold appearance of existence. Already in the Veda, *prāyaścitti* can be effected by means of a completeness, an undivided whole: *tad anena sarveṇa prāyaścittiṃ kurute* "so with this All he makes expiation" (JBr 1, 53: trsl. Bodewitz, p. 164; the "All" is represented by the *vyāhṛti mantra*; cf. also Bodewitz, p. 100). For the human performer, the Śānti effected on the ritual plane thus becomes the function of an integrative experience. The integration concerns a number of manifestations that are unbalanced, unable to effect the good, and even dangerous in themselves. In the category of time they may be the seasons without reference to the year; in that of place: the directions of the sky without reference to the Centre; in the human body: the life-breaths without the Ātman, or the natural elements water, earth, etc. without the Prāṇa or Ātman (cf. MNT 7.97f.). During life, man is an integrative combination of these elements; when someone has died, it is said that he has "fallen asunder into five", *pañcatvaṃ gataḥ*. On the cosmical plane one could say that during creation the Cosmical being has diversified Himself into five : *sa eva māyayā deva pañcadhā saṃsthito Hariḥ* "This same Viṣṇu, O god, exists as fivefold by the agency of the Māyā" (GarPur 32, 4). In the Mahāmāyā fragment, this fivefold appearance of Viṣṇu's Māyā is realized by means of the delusive series of colours. Its aim is not to enable the performer to pick out one of these appearances in order to apply it to an individual act of magic. Its aim is to lead him through a meditative course of supranormal power, a kind of spiritual *pradakṣiṇā*, in order to "release him from all evil" (st. 1) and to create within him that vision of the divine as the harmony of seemingly horrible and contradicting appearances which is called Prāyaścitta. We can compare the symbol of the colours with that of society; the yogin by his position outside the four grades of society (the same word *varṇāḥ*) as it were forms a fifth grade in which the other four are combined, as is said in the HT (ch. 6): "for the man who performs the yoga of Heruka there is association with five varṇas possible; by a combination of these five, one varṇa is constituted, because no difference can be observed between this unique varṇa and a multiplicity of them"[72].

Śānti as the state which results from the integration of the seemingly diffuse world of appearances amounts to ultimate release (*mukti*). But it realizes itself already in this world by the gift of the good life on earth (*bhukti*); also the Mahāmāyā fragment has been applied for "warding off all diseases and calamities" (Stuti & Stava, p. 275). In the Purāṇic and Tantric world view, *bhukti* and *mukti* are always complementary. The adept who realizes Śānti becomes divine; his antagonists are dispersed or annihilated; his place is in the centre of existence; he is *akutobhayaḥ* "without danger from anywhere".

NOTES

Chapter 1

1. J. Gonda, *Māyā*; in: Gonda, 1965, p. 164-197.

2. Gonda, 1965, p.166.

3. Prabhu Dutt Shastri, *The Doctrine of Māyā in the Philosophy of the Vedānta*, London 1911 (Thesis Kiel), p.14.

4. Shastri, *o. c.*, p.30f.; according to Gonda, 1965, p. 166, n. 12.

5. Oldenberg, p.129.

6. Kluckhohn, p.8; it should be noted that, according to Kluckhohn, p. 226, n.7, "the Navaho tend to think of both ceremonial practitioners and 'witches' as, in a larger sense, placed in the same category", so that, in that particular cultural environment, there seems to be little room for the sharp distinction made by E.E. Evans-Pritchard in his study on the Azande between "witchcraft" and "sorcery" (cf. Marwick, p. 24f.). In the present study we do not deal with witchcraft in its more restricted sense and, as a consequence, we shall avoid the use of this term in the sequel.

7. See also Oldenberg, *l.c.*; Devanandan, p. 23.

8. Gonda, 1965, p. 167; māyā is even the Veda of the Asuras according to ŚatBr 13, 4, 3, 11; one might compare the neutrality of magic (Webster, p. 378).

9. Reyna, p. 98, quoting the translation by Hume. On p. 5, Reyna speaks of "the later Upaniṣadic development of the word in the sphere of metaphysics as meaning the power of manifestation of the Absolute".

10. Webster, p. 246.

11. The English place name Grimsdyke still recalls that Woden as Grim "Masked One" once wandered there and built a dyke or mole on the spot. See Sir Frank Stenton, *Anglo-Saxon England,* Oxford 1947, p. 100. In the Edda, Loki could accuse Woden of having performed magic and having wandered on earth disguised as a witch (Julio Caro Baroja, in: Marwick, p. 90).-In Irish mythology, the god of shape-changing is Manannán: M. Dillon / N. K. Chadwick, *The Celtic Realms*, London 1967, p. 151.

12. J. H. Hooykaas—van Leeuwen Boomkamp, *De Goddelijke Gast op Bali, I Bagoes Diarsa,* Bandung 1949.

13. H. Oertel, *Indra in the guise of a woman,* in: JAOS, vol. 26, 1905, p. 176-188, and especially H. Oertel, *Contributions from the Jaiminīya-Brāhmaṇa* in the same volume, p. 192-196.

14. JaimBr 1, 363; SadvBr 1, 6, 9-18. Both texts prescribe a prāyaścitta in the form of a Vyāhṛtimantra.

15. Hillebrandt, in: Wiener Zeitschrift für die Kunde des Morgenlandes, 13, 1899, p. 317f.

16. ŚatBr 3, 3, 4, 15; trsl. Eggeling, vol. II, p.80.

17. Tripathi, p. 42f. According to Tripathi, shape-changing was an inherent part of the divine nature of both Indra and Viṣṇu.

18. Cf. also A.B. Keith, in : JRAS, 1911, p. 989; H. Oldenberg, in : Göttingische Gelehrte Anzeigen, 1911, p. 462.

19. J.A.B. van Buitenen, *The Pravargya*, Poona 1968 (Deccan College Building Centenary and Silver Jubilee Series, 58), p. 147.

20. ŚatBr 3, 2, 1, 26. Cf. Oldenberg, p. 22.

21. Cf. Eggeling's note on ŚatBr 3, 3, 4, 19. A different explanation is given by Sāyaṇa on TAr 1, 12, 4.

22. Wendy Doniger O'Flaherty, in a review of Tripathi's book in BSOAS, 33, 1970, p. 217-220.

23. K. Geldner, *The Ṛgveda*, vol.I, p. 64.

24. H. Oertel, *Indra in the guise of a woman.* (see above, n. 13).

25. Eggeling's trsl. of the ŚatBr, vol. II, p. 81.

26. PD, vol. V, p. 903.

27. AitBr 6, 1, 3; ed. Satyavrata Sāmaśramī, BI, vol. 134, III, 1896.

28. Also gurus may change their shape in order to test their pupils. This was done by Tilopa, the guru of Nāropa. See Wilhelm, p. 57ff.

29. *Stories as told by Swami Ramdas*, Bombay, Bhavan's Book University, 1961, p. 93, title : How Pride Deludes.

30. A. Bergaigne, *Les religions védiques*, repr. 1963. vol. I, p. XXV

31. Oldenberg, p. 25, translating TBr 1, 8, 3, 3. Oldenberg argues that immoral behaviour of the gods is not merely due to a lack of the moral sense in the Vedic period, because the Vedic texts sometimes do betray moral reflexion. Also in the Icelandic Edda the demons are strong, the gods crafty (Zimmer, p. 208f.). Jacques (p. 247) is vague about the morals of the gods.

32. Hillebrandt, *Vedic Mythology*, II, p. 153 and 231.

33. AitBr 7, 28 (adhyāya 35, 2); trsl. A.B. Keith, p. 314.

34. Gonda, 1970, p. 124; 136. For a different view by Tripathi, see above, n. 17.

35. AV 10, 5, 25; Shende, p. 155.

36. Gonda, 1965, p. 173; Devanandan, p. 66.

37. See also J. Estlin Carpenter, *Theism in Medieval India*, London 1921, p. 157, who paraphrases the present passage.

38. Cf. Henry, p. 238.

39. Mrcchakaṭika, act 6; p. 320 in the edition by Ramanuja Ojha, Benares, Haridas Skt. Series, 1962; Engl. trsl. in Winternitz/Jha, vol. III, p. 230.

40. Tripurārahasya, Jñānakhaṇḍa, trsl. A. U. Vasuvada, Benares 1965, p. 76.

41. Translated by Bhandarkar, p. 91.

42. Cf. Kane, 1962, p. 975.

43. Oberhammer, p. 38; 91f.; 130.

44. KūPur 12, 262 (acc. to Jhavery, p. 101); van Kooy, p. 30f.; BrVPur, Kṛṣṇajanmakhaṇḍa, 128, 27; for other instances from the Purāṇas, cf. Kane, 1962, p. 975, who also records a refutation in KulT, 2, 96.

45. See also p. 356, for the idea of *bhramaḥ*.

46. Translation by Surajit Sinha, *Vaiṣṇava influence on a tribal culture*, in: Singer, p. 83. Udayana, in the concluding verse of his Nyāyakusumāñjali, prays that God may attract towards Himself by His supranormal power the sceptics who are not convinced by rational arguments (Chemparathy, p. 156).

47. Cf., in general, Vora, p. 211-221.

48. Cf. Gonda, 1970, p. 128; the same book, p. 212, n. 247, for other references about the subject.

49. Cf. F. Weller, *Duryodhana's Ende*, Stuttgart 1933, p. 19 : "Krischna geht in die verderbenbringende Keule ein wie eine physische oder magische Kraft. . . ."

50. Bhāsa, Dūtavākya, I, 23ff.

51. Cf. Vora, p. 220, who is unable to restrain his indignation with Kṛṣṇa's views.

52. Thus Jīva Goswamin and others; cf. Dimock in Singer, p. 55f. One should consult the latter volume for a closer acquaintance with the motifs of Kṛṣṇa and the cowherdesses.

53. Cf. Gonda, 1970, p. 111, who gives no references. A variant of this legend can be found in Dessigane, 1964, p. 55.

54. Cf. Tripathi, p. 3f.

55. Devanandan, p. 132.

56. For particulars, cf. Tripathi.

57. Bhāsa, Bālacarita, I, 6; ed. Devadhar, *Plays ascribed to Bhāsa*, p. 512: *Māyayā śiśutvam upāgataṃ Trilokeśvaraṃ pragṛhya Vasudevena saha (Devakī) svagṛhān niṣkrāmati.*

58. MtPur 167; BhPur 12, 9, 20ff.

59. "Unfolding" : *vijṛmbhitam*, lit.: "gaping", "yawning"· In Kathās. 12, 25, 51ff., a spell produces an illusory world called *māyāvijṛmbhitam*. Demons summoned are sometimes characterized by this activity of *jṛmbhati* or *jambhati*, e.g. in AgPur 134; Mbh. 3, 23, 18f. See p. 378.

60. Kalkin, most often represented as a mounted horseman; another horse incarnation is Hayagrīva (Gonda, 1970, p. 124ff.). MtPur 93, 69 alludes to the tradition that a white horse came from the ocean when the Water-of-Life was being churned, and identifies this horse with Viṣṇu. According to the DevīBhPur (6, 18, 50ff.), Viṣṇu in horse shape united with Lakṣmī and thus became the ancestor of the tribe of the Haihayas.

61. Gonda, 1970, resp. on p. 125; 151; 153.

62. Gonda, 1970, p. 150.

63. This occurrence is also described in the *Mahimnaḥ stava*, st. 18 (*Rathaḥ kṣoṇī*). A picture is to be found in W. Norman Brown's translation of that hymn.

64. Rājaśekhara, Karpūramañjarī, ed. Konow-Lanman, p. 30, text; p. 238f., trsl., and p. 239, n. 2; Kālidāsa, Mālatimādhava, ed. M. R. Telang V.L.S. Pansikar, 6th ed. 1936, p. 118; KālPur 67, 1 (van Kooy, p. 154).

65. In the version of DevīBhPur 6, 26, 37, the monkey face is due to a curse pronounced by Nārada's friend Parvata.

66. There is some similarity with the seventh of the twelve tests undergone by Nāropa; cf. Wilhelm, p. 63.

67. On Rudra's malevolence in the Veda, cf. Arbman; Gonda, 1970, p. 4.

68. For instance, Pañcabrahma Up 25; Māṇikka Vācakar, Hymn III (Pope, p. 26).

69. For particulars on the Dāruvana legend, cf. Kulke, p. 46-94; for the

epigraphic sources, cf. Pathak, p. 29. Pathak also refers to the Halāyudha-stotra which presents an excuse for Śiva's conduct.

70. Some references have been collected in Gonda, 1970, p. 124f.; p.210, n. 207; n. 212. We add AgPur 3, 18 ff. and BrVPur, Kṛṣṇajanmakhaṇḍa, ch. 31ff., where Mohinī is described as an Apsaras and friend of Rambhā; she falls in love with Brahmā. On the Mohinī legend in the Indonesian Korawāśrama, see J. Gonda, *Śiva in Indonesien*, in : WZKSO, 17, 1970, p. 17.

71. Brahmāṇḍa Purāṇa, according to Adiceam, p. 7. More references in the Āgamas; the Suprabhedāgama also relates that Śiva was seduced by Mohinī at the time of the churning of the ocean: Adiceam, p. 8, and the same book, p. 20, for popular versions.

72. Being a Śākta text, the DevīBhPur extols the Māyā as the possession of the Great Goddess, but this does not essentially affect the argument.

73. This might be considered as a case of siddhi obtained by bathing; for a literary parallel we refer to Kathās. 12, 25, 51ff.

74. The present legend occurs in several Purāṇas, according to Kosambi, p. 77. Zimmer, a master of vagueness, gives a version on p. 37ff. without mentioning its source.

75. Reference and text according to Jhavery, p. 95. Durgā is also called in the stanza in question *Ātharvaṇasya duhite* "Daughter of the Atharvaveda tradition".

76. Dasgupta, p. 362. In another source of the Dharma cult, Lord Dharma after the creation of the world changed himself into a lady and then in his male manifestation united himself with her.

77. Kabīr, *Au cabaret de l'Amour*, trad. Ch. Vaudeville, Paris 1955, p.112f.

78. Bergaigne, p. XVIII; and cf. Gonda, 1965, p.167.

79. Stuti & Stava, Nos. 516, 842, 887. In India, Narasiṃha is still worshipped in the Andhra region (Ramesan, p. 24ff.; 136ff.).

80. Although we have perhaps lost much of our sensitiveness for visions of terror, it is worth recalling that at the time of the explosion of the first atomic bomb above Hiroshima, Robert Oppenheimer, its deviser, is said to have recalled just this vision of the Terrible Viṣṇu "whose fearful rays burn the world'.

81. In Balinese art, this function is discharged in the *wajang* shadow theatre by the Pamurtian, a "many-headed figure representing a transcendental state of anger" (C. Hooykaas, *Pamurtian in Balinese art*, in: Indonesia, No.12, Ithaca, N.Y., Oct. 1971, p.1-20).

Chapter 2

1. The same conviction exists in Tantrism: Gonda, 1963, p. 29f. There is a richly documented tradition of microcosmic-macrocosmic identification by ascetics and yogins; cf. Eliade, p.114, 127.

2. Cf. Hermanns, as summarized by Pinnow in : ZDMG, 119, 1970, p.395-399.

3. Compare the Vaikhānasa *ātmasūktam*, a hymn which is meant to guide the enlargement of the priest's consciousness to cosmic size (edited and translated in IIJ, 12, 1970, p. 212ff.); and also Rangachari. p, 141; C. G.

Diehl, *Instrument and Purpose*, Lund 1956, p. 115, 117; 139; Gonda, 1963, p. 34; van Kooy, p. 14, 17; for Bali: Hooykaas, p. 28f., 36f., 66-85.

4. Cf. Radin, p. 60. In the present book, the term "magic" is used in accordance with the second part of the definition given by Webster, p. 55, quoted here in full: "As a belief, it is the recognition of the existence of occult power, impersonal or only vaguely personal, mystically dangerous and nct lightly to be approached, but capable of being channeled, controlled, and directed by man. As a practice, magic is the utilization of this power for public or private ends, which are good or bad, orthodox or heterodox, licit or illicit, according to the estimate placed upon them by a particular society at a particular time." The magic is practised by individuals for themselves in private, or by specialists for their clients or the rulers of a community (or for that community as a whole). Destructive magic (a term to be preferred to the equivocal "black magic") can be socially approved or disapproved according to the circumstances (for these remarks we refer to R. Firth, *Human Types : An Introduction to Social Anthropology*, 1956, as excerpted in Marwick, p. 38). It should be noted that we feel fully entitled to refer to convictions felt in primitive religions in order to elucidate some features found in practical Hinduism. In Indian religion (we do not speak of other religions now) the elements of the world view which we are wont to call "primitive" were not always destroyed.

5. Many instances are presented by Webster, p. 39-44, among others from the Lushai and the Maria Gonds (in the latter case, the magic came from a Guru; see also Elwin, p. 61). In the mythology of the Korku, the Creator (Bhagwan) created a primeval magician for protecting mankind against demons and sorcerers (Hermanns, p. 207).

6. Iyer, p. 44, quoting Robert Briffault.

7. Iyer, p. 54. The same author describes how another Kerala tribe, the Mannāns, who have come more and more into the sphere of influence of the great tradition of Hinduism, usually invoke blessings of a pure material character (p. 217).

8. Rivers, p. 212. On p. 459, this author says : "these magical formulae of the Todas seem to show us a stage of magic in which religion has been called to its aid".

9. One may compare what Radin (p. 151) has to say on the role of magic in securing the everyday needs of the people even in complex agricultural societies which possess a priesthood proclaiming a spiritualized religion. On p. 154, after discussing instances from the Maori and the Ewe, Radin states that even in the worship of a Supreme Deity there remains an interplay of economic-magical and religious factors.

10. A good example is the PST which constantly refers to both these values.

11. Tattvasaṃgraha, p. 905, as quoted by B. Bhattacharya, p. XVII; also quoted by Kane, 1962, p. 1037. For a case in recent Buddhism, see Bareau, p. 24f.

12. K. Das, p. 72. On p. 42, this author describes how the villagers create their gods "as offsprings of their daily necessities".

13. For a short survey of the theories on this subject, we refer to Heiler, p. 27, repeating that we do not endorse this author's conclusions, nor those of Hermanns which reflect the views of the "Vienna school" of Father W. Schmidt (see Pinnow's recension referred to above in n. 2).

14. In primitive societies, the spirit world is thought to be loaded with magical power. When magic is practised in such a society, powerful spirits are often invoked and presented with sacrificial gifts before the ritual itself is executed (Webster, p. 44f.). On p. 113 Webster speaks about the Maori, whose gods always had to comply with the wishes of those who possessed the know-how necessary for realizing their goals. The Toda sorcerers proceeded in a similar manner; they also were wont to call the gods to their aid during a ritual of magic (Rivers, p. 450; 460).

15. Kluckhohn (p. 31) remarks that a certain chant had been applied in mythical times only against monsters and enemies, but more recently "perversely directed against intra-tribal victims". See also the same work, p. 88f.

16. See Webster, p. 40 (natives of Rossel Island, Western Pacific); p. 44 (the Tlingit of British Columbia; the Buriats); Kluckhohn. p. 25; p. 158ff.; Radin, p. 202 (cult of the Trickster).

17. On Abhicāra, see below, Ch. 6, 8; Henry, p. 220; Shende, p. 153.

18. The political and economic world view of most of the privileged in a modern Western society has been impressively summarized in the form of a fearsome incantation by Breyten Breytenbach in his Afrikaans poem "Breyten bid vir homself".

19. See J. Gonda, *Notes on Brahman*, Utrecht 1950. In concrete situations this brahman was felt to be a supranormal power loaded with magical efficacy "vertu magique" (Henry, p. 224).

20. Some other instances in Shende, p. 201-210; Oldenberg, p. 131ff.; 139.

21. V. Raghavan, in his Preface to the edition of the SVBr by B.R. Sharma, Tirupati 1964, p. 3.

22. Sekoddeśaṭikā, according to Joshi, p. 308; 340, n.61; Poussin, p. 365; Wirz, p. 255.

23. Jhavery, p. 159; 147ff. On p. 198ff. this author relates how Siddhasena Divākara won over various kings to Jainism by showing his magical prowess, especially in overcoming their enemies; similar feats have been told of Hemacandra (p. 220f.); it was said that this authority, notwithstanding his Jain conviction, had caused the death of an inimical king. —One might compare the powers attributed to St. Patrick and St. Columba in Irish legend; see, e.g., Adomnan, *Life of Columba*, 1, 1 (ed. A. O. Anderson and Marjorie Ogilvie Anderson, London a.o., 1961, p. 194ff.)

24. In the JaimBr and ŚatBr, an esoteric doctrine is represented that "speaking the truth is equal to sacrificing" (Bodewitz, p. 236). The Praśnavyākaraṇa, a Jaina canonical text (2, 2, 24), speaks of Truth as the source of all power and the base of all the arts and sciences (Jhavery, p. 274).—On the act of truth as a means for protection and other ends, see M. Dillon, *Celt and Hindu*, in : Vishveshvaranand Indol. Journal, 1, 1963, p. 203-223 (on p. 215f.), who refers to H. Lüders, *Die magische Kraft der Wahrheit im alten*

Indien, in : ZDMG, 98, 1944. For other articles on the subject, see F.B.J. Kuiper, in: IIJ, 14, 1972, p. 144; for Cambodia : Bareau, p. 28.

25. See especially Joan V. Bondurant, *Conquest of Violence. The Gandhian Philosophy of Conflict*, Princeton, N. J., 1958, p. 16-23; 108-111.

26. The magic power of sāmans is also described in ṢaḍvBr 3, 8-11. For instance, the Vajrasāman is the most powerful of thunderbolts. The singers hurl this thunderbolt (especially the *vaṣaṭ* call) towards the sacrificer's rival. The Bṛhat and Rathantara fulfil the same function.

27. Heiler, p. 355. The Gospel, when laid on the head, has been believed to cure headache; during a thunderstorm the prologue to the Gospel of St. John was considered effective.

28. An instructive example, an Algonquin's prayer to a Jesuit missionary, is printed in Radin, p. 186f. In general, see F. Heiler, *Das Gebet* (1918; reprint of the fifth ed., München/Basel, E. Reinhardt Verlag, 1969), p. 41: originally, the motif of a prayer was always "a concrete situation of distress"; Heiler gives a list of the most frequent objectives on p. 65. In the history of religion, the distinction between prayers and spells is a floating one (cf. Webster, p. 111). A prayer to a god can be reinterpreted and adapted in practice as a spell in order to accompany magical actions. For the use of prayers in incantation and exorcism, the reader is referred to Heiler, p. 161-182. Kluckhohn, p. 31: "the incantation may be recited as a prayer...."

29. Heiler, p. 275, who gives other literature in note 28; de Jong, p. 67; J. Gonda, *Notes on names and the name of God in Ancient India Amsterdam* 1970, VKAW, 75, 4.

30. H. Bechert, *Widersprüche im Buddhimus Ceylons*, lecture held in October 1970 for the Theological Faculty of the Catholic University of Nijmegen, p. 7. Magic to be executed with the help of the names of God and of Saints by the mystic orders of Islam is described by Jhavery p. 134ff.

31. Resp. *jñāna, aiśvarya, śakti, bala, vīrya* and *tejas*; on their role in Pāñcarātra speculation, see LT 4, 9ff. (Gupta p. XXV; 20).

32. This shape of the Ṣaḍaṅga formulas is given by N. R. Bhatt in his edition of the Rauravāgama vol. 1 Pondichery 1961 p. 18 n.1—It is added in the note that the "Vedic school" uses the words *namaḥ, svāhā, vauṣat, huṃ, vauṣat* and *phaṭ* in connection with the Six Limbs, i.e. just as in the Vaikhānasa Arcanāsārasaṃgraha. The ISP, which is of post-Āgamic date and character, also records the "Vedic" varieties of the Ṣaḍaṅga formulas (Kriyāpāda, 3, 55); *Oṃ hāṃ Śivāya hṛdayāya namaḥ*; *Oṃ hīṃ Śivāya śirase svāhā*; *Oṃ hūṃ Śivāya śikhāyai vaṣaṭ* (sic); *Oṃ haiṃ Śivāya kavacāya huṃ*; *Oṃ hauṃ Śivāya namaḥ netratrayāya vauṣaṭ*; *Oṃ haṃ Śivāya namaḥ estrāya phaṭ*. In Kriyāpāda 6 after st. 77, in the context of the worship of Śivasūrya the formulas are presented with some variation but with the same six words at the end. Nyāsa should be done to the five fingers of each hand and the two palms; then to the head, mouth, heart, secret part, feet and directions of the compass respectively, and at last to the six parts of the body mentioned in the formulas.

33. Malaviya, p. 45; Hillebrandt, p. 170. AitBr 7, 22, 4 (34, 4, 4) asserts that by uttering *brahmaṇe svāhā* one evokes the Brahman power's friendly disposition (*tad enat prīṇāti*); which means in practice: the Kṣatriya grade evokes the Brahman grade's friendly disposition.

34. De Jong, p. 150, refers to such formulae contained in the papyrus fragments which were recovered from the sands of Egypt, and quotes Iamblichus on the doctrine of their symbolic meaning; they can also lead to the realization of the unio mystica. The Bodhisattvabhūmi (ed. Wogihara, p. 273; also quoted by Dasgupta, p. 22) argues that precisely the meaninglessness of these syllables leads to shaking off worldly opinions and prejudices and leads to the realization of śānti : *nāsty eṣāṃ mantrapadānāṃ kācid arthaparinispattiḥ, nirartha evaite. ayam eva caiṣām artho yad uta nirarthatā. tasmāc ca paraṃ punar anyam arthaṃ na samanveṣate*... (p. 274) *tena bodhisattvena pratilabdhā tāni dhāraṇīpadāny adhiṣṭhāya bodhisattvakṣāṃtir vaktavyā...adhimātrāyām adhimukticaryābhūmikṣāṃtau vartate.*

35. Avalon, 1952, p. 610, who quotes the Yāmala Taṇtra (?) : *devatāyāḥ śarīraṃ tu bījād utpadyate dhruvam.*

36. Gonda, 1963, p. 30. Tantric mantras and bijas are usually given a pseudo-Vedic character by an assignment of a Vedic metre, an ṛṣi, and so on.

37. This remark has been taken from F. D. K. Bosch, *Selected studies in Indonesian archaeology*, The Hague, Nijhoff, 1961, p. 185.

38. See above, n. 34; and De Jong, p. 100.

39. Cf. Kohlbrugge, p. 16, and, in general, Webster, p. 92.

40. F. Bernhard, *Zur Entstehung einer dhāraṇī*, in : ZDMG, 117, 1967, p. 148-168.

41. Cf. Joshi, p. 360, and A. Foucher, *Étude sur l'iconographie bouddhique*, Paris 1905, II, p. 8ff.

42. The *yoga* image is destined for one who strives after the results of yoga; the *bhoga* type is for the obtainment of wealth, dominion or enjoyment; the *vīra* method is for strength (KJ, l.c. : trsl. Goudriaan, p. 161); the *abhicāra* method is for victory over the enemy (KJ, ch. 10). A younger Vaikhānasa source, the Prakirṇādhikāra ascribed to Bhṛgu, distinguishes the image types of *yoga*, *bhoga*, *sṛṣṭi* "creation", "emanation", and *saṃhāra* "dissolution".

43. Ramesan, p. 107. In a copper plate dated 1626 the mentioned village (Akiripalli) is left as an *agrahāra* to god Śobhaneśvara, and put under the guard of one of two bhaktas to whom the god is told to have miraculously revealed his will. On p. 165, Ramesan describes the penance done by Yādava for similar reasons, told in connection with a sanctuary at Yadgiri.

44. On *puraścaraṇa*, see Kane, 1962, p. 1108f. A Buddhist *pūrvasevā* is detailedly described in SM, No. 1.

45. The idea has been developed greatly by the Indians of North America. Radin, p. 156ff., emphasizes ritual fasting (160) and offerings (176). Crooke, p. 148f. describes the precautions to be taken for initiation as a magician.

46. This is described for Ceylon by Gooneratne and Hildburgh.

47. The aim of ruling the animal world is also often stated by texts of this kind. We find it already in TBr 2, 7, 5, 1, where the Pṛthisava is discussed. ĀpŚr 22, 25, 14 advises this *sava* for becoming a lord of cattle: J. Gonda, *The Savayajñas*, p. 15.

48. SCT, ed. Kazi Dawa-Samdup, with English trsl., p. 53 of the trsl, note 8. On p. 66 the mastery of these four kinds of acts is said to be gradually

attained by a course of meditation under the presidence of the Three Kāyas (Nirmāṇakāya, Saṃbhogakāya, Dharmakāya) of Mahāyāna Buddhism.

49. O'Malley, p. 133ff.; Abbott, p. 421-433.

50. Webster, p. 207f. describes how one obtains magical power among the Arapahoes by compelling some spirit. The Angakoks (wizards) of the Eskimos of East Greenland claimed to be masters of the spirit world. The relation of an Angakok to his assisting spirit is more "a purely mechanical mastership" than "a mystical alliance": Webster, p. 232, n. 7, quoting W. Thalbitzer, The heathen priests of East Greenland, Verhandlungen des XVI. Intern. Amerikanisten-Kongresses, I. Hälfte, Wien 1908, p. 448, 454. Webster, p. 209, adds other instances from the Quinault, Lillooet and other tribes.

51. W. H. Skeat, *Malay magic*, London 1900, p. 571, according to Webster, p. 53.

52. A. K. Coomaraswamy, *Yakṣas*, Washington, D.C., 1928, 1931; repr. 1971; Gonda, 1960, p. 323.

53. The Bagalāmukhirahasya (BMR) by Śri-Svāmin; see also below, p. 339.

54. On Jayā, see also Goudriaan, p.——

55. The translation by M. N. Dutt Shastri, Benares 1966 (Chowkhamba Skt. Studies, vol. 54) is unsatisfactory.

56. Van Kooy, p. 34, who refers to publications by G. Tucci and H. Hoffmann.

57. D. Ingalls, *The Brahman tradition*, in : Singer, p. 3-9, esp. p. 7.

58. All kinds of beings or natural powers are liable to be manipulated. The ancient ṛṣis are no exception; according to Iyer, p. 3, "even to this day, the Kanikkār (a tribe in South Travancore) invoke Agastya to bring confusion to their enemies".

59. In religious literature there are instances of the symbolism of the Divine Boatman, for instance in the Dohakośa; cf. A. Bake, *A case of parallel symbolism*, in : *India Antiqua, A Volume of Oriental Studies*, Leiden 1947, p. 10ff.; P. Ch. Bagchi, *Some aspects of Buddhist mysticism in the Caryāpadas*, in; P. Ch. Bagchi, *Studies in the Tantras*, Part I, Calcutta 1939, p. 74-86 (the adept as boatman).—On the *pezegzinatio* of Irish monks in the Early Middle Ages by embarking on a boat, see Nora K. Chandwick, *The Age of the Saints in the Early Celtic Church*, Oxford U. P., 1961, p. 79ff.

Chapter 3

1. The importance of the last thoughts is illustrated by BhGitā 8, 5: *antakāle ca mām eva smaran muktvā kalevaraṃ / yaḥ prayāti sa madbhāvaṃ yāti nāstyatra saṃśayaḥ.*

2. The same is noted by S. C. Mukherji, p. 198. The terracotta relief discussed by V. S. Pathak, *An incantation image of Viṣṇu*, in: Arts Asiatiques, Vol. 6, 1959, p. 235f., seems to me a doubtful case, as well as the image found near Chaitanpur the *abhicāra* nature of which is doubted also by Pathak. o.c.

3. S.C. Mukherji, p. 17; besides, "many Tantric texts describe Jagannātha as Bhairava" (Mahesh P. Dash, *Inter-relation between Vaiṣṇavism and*

Śāktism in Orissa, in : Orissa Historical Research Journal, Vol. XI, No. 4, Bhubaneshwar 1963, pp. 273-281, according to the abstract in *Prāci-Jyoti*, II, 1, Kurukshetra 1964, p. 217).

4. On the importance of Viṣṇuism for the Balinese nobility, see Stuti & Stava, p. 16; C. Hooykaas, *Preliminary remarks on Vaiṣṇavism in Bali*, in : JOIB, Vol. XIV, Nos. 3-4, 1965, p. 326-329.

5. It is not clear which text is Rao's authority for this description. See Kane, 1962, p. 1105, for a few other references.

6. The commentary sums up the Six Acts as *vaśya, ākarṣaṇa, stambhana, mohana, uccāṭana,* and *māraṇa*. They figure here as faculties of a yogin who is on his way to, or has already reached, final release.

7. Edition in : Raghu Vira and Lokesh Chandra (eds.), *Kālacakra Tantra and other texts*, Part I, New Delhi 1966, Śatapiṭaka Ser., Vol 69.

8. For the critical notes on the Skt. text in which also some of the explanations of the paraphrases have been mentioned, the reader is referred to Stuti & Stava, p. 277f.

9. The lotus may, however, function in attacking an adversary; it is called "Kıller of Akṣa.' in the KJ, ch. 74 (trsl. Goudriaan, p. 221); it can also be applied in magical subjugation (see the present work, ch. 6.5, p. 320). The martial character of the Conch appears from Stuti & Stava No. 887 where it figures in a series of aggressive weapons.

10. N. R. Ray, p. 45f.; the author refers to Rao, Icon. I, 1, Plate XVIII (Bhogasthānakamūrti). I could find no instance in this volume of T. G. Rao's work of a Viṣṇu image characterized by disc, conch, mace and sword.

11. An image with the sword in the lower right hand, represented on Plate V, 1 in Coedès' *Bronzes Khmers*, is referred to by K. Bhattacharya on p. 104. For Indian instances of Viṣṇu images bearing the earth instead of the lotus, and not belonging to the Varāha type, Bhattacharya refers to Rao, I, 1, p. 227ff. and to the AgPur, ch. 48. Both references, when checked, turned out to be faulty; a third one, to an article by C. Sivaramamurti, was uncontrollable for me.

12. See KJ, end of ch. 56; Gonda, 1954, p. 234.

13. For the magical manipulation of water, see below, p. 308. Evidence of a similar sort from the Maori tradition is mentioned in Webster, p. 307.

14. H. Mitra, *Sadāśiva worship in Early Bengal*, in: Journal and Proceedings of the Asiatic Soc. of Bengal, XXIX, 1933, pp. 171-242; the essentials of the article have been condensed by Gonda, 1970, p. 163, who refers to other literature in n. 196 and 199. Mitra (p. 230f.) also discusses the description in the MNT of Sadāśiva's five heads in five colours; grey, yellow, pink, white, red (other texts give other colours); also quoted by Banerji, p. 109.

15. There is as yet no comprehensive monograph available on the development of Viṣṇuism in Indonesia; in such a study, its tendency to become a characteristic of the worship of the ruling class should be accentuated. See also n.4 on this chapter.

Chapter 4

1. Jhavery p. 23; O. Garrison, *Tantra, the yoga of sex*, New York, Julian Press, 1964, p. 53-63.

2. M. Alemchiba Ao (publ.), *The arts and crafts of Nagaland*, ed. Naga Institute of Culture, Government of Nagaland, Kohima 1968, p. 7ff.; 18ff., and the photographs.

3. The meaning of *saṃsthānam* seems to be "Anordnung der Teile" (accommodation of parts in a whole); Frauwallner, p. 353.

4. Bedekar bases his argument on the fact that the doctrine is communicated to Vṛtra who is the main antagonist of the Vedic gods, and therefore conceals some authority outside orthodox Hinduism. For the doctrine of the six colours of the soul in Jainism, Bedekar also refers to H. von Glasenapp, *The doctrine of karman in Jaina philosophy*, p. 47f.

5. This case has been discussed by Eliade, p. 198-202.

6. V. W. Turner, in : M. Banton (ed.), *Anthropological approaches to the study of religion*, London 1965. I could not gain access to this paper and had to rely on the recension by J. Blauw, BTLV, 126, 1970, p. 165f. (in Dutch).

7. The reader is referred to Meyer, I, p. 61ff.; Abbott, p. 276ff.

8. A warning by the Church Father Irenaeus against such a belief is discussed by de Jong, p. 117ff.

9. J. L. Motley, *The Rise of the Dutch Republic*, London, Everyman's Library, 1906, repr. 1950, Vol. 2, p. 373, describes how the Spanish king Philip II as it were was cured of his illness by the blood of Dutch rebels massacred by Spanish troops: "The blood of twenty-three hundred of his fellow-creatures....proved for the sanguinary monarch the elixir of life: he drank and was refreshed".

10. For red as a colour of death, see also Meyer, I, p. 83, and Bollée on ṢaḍvBr 3, 8, 22.

11. It is perhaps in connection with this rite and the corresponding passage from the AV that Śiva has been called Nīlalohita "The Red-and-Black One".

12. Cf. Gonda, *Savayajñās*, p. 54, who also gives some further information on the meaning and importance of "four" in the Vedas.

13. The probably best known type of a four-faced (Caturmukha) Viṣṇu is the one with a placid face in front, a terrible one looking backwards, and Varāha and Narasiṃha looking sidewards (Jaiswal, p. 184). Another type, called Vaikuṇṭhanātha, shows a female face looking backwards, while the other faces are as above (Rao, I, 1, p. 256). The Trailokyamohana "Deluding the Threefold World" manifestation should have the same faces, only with Kapila looking backwards, while Ananta and Viśvarūpa have the same faces as Vaikuṇṭhanātha but differ in the number of arms and in their attributes (Rao, I, 1, p. 257f.).

14. Cf. Goudriaan, p.—, based upon P. Ch. Bagchi, *Studies in the Tantras*, Part I, Calcutta 1939, p. 1ff.; K. Bhattacharya, p. 49f.

15. Here I am indebted in some respects to an unpublished study on

the doctrine of the progressive decay of the world based upon the Theravāda Pāli canon and the Mbh: K. van Haasteren, *Het verval der tijden in Pāli Tipiṭaka en Mahābhārata* (Scriptie Nijmegen, 1969). Van Haasteren emphasizes among other aspects that the theory as it is found in the Mbh is a reshaping by Viṣṇuite Brahmans of an older tradition (p.97), while their description of the evils of the Kali age is a veiled criticism of contemporary society (p.100).

16. For instance, in MtPur ch. 144; LiPur, I, ch. 40.

17. Swellengrebel, p. 47; Damais, p. 95f.; Zoetmulder, p. 317f.

18. Stuti & Stava No. 483, called Brahmastava, begins with the words *Namas te bhagavann Agne.* On the Agni-Brahmā relation there is already a reference by H. Kern in his article : *Un dictionnaire Sanskrit-Kavi*, in : *Actes du 6e Congrès International des Orientalistes, tenu en* 1883 *à Leide*, 3e *Partie*; (*Section* 2), Leiden 1885, p. 7. For this information I am indebted to Drs. L. A. van Daalen.

19. Schulte Nordholt remarks that the tradition of the clockwise direction is peculiar because Timor lies South of the equator (the same holds good, for that matter, for Java and Bali). This suggests indebtedness to India.

20. Abbott, p. 295; on the symbolism of this number, cf. Gonda, 1970, p. 45 and notes.

21. On Indonesian evidence, cf. Schulte Nordholt, p. 200; 225ff.

22. Sanjukta Gupta, *The Caturvyūha and the Viśākha-Yūpa in the Pāñcarātra*, in : Adyar Library Bull., 1971, p. 189-204.

23. The reader is referred to a discussion of Kirfel's article by Gonda, 1970, p. 158, n. 53.

24. Parpola, p. 15. This order of the five planets has been deduced by him from the sequence of the weekdays which are presided over by them according to Hindu sources.

25. ViPur 1, 2, 49f.: *ākāśavāyutejāṃsi salilaṃ pṛthivī tathā//śabdādibhir guṇair brahman saṃyuktāny uttarottaraiḥ / śāntā ghorāś ca mūḍhāś ca viśeṣās tena te smṛtāḥ* "the Five Elements : Space, Air, Fire, Water, and Earth, are combined with the qualities of sound, etc., increasing one by one, O brahman, and distinguished further by the three states of being pacified, fearsome and deluded."

26. Avalon, 1958, p. 28, referred to by Mitra, p. 241.

27. See n. 14 on Ch. 3.

28. The system expressed in the Pañcabrahma Up has been mentioned above in Ch. 3.5, p.160.

29. Above, p.193 According to the KJ, ch. 49, Garuḍa consists of earth from his feet up to his knees, of water from knees to navel, of fire from navel to throat, of air from throat to crown. In ch. 35, however, Garuḍa was said to consist of five elements.

30. Lokesh Chandra, *Gaṇeśa in Japan*, in : *Studies in Indo-Asian Art and Culture, Comm. Vol. on the 69th Birthday of Acharya Raghu Vira*, ed. Perala Ratnam, Vol. I, 1972, p. 121ff. (Jōbukuten on p. 125).

31. See Pott, p. 120, and Table II, relying partly upon an article by Moens; Zoetmulder, p. 269 (from the Arjunavijaya).

32. Avalon, 1958; C. W. Leadbeater, *The Chakras*, Madras (Adyar) 1927; repr. 1972.

33. For this reference I am indebted to Mrs. Sanjukta Gupta.

Chapter 5

1. A few instances of this power have been given by PD, s.v. *indrajāla.* On the "sorcerer" or "illusionist", see PD, s.v. *indrajālika.*

2. Celsus seems to regard all such wonderworkers, Jesus included, as degraded people under the influence of an evil genius. Origenes' main argument against Celsus in this matter is that Jesus performed his miracles not in order to make a show of his powers, but out of his desire to lead mankind to greater justice and better understanding of God.

3. Some contributions to the subject—listed here in chronological order—were made by : L. von Schroeder, *Abhicāra in Yajurveda,* in : *Indiens Literatur und Cultur,* Leipzig 1887, p. 121ff.; Hillebrandt, ch. IV, p. 167-186, who also mentions older literature on p. 168, n.1; Bloomfield, *The Atharva-Veda and the Gopatha-Brāhmaṇa,* Strassburg 1899., Grundriss der indo-arischen Philologie und Altertumskunde, II, 1b, p. 57-101; W. Caland, *Altindisches Zauberritual,* Amsterdam 1900 (on the KauśS); V. Henry, *La magie dans l'Inde antique,* Paris 1909; H. Oldenberg, *Vorwissenschaftliche Wissenschaft,* Göttingen 1919, p. 129-149; Shende, p. 153-177; Kane, 1962, p. 1035ff.; and the praiseworthy study by Māyā Mālavīya, *Atharvaveda Śāntipuṣṭikarmāṇi,* Varanasi 1967, which contains more than is suggested by its title, but has, unfortunately for the non-specialist, been written in Sanskrit.

4. The distinction has been clearly made by Baladeva Upadhyaya in his Preface (Prāstāvikam) to Malaviya's book.

5. On the Kṛtyās, see also Shende, p. 161ff.; Macdonell-Keith, p. 118; II, p. 190. An interesting description of the activities of a kṛtyā sent by Hiraṇyakaśipu's court priests against his son Prahlāda is found in ViPur 1, 18, 9; 1, 18, 30ff. Other places from Tantric sources are SST 1, 6, 113 and TSS 18, 63.

6. Cf. the somewhat emotional judgment by Henry, p. 220; 253; and compare Oldenberg, p. 129ff.; 153

7. J. Woodroffe, *Shakti and Shâkta,* Madras 1956; Bagchi, p. 212f.

8. Bagchi, p. 217; see also Ghosh in the same volume, CHI IV, p. 241.

9. Jñātadharmakathāṅga, I, 14, Sūtra 99, according to Jhavery, p. 273; the speaker, a nun called Suvratā, denies that she herself will ever make use of such practices.

10. See J. Gonda, *The Guru,* in : Gonda, 1965, p. 229-283, especially on p. 247, 262; on tribal functionaries, see p. 267 with reference to G. W. Briggs, *The Doms and their near relations,* Mysore 1953, p. 404f.

11. Other cases of the union of the "magic worker" and the "cult leader" in one and the same person outside India, especially in Southeast Asia and Oceania, are presented by Webster, p. 182f.; for India, Webster refers to W. Crooke, *Natives of Northern India,* London 1907, p. 247.—More information on magic in Tribal India can be gathered from : O'Malley, p. 162ff.; Dare, passim; Thurston, p. 224-272; Rivers, p. 255-263; Crooke, Vol. I, p. 143-161; Vol. II, p. 259-286; Bodding, p. 38f.; Elwin, p. 61-81; C. von Fürer-Haimendorf, *Morals and Merit,* London 1967, p. 43 and 47f. The list is far from complete.

12. An interesting case of the self-assertion of the religious specialist against the temporary ruler is AitBr, Pañcikā 7, 19-26, where it is argued that the royal power is dependent on the priestly power and that the king is in consequence thereof not entitled to drink the Soma. In the same text, 8, 24-28, the office of the Purohita is exalted. Cf. Keith's trsl. of the AitBr, p. 29.

13. Of course the function of these remarks is to describe a socio-economic process, not to express some anti-brahmanical or anti-religious bias. A good instance of the same process in Africa is to be found in Marwick, p. 170 (description of a witch-finding movement in the 'thirties in the present Zambia by Audrey Richards).

14. The reason of such inconsequences perhaps also partly lies in a double-sided attitude against sorcery and sorcerers: while destructive rites are at least theoretically considered as disreputable, the performers of such rites may have at the same time been esteemed and secretly dreaded; or people may keep in mind that at a certain moment they may need the services of such performers themselves. Cf. C. von Fürer-Haimendorf, *Morals and Merit*, London 1967, p. 43.

15. In Kathās. 12, 16, 30 (Vetālapañcaviṃśatikā 9, 30), a brahman who claims to possess the power of resuscitation (see below, p. 384) boasts of his being a *vīracaryāsiddha*.—On this subject, see also T. Goudriaan, *Vīrya—and vīra—in Balinese Sanskrit hymns*, in : *Studies in Indo-Asian Art and Culture, Commem. Vol. on the 69th birthday of Acharya Raghu Vira*, ed. Perala Ratnam, Vol. I, 1972, p. 55-61.

16. Political śānti rites are treated in detail in Kane, 1962, p. 719ff.

17. For artificially created supranormal occurrences in Classical Antiquity, see Hippolytus' *Refutation of all sects* (de Jong, p. 164 ff.)

18. On the purohita, see e.g. W. Rau, *Staat und Gesellschaft im alten Indien, nach den Brāhmaṇa-Texten dargestellt*, Wiesbaden 1957, p. 117f.; Fick, p. 156; Jhavery, p. 232 (for the Middle Ages).

19. In the latter passage the magician, who enters the king's audience hall 'like a rain-cloud the earth, bringing confusion by his torrents" and "like a monkey before a tree" (the Skt. commentator adding that the word "monkey" suggests his unfashionable evil bearings and appearance) invites the king to behold a magic trick (*kharolikā*, paraphrased by the commentary with *mithyākautukakrīḍā*) while remaining sitting on his throne, like the moon beholds the earth while residing in the immeasurable space. Having said thus, the man waves a peacock's feather "like the Māyā of the Supreme Self which brings mental confusion"; the result is that a complete illusionary existence is undergone by the king, while for the assistants the incident lasts only a moment. When the magician has made his leave, the councillors conclude that he cannot have been an ordinary illusionist,otherwise he would have asked for money (109, 24 and 28).

20. In Marwick, p. 174, Audrey Richards remarks that in a primitive society the use of magic by a chief against one or more of his subjects may be motivated by a certain weakness of his position. With the Bemba, a Bantu tribe of Africa, the chief, whose authority is traditionally great, does not need to bewitch others (the statement was originally made in 1935).

21. On the Devarāja cult, see the literature noted in Ch. 4, n. 14.

22. This aim is often emphasized in texts like the S.M. For the Jaina tradition the point is stressed by Jhavery, p. 240 and 269.

23. As such a statement we consider for instance PST 14, 78 : *ādhāya bāṇe niśite ca devi Kṣemaṅkarīmantram imaṃ japitvā / tadvedhanād eva vipakṣasenā-diśo diśo dhāvati naṣṭasaṃjñā.* The advertisement made by Cambodian sorcerers is described by Leclère, p. 131f.

24. One may compare what Monier-Williams had to say on the pretensions of the Mantraśāstrins: M. Monier-Williams, *Brahmanism and Hinduism,* p. 201, quoted by Crooke, p. 150f.; or de Jong's remark (de Jong, p. 139) on "overloaded demands" made by the magicians of Classical Antiquity.

25. Or, more probably : "an unguent for the whole world" (unguent being a magical device, cf. p. 317), although this presupposes an incorrect Sanskrit.

26. P. Hacker, *Śraddhā,* in : WZKSOA, Vol. 7, 1963, p. 151ff.

27. Webster, p. 84, quotes other authorities who confirm that among the North American Indians there used to be a belief that an intense concentration of the mind is a necessary preliminary for attaining any important objective.—On "thinking", see also above, p. 69.

28. Among the literature on the subject we mention Avalon, 1952, p. 1144ff.; V. A. Devasenapathi, *Śaiva Siddhānta,* Madras 1960, p. 270; in Pāñcarātra Viṣṇuism: LT, ch. 36 and Gupta, p. 212ff.; Rangachari, p. 141ff.; a few stotras in the BSR and in Aithal, Vol. I, describe mental worship; Nārāyaṇa, Tantrasamuccaya (from Kerala), 7, 6ff.; Trimalla, Pūjāvidhinirūpaṇa, ed. and trsl. by F. Nowotny, IIJ, Vol. 1, 1957, p. 124f. and 136f.

29. Thus executing the famous Advaita image of cosmical illusion. Webster (p. 390) refers to the Mazatec of Mexico, where sorcerers were credited with this particular power. "When thrown into the enemy's direction, it (the snake) goes to him and kills him". Webster refers to J. B. Johnson, *The elements of Mazatec witchcraft,* Göteborg 1939, p. 133, which was inaccessible to me.

30. Identification with gods by the magicians of Classical Antiquity is discussed by de Jong, p. 68f.; 144f.

Chapter 6

1. Cf. Pañcānana Bhaṭṭācārya in his Introduction to the Tārābhaktisudhārṇava, p. 20.

2. Some places collected by Kane, 1962, p. 1064ff., whose concern is to show their immoral character; and see also KCT 3, 97; 4, 124, a. o.; HT 2, 3 a.o.; Wilhelm, p. 61ff. (Nāropa).

3. On this important text we could consult only the article by A. H. Ewing, *The Śāradā-tilaka Tantra,* in : JAOS, vol. 23, 1902, First Half, p. 65-76.

4. On the Kāmyeṣṭis, there is a Dutch publication by W. Caland, *Over de Wenschoffers. Bijdrage tot de kennis van den Veda.* In : *Verslagen en Med. van de Kon. Akad. van Wetenschappen,* 4e Reeks, Vol. 5, Amsterdam 1902, p. 4-36.

5. The development in the relation between rulers and religious specialists is discussed in Kosambi, p. 100; Sharma, 1959, p. 198f.

6. In ViDhPur 3, 51, 10, Yama's buffalo is explained as the "delusion which leads to death" (*moho maraṇe*).

7. The incorporation of the forces of evil into the ritual structuration of space can also be observed in the traditional division of the ground plan of a house or a temple (*vāstuvinyāsaḥ*). The subject is discussed in detail by Stella Kramrisch, *The Hindu Temple*, 2 vols., Calcutta 1946.

8. For example in T, p. 370. On sex of mantras, see also S, p. 186, 46; MMD 24, 92f.; AgPur 293, 3-5; KJ, ch. 4, end.

9. The sources on this subject are BPK 3, 12; K p. 23, st. 16; S p. 192; MMD 25, 42; T p. 372. They are in full agreement only for Vidveṣaṇa and Uccāṭana which should both be accompanied by handling the rosary with thumb and index finger; for Stambhana the thumb and fourth finger are prescribed by both MMD and T, the only sources which mention it.

10. S, p. 192; other sources are MMD 25, 41; T p. 372; T p. 222f. with many particulars on the rosary; BPK 3, 11; HT 2, 10; JT 17, 7ff. The SST, 2, 56, 2 differentiates according to social grade. Reference has also to be made to W. Kirfel, *Der Rosenkranz. Ursprung und Ausbreitung*, Bonn 1949.

11. Cf. Webster, p. 85, and Malinowski, p. 71, on the role of patternized emotions in such circumstances.

12. Some sources on the substances sacrificed in magical Homas : HT 2, 1; PST 7, 53; 13, 45ff.; 14, 65ff.; Second Varadapūrvatāpani Up, in Jacob, p. 131; N p. 272; S p. 193f.; T p. 376; JT 20, 125ff.; MMD 24, 122ff. On Homa of flowers in particular, cf. PST 17, 30; 24; 53; 36, 58ff.; SST 3, 15, 18ff.; 3, 16, 23ff.; 3, 18, 14ff.; 3, 19, 53ff.; JT 20, 122; TSS 27, 16ff.

13. Kluckhohn (p. 40, 177, 181) describes "Frenzy Witchcraft" which was done, or thought to be done, among the Navahos, a predominantly pastoral tribe, in order to procure women, gold, game or rain.

14. See n. 27 on ch. 5.

15. Webster, p. 251, cites a case from the Hidatsa tribe in North America.

16. Webster, p. 344ff.; for the Navaho : Kluckhohn, p. 40, 177f.; 187 by means of an act of flute-playing reminding of Kṛṣṇa; for South East Asia: *Le Monde du Sorcier* (*Sources Orientales*, 7; Paris 1966), p. 313-316 (Pierre Bitard; Cambodge) and p. 343f. (Maurice Durand, Vietnam); in classical Greek and Roman culture: de Jong, p. 29f., 45f., 106, 130ff., 218; with the Baiga: Hermanns, p. 296ff.

17. E. g., 1, 34; 2, 30; 3, 25; 6, 8; 6, 9; 6, 102; cf. KauśS 35, 21-28; 36, 13 and 14.

18. Rājaśekhara, Karpūramañjari, I, 21ff., ed. Konow-Lanman, Harvard Or, Ser., IV, 1901, repr. Delhi 1963, p. 24ff. (text); 235f. (trsl.). In I, 25, the magician says : *Daṃsemi taṃ pi sasiṇaṃ vasuhāvaiṇṇaṃ, thambhemi tassa vi raissa rahaṃ ṇahaddhe, āṇemi jakkhasurasiddhagaṇaṅgaṇāo, taṃ ṇatthi bhūmivalae maha jaṃ ṇa sajjham.*

19. The blue lily acts also as a device of attraction in SST 3, 19, 55 : *nīlotpalakrto homaḥ striyam ākarṣayed dhaṭhāt* (worship of Svapnavārāhi); in the ViDhPur, 3, 52, 14, Rati bears an *utpala* which symbolizes *saubhāgyam*; but its colour is not certain.

20. Caland, l. c., note 5, refers to a regulation in the Roman Laws of the Twelve Tables against the "excantation" of cereals; to an allusion to the

same in Virgil, *Eclogue*, 8, 99; and to a sensational lawsuit conducted against C. Furius Chresimus described by Pliny, *Hist. Naturalis* 18, 8; for the latter, see also de Jong, p. 38f.

21. The classic example in Christian tradition is the splitting of the Red Sea by Moses related in the Old Testament (Exodus 14). Other instances from European literary history have probably been derived from this Biblical tale, such as the dividing of the water of river by the French king Philippe Auguste (1280-1314) for rendering free passage to his army, told by the historian Rigord.

22. Compare the efficacy of the holy man's staff for finding water in the ground or a rock; F. D. K. Bosch, *Guru, drietand en bron*, in : BTLV, Vol. 107, 1951, 117-134; English trsl. in F. D. K. Bosch, *Selected Studies in Indonesian Archaeology*, The Hague 1961, 153-170.

23. Caland cautiously translates literally: "wenn er von überflüssigem Regen gequält wird und wenn er i n u m g e k e h r t e r R i c h t u n g g e z o g e n w i r d....". The Skt. commentaries wisely do not try to explain, at least their explanation does not occur in Bloomfield's selection. In any case the suggestions of Bloomfield ("with dishevelled hair") and of Jolly ("von Missgeschick bedrängt") are to be rejected.

24. TBr 3, 8, 3, 1; P. E. Dumont, *The horse-sacrifice in the Taittirīya-Brāhmaṇa*, Proc. of the American Philos. Soc., 92, 1948, p. 447ff., who on p. 453 somewhat simplifying translates by "rich" and "poor".

25. Kluckhohn, p. 149, refers to such powers in the hands of Navaho magicians; they can get work done by the sun, by thunder, and even by the police.

26. Thus, in Padma Pur. 6, 195, 44 : *ye dāsyena namanti* "those who bow to him while acting as his slaves."

27. The same principle has been expressed more forcibly and beautifully in the stanza *Ātmā tvam*. . quoted by Radhakrishnan in his edition of the BhGītā, *ad locum*; the stanza is also quoted by Nilakaṇṭha in his commentary on Gaṇeśa Gītā 2, 12 : it occurs as stanza 12 in a Śivastotram edited in: *Stotraratnākara*, ed. M. Bāppu Rao, Kollam (Quilon), Śrī Rāmavilāsam Press, on p. 61 (in Malayalam characters).

28. Cf. the Viṣṇuyāga, a sacrifice of a bull made of grains to Viṣṇu described in KJ, ch. 99. The meaning may be that the divine body is strengthened limb by limb through the limb by limb sacrifice of the victim, an act which must have its salutary consequence for the human performers (in the KJ, the context is-Śānti). For the sacrifice of a real buffalo in this way as a substitute for a boy, see K. Das, p. 45. A similar act in another context is discussed in AV 9, 4 (cf. Essers, p. 131).

29. With the Santals, the word *gun* featured in a Bengali mantra recorded by Bodding, p. 101. In some languages, words for "conjurer" or "exorcist" are etymologically connected with this stem; see R. L. Turner, *A comparative dictionary of the Indo-Aryan languages*, London, Oxford U. P., 1962-66, entry 4192, s.v. *guṇin-*. In Indonesian languages, *guna* can have the meaning of "supernatural powers", "sorcery". For Javanese, see Th. Pigeaud, *Javaans-Nederlands Handwoordenboek*, Groningen/Batavia 1938, p. 139; for Indonesian: O. Karow/ I. Hilgers-Hesse, *Indonesisch-Deutsches-Wörterbuch*, Wiesbaden

1962 p. 117 (*guna-guna* "Zaubermittel Schwarze Magie"; *guna-guna pengasih* "Liebeszauber").

30. Wirz p. 248ff. describes Añjana as an important device in Ceylon "eine besondere Zauberkraft....eine Art Hellseherei." Its preparation is a difficult process for which specialists are required (*añjana-kriya*) who among other gods invoke Añjanādévi the mother of Hanuman. The Añjana in such a rite is smeared on a table and the performer makes contact with the deities through the spot.

31. Perhaps the presentation of a flower can be seen as a powerful instance of the winning effect of the presentation of gifts in general; J. Gonda, "Gifts", in : Gonda, 1965, p. 198ff.

32. See, e.g., D. Ingalls, *The Brahman tradition*, in : Singer, p. 3-9, who concentrates upon the possibilities of a literary career. Cf. also P. V. Kane, *History of Dharmaśāstra*, Vol II, p. 117 on the importance of gifts. C. H. Heimsath, *Indian nationalism and Hindu social reform*, Princeton, N. J., 1964, p. 323, quotes an interesting remark made on the subject by R. G. Ranade in 1897.

33. For this inscription and a discussion of its problems, see J. G. de Casparis, *Praśasti Indonesia*, Vol. II, Bandung 1956, p. 15-46; especially on p. 27ff.

34. As has been argued above (p. 312), reduction to the state of a *dāsa*, servant or slave, often occurs as a synonym for subjugation (another case in N, p. 284, st. 3).

35. Caland, p. 117, note 11, quotes Mooney on the subject of young married couples among the Cherokee tribe who by magical means tried to secure each other's affection. Also Ishwaran, p. 107, mentions the use of magic in similar circumstances.

36. We also refer to the acts performed by the primitive hunters to stop the movements of animals (Webster, p. 94). The classic instance from the Bible is the tale of King Jerobeam whose right hand was stiffened as he outstretched it while ordering to arrest an anonymous prophet (1 Kings 13 : 4).

37. O. Bōhtlingk, *Sanskrit-Wörterbuch in kürzerer Fassung*, Vol. III, Repr. Graz 1959, p. 200, records the following meanings for *stabh-* : "1. Feststellen, stützen. 2. Stützen, reichen bis. 3. Anhalten, hemmen, festbannen. 4. (Medium), a. Sich stützen, sich lehnen an. b. Unbeweglich, steif werden. c. Erstarren, zu einem festen Körper werden." *Stabdha-*, its verbal adjective serving as past participle, means : "a Anstossend an, reichend bis. b. Steif, starr, gelähmt, unbeweglich, c. Erstarrt (e.g. water.) d. Aufgeglasen, anspruchsvoll." The causative *stambhayati* means: "1. Befestigen, stützen, aufrichten. 2. Steif, unbeweglich machen, lähmen. 3. Erstarren machen, in einem festen Kōrper verwandlen..". The meanings 2 and 3 for *stambhayati* reflect an act of immobilization applied respectively to animate and inanimate objects. The same pattern of meanings is found for some compound verbs derived from the causative stem, such as *vistambhaya-* and *saṃstambhaya-*.

38. See also my article : *Tumburu and his Sisters*, WZKSO, Vol. 17, 1973, p. 91; and below, p. 373.

39. Bhāsa, Dūtavākya 1, 17 (ed. C. R. Devadhar, *Plays ascribed to Bhāsa*, p. 447) describes how Duryodhana upon the appearance of Kṛṣṇa as messenger falls out of his seat and considers : *Keśavasya prabhāvena calito 'smy āsanād aham / aho bahumāyo 'yaṃ dūtaḥ.*

40. In North America, snake poison was sometimes considered to have been created with an act of magic by the animal (Kluckhohn, p. 133).

41. RV 1, 191; AV 4, 6; 4,7; 5, 13; 6,12; 6, 56; 6, 100, and others; cf. Malaviya, p. 25; Henry, p. 197-203.

42. A fire-walking ceremony is described by H. Whitehead, *The village gods of South India*, Oxford 1916, p. 82f.; 97f.; see also O'Malley, p. 160 (Bihar); Ishwaran, p. 102 (Kanara); K. Das, p. 67f. (Orissa); jumping over a fire : Meyer, p. 191.

43. The early Medieval English historian Bede records a case of Christian masses bringing about the release of a prisoner (Bede, *Historia Eccelesiastica*, 4,22 people who did not know the truth suspected that man to have had *litteras solutorias* "letters (i.e. formulas) of release" with him. Cf. the note by Plummer in his edition of Bede's work, Vol. 2, p. 243.

44. Nilamata Purāṇa, according to P. N. Kaul Bamzai, *A History of Kashmir*, Delhi 1962, p. 50. In Iceland, the first Christian missionaries splitted a huge boulder believed to be inhabited by an ancestor spirit in order to convince the spectators that the God of the Christians was superior: Kristni Saga, ed. B. Kahle, Halle 1905, 2, 2; Thâttr Thorvalds ens vidförla, 2, 6f.; cf A. Heusler, *Germanentum*, Heidelberg 1934, p. 125.

45. Dhātupāṭha *bhedane, vadhe*: Böhtlingk, SW Vol. II, p. 206; MW, p. 382.

46. In an article *Sorcery and native opinion* E. E. Evans Pritchard discussed the role of sorcery "as a legal force upholding the norms and rules of society", a role stressed by Malinowski in his study of a Melanesian community (Marwick, p. 22).

47. "Craziness" is discussed by Kluckhohn (p. 177), but as a feature of Frenzy Witchcraft which is closely associated with love magic.

48. For this use of the term, see the distinction made by E. E. Evans-Pritchard, recorded in Marwick, p. 12, 13 and 25; and see also above, note 6 to Ch. 1.

49. AVPar 36, 2, 5 records a polarization between *vināśana* "destruction" and Śānti. An interesting parallel to the division into Puṣṭi, Śānti and Abhicāra is the threefold division made by R. Firth, *Human Types: An Introduction to Social Anthropology*, 1956, ch. 6, into Productive, Protective and Destructive magic (Marwick, p. 38f.).

50. Webster mentions such acts for the Trobrianders (p. 347) and the Malays (p. 349). Caland (p. 125) compares the Cherokee practice of separating two lovers or married couple.

51. The image and the yantra were very neatly photographed by Prof. C. Hooykaas, who kindly showed me the pictures.

52. Hanuman plays an important role in the charms of the Ojhas, the village magicians, of Mirzapur District and vicinity: Crooke, I, p. 150.

53. One instance: Rāghavabhaṭṭa in his commentary on Kālidāsa's Abhijñānaśākuntalam, 1, 16 prose, describes the beauty of Śakuntalā and her

lady friends with *jagattrayaikamohanaṃ vapuḥ* (ed. N. R. Acharya, 12th edition, NSP, Bombay, 1958, p. 26).

54. A catalogue of instances of abnormal behaviour produced by sorcery is given by Sir W. V. Grigson in his Foreword to Elwin, p. XII.

55. See above, n. 38, and Jhavery, p. 274.

56. "*Oṃ aiṃ*, agitate the stronghold... ". In the variant recorded by K. l.c., there is no mentioning of the "stronghold": *eṃ vatu oṃ kṣobhaya kṣobhaya Bhagavati tvaṃ svāhā*. The "stronghold" presumably means the sense-organs; Indriyavikāraṇī "Disturber of the Sense-organs" is a vague goddess in Viṣṇu's retinue according to KJ, ch. 74 (trsl. Goudriaan, p. 219); Balavikaraṇī and Balapramathinī belong to a group surrounding the Divine Lady according to AgPur 144, 2; LiPur 2, 21, 6f.; AgPur 304; JT 7, 12f., etc.

57. In passages like these, there may be a reference to the famous act of "bone pointing" in which one can cause a person to become sick and wither away by merely pointing at him with a sharp bone (Webster, p. 382 : cases from Australia; Malinowski, p. 71).

58. The transference of disease was also known; see S. Ch. Mitra, *Disease-transference charms*, in : Jn. of the Anthropological Soc. of Bengal, vol. 11, 1917, 3ff. I had no access to this article.

59. Compare what has been said above on the use of sorcery in preserving the social equilibrium (n. 46 on this chapter), and see also Marwick, p. 59 (article by Ph. Mayer).

60. Hermanns, p. 106; from Russell, *Tribes and Castes of the Central Provinces*, Vol. 3, 1916, p. 561f. Similar practices are recorded in Crooke, Vol.2, p. 278f.; Webster, p. 70; for other instances from literature, see below.

61. See, e.g., Elwin, p. 61-81; R. K. Gupta *Witchcraft Murders in the Duars*, in : Man in India, 40, 1960-1. Information from outside India can be found in Webster, p. 250, 269, 273, 380, Caland, p. 158, n.1, again refers to the Cherokees.

62. These psychological and physical effects and their interrelation were discussed by W. B. Cannon, *Voodoo death*, American Anthropologist, vol. 44, 1942, 169-181 (the author does not restrict himself to the Caribbean region).

63. TripR, Māheśvarakhaṇḍa, ch.21; Aithal, No.22, Rājarājeśvaristava, stanza 6 : *yā Lakṣmītanayasya jīvanakarī saṃjīvanavidyayā*.

64. Stuti & Stava, p. 465; J. H. Hooykaas—van Leeuwen Boomkamp, *De Goddelijke Gast op Bali, I Bagoes Diarsa*, Bandung 1949, p. XII.

65. Also in primitive religions, the executors of "white' and "black" magic are sometimes the same persons (Webster, p. 379; Kluckhohn, p. 82f., Marwick, p. 171).

66. Cf. Goudriaan, p. 90.

67. Kane, 1962, p. 721, gives other instances from the Veda; see also the same work on p. 759; 769, note 1239. For the author of the BhāgPur, 12, 10, 27, the multitude of a person's afflictions in saṃsāra is destroyed by the Amṛta of God's words. The LT (49, 59-62; Gupta, p. 325) holds that meditation on Nārāyaṇa Who is an ocean of Amṛta "quietens your mind."

68. J. Gonda, *The Vedic concept of aṃhas*, in : IIJ, vol. 1, 1957, p. 33-60, esp. on p. 37.

69. See Henry, ch. 8; Malaviya, p. 24; 72f.; 108f.; 147-158; Crooke, I. p. 123-174: "the godlings of disease"; Ishwaran, p. 93; professional magicians like the Ojhas specialize in the subject, see e.g. P. K. Bhowmick, *Treatment of diseases among the Lodhas of West Bengal*, in : Man in India, vol. 35, 1955, p. 287-298; an instructive text is the Kumāratantra ascribed to Rāvaṇa which deals with the treatment of children (ed. J. Filliozat, Paris 1926).

70. MtPur 229, 6 classifies Ulkāpāta under the Āntarikṣa phenomena, i.e. those which occur in the intermediate region between the sky and the earth. Falling of meteors and related phenomena are discussed by Kane, 1962, on p. 745; 766f.

71. Hermanns, p. 293, borrowed from V. Elwin, *The Baiga*, p. 349f.; Webster, p. 163 (Panjab); de Jong, p. 41 (Ancient Italy).—The MMK, III, p. 557, gives the synonym *śilāpāta*.

72. With rites destined for securing longevity one may compare other devices taught in the Tantras on Rasāyana (preparing elixirs; cf. Conze, p. 171; D, ch. 13; Mātṛkābheda Tantra); Mṛtyuvañcana ,'deceiving death' or Mṛtyukālajñāna "knowing the time of one's death" in D, ch. 14; and the study of the Riṣṭis "forebodings of death" like in Durgadeva's Riṣṭasamuccaya (ed. A. S. Gopani, Singhi Jain Ser., Vol. 21, Bombay 1945).

73. The structuration of human life as being beset by a succession of magical acts executed by an outside power can be exemplified by the legend from the DevīBhPur (6, 27-30) retold above in ch. 1 (p.44). By the Māyā of Viṣṇu, Nārada experiences an incarnation as a woman of ravishing beauty. A king observes her and falls in love with her: the manifestation of Ākarṣaṇa. The king thereupon even came to neglect his duties because he was "subjugated by amorous play" (Vaśīkaraṇa). The queen obtains many children and grandchildren so that she is wholly absorbed in tending and fondling them and continues doing so, being unable to think of spiritual progress (Stambhana; the text uses the word *mohita*). But in the course of time she developed a feeling of egotism, because she considered herself the happiest of creatures; notwithstanding the fact that sorrow about illness and domestic strife (Vidveṣaṇa) did appear (6, 29, 32ff.). Then fate strikes hard: the family is destroyed by an enemy and only the mother remains weeping lonely on the battlefield (Uccāṭana). At that moment Viṣṇu appears in the guise of a brahman and consoles her by causing her to have insight into the nature of reality (Prāyaścitta). Such a structure resembles the māyic interpretation of the Five Acts of Śiva (above, p.162); and it might be applied also, in a somewhat different way, to the tale of the Two Brothers, the story of a Tamil film very popular in the early fifties, retold by Devanandan (p. 183) as a case of the modern Indian interpretation of Māyā. Woodroffe (*Shakti and Shākta*, 2nd. ed., p. 41, quoted by Jhavery, p. 56) makes the point that in modern society there is plenty of "disguised magic" executed by those who try to rule over other people's minds. And, we may add, modern man who has repudiated magic as being due to a pitiable misapprehension of realities, is more than ever at the mercy of unseen powers who influence and regulate his life and mind. The only act not yet mastered in this modern variety of magic is pacification.

APPENDIX I

SANSKRIT PASSAGES TRANSLATED OR PARAPHRASED

(Referred to in the text by means of square brackets)

Chapter 1

1. RV 1, 51, 13:
   Adadā árbhāṃ mahaté vacasyáve Kakṣívate Vṛcayā́ṃ Indra sunvaté
   Ménābhavo Vṛṣaṇaśvásya sukrato víśvét tā́ te sávaneṣu pravā́cyā
2. KauśBUp 3, 1:
   Triśīrṣāṇaṃ Tvāṣṭram ahanam Arunmukhān yatīn sālāvṛkebhyaḥ prāyacchaṃ, bahviḥ sandhā atikramya divi Prahlādiyān (comm.: anekakoṭisaṅkhyākān mahāmāyān anekacchidraghātino 'surān) atṛnam aham (comm. ātmajñānīndraḥ) antarikṣe Paulomān, pṛthivyāṃ Kālakāñjāṃs, tasya me tatra na loma canāmīyata. Sa yo māṃ veda (comm. asya māṃ...sākṣāt kurvataḥ), na ha vai tasya kena cana karmaṇā loko mīyate na steyena na bhrūṇahatyayā na mātṛvadhena na pitṛvadhena nāsya (comm. madātmajñāninaḥ) pāpaṃ cakruṣo mukhān nīlaṃ (comm. mukhakāntir) vetīti.
3. Mbh 3, 31, 19ff. :

19 Atīva moham āyāti manaś ca paridūyate
niśāmya te duḥkham idam imāṃ cāpadam īdṛśīm
20 Atrāpy udāharantīmam itihāsaṃ purātanam
īśvarasya vaśe lokas tiṣṭhate nātmano yathā
21 Dhātaiva khalu bhūtānāṃ sukhaduḥkhe priyāpriye
dadhāti sarvam īśānaḥ purastāc chukram uccaran
22 Yathā dārumayīṃ yoṣāṃ naro dhīraḥ samāhitaḥ (Southern rec.)
īrayaty aṅgam aṅgāni tathā rājann imāḥ prajāḥ
23 Ākāśa iva bhūtāni vyāpya sarvāṇi Bhārata
īśvaro vidadhātīha kalyāṇaṃ yac ca pāpakam
24 Śakunis tantubaddho vā niyato 'yam anīśvaraḥ
īśvarasya vaśe tiṣṭhan nānyeṣāṃ nātmanaḥ prabhuḥ
25 Maṇiḥ sūtra iva proto nasyota iva govṛṣaḥ
dhātur ādeśam anveti tanmayo hi tadarpaṇaḥ
26 Nātmādhīno manuṣyo 'yaṃ kālaṃ bhavati kaṃ cana
srotaso madhyam āpannaḥ kūlād vṛkṣa iva cyutaḥ
27 Ajño jantur anīśo' yam ātmanaḥ sukhaduḥkhayoḥ
īśvaraprerito gacchet svargaṃ narakam eva ca
28 Yathā vāyos tṛṇāgrāṇi vaśaṃ yānti balīyasaḥ
dhātur evaṃ vaśaṃ yānti sarvabhūtāni Bhārata
29 Āryakarmaṇi yuñjānaḥ pāpe vā punar īśvaraḥ
vyāpya bhūtāni carate na cāyam iti lakṣyate
30 Hetumātram idaṃ dhātuḥ śarīraṃ kṣetrasaṃjñitam
yena kārayate karma śubhāśubhaphalaṃ vibhuḥ

31 Paśya māyāprabhāvo 'yam iśvareṇa yathā kṛtaḥ
yo hanti bhūtair bhūtāni mohayitvātmamāyayā
....
35 Evaṃ sa bhagavān devaḥ svayambhūḥ prapitāmahaḥ
hinasti bhūtair bhūtāni chadma kṛtvā Yudhiṣṭhira
36 Saṃprayojya viyojyāyaṃ kāmakārakaraḥ prabhuḥ
krīḍate bhagavān bhūtair bālaḥ krīḍanakair iva
37 Na mātṛpitṛvad rājan dhātā bhūteṣu vartate
roṣād iva pravṛtto 'yaṃ yathāyam itaro janaḥ
38 Āryāñ chīlavato dṛṣṭvā hrīmato vṛttikarṣitān
anāryān sukhinaś caiva vihvalāmiva cintayā

4. Śūdraka, Mṛcchakaṭikā VI:
Haddhī haddhī : aaṃ pi ṇāma parasampattie santappadi! Bhaavaṃ Kaanta ! Pokkharavattapaḍidajalabindusariser hi kīlasi tumaṃ purisabhāadheehiṃ (hā dhik hā dhik ! ayam api nāma parasampattyā santapyate ! Bhagavan Kṛtānta ! Puṣkarapattrapatitajalabindusadṛśaiḥ krīḍasi tvaṃ puruṣabhāgadheyaiḥ).

5. Mbh 12, 290, 57-60:
Apāṃ phenopamaṃ lokaṃ Viṣṇor māyāśatair vṛtam
cittabhittipratīkāśaṃ nalasāram anarthakam
Tamaḥ śvabhranibhaṃ dṛṣṭvā varṣabudbudasaṃnibham
nāśaprāyaṃ sukhādhīnaṃ nāśottaram abhāvagam
rajas tamasi saṃmagnaṃ paṅke dvīpam ivāvaśam
Sāṃkhyā rājan mahāprājñās tyaktvā dehaṃ prajākṛtam
jñānajñeyena sāṃkhyena vyāpinā mahatā nṛpa
Rājasānuśubhān gandhāṃs tāmasāṃś ca tathāvidhān
puṇyāṃś ca sāttvikān gandhān sparśajān dehasaṃśritān
chittvāśu jñānaśastreṇa tapodaṇḍena Bhārata. . . .

6. BhGītā 7, 13-15:
Tribhir guṇamayair bhāvair ebhiḥ sarvam idaṃ jagat
mohitaṃ nābhijānāti mām ebhyaḥ param avyayam
Daivī hy eṣā guṇamayī mama māyā duratyayā
mām eva ye prapadyante māyām etāṃ taranti te
Na māṃ duṣkṛtino mūḍhāḥ prapadyante narādhamāḥ
māyayāpahṛtajñānā āsuraṃ bhāvam āśritāḥ

7. Mbh 13, 135, 135 and 140 :
Sasurāsuragandharvaṃ sayakṣoragarākṣasam
jagad vaśe vartatedaṃ Kṛṣṇasya sacarācaram
Eko Viṣṇur mahad bhūtaṃ pṛthag bhūtāny anekaśaḥ
trīṃl lokān vyāpya bhūtātmā bhuṅkte viśvabhug avyayaḥ

8. Nīlakaṇṭha, comm. on BhGītā 7, 14 :
...jīveśvaravibhāgaśūnye śuddhacinmātre kalpito māyādarpaṇaś citpratibimbarūpaṃ jīvaṃ vaśīkṛtya bimbacaitanyam anurudhya pracalati.

9. ŚvetUp 4, 9 :
Chandāṃsi yajñāḥ kratavo vratāni
bhūtaṃ bhavyaṃ yac ca vedā vadanti

asmān māyī sṛjate viśvam etat
tasmiṃś cānyo māyayā saṃniruddhaḥ

10. DevīBhPur 6, 31, 46b-47a :
Māyādhīnaṃ jagat sarvaṃ sadevāsuramānuṣam
dehi māyāparādhīnaś ceṣṭate tadvaśānugaḥ

11. Rāmānuja, comm. on BhGītā 7, 14 :
...aindrajālikādiṣv api kenacin mantrauṣadhādinā mithyārthaviṣayāyāḥ pāramārthikyā eva buddher utpādakatvena māyāvīti prayogaḥ... eṣā guṇamayī pāramārthikī bhagavanmāyā eva "māyāṃ tu prakṛtiṃ vidyān māyinaṃ tu maheśvaram" ityādiṣv abhidhīyate. Asyāḥ kāryaṃ bhagavatsvarūpatirodhānaṃ svasvarūpabhogyatvabuddhiś ca, ato bhagavanmāyayā mohitaṃ sarvaṃ jagad bhagavantam anavadhikātiśayānandasvarūpaṃ nābhijānāti.

12. Harivaṃśa 78, 32 Critical note:
Prāpte kāle tu tat karma dṛśyate sarvadehinām
eṣā hy antarhitā māyā durvijñeyā surair api
yathāyaṃ muhyate loko hy atra karmaiva kāraṇam

13. BrVPur Kṛṣṇajanmakhaṇḍa, 78, 19:
Kāmakrodhalobhamohair veṣṭitaḥ sarvakarmasu
māyayā mohitaḥ śaśvaj jñānahīnaś ca durbalaḥ

14. BhPur 8, 12, 38 :
Diṣṭyā tvaṃ...svāṃ niṣṭhām ātmanā sthitaḥ
yan me strīrūpayā svairaṃ mohito 'py aṅga māyayā

8, 12, 43 :
Api vyapaśyas tvam ajasya māyāṃ
parasya puṃsaḥ paradevatāyāḥ
ahaṃ kalānām ṛṣabho vimuhye
yayā vaśo 'nye kim utāsvatantrāḥ

8, 5, 30 :
Na yasya kaś cātititarti māyāṃ
yayā jano muhyati veda nārtham
taṃ nirjitātmātmaguṇaṃ pareśaṃ
namāma bhūteṣu samaṃ carantam

12, 10, 2 :
Prapanno 'smy aṅghrimūlaṃ te prapannābhayadaṃ Hare
yanmāyayāpi vibudhā muhyanti jñānakāśayā

3, 6, 39 :
Ato bhagavato māyā māyinām api mohinī
yat svayaṃ cātmavartmātmā na veda kim utāpare

10, 23, 50 :
Namas tubhyaṃ bhagavate Kṛṣṇāyākuṇṭhamedhase
yanmāyāmohitadhiyo bhramāmaḥ karmavartmasu

15. Marīci, Vimānārcanakalpa, ch. 88 :
Athāyaṃ deho janma kṛtvā bhāryāmayapāśanibandhito bhagavanmāyayā mohitatvāt kāmakrodhalobhamohamadamātsaryahiṃsādini karoti.

16. BNārPur 36, 10 :
Yanmāyayā mohitamānasā ye paśyanti nātmānam api prapannam
ta eva māyāvigatās tadaiva paśyanti sarvātmakam ātmarūpam
17. Śiva Pur, p. 180, st. 25 :
Durjñeyā Śāmbhavī māyā sarveṣāṃ prāṇinām iha
bhaktaṃ vinārpitātmānaṃ tayā saṃmohyate jagat
18. DevīBhPur 6, 25, 24 :
Māyā balavatī brahman dustyajā hy akṛtātmabhiḥ
arūpā ca nirālambā jñāninām api mohinī
6, 26, 2b and 3 :
Saṃsāre 'smin vinā mohaṃ ko 'pi nāsti śarīravān
Brahmā Viṣṇus tathā Rudraḥ Sanakaḥ Kapilas tathā
māyayā veṣṭitāḥ sarve bhramanti bhavavartmani
6, 28, 2 :
Māyayā mohitaṃ sarvaṃ jagat sthāvarajaṅgamam
18a. BhPur 12, 10, 30 :
Naitāvatā bhagavataḥ svamāyāmayavṛttibhiḥ
na duṣyetānubhāvas tair māyinaḥ kuhakaṃ yathā
19. Bhāsa, Ūrubhaṅga, st. 35 :
Yenendrasya sa Pārijātakatarur mānena tulyaṃ hṛto
divyaṃ varṣasahasram arṇavajale suptaś ca yo līlayā
tīvrāṃ Bhīmagadāṃ praviśya sahasā nirvyājayuddhapriyas
tenāhaṃ jagataḥ priyeṇa Hariṇā mṛtyoḥ pratigrāhitaḥ
20. Mbh 7, 164, 99 :
Sa bhavāṃs trātu no Droṇāt satyāj jyāyo 'nṛtaṃ bhavet
anṛtaṃ jīvitasyārthe vadan na spṛśyate 'nṛtaiḥ
21. Mbh 12, 326, 25 :
Paśya devasya māhātmyaṃ mahimānaṃ ca Nārada
śubhāśubhaiḥ karmabhir yo na lipyati kadācana
22. LiPur 1, 80, 19 and 20 :
Dṛṣṭvā nāryas tadā Viṣṇuṃ madaghūrṇitalocanāḥ
viśālajaghanāḥ sadyo nanṛtur mumudur jaguḥ
Kāścid dṛṣṭvā Hariṃ nāryaḥ kiñcitprahasitānanāḥ
kiñcid visrastavastrāś ca srastakāñciguṇā jaguḥ
23. ṚV 7, 100, 6 :
Kím ít te Viṣṇo paricákṣyaṃ bhūt
prá yád vavakṣé śipiviṣṭó asmi
mā́ várpo asmád ápa gūha etád
yád anyárūpaḥ samithé babhū́tha
24. Mbh 5, 109, 5 Crit. Note :
Atra Viṣṇuḥ sahasrākṣaḥ sahasracaraṇo 'vyayaḥ
sahasraśirasaḥ śrīmān anekaḥ (Cr. Ed. ekaḥ) paśyati māyayā
25. Bhāsa, Bālacarita I, 6, prose :
Māyayā śiśutvam upāgataṃ Trilokeśvaraṃ pragṛhya Vasudevena
saha [Devakī] svagṛhān niṣkrāmati. Yaiṣā :
Lokānām abhayakaraṃ guruṃ surāṇāṃ
daityānāṃ nidhanakaraṃ rathāṅgapāṇim
śokārtā śaśivadanā niśi praśāntā
bāhubhyāṃ girim iva Mandaraṃ vahantī...

26. Mbh 12, 47, 38:
Saṃbhakṣya sarvabhūtāni kṛtvā caikārṇavaṃ jagat
bālaḥ svapiti yaś caikas tasmai māyātmane namaḥ
27. Mbh 3, 186, 91-100:
Tato bālena tenāsyaṃ sahasā vivṛtaṃ kṛtam
tasyāham avaśo vaktraṃ daivayogāt praveśitaḥ
Tataḥ praviṣṭas tatkukṣiṃ sahasā manujādhipa
sarāṣṭranagarākirṇāṃ kṛtsnāṃ paśyāmi medinim
Gaṅgāṃ Śatadruṃ Sitāṃ ca Yamunām atha Kauśikim
Carmaṇvatiṃ Vetravatiṃ Candrabhāgāṃ Sarasvatim
Sindhuṃ caiva Vipāśāṃ ca nadiṃ Godāvarim api
vasvokasārāṃ Naliniṃ Narmadāṃ caiva Bhārata
Nadiṃ Tāmrāṃ ca Veṇṇāṃ ca puṇyatoyāṃ śubhāvahām
Suveṇāṃ Kṛṣṇaveṇāṃ ca Irāmāṃ ca mahānadim
Śoṇaṃ ca puruṣavyāghra Viśalyāṃ Kampunām api
(96) Etāś cānyāś ca nadyo 'haṃ pṛthivyāṃ yā narottama
parikrāman prapaśyāmi tasya kukṣau mahātmanaḥ
Tataḥ samudraṃ paśyāmi yādogaṇaniṣevitam
ratnākaram amitraghna nidhānaṃ payaso mahat
Tataḥ paśyāmi gaganaṃ candrasūryavirājitam
jājvalyamānaṃ tejobhiḥ pāvakārkasamaprabhaiḥ
paśyāmi ca mahiṃ rājan kānanair upaśobhitām
Yajante hi tadā rājan brāhmaṇā bahubhiḥ savaiḥ
kṣatriyāś ca pravartante sarvavarṇānurañjane
Vaiśyāḥ kṛṣiṃ yathānyāyaṃ kārayanti narādhipa
śuśrūṣāyāṃ ca niratā dvijānāṃ vṛṣalās tathā
28. Nilakaṇṭha, Comm. on Gaṇeśa Gitā 3,6 :
Anāgatam atitaṃ ca nimeṣaḥ kalpa ity api
tathā dūram adūraṃ ca bhaviṣyat sthūlam aṇv api
cidātmani sthitāny eva paśya māyāvijṛmbhitam
29. Mahāvaṃsa 7, 5-9 :
Tathāgatassa devindo vaco sutvā visārado
devass' Uppalavaṇṇassa Laṅkārakkhaṃ samappayi
Sakkena vuttamatto so Laṅkam āgamma sajjukaṃ
paribbājakavesena rukkhamūlam upāvisi
Vijayappamukhā sabbe tam upecca apucchisuṃ:
"ayaṃ bho ko nu dipo" ti, "Laṅkādipo" ti abruvi
"Na santi manujā ettha, na ca hessati vo bhayaṃ"
iti vatvā kuṇḍikāyaṃ te jalena nisiñciya
Suttañ ca tesaṃ hatthesu laggetvā nabhasāgamā,
dassesi soṇirūpena paricārikayakkhini
30. BrVPur, Gaṇapatikhaṇḍa, 8, 19-22:
Retaḥpatanakāle ca sa Viṣṇur Viṣṇumāyayā
vidhāya viprarūpaṃ tad ājagāma rater gṛham
Jaṭāvantaṃ vinā tailaṃ kucailaṃ bhikṣukaṃ mune
ativa śukladaśanaṃ tṛṣṇayā paripiḍitam
Ativa kṛśagātraṃ ca bibhrat tilakam ujjvalam

bahukākusvaraṃ dinaṃ dainyāt kutsitamūrtimat
Ājuhāva Mahādevam ativṛddho 'nnayācakaḥ
daṇḍāvalambanaṃ kṛtvā ratidvāre 'tidurbalaḥ

31. Ajitāgama, Kriyāpāda 1, 22 :
Bhairave ca tathānyeṣu Paśupāśupatādiṣu
Viṣṇutantre ca Bauddhe ca tathā Dikpāladarśane...
tat tat sa eva deveśaḥ Śivasaṃjñaḥ sanātanaḥ

32. ŚvetUp 3, 1 and comm. by Upaniṣadbrahmayogin:
Ya eko jālavān īśata īśanībhiḥ sarvāṃl lokān īśata īśanībhiḥ
ya evaika udbhave sambhave ca ya etad vidur amṛtās te bhavanti
Jālaśabdena jīvajātamatsyagrāhī māyāśaktir ucyate
tadadhiṣṭhātṛtvena tadvān īśvaraḥ sarvam īśate īśanībhir
māyāśaktibhir iṣṭe.

33. Kaivalya Up 12 :
Sa eva māyāparimohitātmā śarīram āsthāya karoti sarvam
stryannapānādivicitrabhogaiḥ sa eva jāgrat paritṛptim eti

34. Pañcabrahma Up 24 :
Māyayā mohitāḥ Śambhor Mahādevaṃ jagadgurum
na jānanti surāḥ sarve sarvakāraṇakāraṇam

35. BNārPur 15, 74-76:
Mama mūrtyantaraṃ Śambhuṃ yaja stotraiḥ svaśaktitaḥ
sa te samastaśreyāṃsi vidhāsyati na saṃśayaḥ
Aham Adrisutānāthaṃ yajāmi pratyahaṃ nṛpa
tasmād ārādhayeśānaṃ stotraiḥ stutyaṃ sukhapradam
Anādinidhano devaḥ sarvakāmaphalapradaḥ
tvayā saṃpūjito rājaṃs tava śreyo vidhāsyati
Rudrahṛdaya Up 5-7a:
Ye namasyanti Govindaṃ te namasyanti Śaṅkaram
ye 'rcayanti Hariṃ bhaktyā te 'rcayanti Vṛṣadhvajam
Ye dviṣanti Virūpākṣaṃ te dviṣanti Janārdanam
ye Rudraṃ nābhijānanti te na jānanti Keśavam
Rudrāt pravartate bījaṃ bījayonir Janārdanaḥ

36. Skanda Up 9 :
Yathā Śivamayo Viṣṇur evaṃ Viṣṇumayaḥ Śivaḥ
yathāntaraṃ na paśyāmi tathā me svastir āyuṣi
yathāntaraṃ na bhedāḥ syuḥ Śivakeśavayos tathā
deho devālayaḥ proktaḥ sa jīvaḥ kevalaḥ Śivaḥ

37. Mbh 1, 16, 38-40:
Etad atyadbhutaṃ dṛṣṭvā dānavānāṃ samutthitaḥ
amṛtārthe mahān nādo mamedam iti jalpatām
Tato Nārāyaṇo māyām āsthito mohinīṃ prabhuḥ
strīrūpam adbhutaṃ kṛtvā dānavān abhisaṃśritaḥ
Tatas tad amṛtaṃ tasyai dadus te mūḍhacetasaḥ
striyai dānavadaiteyāḥ sarve tadgatamānasāḥ

38. Mbh 1, 17, 2 and 3 :
Tatas tad amṛtaṃ devo Viṣṇur ādāya vīryavān
jahāra dānavendrebhyo Nareṇa sahitaḥ prabhuḥ

35. MMK Vol. I, p. 153 :
He he Mahākrodha, ṣaṇmukha, ṣaṭcaraṇa, sarvavighnaghātaka ! hūṃ hūṃ, kiṃ cirāyasi Vināyaka, jivitāntakara ! duḥṣvapnaṃ me nāśaya, laṅgha[2] samayam anusmara, phaṭ[2] svāhā.

36. MMK Vol. II, p. 298 :
Atha samudrataṭe paścānmukhaṃ paṭaṃ pratiṣṭhāpya nāgakāṣṭhair agniṃ prajvālya samudrasyauddiśya nāgapuṣpāṇāṃ lakṣaṃ juhuyāt. Samudre ūrmaya āgacchanti; siddhinimittaṃ na bhetavyam. Tāvad yāvat samudro brāhmaṇaveṣenāgacchati, braviti : "kiṃ mayā kartavyam ?" Vaktavyam : "vaśyo me bhava" ; tato yad ucyate tat sarvaṃ karoti.

37. Second Varadapūrvatāpani Up (Jacob, p. 131) :
Ya etena caturthiṣu pakṣayor ubhayor api
lakṣaṃ juhuyād apūpānāṃ tatkṣaṇād dhanado bhavet
siddhaudanaṃ trimāsaṃ tu juhvad agnāv ananyadhiḥ
tāvaj juhvat pṛthukān hi sākṣād Vaiśravaṇo bhavet

38. AgPur 302, 6 mantra :
Oṃ hriṃ oṃ namaḥ Kāmāya sarvajanahitāya sarvajanamohanāya prajvalitāya sarvajanahṛdayaṃ mamātmagataṃ kuru kuru oṃ.

Chapter 3

1. Atri-Saṃhitā or Samūrtārcanādhikaraṇa, 20, 17f. :
Śrībhūmibhyāṃ munibhyāṃ ca rahitaṃ vīrahaṃ viduḥ
rahitaṃ śaṅkhacakrābhyāṃ kevalaṃ devam eva vā
Devibhyāṃ rahitaṃ cāpi Bhūmipuṇyārcanāyutam
kaiścid vīraham ity uktam

Marici, Vimānārcanakalpa, ch. 19, p. 81 :
Devaṃ dvibhujaṃ caturbhujaṃ vā dhūmavarṇam śyāmādharaṃ śuṣkavaktraṃ śuṣkāṃgaṃ tamoguṇānvitam ūrdhvanetraṃ brahmādidevair vivarjitaṃ paiśācapadastham ārdrādyanuktanakṣatre śarvaryāṃ cararāśau sthāpitaṃ vimānaṃ ca lakṣaṇahīnaṃ kārayed etad ābhicārikasthānakaṃ syāt.

(p. 83) Devaṃ vedikāsane samāsīnaṃ caturbhujaṃ dvibhujaṃ vā nīlābhaṃ śyāmavastradharaṃ rajoguṇānvitam ūrdhvanetraṃ devyādīn vinā lakṣaṇahīne vimāne śatrudiṅmukhe kṛṣṇāṣṭamyām agnyādyanuktanakṣatre śarvaryāṃ cararāśau garbhālaye paiśācapade sthāpayed etad ābhicārikāsanaṃ bhavet.

(p. 86) Śeṣaṃ lakṣaṇahīnaṃ dviphaṇaṃ dvivalayam anunnataśiraḥpārśvaṃ, devaṃ nīlābhaṃ dvibhujaṃ caturbhujaṃ vā samaśayanaṃ mahānidrāsamāyuktaṃ śuṣkavaktraṃ śuṣkāṅgaṃ śyāmavastradharaṃ sarvadevair vihīnaṃ kārayed etad uttamam ābhicārikaśayanam, ekaphaṇam ekavalayaṃ madhyamaṃ, sarvadehaṃ vinā (?) samasthalaśayanam adhamam.

2. MMD 14, 29 mantra :
Oṃ śrīṃ hrīṃ jaya Lakṣmīpriyāya nityapramuditacetase Lakṣmīśritārdhadehāya śrīṃ hrīṃ namaḥ.

47. DevīBhPur 6, 31, 41 and 42 :
Mādhavo 'pi sadā sattvasaṃśritaḥ sarvathā bhavet
yadā śāntaḥ prītiyukto bhavej jñānasamanvitaḥ
Sa eva raja-ādhikyād aprītisaṃyuto bhavet
ghoraś ca sarvabhūteṣu guṇādhīno Ramāpatiḥ

48. Mbh 12, 47, 37 and 38 :
Yo 'sau yugasahasrānte pradīptārcir vibhāvasuḥ
sambhakṣayati bhūtāni tasmai ghorātmane namaḥ
Sambhakṣya sarvabhūtāni kṛtvā caikārṇavaṃ jagat
bālaḥ svapiti yaś caikas tasmai māyātmane namaḥ
12, 47, 44 :
Yasyāgnir āsyaṃ dyaur mūrdhā khaṃ nābhiś caraṇau kṣitiḥ
Sūryaś cakṣur diśaḥ śrotre tasmai lokātmane namaḥ

49. BhPur 12, 11, 6-8 :
Etad vai pauruṣaṃ rūpaṃ bhūḥ pādau dyauḥ śiro nabhaḥ
nābhiḥ Sūryo 'kṣiṇī nāse Vāyuḥ karṇau diśaḥ prabhoḥ
Prajāpatiḥ prajananam apāno mṛtyur īśituḥ
tadbāhavo lokapālā manaś Candro bhruvau Yamaḥ
Lajjottaro 'dharo lobho dantā jyotsnā smayo bhramaḥ
romāṇi bhūruhā bhūmno meghāḥ puruṣamūrdhajāḥ
12, 11, 11 :
Svamāyāṃ vanamālākhyāṃ nānāguṇamayīṃ dadhat
vāsaś chandomayaṃ pītaṃ brahmasūtraṃ trivṛt svaram
12, 11, 14-16a :
Ojaḥ sahobalayutaṃ mukhyatattvaṃ gadāṃ dadhat
apāṃ tattvaṃ daravaraṃ tejastattvaṃ Sudarśanam
Nabhonibhaṃ nabhas tattvam asiṃ carma tamomayam
Kālarūpaṃ dhanuḥ Śārṅgaṃ tathā karmamayeṣudhim
Indriyāṇi śarān āhur ākūtir asya syandanam

50. DevīBhPur 6, 28, 18b and 19 :
Triyutas tāṃ kathaṃ māyāṃ jetuṃ śaktaḥ pumān bhavet
Kālo 'pi tasya rūpaṃ hi rūpahīnaḥ svarūpakṛt
tadvaśe vartate dehī vidvān mūrkho 'tha madhyamaḥ

51. Stuti & Stava, No. 133, 1 and 2 :
Bhūtarājā mahākrūraḥ sahasrakiraṇaprabhaḥ
ṣaḍvaktrasaṃyutaś caiva...
Mahākṣo ...sarvāstrakarṇadhāraṇaḥ
mahāpretasamārūḍho nāgayajñopaśobhitaḥ
No. 136, 6 :
Daśavaktro mahādevaḥ sahasrabhujabhīṣaṇaḥ
sarvāyudhadharo raudrī daṃṣṭrābālendusaṃnibhaḥ

Chapter 2

1. Tantrasāra, p. 73 (quoting Viśuddheśvara Tantra):
Śarīrākārabhūtānāṃ bhūtānāṃ yad viśodhanam
avyayabrahmasaṃyogād bhūtaśuddhir iyaṃ matā

2. ChUp 4, 5, 3 :
Sa ya etam evaṃ vidvāṃś catuṣkalaṃ pādaṃ Brahmaṇaḥ prakāśavān ity upāste, prakāśavān asmiṃl loke bhavati. Prakāśavato ha lokāñ jayati...
4, 12, 2 :
Sa ya etam evaṃ vidvān upāste, apahate pāpakṛtyām, loki bhavati, sarvam āyur eti, jyog jīvati, nāsyāvarapuruṣāḥ kṣīyante. Upa vayaṃ taṃ bhuñjmo 'smiṃś ca loke 'musmiṃś ca, ya etam evaṃ vidvān upāste.
4, 15, 6 :
Sa enaṃ Brahma gamayati. Eṣa devapathe Brahmapathaḥ. Etena pratipadyamānā imaṃ mānavam āvartaṃ nāvartanta iti....
5, 19, 2 :
...tasyānu tṛptiṃ tṛpyati prajayā paśubhir annādyena tejasā brahmavarcasena.
3. D, Benares ed., 2, 4 :
Brahmātmānaṃ tu vitataṃ dṛṣṭvā vijñānacakṣuṣā
sarvatra māraṇaṃ kāryam anyathā doṣabhāg bhavet
4. Kathās. 12, 22, 25 and 26 :
Tataḥ sa yogagulikāṃ kṣiptvā dhūrtapatir mukhe
Mūladevo vyadhād vṛddhabrāhmaṇākṛtiṃ ātmanaḥ
Dvitīyāṃ gulikāṃ dattvā mukhakṣepyāṃ cakāra ca
sukāntakanyakārūpaṃ taṃ Manaḥsvāminaṃ dvijam
5. Stuti & Stava, No. 636, 2 and 3 :
Naivedyaṃ Brahmā Viṣṇuś ca bhoktā devo Maheśvaraḥ
sarvavyādhin ālabhati sarvakāryāntasiddhāntam
Jayārthī jayam āpnuyād yaśārthī yaśam āpnoti
siddhisakalam āpnuyāt Paramaśivaṃ labhati
6. Stuti & Stava, No. 362, 36 and 37 :
Mantreṇa mokṣam āpnoti mantreṇābhyudayaṃ labhet
hanti mantraṃ mahāśocaṃ pavitraṃ pāpanāśanam
Pāpāni bahudhā kuryād yo naraḥ pitṛmātaraḥ
[tan]mantreṇa viśuddhātmā sarvapāpam utpāvakaḥ
7. AgPur 125, 41 and 42 :
Vaśye jvare tathākarṣe prayogaḥ siddhikārakaḥ
śāntau prītau namaskāro vauṣaṭ puṣṭau vaṣādiṣu
Huṃ mṛtyau prītisannāśe vidveṣoccāṭane ca phaṭ
vaṣaṭ sute ca dīptyādau mantrāṇāṃ jātayaś ca ṣaṭ
8. MMD 24, 92b-95a :
Puṃstrīnapuṃsakāḥ proktā manavas trividhā budhaiḥ
Vaṣaḍantāḥ phaḍantāś ca pumāṃso manavaḥ smṛtāḥ
vauṣaṭsvāhāntagā nāryo huṃ namo 'ntā napuṃsakāḥ
Vaśyoccāṭanarodheṣu pumāṃsaḥ siddhidāyakāḥ
kṣudrakarmarujāṃ nāśe strīmantrāḥ śīghrasiddhidāḥ
Abhicāre smṛtā klībā evaṃ te manavas tridhā
9. KCT 3, 80 :
Puṣṭau svāhāntamantro bhavati narapate
śāntiko 'sau namo 'ntar

ākṛṣṭau vauṣaḍanto bhavati ca vaṣaḍantaś ca vaśye tathaiva
hūṃkārānto 'bhicāre prakṛtiguṇavaśāt kilanādye phaḍantaḥ
śveto raktaś ca kṛṣṇo varakanakanibhaḥ
karmabhedaiś ca mantraḥ

10. MMK Vol. III, p. 662 :
Oṃ hana hana sarvabhayān sādayotsādaya trāsaya moṭaya chinda bhinda jvala jvala huṃ huṃ phaṭ phaṭ svāhā.

11. MMK Vol. III, p. 666 :
Namaḥ sarvatathāgatebhyo arhadbhyaḥ samyaksambuddhebhyaḥ. Oṃ Kumārarūpiṇi viśvasambhava āgacchāgaccha lahu lahu bhrūṃ bhrūṃ hūṃ hūṃ jinajit Mañjuśriya suśriya tāraya māṃ sarvaduḥkhebhyaḥ phaṭ phaṭ śamaya śamaya mṛtodbhavodbhava pāpaṃ me nāśaya svāhā.

12. ṚV 7, 104, 1 :

Indrāsomā tápataṃ rákṣa ubjátaṃ
nyarpayataṃ vṛṣaṇā tamovṛdhaḥ
párā śṛṇitam acíto nyoṣataṃ
hatáṃ nudéthāṃ ní śiśītam atríṇaḥ

13. MtPur 70, 52 and 53 :

Yathāntaraṃ na paśyāmi Kāmakeśavayoḥ sadā
tathaiva sarvakāmāptir astu Viṣṇo sadā mama
Yathā na Kamalā dehāt prayāti tava Keśava
tathā mamāpi deveśa śarīre sve kuru prabho

14. MtPur 93, 151-155 :

Nava (nara?)vāyasaraktāḍhyapātratrayasamanvitāḥ
samidho vāmahastena śyenāsthibalasaṃyutāḥ
hotavyā muktakeśais tu dhyāyadbhir aśivaṃ ripau
Durmitriyās tasmai santu tathā huṃ phaḍ itīti ca
śyenābhicāramantreṇa kṣuraṃ samabhimantrya ca
Pratirūpaṃ ripoḥ kṛtvā kṣureṇa parikartayet
ripurūpasya śakalāny athaivāgnau viniḥkṣipet
Grahayajñavidhānānte sadaivābhicaran punaḥ
vidveṣaṇaṃ tathā kurvann etad eva samācaret
Ihaiva phaladaṃ puṃsām etan nāmutra śobhanam...

15. MMD 12, 139b and 140:
Evaṃ śrīSundarīṃ nityaṃ pūjayan vijitendriyaḥ
navāvṛtiyutāṃ sarvān kāmān iṣṭān avāpnuyāt
atha prayogā vakṣyante sādhakābhīṣṭasiddhidāḥ

16. MMK Vol. I, p. 54 :
Mucyate sarvarogebhyo īpsitam arthaṃ ca sampadyante
aputro labhate putraṃ durbhagaḥ subhago bhavet
Daridro labhate arthān darśanād eva maṇḍalam
striyasya puruṣasyāpi śrāddhasyāpi kalpataḥ
yatheṣṭavividhākārāṃ prāpnuyāt sampadāṃ sadā

17. SM No. 111 (Durgottāraṇīsādhana) :
...Bandhasthena japtavyā; sahasram aṣṭaśataṃ vā dine dine japen mocayati; yadiha muñcati...tadā śirovedanā bhavati, jvaro mahān

bhavati, viṣamā visūcikā bhavati, sādhakasya darśanaṃ dadāti, saptame divase 'vaśyaṃ mocayati.

18. D 12, 13 :
"Devi ! dāridryadagdho 'smi tasya nāśakarī bhava"
dattvārghyaṃ praṇamen mantrī, vadet sā "tvaṃ kim icchasi?"
tato dadāti sā tuṣṭā vittāyuś cirajīvitam

19. MMK Vol. II, p. 293 :
Atha yakṣiṇī-ākarṣayitukāmaḥ tasya nāmaṃ gṛhya saptāham aśoka-puṣpāṇi juhuyāt; āgacchati varaṃ dadāti saptame saptāhe 'vaśyam āgacchati, mātā bhaginī bhāryā yaṃ cārocati. Atha na vā gacchati, mūrdhānam asya sphuṭati.

20. MMK Vol. III, p. 566 :
Oṃ Bhaṭṭe Bhaṭṭe ālokini kiṃ cirāyasi ehy ehi āgaccha āgaccha mama kāryaṃ kuru svāhā.

21. MMK Vol. III, p. 566 :
Namaḥ sarvayakṣīṇām, Oṃ rakte raktāvabhāse raktānulepane svāhā.
Revatyā yakṣiṇīśreṣṭhā lalantyā maithunapriyā
īṣadraktena vastreṇa nīlakuñcitamūrdhajā
Sarvāṅgaśobhanā yakṣī kāmabhogaratā sadā
kāmadā bhogadā nityaṃ varadāṃ tām abhinirdiśet

22. MMD 9, 93 :
Yo me pūrvagataḥ pāpmā pāpakeneha karmaṇā
Indras taṃ devarājo bhañjayatv añjayatu mohayatu nāśayatu
mārayatu kaliṃ tasmai prayacchatu
kṛtaṃ mama śivaṃ mama śāntiḥ svastyayanaṃ cāstu.

23. MMD ch. 10 :
...sādhyam uccāṭaya² śoṣaya² māraya² bhīṣaya² nāśaya² śiraḥ kampaya² mamājñāvartinaṃ kuru² tadvastujātaṃ saṃpādaya² sarvaṃ kuru² svāhā.

24. HT 1, 11 :
Hrīṃkārasaṃbhavā devi raktavarṇā caturbhujā
iṣukārmukahastā ca utpalāṅkuśadhāraṇā
asyā bhāvanāmātreṇa trailokyaṃ vaśam ānayet
lakṣeṇaikena rājānaḥ prajāloko 'yutena ca
paśuyakṣādayaḥ koṭyā saptalakṣeṇa cāsurāḥ
lakṣadvayena devāś ca śatenaikena mantriṇaḥ

25. Kathās 2, 2, 10f. :
Athānyān vīkṣya tān āḍhyān gṛhasthān irṣyayā Śriyam
homaiḥ sa sādhayāmāsa Kālanemiḥ kṛtavrataḥ
Sā ca tuṣṭā satī sākṣād evaṃ Śrīs tam abhāṣata :
....
hutam agnau tvayā yasmād amarṣakaluṣātmanā

26. DevīBhPur 9, 4, 73 :
Śrīṃ hrīṃ Sarasvatyai svāhā śiro me pātu sarvataḥ
Śrīvāgdevatāyai svāhā bhālaṃ me sarvadāvatu

27. MMD 9, 36 :
Gīrvāṇasaṃghārcitapādapaṃkajāruṇaprabhābālaśaśāṅkaśekharā
raktāmbarālepanapuṣpayuṅmude sṛṇiṃ sapāśaṃ dadhatī śivāstu naḥ

28. MMD 18, commentary :

Oṃ aiṃ hrīṃ klīṃ śrīṃ Kāhneśvari sarvajanamanohari sarvamukhastambhani sarvarājavaśaṃkari sarvaduṣṭanirdalani sarvastripuruṣākarṣiṇi vandīśṛṅkhalās troṭaya[2] sarvaśatrūn bhañjaya[2] dveṣṭṛn nirdalaya[2] sarvaṃ stambhaya[2] mohanāstreṇa dveṣiṇa uccāṭaya[2] sarvaṃ vaśaṃ kuru[2] svāhā dehi[2] sarvaṃ Kālarātri kāminīgaṇeśvari namaḥ.

29. MMD 18, 43 :

Oṃ aiṃ klīṃ hrīṃ śrīṃ glauṃ hsauḥ namaḥ Kāhneśvari sarvān mohaya[2] kṛṣṇe kṛṣṇavarṇe kṛṣṇāmbarasamanvite sarvān ākarṣaya[2] śīghra[ṃ]vaśaṃ kuru[2] aiṃ hrīṃ klīṃ śrīṃ.

30. MMD 18, 50 :

Oṃ hlāṃ hlīṃ hlūṃ Kāmākṣi māyārūpiṇi sarvamanohāriṇi stambhaya[2] rodhaya[2] mohaya[2] klāṃ klīṃ klūṃ Kāmākṣe Kāhneśvari huṃ.[2]

31. KCT 4, 163 and 164 :

Pūrṇe home jvalan vai laladaśirasinas tīkṣṇadaṃṣṭras triṇetro
garjan vai sphoṭayan yaḥ kṣitim api caraṇaiḥ
sādhakaṃ bhīṣayan yaḥ
sthitvā kuṇḍāntarāle hasati kahakahaṃ nṛtyate bhīmakāyas
taṃ dṛṣṭvā bhīmamantrī vrajati Yamapuraṃ naṣṭacittaḥ kṣaṇena
Bhetavyaṃ nāsurendrād api citibhuvane mantrasiddhyarthahetor
dṛṣṭvā niḥkampacittaṃ bhavati punar idaṃ sādhito bhūtanāthaḥ
"siddho 'haṃ te suvīra vada sakalam ahaṃ
sāmprataṃ kiṃ karomi?"
ity ukte sādhakena svamanasi rucitaṃ prārthanīyaṃ parārtham

32. KCT 4, 165 and 166 :

Sparśaṃ khaḍgaṃ rasendrāmṛtaphalaguṭikā rocanaṃ cāñjanaṃ ca
yal lepaṃ pādukāṃ vā dadatu samabhavān laukikim aṣṭasiddhim
vidveṣoccāṭanaṃ vai bhuvananidhanatā stambhanākṛṣṭivaśyaṃ
sarvam me yātu siddhim; sa ca vadati punaḥ : "sarvam etat karomi"
Bhūtendraṃ sādhayitvā vrajati narapate sādhako yatra tatra
pātāle cāntarikṣe suravarabhuvane meruśṛṅge 'bdhipāre
tatrārūḍho 'sihastaḥ kṣititalanilaye lokakāryaṃ karoti
tasmāt sattvārthahetoḥ paramakaruṇayā sādhanīyo 'surendraḥ

33. MMK Vol. I, p. 29 :

Namaḥ sarvabuddhabodhisattvānām apratihataśāsanānām. Uṃ, kara[2] kuru[2] mama kāryaṃ, bhañja[2] sarvavighnān, daha[2] sarvavajravināyakam, mūrdhaṭakajīvitāntakara mahāvikṛtarūpiṇe, paca[2] sarvaduṣṭān, mahāgaṇapatijīvitāntakara bandha[2] sarvagrahān. Ṣaṇmukha, ṣaḍbhuja, ṣaṭcaraṇa ! Rudram ānaya, Viṣṇum ānaya, Brahmādyān devān ānaya, mā vilamba mā vilamba, jhal[2] maṇḍalamadhye praveśaya, samayam anusmara, hūṃ[6] phaṭ[2] svāhā.

34. MMK Vol. I, p. 153 :

Ṣaḍbhujo 'tha mahākrodhaḥ ṣaṇmukhaś caiva kalpite
caturakṣaro mahāmantraḥ Kumāre mūrtinisṛtaḥ
ghorarūpā mahāghoro Varāhākārasambhavaḥ
...sarpabhogavilambitaḥ...asihasto...mahaujasaḥ

Tato devagaṇāḥ sarve papus tad amṛtaṃ tadā
Viṣṇoḥ sakāśāt saṃprāpya saṃbhrame tumule sati

39. Mbh 1, 16, 40 Southern Recension :
Sā tu Nārāyaṇī māyā dhārayantī kamaṇḍalum
àsyamāneṣu daityeṣu paṅktyā ca prati dānavaiḥ
devān apāyayad devī na daityāṃs te ca cukruśuḥ
1, 17, 3 Southern Rec. :
Pāyayaty amṛtaṃ devān Harau bāhubalena ca
nirodhayati cāpena dūrīkṛtya dhanurdharān

40. BhPur 8, 12, 39 and 40 :
Ko nu me 'titaren māyāṃ viṣaktas tvad ṛte pumān
tāṃs tān visṛjatīṃ bhāvān dustarām akṛtātmabhiḥ
Seyaṃ guṇamayī māyā na tvām abhibhaviṣyati
mayā sametā kālena kālarūpeṇa bhāgaśaḥ
8, 12, 47 :
...kapaṭayuvativeṣo mohayan yaḥ surārīṃs
tam ahaṃ...nato 'smi

41. DevīBhPur 6, 27, 51b-52a :
gacchan hāsyavinodena strībhāvaṃ gamitaḥ kṣaṇāt
rājapatnītvam āpanno māyābalavimohitaḥ
6, 28, 1 and 2 :
Niśāmaya muniśreṣṭha gadato mama satkathām
māyābalam sudurjñeyaṃ munibhir yogavittamaiḥ
Māyayā mohitaṃ sarvaṃ jagat sthāvarajaṅgamam
Brahmādistambaparyantam ajayā durvibhāvyayā

42. DevīBhPur 6, 29, 51 :
Kiṃ viṣīdasi tanvaṅgi bhramo 'yaṃ prakaṭīkṛtaḥ
mohena kokilālāpe patiputragṛhātmake

43. KūPur 1, 34 :
Māyā mama priyānantā yayedaṃ dhāryate jagat
saiṣā sarvajagatsūtiḥ prakṛtis triguṇātmikā

44. Kṛṣṇa Up, 7 :
Ajayyā Vaiṣṇavī māyāpy ajena sājitā purā
Devakī brahmavidyā sā yā devair upagīyate
Comm.: ...ata eva hi Kṛṣṇarūpabrahmāvirbhāvasambhavaḥ

45. MkPur 81, 41 and 42 :
Tan nātra vismayaḥ kāryo yoganidrā jagatpateḥ
mahāmāyā Hareś caitat tayā sammohyate jagat
Jñāninām api cetāṃsi devī Bhagavatī hi sā
balād ākṛṣya mohāya Mahāmāyā prayacchati

46. DevīBhPur 6, 31, 29b-32 :
Yathendrajālikaḥ kaścit pāñcālīṃ dāravīṃ kare
Kṛtvā nartayate kāmaṃ svecchayā vaśavartinīm
tathā nartayate Māyā jagat sthāvarajaṅgamam
Brahmādistambaparyantaṃ sadevāsuramānuṣam
pañcendriyasamāyuktaṃ manaścittānuvartanam
Guṇās tu kāraṇaṃ rājan...māyāsamudbhavāḥ

3. MMD 14, 111 :
Devakīsuta Govinda Vāsudeva jagatpate
dehi me tanayaṃ Kṛṣṇa tvām ahaṃ śaraṇam gataḥ
4. AgPur 307 mantra (=PST 36, 6ff.)
Oṃ śrīṃ hrīṃ hrūṃ oṃ namaḥ Puruṣottamaḥ Puruṣottamapratirūpa Lakṣmīnivāsa sakalajagatkṣobhaṇa sarvastrīhṛdayadāraṇa tribhuvanamadonmādakara, suramanujasundarījanamanāṃṣi tāpaya[2] dīpaya śoṣaya[2] māraya[2] stambhaya[2] drāvaya[2] ākarṣaya,[2] paramasubhaga sarvasaubhāgyakara kāmaprada, amukaṃ hana[2] cakreṇa gadayā khaḍgeṇa sarvabāṇair bhinda[2] pāśena hatta[2] (PST ghaṭṭaya[2]) aṅkuśena tāḍaya[2]' turu[2] kiṃ tiṣṭhasi yāvat tāvat samīhitaṃ me siddhaṃ bhavati, huṃ phaṭ namaḥ.
5. Second Varadapūrvatāpanī Up (ed. Jacob, p. 123f.) :
Tasya hi ṣaḍ aṅgāni bhavanti : Oṃ hṛdayāya namaḥ śirase svāhā śikhāyai vaṣaṭ kavacāya huṃ netratrayāya vauṣaḍ astrāya phaḍ iti prathamaṃ prathamena. . . . ṣaṣṭhaṃ ṣaṣṭhena pratyakṣaram ubhayato Māyā Lakṣmīś ca bhavati.
6. The OJ Commentary to the Mahāmāyā fragment in the Rotterdam manuscript (No. 19615 Museum Voor Volkenkunde) is as follows:
(1) Saṅ Hyaṅ Māyātattva ajarakna, atyantàmahāpavitranira, ndan èvěkta kapaṅguhanira, mataṅyan rěněn ta kita saṅ yah, kaṅěnaṅěněn sira yan maṅkanā, linuputanirā, ikaṅ sarvvapāpa.
(2) Ndya ta kaṅěnaṅěnanira ? Dvinétra sira, caturbhuja, gadasaṅkācakragiṅgěnira, sarvvajña ta sira, pitavarṇa ikaṅ padma stananira.
(3) Ṣinévita sira déniṅ sarvvadevagaṇa, bhinūśanan ta sira déniṅ sarvvabharaṇa. . . . (mantra). . . . Nihan ta vakyanira muvah :
(4) . . (mantra) . . naṅ mantra.
(5) Yadyan hana ri nusantara, kliṅ hadinya, kahananira saṅ prabhū, i samaṅkanā dohnya, niyata marākirimi saṅ sādhaka, umèhakěn rajyadrvénira, sahāna ni kadatvanira.
(6) Pira gěṅa nikaṅ lvah, tuvi baṅunya kāla niṅ rěṅrěṅ, niyata valuya ni baṅunya muvaha ri saṅkanya ṅuni.
Iti ākarṣaṇaprayoga.
(7) Raktavarṇa raktadhara puṣpadi... (mantra)... naṅ mantra.
(8) Yadyapinyan sḍananyan amaṅkěl rakvaṅ liman, lavan śatru sěk sahā kośa vāhananya, tan vnaṅ inalahakěn, niyata kākavaśanikā kalih, yan Saṅ Hyaṅ Māyā raktavarṇṇa inaradhan.
(9) Pira hayva nikaṅ kanyā, kavaśā ika de saṅ sādhaka, yan inaradhanan Saṅ Hyaṅ Māyā bāṅ.
Iti vaśikaraṇaprayoga.
(10) (11) Pira galakiṅ ula kavdi-vdi, pati sahut-sahutanāvèt niṅ lapanya, inaku māryanya maṅkana, yan inaradhanan Saṅ Hyaṅ Māyā kuniṅ. Múvah piratguhan iṅ ākāśa, ptěṅ pěpět ta déniṅ meghā nila maṅhrū hudan ri kāla niṅ rěṅrěṅ, niyata ṅanti tāya ni Saṅ Hyaṅ Māyā kuniṅ inaradhan. . (mantra) . .
Iti stambana.
(12) . . (mantra) . . . .

(13) Pira kaśa nikaṅ vukir mvaṅ atyanta gĕṅanya, pisaniṅ un polahana mvaṅ kahanan aprāṇa, niyata sivakasa prahāra, yan Saṅ Hyaṅ Māyā kṛṣṇa inaradhana.
Iti uccāṭana prayoga.
(14) Kunaṅ yan prāyaścitta mrayogaknanta, Saṅ Hyaṅ Māyā caturvarṇṇa pūjantārādhananan, caturvarṇṇa sinandaṅnira, tka niṅ vastra puṣpādi, makantaṅ caru, caturvarṇṇa ika kabèh.... (mantra)....naṅ mantra.
(15) Yadyapin sèvu kvèhanikaṅ andaru tumibā riṅ lmah, mvaṅ ikaṅ vintaṅ kukus pira kvèhanikaṅ grahayuddha, pira kvèhanikaṅ hudan vatu, niyata padmanikā kabèh, salviraniṅ hala kavaṅūn dénya, ilaṅ déni prāyaścitta maṅkana.
(16) Lavan sira kvèhaniṅ hala niṅ vvaṅ, piraṅ tavun lavasanyan paṅiḍĕp saṅsāra mvaṅ lara, alupa nara kaharĕpnya, vét nikaśakitanya, niyatanya mulih maluy paripūrṇṇa śarīranya, kadi ṅūni sukacitta, yan pinagavayakĕn prāyaścitta maṅkana. Iti Saṅ Hyaṅ Mahāmāyā, sarvvaprāyaścitta sira, hayva verā, parama[ra]hasya sira.
(17) Nahan ta lvir niṅ prayoga Saṅ Hyaṅ Mahāmāyā.
(18) Makaphala kagavayan iṅ vvaṅ hiriṅvaṅ, mvaṅ bhaktyanya, kadi varṇṇa niṅ sindūra Saṅ Hyaṅ Mantra, vaṣaṭ indikanya : Oṃ hroṃ vaṣaṭ namaḥ vaṣaṭ hruṃ oṃ, i piṅgalā kahanan Saṅ Hyaṅ Mantra. Isĕp tékaṅ sinadya, makavakéki, maññjiṅĕṅ śarīra niṅvaṅ. Kunaṅ yan patya niṅ śatru, hilaṅ varṇṇa Saṅ Hyaṅ Mantra, phaṭ indikānya, Oṃ hroṃ huṃ namaḥ hūṃ hroṃ uṃ, maṅkana.
(19) Yan makadon palayvan iṅ śatru, kukus varṇṇa Saṅ Hyaṅ Mantra, Oṃ indikānya, Oṃ hroṃ huṃ namaḥ hūṃ hroṃ oṃ. Kunaṅ yan makadon huripan i vvaṅ, śvetavarṇṇa (na) S. H. Mantra, vaṣaṭ indikānya, Oṃ hroṃ vaṣaṭ sama voṣaṭ hroṃ oṃ. Kunaṅ yanmakadon tka niṅ śatru, kadi gulū niṅ mrak,....varṇṇa S. H. Mantra, Hūṃ indikānya, upalakṣaṇa.
(20) (21) Oṃ vaṣaṭ oṃ vaṣaṭ namaḥ, riṅ śiraḥ; Oṃ vaṣaṭ aṃ vaṣaṭ namaḥ, riṅ mukamaṇḍala; Oṃ vaṣaṭ ghoṃ vaṣaṭ namaḥ, riṅ hṛdaya; Oṃ hūṃ phaṭ reṃ hūṃ phaṭ namaḥ, riṅ yoni; Oṃ hūṃ phaṭ bhyaḥ hūṃ phaṭ namaḥ, riṅ padakārva; maṅkana nyāsa sarvasiddhi. Iti sarvvaprāyaścitta, inabhyasan sārisāri, tan kaluban rahinĕṅ kulĕm, sarvvaroga hopadrava vināśa, dīrghāyuṣa ta sira.

7. AgPur 308, 10 :
Dhyeyās te padmapattreṣu śaṅkhacakragadādharāḥ
añjanakṣīrakāśmirahemābhās te suvāsasaḥ (TSS : pitavāsasaḥ)
8. MMK Vol. I, p. 44 :
Viṣṇuś cakrapāṇiś caturbhujo gadāśaṅkhāsihasto Garuḍāsanaḥ sarvālaṅkārabhūṣitaś ca.
9. ŚvetUp 3, 5 :
Yā te Rudra śivā tanūr aghorā pāpanāśini
tayā nas tanuvā śantamayā giriśantābhicākaśīhi
10. ŚvetUp 4, 3 :
Tvaṃ strī tvaṃ pumān asi tvaṃ kumāra uta vā kumārī
tvaṃ jīrṇo daṇḍena vañcasi tvaṃ jāto bhavasi viśvatomukhaḥ

11. LiPur 1, 11, 2 and 3a; 1, 12, 1 :
Ekonatriṃśakaḥ kalpo vijñeyaḥ Śvetalohitaḥ
tasmiṃs tat paramaṃ dhyānaṃ dhyāyato Brahmaṇas tadā
Utpannas tu śikhāyuktaḥ kumāraḥ śvetalohitaḥ
....
Tatas triṃśattamaḥ kalpo Rakto nāma prakīrtitaḥ
Brahmā yatra mahātejā raktavarṇam adhārayat

12. LiPur 1, 13, 1-3 :
Ekatriṃśattamaḥ kalpaḥ Pītavāsā iti smṛtaḥ
Brahmā yatra mahābhāgaḥ pītavāsā babhūva ha
Dhyāyataḥ putrakāmasya Brahmaṇaḥ parameṣṭhiṇaḥ
prādurbhūto mahātejāḥ kumāraḥ pītavastradhṛk
Pītagandhānuliptāṅgaḥ pītamālyāmbaro yuvā
hemayajñopavītaś ca pītoṣṇīṣo mahābhujaḥ

13. LiPur 1, 14, 1-6 :
Tatas tasmin gate kalpe pītavarṇe Svayambhuvaḥ
punar anyaḥ pravṛttas tu kalpo nāmnāsitas tu saḥ
Ekārṇave tadā vṛtte divye varṣasahasrake (read : divya-)
sraṣṭukāmaḥ prajā Brahmā cintayāmāsa duḥkhitaḥ
Tasya cintayamānasya putrakāmasya vai prabhoḥ
kṛṣṇaḥ samabhavad varṇo dhyāyataḥ Parameṣṭhiṇaḥ
Athāpaśyan mahātejāḥ prādurbhūtaṃ kumārakam
kṛṣṇavarṇaṃ mahāvīryaṃ dīpyamānaṃ svatejasā
Kṛṣṇāmbaradharoṣṇīṣaṃ kṛṣṇayajñopavītinam
kṛṣṇena maulinā yuktaṃ kṛṣṇasraganulepanam
Sa taṃ dṛṣṭvā mahātmānam Aghoraṃ ghoravikramaṃ
vavande devadeveśam adbhutaṃ kṛṣṇapiṅgalam

14. LiPur 1, 16, 1-5 :
Athānyo Brahmaṇaḥ kalpo vartate munipuṃgavāḥ
Viśvarūpa iti khyāto nāmataḥ paramādbhutaḥ
Vinivṛtte tu saṃhāre punaḥ, sṛṣṭe carācare
Brahmaṇaḥ putrakāmasya dhyāyataḥ parameṣṭhinaḥ
Prādurbhūtā mahānādā Viśvarūpā Sarasvatī
viśvamālyāmbaradharā viśvayajñopavītinī
Viśvoṣṇīṣā viśvagandhā viśvamātā mahoṣṭhikā
tathāvidhaṃ sa bhagavān īśānaṃ parameśvaraṃ
Śuddhasphaṭikasaṃkāśaṃ sarvābharaṇabhūṣitam
atha taṃ manasā dhyātvā yuktātmā vai Pitāmahaḥ....

15. Pañcabrahma Up, st. 25 and 27b-28:
Yena prakāśate viśvaṃ yatraiva pravilīyate
tad Brahma paramaṃ śāntaṃ tad Brahmāsmi paraṃ padam
....
Brahmakāryam iti jñātvā īśānaṃ pratipadyate
Pañcabrahmātmakaṃ sarvaṃ svātmani pravilāpya ca
so 'ham asmīti jānīyād vidvān Brahmāmṛto bhavet

Chapter 4

1. ŚvetUp 4, 1 :
   Ya eko 'varṇo bahudhā śaktiyogād
   varṇān anekān nihitārtho dadhāti
   vi caiti cānte viśvam ādau sa devaḥ
   sa no buddhyā śubhayā saṃyunaktu
2. ŚvetUp 4, 5 :
   Ajām ekāṃ lohitaśuklakṛṣṇām
   bahvīḥ prajāḥ sṛjamānāṃ sarūpāḥ
   ajo hy eko juṣamāṇo 'nuśete
   jahāty enāṃ bhuktabhogām ajo 'nyaḥ
3. Mbh 12, 326, 26 and 27 and 54b :
   Sattvaṃ rajas tamaś caiva guṇān etān pracakṣate
   ete sarvaśarīreṣu tiṣṭhanti vicaranti ca
   Etān guṇāṃs tu kṣetrajño bhuṅkte naibhiḥ sa bhujyate
   nirguṇo guṇabhuk caiva guṇasraṣṭā guṇādhikaḥ
   . . . .
   trīṃś caivemān guṇān paśya matsthān mūrtivivarjitān
   Kṛṣṇa Up, st. 5 :
   Māyā sā trividhā proktā sattvarājasatāmasī
   proktā sāttvī ca Rudre sā bhakte brahmaṇi rājasī
   tāmasī daityapakṣe tu māyā tredhā hy udāhṛtā
4. MMK, Vol. II, p. 538:
   Jātikusumair devīnāṃ pratimāṃ tāḍayet: rājā vaśyo bhavati. Jātikalikair devīnāṃ pratimāṃ tāḍayed, aṣṭaśatavārāṃ pañcakalikābhis trisandhyaṃ sapta divasāni: yam icchati rājakanyāṃ mahādhanopetāṃ varāṅgarūpiṇiṃ tāṃ labhate.
5. JaimBr 1, 80 :
   Sa yaṃ kāmayeta pāpīyān syād iti kṛṣṇam asya pavitre 'pyasyet, pāpīyān eva bhavati. Atha yaṃ kāmayeta nārvāṅ na paraḥ syād iti dhūmram asya pavitre 'pyasyen, naivārvāṅ na paro bhavati. Atha yaṃ kāmayeta śreyān syād rucam aśnuvīteti, phalgunam asya pavitraṃ kuryāc, chreyān eva bhavati rucam aśnute.
6. MMD 5, 82 :
   Karmasu krūrasaumyeṣu dhyāyen mantrī yathā tathā
   evaṃ siddhe manau mantrī girā Vācaspatir bhavet
7. GarPur 50, 36 :
   Pūjyā dvijānāṃ kumudendubhāso ye kṣatriyāṇāṃ jvalanārkavarṇāḥ
   tathā viśāṃ ye kanakāvadātā nīlīprabhāḥ śūdrajanasya ye ca
8. AVPar 70a, 2:
   Viprāṇāṃ bhavati hi śuklam ambudoṣe
   rājānaṃ sapadi nihanti lohitaṃ ca
   pītaṃ ced bhavati nihanti vaiśyavargaṃ
   śūdrāṇāṃ bhavati hi kṛṣṇapiṅgadoṣe
9. Mbh 12, 326, 1-8:
   1 Evaṃ stutaḥ sa bhagavān guhyais tathyaiś ca nāmabhiḥ
   taṃ muniṃ darśayāmāsa Nāradaṃ viśvarūpadhṛk

2 Kiṃcic candraviśuddhātmā kiṃcic candrād viśeṣavān
kṛśānuvarṇaḥ kiṃcic ca kiṃcid dhiṣṇyākṛtiḥ prabhuḥ
3 Śukapatravarṇaḥ kiṃcic ca kiṃcit sphaṭikasaprabhaḥ
nīlāñjanacayaprakhyo jātarūpaprabhaḥ kvacit
4 Pravālāṅkuravarṇaś ca śvetavarṇaḥ kvacid babhau
kvacit suvarṇavarṇābho vaiḍūryasadṛśaḥ kvacit
5 Nīlavaiḍūryasadṛśa indranīlanibhaḥ kvacit
mayūragrīvavarṇābho muktāhāranibhaḥ kvacit
6 Etān varṇān bahuvidhān rūpe bibhrat sanātanaḥ
sahasranayanaḥ śrīmāñ chataśīrṣaḥ sahasrapāt
7 Sahasrodarabāhuś ca Avyakta iti ca kvacit
oṃkāram udgiran vaktrāt sāvitrīṃ ca tadanvayām
8 Śeṣebhyaś caiva vaktrebhyaś caturvedodgataṃ vasu
āraṇyakaṃ jagau devo Harir Nārāyaṇo vaśī

10. Mbh 3, 187, 32-34:

Antakāle ca samprāpte Kālo bhūtvātidāruṇaḥ
trailokyaṃ nāśayāmy ekaḥ kṛtsnaṃ sthāvarajaṅgamam
Ahaṃ trivartmā sarvātmā sarvalokasukhāvahaḥ
abhibhūḥ sarvago 'nanto Hṛṣīkeśa urukramaḥ
Kālacakraṃ nayāmy eko brahmann aham arūpī vai
śamanaṃ sarvabhūtānāṃ sarvalokakṛtodyamam

11. Bhāsa, Bālacarita 1, ed. Devadhar, p. 511 :

Śaṅkhakṣīravapuḥ purā Kṛtayuge nāmnā tu Nārāyaṇas
Tretāyāṃ tripadārpitatribhuvano Viṣṇuḥ suvarṇaprabhaḥ
dūrvāśyāmanibhaḥ sa Rāvaṇavadhe Rāmo yuge Dvāpare
nityaṃ yo 'ñjanasannibhaḥ Kaliyuge vaḥ pātu Dāmodaraḥ

12. BhPur 10, 8, 13:

Āsan varṇās trayo hy asya gṛhṇato 'nuyugaṃ tanuḥ
śuklo raktas tathā pīta idānīṃ kṛṣṇatāṃ gataḥ

13. Mbh 12, 47, 43 :

Brahma vaktraṃ bhujau kṣatraṃ kṛtsnam ūrūdaraṃ viśaḥ
pādau yasyāśritāḥ śūdrās tasmai varṇātmane namaḥ

14. BhPur 3, 6, 34 and 35 :

Ete varṇāḥ svadharmeṇa yajanti svaguruṃ Harim
śraddhayātmaviśuddhyarthaṃ yajjātāḥ saha vṛttibhiḥ
Etat kṣattar bhagavato devakarmātmarūpiṇaḥ
kaḥ śraddadhyād upākartuṃ yogamāyābalodayam

15. PST 22, 35 :

Pītābhā karṇikā syād aruṇataram araṃ śyāmalaṃ cāntarālaṃ
nemiḥ śvetā ca bāhye viracitaśikharekhākulaṃ pārthivāntam
cakradvandvaṃ likhitvā viśadamatiratho saumyayāmyāñ ca mantrī
kumbhaṃ sampūrya saumye praracayatu tathā dakṣiṇe homakarma

AgPur 306, 9b and 10 :

Pītañ cakraṃ gadā raktāḥ svarāḥ śyāmam avāntaram
Nemiḥ śvetā bahiḥ kṛṣṇavarṇarekhā ca pārthivī
madhyetare mare varṇān evaṃ cakradvayaṃ likhet

TSS 18, 7b and 8 :
Pītaṃ cakraṃ ghaṭaṃ raktam araṃ śyāmam arāntaram
Nemiḥ śvetā bahiḥ kṛṣṇavarṇā rekhā ca pārthivī
madhye tāram areṣvarṇān evaṃ cakradvayaṃ likhet

16. SM, No. 194, Vol. II, p. 396 :
..pītāṃ caturmukhāṃ triṇetrām aṣṭabhujāṃ prathamamukhaṃ
pītaṃ dakṣiṇaṃ sitaṃ paścimaṃ nīlaṃ vāmaṃ raktam....

17. HT 2, 1 :
Śukravarṇaṃ bhavec chāntau pītaṃ tu pauṣṭike tathā
māraṇe kṛṣṇavarṇaṃ tu vaśye raktaṃ prakīrtitam
yathā vaśye tathākṛṣṭau dveṣādau yathā māraṇe

18. TSS 47b-50a (=AgPur 301, 15b-17) :
Dhyānaṃ vaśye 'ruṇaṃ stambhe pītam āpyāyane sitam
Abhicāravidhau kṛṣṇaṃ mohane śakracāpavat
yo 'bhiṣekajapadhyānapūjāhomaparaḥ sadā
Tejasvī subhagaḥ śrīmān sa yuddhādau jayaṃ labhet
(AgPur : samudrādau jayaṃ labhet)

19. T, p. 426 :
Raktāṃ dhyāyed imāṃ vaśye stambhe svarṇanibhāṃ smaret
dhūmrām uccāṭane dhyāyet kṛṣṇāṃ māraṇakarmaṇi

20. Māyābījastotra (Jhavery, Appendix 25), st. 4-7 :
Tvāṃ cintayan śvetakarānukāraṃ
jyotsnāmayīṃ paśyati yas trilokīm
śrayanti taṃ tatkṣaṇato 'navadyāḥ
vidyākalāśāntikapauṣṭikāni
Tvām eva bālāruṇamaṇḍalābhaṃ
smṛtvā jagat tvatkarajāladīpram
vilokate yaḥ kila tasya viśvaṃ
viśvaṃ bhaved vaśyam avaśyam eva
Yas taptacāmīkaracārudīpraṃ
piṅgaprabhaṃ tvāṃ kalayet samantāt
sadā mudā tasya gṛhe sahelaṃ
karoti kelīṃ Kamalā calāpi
Yaḥ śyāmalaṃ kajjalamecakābhaṃ
tvāṃ vīkṣate cātuṣadhūmadhūmram
vipakṣapakṣaḥ khalu tasya vātā-
hatāmravad yāty acireṇa nāśam

21. Mbh 1, 55, 28-30 :
Ajayad Bhīmasenas tu diśaṃ prācīṃ mahābalaḥ
udīcīm Arjuno vīraḥ pratīcīṃ Nakulas tathā
Dakṣiṇāṃ Sahadevas tu vijigye paravīrahā
evaṃ cakrur imāṃ sarve vaśe kṛtsnāṃ vasundharām
Pañcabhiḥ Sūryasaṃkāśaiḥ Sūryeṇa ca virājatā
ṣaṭsūryeṇābabhau pṛthvī Pāṇḍavaiḥ satyavikramaiḥ

22. Mbh 1, 62, 3-5 :
Pauravāṇāṃ vaṃśakaro Duḥṣanto nāma vīryavān
pṛthivyāś caturantāyā goptā Bharatasattama
Caturbhāgaṃ bhuvaḥ kṛtsnaṃ sa bhuṅkte manujeśvaraḥ

samudrāvaraṇāṃś cāpi deśān sa Samitiṃjayaḥ
Āmlecchāṭavikān sarvān sa bhuṅkte ripumardanaḥ
ratnākarasamudrāntāṃś cāturvarṇyajanāvṛtān

23. KCT 5, 185 :
Pṛthvī syād dhemadhātur jalam api rajataṃ vahnidhātuś ca tāmraṃ
vāyuś cāyaś ca śūnyaṃ trapu bhujagam idaṃ miśradhātusvabhāvam
pṛthvī syāt pītaratnaṃ sitam api jalajaṃ raktaratnaṃ ca vahniḥ
kṛṣṇaṃ vāyuś ca nīlaṃ haritam api tathā miśradhātūdbhavaṃ tat

24. JT 20, 170 and 171a :
Śvetaṃ dhyānaṃ bhavec chāntyai pītaṃ stambhanakārakam
vaśyākarṣaṇayo raktaṃ kṣobhaṇārthaṃ priyāvaham
Kṛṣṇaṃ ca māraṇe proktaṃ dhūmram uccāṭanādike

25. AVPar 50, 5, 4-6:
Harite śarīre somasya paśūnāṃ vadham ādiśet
kṛṣṇe śarīre somasya śūdrāṇāṃ vadham ādiśet
pīte śarīre somasya vaiśyānāṃ vadham ādiśet
rakte śarīre somasya rājñāṃ tu vadham ādiśet
śukle śarīre somasya brahmavṛddhiṃ vinirdiśet

26. PST 23, 18 :
Jānvor āpādam udyatkanakam iva himaprakhyam ājānunābheḥ
kaṇṭhād ānābhi vahniprabham atha śirasaś cāgalaṃ nīlavarṇam
mauler vyomābham ākaṅkaralasad ariśaṅkhāsikheṭaṃ gadāśakty-
ākhyeṣṭābhītihastaṃ praṇamata vasudhollāsidaṃṣṭraṃ Varāham

27. KCT 4, 182 :
Pādāt kaṭyantapīto Garuḍa iti tathā nābhisīmno himābhaḥ
ākaṇṭhād raktavarṇaḥ gaganaghananibho bhrūlatāṃ yāvad eva
tasmād vai viśvavarṇaḥ phaṇikulasahito mudritaḥ pañcatattvair
dhyātas tanmudrayā vai harati phaṇiviṣaṃ bhūtarogādikaṃ ca

28. PST 30, 54-56; 58; 59; 61; 62 :
54 Pītāyomuṣṭigadahastā mahiṣājyasaṃyutapulākaiḥ
vaibhītakāriṣṭasamitkodravakaiḥ stambhayec ca hutavidhinā
55 Susitā pāśāṅkuśayugvigaladvāripravāhasaṃbhinnā
vaitasasamidāhutyā madhurayujā maṅkṣu vaśayed Durgā
56 Raktā pāśāṅkuśinī niśi phalinīkesarodbhavaiḥ puṣpaiḥ
candanarasasaṃsiktair homād Durgā vaśīkaroti jagat
58 Sakapālaśūlapāśāṅkuśahastāruṇatarā tathā Durgā
ākarṣayec ca lāvaṇaputtalyā trimadhurāktayā homāt
59 Dhyātvā dhūmrāṃ musalatriśikhakarām asthibhiś ca tīkṣṇāktaiḥ
karpāsānāṃ nimbacchadameṣaghṛtair hutāc ca vidveṣaḥ
61 Śikhiśūlakarāgninibhā sarṣapatailāktamattabījaiś ca
marīcair vā rājiyutair homād ahitān vimohayed Durgā
62 Kṛṣṇā śūlāsikarā ripudinavṛkṣodbhavaiḥ samitpravāraiḥ
vraṇakṛdghṛtasaṃsiktair homān mārayati māsato Durgā

29. T, p. 380 :
Utthāya cottare yāme kuṇḍalim āsanaṃ kṛtam
cintayed Ugratārāṃ vai muktibhāgī bhaven naraḥ
śāntyai kundendudhavalāṃ cintayet sādhakottamaḥ

dhūmrābhām pūjayed vāyumaṇḍale pūjitā tathā
unmādayati śatrūṇāṃ balaṃ buddhiṃ na saṃśayaḥ

30. KCT 2, 29 :
Kāye bhāvapraveśaḥ kham iva samaraso bhāvamadhye ca kāyo
jñātavyo yogayuktaiḥ prakṛtiguṇavaśād dhātuvarṇādibhedaiḥ
pītaḥ kṛṣṇaś ca varṇas tv aruṇa iti sito bhūmivātāgnitoye
jñānākāśe ca nīlo bhavati hi haritaḥ kāyabhāvaprabhedāt

31. Jayākhya Saṃhitā 14, 76-78:
Vidhinānena japtavyo mantro dhyānasamanvitaḥ
śāntike sphaṭikābhaṃ ca pītaṃ dhyāyec ca pauṣṭike
vaśye kiṃśukapuṣpābham ākṛṣṭau Nṛpaśailavat
māraṇe kajjalābhaṃ tu vidveṣe cāṣapakṣavat
uccāṭane ca dhūmrābhaṃ mantraṃ dhyāyej japet sadā

Chapter 5

1. Ṛgvidh. 1, 18, 1:
Hiraṇyastūpam Indrasya sūktaṃ karmābhisaṃstavam
taj japan prayataḥ śatrūn ayatnāt pratibādhate

2. ŚatBr 4, 2, 7, 5 :
..yadaivaitena mādhyandinena pavamānena stuvate 'tha vijite bhaye 'nāṣṭre dakṣiṇā nīyante tatho evaiṣa etaiḥ pañcabhir grahaiḥ pāpmano dviṣate bhrātṛvyāya vajraṃ praharati; sa vṛtraṃ pāpmānaṃ hatvā vijite...; tasmād vā etān pañca grahān gṛhṇāti.

3. AgPur 133, 31 :
Hastādyair dhāritā pūrvaṃ Brahmarudrendraviṣṇubhiḥ
gurusaṅgrāmakāle tu vidyayā rakṣitāḥ surāḥ

4. Śāntistava by Tyāgarāja, st. 22 :
Indrajālam idam alpakālikaṃ viśvam evam iti niścayātmanaḥ
bodharūpata ihaiva bhāti yā sā śivāham iti śāntim āśraye

5. YogV, Nirvāṇaprakaraṇa, 1, 20, 23:
Putrāḥ kaccid aparyantavāsanātantuguṇṭhitāt
bhavanto nirgatā nūnam asmāt saṃsārajālakāt ?

6. SkPur 2, 26, 6 and 7a :
Pāpino manujāḥ sarve hy asmāsu snānti yatnataḥ
visṛjya pāpajālāni kṛtārthā yānti vai janāḥ
Asmākaṃ pāpajālaṃ tat kathaṃ naśyati sarvataḥ ?

7. JT 17, 14 :
Pātālatalanāgendrakanyakāḥ kṣā(read : kṣo)bhayanti tam
tāsāṃ kaṭākṣajālais tu na mohaṃ yāti sādhakaḥ

8. Sureśvara, Taittirīyopaniṣadbhāṣyavārttika, 2, 374 :
Vyākṛtir yā tayor Viṣṇoḥ pratyahaṃ nāmarūpayoḥ
bhūyo bhavanaṃ etat syān māyino 'nekatā yathā

9. PST 30, 84 :
Kṛtyā naśyati tasya vīkṣitena grahādayo bhītyā (read : bhītyā)
kartāram eti kupitā kṛtyā sarvātmanā ca nāśayati

10. Manusmṛti 11, 33 and 34 :
Śrutir Atharvāṅgirasiḥ kuryād ity avicārayan

vāk śastraṃ vai brāhmaṇasya tena hanyād arīn dvijaḥ
Kṣatriyo bāhuvīryeṇa tared āpadam ātmanaḥ
dhanena vaiśyaśūdrau tu japahomair dvijottamaḥ

11. GautDh 2, 2, 17 :
Śāntipuṇyāhasvastyayanāyuṣmanmaṅgalasaṃyuktāny ābhyudayikāni vidveṣaṇasaṃvananābhicāradviṣadvyṛddhiyuktāni ca śālāgnau kuryāt.

12. Mitākṣarā, comm. on GautDh 2, 2, 17 :
...uccāṭanādīny etāni ca śālāgnau kuryāt. Kaḥ ? Rājā. Tasya ca kartṛtvam idam eva; yat tat saṃvidhātṛtvam arthasaṃpradānādinā...(aparaḥ) : ābhyudayikāni purohitaḥ svayaṃ kuryād itarāṇi kārayed iti....

13. LiPur 2, 50, 48b and 49 :
Svarāṣṭrapatim uddiśya yaḥ kuryād abhicārikam
Sa ātmānaṃ nihatyaiva svakulaṃ nāśayet kudhīḥ
tasmāt svarāṣṭragoptāraṃ nṛpatiṃ pālayet sadā

14. MMK, Vol. I, p. 49 :
..rājaputraṃ mūrdhābhiṣiktaṃ kṣatriyaputraṃ vā anyaṃ vā mahotsāhamahārājyakāmaṃ vā praveśayet.

15. MMK, Vol. I, p. 51 :
Adhṛṣyaḥ sarvabhūtānām ajitaḥ sarvadehinām
vijayatvaṃ sarvamantrāṇāṃ sādhayastvaṃ (?) yathepsataḥ

16. AV 4, 36, 9 :
Yé mā krodháyanti lapitā́ hastínaṃ maśákā iva
tā́n ahā́ṃ manye dúrhitāṃ jáne àlpaśayūn iva

17. PST 9, 23-27 :
23 Sasurāsurasiddhayakṣavidyādharagandharvabhujaṅgacāraṇānām
pramadā madavegato vikirṇābharaṇāḥ srastadukūlakeśajālāḥ
24 Atiduḥsahamanmathavyathābhir vyathitāntaḥparitāpavepitāṅgyaḥ
ghanagharmajatoyabindumuktāphalasaktorukucāntabahumūlāḥ.
25 Romāñcakañcukitagātralatāghanodyaduttuṅgapīnakucakumbhanipīḍitāṅgyaḥ
autsukyabhāraprthuvepathukhedakhinnapādāravindacalanaskhalitābhighātāḥ
26 Mārasāyakanipātadāritā rāgasāgaranimagnamūrtayaḥ
śvāsamārutataraṅgitādharā bāṣpapūrabharavihvalekṣaṇāḥ
27 Mastakāracitadordvayāñjaliprābhṛtā hariṇaśāvalocanāḥ
vāñcitārthakaraṇodyatāś ca taddṛṣṭipātam api saṃnamanti tāḥ

18. S, p. 200 :
Mūrdhni caiva lalāṭe ca nyasen mantratrayaṃ hṛdi
ārogyaṃ sarvajantūnāṃ yathecchaṃ gacchati svayam

19. S, p. 234 :
Evaṃ dhyātvā tu deveśīṃ śatrustambhanakāriṇīm
mahāvidyāṃ mahāmāyāṃ sādhakasya phalapradām
yasyāḥ smaraṇamātreṇa trailokyaṃ stambhayet kṣaṇāt

20. MMK, Vol. II, p. 322 :
Asahyaṃ sarvabhūtānaṃ sarvalokānuliptakam

adhṛṣyaṃ sarvabhūtānāṃ bhāvamārgaviśodhakam
prāpakaṃ Buddhadharmāṇāṃ sarvaduṣṭanivāraṇam
anumoditaṃ sarvabuddhais tu sarvasampattikārakam
utkṛṣṭaḥ sarvamantrāṇāṃ Mañjughoṣasya śāsane

21. AgPur 302, 6 mantra :
Oṃ hrīṃ oṃ namaḥ Kāmāya sarvajanahitāya sarvajanamohanāya
prajvalitāya sarvajanahṛdayaṃ mamātmagataṃ kuru kuru oṃ.

22. SST 1, 12, 7 :
Sarveśvaraḥ sarvagaś ca sarvamantraparāyaṇaḥ
sarvatantrārthavettā ca sarvatantraparāyaṇaḥ

23. Ṛgvidh. 1, 1, 4 :
Nānārthāni ca karmāṇi śāntipuṣṭyāśrayāṇi ca
siddhayaś ca tapomūlāḥ śraddadhānasya kurvataḥ

Chapter 6

1. T, p. 354 :
Kāmyaprayogakartṛṇāṃ paraloko na vidyate
prayogasiddhir evaiṣāṃ phalam anyan na vidyate
Ekasya hi vidhānasya na kutrāpi phaladvayam
deveśi dṛṣyate yasmān, niṣkāmo devatāṃ bhajet

2. MtPur 93, 140 :
Vaśyakarmābhicārādi tathaivoccāṭanādikam
navagrahamakhaṃ kṛtvā tataḥ kāmyaṃ samācaret

3. Vārāhī Tantra, quoted by Jhavery, p. 51 :
Sṛṣṭiś ca pralayaś caiva devatānāṃ tathārcanam
sādhanaṃ caiva sarveṣāṃ puraścaraṇam eva ca
Ṣaṭkarmasādhanaṃ caiva dhyānayogaś caturvidhaḥ
saptabhir lakṣaṇair yuktam Āgamaṃ tad vidur budhāḥ

4. LiPur 2, 52, 2 and 3 :
Vaśyam ākarṣaṇañ caiva vidveṣaṇam ataḥ param
uccāṭanaṃ stambhanañ ca mocanaṃ (read : mohanaṃ) tāḍanaṃ tathā
Utsādanaṃ tathā chedaṃ māraṇaṃ pratibandhanam
senāstambhanakādīni Sāvitryā sarvam ācaret

5. JT 17, 83-87 :
83 Māsena hanti kaluṣaṃ saptajanmakṛtaṃ naraḥ
pūrvāśābhimukho bhūtvā pītadravyaiḥ samarcayet
84 Pītasthāne samālikhya stambhayet sarvavādinaḥ
uttarāśāmukho bhūtvā sindūrarajasā likhet
85 Pūjayed vidhivad vidvān sarvalokaṃ vaśaṃ nayet
paścimābhimukho bhūtvā candanena samālikhet
86 Sampūjya vidhivad vidvān sarvayoṣinmano haret
vallabho jāyate devi dāsīm iva vaśaṃ nayet
87 Yamāśābhimukho bhūtvā cakraṃ kṛṣṇaṃ yadārcayet
yasya nāmāṅkitaṃ tasya mantrahāniḥ prajāyate

6. KātyŚr 4, 15, 21-26 :
Payasā svargakāmaḥ paśukāmo vā. Yavāgvā grāmakāmaḥ. Taṇḍulair balakāmaḥ. Dadhnendriyakāmaḥ. Ghṛtena tejaskāmaḥ.
7. K, st. 4 and 5a :
vasantaś caiva pūrvāhne grīṣmo madhyāhna ucyate
varṣā jñeyāparāhne tu pradoṣe śiṣiraḥ smṛtaḥ
Ardharātrau śaratkāla ūṣā hemanta ucyate
8. JT 20, 168 and 169 :
Stambhane gajacarmāṇi māraṇe māhiṣaṃ tathā
mṛgacarma tathoccāṭe chāgalaṃ vaśyakarmaṇi
Vidveṣe jambukaṃ proktaṃ gocarma śāntike tathā
nānāsiddhihitārthāya vyāghracarmam udāhṛtam
9. S 1, 31 :
Indre stambhanam uccāṭam Agnau sarvābhicārakam
Yāmye Rakṣasi vidveṣaḥ śāntir Vāruṇavāyave
kulotsādaṃ Marudbhāge Yakṣe kalahavigrahau
10. N, p. 271 :
Śāntike pauṣṭike mokṣe mānasaṃ japam ācaret
vaśyākṛṣṭāv upāṃśu syād vācikaṃ kṣudrakarmaṇi
11. MMK, Vol. III, ch. 52, p. 575 :
Sarve ca samaye ākṛṣṭāḥ iha krodharājena Yamāntakena ānitā grastā samaye sthāpitā Mañjughoṣasyopanāmitā....paricārikā.
12. KCT 3 199 :
Ye sattvā lokadhātau trividhabhavagatā jñānavajrāṅkuśena
ākṛṣṭvā tān samantāt paramakaruṇayā maṇḍale cābhiṣicya
Buddhair vajrāmṛtenāmalaśaśivapuṣā vajriṇo labdhamārgāḥ
svasthāne preṣaṇīyā vyapagatakaluṣā bodhicaryādhirūpaiḥ
13. MMK, Vol. III, ch. 53, 619 :
Kṣaṇena smṛtamātreṇa...huṃkāreṇa mātreṇa Brahmādyān ānayed bhuvi : ākṛṣṭā sarvadevās tu Brahmādyāḥ saśakrakāḥ, hāhākāraṃ pramuñcānā ārtā bhairavanādinaḥ. Kiṃ karoma kim ānītā....
14. N. 6 3 :
Raktavastre likhed yantraṃ lākṣayā raktacandanaiḥ
pūjyaṃ tad dhi taror mūle nikhaned dharaṇītale
trisaptāhaṃ sadā siñcet prātas tat taṇḍulodakaiḥ
dūrād ākarṣayen nārīṃ yadi sā nigaḍānvitā
Oṃ hrīṃ Raktacāmuṇḍe, turu turu amukīm ākarṣaya hrīṃ svāhā
15. JT 17, 28-30 :
Haṭhād ānayate śīghraṃ yakṣiṇīṃ rājakanyakām
nāgakanyām apsarasaṃ khecarīṃ vā surāṅganām
Vidyādharīṃ divyarūpām ṛṣikanyāṃ ripustriyam
madanodbhavasaṃtāpāṃ sphurajjaghanamaṇḍalām
Kāmabāṇaprabhinnāntaḥkaraṇāṃ lolacakṣuṣam
Mahākāmakalādhyānayogāt tu suravandite
16. SM, No. 59, p. 123 :
Iṣuṇā tu kucaṃ viddhvā aśokais tāḍayed dhṛdi
khaḍgena bhīṣayet sādhyāṃ darpaṇaṃ darśayet tataḥ

utpalena padaṃ baddhvā ākarṣayet sa vihvalāṃ muktakeśām iti
Oṃ amukīm ākarṣaya Mañjughoṣa hrīḥ jaḥ

17. MtPur 93, 75 :
Yathā ratneṣu sarveṣu sarve devāḥ pratiṣṭhitāḥ
tathā ratnāni yacchantu ratnadānena me surāḥ

18. AVPar 36, 26, 1-3 (the complete chapter) :
Lakṣajāpottaraṃ gatvā nadīm udadhigāminīm
vālukāsthaṇḍile liṅgaṃ tanmayaṃ tajjasadmani
Padmāṣṭaśatam āhṛtya pūjayitvā vidhānataḥ
udake nābhimātre ca suprabhātaṃ punar japet
Tato māṇḍaliko rājā dīnārāṇāṃ gavāṃ śataṃ
praṇamya śraddhayā tasmai dadyād uddhara mām iti

19. N, p. 363 :
Ardharātre samutthāya sahasraikaṃ japen manum
māsam ekaṃ tato devī nidhiṃ darśayati dhruvam

20. SST 3, 20, 51 :
Annena rahito mārge kṣudhāsaṃpīḍito naraḥ
japed amuṃ mahāmantram aṣṭottarasahasrakam

21. Bhāṣyotkarṣadīpikā on BhGītā 7, 14 :
Māyābimbo vaśīkṛtya tāṃ syāt sarvajña Īśvaraḥ
avidyāvaśagas tv anyas tadvaicitryāt....

22. GarPur, Bareli ed., 107, 43 :
Tṛṇādicaturāsyāntaṃ bhūtagrāmaṃ caturvidham
carācaraṃ jagat sarvaṃ prasuptaṃ māyayā tava

23. GarPur 194, 23b and c :
Yo māṃ paśyati cakṣurbhyāṃ yañ ca paśyāmi cakṣuṣā
sarveṣāṃ pāpaduṣṭānāṃ Viṣṇur badhnāti cakṣuṣī

24. PST 7, 67 :
Anudinam anulimpet tena kiñcit samadyāt tilakam api vidadhyād
uttamāṅge kṣipec ca
anutataduritāpasmārabhūtāpamṛtyugrahaviṣarahitaḥ syāt
prīyate ca prajābhiḥ

25. N 2, 43 mantra (p. 280)
Oṃ namo bhagavate Rudrāya siddharūpiṇe śikhibandha sarveṣāṃ
śivam astu śivam astu hana hana rakṣa rakṣa sarvabhūtebhyaś ca
namaḥ

26. GarPur 178, 6:
Aguruṃ gugguluñ caiva nīlotpalasamanvitam
guḍena dhūpayitvā tu rājadvāre priyo bhavet

27. Inscription of Telaga Batu, line 13 :
ini makalaṅit prāṇa uraṃ marūpabhasmavaidimantraprayoga. Tida
āhāra dari samayaṅku rūpiṇaṅku kuṣṭa kasihan vaśīkaraṇa lai...

28. MtPur 93, 145-148 :
Vaśyakarmaṇi bilvānāṃ padmānāṃ caiva dharmavit
sumitriyā na āpa oṣadhaya iti homayet
Na cātra sthāpanaṃ kāryaṃ na ca kumbhābhiṣecanam
snānaṃ sarvauṣadhaiḥ kṛtvā śuklapuṣpāmbaro gṛhī
Kaṇṭhasūtraiḥ sakanakair viprān samabhipūjayet

sūkṣmavastrāṇi deyāni śuklā gāvaḥ sakāñcanāḥ
Avaśyāni vaśikuryāt sarvaśatrubalāny api
amitrāṇy api mitrāṇi homo'yaṃ pāpanāśanaḥ

29. Kathās, 2, 4, 89 :
Tatra sā Lohajaṅghasya tasya saubhāgyasaṃpadā
vaśikṛtā sati nānyat phalaṃ janmany amanyata

30. GarPur 41, 1 mantra :
Oṃ Viśvāvasur nāma gandharvaḥ kanyānām adhipatir labhāmi te kanyāṃ samutpādya, tasmai Viśvāvasave svāhā.
N 4, 48 mantra (p. 290) :
Oṃ Viśvāvasur nāma gandharvaḥ kanyakānām adhipatiḥ, surūpāṃ sālaṃkārāṃ dehi me, namas tasmai Viśvāvasave svāhā.

31. SM, No. 92, Vaśyādhikāratārāsādhanam :
Tāṃkārajam tāṃkārākrāntamadhyam indivaraṃ dhyātvā tatpariṇatām Āryatārāṃ śyāmavarṇāṃ vāmenotpaladharāṃ dakṣiṇe varadāṃ bhadrāsanasthitām Amoghasiddhimakuṭiṃ dhyātvā jñānasattvenaikikṛtya, Oṃ Tāre tuttāre ture amukam amukiṃ vā vaśam ānaya svāhā iti sādhyanāmasahitam anantaroktena saṃkhyāniyamena japet / śārādicihnābhāve 'pi sādhyāgalam utpalena baddhvā svaśarīrāruṇakiraṇasañcayais taccharīram āpūrya svavaśe sthāpayed iti.

32. GarPur 178, 19 mantra :
Oṃ hriṃ Gauri devi saubhāgyaṃ putravaśyādi dehi me
Oṃ hriṃ Lakṣmi devi saubhāgyaṃ sarvaṃ trailokyamohanaṃ dehi me.

33. JT 17, 53 :
Rājāno vājinaḥ sarpā gajā duṣṭā madotkaṭāḥ
vyāghrāḥ kesariṇo mattā vaśyās tasya bhavanti hi

34. S, p. 241 :
Rājāno harayo madāndhakariṇaḥ sarpā mṛgendrādikā
ete yānti vimohitā ripugaṇā Lakṣmiḥ sthirā siddhayaḥ

35. S, p. 243f., meditation stanzas on Gaṇapati :
Ratnamaṇḍalamadhyasthaṃ ratnasiṃhāsanopari
pitavarṇāṃśukālepamālyābharaṇabhāsvaram
viraṃ vā viditaṃ devaṃ gajavaktraṃ trilocanam
pāśāṅkuśakrodhamudrāṃ paraśuñ cābhayaṃ varam
dadhānaṃ devadeveśaṃ dhyāyed devam ananyadhīḥ

36. BMR, p. 5, meditation stanza :
Sauvarṇāsanasaṃsthitāṃ triṇayanāṃ pitāṃśukollāsinīm
hemabhaṅgaruciṃ śaśāṅkamukuṭāṃ saccampakasragyutām
hastair mudgarapāśavajrarasanāḥ sambibhratiṃ bhūṣaṇair
vyāptāṅgiṃ Bagalāmukhiṃ trijagatāṃ saṃstambhiniṃ cintayet

37. S, p. 239, meditation stanza on Bagalāmukhī :
Madhye sudhābdhimaṇimaṇḍaparatnavedi-
siṃhāsanoparigatāṃ paripitavarṇām
pitāmbarābharaṇamālyavibhūṣitāṅgiṃ
deviṃ smarāmi dhṛtamudgaravairijihvām

38. S, p. 240f. :
Vādī mūkati raṅkati kṣitipatir vaiśvānaraḥ śitati
krodhī śāmyati durjanaḥ sujanati kṣiprānugaḥ khañjati

garvī kharvati sarvavic ca jaḍati tvanmantriṇā yantritaḥ
Śrīnitye Bagalāmukhi pratidinaṃ kalyāṇi tubhyaṃ namaḥ
Duṣṭastambhanam ugravighnaśamanaṃ dāridryavidrāvaṇaṃ
bhūbhṛtstambhanakāraṇaṃ mṛgadṛśāṃ cetaḥsamākarṣaṇam
saubhāgyaikaniketanaṃ mama dṛśoḥ kāruṇyapūrṇāmṛtaṃ
śatror māraṇam āvir astu purato mātas tvadīyaṃ vapuḥ
Mātar bhañjaya me vipakṣavadanaṃ jihvāñ calāṃ kīlaya
brāhmīṃ mudraya nāśayāśu dhiṣaṇām ugrāṃ gatiṃ stambhaya
śatrūṃś cūrṇaya devi tīkṣṇagadayā gaurāṅgi pītāmbare
vighnaughaṃ Bagale hara pratidinaṃ kāruṇyapūrṇekṣaṇe

39. AgPur 125, 48 mantra :
Oṃ namo Mahābhairavāya vikṛtadaṃṣṭrograrūpāya piṅgalākṣāya triśūlakhaḍgadharāya (v.l., -khaṭvāṅgadharāya) vauṣaṭ.

40. AgPur 125, 51 mantra :
Oṃ namo bhagavati Kaumāri lala[2] lālaya[2] ghaṇṭādevi amukaṃ māraya[2] sahasā namo 'stu te bhagavati vidye svāhā.
Anayā vidyayā homād bandhatvaṃ (v.l. dagdhatvaṃ) jāyate ripoḥ

41. AgPur 125, 51 second mantra :
Oṃ vajrakāya vajratuṇḍa kapilapiṅgala karālavadana ūrdhvakeśa mahābala raktamukha taḍijjihva mahāraudra daṃṣṭrotkaṭa kaha karālina mahādṛḍhaprahāra Laṅkeśvara setubandha śailapravāha gaganavara, ehy ehi bhagavan mahābalaparākrama, Bhairavo jñāpayati, ehy ehi mahāraudra, dīrghalāṅgūlena amukaṃ veṣṭaya[2] jambhaya[2] khana[2] vaite hrūṃ phaṭ.

42. N 7, 43 mantra (p. 304) :
Oṃ Himālayottare bhāge Mārīco nāma rākṣasaḥ
tasya mūtrapurīṣābhyāṃ hutāśaṃ stambhayāmy ahaṃ svāhā.

43. AgPur 137, 12b and 13a :
Khararaktasamāyuktahomād uccāṭayed ripum
kākaraktasamāyogād dhomād utsādanaṃ hy areḥ

44. AVPar 7, 1 :
Na suṣvāpa purā Śakro dānavānāṃ purodhasā
prayuktair auṣadhair yogair mantrāṇāṃ japahomataḥ

45. ṢaḍvBr 3, 8, 14 :
...Bṛhadrathaṃtarābhyām evainam ebhyo lokebhya uddhṛtya Plavena praplāvayati parāṃ parāvatam eti na pratitiṣṭhati.

46. AgPur 260, 13 and 14a (=ViDhPur 2, 125, 13 and 14a) :
Ekādaśāṅgulaṃ śaṅkuṃ lauhaṃ khādiram eva ca
dviṣati vadho 'sīti japan nikhaned ripuveśmani
uccāṭanam idaṃ karma śatrūṇāṃ kathitaṃ tava

47. MMK, Vol. II, p. 307 (ch. 27) :
...atha kruddhacittaś caturvarṇyo anyataraṃ vikṛtasthāne vā yāto vikṛṣṭapradhānaliṅgena vā anyadevatābhaktaṃ laukikeṣu yasmin diśi te tiṣṭhanti tad eva veśma so 'sya deśāntaraṃ prakramate / udvignaś ca bhavati / rātrau prapalāyati vā / kuṭumbaṃ vāsya bhidyate / pratyāyanaṃ kṣīrāṣṭasahasrāyutayo hotavyāḥ / svastho bhavati.

48. MMK, Vol. I, p. 33f. :
...tad yathā : Oṃ Garuḍavāhana cakrapāṇi caturbhuja, huṃ huṃ,

samayam anusmara, bodhisattvo jñāpayati svāhā...
Ājñapto Mañjughoṣeṇa kṣipram arthakaraḥ Śivaḥ
vidrāpayati bhūtāni Viṣṇurūpeṇa dehinām

49. S, ch. 8, p. 253f. :
Dhūmravarṇāṃ mahādeviṃ triṇetrāṃ śaśiśekharām
kṛśāṅgim asthimālāñ ca kartṛkāñ ca tathāmbujam
Koṭarākṣiṃ bhīmadaṃṣṭrāṃ pātālasadṛśodarīm
evaṃvidhāñ ca tāṃ dhyātvā kuryād uccāṭanaṃ ripoḥ

50. AV 3, 30, 4 :
Yéna devā́ ná viyánti nó ca vidviṣáte mitháḥ
tát kṛṇmo bráhma vo gṛhé saṃjñānaṃ púruṣebhyaḥ

51. Bhāsa, Abhiṣekanāṭaka 2, 18 (ed. Devadhar, p. 335) :
Devāḥ sendrādayo bhagnā dānavāś ca mayā raṇe
so 'haṃ mohaṃ gato 'smy adya Sītāyās tribhir akṣaraiḥ

52. JT 18, 12 and 26 :
Ekaviṃśatirātreṇa mohayej jagatim imām
devadaityā vaśās tasya jāyante nātra saṃśayaḥ
......
Nāśayen mohayet sarvāṃ samudravalayāṃ dharām

53. ViPur 1, 2, 29 and 31a :
Pradhānapuruṣau cāpi praviśyātmecchayā Hariḥ
kṣobhayāmāsa saṃprāpte sargakāle vyayāpyayau
......
Sa eva kṣobhako brahman kṣobhyaś ca Puruṣottamaḥ

54. T, p. 353 :
Brahmayāmale :
Māraṇe varjayed viprān anyāṃś cāpi sudhārmikān
strījanavyatirekeṣu rājavairiṣu yojayet
Svaroṣato vā lokānāṃ rakṣārthaṃ vā tadācaret
na tu lobhād bhayād vāpi kuryān mantri tu māraṇam
Prāyaścittaṃ ca kartavyaṃ devi taddoṣaśāntaye

55. S, p. 191 :
Yatra na syād upāyo 'nyaḥ śatror bhayanivṛttaye
tadānanyagatitvena māraṇādini kārayet

56. HT, ch. 11 :
Sādhayitvā caturdṛṣṭiṃ sattvāni tārayed budhaḥ
māraṇaṃ nātra kāryaṃ syāt samayabhedaḥ paraṃ bhavet

57. SVBr 3, 6, 12 :
Trirātropoṣitaḥ kṛṣṇacaturdaśyāṃ śavād aṅgāram āhṛtya catuṣpathe bādhakam idhmam upasamādhāya vaibhītakena sruveṇa sarṣapatailenāhutisahasraṃ juhuyāt saṃmīlyena yatra vṛścaśabdaḥ syāt (SV, Āraṇyakagāna, 2, 7, 51, 6), tatra puruṣaḥ śūlahasta uttiṣṭhati. Taṃ brūyād : amuṃ jahīti. Hanty enam.

58. MtPur 93, 155 :
Ihaiva phaladaṃ puṃsām etan nāmutra śobhanam
tasmāc chāntikam evātra kartavyaṃ bhūtim icchatā

For the preceding stanzas, see Quotation No. 14 on Ch. 2.

59. AgPur 285, 1 :
Siddhayogān punar vakṣye mṛtasañjivanikarān
Ātreyabhāṣitān divyān sarvavyādhivimardanān
60. RV 7, 59, 12 :
Tryambakaṃ yajāmahe sugáṃdhiṃ puṣṭivárdhanam
urvārukám iva báṃdhanān mṛtyór mukṣīya mắm ṛtāt
61. MtPur 93, 81 :
Yathā bāṇaprahārāṇāṃ kavacaṃ bhavati vāraṇam
tadvad daivopaghātānāṃ śāntir bhavati vāraṇam
62. KCT 3, 203 :
Śatruḥ siṃho gajendro harir uragapatis taskarāḥ pāśabandhaḥ
kṣubdhāmbhodhiḥ piśācā maraṇabhayakarā vyādhir indropasargaḥ
dāridryaṃ strīviyogaḥ kṣubhitanṛpabhayaṃ vajrapāto 'rthanāśo
nāśāntasya prayāti sphuṭam api caraṇaṃ yaḥ smared Yoginīnām
63. AV 19, 9, 5 :
Imắni yắni páñcendriyắṇi mánaḥṣaṣṭhāní me hṛdi bráhmaṇā sáṃśitāni
yáir evá sasṛjé ghorắṃ táir evá śắntir astu naḥ
64. MtPur 228, 4 and 5a :
Vijigīṣuḥ parān evam abhiyuktas tathā paraiḥ
tathābhicāraśaṅkāyāṃ śatrūṇām abhināśane
Bhaye mahati samprāpte Abhayā śāntir iṣyate
65. For the text, see above, p.—237
66. PST 24, 22 :
Utpāte sati mahati hy upadravāṇāṃ
homo 'yaṃ bhavati ca śāntido narāṇām
yad vānyan nijamanasepsitañ ca kāmaṃ
tat prāpnoty akhilaṃ nṛṇāṃ priyaś ca bhūyāt
67. S, p. 199, meditation stanzas :
Śaṅkhacakradharaṃ devaṃ caturbāhuṃ kiriṭinam
sarvāyudhair upetañ ca Garuḍopari saṃsthitam
Sanakādimunīndrais tu sarvadevair upāsitam
Śrībhūmisahitaṃ devam udayādityasannibham
prātarudyatsahasrāṃśumaṇḍalopari saṃsthitam
sarvalokasya rakṣārtham anantaṃ nityam eva ca
abhayaṃ varadañ caiva prayacchantaṃ mudānvitam
68. SM, No. 270 (Vol. II, p. 532f.) :
Śāntike rocanayā rakṣā bhavati. Sitanetrakarpaṭe bhūrjavaṃśatvacavidhautakarpaṭe vā cakradvayam abhilikhya namaskāravidarbhitam akālamūlādirahite śarāvasampuṭe 'vasthāpya ghṛtamadhumadhye prakṣipya sitasūtreṇa veṣṭayitvā trisandhyaṃ śuklapuṣpeṇārcayitvā pūrvābhimukhaṃ sitavarṇaṃ Yamāntakarūpaṃ dhyātvā purataś candramaṇḍalopaviṣṭaṃ sādhyaṃ dṛṣṭvā sitakalaśaiḥ candrāmṛtaparipūrṇair abhiṣiñcayantaṃ dhyātvā mantraṃ japet : Oṃ hrīḥ strīḥ vikṛtānana Devadattasya śāntiṃ kuru namaḥ svāhā. Śāntikavidhiḥ.

69. TSS 18, 48 :
Kṣudraghnam aśrīpāpaghnaṃ rakṣāyuḥśrījayapradam
gobālagarbhiṇīgrastavyādhitādiṣu śasyate

70. AgPur 302, 25 mantra and 26 :
Oṃ namo bhagavate Tryambakāya upaśamaya^{2} culu^{2} mili^{2} bhida^{2}
gomānini cakriṇi hrūṃ phaṭ. Asmin grāme gokulasya rakṣāṃ kuru^{2}
śāntiṃ kuru^{2}.
Ghaṇṭākarṇo mahāseno vīraḥ prokto mahābalaḥ
Mārīnirṇāśanakaraḥ sa māṃ pātu jagatpatiḥ
ślokau caiva nyased etau mantrau gorakṣakau pṛthak

71. BrVPur, Brahmakhaṇḍa, 19, 67ff. :
67 Idaṃ stotraṃ mahāpuṇyaṃ paṭhed bhaktyā ca yo naraḥ
snānasya sarvatīrthānāṃ phalam āpnoti niścitam
68 Aputro labhate putraṃ varṣam ekaṃ śṛṇoti yaḥ
saṃyataś ca haviṣyāśī praṇamya Śaṅkaraṃ gurum
69 Galatkuṣṭhī mahāśūlī varṣam ekaṃ śṛṇoti yaḥ
avaśyaṃ mucyate rogād Vyāsavākyam iti śrutam
70 Kārāgāre 'pi baddho yo naiva prāpnoti nirvṛtim
stotraṃ śrutvā māsam ekaṃ mucyate bandhanād dhruvam
71 Bhraṣṭarājyo labhed rājyaṃ bhaktyā māsaṃ śṛṇoti yaḥ
māsaṃ śrutvā saṃyataś ca labhed bhraṣṭadhano dhanam
72 Yakṣmagrasto varṣam ekam āstiko yaḥ śṛṇoti cet
niścitaṃ mucyate rogāc Chaṅkarasya prasādataḥ
73 Yaḥ śṛṇoti sadā bhaktyā stavarājam imaṃ dvija
tasyāsādhyaṃ tribhuvane nāsti kiṃcic ca Śaunaka
74 Kadācid bandhuvicchedo na bhavet tasya Bhārate
acalaṃ param aiśvaryaṃ labhate nātra saṃśayaḥ
75 Susaṃyato 'tibhaktyā ca māsam ekaṃ śṛṇoti yaḥ
abhāryo labhate bhāryāṃ suvinītāṃ satīṃ varām
76 Mahāmūrkhaś ca durmedhā māsam ekaṃ śṛṇoti yaḥ
buddhiṃ vidyāṃ ca labhate gurūpadeśamātrataḥ
77 Karmaduḥkhī daridraś ca māsaṃ bhaktyā śṛṇoti yaḥ
dhruvaṃ vittaṃ bhavet tasya Śaṅkarasya prasādataḥ
78 Iha loke sukhaṃ bhuktvā kṛtvā kīrtiṃ sudurlabhām
nānāprakāradharmaṃ ca yāty ante Śaṅkarālayam....

72. HT, Ch. 6 :
Herukayogasya puṃso vihāraḥ pañcavarṇeṣu
pañcavarṇasamāyuktam ekavarṇaṃ tu kalpitam
anekenaikavarṇena yasmād bhedo na lakṣyate

APPENDIX 2

A SELECTION OF REFERENCES TO TEXT-PLACES QUOTED OR DISCUSSED

(For explanation of abbreviated titles, see the Bibliography)

APPENDIX 3

REFERENCES TO THE BALINESE COLLECTION OF HYMNS, "STUTI & STAVA"

Number of hymns in "Stuti & Stava"	Title(s) of hymn	Referred to on p.
040	Ākāśastava	247
073	Dvādaśa-Smarastava	303
097	Akṣamā Pañcarakṣā; Vīramantra	71,328
100	Narasiṃhāṣṭaka; Rudrakavaca	51,126
103	Saptoṃkāra; Mantra-n Kajaṅ	166,207
121	Bhasma Āgama-tīrtha	80
133	Bhūtarājastava	54,118
136	Khaḍga-Rāvaṇa[stava]	54
145	Brahmākavaca; Lokanātha	57,62,201
148	Dvijendrastava	247
151	Brahmāstava	175
223	Praṇavabheda[stuti]	194
229	Rāmakavaca	70
314	[Gurupādapraśaṃsā]	73
325	Trailokyavijayā[stuti]	108f.
330	Aṣṭapūjā; Saptapūjā	248
336	Bhairavanaramāṃsaśūnyastava	68
360	Brahmāstava; Śivastava, a.o.	155
362	[Śivālayatattva]	69,160
366	Īśvarastava	175
372	Caturkumbha; Caturdevastava	186
381	Vedasāra	19,126
384	Stava Bhaṭṭāra	126
402	Cakṣuṣo Vidyādhara	298
441	Gāruḍeyamantra; Bhairavastava	199,441f.
450	Mahāmāyā; Caturvarṇaprāyaścitta	133f,242,251, 394, 412
456	Saptātmā	166
471	Śivastava	37
477	Nāgavāyustava; Pañcabuddhastava	200

Number of hymn in "Stuti & Stava"	Title (s) of hymn	Referred to on p.
483	Brahmāstava	174
504	Aṣṭamahābhaya Kliṅ	68,351
507	Vīramantra; Aṣṭakamantra	65,68
519	Gaṇapatistava	117
528	Buddhastava	55
534	[Viṣṇustava]	175
540	Ardhanārīśvarastava	25
594	Rudrānalāgni	198
600	Śrīstava	185
636	Tribhuvana	40,68
642	Śambhustava	247
658	[Bharāli-Prajñāpāramitāstava]	201
676	Rudrakavaca	250
787	Viṣṇupañjara	213
800	Pañcasarasvatīmantra	201
801	Pañcatathāgatastuti	201
802	Caturvedastuti	201
803	Pañcasarasvatīmantra (Buddhist version)	201
809	[Ṣaḍakṣarastava]	77
815	Yamarājastava	61
842	Lokamantra	126f,155
887	Narasiṃhāṣṭaka	127
941	Eka-Yamarājastava	368
Phalaśrutis to various hymns		94

BIBLIOGRAPHY

I : Sanskrit and Pali Texts

AgPur — Agni-Purāṇa, ed. Baladev Upadhyaya, Benares 1966 (KSS, 174).

AitBr — Aitareya-Brāhmaṇa, ed. Satyavrata Sāmaśramī, Calcutta 1896 (BI, 134-III); trsl. A. B. Keith, Cambridge, Mass., 1920 (HOS, 25).

Ajitāgama — Ajitāgama, Kriyāpāda, ed. N. R. Bhatt, Pondichéry 1964 (PIFI, 24).

Ambikāstuti — Ambikāstuti by Hanuman, ed. K. P. Aithal, in : *Stotrasamuccaya*, vol. I, Madras-Adyar 1969, as No. 10.

AṅgN — Aṅguttara-Nikāya, ed. R. Morris, London 1955 (PTS).

ĀpGṛh — Āpastamba-Gṛhyasūtra, ed. M. Winternitz, Wien 1887.

ĀpŚr — Āpastamba-Śrautasūtra, ed. R. Garbe, Calcutta 1882-1892 (BI, 92, vol. 1-3).

Atri Saṃhitā — Samūrtārcanādhikaraṇa (Atri Saṃhitā) by Maharshi Atri, ed. M. Ramakrishna Kavi, Tirupati 1943 (SVOS, No. 6).

AV — Atharvaveda, ed. R. Roth — W. D. Whitney, rev. ed. by M. Lindenau, Berlin 1924 : trsl. W. D. Whitney, rev. by Ch. R. Lanman, Cambridge, Mass., 1905 (HOS 7 and 8).

AVPar — Atharvavedapariśiṣṭāni, ed. G. M. Bolling — J. von Negelein, Leipzig 1909.

Bagalāmukhīrahasya, — see BMR

BaudhŚr — Baudhāyana-Śrautasūtra, ed. W. Caland, Calcutta 1904-13 (BI, 163, vol. 1-3).

BAUp — Bṛhadāraṇyaka-Upaniṣad, ed. E. Senart, Paris 1934.

BhārGṛh — Bhāradvāja-Gṛhyasūtra, ed. H.J.W. Salomons, Leiden 1913 (Thesis Utrecht).

Bhāsa — "Plays ascribed to Bhāsa", ed. C. R. Devadhar, Poona 1962 (Poona Or. Ser., No. 54).

BhGītā — Bhagavad-Gītā, ed. F. Edgerton, 2 vols., Cambridge, Mass., 1952 (HOS, 38 and 39); ed. with 8 commentaries by V.L.S. Pansikar, Bombay [2]1936.

BhPur — Bhāgavata-Purāṇa, ed. V.L.S. Pansikar, rev. by N.R. Acharya,[9] Bombay 1950 (NSP).

Bhṛgu-Yajñādhikāra, — ed. D. Rangacharya, n.p., 1931 (Śrīvaikhānasagranthamālā, 19).

BJUp — Bṛhajjābāla-Upaniṣad, ed. A. Mahadeva Sastri, in: *Śaiva Upaniṣads*, Adyar 1950, p. 87-128.

BMR — Bagalāmukhīrahasya by Śrī-Svāmin, ed. R. N. Sharma, Datia, 1965.

BNārPur — Bṛhannāradīya-Purāṇa, ed. Hṛṣīkeśa Śāstrī, Calcutta 1891 (BI, 107).

Bodhisattvabhūmi by — Asaṅga, ed. U. Wogihara.

BPK — Bhairavapadmāvatīkalpa, ed. by M. B. Jhavery, *Comparative and Critical Study of Mantrashastra*, Ahmedabad 1944, as an Appendix.

BṛhSaṃh — Bṛhatsaṃhitā by Varāhamihira, ed. Acyutānanda Jhā, Benares 1959 (Vidyabhavan Skt. Ser., 41).

BṛVPur — Brahmavaivarta-Purāṇa, ed. V.S. Marathe — V. G. Apte, Poona 1935 (ASS, 102).

BŚR — Bṛhatstotraratnākara, ed. Śivarāma Śarma Vasiṣṭha, Benares 1960.

ChUp — Chāndogya-Upaniṣad, ed. E. Senart, Paris 1930.

D — Dattātreya-Tantra, ed. J. Vidyasagar's sons, in: *Indrajālavidyāsaṃgraha*, Calcutta 1915, p. 132-179; ed. B. M. Pandey, Benares Saṃvat 2019 (1962-63).

DevīBhPur — Devībhāgavata-Purāṇa, ed. R. T. Pandey, Benares 1963.

DN — Dīgha-Nikāya, ed. T. W. Rhys Davids-J. Estlin Carpenter, 3 vols., London 1890-1911 (PTS).

GaṇGītā — Gaṇeśa-Gītā, ed. with the commentary of Nīlakaṇṭha by H. N. Apte, Poona 1906 (ASS, 52); trsl. K. Yoroi, Thesis Utrecht 1968.

GarPur — Garuḍa-Purāṇa, ed.Ramshankar Bhattacharya, Benares 1964 (KSS, 165); ed. by Śrīrāma Śarma, 2 vols., Bareli 1968.

GautDh — Gautama-Dharmasūtra, ed. with the comm. Mitākṣarā by U. Ch. Pandey, Benares 1966 (KSS, 172).

GopBr — Gopatha-Brāhmaṇa, ed. D. Gaastra, Leiden 1919.

GST — Guhyasamāja-Tantra, ed. B. Bhattacharya, Baroda 1931, [2]1967 (GOS, 53).

GT — Gāyatrī-Tantra, ed. T. Bhattacharya, Benares 1946 (KSS, 143).

HirŚr — Hiraṇyakeśi-Śrautasūtra, ed. C. B. Agashe, 5 vols., Poona 1907-30 (ASS, 53).

HT — Hevajra-Tantra, ed. Raghu Vira—Lokesh Chandra, in: *Kālacakratantra and other texts*, New Delhi 1966 (Śata-Piṭaka Ser., 69), Vol. II, pp. 683-698; ed.D. L. Snellgrove, 2 vols., London 1959.

Is — Indrajālaśāstra, ed. J. Vidyasagar's sons, in : *Indrajālavidyāsaṃgraha*, Calcutta 1915, pp. 1-21.

ISP — Īśānaśivagurudevapaddhati by Īśānaśiva, ed. T. Gaṇapati Śāstrī, Vol. III, Kriyāpāda, Trivandrum 1922 (TrivSS, 77).

JainBr — Jaiminīya-Brāhmaṇa, edition of fragments by W. Caland, *Das Jaiminīya-*

Brāhmaṇa in Auswahl, Amsterdam 1919 (VKAW, 19).

Jayākhya Saṃhitā, ed. V. Krishnamacharya, Baroda 1931.

JT — Jñānārṇava-Tantra, ed. G. S. Gokhale, Poona (ASS, 69).

K — Kāmaratna, ed. J. Vidyasagar's sons, in: *Indrajālavidyāsaṃgraha*, Calcutta 1915, p. 22-131.

KA — Kāmaratna, Assamese version, ed. and trsl. H. Goswami Tattvabhusan, Shillong 1928.

Kaivalya Up — Kaivalya-Upaniṣad, ed. A. Mahadeva Sastri, in: *Śaiva Upaniṣads*, Adyar 1950, p. 51ff.

KālPur — Kālikā-Purāṇa, trsl. by K. R. van Kooy of chs. 54-69, Thesis Utrecht, Leiden 1972.

Karpūramañjarī by Rājaśekhara, ed. S. Konow—Ch. R. Lanman, Cambridge, Mass., 1901 (HOS, 4); repr. Delhi 1963.

Kathās — Kathāsaritsāgara by Somadeva, ed. J. L. Shastri, Delhi 1970.

Kaṭha Up — Kaṭha-Upaniṣad, ed. S. Radhakrishnan, in : *The Principal Upaniṣads*, London ²1968.

KātyŚr — Kātyāyana-Śrautasūtra, ed. A. Weber, Berlin-London 1859.

KauśBUp — Kauśītaki-Brāhmaṇa-Upaniṣad, ed. E. B. Cowell, Calcutta 1861; repr. Benares 1968 (Chowkhamba Skt. Studies, 64).

KauśS — Kauśika-Sūtra, ed. M. Bloomfield, New Haven, Conn. 1890; partly trsl. by W. Caland, *Altindisches Zauberritual*, Amsterdam 1900 (VKAW 3, 2), repr. Wiesbaden 1967.

KCT — Kālacakra-Tantra; ed. Raghu Vira—Lokesh Chandra, in: *Kālacakratantra and other texts*, Vol. 1, New Delhi 1966 (Śata-Piṭaka Ser., 69), p. 332-378.

KJ — Kāśyapa-Jñānakāṇḍa, ed. R.B. Parthasarathi Bhattacharya, Tirupati 1950 (SVOS, 12); 2nd. ed., 1960.

Kṛṣṇa Up — Kṛṣṇa-Upaniṣad, ed. G.A. Jacob, in: *Eleven Ātharvaṇa Upanishads*, Bombay ²1916, p. 3-13.

KS — Kaṭha Saṃhitā, ed. L. von Schroeder, 4 vols., Leipzig 1900-1910.

KulaCT — Kulacūḍāmaṇi-Tantra, ed. G. Ch. Vedāntatīrtha, Calcutta-London 1915 (Tantrik Texts, 4).

KulT — Kulārṇava-Tantra, ed. J. Woodroffe—M. P. Pandit, Madras 1965.

Kumāratattva (Bal.) — "Koemaratatwa", ms. No. 2322 in the collection of the Geḍong Kīrtya, Singaradja, Bali; copy in the Leiden University Library (see Th. Pigeaud, Literature of Java, vol. I, The Hague 1967, p. 56).

KūPur — Kūrma-Purāṇa, ed. N. Mukhopadhyaya, Calcutta 1890 (BI, 106).

KVT — Kālīvilāsa-Tantra, ed. P. Ch. Tarkaūrtha, London 1917 (Tantrik Texts, 6).

LāṭyŚr — Lāṭyāyana-Śrautasūtra, ed. A. Vedāntavāgīśa, Calcutta 1870-72 (BI).

LiPur — Liṅga-Purāṇa, ed. P. Tarkaratna, Calcutta 1889; ed. Khemarāja Śrīkṛṣṇadāsa, Bombay 1906.

LT — Lakṣmī-Tantra, ed. V. Krishnamacharya, Adyar 1959; trsl. Sanjukta Gupta, Leiden 1972 (Thesis Utrecht).

Mahāmāyā fragment = Stuti & Stava, No. 450.

Mahāṣoḍaśīvarṇaratnāvalīstotra, ed. K. P. Aithal, in : *Stotrasamuccaya*, Vol. I, Adyar 1969, as No. 15.

Mahāvaṃsa, ed. W. Geiger, London 1908 (PTS), repr. 1958.

MajN — Majjhima-Nikāya, ed. V. Trenckner—R. Chalmers, 4 vols., London 1888-1902 (PTS).

Mālatīmādhava by Bhavabhūti, ed. M. R. Telang—V.L.S. Pansikar, Bombay 1936 (NSP).

Mañjuśrīmūlakalpa, see MMK.
Mantramahodadhi, see MMD.
Manu Manusmṛti, ed. J. Jolly, London 1887.
Marīci-Vimānārcanakalpa, ed. as No. 15 in the Śrīvaikhānasagranthamālā, Egavaripalem 1927.
Māyābījastotra, ed. M. B. Jhavery, in: *Comparative and Critical Study of Mantrashastra*, Ahmedabad 1944, as Appendix 25.
Mbh Mahābhārata, Crit. ed. by V.S. Sukthankar a.o., Poona 1933-1966.
MkPur Mārkaṇḍeya-Purāṇa, ed. K.M. Banerjea, Calcutta 1862 (BI, 29).
MMD Mantramahodadhi by Mahīdhara, ed. Khemarāja Śrīkṛṣṇadāsa, Bombay 1962.
MMK Mañjuśrīmūlakalpa, ed. T. Gaṇapati Śāstrī, Trivandrum 1920-25 (TrivSS, 70, 76, 84).
MNT Mahānirvāṇa-Tantra, ed. J. Vidyasagar, Calcutta 1884.
MNUp Mahānārāyaṇa-Upaniṣad, ed. and trsl. J. Varenne, Paris 1960 (in French).
MPN Mañjuśrījñānasattvasya paramārthā nāma saṃgītiḥ, ed. Raghu Vira—Lokesh Chandra, in: *Kālacakratantra and other texts*, vol. I, New Delhi 1966 (Śata-Piṭaka Ser., 69), p. 31f.
Mṛcchakaṭika by Śūdraka, ed. R. Ojha, Benares 1962 (Haridas Skt. Ser.).
MS Maitrāyaṇī-Saṃhitā, ed. L. von Schroeder, 2 vols., Leipzig 1881-86.
MtPur Matsya-Purāṇa, ed. by Pandits of the Ānandāśrama, Poona 1907 (ASS, 54).
MuUp Muṇḍaka-Upaniṣad, ed. with French trsl. Jacq. Maury, Paris 1943 ("Les Upanishad", 4).
N Siddhanāgārjunakakṣapuṭa, ed. J. Vidyasagar's sons, in: *Indrajālavidyāsaṃgraha*, Calcutta 1915, p. 264-390.
NiṣpY Niṣpannayogāvali, ed. B. Bhattacharya, Baroda 1949 (GOS, 109).

Pañcabrahma Up — Pañcabrahma-Upaniṣad, ed. A. Mahadeva Sastri, in: *The Śaiva Upaniṣads*, Adyar 1950, p. 79-86.

Pañcaviṃśa Br, see PVBr.

Praśna Up — Praśna-Upaniṣad, ed. O. Böhtlingk, Leipzig 1890.

PST — Prapañcasāra-Tantra, ed. T. Vidyāratna, Calcutta-London 1914 (Tantrik Texts, 3).

PVBr — Pañcaviṃśa-Brāhmaṇa, ed. A. Chinnaswami Sastri, 2 vols., Benares 1935 (KSS, 105).

Rām. — Rāmāyaṇa, Crit. Ed. by G.H. Bhatt a. o., Baroda 1960.

Ṛgvidh. — Ṛgvidhāna, ed. R. Meyer, Berlin 1878; trsl. J. Gonda, Utrecht 1951.

Rudrahṛdaya Up. — Rudrahṛdaya-Upaniṣad, ed. A. Mahadeva Sastri, in: *Śaiva Upaniṣads*, Adyar 1950, p. 149f.

ṚV — Ṛgveda, ed. F. Max Müller, repr. in 2 vols., Benares 1965 (KSS, 167).

S — Ṣaṭkarmadīpikā, ed. J. Vidyasagar's sons, in : *Indrajālavidyāsaṃgraha*, Calcutta 1915, p. 179-264.

Sādhanamālā, see SM.

ṢaḍvBr — Ṣaḍviṃśa-Brāhmaṇa, ed. H.F. Eelsingh, Leiden 1908 (thesis Utrecht); trsl. W. B. Bollée, Thesis Utrecht 1956.

Śaiva Ups — Śaiva Upaniṣads, ed. A. Mahadeva Sastri, Adyar 1950.

Śaktisaṅgamatantra, see SST.

Sāmavidhānabrāhmaṇa, see SVBr.

Śāntistava by Tyāgarāja, ed. K. P. Aithal, in : *Stotrasamuccaya*, vol.1, Adyar 1969, as No. 23.

Śarabha Up — Śarabha-Upaniṣad, ed. A. Mahadeva Sastri, in : *Śaiva Upaniṣads*, Adyar 1950, p. 165ff.

ŚārTil — Śāradā-Tilaka, only in references (cf. the article by Ewing).

ŚatBr Śatapatha-Brāhmaṇa, ed. A. Weber, Berlin-London 1855, repr. Darmstadt 1963, Benares 1964; trsl. J. Eggeling, 5 vols., repr. Delhi 1964 (Sacred Books of the East, vols 12, 26, 41, 43, 44).

Ṣaṭkarmadīpikā, see S.

SCT Śrīcakrasaṃbhāra-Tantra, ed. and trsl. Kazi Dawa-Samdup, Calcutta-London 1919 (Tantrik Texts, 7).

Siddhanāgārjunakakṣapuṭa, see N.

Śivagaurīstotra by Jñānaśiva, ed. K. P. Aithal, in : *Stotrasamuccaya*, vol. 1, Adyar 1969, as No. 40.

Śivajñānabodham, trsl. G. Matthews, Oxford 1948.

Śivapūjāstava by Jñānaśiva, ed. K. P. Aithal, in : *Stotrasamuccaya*, vol. 1, Adyar 1969, as No. 41.

Śiva Pur Śiva-Purāṇa, ed. R. Sh. Acharya, Bareli 1966.

Skanda Up Skanda-Upaniṣad, ed. G.A. Jacob, in : *Eleven Ātharvaṇa Upaniṣads*, Bombay 1916, p. 161f.

SkPur Skanda-Purāṇa, ed. Khemarāja Śrīkṛṣṇadāsa, 7 vols., Bombay 1909-10.

SM Sādhanamālā, ed. B. Bhattacharya, 2 vols., Baroda 1925, repr. 1968 (GOS, 26 and 41).

Śrīcakrasaṃbhāratantra, see SCT.

SST Śaktisaṃgama-Tantra, ed. B. Bhattacharya, 3 vols., Baroda 1932-1947 (GOS 61, 94, 104).

Stuti & Stava Stuti and Stava (Bauddha, Śaiva and Vaiṣṇava) of Balinese brahman priests, ed. and trsl. by T. Goudriaan and C. Hooykaas, Amsterdam 1971 (VKAW, 76).

SV Sāmaveda (only in references).

SVBr Sāmavidhāna-Brāhmaṇa, ed. with the commentaries of Sāyaṇa and Bharatasvāmin by B. R. Sharma, Tirupati 1964 (Kendriya Skt. Vidyapeetha Ser., 1).

ŚvetUp — Śvetāśvatara-Upaniṣad, ed. R. Hauschild, Leipzig 1927.

T — Tārābhaktisudhārṇava by Narasiṃha, ed. Panchanana Bhattacharya, Calcutta-London 1940 (Tantrik Texts, 21).

Taittirīya-Upaniṣad-bhāṣyavārttikam by Sureśvara, trsl. J.M. van Boetzelaer, Leiden 1971 (Thesis Utrecht).

Tantrasāra by Kṛṣṇānandavāgīśabhaṭṭācārya, ed. as CSS, Work No. 491.

Tantrasārasaṃgraha, see TSS.

TAr — Taittirīya-Āraṇyaka (only in references).

Tattvasaṃgraha by Śāntarakṣita, ed. D. Shastri. vol. 1, Varanasi 1968 (Bauddha Bhārati Ser., 1).

TBr — Taittirīya-Brāhmaṇa, ed. N. Apte, Poona 1898, reed. 1938 (ASS, 37).

Tiruvacakam — Tiruvaśagam by Māṇikka-Vāśagar, ed. with trsl. by G. U. Pope, Oxford 1900.

TripR — Tripurārahasya. Jñānakhaṇḍa: trsl. by A.U. Vasavada, Benares 1965 (Chowkhamba Skt. Studies, 50); Māhātmyakhaṇḍa, ed. M. L. Shastri, Benares 1932 (KSS, 92).

TS — Taittirīya-Saṃhitā, ed. D. Satvalekar, Pardi 1957.

TSS — Tantrasārasaṃgraha by Nārāyaṇa, ed. M. Duraiswami Aiyangar, Madras 1950 (Madras Govt. Or. Ser., 15).

TSSC — Anonymous commentary on the TSS, see above.

Uttararāmacarita by Bhavabhūti, ed. T.R.R. Aiyar—V.L.S. Pansikar, 10th ed. rev. by N.R. Acharya, Bombay 1949 (NSP).

Varadapūrvatāpanī-Upaniṣad, ed. G.A. Jacob, in : *Eleven Ātharvaṇa Upaniṣads*, Bombay 1916, p. 111-133.

Varāhamukhīstava, ed. K. P. Aithal, in : *Stotrasamuccaya*, vol. 1, Adyar 1969, as No. 18.

Vāyu Pur — Vāyu-Purāṇa, ed. R. Mitra, Calcutta 1880-89 (BI).

ViDhPur — Viṣṇudharmottara-Purāṇa, ed. Khemarāja Śrīkṛṣṇadāsa, 2 vols., Bombay 1912-13.

ViPur — Viṣṇu-Purāṇa, ed. M. Gupta, Gorakhpur 1952.

Viṣṇusmṛti, ed. J. Jolly, repr. Benares 1962 (CSS, 95).

YogV — Yogavāsiṣṭha, ed. V.L.S. Pansikar, 3rd ed. rev. by N.R. Acharya, Bombay 1937 (NSP).

YV — Yajurveda (only in references).

II: Books and Articles by Modern Authors

Abbott — Abbott, J., *The Keys of Power*, London 1932.

Adiceam — Adiceam, Marg. E., *Contribution à l'étude d' Aiyanār-Śāstā*, Pondichéry 1967 (PIFI, 32).

Aithal — Aithal, K. Parameswara, *Stotrasamuccaya, a Collection of Rare and Unpublished Stotras*, vol. 1, Adyar 1969 (Adyar Library Ser., 99).e

Arbman — Arbman, E., *Rudra, Untersuchungen zum altindischen Glauben und Kultus*, Thesis Uppsala 1922.

Avalon 1952 — Avalon, A., *Principles of Tantra* (a translation of the Tantra Tattva by Pandit Shiva Chandra Vidyārṇava Bhattacharya), Madras 1914, 1952.

Avalon 1958 — Avalon, A., *The Serpent Power*, Madras 1958.

Awasthi — Awasthi, A.B.L., *Studies in Skanda Purāṇa*, vol. I, Lucknow 1965.

Bagchi — Bagchi, P.Ch., "Evolution of the Tantras", CHI, vol.4, Calcutta 1956, p. 211-226.

Banerji — Banerji, R.D., *Eastern Indian School of Medieval Sculpture*, Delhi 1933 (Archaeological Survey of India, New Imperial Ser., vol. XLVII).

Bareau — Bareau, A., "Les idées sous-jacentes aux pratiques cultuelles bouddhiques dans le Cambodge actuel", in : *Beiträge zur Geistesgeschichte Indiens* (Festschrift Frauwallner), Leiden 1968, p. 23-32.

Bedekar — Bedekar, V.M., "The Doctrine of the Colours of Souls in the Mahābhārata: its Characteristics and Implications", in : ABORI, 48 and 49, 1968, p. 329ff.

van den Berg — Berg OSA, P.J.M. van den, *Upanayana volgens de Gṛhyasūtras van de Taittirīya-school* (unpublished study made for the doctoral examination in Theology at the University of Nijmegen, 1970).

Bergaigne — Bergaigne, A., *La religion védique d'après les hymnes du Rig-Veda*, 4 vols., Paris 1963.

Bernhard — Bernhard, F., "Zur Entstehung einer Dhāraṇī", in : ZDMG, 117, 1967, p. 148-168.

Bhandarkar — Bhandarkar, R.G., *Vaiṣṇavism, Śaivism and Minor Religious Systems*, Strassburg 1913, repr. Varanasi 1965.

Bharati — Bharati, Agehananda, *The Tantric Tradition*, London 1965.

B. Bhattacharya — Bhattacharya, B., *Introduction* to : *Sādhanamālā*, ed. by B. Bhattacharya, 2 vols., Baroda 1925, repr. 1968 (GOS, 26 and 41).

K. Bhattacharya — Bhattacharya, K., *Les religions brahmaniques dans l'Ancien Cambodge*, Paris 1961.

Bodding — Bodding, P. O., "The Santals and Disease", in : Memoirs of the As. Soc. of Bengal, 10, 1, n.d.

Bodewitz — Bodewitz, H.W., *Jaiminīya Brāhmaṇa I, 1-65, Translation and Commentary, with a study : Agnihotra and Prāṇāgnihotra*, Leiden 1973 (Thesis Utrecht).

van Boetzelaer — Boetzelaer, J. M. van (trsl.), *Sureśvara's Taittirīyopaniṣadbhāṣyavārttikam*, Leiden 1971 (Thesis Utrecht).

Böhtlingk, SW	Böhtlingk, O., *Sanskrit-Wörterbuch in kürzerer Fassung*, 3 vols.
Bollée	Bollée, W.B., *Ṣaḍviṃśa-Brāhmaṇa* (Introd., trsl. and notes), Thesis Utrecht 1956.
Caland	Caland, W., *Altindisches Zauberritual. Probe einer Übersetzung der wichtigsten Theile des Kauśika Sūtra*, Amsterdam 1900 (VKAW, 3, 2).
de Casparis	Casparis, J.G. de, *Praśasti Indonesia*, vol. II, Bandung 1956.
Chemparathy	Chemparathy, G., *An Indian Rational Theology. Introduction to Udayana's Nyāyakusumāñjali*, Wien 1972 (Thesis Utrecht).
Conze	Conze, E., *Der Buddhismus, Wesen und Entwicklung*, Stuttgart 1953 (Urban-Bücher).
Crooke	Crooke, W., *The Popular Religion and Folklore of Northern India*, 2 vols., 1894-96, repr. Delhi 1968.
Damais	Damais, L.-Ch., "A propos des couleurs symboliques des points cardinaux" (Etudes Javanaises, III), in : BEFEO, 56, 1969, p. 75-118.
Daniélou	Daniélou, A., *Le polythéisme hindou*, Paris 1960.
Dare	Dare, P. *Magie blanche et magie noire aux Indes*, Paris 1947.
K. Das	Das, K., *A Study of Orissan Folklore*, Santiniketan 1953.
Dasgupta	Dasgupta, S.B., *Obscure Religious Cults as Background of Bengali Literature*, Calcutta 1946.
Dessigane 1960	Dessigane, R., Pattabiramin, P.Z., Filliozat, J., *La Légende des jeux de Śiva à Madurai d'après les textes et les peintures*, Pondichéry 1960 (PIFI, 19).
Dessigane 1964	Dessigane, R., Pattabiramin, P.Z., Filliozat, J., *Les légendes Śivaites de Kāñci-*

puram. Analyse de textes et iconographie, Pondichéry 1964 (PIFI, 27).

Devanandan — Devanandan, P. D., *The Concept of Māyā*, Calcutta-London, 1954.

Dumont — Dumont, P. E., *L'Agnihotra*, Baltimore 1935.

Eggeling, cf. ŚatBr.

Eliade — Eliade, M., *Le Yoga, immortalité et liberté*, Paris 1954.

Elwin — Elwin, V., *Maria Murder and Suicide*, Oxford U.P., 1943, 1950.

Eracle — Eracle, J., *L'art des Thanka et le bouddhisme tantrique*, Genève 1970.

Essers — Essers, B., *Een oudindische symboliek van het geluid*, Assen 1952 (Thesis Groningen).

Ewing — Ewing, A. H., "The Śāradā-tilaka Tantra", in : JAOS, 23, 1902, p. 65-76.

Fick — Fick, R., *Die soziale Gliederung im Nordosten Indiens zu Buddhas Zeit*, Kiel 1897 (Thesis).

Frauwallner — Frauwallner, E. *Geschichte der indischen Philosophie*, I. Band, Salzburg 1953.

Ghurye — Ghurye, G.S., *Gods and Men*, Bombay 1962.

Goldstücker — Goldstücker, Th., *Dictionary English and Sanskrit*.

Gonda 1954 — Gonda, J., *Aspects of Early Viṣṇuism*, Utrecht 1954

Gonda 1960 — Gonda, J., *Die Religionen Indiens. I : Veda und älterer Hinduismus*, Stuttgart 1960 (Die Religionen der Menschheit, Band 11).

Gonda 1963 — Gonda, J., *Die Religionen Indiens. II : Der jüngere Hinduismus*, Stuttgart 1963 (Die Rel. der Menschheit, Band 12).

Gonda 1965 — Gonda, J., *Change and Continuity in Indian Religion*, The Hague 1965 (Disputationes Rheno-Trajectinae, 9). Within this book : *Māyā* (p. 164-197); *The Guru* (p. 229-283); *Dikṣā* (p. 315-462).

Gonda, Savayajñas — Gonda, J., *The Savayajñas* (*Kauśikasūtra* 60-68), *Translation, Introduction, Commentary*, Amsterdam 1965 (VKAW, 71, 2).

Gonda 1970 — Gonda, J., *Viṣṇuism and Śivaism, A Comparison*, London 1970.

Gooneratne — Gooneratne, D. de Silva, "On Witchcraft and Demonology in Ceylon", in: Jn. of the Ceylon Branch of the R. A. S., 4, 1865-66, p. 1-118 (this article was available to me only in a Dutch excerpt prepared by Kees van Esch, Nijmegen 1971).

Goudriaan — Goudriaan, T., "Tumburu and his Sisters", in: WZKSOA, 15, 1973, p. 49-95.

Gupta — Gupta, S., *Lakṣmī Tantra, A Pāñcarātra Text, Translation and Notes*, Leiden 1972 (Thesis Utrecht).

Heiler — Heiler, F., *Die Religionen der Menschheit*, Stuttgart 1959.

Henry — Henry, V., *La magie dans l'Inde antique*, Paris 1909.

Hermanns — Hermanns, M., *Die religiös-magische Weltanschauung der Primitivstämme Indiens. Band* 2 : *Die Bhilala, Korku, Gond, Baiga*, Wiesbaden 1966.

Hildburgh — Hildburgh, W. L., "Notes on Sinhalese Magic", in : Jn. of the Royal Anthropological Institute, 38, 1908, p. 148-205 (this article was available to me only in a Dutch excerpt prepared by Wim Dijkstra, Nijmegen 1971).

Hillebrandt — Hillebrandt, A., *Ritualliteratur—Vedische Opfer und Zauber*, Strassburg 1897 (Grundriss der Indo-Arischen Philologie und Altertumskunde, 3, 2).

Hoens — Hoens, D. J., *Śānti. A Contribution to Ancient Indian Religious Terminology*. The Hague 1951 (Thesis Utrecht).

Hooykaas	Hooykaas, C., *Sūrya-Sevanā. The Way to God of a Balinese Śiva Priest*, Amsterdam 1966 (VKAW, 72, 3).
Hopkins	Hopkins, E. W., "The Social and Military Position of the Ruling Caste in Ancient India as represented by the Sanskrit Epics", in: JAOS, 13, 1889, p. 57-376.
Inde Cl.	Renou, L. et Filliozat, J., *l'Inde Classique. Manuel des études indiennes*, 2 vols., Paris 1947. 1953.
Ishwaran	Ishwaran, K., *Shivapur, a South Indian Village*, London 1968.
Iyer	Iyer, L.A. Krishna, *The Travancore Tribes and Castes*, vol. 1, Trivandrum 1937.
Jacob	Jacob, G.A. (ed.), *Eleven Ātharvaṇa Upaniṣads with Dīpikās*, Bombay [2]1916 (Bombay Skt. and Prakrit Ser., 40).
Jacques	Jacques, C., "Le monde du sorcier en Inde", in: *Le monde du sorcier*, Paris 1966 (Sources Orientales, 7).
Jaiswal	Jaiswal, Suvīrā, *The Origin and Development of Vaiṣṇavism (from 200 B.C. to A.D.* 500), Delhi 1967.
Jhavery	Jhavery, Mohanlal B. *Comparative and Critical Study of Mantraśāstra (with Special Treatment of Jain Mantravāda)*, Ahmedabad 1944.
de Jong	Jong, K.H.E. de, *De magie bij de Grieken en Romeinen*, Haarlem 1948.
Joshi	Joshi, L. M., *Studies in the Buddhistic Culture of India (during the 7th and 8th Centuries A.D.)*, Delhi 1967.
Kane 1958	Kane, P. V., *History of Dharmaśāstra*, vol. V, Part 1, Poona 1958.
Kane 1962	Kane, P. V., *History of Dharmaśāstra*, vol. V, Part 2, Poona 1962.
Kluckhohn	Kluckhohn, C., *Navaho Witchcraft*, Boston, Mass., 1967, 1968 (Beacon Press Edition; originally published, 1944).

Kohlbrugge — Kohlbrugge, D. J., *Atharvavedapariśiṣṭa über Omina*, Utrecht 1938 (Thesis).

van Kooy — Kooy, K. R. van, *Worship of the Goddess According to the Kālikāpurāṇa*. Part I: A Translation with an Introduction and Notes of Chapters 54-69, Leiden 1972 (Thesis Utrecht).

Kosambi — Kosambi, D.D., *An Introduction to the Study of Indian History*, Bombay, 1956.

Kulke — Kulke, H., *Cidambaramāhātmya. Eine Untersuchung der religionsgeschichtlichen und historischen Hintergründe für die Entstehung der Tradition einer südindischen Tempelstadt*, Wiesbaden 1970 (Freiburger Beiträge zur Indologie, 3).

Leclère — Leclère, A., "La sorcellerie chez les Cambodgiens", in: *Revue Scientifique*, Série 4, III, 1895, p. 129-136.

Lévi — Lévi, S., *Sanskrit Texts from Bali* (*Bālidvipagranthāḥ*), Baroda 1933 (GOS, 67).

Macdonell-Keith — Macdonell, A.A., and Keith, A.B., *Vedic Index of Names and Subjects*, 2 vols., 1912, repr. Delhi 1967.

Majumdar/Altekar — Majumdar, R. Ch., and Altekar, A.S., *The Vākāṭaka-Gupta Age* (*Circa* 200-550 *A.D.*), Delhi 1967 (A New History of the Indian People, vol. 6).

Malaviya — Mālavīyā, Māyā, *Atharvaveda Śāntipuṣṭikarmāṇi*, Varanasi 1967 (Sarasvati Bhavana Studies, 17).

Malinowski — Malinowski, B., *Magic, Science and Religion*, ed. R. Redfield, New York 1954 (Doubleday Anchor Book; originally published, 1925).

Marwick — Marwick, M. (ed.), *Witchcraft and Sorcery*, Harmondsworth 1970 (Penguin Modern Sociology Readings).

Mayrhofer — Mayrhofer, M., *Kurzgefasstes Etymologisches Wörterbuch des Altindischen*, Heidelberg 1956.

Meyer	Meyer, J. J., *Trilogie altindischer Mächte und Feste der Vegetation*, Zürich 1937.
Mitra	Mitra, H., "Sadāśiva Worship in Early Bengal", in: Jn. of the As. Soc. of Bengal, New Ser., 29, 1933, p. 171-242.
Monier-Williams	Monier-Williams, Sir M., *Hinduism*, Calcutta ed., 1951.
Mookerjee	Mookerjee, Ajit, *Tantra Art*, New Delhi a.o., 1966.
Mukherji	Mukherji, S.C., *A Study of Vaiṣṇavism in Ancient and Medieval Bengal*, Calcutta 1966.
Nowotny	Nowotny, Fausta, "Das Pūjāvidhinirūpaṇa des Trimalla", in: IIJ, 1, 1957, p. 109-154.
Oberhammer	Oberhammer, G., *Yāmunamunis Interpretation von Brahmasūtram* 2, 2, 42-45 (*Eine Untersuchung zur Pāñcarātra-Tradition der Rāmānuja-Schule*), Wien 1971 (Österreich. Ak. der Wiss.).
Oertel	Oertel, H., "Indra in the Guise of a Woman", in: JAOS, 26, 1905, p. 166-178; the same, "Contributions from the Jaiminīya-Brāhmaṇa", in: JAOS, 26, 1905, p. 192-196.
Oldenberg	Oldenberg, H., *Vorwissenschaftliche Wissenschaft. Die Weltanschauung der Brāhmaṇa-Texte*, Göttingen 1919.
O'Malley	O'Malley, L.S.S., *Popular Hinduism. The Religion of the Masses*, Cambridge 1935.
Paranjoti	Paranjoti, V., *Śaiva Siddhānta*, London [2]1954.
Parpola	Parpola, Asko, a.o., *Further Progress in the Indus Script Decipherment*, Copenhagen 1970 (Scandinavian Inst. of Asian Studies, Special Publs., 3).
Pathak	Pathak, V.S., *Śaiva Cults in Northern India (from inscriptions 700 A. D. to 1200 A.D.)*, Benares 1960.

PD — Böhtlingk, O., and Roth, R., *Sanskrit-Wörterbuch*, 7 vols., St. Petersburg 1852-1875.

Pope — Pope, G. U., *The Tiruvāśagam or "Sacred Utterances" of... Māṇikka-Vāśagar* (text, translation, notes), Oxford 1900.

Pott — Pott, P.H., *Yoga en Yantra in hunne beteekenis voor de Indische archaeologie*, Leiden 1946 (Thesis).

Poussin — Poussin, L. de la Vallée, *Bouddhisme, Opinions sur l'histoire de la dogmatique*, Paris 1925.

Radin — Radin, P., *Primitive Religion, its Nature and Origin*, New York, N.Y., 1957 (Dover Paperback; copyright 1937).

Ramesan — Ramesan, N., *Temples and Legends of Andhra Pradesh*, Bombay 1962 (Bhavan's book Univ., 98).

Ram Gopal — Ram Gopal, India of Vedic Kalpa-sūtras, Delhi 1959.

Rangachari — Rangachari, K., The Śrī Vaiṣṇava Brahmans, Madras 1931 (Bulletin of the Madras Govt. Museum, New Ser., Gen. Section, II, 2).

Rao — Rao, T.A. Gopinath, Elements of Hindu Iconography, 2 vols., Madras 1914.

N.R. Ray — Ray, N.R., Brahmanical Gods in Burma, Calcutta 1932.

S.K. Ray — Ray, S.K., The Ritual Art of the Bratas of Bengal, Calcutta 1961.

Regmi — Regmi, D.R., Medieval Nepal, Part III: Source Materials, Calcutta 1966.

Reyna — Reyna, Ruth, The Concept of Māyā, London 1962.

Rivers — Rivers, W.H.R., The Todas, London 1906, repr. Oosterhout 1967.

Schulte Nordholt — Schulte Nordholt, H.G., Het politieke systeem van de Atoni van Timor, Amsterdams 1966 (Thesi VU).

Segal	Segal, R., The Crisis of India, London 1965.
Sharma 1958	Sharma, R.S., Śūdras in Ancient India (A Survey of the Position of the Lower Orders Down to C. A.D. 500), Delhi 1958.
Sharma 1959	Sharma, R.S., Aspects of Political Ideas and Institutions in Ancient India, Delhi 1959.
Shende	Shende, N.J., The Religion and Philosophy of the Atharvaveda, Poona 1952 (Bhandarkar Or. Ser., 8).
Singer	Singer, M. (ed.), Krishna: Myths, Rites and Attitudes, Honolulu 1966.
Soerensen	Soerensen, S., An Index to the Names in the Mahābhārata, First ed., 1904; repr. Delhi 1963.
Swellengrebel	Swellengrebel, J. L. (ed.), Bali, Studies on Life, Thought, and Ritual, The Hague 1960 (Introduction by J.L. Swellengrebel, p. 3-76).
Thomas	Thomas, E.J., The Life of Buddha as Legend and History, London 1927, rev. ed., 1949, repr. 1956.
Thurston	Thurston, E., *Omens and Superstitions of Southern India*, London 1912.
Tripathi	Tripathi, G. Ch., *Der Ursprung und die Entwicklung der Vāmana-Legende in der indischen Literatur*, Wiesbaden 1968 (Freiburger Beitr. zur Indologie, 1).
Vaudeville	Kabīr, *Au Cabaret de l'Amour* trad. par Charlotte Vaudeville, Paris 1955.
Vora	Vora, D. P., *Evolution of Morals in the Epics*, Bombay 1959.
Weber	Weber, A., *Verzeichnis der Skt.-und Prakrit-HSS. der Königlichen Bibliothek zu Berlin, II. Band, Dritte Abteilung*, Berlin 1892.
Webster	Webster, H., *Magic. A Sociological Study*, Stanford Univ. Press, Cal., 1948.

Wilhelm — Wilhelm, F., *Prüfung und Initiation im Buche Pauṣya und in der Biographie des Nāropa*, Wiesbaden 1965 (Münchener Indol. Studien, Band 3).

Winternitz/Jha — Winternitz, M., *A History of Indian Literature*, vol. III, translated by Subhadra Jhā. Part I : *Classical Skt. Literature*, Delhi 1963. Part II : *Scientific Literature*, Delhi 1967.

Wirz — Wirz, P., *Exorzismus und Heilkunde auf Ceylon*, Bern, 1941.

Woodroffe — Woodroffe, J., *Introduction to Tantra Śāstra*, Madras 1963.

Zimmer — Zimmer, H., *Maya, der indische Mythos*, Stuttgart-Berlin 1936.

Zoetmulder — Zoetmulder S.J., P. J., "Die Hochreligionen Indonesiens", in : W. Stöhr and P. J. Zoetmulder, *Die Religionen Indonesiens*, Stuttgart 1965 (Die Religionen der Menschheit, 5, 1), p. 223-354.

INDEX